Beginning Ubuntu Linux

Second Edition

A

ARDED

Keir Thomas

Apress®

Beginning Ubuntu Linux, Second Edition

Copyright © 2007 by Keir Thomas

Ubuntu is a registered trademark of Canonical Limited.

ISBN-13 (pbk): 978-1-59059-820-7

ISBN-10 (pbk): 1-59059-820-2

Printed and bound in the United States of America 9 8 7 6 5 4 3 2 1

Lead Editor: Jason Gilmore
Technical Reviewer: Eric Hewitt
Editorial Board: Steve Anglin, Ewan Buckingham, Gary Cornell, Jason Gilmore, Jonathan Gennick,
    Jonathan Hassell, James Huddleston, Chris Mills, Matthew Moodie, Jeff Pepper, Paul Sarknas,
    Dominic Shakeshaft, Jim Sumser, Matt Wade
Project Manager: Richard Dal Porto
Copy Edit Manager: Nicole Flores
Copy Editor: Heather Lang
Assistant Production Director: Kari Brooks-Copony
Production Editor: Ellie Fountain
Compositor: Susan Glinert
Proofreader: Nancy Riddiough
Indexer: Broccoli Information Management
Artist: Kinetic Publishing Services, LLC
Cover Designer: Kurt Krames
Manufacturing Director: Tom Debolski

Distributed to the book trade worldwide by Springer-Verlag New York, Inc., 233 Spring Street, 6th Floor, New York, NY 10013. Phone 1-800-SPRINGER, fax 201-348-4505, e-mail orders-ny@springer-sbm.com, or visit http://www.springeronline.com.

For information on translations, please contact Apress directly at 2560 Ninth Street, Suite 219, Berkeley, CA 94710. Phone 510-549-5930, fax 510-549-5939, e-mail info@apress.com, or visit http://www.apress.com.

Dedicated to the muse

Contents at a Glance

PART 1 ■■■ Introducing the World of Linux

PART 2 ■■■ Installing Ubuntu

PART 3 ■■■ The No-Nonsense Getting Started Guide

PART 4 ■■■ The Shell and Beyond

PART 5 ■■■ Multimedia

PART 6 ■■■ Office Tasks

PART 7 ■■■ Keeping Your System Running

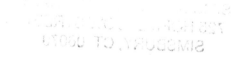

PART 8 ■■■ Appendixes

Contents

PART 1 ■■■ Introducing the World of Linux

PART 2 ■■■ Installing Ubuntu

PART 3 ■■■ The No-Nonsense Getting Started Guide

PART 4 ■■■ **The Shell and Beyond**

PART 5 ■■■ Multimedia

PART 6 ■■■ Office Tasks

PART 7 ■■■ Keeping Your System Running

PART 8 ■■■ Appendixes

About the Author

KEIR THOMAS is an award-winning author who has written several best-selling Linux titles for Apress. A former computer magazine editor, he has been writing about computers, operating systems, and software for a decade. He has also served as editor on several computer books. His works have been translated into many languages.

Thomas works as a full-time author and has written four books for Apress. He lives on the side of a mountain in England, and his hobbies include hiking and playing musical instruments.

About the Technical Reviewer

 **ERIC HEWITT** is an Ubuntu community member and developer. He's involved in the development and testing of BUMPS, the Ubuntu multimedia metapackage project, and is the sole developer for Vive, the ffmpeg front end. He will graduate, in May 2007, from the Carroll School of Management at Boston College with a concentration in economics and then return to his home in central New York.

Acknowledgments

Books like the one you're holding now take an enormous amount of work by a lot of people to come into fruition. To this end, I'd like to acknowledge the help of the following individuals who have contributed to this edition, as well as various earlier editions: Chris Mills, Emily Wolman, Marilyn Smith, Heather Lang, Ellie Fountain, Jason Gilmore, Sofia Marchant, Richard Dal Porto, and Julie Miller. I'd also like to thank the technical reviewers who have been involved with editions of this book: Eric Hewitt, Frank Pohlmann, and John Hornbeck.

Introduction

Linux has come a long way in a short time. Computing itself is still relatively young by any standard; if the era of modern computing started with the invention of the microchip, it's still less than 50 years old. But Linux is a youngster compared even to this; it has been around for only 16 of those years.

In that brief time span, a student's personal project has grown to where it now runs many computers throughout the world. It has rampaged through the computing industry, providing an alternative to commercial solutions such as those offered by Microsoft, and toppling long-held beliefs about the way things should be done. This is all by virtue of the fact that Linux is simply better than every other choice out there. Many argue that it's more secure and faster than other operating systems. But here's the kicker—Linux is free of charge. Yes, that's right. It doesn't have to cost a penny. It is one of the computing industry's best-kept secrets.

I was bitten by the Linux bug in the mid-1990s. I was introduced to it by a friend who sold it to me as a kind of alternative to DOS. At that time, I typed a few commands at the prompt and was greeted by error messages. I must admit that I was put off. But shortly afterwards, I revisited Linux and quickly became hooked.

Yet getting used to Linux wasn't easy. I read as many books as I could, but they weren't very helpful to me. They were usually overly complicated or simply irrelevant. To start off, I didn't want to know how to create a program that could parse text files. I just wanted to know how to copy and delete files. I didn't want to set up a web server. I just wanted to know how to play my MP3 tracks and browse the Web.

This book is my answer to the need for a fundamental, authoritative, and down-to-earth guide to Linux, done in the context of one of the most popular flavors of Linux in existence today. It's a book that is desperately needed in our modern world, especially as Linux becomes more and more popular and enters homes and workplaces.

Beginning Ubuntu Linux, Second Edition purely and simply focuses on what you need to know to use Linux. It's concise and to the point, aiming to re-create under Linux all the stuff you used to do under Windows, or even Apple Macintosh. But don't think that this means *Beginning Ubuntu Linux, Second Edition* cuts corners. Wherever justified, this book spends time examining the topics you need to know in order to gain a complete and comprehensive understanding. For example, you'll find a hefty chapter looking at the command-line prompt—arguably the heart of Linux and the element that gives Linux most of its power. There's also an entire chapter discussing (and illustrating) how to initially install Ubuntu on your computer. *Beginning Ubuntu Linux, Second Edition* really is a complete guide.

About Ubuntu

Linux applies an alternative philosophy to computing that revolves around the sharing of not only software but also knowledge. To use Linux is to become part of a huge global community of people who have caught on to a phenomenon that is changing the world.

Ubuntu (www.ubuntulinux.org) is the natural continuation of these goals. It's a project founded by entrepreneur businessman Mark Shuttleworth with the intention of bringing a freely available, high-quality operating system to the world. To this end, Shuttleworth invested $10 million of his own money to guarantee that this will be the case for many years to come.

The fundamental concept is that Ubuntu is available for use by anyone in the world, no matter who they are or where they are. As such, many different languages are supported, and the operating system can also be accessed by those with disabilities, such as partial sight or hearing. Ubuntu might just as easily be found on a Wall Street banker's laptop as on a battered, old computer in a Brazilian favela.

Ubuntu is built around one of the most established versions of Linux: Debian (www.debian.org). The Debian Project was started back in 1993, shortly after the very first version of the Linux software was released, and has become one of the pioneering varieties of Linux.

Ubuntu and Debian Linux both share common goals and are closely allied, but Ubuntu focuses largely on the desktop. It provides a powerful office suite by default, for example, as well as some excellent pieces of Internet software.

It's also very easy to use. Ubuntu works straight out of the box. As soon as it's installed, you should be ready to start using it without any further work. In addition, tasks such as updating your software are as easy under Ubuntu as they are under Windows.

Above all, however, Ubuntu is designed to be shared. You can take the DVD-ROM included with this book and install Ubuntu on as many computers as you want. You can also copy it as many times as you want and give those copies to your friends. I'm serious! This isn't some kind of trick either—Ubuntu isn't a trial version that will quit running in a month. You will *never* find yourself having to pay a fee further down the line, even if you want to install additional software. Ubuntu will always be free of charge.

What You'll Find in This Book

Beginning Ubuntu Linux, Second Edition is split into seven parts, each of which contains chapters about a certain aspect of Ubuntu use. These parts can be read in sequence, or you can dip in and out of them at will. Whenever a technical term is mentioned, a reference is made to the chapter where that term is explained.

Part 1 examines the history and philosophy behind the Linux operating system. I aim to answer many of the common questions about Linux. Such knowledge is considered to be as important, if not more so, than understanding the technical details on how Linux works.

But while these chapters should be read sooner rather than later, they don't contain any technical information that you absolutely require to get started with Ubuntu.

Part 2 covers installing Ubuntu on your computer. An illustrated guide is provided, and all installation choices are explained in depth. Additionally, you'll find a problem-solving chapter to help, just in case anything goes wrong.

Part 3 focuses on getting started with Ubuntu. It covers setting up the Linux system so that it's ready to use. One chapter is dedicated to setting up common hardware devices, such as printers and modems, and another explains how you can secure your system. Other chapters in this part explore the desktop, explaining what you need to know to begin using Ubuntu on a daily basis.

In Part 4, we take a look at how the underlying technology behind Linux functions. You're introduced to the command-line prompt, and you learn how the file system works. It's in these chapters that you'll really master controlling Linux!

Part 5 covers multimedia functions available for Ubuntu users, which let you watch movies and play back music. We also take a look at the image-editing software built into Ubuntu.

Part 6 moves on to explain how typical office tasks can be accomplished under Ubuntu. We investigate OpenOffice.org, the complete office suite built into Ubuntu. After an introduction to OpenOffice.org, separate chapters explore its word processor, spreadsheet, database, and presentation package. You also learn how to use the Evolution e-mail and personal information manager program.

Part 7 carries on from Part 4 and takes an even more in-depth look at the underlying technology behind Ubuntu. This time, the emphasis is on giving you the skills you need to keep your system running smoothly. You learn how to install software, manage users, optimize your system, back up essential data, schedule tasks, and access computers remotely.

Finally, Part 8 contains four appendixes. The first is a glossary of Linux terms used not only in this book but also in the Linux and Unix worlds. The second appendix is a quick reference to commands typically used at the command-line prompt under Linux. The third appendix explains how to get further help when using Ubuntu, and the fourth explains how to use the DVD-ROM and the differences between the various versions of Ubuntu.

What's New in the Second Edition

This second edition of *Beginning Ubuntu Linux* has been thoroughly updated and revised to take into account improvements introduced with the 6.10 release of Ubuntu (code-named Edgy Eft). The previous edition covered the 5.10 release, and the changes introduced with the 6.10 release, though often subtle, make a dramatic difference in the Ubuntu experience.

In many cases in this second edition, I've attempted to make the book more robust by adding extra content. Chapter 9, which examines how to make your Ubuntu setup secure, now includes a section that looks at installing an antivirus program, for example. Chapter 28, covering software management, now includes a section that looks at managing software repositories—thanks to a new tool offered with the 6.10 release. There are many other small but important changes like this throughout the book.

About the DVD-ROM Supplied with This Book

The DVD-ROM attached to the book is completely new, compared to the CD-ROM offered on the first edition. This edition offers a double-sided DVD-ROM that contains both the latest Ubuntu 6.10 release and the older 6.06.1 release. You can opt to install either version or run in "live" mode, which means that the entire operating system boots from the disc and doesn't touch your hard disk. This can be useful for those who wish to "try out" Ubuntu, but there are a handful of caveats, which I explain in Chapter 5.

The 6.06.1 and 6.10 releases are included to give you the best choice of Ubuntu experience. Some users might prefer the long-term support package offered by the 6.06.1 release rather than the cutting-edge features in the 6.10 release. In Appendix D, I explain more about the differences between versions of Ubuntu.

The DVD-ROM also contains the Ubuntu spin-off projects: Kubuntu, Edubuntu, and Xubuntu, in both the 6.06.1 and 6.10 releases. You'll also find the PowerPC version of Ubuntu on the disc for users of older Apple Macintosh computers, as well as the alternate install version of Ubuntu, which can help if you run into problems installing Ubuntu. Again, you'll find more details in Appendix D.

Conventions Used in This Book

The goal when writing *Beginning Ubuntu Linux* was to make it as readable as possible while providing the facility for readers to learn at their own pace.

Throughout the book, you'll find various types of notes and sidebars complementing the regular text. These are designed to provide handy information to help further your knowledge. They also make reading the book a bit easier.

▪**Note** A note is designed to provide an important piece of information that you should know and that will help your understanding of the topic being discussed.

▪**Tip** A tip is something that will help when you need to perform the task being described. Alternatively, it might be something that can make your life easier when using Ubuntu.

Caution A caution is something you should certainly pay attention to, because it warns of a hidden danger or particular caveat that applies to the topic being discussed.

In the sidebars, I take a moment to explain something that you should know, but that isn't vital to an understanding of the main topic being discussed. You don't need to read the sidebars there and then; you can return to them later if you wish.

PART 1

■■■

Introducing the World of Linux

CHAPTER 1

■■■

Welcome!

If you're an avid computer user, there's a good chance that you've heard of Linux. You might have read about it, or perhaps you've seen TV ads that refer to it.

One of the odd things about Linux is that the more you learn about it, the more questions you have. For instance, it's generally thought that Linux is free of charge, but this then raises the question of how, in our modern world, something like an entire computer operating system can cost nothing. Who pays the programmers?

Over the following introductory chapters, I'm going to try to answer some of these questions. In this chapter, I'll explain what Linux is and its benefits compared to Windows.

What Is Linux?

There are two ways of looking at a PC. The first is to see it as a magical box, which lets you do cool stuff like browse the Internet or play games. Seen in this way, it's like a VCR—put in a tape, press a button, and a picture appears on your TV. On your PC, you click the Internet Explorer icon, type a web address, and a web site somehow appears. The astonishing technical complexity behind these simple procedures isn't important to most people.

The other way of looking at a PC is as a collection of components that are made by various manufacturers. You might be familiar with this way of thinking if you're ever tried to upgrade your PC's hardware. In that case, you'll know that your PC consists of a CPU, a hard disk, a graphics card, and so on. You can swap any of these out to put in newer and better components that upgrade your PC's performance or allow more data storage.

What almost no one realizes is that the operating system is just another component of your PC. It, too, can be swapped out for a better replacement. Windows doesn't come free of charge, and Microsoft isn't performing a public service by providing it. Around $50 to $100 of the price you pay for a PC goes straight into Microsoft's pocket. Bearing in mind that hundreds of millions of PCs are made each year, it's not hard to see why Microsoft is one of the world's richest corporations.

It would be difficult to question this state of affairs if Microsoft gave us our money's worth. But it often falls far short. Its products are full of serious security holes, which at best inconvenience us and at worst make us lose data.

Microsoft became rich, and maintains its wealth, by a virtual monopoly over PC manufacturers. While the intelligent computer buyer can choose between components to put together a better PC—deciding between an AMD or Intel processor, for example—you usually have little choice but to buy Windows with a new PC. Try it now. Phone your favorite big-name computer retailer. Say that you want a PC but you *don't* want Windows installed. Then listen as the salesperson on the other end of the phone struggles to understand.

■Note Some PC manufacturers actually will sell you a PC without Windows installed on it. All you have to do is ask, although you might need to speak to a senior salesperson to get through to someone who understands your request. Smaller local companies, in particular, will be more than willing to sell you a PC without Windows. Some larger multinational companies, such as Hewlett-Packard, sell workstations with Linux preinstalled instead of Windows. However, these computers are usually aimed at businesses rather than home users.

Wouldn't it be terrific if you could get rid of Windows? Would you like to finally say goodbye to all those security holes and not have to worry about virus infections anymore, yet not lose out on any features or need to make sacrifices or compromises?

There is an alternative. Welcome to the world of Linux.

Linux is an operating system, which is to say that it's a bit like Windows. It's the core software that runs your computer and lets you do stuff on it. By the strictest definition of the term, an *operating system* is the fundamental software that's needed to make your PC work. Without an operating system installed on your PC, it would merely be an expensive doorstop. When you turned it on, it would beep in annoyance—its way of telling you that it can't do much without a whole set of programs to tell it what to do next.

An operating system allows your PC's hardware to communicate with the software you run on it. It's hundreds of programs, system libraries, drivers, and more, all tightly integrated into a whole. In addition, an operating system lets programs talk to other programs and, of course, communicate with you, the user. In other words, the operating system runs everything and allows everything to work.

■Note Some companies and individuals, including Microsoft, define an operating system as much more than this fundamental software. They add in the basic tools you run on an operating system, such as web browsers and file management programs.

Linux consists of a central set of programs that run the PC on a low level, referred to as the *kernel*, and hundreds (if not thousands) of additional programs provided by other people and various companies. Technically speaking, the word "Linux" refers explicitly to the core kernel program. However, most people generally refer to the entire bundle of programs that make up the operating system as "Linux."

GNU/LINUX

Although most of us refer to Linux as a complete operating system, the title "Linux" hides a lot of confusing but rather important details. Technically speaking, the word "Linux" refers merely to the kernel file: the central set of programs that lie at the heart of the operating system. Everything else that comes with a typical version of Linux, such as programs to display graphics on the screen or let the user input data, is supplied by other people, organizations, or companies. The Linux operating system is the combination of many disparate projects. (I'll explain how this works in the next chapter.)

The GNU organization, in particular, supplies a lot of vital programs and also system library files, without which Linux wouldn't run. These programs and files were vital to the acceptance of Linux as an operating system in its early days. Because of this, and the fact that Linux completed a long-running goal of the GNU project to create a Unix-like operating system, some people choose to refer to Linux as GNU/Linux.

A fierce debate rages over the correct way to refer to the Linux operating system and whether the GNU prefix should be used. For what it's worth, an equally fierce debate rages over how we should define an operating system. It can all get very confusing. It's also very easy to accidentally offend someone by not using the correct terminology!

It's not the purpose of this book to get involved in this debate. Suffice it to say that I acknowledge the vital input of the GNU project into the operating system many people refer to simply as Linux, as well as that of other vital projects. However, readers should note that when I refer to Linux throughout this book, I mean the entire operating system. If I intend to refer simply to the kernel programs, I will make that clear.

The Age of Linux

At the time of writing this book, Linux is a little over 15 years old. It has gone from a hobbyist project maintained by just one man to a professional and corporate-sponsored solution for virtually every level of computer user.

Linux has also gone from being a server operating system, designed for central computers that hand out files and other computer resources to other computers, to becoming a full-fledged graphical desktop operating system like Windows. In fact, it's gone even further. Today, it's very likely that you'll find Linux running your digital video recorder and other computerized household gadgets.

Getting technical for a moment, Linux is a 32-bit and 64-bit, multitasking, multiuser operating system. This is a complicated way of saying that it's pretty darn powerful. Linux is as capable of running supercomputers as it is of running a desktop PC. Linux builds on the foundation laid by Unix, which itself was based on Multics, which was one of the first modern computer operating systems. It's not an exaggeration to say that Linux can trace its family tree all the way back to the pioneering days of computing.

CORRECT PRONUNCIATION

What most people refer to as the Linux operating system takes its name from the kernel program, one of its most important system components. This, in turn, was named after its creator, Linus Torvalds.

The name Linus is commonly pronounced "Lie-nus" in many English-speaking countries, but Torvalds speaks Swedish. He pronounces his name "Leen-us" (imagine this spoken with a gentle Scandinavian lilt, and you've got it about right).

Because of this, he pronounces Linux as "Lin-ux", and most people copy this pronunciation. You can hear this spoken by Torvalds himself by visiting www.paul.sladen.org/pronunciation/.

Some people refer to the Linux operating system by its full title of GNU/Linux. In this case, GNU is pronounced as in the name of the animal, with a hard G: "G-noo." The full pronunciation is therefore "G-noo Lin-ux."

Finally, the DVD that comes with this book contains a version of Linux called Ubuntu. This is an African word that, in its country of origin, is pronounced in three separate short syllables: "oo-bu-ntoo." However, most western English speakers pronounce the word "oo-bunt-oo," which is perfectly acceptable!

The Problems with Windows

The world's most popular operating system is Windows, which is made by the Microsoft Corporation. Linux has no links with Windows at all. Microsoft doesn't contribute anything to Linux and, in fact, is rather hostile toward it, because it threatens Microsoft's market dominance. This means that installing Linux can give you an entirely Microsoft-free PC. How enticing does *that* sound?

Windows is used on 91 percent of the world's desktop computers. In other words, it must be doing a good job for it to be so popular, right?

Let's face facts. On many levels, Windows is a great operating system, and since the release of Windows XP in particular, Microsoft has cleaned up its act. Windows XP does a much better job compared to previous versions of Windows (and Vista makes even more improvements). But the situation is far from perfect. Windows XP is notoriously insecure and virtually every day a new security hole is uncovered. The United States Computer Emergency Readiness Team (www.us-cert.gov) reported 812 security vulnerabilities for Microsoft Windows during 2005. That's 15 vulnerabilities *per week*! In June 2005, the computer security company Sophos (www.sophos.com) advertised that its Windows anti-virus program defended against over 103,000 viruses!

This has led to an entire industry that creates antivirus programs, which are additional pieces of software you *have to install* once your computer is up and running for it to run without the risk of data loss or data theft.

■**Note** Unlike many books, *Beginning Ubuntu Linux* doesn't ignore Windows. Throughout its pages, you'll find frequent references to Windows and the software that runs under it. You'll find direct comparisons with actual Windows programs, and you'll learn how to work with Windows files. The intention is that anyone with prior experience will be able to get started with Ubuntu much more quickly.

So is Linux the solution to these problems? Most would agree that it's a step in the right direction, at the very least. Most Linux users don't install antivirus programs, because there are virtually no Linux-specific viruses. As with all software, security holes are occasionally discovered in Linux, but the way it is built means exploiting those holes is much more difficult.

■**Note** There have been a couple of viruses for Linux, but they're no longer "in the wild" (that is, they are no longer infecting PCs). This is because the security holes they exploited were quickly patched, causing the viruses to die out. This happened because the majority of Linux users update their systems regularly, so any security holes that viruses might exploit are patched promptly. Compare that to Windows, where most users aren't even aware they can update their systems, even when Microsoft gets around to issuing a patch (which has been known to take months).

There's also the fact that Linux encourages you to take control of your computer, as opposed to treating it like a magical box. As soon as you install Linux, you become a power user. Every aspect of your PC is under your control, unlike with Windows. This means fixing problems is a lot easier, and optimizing your system becomes part and parcel of the user experience.

■**Tip** There's no reason why Linux and Windows can't live side-by-side on the same computer. This can be done by dual-booting, and I explain how in Chapter 5.

WINDOWS COMPATIBLE?

One of the biggest questions asked by most newcomers to Linux is whether it can run Windows software. The answer is yes . . . and no.

Linux is completely different from Windows on a fundamental technical level. Its creators based it on Unix, an industrial-strength operating system, and deliberately steered clear of emulating Windows. This means that Linux isn't a swap-in replacement for Windows. You cannot take the installation CD of a Windows program and use it to install that program on Linux, in the same way that you cannot install an Apple Mac program on Windows.

However, several current projects let you run Windows programs on Linux. Wine (`www.winehq.com`) is an example of such a project, and you can download a commercial and easy-to-use variation of it from `www.codeweavers.com`. You can also use programs like VMware (`www.vmware.com`) to create a "virtual PC" running on Linux. Then you can install the Windows operating system and, therefore, any Windows software you like.

In most cases, however, you'll find that there's a Linux equivalent of your favorite Windows software. Frequently, you'll find that this Linux version is actually superior to the Windows program you've been using. I'll discuss many of these in Chapter 11.

The Benefits of Linux

People have been known to exaggerate about Linux when singing its praises, and there's certainly some hyperbole around. But there are a couple of cast-iron facts about its benefits.

Fewer Crashes

The experiences of different people vary but, in my extensive experience, Linux very rarely crashes. My mouse cursor has never frozen on screen. A strange error box has never appeared and remained until I've rebooted. Program windows don't freeze and leave trails as I drag them around. It's possible to leave a Linux system running for years without ever needing to reboot (although most desktop Ubuntu users shut down their PCs when they won't be using them for a while, just like the rest of us).

Of course, programs that run on top of Linux sometimes crash, but they don't take the rest of the system down with them. Instead, you can clean up after a crash and just carry on.

Security

The next benefit is that Linux is very secure. It's built from the ground up to be secure, in fact, and Linux is based on years of proven computer science research. It works on the principle of users who have permissions to undertake various tasks on the system. If you don't have the correct permission, you cannot, for example, access a particular piece of hardware. Additionally, privacy can be ensured, because the files on the PC are "owned" by individual users, who can permit or deny others access to those files.

Free and Shareable

Another big benefit is that Linux can be obtained free of charge. Once it's installed, the latest updates for all your programs are also free of charge. Not only that, but if you want any new software, it will also usually be free of charge (and normally just a download away). Is this starting to sound attractive yet?

The software is also released under a license that means you can share it with anybody you want. Suppose that you find a really great image editor. You mention it to a friend, and he asks for a copy. Under Windows, copying the program is strictly illegal—to do so turns you into a software pirate! Unless that image editor is freeware, your friend will need to buy the software himself. Under Linux, sharing software is normally entirely legal. In fact, it's encouraged! I'll explain why in Chapter 2.

This philosophy of sharing applies to the entire operating system. You can install the software contained on the DVD on the computer of your friends, relatives, or neighbors. You can even give them copies of the DVD. All this can be done entirely legally!

In fact, this redistribution is what the makers of Ubuntu want. They created Ubuntu so that it would be shared and used by anybody, anywhere in the world. They'll even send you or somebody you know free copies of the installation CD if you want; see the ShipIt page of the Ubuntu website: `https://shipit.ubuntu.com`.

No Annoying Copy Protection or Usage Restrictions

A happy side effect of the sharing culture that surrounds Linux is that you'll never need a software registration code to install it. There's no scheme like Windows Product Activation (WPA), or Windows Genuine Advantage, whereby the software must "phone home" over the Internet to be "activated."

This kind of approach to software, where the creators attempt to fundamentally limit what users can do with the software they've bought, is anathema to all those involved in Linux. Linux users are encouraged to play with the software in order to find or create more uses for programs, since Linux is about freedom, rather than restrictions.

The Linux Community

We've established that Linux is powerful, secure, and flexible. It doesn't nag you to register or ask you to type in lengthy registration codes.

But I've saved the best for last. Linux is more than a computer operating system. It's an entire community of users spread across the globe. When you start to use Linux, you become part of this community (whether you like it or not!).

One of the benefits of membership is that you're never far from finding a solution to a problem. The community likes to congregate online around forums and newsgroups, which you can join in order to find help.

Your placement in the ranks of the community is "newbie." This is a popular way of describing someone who is new to Linux. Although this sounds derisory, it will actually help when you talk to others. Advertising your newbie status will encourage people to take the time to help you. After all, they were newbies once upon a time!

There's another reason not to be disheartened by your newbie tag: you'll outgrow it very quickly. By the time you reach the end of this book, you'll have advanced to the other end of the spectrum—"guru." You'll be one of those giving out the advice to those poor, clueless newbies, and you'll be 100 percent confident in your skills.

■Tip One of the best ways to learn about Linux is under the auspices of a knowledgeable friend. It's very beneficial to have your own guru to help you along when you get stuck—someone who is just an e-mail message or phone call away. If you have a friend who uses Linux, consider taking him or her out for a drink and getting more friendly!

But being part of a community is not just about getting free technical support. It's about sharing knowledge. Linux is as much about an ideal as it is about software. It was created to be shared among those who want to use it. There are no restrictions, apart from one: any changes you make and distribute must also be made available to others.

The spirit of sharing and collaboration has been there since day one. One of the first things Linus Torvalds did when he produced an early version of Linux was to ask for help from others. And he got it. Complete strangers e-mailed him and said they would contribute their time, skills, and effort to help his project. This has been the way Linux has been developed ever since. Thousands of people around the world contribute their own small pieces, rather than there being one overall company in charge. And the same concept applies to knowledge of Linux. When you learn something, don't be afraid to share this knowledge with others. "Giving something back" is a very important part of the way of the Linux community.

To understand why Linux is shared, you need to understand its history, as well as the history of what came before it. This is the topic of Chapter 2.

Summary

This chapter provided an introduction to Linux. It explained what Linux can be used for and also its many advantages when compared to Microsoft Windows. It also introduced the community surrounding Linux, which adds to its benefits. You should be starting to realize what makes millions of people around the world use Linux as the operating system of choice.

The next chapter covers the history of Linux. It also discusses another curious aspect: the political scene that drives the operating system forward.

## CHAPTER 2

A History and Politics Lesson

Linux is more than just software. It's an entire community of users, and as such, there's a detailed social history behind it. In this chapter, we'll look at the origins of Linux, both in terms of where it came from and the people who make it.

You might be tempted to skip this chapter and move on to the information about installing Ubuntu. To be fair, nothing of vital technical importance is mentioned here. But it's important that you read this chapter at some stage, because Linux is more than simply the sum of its parts. It's far more than simply a set of computer programs.

If nothing else, this chapter explains the fundamental philosophies behind Linux and attempts to answer some of the often-baffling questions that arise when Linux is considered as a whole.

In the Beginning

Linux was created 16 years ago, in 1991. A period of 16 years is considered a lifetime in the world of computing, but the origin of Linux actually harks back even further, into the early days of modern computing in the mid-1970s.

Linux was created by a Finnish national named Linus Torvalds. At the time, he was studying in Helsinki and had bought a desktop PC. His new computer needed an operating system. Torvalds's operating system choices were limited: there were various versions of DOS and something called Minix. It was the latter that Torvalds decided to use.

Minix was a clone of the popular Unix operating system. Unix was used on huge computers in businesses and universities, including those at Torvalds's university. Unix was created in the early 1970s and has evolved since then to become what many considered the cutting edge of computing. Unix brought to fruition a large number of computing concepts in use today and, many agree, got almost everything just right in terms of features and usability.

Versions of Unix were available for smaller computers like Torvalds's PC, but they were considered professional tools and were very expensive. This was in the early days of the home computer craze, and the only people who used IBM PCs were businesspeople and hobbyists.

■**Note** Linux is a pretty faithful clone of Unix. If you were to travel back in time 20 or 30 years, you would find that using Unix on those old mainframe computers, complete with their teletype interfaces, would be similar to using Linux on your home PC. Many of the fundamental concepts of Linux, such as the file system hierarchy and user permissions, are taken directly from Unix.

Torvalds liked Unix because of its power, and he liked Minix because it ran on his computer. Minix was created by Andrew Tanenbaum, a professor of computing, to demonstrate the principles of operating system design to his students. Because Minix was also a learning tool, people could also view the *source code* of the program—the original listings that Tanenbaum had entered to create the software.

But Torvalds had a number of issues with Minix. Although it's now available free of charge, at the time Minix was only available for a fee, although in many universities, it was possible to obtain copies free of charge from professors who paid a group licensing fee. Nevertheless, the copyright issue meant that using Minix in the wider world was difficult, and this, along with a handful of technical issues, inspired Torvalds to create from scratch his own version of Unix, just as Tanenbaum had done with Minix.

■**Note** Most clones or implementations of Unix are named so that they end in an "x." One story has it that Torvalds wanted to call his creation Freax, but a containing directory was accidentally renamed Linux on an Internet server. The name stuck.

From day one, Torvalds intended his creation to be shared among everyone who wanted to use it. He encouraged people to copy it and give it to friends. He didn't charge any money for it, and he also made the source code freely available. The idea was that people could take the code and improve it.

This was a master stroke. Many people contacted Torvalds, offering to help out. Because they could see the program code, they realized he was onto a good thing. Soon, Torvalds wasn't the only person developing Linux. He became the leader of a team that used the fledgling Internet to communicate and share improvements.

■**Note** The popular conception of Linux is that it is created by a few hobbyists who work on it in their spare time. This might have been true in the very early days. Nowadays, in addition to these "bedroom programmers," Linux is programmed by hundreds of professionals around the world, many of whom are employed specifically for the task. Torvalds adds to the effort himself and also coordinates the work.

It's important to note that when we talk here about Linux, we're actually talking about the kernel—the central program that runs the PC hardware and keeps the computer ticking. This is all that Torvalds initially produced back in 1991. It was an impressive achievement, but needed a lot of extra add-on programs to take care of even the most basic tasks. Torvalds's kernel needed additional software so that users could enter data, for example. It needed a way for users to be able to enter commands so they could manipulate files, such as deleting or copying them. And that's before you even consider more complicated stuff like displaying graphics on the screen or printing documents.

Linux itself didn't offer these functions. It simply ran the computer's hardware. Once it booted up, it expected to find other programs. If they weren't present, then all you saw was a blank screen.

LINUS TORVALDS

Linus Benedict Torvalds was born in Helsinki, Finland, in 1969. A member of the minority Swedish-speaking population, he attended the University of Helsinki from 1988 to 1996, graduating with a Masters degree in Computer Science.

He started Linux not through a desire to give the world a first-class operating system but with other goals in mind. Its inspiration is in part due to Helsinki winters being so cold. Rather than leave his warm flat and trudge through the snow to the university's campus in order to use its powerful minicomputer, he wanted to be able to connect to it from home! He also wanted to have a platform to use to experiment with the properties of the Intel 386, but that's another story. Torvalds needed an operating system capable of such tasks. Linux was born.

It took Torvalds the better part of a year to come up with the very first version of Linux, during which he worked alone in a darkened room. In 1991, he announced his creation to the world, describing Linux as "just a hobby," and saying it would never be big. It wouldn't be until 1994 that it reached version 1.0.

In the early days, Torvalds's creation was fairly primitive. He was passionate that it should be free for everyone to use, and so he released it under a software license that said that no one could ever sell it. However, he quickly changed his mind, adopting the GNU Public License.

Torvalds was made wealthy by his creation, courtesy of the dot.com boom of the late 1990s, even though this was never his intention; he was driven by altruism. Nowadays, he lives in Portland, Oregon, with his wife and children, having moved to the United States from Finland in the late 1990s.

Initially, Torvalds worked for Transmeta, developing CPU architectures as well as overseeing kernel development, although this wasn't part of his official work. He still programs the kernel, but currently he oversees the Open Source Development Lab, an organization created to encourage open source adoption in industry and which is also referred to as the home of Linux.

The GNU Project

Around the time Linus created Linux, another project, called GNU, also existed. This project team also hoped to create an operating system that used Unix as its inspiration, while avoiding some of the pitfalls that had blighted that operating system, both technically and in terms of its licensing. GNU is a so-called recursive acronym that stands for "GNU's Not Unix," a play on words favored by computer programmers.

GNU's parent organization, the Free Software Foundation (FSF), had been formed eight years prior to Torvalds's effort, and since that time, had produced the majority of the core software that Linux desperately needed. However, as luck would have it, FSF lacked the essential functionality of the kernel. The developers were in the process of creating their own kernel, but it had not come to fruition.

The GNU software was distributed for free to anyone who wanted it. The source code was also made available, so users could adapt and change the programs to meet their own needs (in fact, Torvalds had used the GNU model when deciding how to distribute Linux).

Richard Stallman is the man behind GNU and, along with Linus Torvalds, is the second accidental hero in our story. Stallman had been around since the Dark Ages of computing, back when wardrobe-sized computers were "time-shared" among users who used small desktop terminals to access them. Like Torvalds, Stallman started GNU as a personal project, but then found others who were more than willing to join his cause.

■**Note** Stallman created the Emacs text editor and the GNU C Compiler (GCC). Together, they allow the creation of yet more software, so it's no surprise that one of the very first programs Torvalds used in the early days to create Linux was Stallman's GCC.

Back in Stallman's day at the legendary Massachusetts Institute of Technology (MIT), computer software was shared. If you created a program to perform a particular task, you offered it to practically anyone who wanted it. Alternatively, if you found an existing program wasn't adequate or had a bug, you improved it yourself, and then made the resulting program available to others. People might use your improved version, or they might not; it was up to them.

This way of sharing software was disorganized and done on an ad hoc basis, but came about of its own accord. Nobody questioned it, and it seemed the best way of doing things. There certainly wasn't any money involved, any more than there would be money involved in one friend explaining an idea to another.

RICHARD STALLMAN

Richard Matthew Stallman, usually referred to as RMS, was born in 1953 in Manhattan. He comes from the old school of computing forged during the 1970s and was a member of MIT's legendary Artificial Intelligence Lab.

Seemingly destined for a life in academia, Stallman left MIT in 1984 to found the GNU Project. This was as a reaction to the increasing commercialization of computer software. Whereas once all hackers (that is, programmers) had shared ideas and program code, the trend in the 1980s was toward proprietary, nonshared code, as well as legal contracts, which forced programmers to keep secrets from one another.

Stallman is a very talented programmer and is considered a genius by many observers. He single-handedly created many essential programming tools in his initial efforts to get GNU off the ground. Many of these find a home in Linux.

Stallman is also widely applauded for the creation of the GNU Public License. This is a legal document that lets people share software. It introduces the concept of *copyleft* and is opposed to the legal concept of copyright, which attempts to limit the freedom of individuals when using a piece of software (or any other creative work). Nowadays, the concept of copyleft has been applied to literature, music, and other arts in an attempt to avoid restricting who can and cannot access various items, as well as to encourage a collaborative working environment.

Proprietary Software and the GPL

In the 1980s, everything changed. The world became more corporate, and with the rise of the desktop PC, the concept of proprietary software became prevalent. More and more companies started to sell software. They reasoned that this was impossible to do if they shared it with everybody else, so they kept it secret. Microsoft led this charge and did very well with its proprietary software.

To Stallman, this "trade secrets" approach to software was anathema. He had nothing against software being sold for a profit, but he hated the fundamental ideas behind software being kept secret. He felt passionately that sharing software and being able to understand how it worked was akin to free speech—necessary and vital for the furthering of technology, and therefore society itself. How could the new generation of programmers improve on the previous generation's work if they were unable to see how it worked? It was absurd to need to create software from scratch each time, rather than taking something that already existed and making it better.

Because of his beliefs, Stallman resigned from his job in the MIT Artificial Intelligence Lab and founded GNU. His aim initially was to produce a complete clone of Unix that would be shared in the ways he knew from the early days of computing. This software would be available for everyone to use, to study, and to adapt. It would be free, in the same sense as free speech— shared and unrestricted. This gave rise to the vital concept of "free software" and soon GNU, and the FSF, became not just a programming venture, but also a political movement.

■**Note** A very common misconception of "free software" is that it is always free of charge. This isn't correct. The word *free* is used here in its political sense, as in "free speech." Many companies and individuals make a healthy profit from selling free software and, in fact, selling free software is encouraged by the GNU Project.

To protect the rights of people to share and adapt the GNU software, Stallman came up with the GNU Public License (GPL). Various drafts of this license were produced over time, until it became a completely watertight legal contract, which furthered the concept of free software.

Most software you buy comes with a license agreement—that big chunk of text you must agree to when installing software (in the case of Windows desktop software, it's frequently referred to as the End-User License Agreement, or EULA). The license agreement usually says that you cannot copy the software or share it with friends. If others want to use the software, they must buy their own version.

The GPL turns this on its head. Rather than restricting what people can do with the software, it gives them permission to share the software with whomever they wish. However, if they modify the program in any way, and then distribute it to others, the program they come up with must also be licensed under the GPL. In other words, people cannot make changes to a program that has a GPL, and then sell the modified program, keeping their improvements secret.

■**Note** An interesting side note is that the actual wording of the GPL says that any changes you make should be shared with others *only if the software is redistributed*. This means that if you modify some GPL software and don't give it to anyone else, there's no need for you to publish your changes or make others aware of those changes.

GNU and Linux Together

The Linux kernel, developed by Torvalds, and the GNU software, developed by Stallman, were a perfect match. It's important to note that this doesn't mean the two projects joined forces. It simply means that the Linux project took some of the GNU software and gave it a good home. This was done with Stallman's blessing, but there wasn't any official union between the two groups. Remember that Stallman had intended everyone to freely share and use the GNU tools. Linux represented a set of people doing just that. GNU is still working on its own kernel, called Hurd, which may provide an alternative to using Torvalds's Linux kernel.

Note Hurd was first planned back in the 1980s and, at the time of writing, still has yet to see the light of day (although testing versions are available). Hurd is a hugely ambitious project and will set a gold standard when it is released.

GNU and Linux together formed a complete operating system, which mimicked the way Unix operated. Other projects and individuals spotted the success of Linux and came onboard, and it wasn't long before Linux realized the potential for a graphical user interface (GUI), the fundamentals of which were provided by the XFree86 Project. A lot of additional software was also provided by individuals and organizations, all using the same "share and share alike" example set by Stallman, with the GNU tools, and Torvalds, with his kernel.

Many people refer to Linux as GNU/Linux. This gives credit to the GNU Project that provided the majority of tools vital to making Linux into a usable operating system. However, like the majority of people in the computing world, I use the term "Linux" throughout this book to avoid confusion.

Different Flavors of Linux

All the pieces of GNU software were available for free download and were therefore free of charge. But this brought its own problems. Not everyone had the know-how to put all the bits and pieces together into a complete operating system. Those who could do this didn't necessarily have the time for it.

Because of this, a number of companies stepped in to do the hard work. They put together versions of Linux, complete with all the software from the GNU Project, which they then sold for a fee on floppy disks, CDs, or DVDs. They also added in bits of their own software, which made it possible to install Linux easily onto a computer's hard disk, for example. They produced their own manuals and documentation, too, and did other things such as bug testing to ensure it all worked well.

What they came up with became known as *distributions* of Linux, or *distros* for short. Examples of these companies include Red Hat, SUSE, Mandrake, and many others around the world. Additionally, a number of enthusiasts got together and formed organizations to create their own distros, such as Debian and Slackware.

Modern distros are very advanced. They make it easy to install Linux on your PC, and they usually come with everything you need, so you can get started immediately. Additionally, they have their own look and feel, as well as unique ways of working and operating.

This means that Ubuntu is not the same as Red Hat Linux, for example, although they share a lot of common features and, of course, they all share the core GNU software.

Linux Today

Nowadays, Linux is a thoroughly modern and capable operating system, considered cutting edge by many. It also runs on many different types of computer hardware, including Apple Macintosh computers, Sun SPARC machines, and the ubiquitous desktop PCs equipped with Intel or AMD processors. One of the ironies is that, although Linux was based on Unix, it has slowly come to dominate the computer operating system market. According to industry sources, Linux is on its way to making commercial varieties of Unix redundant. Companies that sell their own versions of Unix, such as Hewlett Packard and IBM, have added Linux to their traditional product range.

Recent innovations in the latest versions of the kernel mean that it finds uses on the smallest computers in the world, as well as on the biggest. Several of the top supercomputers in the world run Linux and, ironically, it can also be used on handheld PDAs or even digital watches! You'll even find it running things like digital video recorders or other household goods, where it sits invisibly in the background and makes everything work. Remember that one of the fundamental principles of Linux is that you can use it for whatever you want. You don't need to ask for permission first or tell anyone what you're doing.

Linux initially found mainstream use by software developers, and on server computers, such as those that run the Internet. However, in recent years, it has become increasingly popular on desktop computers. This is the area where experts suggest it will see massive growth over the coming years.

Modern Linux Development

Nowadays, Linux is developed not only by Torvalds, who manages the huge project, but also by hundreds of volunteers and corporations who contribute resources. Most recently, IBM and Novell have gotten involved and contribute hundreds of people to the effort of creating Linux. Sun contributes the OpenOffice.org office suite and sells its own version of Unix. Corporations like Computer Associates contribute their own software, too.

These companies have realized that the best way of producing software is to share and share alike, rather than develop their own proprietary software and keep it secret. The proprietary ways of the 1980s are starting to seem like an ill-conceived flash in the pan.

Most recently, Novell found that by embracing Linux, it could massively enhance the functions of its aging NetWare product, without needing to return to the drawing board and start from scratch. It could just take what it wanted from the pile of Linux software. This shows the philosophy of Linux in action.

Linux has software for just about every need, ranging from simply receiving e-mail to running a huge e-mail server. There are databases, office suites, web browsers, video games, movie players, audio tools, and more, as well as thousands of pieces of specialized software used in various niches of industry (and too boring to mention here). Most of this software is available to anyone who wants it, free of charge.

What more could you want?

Summary

This chapter has detailed the history of Linux and explained its origins. It also explained *why* Linux came into being. We looked at how Linux formed one of the building blocks of a political movement geared toward producing software that can be shared.

We discussed the creator of Linux, Linus Torvalds. We've also looked at the massive input the GNU Project has made and, in particular, that of its philosopher king, Richard Stallman.

In the next chapter, we move on to look at what you can expect from day-to-day use of Linux.

■■■

## CHAPTER 3

The Realities of Running Linux

So now that you've learned about the politics, history, and personalities behind Linux, only one question remains: what's Linux actually like when used day to day? What should the average user expect from the experience?

These are the questions I hope to answer in this brief chapter.

Learning to Use Linux

What should you expect from Linux once you've installed it? Well, it's a little like running Windows, except there are no viruses, fewer crashes, and no inexplicable slowdowns.

In addition, you have complete control over the system. This doesn't mean Linux is necessarily complicated. It's just that you have the control if you wish to make use of it. We'll look into this in the later chapters of this book.

Most software you use under Windows has at least one equivalent under Ubuntu, installed by default. It's unlikely that you'll need to download or install any additional software and, even if you do, you'll probably find it's available for free.

In most cases, the Linux swap-ins are at least as powerful and easy to use as their Windows alternatives. Tabbed browsing in the Mozilla Firefox web browser lets you visit more than one site at once, for example, without needing to have a lot of browser instances running, as you do with Microsoft Internet Explorer. The Evolution program has a search routine that lets you look through your e-mail messages quickly for a variety of criteria, and it puts the features in a similar Microsoft product to shame.

Does this sound too good to be true? There is just one caveat. Linux isn't a clone of Windows and doesn't aim to be. It has its own way of doing certain things, and sometimes works differently from Windows. This means that many people experience a learning curve when they first begin using Linux.

■**Note** Several Linux distributions aim to mimic Windows pretty faithfully. For example, Xandros and Linspire copy the look and feel of Windows to the extent that (allegedly) some people are unable to tell the difference.

But in just a few weeks after your move to Linux, everything will start to seem entirely normal. Most of the time, you won't even be aware you're running Linux. Of course, some patience is required during those initial few weeks. Linux can be illogical and frustrating; on the other hand, so can Windows. We simply got used to it.

Who Uses Linux?

Who uses Linux? The myth from the old days is that it's only for techies and power users. When you needed to put everything together by hand, this was clearly true. But modern distributions make Linux accessible to all. It's no exaggeration to say that you could install Linux on a computer Luddite's PC and have that person use it in preference to Windows.

Up until quite recently, Linux was largely seen as a developer's tool and a server operating system. It was geared toward programmers or was destined for a life running backroom computers, serving data, and making other computer resources available to users.

To this end, Linux continues to run a sizable proportion of the computers that make the Internet work, largely because it provides an ideal platform for the Apache web server, as well as various databases and web-based programming languages. This has lead to the LAMP acronym, which stands for Linux, Apache (a web server), MySQL (a database), and PHP, Python, or Perl (three programming languages that can be used in an online environment).

Despite its technical origins, recent years have seen a strong push for Linux on desktop computers. Linux has stepped out of the dark backrooms, with the goal of pushing aside Microsoft Windows and Mac OS in order to dominate the corporate workstation and home user market.

Running Linux on the desktop has always been possible, but the level of knowledge required was often prohibitively high, putting Linux out of the reach of most ordinary users. It's only comparatively recently that the companies behind the distributions of Linux have taken a long, hard look at Windows and attempted to mirror its user-friendly approach. In addition, the configuration software in distributions like Ubuntu has progressed in leaps and bounds. Now, it's no longer necessary to know arcane commands in order to do something as simple as switch the screen resolution. The situation has also been helped by the development of extremely powerful office software, such as OpenOffice.org and Koffice.

Is Linux for you? There's only one way of finding out, and that's to give it a go. Linux doesn't require much of you except an open mind and the will to learn new ways of doing things. You shouldn't see learning to use Linux as a chore. Instead, you should see it as an adventure—a way of finally getting the most from your PC and not having to worry about things going wrong for reasons outside your control.

Linux puts you in charge. You're the mechanic of the car as well as its driver, and you'll be expected to get your hands dirty every now and then. Unlike Windows, Linux doesn't hide any of its settings or stop you from doing things for your own protection; everything is available to tweak. Using Linux requires commitment and the realization that there are probably going to be problems, and they're going to need to be overcome.

However, using Linux should be enjoyable. In his initial newsgroup posting announcing Linux back in 1992, Linus Torvalds said that he was creating Linux "just for fun." This is what it should be for you.

Getting Hold of Linux

Getting hold of Linux is easy. You'll already have spotted the version of Ubuntu packaged with this book. Ubuntu is the main focus of this book, and I consider it to be one of the very best versions of Linux out there. It's ideal for both beginners and power users, and it really does match the functionality offered in Windows. It includes several easy-to-use configuration tools, which makes changing your system settings a breeze. For example, a tool known as the Synaptic Package Manager can automate the download and installation of new software with just a few clicks.

Ubuntu is also a very good-looking distribution. You'll find your friends and colleagues "wowing" when they happen to pass by and glance at your PC!

Quite a number of Linux distributions are available. If you want to explore other Linux distributions as well as Ubuntu, by far the most fuss-free method of getting hold of Linux is to pop over to your local computer store (or online retailer) and buy a boxed copy. You can choose from Red Hat, SUSE, Mandrake, Libranet, TurboLinux (if you want foreign language support, although nearly all commercial distributions do a good job of supporting mainstream languages), and many others. Many distributions come on more than a single CD—typically up to four CDs at the moment. Some versions of Linux come on DVD.

■**Caution** Bearing in mind what I've said about the sharing nature of Linux, you might think it possible to buy a boxed copy of Linux and run off copies for friends, or even sell them for a profit. However, you shouldn't assume this is the case. A minority of distribution companies, such as Xandros and Linspire, incorporate copyrighted corporate logos into their distributions that place restrictions on redistribution. Sometimes they include proprietary software along with the Linux tools, which you cannot copy without prior permission. However, in many cases, reproducing the CDs in small volumes for friends or for use on workstations in a company environment is permitted.

Many of the Linux distributions are also available to download free of charge. In fact, many community-run distributions—such as Slackware, Debian, Fedora, and Gentoo—are *only* available this way (although you can often buy "homemade" CDs from small retailers, who effectively burn the CDs for you and produce makeshift packaging). If your PC has a CD-R/RW drive and you have some CD-burning software under Windows (such as Nero), you can download an ISO image and make your own installation CD from it.

■**Note** An *ISO image* is a very large file (typically 700MB for a CD or 4.3GB for a DVD), which you can burn to CD or DVD. This CD or DVD is then used to install Linux.

Using Ubuntu

Ubuntu is a relatively young Linux distribution. It is based on and is still closely allied with the Debian distribution (www.debian.org), like many versions of Linux. Debian has been in existence since 1993—almost as long as the Linux kernel—and embraces the spirit and philosophy of Linux, which says software should be shared and made available to anyone who wants it.

Ubuntu takes this one step further. Its goal is to give anyone in the world access to an easy-to-use version of Linux, regardless of geographical location or physical abilities. Ubuntu supports a large number of languages, so it can be used in most countries around the world. In addition, it includes accessibility tools, so it can be used by partially sighted, deaf, or disabled people.

From the very start, Mark Shuttleworth, Ubuntu's creator, decided it would always be free of charge and would always be freely available. Unlike many versions of Linux, no commercial version of Ubuntu exists (although it is possible to pay for various services, such as support, if you wish).

But perhaps Ubuntu's greatest strength is its community, which extends across the world. If you have a question about Ubuntu, you'll find hundreds of people willing to help. Just as the software is designed to be shared, a strong belief within the Ubuntu community is that knowledge should be shared, too.

It might come as no surprise that *Ubuntu* is an ancient African word that roughly translates as "humanity to others." In Shuttleworth's native South Africa in particular, "Ubuntu" is a way of life that advocates acceptance and compassion toward others. The Ubuntu philosophy is one of the underpinnings of post-apartheid South Africa and spreads into political spheres as well as everyday life. The Ubuntu version of Linux is an attempt to bring this spirit to the world of computer software.

Ubuntu is primarily geared toward desktop users, although with a little adapting, it can also be used to run server computers.

Ubuntu is designed to be easy to use. Anyone who has used Windows or Mac OS will feel right at home. It features every piece of software you could wish for or would find within a well-equipped modern operating system. It includes a web browser, an e-mail client, instant messaging software, an office suite, a graphics editor, and much more. And don't think that these are cut-down versions designed to lure you into purchasing the full version later on. In every case, they're full-featured pieces of software that give proprietary programs a run for their money.

Perhaps more importantly, Ubuntu is very user-friendly. Updating the system can be done with just a few clicks of the mouse, as can downloading and installing new software.

Summary

This chapter explained what you can realistically expect when using Linux every day. It also discussed the kind of company you'll be keeping in terms of fellow users.

You learned how people usually get hold of Linux. Of course, with this book, you already have a version of Linux, Ubuntu, which was introduced in this chapter.

This completes the general overview of the world of Linux. In the next part of the book, you'll move on to actually installing Linux on your hard disk. This sounds more daunting than it actually is. The next chapter gets you started by explaining a few basic preinstallation steps.

PART 2

■■■

Installing Ubuntu

CHAPTER 4

■■■

Preinstallation Steps

The first part of this book discussed using Linux as part of your day-to-day life. It was intended to help you evaluate Linux and understand what you're buying into should you decide to make it your operating system of choice. Now we move on to actually installing Linux and, specifically, Ubuntu, which is included with this book on a DVD-ROM.

Installing any kind of operating system is a big move and can come as something of a shock to your PC. However, Ubuntu makes this complicated maneuver as easy as it's possible to be. Its installation routines are very advanced compared to previous versions of Linux, and even compared to other current distributions.

What does saying that you're going to install Ubuntu actually mean? This effectively implies three things:

- Somehow, all the files necessary to run Ubuntu are going to be put onto your hard disk.

- The PC will be configured so that it knows where to find these files when it first boots up.

- The Ubuntu operating system will be set up so that you can use it.

However, in order to do all this and get Ubuntu onto your PC, you must undertake some preparatory work, which is the focus of this chapter.

Understanding Partitioning

Chances are your PC already has Windows installed on it. This won't present a problem. In most cases, Ubuntu can live happily alongside Windows in what's called a *dual-boot setup*, where you can choose at startup which operating system to run. However, installing Ubuntu means that Windows must make certain compromises. Windows is forced to cohabit on your hard disk with another operating system—something it isn't designed to do.

The main issue with such a situation is that Windows needs to shrink and make some space available for Ubuntu (unless you install a second hard disk, which is discussed later in this chapter). Ubuntu isn't able to use the same file system as Windows, and it needs its own separately defined part of the disk, which is referred to as a *partition*. All of this can be handled automatically by the Ubuntu installation routine, but it's important that you know what happens.

All hard disks are split into partitions, which are large chunks of the disk created to hold operating systems (just like a large farm is partitioned into separate fields). A partition is usually multiple gigabytes in size, although it can be smaller.

■**Note** If you use a Macintosh then don't feel left out! In the next chapter I include a sidebar explaining the options for installing Ubuntu on your computer.

You can view your disk's partitions using the Disk Management tool in Windows XP, 2000, and Vista, as shown in Figure 4-1. You can access this tool by opening the Control Panel, switching to Classic View, clicking the Administrative Tools icon, selecting Computer Management, selecting Storage, and then choosing Disk Management.

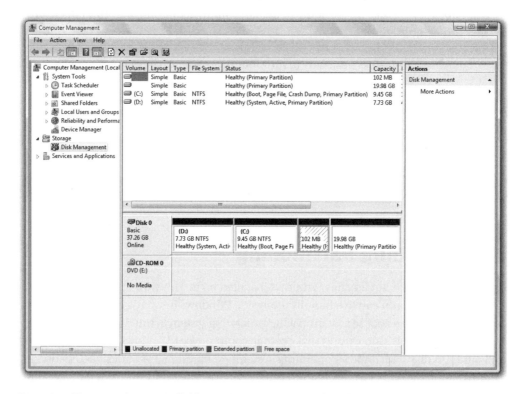

Figure 4-1. *You can view your disk's partitions using Windows's Disk Management tool.*

Most desktop PC systems have just one partition, unless the user has specifically created new partitions. As mentioned, Ubuntu needs a partition of its own. During installation, Ubuntu needs to shrink the main Windows partition and create a fresh partition alongside it (actually, it creates two partitions; the extra one is used to hold the swap file).

In addition, the Ubuntu installation routine writes a new boot sector (also known as a boot loader). The boot sector is located at the very beginning of the disk and contains a small program that then runs another program that lets you choose between operating systems (and therefore partitions) when you first boot up.

■**Note** Not all Linux distributions have the ability to repartition the hard disk. In fact, at the time of writing, it's pretty rare. Most expect to simply take over the entire hard disk, wiping Windows in the process (although they'll always ask the user to confirm this beforehand). The ability to repartition a disk is just one of the reasons that Ubuntu is among the best Linux distributions currently available.

Of course, Ubuntu cannot shrink a Windows partition that is packed full of data, because no space is available for it to reclaim.

UBUNTU AND WINDOWS FILE SYSTEMS

One of the benefits of dual-booting Linux and Windows is that Ubuntu lets you access the files on the Windows partition. This is quite handy and facilitates the easy exchange of data.

If the Windows partition is FAT32—used on Windows 95, 98, Me, and (sometimes) XP—then Ubuntu can both read and write files to the partition. However, if the file system is NTFS—used with Windows NT, 2000, XP, and Vista—Ubuntu will make the file system available as read-only.

Because of this, if you run Windows XP, you might consider converting your NTFS Windows partition to FAT32 before you install Ubuntu (but be aware that doing so means you lose some of the security and performance features of NTFS). Microsoft doesn't include a tool that lets you do this automatically, but you can use third-party disk partitioning programs like Norton's Partition Magic (www.powerquest.com) to convert your file system.

Freeing Up Space

The first step before installing Ubuntu alongside Windows is to check how much free space you have in your Windows partition. To see the amount of free space you have under Windows Vista, click the Start button, click Computer, and look at the bar graph next to your hard disk drive, as shown in Figure 4-2. With older versions of Windows, you should double-click My Computer, right-click your boot drive, and select Properties. The free space is usually indicated in purple on a pie chart.

In both cases, look for how much free space you have. In Windows Vista, this is the first figure underneath the bar graph.

You need to have at least 3GB of free space in your Windows partition for Ubuntu to use. You'll need more space if you wish to install a lot of programs. If you don't have enough free space, you have several options: reclaim space, remove Windows, or use a second hard disk.

Figure 4-2. *Ubuntu needs free disk space in which to install, so you might need to clean up your Windows partition.*

Reclaiming Space

In Windows Vista and XP, you can run the Disk Cleanup tool to free some space on your hard disk. Under Windows Vista, click Start ➤ Computer, and right-click the icon representing your hard disk. Select Properties from the menu that appears, and click the Disk Cleanup button. On Windows XP, click the Disk Cleanup button beneath the pie chart showing the free disk space. Disk Cleanup is also accessible by clicking Start ➤ All Programs ➤ Accessories ➤ System Tools ➤ Disk Cleanup.

You might also consider turning off System Restore. This consumes a lot of disk space, which you can therefore reclaim. However, deactivating System Restore will mean that you lose the possibility of returning your system to a previous state should anything go wrong. To access the System Restore under Vista, click the Start button, and then right-click Computer in the menu. Select Properties, and click the System Protection link on the left of the window that appears. Next, remove the check alongside the drives under the Available Disk list, confirm that you want to turn off System Restore, and click the OK button on the System Properties dialog box. Under Windows XP, right-click My Computer, click Properties, and then click the System Restore tab. Next, put a check alongside Turn Off System Restore on all Drives, and click OK.

If you still cannot free up enough disk space, consider uninstalling unused software via the Add/Remove Programs applet within Control Panel. If you have any large games installed, consider removing them first, because they usually take up substantial amounts of hard disk space. You might also consider deleting movie and MP3 music files, which are renowned for eating up hard disk space. The average MP3 is around 4MB, for example, and one minute of video typically takes up 1MB of disk space!

Removing Windows

Some users might prefer a second, more radical option: getting rid of Windows completely and letting Ubuntu take over the entire hard disk. If you feel confident that Ubuntu will fulfill your needs, this is undoubtedly the most straightforward solution. You'll be able to do this during installation. However, this will also mean that any personal data you have will be lost, so you should first back up your data (as described shortly).

Caution You should be aware that installing Windows back onto a hard disk that has Ubuntu on it is trouble-some. Windows has a Darwinian desire to wipe out the competition. If you attempt to install Windows on an Ubuntu hard disk, it will overwrite Linux.

Using Another Hard Disk

A third option for making room for Ubuntu is attractive and somewhat safer in terms of avoiding the potential for data loss, but also potentially expensive: fitting a second hard disk to your PC. You can then install Ubuntu on this other hard disk, letting it take up the entire disk. Unlike Windows, Ubuntu doesn't need to be installed on the primary hard disk and is happy on a secondary drive.

A second hard disk is perhaps the best solution if you're low on disk space and want to retain Windows on your system. However, you'll need to know how to install the new drive or find someone to do it for you (although step-by-step guides can be found on the Web—just search using Google or another search engine). In addition, if your PC is less than 12 months old, there is a possibility that you'll invalidate your warranty by opening up your PC.

If you have an old PC lying around, you might also consider installing Ubuntu on it, at least until you're sure that you want to run it on your main PC.

VIRTUALIZATION

If you don't want to repartition your disk or add another disk drive, there's another way you can run Ubuntu under Windows: using virtualization software.

Put simply, virtualization software lets you run a "computer within a computer" (or, in fact, several computers within a computer!). It does this by cleverly sharing system resources between the real computer and the one that's being virtualized.

When the virtualization software is run, the virtual computer appears in a program window. A BIOS-like startup screen appears, just like on a real computer, and then the virtual hard disk (usually a file on the main hard disk) is booted. An operating system may then be installed onto the virtual hard disk or, alternatively, it's possible to download entire virtual machines from various sites, for which the hard work of installing the operating system has been done for you!

There are a wide variety of virtualization software packages available. Perhaps the most popular are those offered by VMWare, including VMWare Server and VMWare Player. Although proprietary software, both of these two products are entirely free of charge and can be downloaded from www.vmware.com. Another version of VMWare, called Workstation, which is available for a charge, is also highly praised by many. You might investigate Microsoft Virtual PC 2004 too, which is also free of charge and can be downloaded from www.microsoft.com/windows/virtualpc/default.mspx.

You can also obtain open-source renditions of virtualization software, such as QEMU (http://fabrice.bellard.free.fr/qemu), although also worth downloading is QEMU Manager, which provides a GUI-based configuration front end for QEMU: see www.davereyn.co.uk/download.htm.

Using a virtualized computer is useful for testing software but, obviously, the experience isn't seamless. Operating systems running within virtual computers tend to operate more slowly compared to running natively on a computer, and the virtualized hardware is often very simple (you are usually unable to access your computer's 3D graphics hardware, for example). Setting up a virtual computer can also be difficult for those who are new to it.

One final note: virtualization software doesn't just run on Windows. You can download several virtualization software packages for Ubuntu, which means you could install and run Windows within a virtual machine running on Ubuntu! QEMU, mentioned previously, runs on Ubuntu, as does Xen: www.xensource.com/products/downloads.

Backing Up Your Data

Whichever route you decide to take when installing Ubuntu, you should back up the data currently on your computer beforehand. Possibly the easiest way of doing this is to burn the data to CD-R/RW discs using a program like Nero and a CD-R/RW or DVD+-R/RW drive.

If you take the coexistence route, installing Ubuntu alongside Windows, backing up your data should be done for insurance purposes. Although the people behind Ubuntu test all their software thoroughly and rely on community reporting of bugs, there's always the chance that something will go wrong. Repartitioning a hard disk is a major operation and carries with it the potential for data loss.

If you intend to erase the hard disk when installing Ubuntu (thereby removing Windows), you can back up your data and then import it into Ubuntu.

Table 4-1 shows a list of common personal data file types, their file extensions, where they can be typically found on a Windows system, and notes on importing the data into Ubuntu. Note that earlier versions of Windows (95, 98, and Me) may differ when it comes to data storage locations.

Table 4-1. *Data That Should Be Backed Up*

Type of File	File Extensions	Typical Location (Vista)	Typical Location (XP)	Notes
Office files	`.doc`, `.xls`, `.ppt`, `.pdf`, etc.	`\Users\`*`<username>`*`\ Documents`	`\Documents and Settings\` *`<username>`*`\ My Documents`	Microsoft Office files can be opened, edited, and saved under Ubuntu using the `OpenOffice.org` suite. PDF documents can be viewed with the Evince program.
E-mail files	N/A	N/A	N/A	The Evolution mail client used by Ubuntu cannot import data directly from Microsoft Outlook or Outlook Express. However, there is a convoluted but effective workaround, which is described in the next section.
Digital images	`.jpg`, `.bmp`, `.tif`, `.png`, `.gif`, etc.	`\Users\`*`<username>`*`\ Documents\Pictures`	`\Documents and Settings\` *`<username>`*`\ My Pictures`	Ubuntu includes a variety of programs to both view and edit image files.
Multimedia files	`.mp3`, `.mpg`, `.avi`, `.wma`, etc.	Various within `Documents`	Various within `My Documents`	With some additional downloads, discussed in Chapter 18, programs under Ubuntu can play MP3 music files and most movie file formats.

Table 4-1. *Data That Should Be Backed Up (Continued)*

Type of File	File Extensions	Typical Location (Vista)	Typical Location (XP)	Notes
Internet Explorer Favorites	None	\Users*<username>*\ Favorites	\Documents and Settings\ *<username>*\ Favorites	Your Favorites list cannot be imported into Ubuntu, but the individual files can be opened in a text editor in order to view their URLs, which can then be opened in the Ubuntu web browser.
Mozilla Firefox Bookmarks	.html	N/A	N/A	If you use Mozilla Firefox under Windows, you can manually export your bookmarks for import under Firefox when Ubuntu is installed. Click Bookmarks ➤ Organize bookmarks, and click File ➤ Export in the window that appears. To import the bookmarks into Ubuntu's version of Firefox, repeat the steps, but click File ➤ Import instead, and then locate the .html file you saved.
Miscellaneous Internet files	Various	Various	Various	You might also want to back up web site archives or instant messenger chat logs, although hidden data such as cookies cannot be imported.

Backing Up E-Mail Files

Microsoft e-mail cannot be easily imported into Ubuntu. Most e-mail programs use the MBOX format, and this is true of Ubuntu as well as programs created by the Mozilla Foundation (the organization behind the Firefox web browser). However, Microsoft uses its own DBX file format for Outlook Express and PST format for Outlook.

As a workaround, you can download and install the free Mozilla Thunderbird e-mail client (available from www.mozilla.com/en-US/thunderbird) on your Windows system. In Thunderbird, select Tools ➤ Import to import your messages from Outlook, Outlook Express, or even the popular Eudora mail client. You will then be able to back up Thunderbird's mail files and import them into Evolution under Ubuntu, as described in Chapter 27.

To find where the mail files are stored, in Thunderbird, select Tools ➤ Account Settings, and then look in the Local Directory box. Back up each file that corresponds to a folder within your mail program (for example, Inbox, Sent, and so on). Note that you only need to back up the files *without* file extensions. You can ignore the `.sdb` folders as well as the `.msf` files.

■Tip To quickly go to the location of the Thunderbird e-mail files under Windows, copy the address in the Local Directory text box. Then, under Windows XP, click Start ➤ Run, paste the address straight into the Open box, and click OK. Under Windows Vista, paste the address into the Start Search text box, and press Enter.

Making Notes

When you're backing up data, a pencil and paper come in handy, too. You should write down any important usernames and passwords, such as those for your e-mail account and other online services. You might want to write down the phone number of your dial-up connection, for example, or your DSL/cable modem technical settings. Figure 4-3 shows an example of some information you might want to record.

In addition, don't forget to jot down essential technical details, such as your IP address if you are part of a network of computers using static addresses (this will usually be relevant only if you work in an office environment).

■Tip If you've forgotten any passwords, several freeware/shareware applications are able to "decode" the asterisks that obscure Windows passwords and show what's beneath them. A good example is Asterisk Password Reveal, which you can download from `www.paqtool.com/product/pass/pass_001.htm`. Shareware sites like `www.download.com` offer similar applications.

Note that you don't need to write down information such as hardware interrupt (IRQ) or memory addresses, because hardware is configured automatically by Ubuntu. However, it might be worth making a note of the make and model of some items of internal hardware, such as your graphics card, modem (dial-up, DSL, or cable), and sound card. This will help if Ubuntu is unable to automatically detect your hardware, although such a situation is fairly unlikely to arise. Under Windows Vista, you can find out this information by clicking the Start button and right-clicking Computer. Click Properties in the menu that appears, and click the Device Manager link on the left of the window that appears. Under Windows XP, right-click My Computer on the desktop (or on your Start menu), select Properties, and click the Hardware tab. Then click the Device Manager button.

Instead of writing everything down, you might consider taking a screenshot by pressing the Print Scr button and using your favorite image editor to print it.

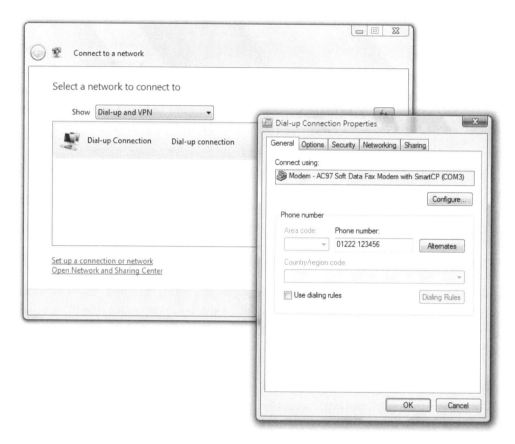

Figure 4-3. *Don't forget to back up "hidden" data, such as ISP dial-up phone numbers.*

■**Tip** Ubuntu works with a wide variety of hardware, and in most cases, it will automatically detect your system components. If you're in any doubt, you can consult the forums at http://ubuntuforums.org, in particular, the Hardware Help forums under the Main Support Categories heading. You might also consider subscribing to one or more of the Ubuntu mailing lists at https://lists.ubuntu.com. Remember that an important element of Ubuntu is its community of users, many of whom will be very willing to answer any questions you might have!

Once you're certain that all your data is backed up, you can move on to the next chapter, which provides a step-by-step guide to installing the operating system.

Summary

The aim of this chapter has been to prepare both you and your computer for the installation of Ubuntu. We've looked at how your hard disk will be partitioned prior to installation and the preparations you should make to ensure your hard disk has sufficient free space. You also learned about the types of files you might choose to back up, in addition to vital details you should record, such as usernames and passwords for your online accounts.

In the next chapter, we move on to a full description of the Ubuntu installation procedure. The chapter guides you through getting Ubuntu onto your computer.

CHAPTER 5

■■■

Installing Ubuntu

I t's now time to install Ubuntu. This is a surprisingly quick task and shouldn't take more than 30 minutes on a modern PC. It's also relatively simple, with very few decisions to make throughout. Ubuntu's installation program automates the task to a high degree.

However, you should examine all the options you're offered to make sure they're correct. Installing an operating system involves a couple of serious maneuvers that, via an incorrect click of the mouse or accidental keystroke, bring with them the possibility of data loss. Read and consider every warning message you see, and be sure to keep your wits about you. Above all, make a backup of your data, as described in the previous chapter.

An Overview of the Installation Process

The DVD-ROM disc supplied with this book is double-sided. This means it's like a vinyl LP record. To play side A, simply insert the disc with the Side A label topmost (the label is located around the hole in the middle). To play side B, insert the disc with the Side B label topmost.

Side A contains Ubuntu 6.10, codename Edgy Eft. This is the most recent version of Ubuntu at the time of writing. Side B contains the previous version of Ubuntu—6.06.1 LTS, codename Dapper Drake. There are some advantages to using this older version if you're a business user, and I explain what these are in Appendix D.

However, most will want to install the most recent version of Ubuntu, so to start things rolling, insert Side A of the DVD-ROM drive and boot your computer. You might have to set your BIOS to boot from DVD, as I explain in the second step of the guide later in this chapter.

If you've ever installed Windows from scratch on a computer, you might be used to working with the Windows installation program. This appears when you boot from a Windows CD or DVD or run the `setup.exe` program from the desktop, and it guides you through installing Windows onto your hard disk.

Ubuntu is a little different. Once you've inserted the DVD-ROM, it will boot straight to the Ubuntu desktop, and the entire operating system will run from the DVD-ROM. You can then choose to install Ubuntu or, if you wish, simply try it out. If you choose the latter, most programs will still be fully functional.

Using Ubuntu without installing it to the hard disk is known as running in *live distro mode*. Although this is a great way to take a sneak peak at what Ubuntu offers, there are a handful of practical drawbacks, which I discuss in the sidebar titled "Running in Live Distro Mode."

To install Ubuntu to your computer, double-click the Install icon on the Ubuntu desktop. This will run the dedicated installation program, which will work through a few stages to get Linux on your computer's hard disk; during the installation stages, you'll be asked a handful of essential questions. You'll then be prompted to repartition your hard disk in order to create space for Ubuntu. After this, Ubuntu is installed onto your hard disk.

At the end of the procedure, your PC will boot straight into the Ubuntu login screen, and you're set to go. There's no need to mess around configuring hardware, because that's done automatically. Neat, eh?

In most cases, the installation process will run smoothly without a hitch. But if you do run into problems, head over to Chapter 6, which addresses many of the most-common issues and provides solutions.

RUNNING IN LIVE DISTRO MODE

If you don't want to install Ubuntu just yet, you can try it out by booting the operating system straight from the DVD supplied with this book. To do this, simply insert the DVD-ROM, and then reboot your computer. Make sure the computer is set to boot from DVD (see stage 2 of the installation guide in this chapter to learn how), and after a few moments, the Ubuntu desktop will appear. You can follow most of the chapters in this book when running in live distro mode. However, there a number of issues you should be aware of:

- **Settings:** Any changes you make to the system will be forgotten as soon as you shut down your PC or reboot. In other words, each time you run in live distro mode, it will be as if Ubuntu has been freshly installed. For example, if you've configured a network card or rearranged the desktop, those changes will be lost. There are ways around losing settings on each reboot, but they involve partitioning your hard disk, which, frankly, is as much effort as installing Ubuntu from scratch. So there's little to be gained by doing so.

- **Performance:** Because the data must be read from DVD-ROM, running Ubuntu in live distro mode is a slow and, therefore, frustrating experience. It can also be noisy if your DVD-ROM is a model that makes a whirring noise as it spins.

- **System:** As strange as it sounds, Ubuntu is largely unaware of when it's running in live distro mode. For example, if you were to follow the instructions in Chapter 9, which discuss how to update your system, Ubuntu will attempt to update, even though it's running in live distro mode! Of course, it can't do this, because, as far as it is concerned, the DVD-ROM is the hard disk, and it's therefore impossible to write data to it. This can create confusing error messages.

- **Root:** When running in live distro mode, you're automatically given root-user powers. I explain the significance of this in Chapter 7, but for the moment, it's enough to know that the root user has unlimited power over the system. This means that you could repartition the hard disk, for example, or even wipe the hard disk entirely, all without any password prompt or warning. This can be useful in certain circumstances—you can attempt to "rescue" a hard disk that's having problems using the live distro mode of the Ubuntu disc. But using it for everyday tasks is a huge risk, and the potential for accidental damage is high.

In short, I would recommend that you use live distro mode sparingly and only to get a taste of what Ubuntu is like. If you intend to use Ubuntu for any significant period of time, you should install it to your hard disk.

Step-by-Step Guide

As outlined in Chapter 4, you shouldn't start the installation process until you've made sure there is enough space for Ubuntu on your hard disk and you have backed up all the data. With those preparations complete, you're ready to install Ubuntu. The remainder of this chapter guides you through the process.

Stage 1: Prepare the Windows Partition for Resizing

If you're installing Ubuntu on a computer that already contains Windows, it's a good idea to perform three additional steps before actually installing Ubuntu. These steps will ensure Ubuntu will be able to resize the Windows partition successfully.

If your computer doesn't contain Windows, or if you're installing Ubuntu onto a second hard disk, then you can skip straight to stage 2.

The steps that should be carried out follow:

1. Scan the disk for errors.

2. Defragment the hard disk.

3. Ensure Windows is shut down correctly.

To scan the disk, open My Computer (or Computer if you're running Windows Vista), and right-click your Windows drive (usually C:\). Select Properties; in the window that appears, click the Tools tab, and click the Check Now button under the Error Checking heading. Ensure there's a check alongside Automatically Fix File System Errors, as shown in Figure 5-1, and click the Start button. You will then be prompted to schedule the disk check the next time your computer restarts. Select to do so, and reboot your computer, so the disk check can take place.

When the computer has rebooted, repeat the previous steps to view the Tools tab of the drive's Properties dialog box, and click the Defragment Now button. Then work through the defragmentation program's options in order to defragment the Windows disk (usually this involves simply clicking the Defragment button; this button is labeled Defragment Now under Windows Vista).

Once that has completed—it make take several hours if your computer has not been defragmented before—shut down the computer as usual, and proceed to stage 2 of the installation process.

It's vital that the computer shuts itself down properly. If the computer doesn't cleanly shut down, then Ubuntu's installation program might stop with an error message about not being able to resize the partition.

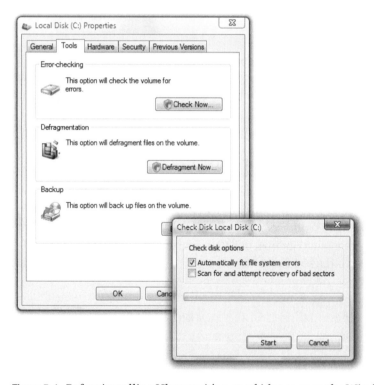

Figure 5-1. *Before installing Ubuntu, it's a good idea to scan the Windows partition for errors and to defragment it.*

Stage 2: Boot from the DVD-ROM

With your computer booted up, insert the Ubuntu disc into the DVD-ROM drive, with Side A topmost. Close the tray, and reboot your computer. The disc will automatically run, opening a browser window with some details about Ubuntu, but you can ignore this.

Because we need to boot from the DVD-ROM disc in order to run the Ubuntu installer, the first step is to make sure your computer's BIOS is set correctly.

Many modern computers let you press a particular key during the initial boot phase of your computer, during the memory testing and drive identification period, to make a boot menu appear. On the boot menu, you can choose to boot from the CD- or DVD-ROM drive from the list. On my test PC and on my notebook computer, hitting the Esc key causes this menu to appear, but your computer may be different. Your computer's boot screen should indicate which key to press.

If you do not have an option to boot from the CD/DVD drive, you'll need to enter the BIOS setup program and change the boot priority of your computer. To do this, press the Delete key just after the computer is first activated. Again, some computers use another key or key combination, and your boot screen should indicate which key to press.

When the BIOS menu appears, look for a menu option such as Boot and select it (you can usually navigate around the screen of the BIOS menu using the cursor keys and select options by pressing Enter). On the new menu, look for a separate entry such as Boot Device Priority or perhaps Boot Sequence. Make sure that the entry for the CD/DVD-ROM is at the top of the list, as shown in the example in Figure 5-2. Arrange the list so that CD/DVD-ROM is followed by the floppy drive and then your main hard disk (which will probably be identified as "IDE-0" or "First hard disk"). You can usually press the F1 key for help on how the menu selection system works.

Once you've made the changes, be sure to select the Exit Saving Changes option. Your PC will then reset and boot from the Ubuntu DVD-ROM, and you'll be greeted by the Ubuntu DVD boot menu.

■**Note** After Ubuntu has been installed on your computer, you might choose to repeat this step and rearrange the boot order once more to make the hard disk appear at the top of the list. Then your computer won't waste time checking the DVD-ROM drive for a boot disc every time it starts.

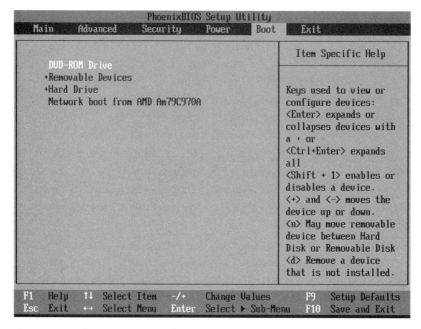

Figure 5-2. *Before starting, make sure your computer can boot the CD-ROM.*

Stage 3: Select from the Boot Menu

When the DVD-ROM boot menu appears, you'll be offered a number of options. You should select the first—"Start or install Ubuntu 6.10," as shown in Figure 5-3.

The other options are designed for problem-solving purposes, and you can move between them using the up and down arrow keys. The second option—"Start Ubuntu in safe graphics mode"—will start Ubuntu using graphics drivers that are known to be widely compatible with most computers. You should use this mode if you experience graphical glitches.

The third option—"Memory test"—will start a simple but thorough memory testing program called Memtest86. This is useful if you think your computer's memory might have a fault that means it can't install Ubuntu. For more details about how to use Memtest86, see www.memtest86.com. To quit Memtest86 once it's running and reboot your computer, press Esc.

The fourth option—"Boot from first hard disk"—will cause the computer to boot from the default hard disk, thereby bypassing Ubuntu. If your computer has Windows installed on it, this will mean Windows is booted.

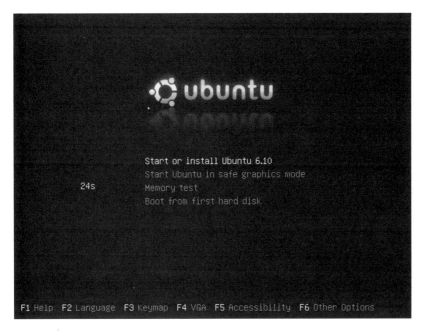

Figure 5-3. *Select "Start or install Ubuntu," and press Enter.*

Stage 4: Start the Install Program

After some time, the Ubuntu desktop will appear. At this stage, you can audition the Ubuntu software and play around, but to install Ubuntu, double-click the Install icon on the desktop, shown in Figure 5-4.

■**Caution** Generally speaking, damaging your computer at this stage requires determined effort, and most of the Ubuntu software packages are safe to use. But, if you do decide to audition Ubuntu prior to installation, steer clear of using the GNOME Partition Editor program on the System ➤ Administration menu. This is a disk repartitioning program and has the power to wipe your hard disk!

Figure 5-4. *Double-click the Install icon on the Ubuntu desktop to start the installation program.*

Stage 5: Select Your Language

One of the design goals of Ubuntu is to be usable by just about anyone in the world. Ubuntu supports a massive list of languages, and the first step in the installation routine is to select one, as shown in Figure 5-5. It offers many eastern and western European languages, as well as Asian languages. The default is English.

Once you've made the choice, click the Forward button.

Figure 5-5. *Choose your language, and then click the Forward button.*

Stage 6: Select Your Country and Time Zone

Ubuntu will next ask you to choose your time zone. Choices include American time zones, such as Eastern Standard Time (EST), and European/Asian time zones, such as Greenwich Mean Time (GMT). The selection can be made either by clicking your location on the world map that's displayed or by selecting the nearest city from the Selected City dropdown list.

When you click the map, you should find that it zooms in; clicking anywhere within the mainland United States, for example, should enlarge the continent, allowing for more-accurate selection. See Figure 5-6 for an example.

Regardless of where you live, you should see dots on the map representing major cities in your locality. Click the one closest to you that's in the same time zone. In some cases, the choice is limited—those in the UK can only click London, for example!

■Note Actually, this isn't quite true. Look closely and you'll see that, in addition to London, you can also click on the Isle of Man, a small island off the northwest coast of England. Why is such attention paid to this location? Well, it so happens that this is where the registered offices of Canonical, the company behind Ubuntu, are located!

The city you choose doesn't matter a great deal—the purpose of this step is to ensure Ubuntu selects the correct time zone for your location, which it does by looking up the city in a database of time zones.

Once the time zone is selected, you should see the correct time in the Current Time section of the window. If the time is incorrect, you can click the Set Time button to change it. However, you should only do this if your PC's hardware clock is incorrectly set. Don't do this if the time was previously correct under Windows but you now find the hourly offset is wrong—if that's the case, then clearly you haven't selected the correct city location.

When you've made your selection, click the Forward button.

Figure 5-6. *When you click on the time zone map, you should find it zooms in and allows for easier selection of the nearest city to your location.*

Stage 7: Confirm Your Keyboard Layout

Next, you'll be asked to confirm the keyboard layout you'll be using. This should correspond to your language and locale settings and will be automatically selected, so you can just click the Forward button.

Note Keyboard layouts can differ from country to country even if they speak the same language. This is to allow for local necessities. The UK keyboard layout has the pound sterling symbol (£) above the number 3, for example, and swaps around the locations of a handful of other symbols too.

If you're unsure whether Ubuntu has guessed the correct keyboard layout, you can click the test text field and type some characters, as shown in Figure 5-7. Once done, click the Forward button.

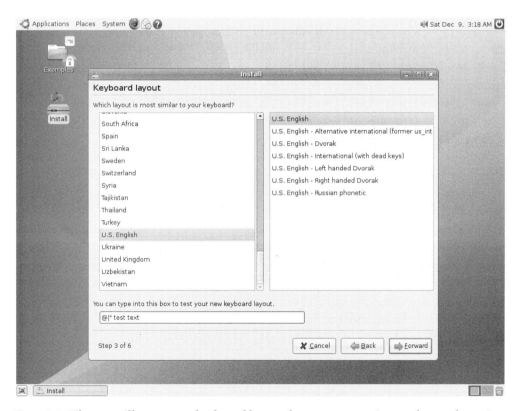

Figure 5-7. *Ubuntu will guess your keyboard layout, but you can test it to make sure by typing in the test text field at the bottom left of the dialog box.*

Stage 8: Enter a Username

Next, you'll be prompted to enter your real name and your username. The *real name* is how you'll be formally identified on the system to anyone who uses the system and should be typed into the first text field headed "What Is Your Name?" The standard practice is to use your full name, including first and last names, separated by a space.

The *username* is how the computer itself will identify you, and this should be typed into the second text field headed "What Name Do You Want to Use To Log In?" This needs to be unique—two users on the same computer cannot have the same username.

There are rules about which characters you can use for the username. It should be one word without any spaces in it. You can choose any username consisting of uppercase and lowercase letters and numbers, but not symbols and punctuation. Additionally, the username cannot begin with an uppercase letter, although you can use uppercase in the rest of the username.

The simplest procedure for choosing a username is to use your own first name, typed entirely in lowercase letters. For example, I typed my real name as **Keir Thomas** and chose **keir** as my username, as shown in Figure 5-8.

Following this, you'll be asked to enter a password. Here, the rules are the inverse of those for your username. A good password contains numbers, uppercase and lowercase letters, punctuation marks, and anything else you can get in there! This helps make your password almost impossible for someone else to guess, and thus makes your system more secure. (If you want to be *really* secure, create a password that's ten or more characters long.) You'll need to enter the password twice; the second time confirms that you didn't make a typo the first time around.

You can also set a hostname for the computer, which is how the computer is identified on certain types of networks, if you choose to share files or resources with other computers. It is also the name that will appear at the front of the command-line prompt, as described in Part 4 of this book.

Ubuntu will fill in this field automatically based on your username, but you can choose to type something else more personal. For example, if your computer is a Dell PC, then you might type **Office_Dell** (note that you can use an underscore character in place of a space character). The rules for the hostname are broadly similar to those for the username—you should type something without spaces or symbols.

Once you're finished, click the Forward button.

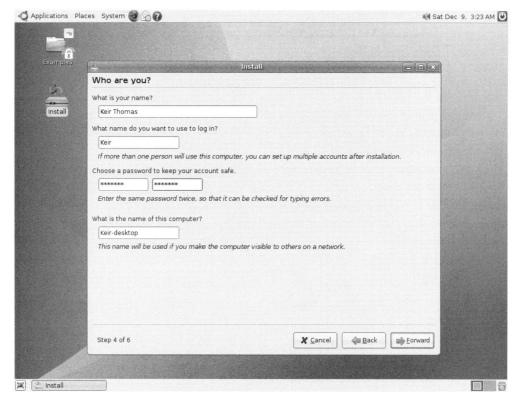

Figure 5-8. *You should enter a real name, a username, a password and, if you wish, a name to give your computer.*

Stage 9: Repartition Your Hard Disk

Partitioning the disk is one of the most important steps during installation, although, unfortunately, it's one that can be couched in difficult terminology. Ubuntu does its best to make partitioning easy.

The Ubuntu installation routine offers up to six options when it comes to disk partitioning:

1. Use the entire disk, if there is nothing else installed therein (that is, if the computer or hard disk is new).

2. Erase the existing partition(s), and use the entire hard disk.

3. Resize the existing Windows partition on the hard disk, and install Ubuntu alongside it in the newly created free space.

4. Use any free space that might already exist on the hard disk (perhaps if you've already manually repartitioned the disk earlier).

5. Manually edit the partition table, that is, resize/delete any existing partitons by hand and create the Ubuntu partitions.

6. Perform any of the previous options on a second hard disk that you have installed in your computer, leaving the first hard disk untouched.

For most people who are installing Ubuntu on a computer that already has Windows on it, the third option is the one they want, and they can skip straight to the "Resizing the Main Partition" subheading.

If you're installing Ubuntu on a computer that has no operating system installed or has one that you'd like to completely erase from the computer, you should skip to the "Erasing Entire Disk" subheading. Although the hard disk is empty, and therefore nothing will actually be erased, Ubuntu still refers to it as "erasing the disk."

Resize the Main Partition

This is the default partitioning option if your computer already has Windows installed on it. Ubuntu will detect the main Windows partition and suggest the amount by which it must be resized.

Caution Remember what I said in Chapter 4—if there's not enough free space within the Windows partition, you won't be able to resize it to make space for Ubuntu. If this is the case, then the Ubuntu installer will tell you.

You can alter the degree of resizing by clicking and dragging the New Partition Size slider. By default, Ubuntu attempts to divide the space equally between the existing partition and what its needs for itself, so you should find the slider approximately halfway along. On my test system, the slider was set at 69 percent, as shown in Figure 5-9. This means that the existing partition would be shrunk to 69 percent of its previous size. However, you can drag the slider to the left to shrink the existing partition even further, or drag it to the right to decrease the amount of free space created for Ubuntu. The Ubuntu installer is intelligent enough not to let you set an impossible value for shrinking the existing partition. On my test system, I couldn't set a size for the existing partition lower than 39 percent, because the existing data on the partition occupied around 39 percent of the space.

Note Actually, the Ubuntu installer is even more clever than that. It knows that Windows needs some free space within its partition to operate effectively—to write temporary and system files, for example, or user-created files such as Word documents. The 39 percent on my test system wasn't just data but also this allocation of free space. You can override this protection by manually partitioning, as described later in this chapter.

In a similar way, the installer wouldn't let me create an inadequate amount of free space for Ubuntu when dragging the slider to the right. The amount of free space Ubuntu demands varies, depending on the quantity of physical RAM installed in your computer.

Note Bear in mind that the gigabyte figure quoted above the slider is the new size of the existing partition, and *not* the size of the new Ubuntu partition.

Once you've made your selection, click the Forward button. The resizing of the partition will then take place. You should wait for this to complete; it might take a few moments.

Caution If you're resizing a partition on a notebook computer, ensure that you have the main power connected. If the power goes off during the resizing procedure because of a failing battery, there's a very good chance your Windows partition will be destroyed.

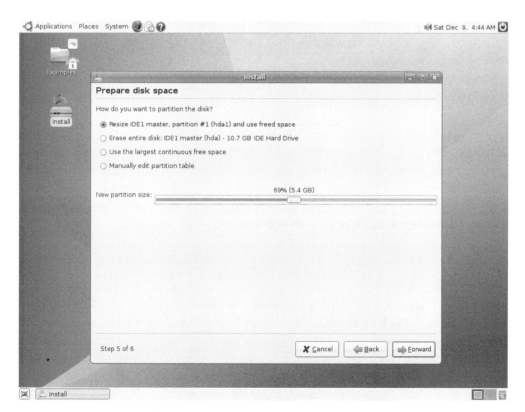

Figure 5-9. *You can resize the existing partition on the hard disk by clicking and dragging the New Partition Size slider.*

Erase the Entire Disk

If the hard disk is empty, or if you've decided to eradicate Windows and use only Ubuntu on your computer, you can choose the Erase Entire Disk option. Even though the hard disk might be entirely new and devoid of contents, Ubuntu still refers to it as erasing.

If the disk does have contents, this option will remove them and then use the entire disk to install Ubuntu. As mentioned in Chapter 4, before undertaking this move, you should back up essential data on the Windows partition (or any others on the hard disk). There is no way of undoing the partition erasure, so you should proceed with caution.

Once you've made the choice, click the Forward button. The deletion should take place quickly, after which you can proceed straight to the next stage in this guide.

Use Existing Free Space

If you've already repartitioned your hard disk using a third-party utility, or if you deliberately created a smaller Windows partition in order to leave free space for another operating system, then you can select the option headed Use the Largest Continuous Free Space. This will cause the Ubuntu installation program to utilize the *largest amount of free space* for the Ubuntu partitions. This is an important point—if you have more than one area of free space, the largest will be used. The Ubuntu installation routine is unable to automatically utilize any smaller amounts of free space, and if you wish this to be the case, the only option is to manually partition, as described later. However, only advanced users will need to make use of this.

When you've made your choice, click the Forward button, and proceed to the next stage in this guide.

■**Caution** Unfortunately, in my tests, it appeared the partitioning tool wasn't able to correctly evaluate smaller quantities of free space. On one occasion, the installation program detected a very small amount of free space (around 100MB or so) and assumed it was enough to install Ubuntu into, despite the fact that it was 2.9GB too small! This caused the installation program to quit with an error message later on. However, if there is enough free space, then everything works correctly.

Use a Second Hard Disk

If there is more than one hard disk within your computer—perhaps if you've installed a second hard disk on which to install Ubuntu, as described in Chapter 4, or if you simply wish to utilize a second hard disk already installed in your computer—you'll be asked to select which disk you'd like to use when the partitioning component of the Ubuntu installer starts, as shown in Figure 5-10. The way Ubuntu identifies your hard disks might seem a little complicated at first but is actually straightforward.

Figure 5-10. *If there's more than one hard disk installed, you'll be prompted to choose between them when the partitioning tool starts.*

If your computer uses IDE-based hard disks, the drives will be identified as /dev/hda, /dev/hdb, and so on. Look at the last letter in each case—the primary master drive in the system is identified as hda, the primary slave as hdb, the secondary master as hdc, and so on. See Table 5-1 for more details. The drive will also be identified by make and model, which may help you identify it.

Assuming the second hard disk is installed as a slave on the primary channel, as is the standard configuration for an additional hard disk, it will be identified as /dev/hdb, so make that selection. If the disk is installed as the slave on the *secondary* channel (that is, the same channel as the DVD-ROM drive), it will be identified as /dev/hdd.

Table 5-1. *IDE Hard Disk Identifiers*

Identifier	Hardware Description	Notes
/dev/hda	Primary master	The main hard disk in the computer and the one that is booted by default.
/dev/hdb	Primary slave	A hard disk connected to the same IDE cable as the main hard disk. On some budget computers, the CD/DVD drive is connected to the primary slave.
/dev/hdc	Secondary master	Usually, this is the CD/DVD drive.
/dev/hdd	Secondary slave	A hard disk connected to the same IDE cable as the CD/DVD drive.

If your computer uses SATA hard disks, they will be identified as /dev/sda, /dev/sdb, /dev/sdc, and so on. Therefore, a second hard disk will most likely be identified as /dev/sdb, and you should make that selection.

Once the disk selection has been made, click the Forward button. You will then be faced with the same choices as mentioned previously—to either resize an existing partition, if one exists on the disk, or use the entire disk in order to install Ubuntu.

■**Caution** After clicking the Forward button, if you're given the option of resizing a partition, but you anticipated that the disk would be completely empty, then you've probably chosen the wrong disk. Click the Back button, and try again.

Manually Edit the Partitioning Table

If, for any reason, you find that Ubuntu's default partitioning choices are not for you, you can opt to manually edit the partition table.

There are essentially two stages to work through if you choose this option:

1. You're given the chance to repartition the disk manually, using a utility called GParted. Using this tool, you can resize or delete any existing partitions and create the partitions Ubuntu needs.

2. After partitioning has taken place, you'll be asked to assign *mount points*—you'll be prompted to tell Ubuntu which of the partitions on the disk it should use for the *root file system* (that is, the main partition for Ubuntu's use), and which should be used for the *swap partition.*

Manually partitioning offers ultimate flexibility but requires a relatively high level of knowledge of how Ubuntu works. Therefore, I would recommend that only experts undertake this step, unless you have no other choice, because the default Ubuntu partitioning choices do not offer what you need or do not work properly for you.

In the following steps, I explain how to resize an existing partition, create the new partitions that Ubuntu needs, and assign mount points so that Ubuntu is able to utilize them.

1. When the disk partitioning choices appear, select Manually Edit Partition Table, and click Forward.

2. This will start the GParted utility. If you've used a third-party disk partitioning utility under Windows, such as Partition Magic, this utility may look familiar. At the top of the window is a graphical representation of the partition(s) on your hard disk, and beneath that is a table describing each partition. Right-clicking a partition, either in the graphical display or in the list, will reveal a variety of options. You want to resize the main NTFS (Windows) partition, so right-click its entry in the list, and select Resize/Move, as shown in Figure 5-11.

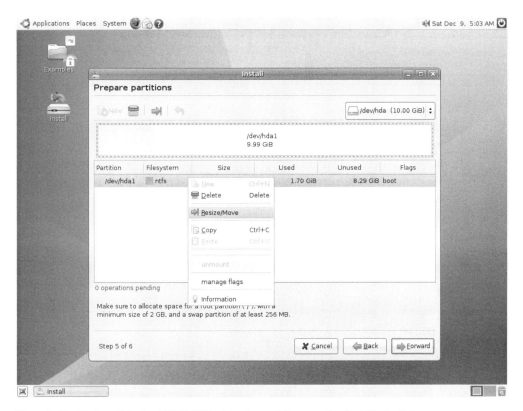

Figure 5-11. *Right-click the NTFS (Windows) partition, and select Resize/Move.*

3. The Resize dialog box will appear. Here you can resize the partition either by typing a new value into the New Size (MiB) box (press Enter afterwards), or by clicking and

dragging the right-hand edge of the partition, which is marked with a right-facing arrow. The new size of the partition will be listed in the New Size box.

■**Note** The figures quoted within GParted are actually MiB, which stands for *mebibytes.* This is a more precise description of what most of us refer to as a megabyte. A mebibyte refers specifically to 1024KB, whereas a megabyte can refer to either 1024KB or 1000KB, depending on the context. However, there's no need for you to worry about this distinction. In this chapter, the terms MB and MiB are interchangeable, and 1MB = 1024KB.

Within the graphical display of the partition, the yellow block represents data, and the white block represents free space. For obvious reasons, you will not be able to resize the partition beyond the yellow block.

■**Caution** Remember to leave some free space after the data, so that Windows can save temporary data and operate effectively.

You should free up as much space as possible for Ubuntu, but I would advise you create at least 2.5GB (2560MB) for the main partition (known as the *root* partition), plus some additional space for the swap partition, the size of which is defined by the quantity of RAM in your computer. Working out the total free space you need to create can be confusing, but in Table 5-2, I've listed the *minimum* amount of total free space you should create.

Table 5-2. *Minimum Quantities of Free Space for Typical Systems*

Physical RAM Size	Minimum Free Space You Should Create (MiB)
512MB	3072
1GB (1024MB)	3584
1.5GB (1536MB)	4096
2GB (2048MB)	4608

■**Caution** Remember that in the context of RAM, one gigabyte is 1024 megabytes, *not* 1000 megabytes.

For example, if your computer has 1GB of RAM (1024MB), then the minimum amount of free space you should create is 3584MB. A quick way of doing this is to type this value into the Free Space Following (MiB) box. Once you've made your choice, click the Resize button. Don't worry—the resizing won't take place until you've confirmed your partitioning choices later on.

4. Back in the main partitioning window, you should now find a preview of the smaller partition plus the free space you created, which will be indicated by a dark gray area marked as Unallocated. The next step is to create the partitions for Ubuntu, so right-click the free space, and select New.

5. First, you should create the *swap partition*. This is similar to the swap file under Windows (sometimes referred to as *virtual memory* or the *paging file*), except that it lives on its own partition. The swap partition acts as additional memory should the main memory become full. Because accessing the hard disk takes longer than accessing the RAM, using the swap file is undesirable and is a last resort. However, all operating systems need them just in case. The rules for the size of the swap partition vary depending on the size of the physical memory that your computer has. See Table 5-3 for some typical values. Most of the other settings in the Create New Partition dialog box can remain as they are, but you should click the Filesystem drop-down list and select linux-swap. Then, in the New Size (MiB) box, type the size of the swap partition, in megabytes.

■**Note** You can create larger or smaller swap partitions than my recommendations, depending on your personal preference. Indeed, there are various competing theories about precisely how much swap space you need, and I've erred toward smaller sizes. If you intend to manipulate very large files, perhaps if you intend to use Ubuntu for video editing, then you should certainly choose larger swap files. But, whatever size you choose, beware that the Hibernate feature of Ubuntu—which allows Ubuntu to suspend to disk—saves the contents of the RAM to the swap partition. Therefore, for Hibernate to work, you'll need a partition at least as big as the quantity of RAM installed in your computer.

Table 5-3. *Suggested Swap Partition Sizes for a Desktop Ubuntu System*

Physical RAM Size	Swap Partition Size (MiB)
512MB	768
1024MB (1GB)	1024
1536MB (1.5GB)	1536
2048MB (2GB)	2048

Once you've finished, click the Add button. As before, no changes will be made to the disk until you confirm your choices later on.

6. Next, you should create the primary Ubuntu partition. Right-click again in the unallocated space, and click New. This time around, the default choices will be correct, and GParted will automatically set the entire amount of free space as the new partition size. So all you have to do is click the Add button.

7. Check your choices to make sure they're correct, and make a mental or written note of your new partition numbers, because you'll need to know them later. For example, on my system, the swap partition was named New Partition #1, and the main Ubuntu partition was identified as New Partition #2, as shown in Figure 5-12.

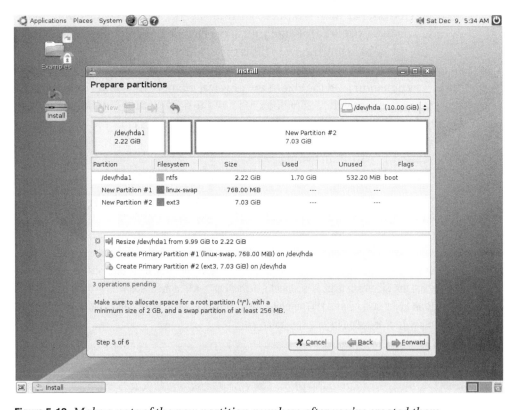

Figure 5-12. *Make a note of the new partition numbers after you've created them.*

8. Click the Forward button at the bottom-right corner of the window. This will cause the resizing and creation of the new partitions, but first, you'll be asked to confirm that you want the changes to take place. Click the Apply button in the dialog box, and then sit back and wait while partitioning takes place.

■**Caution** If you're undertaking this procedure on a notebook computer, ensure the main power is connected. If you lose power during partitioning, perhaps if the battery dies, then the results could be catastrophic, and you might lose *all* the data on the hard disk.

9. When the partitioning has finished, click the Close button on the Applying Pending Operations dialog box.

10. Following the partition resizing and creation, you'll be asked to prepare mount points. This sounds complicated but is very simple—all you have to do is tell Ubuntu which partitions you'd like it to use. In my tests, the installation program selected the new partitions automatically, and all I had to do was click the Forward button, but you should check that, under the Mount Point heading, the swap entry lines up with the swap partition you created, and that the forward slash (/) lines up with the main Ubuntu partition you created. The entries under the Partition heading will be numbered, and you can compare them to the notes you made prior to the partitioning work taking place. If there's any mismatch, click the drop-down menus under the Partition heading and reassign them. Assuming that you're happy with the choices, click the Forward button.

■**Caution** The Windows partition, which will probably be the first on the disk, will also be in the list of mount points, probably as /media/hda1 (/media/sda1 if your computer uses a SATA hard disk). This is fine—it simply means that you'll be able to access the Windows partition under Ubuntu. If you have any other partitions on the disk, then they will also appear in the list, and therefore will also be available within Ubuntu. But you should ensure the Reformat? check box alongside these partition(s) *doesn't* have a check in it—this will cause Ubuntu to format the partition, thereby wiping it!

Stage 10: Confirm Installation Choices

Once partitioning has taken place, you'll be shown the Ready To Install screen (see Figure 5-13), where you'll see confirmation of the choices you made earlier. It's a good idea to check to make sure everything is correct before clicking the Install button. This will start the installation procedure—the new partitions you created will be formatted, and the Ubuntu files will be copied across.

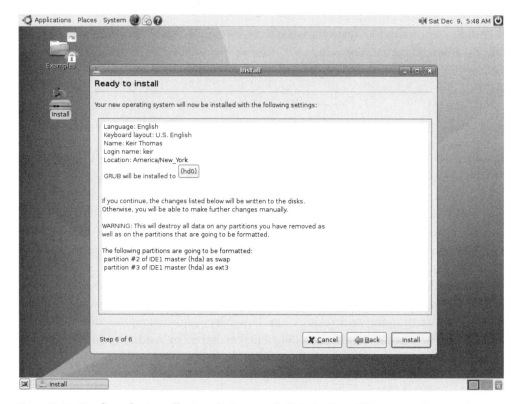

Figure 5-13. *Confirm the installation choices, and click the Install button to format the new partitions and copy the Ubuntu files across.*

Stage 11: Wait During Installation

Now all you have to do is wait! The Ubuntu installation routine will copy the necessary files and install Ubuntu, as shown in Figure 5-14. It won't require any further prompting from you, unless something goes wrong. For example, if you've created partitions that are too small in the previous section, this is the point at which you'll be told. If you do encounter an error, the installation program will quit, and you will have to start it again by clicking the icon on the desktop, this time altering your choices accordingly.

Installation should take no more than 30 minutes and completed in half that time on most of my test systems.

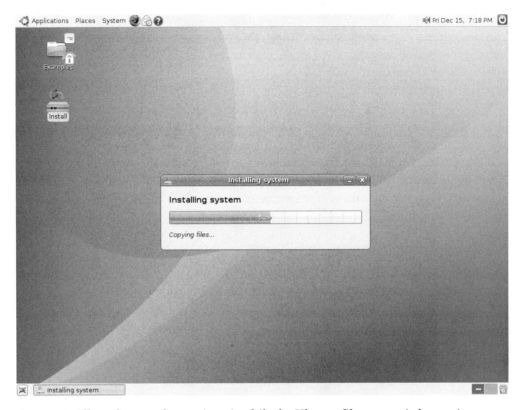

Figure 5-14. *All you have to do now is wait while the Ubuntu files are copied across!*

Stage 12: Reboot and Enjoy Ubuntu!

When installation has finished, a dialog box will appear asking if you want to continue running in live distro mode, or if you want to restart your computer and boot your new Ubuntu installation. You'll probably be eager to use your new Ubuntu setup, so click the Restart Now button.

The DVD disc will automatically be ejected, and it's important that you remove it, so that you don't accidentally boot Ubuntu's live distro mode again when you restart. In fact, Ubuntu will ask you to remove the disk and press Enter to confirm the removal.

Following this, the system will restart. If you've installed Ubuntu on a computer that contains Windows, you'll first see the GRUB boot menu. This offers a number of choices, including the chance to boot Ubuntu into recovery mode, which can help fix your computer and which I discuss in Chapter 6. You can also choose to boot into Windows. You can switch between the menu choices by using the arrow keys; press Enter to make your selection.

You can also run Memtest86, as described previously in stage 3. However, most users can simply press Enter when the menu appears, which will select the top-most entry, thereby booting Ubuntu in normal mode. Alternatively, after 10 seconds, the default choice will be automatically selected.

If you installed Ubuntu onto a computer or hard disk without any other operating system, you'll see a brief countdown timer, during which you can press any key to make the boot menu appear. Otherwise, it will be hidden, and after the countdown has finished, Ubuntu will start its boot procedure.

Once the boot menu is out of the way and after a few seconds have passed while Ubuntu loads, you'll see the Ubuntu login screen, as shown in Figure 5-15. From here, you can progress to Chapter 7 to learn how to get started. Alternatively, if you've run into any problems, see Chapter 6.

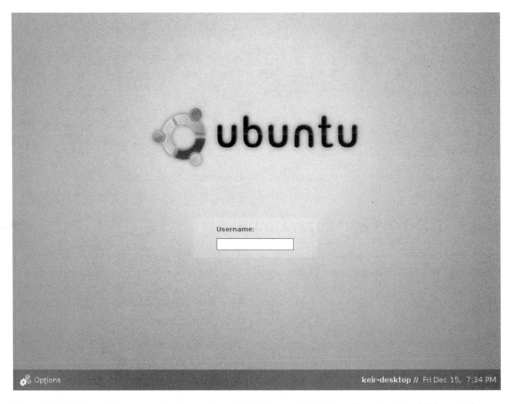

Figure 5-15. *When the computer has rebooted after installation, the standard Ubuntu login screen will appear.*

INSTALLING UBUNTU ON AN APPLE MAC

Ubuntu can also run on Apple Macintosh computers, as well as PCs, and the DVD-ROM supplied with this book contains everything you need. However, the instructions vary depending on what processor is installed in your Macintosh. To find out what type of processor your Mac uses, click the Apple menu and select About This Mac. In the summary dialog box, look for the Processor heading. If the line reads "PowerPC," then skip to the relevant heading following. If the line contains "Intel" in combination with any other words, such as "Intel Core Duo," then skip to the Intel heading.

Intel

If your Mac contains an Intel processor, you can boot from the DVD-ROM supplied with this book and use it to install Ubuntu. However, some extra steps are necessary. If you're running OS 10.4, also known as Tiger, you'll need to install Apple's Boot Camp utility (`www.apple.com/macosx/bootcamp/`), which allows you to resize the existing OS X partition, so you can install Ubuntu alongside. It also provides a boot menu to let you switch between OS X and Ubuntu. If you're using OS 10.5, also known as Leopard, Boot Camp will be installed by default. However, Boot Camp is designed to allow Windows to be installed alongside OS X, so some additional steps are necessary to make it work with Ubuntu. A full guide is provided at the official Ubuntu wiki: `https://wiki.ubuntu.com/MacBook`.

Once the computer has been correctly configured by following the guide, you can boot from the DVD-ROM and follow the instructions in the rest of this chapter. Hold down the C key when the Apple symbol appears during booting to boot from the DVD-ROM disc.

PowerPC

If your Mac contains a PowerPC processor you can use the special PowerPC version of Ubuntu that's supplied on the DVD-ROM as an `.iso` image. You'll have to manually burn this to a blank CD-R or CD-RW disc and then boot from it to install Ubuntu. However, first you must create some free space on the hard disk, so you can install Ubuntu alongside (assuming you want to dual-boot OS X and Ubuntu; if you want to let Ubuntu use the entire hard disk, the Ubuntu installer will be able to wipe the existing partitions and no further action is necessary). To create the free space, you can either use a third-party disk repartitioning utility, such as VolumeWorks (`www.subrosasoft.com/OSXSoftware/index.php?main_page=product_info&products_id=6`), or simply reinstall OS X on the hard disk but choose a smaller partition size, allowing free space for Ubuntu to utilize later on.

To create the Ubuntu install CD, boot to OS X. Next, navigate to the `ubuntu_alternatives` directory on the DVD-ROM, and copy the `ubuntu-6.10-desktop-powerpc.iso` file to the desktop. Insert a blank CD-R or CD-RW and then, again using Finder, click Applications ➤ Utilities ➤ Disc Utility. When the program starts, click Images on the menu and then Burn. Navigate to the `ubuntu-6.10-desktop-powerpc.iso` file on the desktop, and then click the Burn button. Then, when the burn has finished, use the disc to boot from and install Ubuntu, following the instructions provided in this chapter. Hold down the C key when the Apple symbol appears during booting to boot from the CD.

Summary

By following the steps outlined in this chapter, you should now have Ubuntu installed on your computer. I've tried to provide you with enough information to get around any problems, as well as explain exactly what's happening every step of the way.

Alas, it's still possible that you encountered hurdles that weren't addressed here. In the next chapter, you'll find solutions to common problems associated with Ubuntu installation.

CHAPTER 6

■■■

Solving Installation Problems

Chances are that your installation of Ubuntu will complete without a hitch, and you'll find yourself with a first-rate operating system up and running within just a few minutes. However, if a problem rears its ugly head, you should be able to find the solution in this chapter, which addresses the most common installation problems. These problems are organized by when they occur: before you start Ubuntu's live distro mode, while running the installation program, and after the installation when you boot for the first time. The final section of the chapter describes how to configure the graphical subsystem with the X.org configuration utility, which can be useful if graphical glitches arise.

Preinstallation Problems

Some problems might arise before you even boot Ubuntu's live distro mode in order to run the installation program. This section addresses such issues.

Problem

When I boot from the Ubuntu DVD-ROM, the drive spins up as if something is happening, but I see nothing. (Alternatively, I see on-screen graphical corruption.)

Solution

It's possible the DVD-ROM disc is either dirty or faulty. Examine its surface for scratches, or try cleaning it with a moist tissue. A typical indicator of a dirty or damaged disc is that the drive spins up and then instantly spins down several times in succession—listen to the whir of the drive's motor to tell if this is the case.

If the disc seems OK, it might be that your computer is unable to display the Ubuntu boot menu. To get around this, when you see the blank screen blank or graphical corruption, press the Esc key. Then press Enter. You'll see the word boot: at the top left of the screen, along with a prompt at which you can enter commands. Type **live**, and press Enter.

Problem

The computer boots from the DVD-ROM, but when the boot menu appears, pressing Enter doesn't start the installation. In fact, nothing happens at all! I'm unable to move up and down through the menu choices either—the keyboard is totally unresponsive.

Solution

If your PC uses a USB keyboard, it might be that it's not being recognized by the Ubuntu boot loader. To get around this, it's possible to make most computers pretend that USB keyboards are older PS/2 keyboards. This is done on a fundamental hardware level and is invisible to the operating system. Here are the steps:

1. Enter the BIOS setup program by pressing Delete during the initial stages of your computer's boot routine (while memory testing and drive identification are still taking place). Some computers might use a different key combination to enter BIOS setup, such as Ctrl+Insert, but this information will be displayed on screen.

2. Use the cursor keys to navigate to the Integrated Peripherals section, and then look for an entry along the lines of USB Legacy Support. Set it to Enabled.

3. Press Escape to return to the main menu, and opt to save the changes.

4. Reboot the computer.

Note that you should repeat this procedure and deactivate USB Legacy Support once Ubuntu has been installed. At that stage, Ubuntu should be able to recognize the USB keyboard properly.

Problem

I'm using the same keyboard, mouse, and monitor across several computers courtesy of a keyboard, video, and mouse (KVM) switch. When Ubuntu boots, the resolution is wrong and the graphics are corrupted. (Also, my keyboard or mouse doesn't work correctly.)

Solution

A KVM switch doesn't allow Ubuntu to correctly probe the attached hardware. Consider attaching the keyboard, monitor, and mouse directly to the computer for the duration of the installation.

Problem

After I've pressed Enter at the boot menu to start booting Ubuntu's live distro mode, the computer freezes and eventually displays a message along the lines of Kernel Panic.

Solution

Kernel Panic errors occur when Ubuntu cannot continue to load for various reasons. In this context, it's likely that either the DVD is faulty (or dirty) or that your PC has a defective item of hardware.

First, check to make sure the DVD is clean and not scratched. If possible, try it on a different computer. If it works, then it's clearly not at fault, and your computer most likely has a hardware issue. In particular, bad memory can cause problems. Does the computer already have an operating system installed? Does this run without problems? If not, consider replacing your memory modules.

To thoroughly test your computer's memory, boot from the Ubuntu CD-ROM, and select the Memory Test option on the menu (use the arrow keys to move up or down in the list, and press Enter to make a selection). This will run the Memtest86 program, and any problems with your memory will be reported in the Errors column on the right side of the program screen. For more details about how to use Memtest86, see `www.memtest86.com`.

Problem

Immediately after I press Enter at the boot menu to start Ubuntu's live distro mode, the computer looks like it's crashed—the graphics are corrupted!

Solution

Your graphics card may be incompatible with the framebuffer graphical mode used by Ubuntu's boot routine. You can overcome this problem by following these steps:

1. Reboot and, when you would normally press Enter to start the Ubuntu installation routine, instead press the F6 key (the Function keys run across the top of the keyboard).

2. You should see a line of text appear below the menu that begins `Boot Options`. Using the Backspace key, delete `quiet splash --` from the end of the line. Then press Enter.

If you continue to see graphical corruption, try using the solution to the next problem.

Problem

When I select the Start or Install Ubuntu option and press Enter, I see a status bar, but when the Ubuntu desktop should appear, it looks like my computer has crashed—all I see is graphical corruption.

Solution

Reboot the computer, and when the Ubuntu boot menu appears, select the Start Ubuntu in Safe Graphics Mode entry. Then press Enter. This will start Ubuntu using Vesa graphics drivers, which are compatible with practically every graphics card made within the last ten years.

If you're trying this solution after trying the solution to the previous problem, select Start Ubuntu in Safe Graphics Mode, and before pressing Enter, repeat the steps in the previous solution: press F6 and then delete the text at the end of the Boot Options line.

If, after installing Ubuntu onto your computer's hard disk, you find that there's still graphical corruption when you boot Ubuntu, see the instructions under the "Graphical Problems" heading toward the end of this chapter.

Problem

After I've selected the Start or Install Ubuntu option on the menu, the status bar appears, but then the computer freezes.

Solution

It's possible the power-saving feature or the advanced programmable interrupt controller (APIC) in your computer is causing problems. Press the F6 key, and type the following at the end of the Boot Options line that appears:

```
acpi=off noapic nolapic
```

Press Enter when you've finished to boot Ubuntu.

Problem

I'm attempting to install Ubuntu onto a notebook computer. After I select the Start or Install Ubuntu option and press Enter, the screen is filled with graphical corruption, and it looks like Ubuntu has crashed. (Alternatively, the screen looks squashed, or some elements are off-center or off the edge of the screen.)

Solution

When the Ubuntu boot menu appears, press the Escape key and press Enter. At the `boot:` prompt, type **live vga=771**. Then press Enter.

Problem

During booting, my computer hangs. On screen I see a lot of output, but at the bottom of it are the words `aec671x-detect....`

Solution

When the Ubuntu boot menu appears, press the Escape key and press Enter. At the `boot:` prompt, type **live gdth=disable:y**. Then press Enter.

Problem

The Ubuntu DVD-ROM seems to boot into live distro mode, but then the screen goes blank, and my monitor flashes an error along the lines of "Cannot display this mode" or "Out of mode". (This problem might affect users of wide-screen monitors in particular.)

Solution

It sounds like the graphical configuration Ubuntu automatically generates for your computer isn't correct. Reboot the computer, and when the Ubuntu boot menu appears, select the Start Ubuntu in Safe Graphics Mode entry. Then press Enter. This will start Ubuntu using Vesa graphics drivers, which are compatible with practically every graphics card made within the last ten years.

Alternatively, it's possible that, although the screen is blank, the Ubuntu login screen is running in the background. You can, therefore, try logging in "blind" (that is, without any visual feedback on screen). Type your username, press Enter, type your password, and press Enter again. At this point, you may find that the desktop appears as it should. This should allow you to run the Ubuntu installation program.

NONE OF THESE SOLUTIONS WORK!

If you run into installation problems for which you can't find a solution here, you can try installing Ubuntu using the alternate install disc.

The alternate install disc doesn't boot into live distro mode; instead, it boots to an older but reliable text-mode installation program. From there, you can follow the prompts to install Ubuntu. Unfortunately, there isn't space to provide a full installation guide here, although most installation options should correspond loosely to those discussed in Chapter 5.

The alternate install disc is supplied on the DVD-ROM supplied with this book as an `.iso` file, and you'll have to manually burn it to a blank CD-R or CD-RW, which you should then boot from to install Ubuntu. You can burn the disc from within Windows using most of the commercially available CD/DVD burning packages, such as Nero, or you can download the freeware ISO Recorder tool from `http://isorecorder.alexfeinman.com/isorecorder.htm`. Versions are available for both Windows XP and Vista.

Assuming you're using ISO Recorder to burn the alternate install `.iso` image, copy the `ubuntu-6.10-alternate-i386.iso` file from the `ubuntu_alternatives` directory to your desktop. Then, insert a blank CD-R or CD-RW into your drive, right-click the `.iso` file on the desktop, and select Open With ➤ ISO Recorder.

Before burning, click the Properties button on the ISO Recorder program window, and click and drag the recording speed slider so that the middle number under the slider is 1 (or to the lowest possible number if 1 isn't available). This will ensure your `.iso` image is burned slowly, reducing the risk of data error. Note that it's very important that the `.iso` image is burned at a slow speed, regardless of the potential high write speeds of your CD/DVD writer; it probably won't work otherwise.

Click OK on the Properties dialog box, and click the Next button on the main ISO Recorder program window. This will start the burning procedure, which might take some time, during which you should avoid using your PC.

Once the burn has finished, the disc will automatically be ejected. Once this happens, reinsert the disc, and reboot your computer from the new disc. Then, select to install Ubuntu from the boot menu that appears.

Installation Problems

Once the DVD-ROM has booted in live distro mode, and you've run the installation program, you may get error messages or experience other difficulties. This section offers some solutions to common installation problems.

Problem

I've partitioned my disk and clicked to start the installation, after which the Installing System progress bar appears. However, it stops at a certain percentage with an error message. If I click the Continue button, everything continues, and at the end, I'm offered the chance to reboot into the new installation. However, when I reboot, the Ubuntu desktop doesn't appear. Instead, all I see is a black screen with a text-mode login prompt.

Solution

For some reason vital Ubuntu software hasn't been correctly copied to the machine. At the login prompt, type your username, and type your password when it's requested. Then, at the command prompt, type the following:

```
sudo apt-get update
  [At this point you'll need to type your password; do so]
sudo apt-get -f install
sudo apt-get install ubuntu-desktop
```

You should ensure the DVD-ROM is inserted. If you find this doesn't work, follow the instructions in the "None of These Solutions Work!" sidebar, and install Ubuntu using the alternate install CD.

Problem

When the Ubuntu installation program gets to the Starting Up the Partitioner stage, it reports that it can't find any hard disk in my computer.

Solution

There are many possible reasons for this, but here are three potential solutions that you might try in sequence:

1. Click Manually Edit Partition Table, and click the Forward button. At the top-right corner of the window, in the drive selection drop-down list, ensure the correct hard disk is selected. Once you select the disk, you should find the partitions are displayed, and you should then be able to follow the instructions under the "Manually Editing the Partition Table" heading in Chapter 5.

2. Ensure the jumpers are set correctly on the hard disk (consult the hard disk's documentation if necessary). This is particularly worth checking if you have more than one hard disk. If this doesn't solve the problem, and your second hard disk is nonbootable (that is, it's used only for data storage), try temporarily removing it, and then install Ubuntu. Reconnect it after installation has completed.

3. See the "None of These Solutions Work!" sidebar to learn how to use the alternate install CD. This contains an older installation program that many consider more reliable on some problematic computers.

Problem

When I try to install Ubuntu, the Prepare Disk Space screen shows one (or several) additional small hard disks, usually identified as /dev/sda followed by a number.

Solution

If you have a USB memory stick inserted, or a photographic card reader, it will be identified by the Ubuntu installer in this way. You can ignore this or, if you want to avoid confusion, quit the installer, remove the memory stick or card reader, and restart the installer program.

Problem

When manually partitioning, I see an error message to the effect that I can't have more than four primary partitions.

Solution

This is a limitation in how hard disks work and not an issue with Ubuntu. You will have to create an extended partition to contain your new Ubuntu partitions. To do this, right-click the free space, click New, and select Extended Partition from the Create As drop-down list. By default, all the free space should be used, so click the Add button. Then, click in the new, extended partition, and create the Ubuntu partitions, as explained in the previous chapter.

For more details about primary and extended hard disk partitioning, see http://en.wikipedia.org/wiki/Disk_partitioning.

Problem

When I try to install Ubuntu into partitions that have previously contained Ubuntu (or another version of Linux), in order to wipe them and install Ubuntu into them, I get the error message "No root file system" on the Prepare Mount Points screen. (Alternatively, I created the Ubuntu partitions and then quit the installer before package installation had taken place. When I started it again later and attempted to use the partitions I'd created, I received the "No root file system" message.)

Solution

Unfortunately there's a bug in the Ubuntu installer, which appears on a minority of computers, that means it's unable to utilize partitions that already exist when the installer starts. It seems the Ubuntu installer will only utilize partitions that it's created. The solution is simple—go back to the manual partitioning screen by clicking the Back button, delete the existing partition that you intended to use, and then recreate it, as described in the "Manually Editing the Partition Table" section of Chapter 5.

Postinstallation Problems

Problems might also occur after you install Ubuntu. This section addresses several possible postinstallation problems. This section covers only problems that appear immediately after installation—those that prevent Ubuntu from working correctly right after its first boot. Issues surrounding the configuration of hardware or software are dealt with in Chapter 8 of this book.

Problem

I use a wide-screen monitor (or a wide-screen notebook). When I boot to the desktop, the resolution is set too low. When I try to switch resolutions (by clicking System ➤ Preferences ➤ Screen Resolution), the resolution my monitor usually runs at isn't available in the list.

Solution

It a minority of cases, the open source drivers for ATI and NVIDIA cards can't support certain resolutions on particular monitors. One solution is to install proprietary graphics drivers, as discussed in Chapter 8, although you should also update your system online as soon as possible (see Chapter 9) to see if the open source graphics drivers have been updated and improved. In both cases, you'll need to configure your computer to go online, which is also explained in Chapter 8.

Problem

After booting up, my USB mouse and/or USB keyboard are not recognized.

Solution

Try unplugging the keyboard and/or mouse, and then reattaching them. If you find they now work, log in to Ubuntu, and perform an online system upgrade. See Chapter 9 for more information about this task.

If this fails to solve the problem, you can configure your BIOS to pretend your mouse and keyboard are traditional PS/2-style devices, as follows:

1. Enter the BIOS setup program by pressing Delete during the initial stages of your computer boot routine (while memory testing and drive identification are still taking place). Some computers might use a different key combination to enter BIOS setup, such as Ctrl+Insert, but this information will be displayed on screen.

2. Use the cursor keys to navigate to the Integrated Peripherals section, and then look for an entry along the lines of USB Legacy Support. Set it to Enabled.

3. Press Escape to return to the main menu, and opt to save the changes.

4. Reboot the computer.

Problem

When I boot for the first time, I see an error message along the lines of "No operating system could be found on the hard disk."

Solution

It seems that, for whatever reason, the GRUB boot loader wasn't installed correctly. Boot from the DVD-ROM, and select to Enter or Install Ubuntu when prompted. When the Ubuntu desktop appears, click Applications ➤ Accessories ➤ Terminal. This will open a command-prompt window. Type the following commands in sequence:

```
sudo grub
    [At this point you'll need to type your password; do so]
root (hd0,1)
setup (hd0)
quit
```

Then restart Ubuntu (click System ➤ Quit). Ensure you remove the DVD-ROM when prompted. You should find that the Ubuntu boot menu now appears when you boot.

Problem

After I've installed Ubuntu, Windows will no longer boot, although Ubuntu works fine. After I select Windows from the boot menu, the Windows boot procedure either freezes when "Starting Windows . . ." appears, or the boot status bar is shown, but the desktop never appears.

Solution

Try repairing your Windows disk using the Windows command-line tool `chkdsk`. This can be done from the recovery mode of the Windows installation CD/DVD, but the instructions for how to do this vary depending on if you're running Windows Vista or XP.

Windows Vista

If you're running Windows Vista, follow these steps to run `chkdsk`:

1. Insert the Windows Vista installation DVD, and select to boot from it. For details of how to configure your computer to boot from DVD, see stage 2 of the Ubuntu installation guide in Chapter 5.

2. For some time, you'll see the message Windows is Loading Files, along with a progress bar. Once this has cleared, select your language/locale settings from the Install Windows dialog box, and click Next.

3. On the next screen, *don't* click the Install Now button. Instead, click the Repair Your Computer link at the bottom-left corner of the window.

4. In the System Recovery Options dialog box, select your Windows Vista partition, and click Next.

5. On the next screen, select Command Prompt.

6. In the command-prompt window that appears, type the following (this assumes Vista is installed on drive `C:`):

   ```
   chkdsk c: /R
   ```

7. Wait until the check has completed, and type **exit** at the prompt.

8. Back in the System Recovery Options dialog box, click Restart. This will reboot your computer. Be sure to eject the Windows Vista DVD before doing so.

Windows XP

1. Insert the Windows XP installation CD, and select to boot from it. For details of how to configure your computer to boot from CD, see stage 2 of the Ubuntu installation guide in Chapter 5.

2. For some time, you'll see status messages that Windows is loading driver files. Eventually the Windows Setup menu will appear. Press R to start the Recovery Console.

3. You'll be asked to confirm which Window installation you'd like to boot into; do so.

4. You'll then be prompted for the administrator's password. If you don't have one, simply press Enter.

5. At the command prompt, type the following:

   ```
   chkdsk c: /R
   ```

6. Wait until the check has completed, and then type **exit** at the prompt. This will reboot your computer. Be sure to eject the Windows XP CD before rebooting.

Problem

When I boot for the first time, all I see is a black screen with some text at the top saying `Ubuntu 6.10 'Edgy Eft' Ubuntu tty1` and, beneath that, `ubuntu login:`.

Solution

For some reason, the automatic configuration of your graphics card failed during installation. See the following section for instructions on configuring your GUI manually.

Graphical Problems

Although Ubuntu is extremely adept at automatically detecting and configuring your PC's graphics hardware, it sometimes gets things wrong. Such problems are characterized by one of the following:

- Ubuntu freezes when the desktop would normally appear.

- You see on-screen graphical corruption, of either text or graphics.

- The resolution is set too low or too high, and you can't change it to the correct resolution because it isn't offered.

- You see a message that the X server isn't working.

- You see a black screen with only with a text login prompt.

If this happens when you're attempting to boot into Ubuntu's live distro mode to install Ubuntu, the solution is to select the second option on the DVD-ROM boot menu: Start Ubuntu in Safe Graphics Mode. This will use Vesa-mode graphics drivers, which are known to work with the majority of graphics cards in use today.

If you run into graphical problems *after* Ubuntu has been installed, you can reconfigure X.org, Ubuntu's graphical subsystem (often referred to simply as X). This can be done using Ubuntu's `dpkg-reconfigure` tool at the command prompt.

Additionally, if your computer utilizes a recent NVIDIA or ATI 3D graphics card, you can try installing the proprietary drivers. This is recommended if your computer utilizes a wide-screen display of some kind, and you are unable to set the resolution correctly. You might also find you are unable to set the correct resolution if you're using a very new model graphics card that isn't yet fully supported by Ubuntu's built-in drivers.

However, the proprietary graphics drivers need to be downloaded via Ubuntu's package management system, and this means your computer needs to be online. Configuring your computer to go online is best done when some kind of GUI is up and running. Therefore, you should follow the instructions in the next section to reconfigure X.org to get *some* kind of graphical system up and running, even if it's the wrong resolution or otherwise less than ideal, before following the instructions in Chapter 8 that describe how to get your system online. In that chapter, you can also find out how to install proprietary graphics drivers.

Using Ubuntu's Reconfiguration Tool

To start Ubuntu's graphical subsystem reconfiguration program, first boot into Ubuntu's recovery mode. This provides a simple command-line prompt and is designed to let you fix the system if anything goes wrong. To do this, ensure the installation DVD-ROM is removed from your computer's DVD-ROM drive, and switch on your computer. If you dual-boot your computer with Windows, you'll need to select the "Ubuntu [. . .] (recovery mode)" option from the menu that appears just after your computer boots. If your computer has only Ubuntu installed on it, you'll need to press a key to enter the boot menu when prompted; then select the "Ubuntu [. . .] (recovery mode)" option.

Eventually, a command prompt will appear, and you'll see root@*hostname*:~#, followed by a cursor (in place of *hostname* will be the hostname you entered during installation). At the prompt, type the following:

```
dpkg-reconfigure xserver-xorg
```

This will start the configuration program, which runs in text mode. Reconfiguring X.org simply requires answering some basic questions, as outlined in the following steps. The configuration program guides you through selections for your graphics card, input devices, and monitor. Although the steps are separated into subsections for clarity, note that the program actually presents one long series of questions that moves seamlessly from topic to topic.

Graphics Card Configuration

The X.org configuration program begins with graphics card setup. Note that the configuration program does not use the mouse. Instead you should use the keyboard—use the arrow keys to move among options on a menu, and Tab to move the selection between on-screen options. Press Enter to select an option.

1. The first question asks you to choose a driver from a list. If you wish, you can select the driver that seems appropriate to your hardware (the `ati` option for an ATI-based card, for example), but the safest choice is to choose the Vesa option. This driver works on virtually every graphics card. Press Enter when you've made your choice.

■Note Using the Vesa driver entails a slight performance penalty, particularly when it comes to video playback. Therefore, you might choose to reconfigure X.org again in the future when your knowledge of Linux improves.

---

2. You're asked to enter an identifier for your graphics card. This is merely for reference purposes, and anything will do. The default that Ubuntu suggests is fine, and you can simply press Enter.

3. An information screen outlining the next step, which is to identify the bus ID of the card, appears. This is a technical setting needed for Ubuntu to use the card. Highlight the OK button using the Tab key, and press Enter.

4. Next, you'll be invited to fill in the bus ID details. The default suggested by Ubuntu should be automatically filled in and should work for most people, so simply press Enter.

5. You're invited to enter the amount of memory your graphics card contains. Once again, Ubuntu is able to autodetect this. It's acceptable to leave the field blank and press Enter.

6. You're asked whether you want to use your graphics card's framebuffer. This is a method of accessing the graphics card memory, and nearly all modern graphics cards are compatible with it, so you can select Yes and press Enter. However, if after completing these steps you find that you still have problems with your display, start again from step 1, and choose not to use the framebuffer.

Keyboard and Mouse Configuration

Following the graphical configuration, the configuration program will move on to configure your mouse and keyboard. Although your keyboard and mouse might work just fine, X.org handles the input devices as well as the graphics subsystem, and you now need to reconfigure them.

1. You're asked whether you want the configuration program to autodetect your keyboard layout. This is perfectly acceptable, so select Yes and press Enter.

2. You're invited to enter your keyboard layout. This takes the form of two-letter country codes, the type used throughout the world. For example, a United States keyboard layout is indicated by typing **US**. United Kingdom users will want to type **UK**. Australian users should type **AU**. For a complete list of world country codes, see `www.iso.org/iso/en/prods-services/iso3166ma/02iso-3166-code-lists/list-en1.html`. Once finished, press Enter.

3. You're asked to enter the XKB rule set you wish to use. The default answer is fine for most users, so press Enter.

4. You see an information screen describing keyboard models, which you'll be invited to enter in a moment. In a nutshell, most recent English-based keyboards are pc104 models, which is to say they have 104 keys. If you're using an older keyboard that does not have the Windows keys to the left and right of the spacebar, you should enter **pc101**. Once done, highlight OK, and press Enter.

■**Note** There are some special rules regarding Macintosh keyboards—see the on-screen instructions for more details.

---

5. Now you're asked to enter the keyboard model; do so. The default is pc105, but in my case, I deleted this and typed **pc104**. Once this is done, press Enter.

6. Next is another information screen discussing the use of additional keyboard rules. If you have an English-based keyboard, you can ignore this. Highlight OK, and press Enter.

7. The Keyboard Variant field will appear. As described in step 6, leave this empty, and press Enter.

8. You're shown an information page about special keyboard definitions. This is an interesting option you might like to explore in the future, but you can ignore it for now. Highlight OK, and press Enter.

9. You now see the Keyboard Options text field. Leave the default contents as they are, and press Enter.

10. You're now asked to select the mouse protocol. There are two choices: ImPS/2 and ExplorerPS/2. The first should be selected for most mice of any make or model. The latter should be selected if you're using a mouse from the Microsoft Intelli-Mouse range. Highlight the option you require, and press Enter. If, when Ubuntu is up and running, you find your scroll wheel doesn't work, or the mouse acts in any other strange way, repeat the configuration steps here, and try the other option.

11. You're asked if you want to emulate a three-button mouse. Linux is designed around a three-button mouse system, rather than the two-button mouse used with Windows (or the single button used on the Apple Macintosh). Emulation of a three-button mouse means that when the left and right buttons are clicked at the same time, the computer thinks a third button has been pressed. Emulation isn't necessary with most modern mice, because the scroll wheel is configured as the third button, so you should select No here. Then press Enter.

12. Next, you see an information screen describing various modules that can be enabled to add additional functionality to X.org. This is only for advanced users. Highlight OK, and press Enter.

13. Now, you can choose from the list of modules. Once again, Ubuntu does the hard work for you, and the modules will be automatically selected, so highlight OK, and press Enter.

14. You're asked to confirm that you want to write the Files section to your X.org configuration file. You should certainly select Yes here, and press Enter.

Monitor Configuration

Following the keyboard and mouse setup, it is time to configure your monitor.

1. The first monitor setup question asks if you want to autodetect the monitor. If your graphical system isn't working, there's a chance that this feature is incompatible with your system. Therefore, you should opt not to autodetect—highlight No, and press Enter.

2. You're asked to enter an identifier for your monitor. Anything will do, and the default Ubuntu suggests is usually fine, so press Enter.

3. Select from the list the resolutions you would like to be available to use under Ubuntu. You can move up and down the list using the arrow keys. Highlight each entry in the list that you want, and press the spacebar, so that an asterisk appears alongside it. See Table 6-1 for guidance on typical resolutions for monitors, although you should refer to your monitor documentation as well, especially if you're using a wide-screen monitor (or a notebook with a wide-screen panel). When you're finished, highlight OK, and press Enter.

Note TFT screens are designed to run at a single optimal resolution, rather than at a range of resolutions. Therefore, you should select only one resolution from the list if you have this type of monitor.

---

4. Next, you see an information screen explaining that you'll be asked to enter some technical characteristics of your monitor. You can choose the Simple, Medium, or Advanced option; each requires you to enter progressively more information. In most cases, the Simple option should suffice and simply involves entering the physical size of your screen (such as 15 or 17 inches). However, if after completing these steps you find you still have problems, you might try repeating the configuration and choosing the Advanced option, which will ask for the horizontal and vertical scan rates of the monitor. You can find this information in the monitor's manual or, if that's not available, by searching online for the specification list of your model at the manufacturer's web site. When you've read the information, highlight OK, and press Enter.

5. Now you're asked to choose which mode you want. Select Simple, and press Enter.

6. Following that, you're asked to select the approximate size of your screen. Do so, and then press Enter.

7. You're asked to confirm that you want to write the monitor synchronization ranges to the configuration file. Highlight Yes, and then press Enter.

8. You're asked to enter the color depth you wish to use. All modern graphics cards are capable of 24-bit color, but if you have an older card with less memory, you might choose 16 from the list. Once again, if you find that the graphical configuration doesn't work after completing these steps, you might wish to return to this step and try decreasing the value. Once you've made your choice, press Enter.

9. After selecting the color depth, the configuration file will be written to disk, and you'll be returned to the command prompt. You can now reboot by simply typing **reboot** at the command prompt.

Table 6-1. *Typical Monitor Resolutions*

Monitor Size	Typical Resolutions
CRT Monitors	
14 inches	800×600, 640×480
15 inches	800×600, 640×480
17 inches	1024×768, 800×600, 640×480
19 inches	1280×1024, 1024×768, 800×600, 640×480
20 inches	1600×1200, 1280×1024, 1024×768, 800×600, 640×480
TFT Screens	
14 inches	1024×768
15 inches	1024×768
17 inches	1280×1024
19 inches	1280×1024

Summary

This chapter's goal was to address problems that might occur during the installation of Ubuntu. It discussed preinstallation, installation, and postinstallation issues. It also covered how to use the X.org reconfiguration utility to configure the graphics subsystem, which may be necessary if the installation program failed to properly recognize your graphics card or monitor.

You should now have Ubuntu installed. The next part of this book focuses on helping you get everything up and running. You'll learn essential skills and become a confident Linux user.

PART 3

■ ■ ■

The No-Nonsense Getting Started Guide

CHAPTER 7

■ ■ ■

Booting Ubuntu for the First Time

Now that Ubuntu is installed, you'll no doubt want to get started immediately, and that's what Part 3 of this book is all about. In later chapters, we'll examine specific details of using Ubuntu and getting essential hardware up and running. We'll also look at personalizing Ubuntu so that it works in a way that's best for you on a day-to-day basis. But right now, the goal of this chapter is to get you doing the same things you did under Windows as quickly as possible.

This chapter explains how to start up Ubuntu for the first time and work with the desktop. It also looks at how some familiar aspects of your computer, such as using the mouse, are slightly enhanced under Ubuntu.

Starting Up

If you've chosen to dual-boot with Windows, the first Ubuntu screen you'll see is the boot loader menu, which appears shortly after you switch on your PC. If Ubuntu is the only operating system on your hard disk, you'll see a brief one-line message pointing out that if you press a key, you can access this boot menu. You won't need to do so unless you want to access the recovery mode boot settings. In fact, if Ubuntu is the only operating system on your computer, you can skip to the next section of this chapter.

■**Note** The boot loader is actually a separate program called GRUB. This program kicks off everything and starts Ubuntu.

The boot loader menu you see when your PC is set to dual-boot has three or four choices, as shown in Figure 7-1. The top one is what you need to boot Ubuntu. The Ubuntu option will be selected automatically within 10 seconds, but you can press Enter to start immediately.

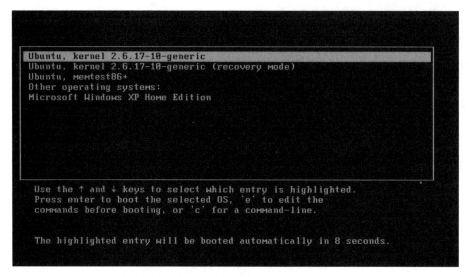

```
Ubuntu, kernel 2.6.17-10-generic
Ubuntu, kernel 2.6.17-10-generic (recovery mode)
Ubuntu, memtest86+
Other operating systems:
Microsoft Windows XP Home Edition




    Use the ↑ and ↓ keys to select which entry is highlighted.
    Press enter to boot the selected OS, 'e' to edit the
    commands before booting, or 'c' for a command-line.


    The highlighted entry will be booted automatically in 8 seconds.
```

Figure 7-1. *The default choice is fine on the boot menu, so press Enter to start Ubuntu.*

You should find that you also have an entry for Windows, located at the bottom of the list. To boot into Windows, simply use the cursor keys to move the selection to the appropriate option, and then press Enter.

You should also see an entry ending in "(recovery mode)". This is a little like Safe Mode within Windows, in that the system boots with conservative system settings, and you should be able to make repairs to the system if something has gone wrong. However, in Ubuntu's recovery mode, you're presented with a command-line prompt.

When you update your system software, you might find new entries are added to the boot menu list. This is because the kernel has been updated. The *kernel* is the central system file that Ubuntu relies upon, and essentially, the boot menu exists to let you choose between different kernels.

Without exception, the topmost entry is the one you'll want each time to boot Ubuntu, because this will always use the most recent version of the kernel, along with the latest versions of other system software. The entries beneath this will start the system with older versions of the kernel and are provided in the unlikely situation that the latest kernel causes problems.

■**Note** All operating systems need a boot loader—even Windows. However, the Windows boot loader is hidden and simply starts the operating system. Under Ubuntu, the boot loader usually has a menu, so you can select Linux or perhaps an option that lets you access your PC for troubleshooting problems. When you gain some experience with Ubuntu, you might choose to install two or more versions of Linux on the same hard disk, and you'll be able to select among them using the boot menu.

Logging In

After Ubuntu has booted, you should see the login screen, as shown in Figure 7-2. Here, you enter the username and the password you created during the installation process. By clicking the Options button in the bottom-left corner of the screen, a menu will appear from which you can opt to reboot the system or shut it down.

Figure 7-2. *Type your username, enter your password, and then press Enter to log in.*

The user account you created during installation is similar to what Windows Vista and XP refer to as an "administrator" account. This means that the account you use on a day-to-day basis can also change important system settings and reconfigure the system. However, the main difference between Ubuntu and Windows is that you'll need to enter your password to make any serious changes, rather than clicking on a confirmation dialog, as you do with Vista (of course, XP doesn't have any kind of confirmation dialog at all!).

Don't worry about damaging anything accidentally; trying to reconfigure the system or access a serious system setting will invariably bring up a password prompt. You can simply click the Cancel button if you don't want to continue.

Note Unlike some versions of Linux, Ubuntu doesn't encourage the user to use an actual root (or administrator) account. Instead, it operates on the principle of certain ordinary users adopting superuser privileges that allow them to administer the system when they need to. The user account you create during setup has these privileges.

Exploring the Desktop

After you've logged in, you'll see the welcoming theme of the Ubuntu desktop, as shown in Figure 7-3. Feel free to click around and see what you can discover. There's little chance of you doing serious damage, so let yourself go wild and play around with your new operating system! However, be careful if any dialog boxes ask you to type your password—this indicates that you've clicked an action that has the potential to change the system in a fundamental way.

Tip Although you can't damage the system by messing around, you might find that you somehow cause programs to work incorrectly. Don't worry if this happens. You can always create a new account for yourself following the instructions in Chapter 29. When using this new account, you should find all the settings are returned to normal, and you'll be back to square one!

Figure 7-3. *Feel free to experiment with the Ubuntu desktop and see what you can discover.*

First Impressions

The first thing you'll notice is that the desktop is clean compared to Windows. You don't have a lot of icons littering the screen.

Of course, you can fill the desktop with all of the icons you please. As with Windows, you can save files to the desktop for easy access. In addition, you can click and drag icons from any of the menus onto the desktop in order to create shortcuts.

Along the top of the desktop, you see three menus:

The **Applications** menu is the equivalent of the Windows Start ➤ Programs menu. Here, you'll find access to all the software available under Ubuntu.

The **Places** menu is somewhat like My Computer in Windows, in that it gives quick access to locations within the file system. However, the Places menu also provides access to network locations, such as file servers (this will probably only be important if you use Ubuntu in a business context).

The **System** menu is a little like the Windows Control Panel, in that it allows you to change various system settings.

The counterpart of the Windows Recycle Bin lives at the bottom-right corner of the screen as a small icon and is called the Trash. Although diminished in stature compared to the Windows representation, it works in a similar way: you can drag icons and files onto the icon to delete them, and you can click it to open the Trash and salvage files.

■**Note** There's one important difference between Windows' Recycle Bin and Ubuntu's Trash. By default, the Recycle Bin only uses 10 percent of the remaining space on a hard disk. After this, the oldest items are automatically deleted. With Ubuntu's Trash, the only limit on the contents is the remaining free space on the disk. Nothing will ever be removed from the Trash unless you specifically choose to do so.

The mouse works largely as it does in Windows, in that you can move it around and click on things. You can also right-click virtually everything and everywhere to bring up context menus, which usually let you alter settings. And you should find that the scroll wheel in between the mouse buttons lets you scroll windows.

Whenever Ubuntu is busy, an animated circular icon will appear that is similar in principle to the hourglass icon used in Windows. It also appears when programs are being launched.

■**Caution** Bear in mind that Ubuntu isn't a clone of Windows and doesn't try to be. Although it works in a similar way—by providing menus, icons, and containing programs within windows—there are various potholes in the road that can trip up the unwary.

Shutting Down or Restarting Ubuntu

You can shut down or reboot your PC by selecting the System ➤ Quit menu option. Alternatively, you can click the icon at the top-right corner of the screen. Either method will open a dialog box showing icons for various options, as follows and as shown in Figure 7-4:

Log Out: This option will log you out of the current user account and return you to the Ubuntu login screen. Any open programs will automatically be shut down.

■**Note** During shutdown or logout operations, Ubuntu sometimes automatically shuts down applications that contain unsaved data without prompting you, so you should always save files prior to selecting any of the options here.

Lock Screen: This will enable the screensaver and password protect the system. The only way to leave Lock Screen mode is to enter the user's password into the dialog box that will appear whenever you move the mouse or press a key.

Switch User: This will let you switch between two or more user accounts, if they're set up on the system (Chapter 29 discusses how to add additional user accounts). Therefore, you'll be returned to the Ubuntu login screen. Unlike the Log Out option, the user's session *will continue running in the background* while the computer is used to log in to a different user account. To switch back to the original user, select Switch User again, and type the original username and password. You'll be asked if you want to return to the previous session or create another session for the user. Be careful, however, because any new session will automatically terminate the old session.

Suspend: This will make use of your computer's Suspend mode, in which most of the PC's systems are powered down except for the computer's memory. This is designed to save power and allow a quick reactivation of the PC. Not all computers are compatible with Suspend, however, and you should experiment to see if your computer works correctly. Ensure you save any open files before doing so.

Hibernate: This saves the contents of the computer's memory to the hard disk and then completely powers down the computer. When the computer is reactivated, the user chooses to start Ubuntu as normal, and the memory contents are read in from disk. This allows a faster start-up and allows the user to resume from where he/she was last working. For Hibernate to work, the swap file needs to be as large or larger than the main memory. Ubuntu's installation program should have automatically done this, but if you didn't dedicate enough disk space to Ubuntu when repartitioning, it might not have been able to do so. The only way to find out is to attempt to hibernate and see if it works.

■**Caution** Some users have reported that their computer is sometimes unable to "wake" from hibernation, so you should save any open files before hibernating as insurance against the unlikely prospect that this happens. I've had this happen a few times, although hundreds of other times it's worked fine.

Restart: This option will shut down Ubuntu and then restart the computer.

Shut Down: This will shut down Ubuntu and then power off your computer, provided its BIOS is compatible with the standard shutdown commands (all computers bought within the last five years are; if you find that the computer hangs at the end of the Ubuntu shutdown procedure, simply turn it off manually via the power switch).

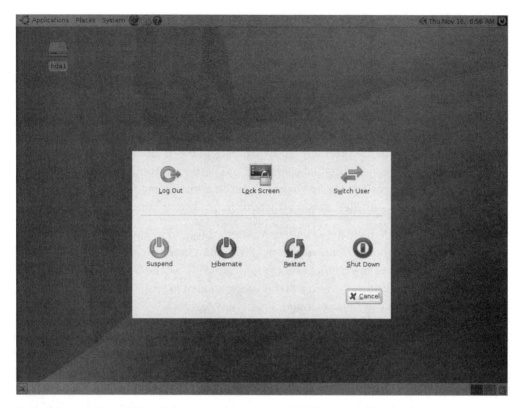

Figure 7-4. *A variety of shutdown operations are available, some allowing for a quick resumption later on.*

WRONG RESOLUTION!

You might find when you boot up that Ubuntu has defaulted to the wrong resolution. In other words, everything might be a little too large or too small. You might have trouble reading text, for example, or you might find that program windows fill the screen to the extent that their contents partially disappear off the edges.

Changing the resolution is simple. Select System ➤ Preferences ➤ Screen Resolution from the menu (at the top of the screen). In the Resolution drop-down list, select the appropriate setting for your monitor. For a 17-inch CRT monitor, the standard resolution is 1024 × 768 (although some people prefer 800 × 600). Most 17-inch TFT screens run at 1280 × 1024 resolution. If you have a 15-inch CRT monitor (common on PCs made before 2000), you'll probably find 800 × 600 a maximum setting; others prefer 640 × 480. A 15-inch TFT screen will usually run at 1024 × 768 resolution. If you're in doubt as to your monitor's resolution, consult your monitor's manual for more information.

If the resolution you want isn't available, Ubuntu might have incorrectly set up your graphics card. See the "Graphical Problems" section in Chapter 6 to learn how to reconfigure the graphical subsystem.

Desktop Elements

The Ubuntu desktop is similar to that of Windows. It has the following elements:

Menus: The three menus at the top left of the screen provide access to all of Ubuntu's functionality. As noted earlier, the Applications menu provides access to programs; the Places menu provides access to the file system, and the System menu provides access to configuration settings (as well as the Log Out option). You can click and drag practically every menu entry onto the desktop in order to create a shortcut.

Icons: Although the Ubuntu desktop is largely clean, some icons are tucked away at the top and bottom of the screen. Those at the top are located to the right of the menus and allow you to start the browser, e-mail client, and help system (and they are arranged in that order). At the top right is a speaker icon that lets you alter the sound volume, along with the Quit icon (additionally, if your system is online, you might see the System Update icon—this is explained in Chapter 9). At the bottom left is the Hide Windows button that instantly minimizes all open windows to give access to the desktop underneath. At the bottom right are the two virtual desktop buttons, which I'll discuss in the "Working with Virtual Desktops" section later in this chapter, and also the Trash icon.

■**Note** If you're dual-booting with Windows, you might see an icon at the top left of the desktop that will let you access your Windows files. On my system, this was identified has hda1. Double-click the icon to view the Windows file system. Similarly, if you have a memory card reader or digital camera plugged into your PC, you might see desktop icons for them too, and any inserted CD/DVD discs will also be represented by desktop icons.

Window List: The bar at the bottom of the screen, called the Window List, shows which programs are currently running (if any). As with Windows, you can simply click the button for any program to bring that window "to the top." Alternatively, you can right-click each entry to instantly minimize or maximize that particular window.

Clock: The clock is located in the top right of the screen. Clicking it brings up a handy monthly calendar (click it again to hide it). Right-clicking it brings up a context menu. On this menu, the Preferences option lets you alter the way the date and time are displayed. The Adjust Date & Time option lets you change the time and/or date if they're incorrect.

Notification area: The speaker icon and clock are located in the notification area, which is similar to the Windows system tray. Programs that like to hang around in memory, such as the Rhythmbox media player, will add an icon in this top-right area, to allow quick access to their functions. Usually, you simply need to click (or right-click) their icons to access the program features.

Tip The small bar marks the leftmost boundary of the notification area. To resize the notification area, right-click this bar and remove the tick from the Lock to Panel menu entry. Then you can click and drag the bar to a different size. This might be handy if the notification area starts to fill up with icons!

BEHIND THE DESKTOP: GNOME

Although I refer to the Ubuntu desktop, the fundamental software behind it is created by GNOME: The Free Software Desktop Project. This is one of the most well-established organizations currently producing desktop interfaces for Linux, as well as for other versions of Unix. Its home page is www.gnome.org.

Although it's based on GNOME, Ubuntu's desktop has its own set of individual features and programs, as well as a unique look and feel. That said, it works in an almost identical way to versions of GNOME that are used in other Linux distributions, such as Red Hat Fedora.

The nature of open source software—whereby anyone can take the source code and create his/her own version of a program—makes Ubuntu's remodeling of the GNOME desktop possible. Unlike with Windows software, more than one current version of a particular program or software suite can exist, and each is usually tailored to the particular needs of one of the various Linux distributions.

There are also versions of Ubuntu built around KDE (www.kde.org) and Xfce 4 (www.xfce.org), two similar desktop environments. They're called Kubuntu and Xubuntu, respectively, and they're supplied on the DVD-ROM that comes with this book. For more details, including installation instructions, see Appendix D.

Quick Desktop Guides

Refer to Figure 7-5 for an annotated diagram of the desktop. The figure includes an open menu, browser window, and program window, so you can get an idea of working from the desktop.

As another handy reference, Table 7-1 lists standard Windows desktop features and where similar functionality can be found on the Ubuntu desktop.

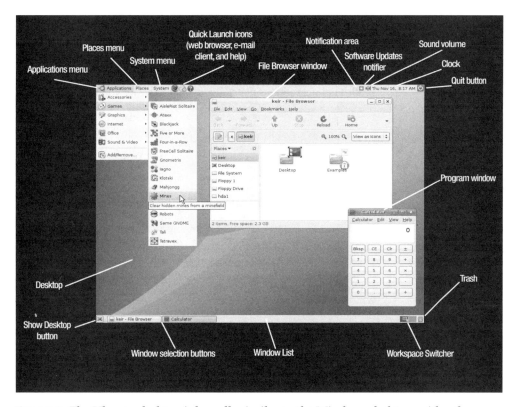

Figure 7-5. *The Ubuntu desktop is broadly similar to the Windows desktop, with a few minor differences.*

Table 7-1. *Windows Desktop Features Equivalents Under Ubuntu*

Windows Function	Description	Ubuntu Equivalent
My Computer/ Computer	Double-clicking the My Computer/ Computer icon gives you access to the PC system. In particular, it lets you browse the file system.	Click Places ➤ Computer to see all the drives attached to the computer in the file browser window. If you wish to browse the file system, double-click File System in the list on the left side of the file browser window.
Recycle Bin	The Recycle Bin is the repository of deleted files.	Click the small Trash icon located at the bottom-right corner of the Ubuntu desktop.

Table 7-1. *Windows Desktop Features Equivalents Under Ubuntu (Continued)*

Windows Function	Description	Ubuntu Equivalent
Start menu	The Start menu provides access to many computer functions, as well as a list of the programs installed on the system.	This function is split between the Applications and System menus. The Applications menu provides access to software installed under Ubuntu. The System menu lets you configure and administer the system, rather like the Windows Control Panel.
Quick Launch toolbar	Located just to the right of the Start button, these small icons let you launch popular programs with a single click.	Similar icons are located to the right of the main menus at the top of the Ubuntu desktop. You can add you own entries here by clicking and dragging program icons from the Applications menu.
My Network Places/ Network Neighborhood	This icon is used to access network services, usually within a business environment (on newer versions of Windows, this icon is often hidden by default).	To browse the local network, click Places ➤ Network Servers.
My Documents/ Documents	The My Documents/Documents folder, accessed via its icon on the Windows desktop, is a storage space set aside for a user's documents.	The user's Home folder serves this purpose and can be accessed by clicking Places ➤ Home Folder.
Control Panel	The Windows Control Panel, located off the Start menu, allows the user to change system settings and preferences.	Similar functionality can be found under the System ➤ Administration and System ➤ Preferences menu options.
Find Files/ Start Search	Located on the Start menu, the Find Files/Start Search function lets a user search the file system for missing items.	To find files, click Places ➤ Search for Files.
Shutdown/Reboot	At the bottom of the Start menu within Windows is the Shutdown/ Reboot button.	Clicking System ➤ Quit brings up a dialog box that is almost identical to the one displayed in Windows XP and offers the same options as the Windows Vista shutdown submenu.

It will take some time to get used to the look and feel of Ubuntu; everything will initially seem odd. You'll find that the on-screen fonts look a little different from those in Windows, for example. The icons also won't be the same as you're used to in Windows. This can be a little disconcerting, but that feeling will quickly pass, and everything will become second nature. We'll look at how you can personalize the desktop in Chapter 10.

UBUNTU FOR MACINTOSH OS X USERS

Migrating to Ubuntu from Mac OS X shouldn't present too many surprises and, in some ways, Ubuntu has more in common with OS X than it does with Windows. After all, both Linux and OS X are versions of Unix. Here is a list of OS X functions alongside details of where they can be found within Ubuntu:

- **Finder (File Browsing):** Finder under OS X offers access to files, applications, and much more and is represented on the Dock by the Mac smiley face icon. In terms of file browsing functionality, clicking Places ➤ Home under Ubuntu is all that's needed for similar behavior.

- **Finder (Applications):** The Applications option within Finder shows a list of all installed programs. Exactly the same thing can be found by clicking the Applications button under Ubuntu, although the programs are arranged into submenus to make finding what you're looking for easier.

- **Finder (Network Locations):** Clicking the Network button in Finder allows the user to browse the local area network or access remote file servers. This functionality can be found on the Places menu—click Places ➤ Network Servers to browse the local network and Places ➤ Connect to Server to access a remote server, such as FTP (this function also allows the user to connect to local servers by specifying their addresses).

- **Macintosh HD:** Double-clicking this icon on the desktop allows the user to access the root of the Macintosh file system. To access the root file system under Ubuntu, click Places ➤ Computer, and then click the File System link in the left-hand pane of the file-browsing window.

- **Dock:** There is no direct analogy to the dock under Ubuntu, but the Quick Launch icons to the right of the Applications/Places/System menus offer quick access to the Web browser, e-mail client, and help system. Additional programs can be added to the Quick Launch toolbar by clicking and dragging them from the Applications menu, while the Window List controls the active window.

- **Trash:** Located on the Dock, the Trash icon lets OS X users salvage deleted files. The same functionality is offered by the Ubuntu Trash icon, which is located at the bottom-right corner of the screen.

- **System Preferences:** Located on the Dock and in the Applications menu, the System Preferences icon offers access to all of OS X's configuration utilities. Similar functionality can be found on the System ➤ Preferences and System ➤ Administration menus.

- **Spotlight (version 10.4 and above):** Spotlight allows users to search their hard disk for files. To access Ubuntu's search function, click Places ➤ Search for Files.

Running Programs

Starting a new program is easy. Just click the Applications menu, and then choose a program from the list as you would in Windows using the Start ➤ Programs menu. The menu, shown in Figure 7-6, is split into various subcategories of programs, such as office tools, graphics programs, and even games!

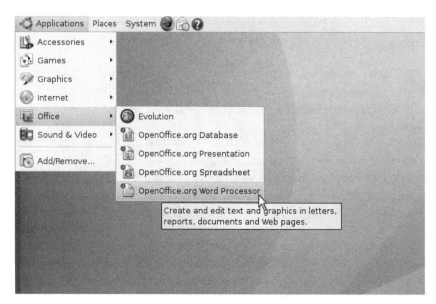

Figure 7-6. *The programs on the Applications menu are split into various categories.*

If you want to start the web browser or e-mail client (arguably two of the most popular programs offered by Ubuntu), you can click their icons on the top panel bar, just to the right of the menus at the top of the screen (see Figure 7-6).

At the top right of every program window under Ubuntu, you'll see the familiar Close, Minimize, and Maximize buttons, albeit with a slightly different look and feel than you're used to. Clicking Close will end each program, as in Windows.

Working with Virtual Desktops

Windows works on the premise of everything taking place on top of a desktop. When you start a new program, it runs on top of the desktop, effectively covering up the desktop. In fact, all programs are run on this desktop, so it can get a bit confusing when you have more than a couple of programs running at the same time. Which Microsoft Word window contains the document you're working on, rather than the one you've opened to take notes from? Where is that My Computer window you were using to copy files?

Ubuntu overcomes this problem by having more than one desktop area. By using the Workspace Switcher tool, located at the bottom right of the desktop, you can switch between two virtual desktops. This is best explained by a demonstration.

1. Make sure that you're currently on the first virtual desktop (click the leftmost square on the Workspace Switcher), and start up the web browser by clicking its icon at the top of the screen (the globe icon located to the right of the menus).

2. Click the second square on the Workspace Switcher. This will switch you to a clean desktop, where no programs are running—desktop number two.

3. Start up the file browser by selecting the Places ➤ Home menu option. A file browser window appears.

4. Click the first square in the Workspace Switcher again. You should switch back to the desktop that is running the web browser.

5. Click the second square, and you'll switch back to the other desktop, which is running the file browser.

■**Tip** Right-clicking any of the program entries in the Window List will bring up a menu where you can move a program from one virtual desktop to another. Just select Move to Another Workspace.

See how it works? You can create more than two virtual desktops—as many as 36, in fact! To set the number of workspaces, right-click the Workspace Switcher and select Preferences. In the window that appears, click the up arrow next to the Number of Workspaces entry, as shown in Figure 7-7.

You can also rename each virtual desktop by double-clicking its entry in the list in the Workspace Names list. This allows you to be even more organized. For example, you might reserve desktop 1 for running Internet programs and give it a name that indicates this, such as Net Programs. You might then use desktop 2 to run office programs, giving it an appropriate title; use desktop 3 for file browsing; and so on. This name will appear whenever you right-click a program's entry on the Panel and attempt to move it to a different desktop. Additionally, these titles will appear whenever you right-click and choose to send each program window to a different desktop.

■**Tip** Putting your mouse over the Workspace Switcher and scrolling the mouse wheel switches between the various virtual desktops instantly. Alternatively, you can hold down Ctrl+Alt and press the left and right cursor keys to switch between virtual desktops.

Figure 7-7. *Four virtual desktops are set up by default, but you can have as many as 36.*

The Workspace Switcher provides a way of organizing your programs and also reducing the clutter. You can experiment with virtual desktops to see if you want to organize your work this way. Some people swear by them. Experienced Ubuntu users may have in excess of ten virtual desktops, although clearly this will appeal only to organizational geniuses! Other users think multiple desktops are a waste of time. They're certainly worth trying out to see if they suit the way you work.

Using the Mouse

As noted earlier, the mouse works mostly the same under Ubuntu as it does under Windows: a left-click selects things, and a right-click usually brings up a context menu. Try right-clicking various items, such as icons on the desktop or even the desktop itself.

■**Tip** Right-clicking a blank spot on the desktop and selecting Create Launcher lets you create shortcuts to applications. Clicking Create Folder lets you create new empty folders.

You can use the mouse to drag icons on top of other icons. For example, you can drag a file onto a program icon in order to run it. You can also click and drag in certain areas to create an elastic band and, as in Windows, this lets you select more than one icon at once.

You can resize windows using the mouse in much the same way as in Windows. Just click and drag the edges and corners of the windows. In addition, you can double-click the title bar to maximize and subsequently restore windows.

Ubuntu also makes use of the third mouse button for middle-clicking. You might not think your mouse has one of these but, actually, if it's relatively modern, it probably does. Such mice have a scroll wheel between the buttons, and this can act as a third button when pressed.

In Ubuntu, the main use of the middle mouse button is in copying and pasting, as described in the next section. Middle-clicking also has a handful of other functions; for example, middle-clicking the title bar of any open window will switch to the window underneath.

Tip If your mouse doesn't have a scroll wheel, or if it has one that doesn't click, you can still middle-click. Simply press the left and right mouse buttons at the same time. This emulates a middle-click, although it takes a little skill to get right. Generally speaking, you need to press one button a fraction of a second before you press the other button.

Cutting and Pasting Text

Ubuntu offers two separate methods of cutting and pasting text. The first method is identical to that under Windows. In a word processor or another application that deals with text, you can click and drag the mouse to highlight text, right-click anywhere on it, and then select to copy or cut the text. In many programs, you can also use the keyboard shortcuts of Ctrl+X to cut, Ctrl+C to copy, and Ctrl+V to paste.

However, there's a quicker method of copying and pasting. Simply click and drag to highlight some text, and then immediately click the middle mouse button where you want the text to appear. This will copy and paste the highlighted text automatically, as shown in Figure 7-8.

This special method of cutting and pasting bypasses the usual clipboard, so you should find that any text you've copied or cut previously should still be there. The downside is that it doesn't work across all applications within Ubuntu, although it does work with the majority of them.

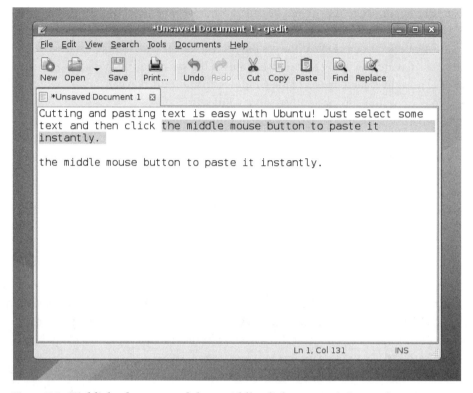

Figure 7-8. *Highlight the text, and then middle-click to paste it instantly.*

Summary

This chapter covered booting into Ubuntu for the first time and discovering the desktop.
We've looked at starting programs, working with virtual desktops, using the mouse on the
Ubuntu desktop, and much more. You should have become confident in some basic Ubuntu
skills and should now be ready to learn more!

In the next chapter, we'll look at getting your system up and running, focusing in
particular on items of hardware that experience day-to-day use.

CHAPTER 8

∎∎∎

Getting Everything Up and Running

This chapter guides you through setting up all the essential components of your Ubuntu installation. This includes hardware configuration, as well as setting up e-mail and online software repositories. It covers the post-installation steps necessary to get your system up and running efficiently.

Like all modern Linux distributions, Ubuntu is practically automated when it comes to setting up key hardware and software components. Key software will work from the start, and most hardware will be automatically configured. However, you might need to tweak a few settings to make everything work correctly. Read on to learn more.

Ubuntu Hardware Support

The age-old criticism that the Linux operating system lags behind Windows in terms of hardware support is long dead. The majority of add-ins, such as digital cameras and printers, will all work with Ubuntu immediately, with little, if any, configuration.

In fact, most underlying PC hardware is preconfigured during installation without your knowledge and without requiring further work. Both your graphics and sound cards should work without a hitch, for example. In addition, nearly all USB and FireWire devices you plug in after installation will be supported.

Ubuntu doesn't support a few hardware items. Generally, it's a black or white situation; Ubuntu either works with a piece of hardware or it doesn't.

The types of hardware that Ubuntu doesn't support tend to be esoteric devices that rely on custom software provided by the hardware manufacturer. It's also sometimes the case that brand-new models of hardware won't work with Ubuntu because support has yet to be added. However, as soon as a new piece of hardware comes out, work is usually undertaken to ensure that Linux is made compatible with it. This is especially true of hardware such as printers or scanners, and it's one more reason why you should regularly update your system online, as explained in Chapter 9.

■**Tip** Before you buy a new piece of hardware, why not ask the salesperson if it runs under Linux? You can only hope that the salesperson knows or can find out for you. Also, compatibility with Linux is often listed on the hardware box or at the manufacturer's web site (even if you sometimes need to search through the FAQ section to find out about it!).

Unfortunately, unlike with Windows, it's rare to find Linux drivers on the CD that comes with the hardware. Even if you do find a Linux driver supplied, chances are that it will work with only certain versions of Linux, such as Red Hat or SUSE Linux. At the time of this writing, Ubuntu has yet to gain the kind of momentum where manufacturers specifically produce drivers for it. But this may change in the future.

■**Note** It's possible to use a program called `alien` to convert software installation packages designed for other distributions into Ubuntu installation files. Doing so isn't very complicated but may not work very well with driver files because of the subtle differences in where system files are stored across different Linux distributions. You can find more information about `alien` at `http://kitenet.net/~joey/code/alien.html`. It's contained within the Ubuntu software repositories and can be downloaded using the Synaptic Package Manager, as explained Chapter 28.

Proprietary vs. Open-Source Drivers

As discussed earlier in this book, Linux is an open-source operating system. This means that the source code underlying Linux programs is available for study and even reuse. This is a good thing when it comes to hardware drivers, because bugs in the code can be spotted and repaired by anyone with an interest in doing so. If you consider that a bug in a graphics driver could mean your PC crashes every five minutes, the value of such an approach is abundantly clear.

Unfortunately, some hardware manufacturers don't like to disclose how their hardware works, because they want to protect their trade secrets. This makes it impossible for them to release open-source drivers, because such drivers would expose exactly how the hardware operates. Because such companies are aware of the fact that growing numbers of people use Linux, they release *proprietary drivers*, whose source code is not made publicly available.

Aside from ethical issues surrounding not being able to study the source code, the biggest issue with proprietary drivers relates to bug fixing. To use a proprietary driver is to be at the mercy of the hardware manufacturer's own development and release schedule. If the driver has a serious bug, you'll either have to work around it or put up with troubling issues until the manufacturer offers an update. Recently a proprietary driver for a 3D graphics card stopped any computer it was installed on from going into hibernation mode (that is, suspending to disk). Those using the drivers had to wait months until the fix was released.

Despite this and although the folks behind Ubuntu strongly support open-source software, they realize proprietary drivers need to be used in certain situations. For example, it's impossible to use the 3D graphics elements of most modern graphics cards unless you have a proprietary driver. Because of this, it's often possible to grab proprietary drivers from the Ubuntu online software repositories. You'll also learn how to download 3D graphics card drivers, in the "Installing 3D Graphics Card Drivers" section. Additionally, Ubuntu installs proprietary drivers for some wireless network devices automatically.

Note Linux sees hardware in a technical way, rather than in the way humans do. If you attach something like a USB CD-R/RW drive, Linux will recognize the drive hardware and attempt to make it work. It won't try to find a driver for that specific make and model of CD-R/RW drive. Thus, Linux is able to work with a wide range of hardware, because a lot of hardware is actually very similar on a technical level, despite the differences in case design, model names, and even prices!

WHAT HARDWARE WORKS?

The question of what hardware works under Ubuntu is one that's not easily answered. However, you can take a look at `http://doc.gwos.org/index.php/HCL` to see if your hardware is listed. This is an informal list created by the Ubuntu community, and it's not comprehensive (which is to say that there may be hardware that works fine that isn't mentioned). Nor is the list guaranteed to be 100% accurate. But it's certainly worth a look.

Perhaps even more useful is the Hardware *Incompatibility* List, which partners the previous one and can be found at `http://doc.gwos.org/index.php/AntiHCL`. This lists hardware that users have found definitely doesn't work or that works in a buggy way.

A search engine like Google is your best friend if the two Ubuntu hardware lists don't help. Simply search for the brand and model of your hardware and add "Ubuntu" to the search string. This should return results, usually from the Ubuntu forums (`www.ubuntuforms.org`) or an individual's blog, written by those who have found a way to make that type of hardware work.

How to Configure Ubuntu

Throughout this chapter, I'll ask you to use various Ubuntu configuration software, as follows.

Device Manager

When using Windows, you might have come across Device Manager, the handy tool that lists your PC's hardware. Ubuntu contains a similar piece of software, shown in Figure 8-1, which you can open by selecting System ➤ Administration ➤ Device Manager.

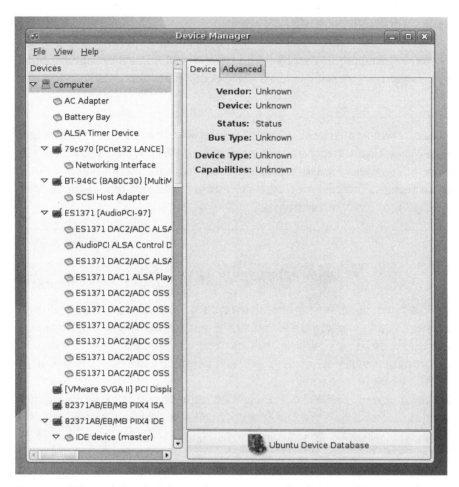

Figure 8-1. *Ubuntu's Device Manager program can display just about everything you need to know about attached hardware.*

You should be aware of a few important differences between the Windows and Ubuntu versions of Device Manager. Under Ubuntu, the list is for information only. You can't tweak any settings and must instead rely on separate pieces of configuration software. On the other hand, Ubuntu's list is far more comprehensive than that in Windows. In Ubuntu, Device Manager thoroughly probes the hardware to discover its capabilities.

Perhaps the biggest difference, however, is that just because a piece of hardware is listed within Ubuntu's Device Manager, it doesn't mean that the hardware is configured to work with Ubuntu. In fact, it doesn't even imply that the hardware will *ever* work under Ubuntu. Device Manager's list is simply the result of probing devices attached to the various system buses (PCI, AGP, USB, and so on) and reporting the data.

Nonetheless, Device Manager is the best starting place if you find that a certain piece of hardware isn't working. If a piece of hardware is listed, then it proves, if nothing else, that the system recognizes that the hardware is attached. For example, later in this chapter, I'll describe how you can use Device Manager to discover crucial details about wireless network devices, which we will then use to install drivers.

Individual Configuration Programs

Unlike some versions of Linux, Ubuntu doesn't rely on a centralized configuration software package. Instead it uses smaller programs to configure hardware. For example, the network configuration tool can be found on the System ➤ Administration menu, as can the separate printer configuration program. However, because using such software involves reconfiguring your entire system, doing so requires administrator privileges. Therefore, you'll be prompted for your login password each time you use such programs.

In some cases, after you've made changes, you'll need to click the Apply button to put the changes into operation. When you've finished configuration, simply close the program window by clicking the Close button.

■**Note** For five minutes after you enter your password, Ubuntu remembers it, so if you open the same application or another that requires administrator privileges, you won't be prompted.

Using the Command Line

For some configuration steps discussed later I ask that you open a terminal window. This will give access to the command-line prompt, by which you can issue commands directly to Ubuntu. The Linux command-line prompt is a little like MS-DOS that you might have used in the early days of Windows, except it's a lot more powerful. As with DOS, you should press Enter after typing each command. Nearly all the commands affect your system, so they will require you to enter your password when prompted.

I explain all about the command-line prompt in Part 4 of this book, beginning with Chapter 13, but for the moment you should bear in mind the following points:

- Type any commands exactly as they're written, including lowercase and uppercase letters.

- Check the command once you've typed it to ensure it reads as is printed on the page; even a stray space in the command could cause havoc.

- Don't be tempted to experiment at the prompt at this stage of your Linux learning curve; this is especially true should you use administrator powers, which you'll be doing for nearly all the commands.

To enter commands at the prompt, you'll need to open a terminal window. This can be done by clicking Applications ➤ Accessories ➤ Terminal. After you've finished entering the commands and they have completed, simply close the program window.

Installing Software

Throughout this chapter and in other chapters in this book, I might ask that you install software packages using Ubuntu's software configuration tool, Synaptic Package Manager. Some software packages might be installed from the DVD-ROM disc, so you'll need to keep this handy, but the majority will be automatically downloaded from online repositories once you've configured your computer to go online.

I explain all about software installation in Chapter 28 of this book, but here's a brief primer on what to do. Synaptic Package Manager can be started by clicking System ➤ Administration ➤ Synaptic Package Manager. Because you're reconfiguring your system, you'll need to enter your login password when prompted.

Every time you use Synaptic Package Manager, you should click the Reload button, at the left of the toolbar running across the top of the screen. This will grab the most up-to-date list of software from the online servers. To search for software, click the Search button on the toolbar, and type the name into the Search field of the dialog box. Then click the dialog box's Search button.

To install a software package, click the check box alongside it in the list of results, and click Mark for Installation on the menu that pops up. Sometimes you might be informed that extra software packages need to be installed. This is fine, and they will automatically be added to the list. When you've finished making your choices, click the Apply button on the main toolbar. Click Apply once more in the dialog box that appears to confirm your choices. When installation has finished, click the Close button in the dialog box, and close Synaptic Package Manager.

■**Note** Later in this chapter, I explain how to add additional software repositories to your Ubuntu setup to give you the widest choice of software. Adding the repositories is an essential step that you should undertake as soon as you configure your system to go online.

MAKING USE OF THE COMMUNITY

Configuring hardware is one area where the value of the Ubuntu community becomes very apparent. If you run into a problem, it's unlikely your situation will be unique. Somebody else will probably have encountered the same problem and may well have figured out a solution. If so, they may have posted it online. If nothing else, you might find sufficient clues to be able to solve the problem by yourself. The sharing of information in this way is part of the spirit of Ubuntu and also Linux.

I've tried to provide complete guides to most hardware configuration in this chapter, but if you run into problems, your first port of call should be the Ubuntu forums—www.ubuntuforums.org. This is the central meeting place for the Ubuntu community. You can search through existing forum postings or start your own thread asking for help. I explain a little more about the protocols of asking for help in Appendix C of this book.

Also worth visiting in times of trouble is the community-written wiki, which can be found at https://help.ubuntu.com/community. Here you'll find a range of guides to help configure various aspects of Ubuntu. A *wiki* is a form of web site that anybody can edit or contribute to. The idea is that it's constructed by its readers.

I would also advise you take a look at the Ubuntu Guide—http://ubuntuguide.org/wiki/Ubuntu_Edgy—which is also community-written. The Ubuntu Guide can be very concise, and often expects a relatively high degree of technical knowledge, but it is also very comprehensive.

Finally, don't forget that you're a member of the community too. If you encounter and subsequently solve a configuration problem, share the solution with others. You can do this by editing the wiki, mentioned previously, or by posting to the Ubuntu forums.

Getting Online

Getting online is vital in our modern Internet age, and Ubuntu caters to all the standard ways of doing so. Linux was built from the ground up to be an online operating system and is based on Unix, which pioneered the concept of networking computers together to share data back in the 1970s. However, none of this is to say that getting online with Ubuntu is difficult! In fact, it's very easy.

Regardless of whether you use a modem, standard ethernet network device, or wireless network device, the same program is used to configure your network settings under Ubuntu. Support for many makes and models of equipment is built in, so in most cases, all you need to do is enter a few configuration details.

■**Note** Linux actually runs around 60% of the computers that make the Internet work! Whenever you visit a web site, there's a strong chance that it's run using Linux. As your Linux skills increase, you'll eventually get to a stage where you, too, can run your own Internet servers. It sounds difficult, but can be quite easy.

Using an Ethernet Network Device

Ethernet is one of the oldest and most established network technologies. When we talk of ethernet, we refer to wired networks—all the computers on the network are connected by cabling to a central hub or router. (The other form of networking technology, which works without wires, is covered in the next section.)

You might go online via ethernet in a variety of situations. If you have DSL or cable broadband service at your home or workplace, for example, you might use a DSL router. Your computer will then connect to this router via an ethernet cable, and all you need to worry about on your PC is getting your ethernet network device up and running.

If you're running Ubuntu on a PC in an office environment, it's likely that you will connect to the local area network using ethernet. This lets your computer communicate with other computers, as well as with shared printers. In some offices in which an Internet connection is provided, this connection might also allow you to go online.

Configuring a Network Device via DHCP

Practically all computers that connect to a broadband router or an office network receive their configuration data via the Dynamic Host Control Protocol (DHCP), which is to say that your computer receives its IP, gateway, subnet mask, and DNS addresses automatically.

If your network offers this functionality then, congratulations, you should find yourself already online! You can test this by opening a web browsing window and visiting a site, if your network provides Internet access, or by attempting to look for other computers on the network by clicking Places ➤ Network Servers.

If, for any reason, you find you're not online, you can manually configure your network device to work via DHCP by following these steps:

1. Select System ➤ Administration ➤ Networking to open the Network Settings dialog box.

2. You should find your Ethernet device at the top of the list. It will be identified as Wired Connection. Click the entry, and then click Properties.

■**Note** Listed beneath the ethernet device will be any other networking devices your computer might have, such as a dial-up modem. If you don't want to use these, you can leave them unconfigured.

3. In the dialog box, put a check in the Enable This Connection check box, and make sure the Configuration drop-down list reads Automatic Configuration (DHCP). Then click OK.

4. In the Network Settings dialog box, ensure there's a check alongside the Wired Connection entry in the list. If there's already a check there, remove it, and then click again to check the box.

5. After a few seconds, your network device should be up and running.

From this point on, your network device should automatically activate each time you boot, so you should not need to return to the Network Settings applet.

Configuring a Static IP Address

On some networks, you might have been assigned an IP address, which you must enter manually, along with a few other networking addresses. This is referred to as a *static IP address.*

You should speak to your system administrator or technical support person to determine these settings. Ask the administrator for your IP address, DNS server addresses (there are usually two or three of these), your subnet mask, and the router address (sometimes referred to as the gateway address). The settings you will get from your system administrator will usually be in the form of a series of four numbers separated by dots, something like 192.168.0.233.

Once you know your settings, proceed as follows:

1. Select System ➤ Administration ➤ Networking to open the Network Settings dialog box.

2. Find your network device in the list (it should be referred to as Wired Connection), click its entry, and click Properties.

3. In the dialog box that appears, put a check in the Enable This Connection check box. In the Configuration drop-down list, make sure Static IP Address is highlighted. In the IP Address, Subnet Mask, and Gateway Address text boxes, fill in the relevant details. Figure 8-2 shows an example of a completed Interface Properties dialog box. Click OK after filling in the information.

4. Click the DNS tab in the Network Settings window.

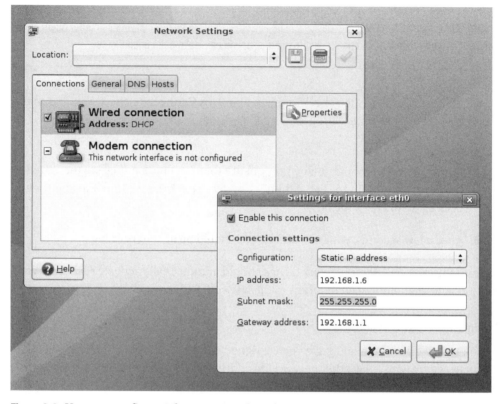

Figure 8-2. *You can configure Ubuntu to work with DHCP networks, or you can define a static IP address.*

5. Click the Add button, and then type the first DNS address. Press Enter when you've finished. Click Add again, and enter the second DNS address, if you have been given one (and then enter a third if you were given one).

■**Tip** If you're using a static IP address with a router, such as that provided by a DSL modem, the DNS address will probably be the same as the router/gateway address.

---

6. Click the Close button.

7. Click the Connections tab again, and remove the check alongside the Wired Connection entry. Then click again to recheck the box, thereby activating the device with the new configuration.

Your network connection should now work. If you find it isn't working, try rebooting. However, if your system administrator mentioned that a proxy must also be configured, you'll also need to follow the instructions in the "Working with a Proxy Server" section later in this chapter.

Joining a Wireless Network

A wireless (also referred to as Wi-Fi) network is, as its name suggests, a network that does away with cabling and uses radio frequencies to communicate. It's more common for notebooks and handheld computers to use wireless connections, but some desktop computers also do. Indeed, it's increasingly the case that many workplaces are switching to wireless networking, eschewing old-fashioned, cable-based networking.

Notebooks and PDAs typically use built-in wireless network devices, with an antenna built into the case. However, some notebooks might use PCMCIA cards, which will have an external square antenna, and some desktop computers might use PCI-based wireless cards, that have external rubber/plastic antennas, in the style of old cell phones.

Ubuntu includes support for some, but not all, wireless network devices. This is because Linux drivers simply aren't available for all makes and models of wireless hardware. However, it's possible to use Windows drivers for the unsupported hardware, and this is described under the "Using NdisWrapper to Install Windows Wireless Network Device Drivers" heading later in this chapter.

Sometimes Ubuntu appears to support a wireless network device, in that it identifies it and lets you configure it, but you might find that it simply doesn't work (or works very badly, perhaps with an intermittent connection). In this situation, you can also try installing Windows network device drivers.

Configuring Wireless Hardware

Configuring a wireless network device is quite similar to configuring a standard ethernet device, except that you'll need to tell Ubuntu which wireless base station to utilize. The name of the base station is known as its Service Set Identifier (SSID) or sometimes ESSID, with E standing for Extended. You should, therefore, find out the SSID before undertaking the following steps. Note that these instructions assume WEP/WPA isn't in use. Additional instructions are provided later for networks utilizing such protection:

1. Click System ➤ Administration ➤ Networking to start the Network Settings configuration tool.

2. The wireless device will be identified as Wireless Connection. Select this, and then click the Properties button. If your computer also has a standard ethernet adapter in addition to wireless capabilities, it will also be mentioned in the list as Wired Connection. Ensure you select the correct entry.

3. Click Enable This Connection, and then, in the Network Name (ESSID) field, type the SSID of your base station. Alternatively, if you click the drop-down list, you might find you can select it, because Ubuntu may have autodetected it. However, this obviously won't be the case if your wireless base station isn't set to broadcast its SSID.

4. In most instances, wireless network devices are configured with DHCP, so that they grab a network address automatically. Therefore, you should ensure the Configuration drop-down list reads Automatic Configuration (DHCP), as it should by default. If your wireless network uses static IP addresses, see the instructions under the previous "Configuring a Static IP Address" heading.

5. Once finished, click the OK button. Back in the Network Settings program window, ensure there's a check alongside the Wireless Connection entry in the list. If there's already a check there, remove the check, and click again to activate the device.

Configuring Wireless Hardware with WEP Encryption

Some wireless networks use the Wired Equivalency Privacy (WEP) system. These systems encrypt the data being transmitted on the network, so it cannot be stolen by hackers with special equipment. Also, people can't join the wireless network unless they know the encryption key, which is basically an access code. This prevents unauthorized people from accessing the network.

WEP keys come in either hexadecimal (hex) or plain text (passphrase) varieties. Hex keys look similar to this in their 128-bit form: CB4C4189B1861E19BC9A9BDA59. In their 64-bit form, they will be shorter and may look similar to 4D9ED51E23. A passphrase will take the form of a single short sentence. Ubuntu can work with both 64- and 128-bit keys, as well as passphrases.

■**Tip** If you find that you can't connect using a passphrase, try reconfiguring your router or wireless base station to use 64- or 128-bit hex.

Follow the steps under the "Configuring Wireless Hardware" heading to configure your wireless device. However, before clicking the OK button, follow these extra steps:

1. In the Key Type drop-down list, select Hexadecimal if you have a hex key, or select Plain (ASCII) if you have a passphrase.

2. In the WEP Key box, type the key or passphrase, as shown in Figure 8-3. It will be obscured by circle characters, to discourage anybody who might be looking over your shoulder, so type slowly to ensure you don't make a mistake. Then click OK.

3. In the main Network Settings program window, remove the check alongside the wireless device entry in the list, and click again to check the box. This will deactivate and then reactive the device with the new settings.

If you find your hardware doesn't seem to work after you enter new WEP settings, try rebooting. Then open the Network Settings applet, and make sure your device is activated.

If the hardware doesn't work after this, it might be that the drivers Ubuntu installed by default are incompatible with your network device. See the "Using NdisWrapper to Install Windows Wireless Network Device Drivers" heading.

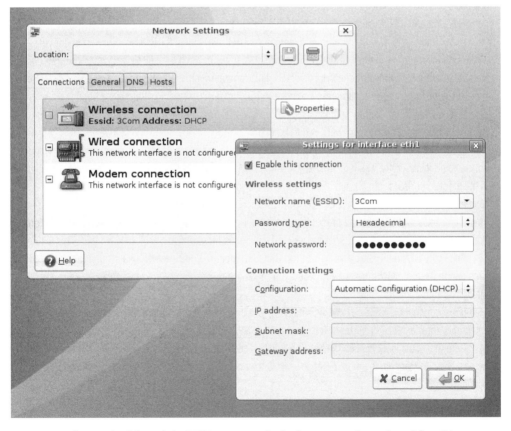

Figure 8-3. *Ubuntu is able to join WEP-protected wireless networks, using either 64- or 128-bit keys.*

INSTALLING NETWORKMANAGER

NetworkManager is a new piece of Linux software designed to let users easily manage network connections. Once up and running, NetworkManager sits in the system tray and detects any wireless networks that are in range. Clicking the icon will show a list of networks that the system has detected. By selecting the entry in the list, you can then connect to the network, and you'll be prompted to configure WEP/WPA protection, if applicable. Following this, the NetworkManager icon will display the signal strength of the connection for as long as you're connected, and by clicking it, you'll be able to see at a glance what network you're connected to.

NetworkManager settings persist across reboots provided the network you last configured is in range. This means that NetworkManager is ideal for all kinds of wireless network users, from those who frequently switch between different networks (that is, mobile workers), to those who only ever use a single wireless network connection, such as that provided by a wireless network broadband router in a home/small office environment. Additionally, NetworkManager will also let you switch to a wired (ethernet) connection, if and when you attach one to your computer.

Unfortunately, NetworkManager isn't installed by default. This is for good reason—it is not yet 100% integrated with Ubuntu's underlying systems. This was borne out in my testing when I couldn't get NetworkManager to work satisfactorily on one of my computers, although it worked well on another. But there are also many reports within the Ubuntu community of people using it without a hitch.

If you'd like to try it, start by installing the `network-manager-gnome` package using Synaptic Package Manager. Your system will need to be online in order to download the software.

For NetworkManager to work, you need to give it control of your network devices, and this involves editing a configuration file. Open a terminal window and type `gksu gedit /etc/network/interfaces`. In the file that appears, put a hash symbol (#) at the beginning of all lines in the file *except* those that read `auto lo` and `iface lo inet loopback`. These two lines will probably be at the top of the file. Ignore any lines that are already preceded by a hash. Note that, with some Ubuntu setups, there might not be any other lines in the file, so there won't be any lines for you to put hashes in front of! This is fine.

Save the file, and restart your computer. Once it's rebooted, click the NetworkManager icon in the Notification Area to select the network you want to join, and reconfigure your network device in the dialog box that appears.

If the connection uses WEP/WPA protection, you'll be invited to create a Keyring password when you first enter the password. This will store the WEP/WPA password in encrypted form on the hard disk.

Note that you should *not* use the Network Settings configuration tool on the System ➤ Administration menu if NetworkManager is running. Not only will it not work, it will also damage your NetworkManager configuration.

Configuring Wireless Hardware with WPA Protection

Some networks utilize Wi-Fi Protected Access (WPA). This is effectively an updated version of WEP, and offers stronger protection. However, support for WPA has yet to be officially added to Ubuntu. It's possible to join networks using WPA with a little work, but support is patchy—not all the wireless drivers installed by Ubuntu support WPA, for example, so you may find that even when follow the steps in this section, you're simply unable to utilize WPA.

Rather than undertake these steps, I advise that you configure your wireless base station to use the older WEP standard instead. Using WEP with Ubuntu has an almost 100% success rate.

In most home and offices, WEP and WPA are used merely to stop unauthorized users connecting to the wireless network. In nearly all situations, WEP offers enough protection to prevent this. Critics point out that WEP has been proven to be insecure, in that a determined hacker can easily eavesdrop or break into the network, but this still requires special skillls that are beyond the range of many people. Consider your immediate environment. If your wireless network is within your home, is it likely that your neighbors will have the know-how to crack a wireless network connection? Are they likely to want to do so? What is the genuine likelihood that somebody will attempt to eavesdrop?

If you must have WPA, follow these steps:

1. The easiest way to configure WPA is to use the NetworkManager applet. This is an extra piece of software that makes it easy to configure your network connections. See the "Installing NetworkManager" sidebar describing how to install Network-Manager. Move to Step 2 after it's installed and your computer has rebooted.

2. Click the NetworkManager icon in the Notification Area, and select your wireless network from the list.

3. Type your password into the relevant field. Check the Wireless Security drop-down list to ensure the correct entry is selected. The Type drop-down list can be left so that it reads Automatic.

4. When finished, click the Connect button. After a few seconds, you'll be prompted to create a Keyring, which requires entering a password. When finished, click the OK button.

5. After a few seconds, you should find yourself online.

Using NdisWrapper to Install Windows XP Network Device Drivers

NdisWrapper is effectively an open-source driver (technically described as a *kernel module*) that allows Linux to use standard Windows XP drivers for wireless network devices. You might describe NdisWrapper as being a translation layer between the Linux kernel and the Windows drivers, which can be installed using NdisWrapper's configuration tools.

You should only use NdisWrapper in one of two situations:

- Your wireless network hardware simply isn't recognized by Ubuntu, which is to say, no entry for the wireless hardware appears in the list of network devices in the Network Settings configuration dialog.

- Your network hardware *is* recognized by Ubuntu but fails to work correctly when you configure it. Perhaps it is unable to associate with wireless base stations, for example. If this is the case, in addition to installing NdisWrapper, you'll have to undertake an additional step in order to blacklist the existing Ubuntu driver. This is explained later.

Using NdisWrapper is relatively simple and just a handful of commands are required. However, getting hold of the necessary Windows driver files is harder work because, unfortunately, NdisWrapper isn't designed to work with the usual method of driver distribution: .exe files. Instead, NdisWrapper needs the specific .inf and .sys files that constitute the driver—effectively, the Windows system files. These are contained within the .exe file and must be manually extracted.

■**Note** Of course, sometimes drivers are distributed as .zip files, in which case the relevant files are easy to get at. Keep your fingers crossed that this will be the case for your particular hardware!

NdisWrapper is far from perfect. Not all wireless devices have been proven to work with it, and it's not necessarily the case that a driver available for Windows will work under Linux. Sometimes trial and error is required. Annoyingly, Windows drivers sometimes appear to work but then prove unreliable. Some might stop working. Some might even crash your system. The best plan is simply to give it a try.

■**Tip** NdisWrapper gets better and better with every new release. This is why it's a good idea to update your system on a regular basis, as described in Chapter 9.

In the instructions in this section, I explain how to make an Asus 802.11g wireless network device that's built into an Asus A6R notebook work under Ubuntu using NdisWrapper. The instructions remain essentially the same for all types of wireless network hardware. However, some specific details, such as download addresses, will obviously differ.

First, I explain how to install the NdisWrapper software. Next, I explain how to discover what Windows drivers you need. Following this, I explain how to extract the necessary files from the driver archive, and finally, how to actually install the Windows drivers under Ubuntu. You might also need to blacklist the existing driver, which I also cover.

These steps merely make your wireless network device available under Ubuntu. Once completed, you should see the previous steps regarding configuring your wireless network hardware, such as connecting to a wireless base station, and, if necessary, configuring WEP/WPA protection.

■**Note** Ensure that you select `ndiswrapper-utils-1.8` and not any other version of `ndiswrapper`! A packaging bug means that other versions won't work correctly.

Installing the NdisWrapper Configuration Tools

NdisWrapper consists of two components: a kernel module and configuration tools. The kernel module comes as part of the default kernel package, so is installed by default. Therefore, all you have to do is install the configuration tools. Start Synaptic Package Manager, and search for and install `ndiswrapper-utils-1.8`. You'll be told that `ndiswrapper-common` also needs to be installed. This is fine.

Installing the Windows XP Drivers

Once the NdisWrapper configuration software is installed, you can install the Windows XP wireless network device drivers. There are three parts to the procedure:

1. Identify the wireless network hardware and then source the appropriate Windows driver.

2. Extract the necessary `.sys` and `.inf` files from the driver archive (and possibly `.bin` files, although this is rare).

3. Use the NdisWrapper configuration tools to install the Windows driver, and tweak a configuration file so that the NdisWrapper kernel module loads each time you boot.

All three steps are dealt with separately in the following sections. In later stages, you will need another computer that's already online to download some files and check the NdisWrapper web site for information. If your computer dual-boots, you can use your Windows setup to do this.

Identifying Your Wireless Network Hardware and Sourcing Drivers

To identify the wireless network hardware for use with NdisWrapper, it's necessary to discover two pieces of information: the make and model of the hardware and the PCI ID number.

The former is the make and model of the hardware, as identified by Ubuntu as a result of system probing, rather than what's quoted on the packaging for the wireless network device or in its documentation. These details discovered by Ubuntu will usually relate to the manufacturer of the underlying components, rather than the company that manufactured the hardware.

The PCI ID is two four-digit hexadecimal numbers used by your computer to identify the device internally. The same PCI ID numbering system is used by both Windows and Ubuntu, which is why it's so useful in this instance.

Follow these instructions to discover the information you need:

1. You can find both the PCI ID and the make/model information using the Device Manager tool. Start System ➤ Administration ➤ Device Manager.

2. What you do now depends on whether your wireless hardware is recognized by Ubuntu (which is to say, it appears in Network Settings but doesn't work properly). If the device *isn't* recognized, skip to the next step. If it *is* recognized, look in the list of hardware that appears, and find the entry that reads WLAN Interface. Then look at the entry immediately above this in the list, where you'll find listed the make and model of the hardware. Write this down. On my test notebook, containing an ASUS wireless network device, this read BCM4318 [AirForce One 54g] 802.11g Wireless Lan Controller. As anticipated, these details don't relate to those listed in the wireless network device's documentation (the notebook's manual lists the hardware simply as an ASUS 802.11g device). This is because Ubuntu is identifying the hardware generically, reading information from its component hardware. Select the WLAN Interface entry, and click the Advanced tab on the right side of the program window. Then look through the information there for the line that begins net.physical_device. Look at the end of the line, and make a note of the two sets of letters and numbers that are separated by underscore characters and are preceded by pci_. On my test notebook, these were 14e4 and 4318, as shown in Figure 8-4, in which the relevant areas are highlighted.

3. If the wireless hardware *isn't* recognized by Ubuntu (which is to say, it doesn't appear in the Network Settings dialog box), look in the Device Manager list of hardware for an entry mentioning 802.11, WLAN, or possibly wireless. This entry in the list will be the make and model details you need, so write them down. Next, select the wireless device's entry in the list, and click the Advanced tab on the right side of the window. Look through the information there for a line that reads info.udi. Look at the end of the line, and make a note of the two sets of letters and numbers that are separated by underscore characters and are preceded by pci_. Look at Figure 8-4 for guidance.

■**Note** These two clusters of letters and numbers are actually *hexadecimal digits*. For more details on hexadecimal, see http://en.wikipedia.org/wiki/Hexadecimal.

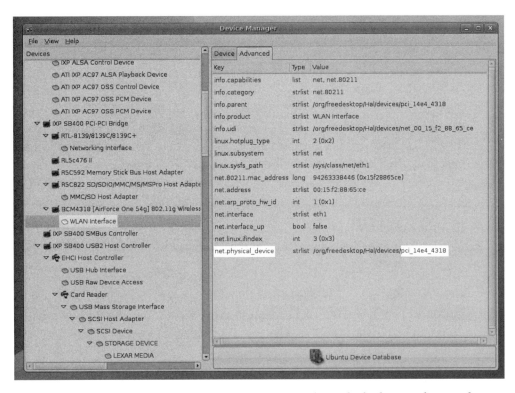

Figure 8-4. *Find the PCI ID of your wireless network hardware by looking at the two clusters of numbers and letters at the end of the* net.physical_device *line.*

4. When written alongside each other, the two sets of digits you noted in step 2 or 3 become the PCI ID number. In written form, they're usually separated by a colon, so in my case, the PCI ID of the wireless network device is 14e4:4318. If either of the sets of letters or numbers is less than four characters long, simply add zeros before them in order to make four characters. For example, on my desktop PC, the end of the net.physical_device line read 1814_201. I added a zero before 201, making the complete PCI ID of 1814:0201. On another of my test PCs, the end of the line read 168c_13. I, therefore, added two zeros before the 13 to make a PCI ID of 168c:0013.

5. Using another computer that's able to go online, visit http://ndiswrapper. sourceforge.net/mediawiki/index.php/List. This is a community-generated listing of the wireless network devices that have been proven to work with NdisWrapper.

■**Tip** The URL in step 5 was correct as this book went to press. If you find it no longer accurate, search Google using "NdisWrapper list" as a search term.

---

6. Using the search function of your browser (Ctrl+F within Firefox), look for the PCI ID number you noted earlier, in the format described in step 4. For example, with the PCI ID I discovered on my test notebook, I searched for 14e4:4318. In the list, look to match the following things, presented in order of importance:

   • The PCI ID.

   • The manufacturer and model name of the wireless hardware, as reported by Device Manager; this will be listed in the Card: part of the entry in the list and/or within the Chipset: section too.

   • The manufacturer and model of the notebook, as mentioned on its case or within its documentation. This will be mentioned in the Card: or Chipset: sections or possibly within the Other: section.

   It's likely many entries in the list may match your PCI ID, so search until you find the one that best matches the manufacturer and model of the hardware. If there are *still* many matches, search until you find an entry that matches the manufacturer and model of the notebook. You might not be lucky enough to find an exact match for the notebook manufacturer and model, however, and you might have to select the most likely choice. Use your common sense and judgment. If your notebook is manufactured by Asus, for example, but you can't find the drivers for the exact model, then choose drivers for another Asus model.

■**Caution** Watch out for any mention of x86_64 in the description of the driver file. This indicates the entry in the list relates to 64-bit Linux. The version of Ubuntu supplied with this book is 32-bit. If you encounter an entry relating to x86_64, keep searching.

---

7. Look within the entry in the list for a direct link to the driver file. Sometimes this isn't given, and a manufacturer web site address will be mentioned, which you can visit and navigate through to the driver download section (usually under the Support section within the web site). Download the Windows XP driver release.

Extracting the Driver Components

Once the drivers are downloaded, you'll have to extract the `.sys` and `.inf` file relevant to your wireless network hardware. These are all that NdisWrapper needs, and the rest of the driver files can be discarded. However, extracting the files can be hard to do, because often they're contained within an `.exe` file.

■**Note** Most driver `.exe` files are actually self-extracting archive files.

Additionally, the driver file might contain drivers for several different models of hardware, and it's necessary to identify the particular driver `.inf` file relevant to your wireless network device:

1. If the driver you've downloaded is a `.zip` file, then your task will probably be much easier. Simply double-click the downloaded `.zip` file to look within it for the directory containing the actual driver files. Often this directory is called `driver`, or sometimes it's named after the OS for which it contains files, such as `Win_XP`. If you've ever installed Windows drivers then this will sound familiar. Once you've found the relevant directory, click and drag the `.inf`, `.sys`, and `.bin` files to a separate folder (there probably won't be any `.bin` files, however). You can ignore any other files, such as `.cab` and `.cat` files. Then go to step 4.

2. If the driver is an `.exe` file, it's necessary to extract the files within it. With any luck you might be able to do this using an archive tool like WinZip (`www.winzip.com`), assuming that you've downloaded the file using Windows. Simply open the archive using the File ➤ Open menu option within WinZip. You may have to select All Files from the File Type drop-down list in order for the `.exe` file to show up in the file list. However, if you're using Windows, I recommend an open-source and free of charge program called Universal Extractor, which can be downloaded from `http://tinyurl.com/qzm5p`. This program can extract files from virtually every kind of archive, including most driver installation files. Once it is installed, simply right-click the installation `.exe` file, and select UniExtract to Subdir. This will then create a new folder in the same directory as the downloaded file, containing the contents of the installer file.

3. As mentioned in step 1, it's likely the driver files you need will be contained in a folder called something like `Driver` or `Win_XP`. Once you've found the relevant directory, look for `.inf`, `.sys`, and `.bin` files (although you may not find any `.bin` files; they're only used in a handful of drivers). Click and drag the files to a separate folder. You can ignore any other files, such as `.cab` and `.cat` files.

4. The task now is to find the .inf file for your hardware. If there's only one .inf file, then you can move to the next step. If there's more than one, you'll need to search each until you find the one you need. You need to look for text that corresponds to the PCI ID you noted earlier. Open the first .inf file in a text editor (double-clicking will do this in Windows), and using the search tool, search for the first part of the PCI ID, as discovered earlier. For example, I searched for 14e4. If this isn't found within the file, move on to the next .inf file, and search again. When you get a search match, it will probably be in a long line of text and to the right of the text VEN_. Then, look further along that line to see if the second part of the PCI ID is mentioned, probably to the right of text that reads DEV_. In the case of the driver file I downloaded, the entire line within the .inf file read as follows (I've highlighted the two component PCI ID parts in bold):

```
%BCM430B_DeviceDesc% = BCM43XX, PCI\VEN_14E4&DEV_4318&SUBSYS_12F3103C
```

If you find both component parts of the PCI ID in the line, as in my example, then you've found the .inf file you need. (In actual fact, you'll probably find *many* lines matching what you need; this is no issue.)

5. You must now transfer the .inf file, along with the .sys and .bin files (if any .bin files were included with the driver) to the computer on which you want to install the drivers. This can be done by putting them onto a floppy disk, by burning them onto CD, or using a USB memory stick.

Blacklisting Existing Drivers

Your progress from this point onward depends on if Ubuntu recognized your wireless networking device when you first booted but was unable to make it work correctly. If it *did* then you will have to blacklist the built-in driver, so that NdisWrapper can associate with the hardware. If the device *wasn't* recognized, you can skip straight to the "Using Ndis-Wrapper to Install the Drivers" heading.

To blacklist the existing driver, you need to find out the name of the kernel module and then add it to the /etc/modprobe.d/blacklist file. Here are the steps:

1. Open Device Manager (System ➤ Administration ➤ Device Manager), and select the entry in the list for your wireless network device. Click the entry mentioning the make and model of your network hardware.

2. Click the Advanced tab on the right-hand side of the window, and look for the line that begins info.linux.driver. Then look in the value column, and make a note of what's there. For example, on my test notebook, the value column read bcm43xx.

3. Close Device Manager, and open a terminal window (Applications ➤ Accessories ➤ Terminal). Type the following to open the blacklist configuration file in the Gedit text editor:

```
gksu gedit /etc/modprobe.d/blacklist
```

4. At the bottom of the file, type the following on a new line:

```
blacklist modulename
```

Replace *modulename* with the name of the module you discovered earlier. For example, on my test system, I typed the following (as shown in Figure 8-5):

```
blacklist bcm43xx
```

Save the file, and reboot your computer. You should now find that the wireless network device is no longer visible in the Network Settings program window. This is good, because it means the hardware no longer has a driver attached, and we can now tell NdisWrapper to make use of the hardware.

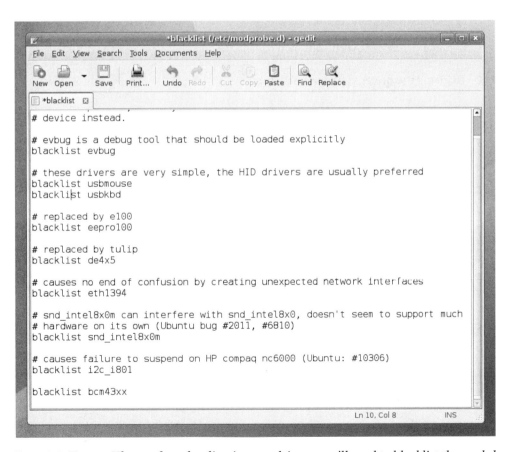

Figure 8-5. *To stop Ubuntu from loading its own drivers, you'll need to blacklist the module.*

Using NdisWrapper to Install the Drivers

On the Ubuntu computer on which you wish to install the drivers, you should now have the `.inf` file from the previous steps, plus the `.sys` and possibly `.bin` files that constitute the driver. Copy the files from the removable storage device into an empty folder on the desktop. Name the new folder `driver`.

▓**Note** If you've used a USB memory stick to transfer the files, it should appear automatically on the desktop as soon as it's inserted. When you've finished with it, right-click the desktop icon, and select Eject. You must do this before physically removing any kind of USB memory device, as explained later in this chapter.

To install the driver using NdisWrapper, follow these instructions:

1. Open a terminal window (Applications ➤ Accessories ➤ Terminal). In the window, type the following to switch to the directory containing the driver files:

   ```
   cd /home/<username>/Desktop/driver
   ```

   Replace *<username>* with your own username.

2. To install the driver, type the following:

   ```
   sudo ndiswrapper -i filename.inf
   ```

   Replace *filename.inf* with the name of the `.inf` file you discovered in the previous steps.

3. Next, type the following:

   ```
   sudo ndiswrapper -m
   gksu gedit /etc/modules
   ```

   This will open the `modules` configuration file for editing. On a new line at the bottom, add the following:

   ```
   ndiswrapper
   ```

   Ensure you press Enter after adding the line.

4. Save the file, close Gedit, and reboot your computer.

Following this, you should find the network device is available for configuration, such as associating with a wireless base station and configuring WEP/WPA. Follow the instructions under the previous "Joining a Wireless Network" heading.

Removing NdisWrapper Drivers

As mentioned earlier, although NdisWrapper can solve a lot of headaches with nonworking wireless hardware, it isn't perfect. You might find that the Windows driver you install simply doesn't work. In such a case, you can download a different version of the driver and try again. But first you'll need to uninstall the existing driver.

Open a terminal window, and type the following, which will cause NdisWrapper to list currently installed Windows drivers:

```
sudo ndiswrapper -l
```

Look for the first component of the line that's returned. On my test notebook, the line read:

```
bcmwl5    driver installer, hardware present
```

The first component of the line will be the name of the driver that you need to remove. To remove it, type the following line:

```
sudo ndiswrapper -e <drivername>
```

Replace *<drivername>* with the name of the driver. For example, I typed the following:

```
sudo ndiswrapper -e bcmwl5
```

Now, you can repeat the preceding step discussing sourcing the Windows driver. Note that there's no need to repeat all of the steps under the "Using NdisWrapper to Install Drivers" heading discussing installing the NdisWrapper modules. All that's necessary once you grab the new driver file is to issue the sudo ndiswrapper -i command, specifying the new driver .inf file.

■**Note**   The Broadcom BCM4318 wireless device, used as an example here, is extremely common in modern notebooks. Although work is being undertaken to make it work under Ubuntu, at the time of this writing, support is patchy. Therefore, a lot of Ubuntu users with notebooks containing this hardware utilize NdisWrapper to make it work. In fact, a handful of community members got together and created an installation script to make the process a lot easier. The script will automatically blacklist the existing driver and install a new one. You can find more information at the Ubuntu Forums: http://ubuntuforums.org/showthread.php?t=197102.

SECURE CONNECTIONS ON THE NET

For home users, the use of online banking services involves the transfer of confidential data. So is this a good reason to use the strongest form of wireless network encryption with your broadband router? No it isn't. In fact, it makes no difference.

This is because the transfer of confidential or financial data across the Web—to and from online banking sites, for example—is nearly always protected by Secure Socket Layer (SSL) HTTP. This works across any type of network connection, including wireless and ethernet, regardless of whether the connection has its own protection.

You can tell you're browsing a site that's using SSL because the address will begin with `https://`. Additionally, most browsers display a padlock symbol at the bottom of the screen (the Firefox browser will also turn the background of the address bar yellow). Accessing such sites should be safe, even if your wireless network connection is "open," which is to say it isn't protected with either WEP or WPA.

Similarly, although online shopping sites might not use SSL while you're browsing, when it's time to pay, they always use SSL. This ensures your credit card details are encrypted. If the store doesn't adopt an `https://` address when you click to visit the virtual checkout, you shouldn't shop there!

So do you even need WEP or WPA protection if you simply use your wireless connection to browse the Internet? Yes. In addition to the risk of unauthorized users hopping onto your connection if it isn't protected, some web mail services transfer your username and password "in the clear," which is to say without using SSL. This means your information could be picked up by an eavesdropper. In the case of Hotmail and Yahoo Mail, you can select secure login, but it isn't activated by default. Google Mail appears to use SSL all the time for login, but after this, your e-mail messages are transmitted across the Internet in the clear and, in theory, anyone, anywhere can eavesdrop.

Using Dial-up Telephone Modems

In our world of high-speed broadband connections, we sometimes forget that a sizeable minority of people use telephone dial-up to connect to an ISP.

For such people, Ubuntu offers good and bad news. The good news is that the Ubuntu software repository includes fuss-free software that can be used to configure connections and dial-up with the click of a mouse. The bad news is that, taken as a whole, Ubuntu support for dial-up modems isn't very strong.

If your modem is external and connects to the serial port, then there's a very good chance Ubuntu will work fine with it. However, if the modem connects to the USB port, is built into your computer, or is provided on a PCMCIA card, then Ubuntu support is less certain. This is because many modems need additional and specialized configuration. See the sidebar titled "Winmodems."

There's no quick way to find out if your modem is supported, other than to follow the instructions later in this section and attempt to use it. To follow the instructions, you'll need access to a computer that's already online to download a software package. If you dual-boot with Windows, then you can use it to download the software.

To configure your modem once the software is downloaded, you will need three pieces of information: the telephone number you should use to dial up, your username, and your password for your ISP (*not* your Ubuntu login username and password!).

WINMODEMS

Some years ago, hardware manufacturers realized that they could produce dial-up modems more cheaply if they shifted the hard work of decoding the signal onto the computer's operating system. With the work off-loaded, the modem's circuitry could contain fewer and simpler components, thus saving money.

For this to work, a special hardware driver was needed that effectively works as a middle-man, handing the decoding work to the computer's CPU. Unlike with other hardware drivers, these modem drivers aren't around simply to make the hardware work with the operating system. Effectively, the drivers for such modems are a separate piece of software within themselves.

Because of their need for this special driver software, which usually only runs on Windows, the modems are known as *winmodems*.

As you might anticipate, using the modems under Linux presents many problems, chief among them being that Windows and Linux are two separate operating systems and, generally speaking, are incompatible. Although solutions exist and the problems aren't insurmountable, setting up a winmodem under Linux often involves quite a lot of additional configuration.

It's impossible to provide a guide to getting winmodems working within this chapter, because there are simply too many types of winmodems, all of which need to be configured in different ways. However, an excellent web site exists that provides both step-by-step information and the necessary software. Using a computer that can get online, visit `http://linmodems.org`. Additionally, the user-friendly guide at `http://linmodems.technion.ac.il/first.html` might also be of help. As always, searching the Ubuntu forums (`www.ubuntoforums.org`) and specifying the make and model of your modem is also a good idea, because it's almost certain that at least one other person will have tried to make the modem work under Ubuntu.

Here are the steps necessary to configure a modem to dial up. You should ensure that your modem is plugged into the phone socket and is powered up. These instructions involve downloading the GNOME PPP dial-up tool, which will handle your dial-up requests.

1. Using another computer that's already online (or by switching to Windows XP if you dual-boot), visit the following address using a web browser. You'll be prompted to download a file. Save the file to a floppy disk or USB memory stick or burn it to a blank CD-R/RW disk. This is necessary because you'll need to transfer the file to your Ubuntu computer.

   ```
   http://us.archive.ubuntu.com/ubuntu/pool/universe/g/gnome-ppp/
   gnome-ppp_0.3.23-0ubuntu2_i386.deb
   ```

2. On the Ubuntu computer, copy the downloaded file to the desktop. Then open a terminal window (Applications ➤ Accessories ➤ Terminal), and type the following:

```
sudo dpkg -i Desktop/gnome-ppp_0.3.23-0ubuntu2_i386.deb
```

You'll need to enter your password when prompted.

3. You'll find GNOME PPP on the Applications ➤ Internet menu. When the program starts, click the Setup button.

4. In the Setup window, click the Detect button. This will probe your modem, and change GNOME PPP's configuration settings to match. Once probing is complete, remove the check from Wait for Dialtone, but don't change any other settings on the Modem tab.

5. Click the Options tab. Put a check alongside Dock in Notification Area. Then click the Close button.

6. In the Username, Password, and Phone Number fields, enter the relevant details, as illustrated in Figure 8-6. Remember that you should enter your dial-up username and password here, and not your Ubuntu username and password! Don't forget to add any additional numbers to the front of the phone number if it's necessary to deactivate call waiting or similar services on your phone line. It's also wise to put a check in the Remember Password box, so you won't be prompted for your password each time you dial up.

7. Click the Connect button to dial up. Once you're connected, you'll see a new icon appear in the notification area. When you want to disconnect, right-click this icon, and select the relevant option.

Following the initial setup, it makes sense to create a desktop shortcut for GNOME PPP. This can be done by clicking and dragging the icon from the menu to a convenient spot.

Figure 8-6. *GNOME PPP can be used to connect to the Internet if you use a dial-up modem.*

Working with a Proxy Server

Some networks in offices require that you use a web proxy (often referred to as an *HTTP proxy*). A *proxy* is a server computer that does two things. First, it provides additional security by providing a single portal to all web pages. Second, it helps speed up Internet access by storing frequently accessed pages. This means that if ten people request the same web page, there's no need to get the same ten pieces of data from the Internet. The proxy computer can send them its own copies. For various reasons, proxies are becoming less popular nowadays, but larger organizations might still use them.

You'll need to speak to your system administrator to see if your office uses a proxy. If it does, your administrator will most likely give you an address, which may take the form of a web address or an IP address. Once you have this information, follow these steps to configure the proxy:

1. Open a GNOME Terminal window (Applications ➤ Accessories ➤ Terminal).

2. At the prompt, type the following to open the bash.bashrc file in Gedit:

   ```
   gksu gedit /etc/bash.bashrc
   ```

3. Scroll to the bottom, create a new line, and add the following:

   ```
   export http_proxy="http://username:password@address:port_number/"
   ```

   Replace *username*, *password*, *address*, and *port_number* with your own details. If your proxy doesn't use usernames and passwords, simply leave them out (type http_proxy="http://*address*:*port_number*/").

4. Save the file, and then log out and back in again.

■Tip Some ISPs run proxy servers, too. However, unlike proxies in offices, it's normally up to you whether you choose to use them. You might find that using a proxy speeds up your connection, especially when you access popular sites, so it's worth trying out. To find out if your ISP offers a proxy, visit its technical support web pages or phone its technical support line.

Setting Up Online Software Repositories

The installation, removal, and updating of software under Ubuntu is normally handled by the Synaptic Package Manager. This is a little like the Add/Remove Programs applet within the Windows Control Panel, except that it will automatically search for, download (if necessary), and install any new software you require.

Ubuntu can grab new software from the installation DVD-ROM if need be, but it would rather download them. This guarantees the latest version of each package. Out of the box, Ubuntu is preconfigured to access a couple of online *repositories* (collections) of software that match the software on the DVD-ROM. But these repositories don't give you the fullest choice of software. I explain more about this in Chapter 28, when I fully describe software installation under Ubuntu, but for the moment, it's enough to know that a fresh Ubuntu installation is subscribed only to the Main and Restricted online software repositories. Subscribing also to the Universe and Multiverse repositories is advisable, especially if you want to follow some of the steps in later chapters of this book that describe installing software.

■**Note** A fresh installation of Ubuntu isn't subscribed to these repositories, because the software they offer isn't supported by Canonical, the company behind Ubuntu. In addition, some of the software offered doesn't comply with the wording or spirit of the GPL software license, which governs most of the Ubuntu software. If you've purchased a support contract from Canonical, then the lack of support might be an important note, but if you rely on the community for support—via the `www.ubuntuforums.org` web site, for example—then this shouldn't be an issue.

Luckily, adding these extra repositories can be done using the Software Sources program, and takes no more than a few clicks of the mouse, as follows:

1. Click System ➤ Administration ➤ Software Sources.

2. Ensure the Ubuntu 6.10 tab is selected, and then put a check alongside Community Maintained Open Source Software (Universe), and Software Restricted by Copyright or Legal Issues (Multiverse). When you've finished, all the boxes in the Ubuntu 6.10 tab should be checked, as shown in Figure 8-7.

3. Click the Close button. A dialog box will appear mentioning that your information about available software is out of date. Click the Reload button. Ubuntu will then download the latest package information, which may take a few minutes, depending on the speed of your Internet connection. Note that the reloading can't take place if you've got Synaptic Package Manager open, so close that before clicking the Close button in Software Sources.

When the updating has finished, Software Sources will automatically close. You can then install software using Synaptic Package Manager.

Figure 8-7. *Adding the Universe and Multiverse repositories gives you the widest selection of software.*

ADDITIONAL NOTEBOOK CONFIGURATION

Generally speaking, a notebook computer will not need any configuration above and beyond what's outlined in this chapter. For example, if you have a wireless network card, you can simply follow the instructions under the "Configuring a Wireless Card" heading. However, you might want to make use of the GNOME CPU Frequency Scaling Monitor. If you have a compatible CPU in your notebook (or even some desktop PCs), this tool lets you adjust the speed of the chip to save power. Most modern mobile-oriented CPUs support this function. Unfortunately, because of the possibility of crackers using it to slow down your system, the applet is considered a security risk. Before you use it, you must reconfigure your system to allow it to work.

Open a GNOME Terminal window (Applications ➤ Accessories ➤ Terminal), and type `sudo dpkg-reconfigure gnome-applets`. You'll then be asked if you want to set SUID root for the cpufreq-selector applet. Select Yes using the arrow keys, and press Enter. Reboot your computer, and then right-click a blank spot on the panel at the top of the screen. Click Add to Panel and, in the dialog box that appears, scroll down to the System & Hardware heading. Click the CPU Frequency Scaling Monitor icon, and click the Add button. To alter your CPU frequency, click the applet, and choose the clock speed setting you desire.

Configuring Power-Saving Features

Ubuntu includes a number of features that can utilize the power-saving features of your computer, including switching off the monitor after a set period of inactivity and placing the computer into standby mode, whereby only the RAM subsystem is kept powered. However, some quick configuration is necessary to set up the system just the way you want it.

■**Tip** If your computer has a CPU that can adjust its clock speed on the fly, such as a mobile processor or an AMD chip with the PowerNow! function, Ubuntu will automatically install software that will make this work. This will run in the background. To see a live view showing the speed of your processor, right-click the Panel, select Add to Panel, and choose the CPU Frequency Scaling Monitor under the System & Hardware heading. Note that, to manually control the speed of the processor, you might need to undertake the steps described in the "Additional Notebook Configuration" sidebar. If you find that the computer subsequently crashes when you attempt to scale the processor speed, use Synaptic Package Manager to install `cpufreqd`. This should fix the issue. As always, updating online might also provide a cure.

Using Power-Management Preferences

Depending on the degree to which your computer supports power-saving functionality, Ubuntu will let you configure your display to go into standby mode after a certain amount of time and will also allow you to configure your notebook to enter "sleep" (standby) mode. In addition, if you use a notebook computer, Ubuntu might let you configure additional aspects of your computer, such as the display brightness. These functions are controlled using the Power Management applet. To start this, click System ➤ Preferences ➤ Power Management. If Ubuntu is installed on a notebook computer, you'll see three tabs in the program window: Running on AC, Running on Battery, and General. If Ubuntu is installed on a desktop computer, you'll see just the Running on AC and General tabs.

■**Note** Not all PCs are created equal when it comes to power-saving features. Some support more functionality than others. In addition, Ubuntu is compatible with most but not all power management systems, and it might not be able to support certain power-management functionality on your system, even if such functionality normally works under Windows.

Notebooks have the additional tab because it's possible to define two separate power management profiles: one for when the computer is plugged in and one for running on battery power. This makes sense, because you might never want your display to switch off when connected to an outlet, but it's advisable that it should deactivate within, say, 15 minutes of inactivity if the computer is running on battery power to extend the life of the battery.

The three tabs of the Power Management applet are explained in the following sections.

Running on AC

If your computer is a desktop PC without a battery, then you'll see two options under the Running on AC tab: Put Display To Sleep When Computer is Inactive For and Put Computer to Sleep When It Is Inactive For. By clicking and dragging the sliders beneath both headings you can control the amount of time before each feature kicks in. By dragging each to the far right, you can set a value of Never, which will deactivate that feature.

■**Note** The sleep mode can be to either suspend to RAM (that is, standby) or hibernate. You can set this under the General tab, as discussed in a moment.

If your computer is a notebook computer, you'll see some extra options. Depending on the technology used in your computer, you might see a slider headed Set Display Brightness To, which you can use to set the brightness of the screen when the power is connected (you'll see a similar slider under the Running on Battery tab, which I'll discuss in a moment). Whenever AC power is connected, the display brightness will be changed to match this setting.

Additionally, you may see a drop-down list headed When Laptop Lid Is Closed. As it suggests, this will control what happens when the notebook is closed. Depending on the hardware contained in your computer, you might have the choice of blanking the screen, suspending the computer (shutting down all systems but RAM), and hibernating (suspending RAM to disk and turning off the notebook). However, not all computers support each of these modes, so the choices you see might vary.

Finally, at the bottom, those with a notebook computer will see a check box headed Prefer Power Savings Over Performance. This switches on extra power saving features of some notebooks. However, it shouldn't be activated under the Running on AC tab because, with AC power, there's no need to activate power saving features above and beyond deactivating the computer when it's idle.

Running on Battery

The options under the Running on Battery tab, which will only be present on a notebook computer, are largely the same as those under the Running on AC tab, as you can see in Figure 8-8. These settings come into operation the instant the main power is disconnected from your notebook and the battery kicks in.

You might choose to set screen brightness low, for example, because screen backlighting is one of the biggest drains on battery power. Even setting the brightness to 75% could lead to your notebook lasting longer before the battery needs recharging.

■**Note** Some notebooks set screen dimming via the BIOS, and Ubuntu is unable to override this. You might find the slider has no effect.

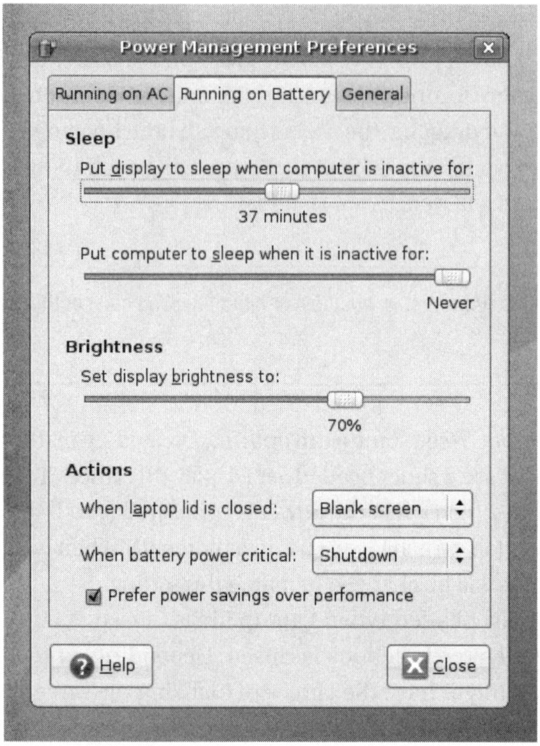

Figure 8-8. *Notebook users can define an additional power profile that will kick in when the battery is in use.*

There will also be an extra option near the bottom of the dialog box: When Battery Power Critical. Here you can set what happens to the notebook when the battery power reaches a very low level. You can make the computer hibernate, for example, or enter sleep mode (suspend).

■**Caution** Be aware that sleep mode requires a little battery power to work and will eventually drain your battery, especially if it's already on its last legs!

General

Under the General tab, you can set the default sleep mode for the computer, which is to say, the sleep mode the computer will use when the times specified under the Running on AC and Running on Battery headings are reached. The choices will probably be to either hibernate or suspend, although some users might not see either or both options, depending on whether your computer supports suspend and hibernate functionality.

Hibernate will write the contents of RAM to the hard disk and then shut down the computer. Suspend will shut down most systems of the computer except for the RAM, which will be kept active. Then, when you press a key or move the mouse, the computer will wake up almost instantly as the subsystems are reactivated.

■**Caution** Hibernate doesn't work on all systems. The best plan is to test it by selecting System ➤ Quit and selecting Hibernate. Even if Hibernate appears to work, there are reports of it being unreliable. Some users report that their computer occasionally fails to wake up, causing a loss of data. Therefore, you should always save any open files before using the Hibernate function or before leaving your computer unattended for any period in which Hibernate mode might kick in automatically.

Beneath the controls for the default sleep mode, you can set what happens when the power button is pressed once the computer is active. Effectively, this controls whether or not pressing the button when Ubuntu is running should shut down the computer, suspend it, or hibernate it. You can also select Ask Me, which will cause the standard Quit dialog box to appear (that is, the same dialog that appears if you click System ➤ Quit).

Notebook users will see an extra option under this, by which the notebook screen can be dimmed after a period of inactivity. This can help save battery power by leaving the screen visible with reduced backlighting, thereby saving power. It's preferable to turning the screen off, because that can sometimes cause confusion as to whether the notebook is active or not.

Finally, the General tab lets you select whether the power icon is visible in the Notification Area. For desktop PC users, there's no need for this icon to be visible, but for notebook users, it can show the current battery charge, expressed graphically, as well as whether main power is connected. The most fuss-free option is perhaps Only Display When Charging or Discharging, and this is what's selected by default.

■**Tip** Right-clicking the power icon in the Notification Area lets you quickly hibernate the computer. Just select the entry from the menu that appears.

Spinning Down the Hard Disk

All modern hard disks come with the ability to spin down their motors to save energy. Then, when data is requested, the motors spin up again. There may be a slight delay while this happens, and some people dislike using disk spin-down because of this. However, on a notebook, it can lead to a substantial increase in battery life. On a desktop system, it's worth considering, because over the lifetime of a computer, it can save a lot of electricity (and therefore money!).

The spin-down settings are contained in the /etc/hdparm.conf file, which you'll need to edit by hand. Follow these steps to adjust the spin-down settings:

1. Open a GNOME Terminal window (Applications ➤ Accessories ➤ Terminal).

2. Type the following in the terminal window:

   ```
   gksu gedit /etc/hdparm.conf
   ```

3. Click Search ➤ Find, and in the box, type spindown_time.

4. Click the Find button. You should find that a line in the file is now highlighted. Close the Search dialog box.

5. Change the line to remove the hash mark from the beginning, so it reads like this:

   ```
   spindown_time = 24
   ```

   You can alter the value to anything you want. Each time unit is five seconds, so 24 equates to 120 seconds (24×5 seconds) or 2 minutes. To set a time of 20 minutes, enter 240 (240×5 seconds). If you specify a number above 240, the time units are increased to 30 minutes. In other words, a value of 241 will equate to 30 minutes, a value of 242 will equate to 60 minutes, and so on.

6. When you've finished, save the file.

7. Reboot for the settings to take effect.

POWER SAVING: IS IT WORTH IT?

An average computer draws anywhere between 100 to 500 watts of power. An average light bulb draws around 150 watts of power, so you can see that, relatively speaking, computers are low power consumers compared to many household devices. However, it's still worth considering employing power-saving techniques. You might not save yourself a lot of money, but if you switch on power saving, and your neighbor does too, and her neighbor does, then the cumulative effect will add up, and we can all contribute less toward global warming.

Try to avoid leaving your computer turned on overnight or when you're away from it for long periods. As well as saving power, switching off your computer will avoid wear and tear on its components. Although the CPU can work 24/7 without trouble, it's cooled by a fan that's a simple mechanical device. There are other fans in your computer too, such as the graphics card fan and case fan. Each of these will eventually wear out. If your graphics card fan stops working, the card itself will overheat and might burn out. The same is true of the CPU fan. However, by shutting down your computer overnight, you can effectively double the life of the fans and radically reduce the risk of catastrophic failure. Isn't that worth considering?

Adding a Printer

Most people have a printer nowadays, and Ubuntu supports a wide variety of models—everything from laser printers to color ink-jet models, and even some of the very old dot-matrix printers.

If you work in an office environment, you might be expected to access a shared printer. Sharing a printer is usually achieved by connecting the device directly to the network. The printer itself normally has special built-in hardware to allow this to happen. Alternatively, the printer might be plugged into a Windows computer, such as a Windows NT, 2000, or XP server (or even simply someone's desktop PC), and shared so that other users can access it, a setup that is known as *Windows printer sharing*. Ubuntu will work with network printers of both types.

■**Note** These instructions will let you set up a printer for use by most of Ubuntu's applications. However, if you intend to print from The GIMP, you'll need to follow some additional instructions under the "Administering a Printer" heading.

Configuring a Local Printer

A *local printer* is one that's directly connected to your computer, normally via USB, although if the printer is a number of years old, it might connect via the parallel port. To set up a local printer, follow these instructions:

1. Click System ➤ Administration ➤ Printing. In the Printers window, double-click the New Printer icon. A dialog box will appear, saying Reading Printer Database. This might take a few moments to work through.

2. In the Add a Printer dialog box, ensure Local Printer is selected. With any luck, your printer will have been automatically detected, which you'll see under the Use a Detected Printer heading. In this case, click the Forward button to continue. If the printer isn't detected, ensure Use Another Printer by Specifying a Port is selected, click the Printer Port drop-down list, and select USB Printer #1 for a USB printer or Parallel Port #1 for a parallel-port based printer. Click the Forward button to continue.

3. The next step is to select your printer driver. Choose your printer manufacturer from the drop-down list, and the printer model from the list below. If your printer was detected automatically, these details should already have been filled in. If you find yourself manually selecting the details, it might help to know that the printer will be referred to by its full title, rather than just its model number. This includes any prefixes, such as *Optra* or *Stylus Color*. If your printer isn't listed, look for the

next best match. For example, for an Epson Stylus Color 3600, I could select the Epson Stylus Color 3200. I knew it would be compatible, because the 3200 is similar to the 3600, and they also share the same Windows driver file. When you've finished, click Forward.

Tip If you can't find your printer, or any mention of it, try visiting the manufacturer's web site and looking on its support pages for a Postscript Printer Driver (PPD) file. You might also take a look at www.linuxprinting.org/download/PPD and www.adobe.com/products/printerdrivers/winppd.html, which offer many printer drivers available for download. If you find one, download it, and then click the Install Driver button to install it.

---

4. Next you'll be invited to give the printer a name. The default should be OK. You can fill in the Description and Location fields if you want, but these are only necessary if you intend to share the printer across a network. Click Apply when you've finished.

Once installation has finished, the printer will then appear in the Printers window, as shown in Figure 8-9. To see whether it's working correctly, right-click its icon, select Properties, and then click the Print a Test Page button.

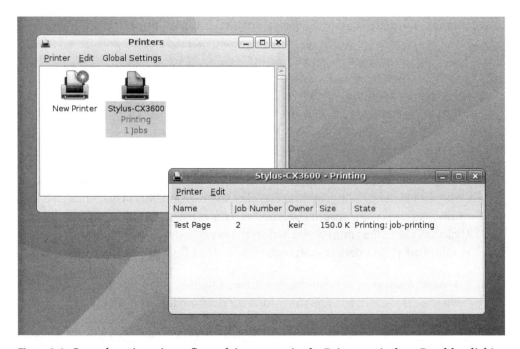

Figure 8-9. *Once the printer is configured, it appears in the Printers window. Double-clicking its icon will show queued printing jobs.*

If the printer is installed correctly, you should find yourself with a test page showing color gradations.

If the printer hasn't been installed correctly, it either won't work at all or will start spewing out page after page of junk text. If this is the case, turn off the printer, and double-click the printer icon. In the window that appears, right-click the printer job, and select Cancel. You have either selected the wrong port or, more likely, installed incompatible printer drivers. Right-click the new printer's icon and select Remove. Then repeat the installation steps, this time trying different settings.

Configuring a Network Printer

A *network printer* is one that is not directly connected to any computer. Instead, it connects to the network via an ethernet cable. In this way, all computers in the office will be able to use it. If the network printer is directly connected to a computer, it will very probably be shared via Windows/SMB. In this case, follow the instructions in the next section.

Some printers have the required server hardware built in, but others might use a special print server module that attaches to the printer's USB or parallel printer port. Ubuntu can work with both types of hardware.

Ubuntu is compatible with Unix (LPD), HP JetDirect, and Internet Printing Protocol (IPP) server types. These are the most ubiquitous types currently in use for stand-alone printer servers.

Before beginning, you'll need to find out the printer's network address and, if relevant, the queue name or the port number. You should be able to find out these details by speaking to your network administrator or the person who configured the printer.

Follow these steps to configure a network printer:

1. Click System ➤ Administration ➤ Printing. In the Printers window, double-click the New Printer icon.

■**Tip** You can add as many printers as you want. You could configure a local printer (that is, one attached to your computer) and then configure a network printer too.

---

2. In the Add a Printer dialog box, click Network Printer.

3. In the drop-down list, select the type of printer server. If you're unsure of which to choose, try CUPS Printer (IPP). If you wish to connect to a Hewlett Packard printer with a HP print server attached, select HP JetDirect.

4. In the URI/Host field, enter the network address of the printer. In the case of HP JetDirect, the default port number should be okay, unless you have been specifically told to enter a different number. Depending on which server option you chose, you may also need to enter the queue name. Click Forward.

5. In the next screen, choose the printer make and model, just as if you were configuring a local printer. See steps 3 and 4 in the previous section for guidance. Then click Apply.

When the printer is installed, right-click its icon in the Printers window, select Properties, and click Print a Test Page.

If the printer doesn't work, it's likely that you set the wrong server type. Try an alternative type; if you chose CUPS the first time, try HP JetDirect the second time. Many print servers can emulate a variety of modes, so trying a different setting may work.

If the printer starts spewing out page after page of text, it's likely that you selected an incorrect printer driver. Cancel the job at the printer. Next, double-click the printer icon, right-click the job, and select Cancel. Then, right-click the printer, select Remove, and repeat the installation steps, this time trying an alternative driver.

Configuring a Windows/SMB Shared Printer

A Windows (or SMB) printer is one that's directly connected to a computer, and then made available across the network via the network sharing function of the operating system. Effectively, the computer acts as the printer server. Often, in corporate environments, such printers are attached to server computers, but an individual may share the printer attached to a workstation.

In a home situation, a Windows/SMB share is an excellent and inexpensive way of sharing a printer among many computers. The printer is attached to one PC, and, as long as that computer is switched on, the printer will be available to the other computers in the household.

Assuming that the printer has been correctly set up to be shared on the host computer, connecting to a Windows/SMB printer share is easy. In most cases, Ubuntu will do the hard work for you.

Follow these steps to set up a Windows/SMB shared printer:

1. Click System ➤ Administration ➤ Printing. In the Printers window, double-click the New Printer icon.

2. In the Add a Printer dialog box, click Network Printer.

3. In the drop-down list, select Windows Printer (SMB), as shown in Figure 8-10.

4. Wait for a minute or two while Ubuntu probes the network to see if any shared printers are available. When Ubuntu discovers a printer, you might find an Authentication dialog box appears. Here, you should type the username and password (if applicable) for the shared printer. Ask the person who administers the computer that's sharing the printer for this information. (When connecting to the shared printer attached to a Windows XP Home machine, I was able to click the Cancel button in the Authentication dialog box.)

Figure 8-10. *Ubuntu should be able to automatically detect any Windows or SMB shared printers on your network.*

5. In the Host drop-down list, select the computer to which the printer is attached. If there is more than one shared printer on the network, you may need to choose among several options, so make sure that you know the correct network name of the machine sharing the printer. The best way to do this is to speak to your system administrator or the person who set up the printer share.

6. Wait a few more seconds, and then, in the Printer drop-down list, select the shared printer. Once again, this should be detected automatically.

Note If you find that the Host and Printer details aren't automatically configured, you will need to enter them manually. Speak to the system administrator or the individual in charge of the shared printer to find out what these are.

---

7. In the Username and Password fields, type the username and password that might be required to access the shared printer, if they haven't already been filled in automatically. With a Windows XP Home host I used for testing, I found that I could type any username and leave the Password field blank. To connect to a Windows XP Professional or Windows 2000 host, you will most likely need to enter both a username and password. These can be the login details of any user of the computer or, if the shared computer and printer are configured for Guest access, you can try typing Guest for the username and leaving the Password field blank. Once the details have been filled in, click Forward.

8. Select the printer driver as if you were configuring a printer attached to your computer; see steps 3 and 4 in the "Configuring a Local Printer" section for guidance. Note that it is unlikely the printer will be automatically recognized—you will have to manually select the manufacturer and model details. When the details have been supplied, click the Forward and Apply buttons on the Printer Information screen.

When the printer is installed, right-click its icon in the Printers window, select Properties, and click Print a Test Page.

If the printer doesn't work at all, the username and password details may be wrong. Alternatively, if you entered the printer network address manually, you might have entered it incorrectly. Try repeating the installation steps and using alternative settings.

If the printer makes a noise as if to start printing but then decides not to, you might need to change a setting *on the Windows machine*. Click Start ➤ Settings ➤ Printers and Faxes, and then right-click the shared printer's icon. Select Properties, and click the Ports tab in the window that appears. Remove the check on the Enable Bidirectional Support box, and click OK. Then restart both the Windows and Ubuntu computers.

If the printer starts spewing out page after page of text instead of the test page, it's likely that you selected an incorrect printer driver. Cancel the job at the printer. Then double-click the printer icon in Ubuntu, right-click the job, and select Cancel. Next, right-click the printer, and select Remove. Repeat the installation steps, this time trying an alternative driver.

Administering a Printer

Like Windows, Ubuntu uses the concepts of print queues to handle printing. When you print from an application, the print job is actually held in the print queue. If the queue is empty, then the job is printed immediately. If there are already jobs waiting to be printed, or if a print job is already in progress, then the new job is added to the queue.

To view and otherwise manipulate the print queue, click System ➤ Administration ➤ Printers. Then double-click the entry for your printer. In the window that appears, you should see the jobs waiting to be printed, if any. Right-clicking them will let you delete jobs, by clicking Cancel, pause them, and resume them.

However, the similarities with Windows end there. Ubuntu doesn't offer a unified printer interface, as you might be used to. Instead various applications offer differing options when it comes to setting print quality, paper size, and so on. Some applications don't offer any options at all and rely on the default settings.

Here's how to alter settings for applications people commonly print from in Ubuntu.

OpenOffice.org

To change print settings within any OpenOffice.org application, click File ➤ Printer Settings. Next, click the Properties button. You can select the paper size and scaling of the print in the dialog box that appears. Click the Device tab to access a range of printer configuration options; you should be able to change the print quality settings, as well as various other options, depending on the make and model of printer in use (see Figure 8-11). Select the category on the left side of the window and the details on the right.

The changes you make last only as long as the OpenOffice.org application is open. Once the application is closed the settings revert back to their default settings.

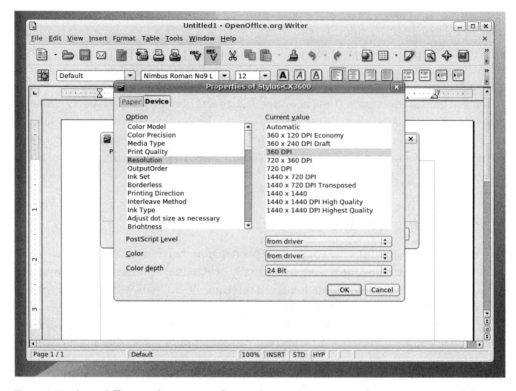

Figure 8-11. *OpenOffice.org lets you configure the same printer preferences presented during initial configuration.*

The Gimp

The GIMP offers by far the most control over printing. This is at least partially because many of the printer drivers used by Ubuntu originated within the GIMP-Print project (http://gimp-print.sourceforge.net).

■**Note** Gimp-Print has since been given a more nonspecific name and is now known as Guttenprint.

However, perhaps ironically, The GIMP needs extra configuration before it can print. This is because it assumes your printer is PostScript compatible. Most nonprofessional printers aren't. If you're in doubt about whether your model supports PostScript, you should check the documentation that came with your printer, as well as the packaging, and look for the PostScript logo. However, unless you specifically opted to purchase a PostScript-compatible model, it's unlikely the function will be supported.

Follow these steps to configure The GIMP to use your printer if it's not PostScript compatible. These steps only have to be carried out once in order to configure the printer.

1. Right-click on the image you want to print within The GIMP, and select File ➤ Print.

2. In the Print dialog that appears, click the New Printer button. Enter a memorable name into the dialog box that appears, and click OK. Then click the Setup Printer button.

3. In the Setup Printer dialog that appears, choose your printer from the list. As when setting up your printer earlier, if you can't find an exact match, choose the nearest match.

4. Still in the Setup Printer dialog box, select the printer you set up earlier from the Printer Queue drop-down list. Then click OK.

5. In the main print dialog box, click the Save Settings button, which is located near the bottom. You can then click the Print button to print the image you're working on, or simply click Cancel to end configuration.

Following this, and each time you print, you can select the print quality settings in the Print dialog box. Perhaps the most important control is the Image Size slider, at the bottom of the window, that controls the size of the printed image relative to the size of the paper. Under the Printer Settings tab, at the top right of the window, you can select the paper type from the Media Type drop-down list.

■**Note** You might be accustomed to using color profiles within Windows. By applying a color profile to every output device, including your monitor, these aim to match up what you see on screen with what is eventually printed out. Unfortunately, Ubuntu currently doesn't support this functionality.

Mozilla Firefox

Mozilla Firefox doesn't offer much control over print quality and works according to the default printer settings. To print, simply click File ➤ Print. Clicking the Properties button in the Print dialog offers a chance to set the paper size, alter the margins, and switch between color and grayscale printing, but that's all there is.

To switch to landscape mode, click Print ➤ Page Setup. Here you can also alter the scale of the web site print, which can be useful if the web page won't print correctly because it's simply too large. Removing the check from the Shrink To Fit Page Width button and setting a value of less than 100% will shrink images and text by a corresponding percentage. You can preview the results by clicking OK in the dialog box and then clicking File ➤ Print Preview.

Using Digital Cameras, MP3 Players, and USB Memory Sticks

Removable storage is the term applied to peripherals that you might attach to your computer that contain their own storage. Examples include USB memory sticks and external hard drives, and also MP3 players, digital cameras, and photographic memory card readers. You might also find some devices like mobile phones are treated like removable storage devices should you directly attach them to your computer.

Upon attaching any removable storage device, Ubuntu does exactly the same thing, which is to say that it will do the following:

1. Automatically open a Nautilus file browsing window displaying the contents of the removable storage device so you can access the files.

2. Display an icon on the desktop, which you can double-click to view the removable storage device contents, as described in step 1.

3. Add an icon to Nautilus' Computer view, which can be accessed by clicking Places ➤ Computer (or Go ➤ Computer in a currently open Nautilus window). As with the desktop icon, double-clicking this will display the contents of the removable storage device. The Computer view is a good way to see at a glance *all* removable storage devices attached to your computer.

4. In addition, if the removable storage device contains digital images (if it's a digital camera, for example), a dialog box will appear asking if you want to import the images. Clicking this button will start the gThumb program. I discuss more about this in Chapter 20, when I provide a concise guide to cataloging and manipulating your digital images.

The contents of the removable storage device will be accessible in exactly the same way as any other files on your system. You should be able to copy, delete, and create files on the device, provided the device isn't read-only (if the read-only switch isn't set on a USB memory stick, for example). If the device contains MP3 tunes, for example, then you should be able to double-click them to play them, provided the playback codecs are installed (see Chapter 18).

■**Note** iPods are included in the list of MP3 players you can access under Ubuntu, but you won't be able to access an iPod that's Mac formatted. Ubuntu can only access the iPod if it uses Windows format. You should be able to change the formatting using the iTunes software under Windows or Mac.

However, a very important rule must be followed when you've finished with removable storage devices under Ubuntu: the device must be *ejected* before you physically remove it.

This applies also to memory cards that are inserted into a card reader—before removing any card from the card reader, it must be ejected.

This is quite simple to do. Just right-click the icon on the desktop or within the Computer window, and select Eject. Make sure that you save and close any files that you may have been working on before you do so, or you may see an error message. You'll need to close any Nautilus windows that might have been browsing the storage device too.

If you've used the command line to manipulate files on the removable storage, remember to close any running programs in the terminal window. You'll also need to cd out of the removable storage device directory before you'll be allowed to eject it (alternatively, you can simply close the terminal window).

Following this, you can safely physically remove the card or unattach the device. Reinserting it will make it available once again.

■**Caution** Be very careful not to remove a memory card from a card reader while you're writing or reading from it on your PC. This will most likely damage the card irreparably. At the very least, it will wipe the contents of the card, so you'll lose your photographs.

Configuring a Scanner

Although scanners have fallen out of favor recently with the advent of digital photography, they're vital for getting nondigital photos and old documents onto your PC.

A lot of flatbed scanners can be made to work under Ubuntu, but not all types are supported. You can check the list of currently supported scanners by visiting www.sane-project.org. Additional models are added to the list all the time, and this is another reason to make sure your system is completely up-to-date (see Chapter 9 and Appendix D; the former explains how to update your system software, while the latter explains how to update to the latest version of Ubuntu).

The best test of whether your scanner is supported under Ubuntu is simply to see if it will work. Scanning within Ubuntu is handled by the XSane utility. This is a stand-alone program that operates like the TWAIN drivers that you might have used under Windows.

■**Tip** XSane is even capable of optical character recognition! Simply use the Synaptic Package Manager to download and install the gocr program. Then select the OCR button on the toolbar of XSane's image preview window. Note that gocr is in the Universe repository, so you'll need to add this to your Ubuntu setup by following the instructions under the "Setting Up Online Software Repositories" heading.

To configure a scanner and scan images, follow these steps:

1. Select Applications ➤ Graphics ➤ XSane Image Scanning Program. On startup, the program will attempt to detect your scanner. If it finds a compatible model, XSane will start. If the scanner isn't recognized, a dialog box will appear telling you so.

2. XSane consists of a handful of windows, including the main program window, the Standard Options dialog, the Histogram window, and the Preview window. You can close the Standard Options and Histogram windows for the moment and concentrate on the main XSane program window, which should be similar in appearance to the TWAIN scanner drivers you might have used under Windows. At the top of the window is the XSane mode drop-down list. Here, you can select from a variety of scanning modes, such as those to scan documents for faxing. However, in most cases, the Save setting is best. This lets you preview your scans and then save them to disk if you're happy with them.

3. Beneath this is the filename field. Here you should type the filename you wish to use for the scanned file. XSane can save in a variety of file formats, and it detects which you want to use from the file extension you choose. For example, typing `picture.jpg` will cause the picture to be saved as a JPEG image. Typing `picture.tif` will cause the image to be saved as a TIFF file.

4. Beneath the filename field, on the left, is the filename number count. This is used if you wish to scan many images in succession—a number is added to the end of the filename, and this control configures the increment. A setting of +1 is fine.

5. Beneath the filename field, and to the right, is the Type drop-down list, by which you can force a certain file type to be used when saving files. However, leaving this at the default By Ext is best. This means that, as mentioned previously, you can define the type of image saved by the filename extension.

6. Next down is the color/monochrome drop-down list. Here, you can select to scan Binary (line-art), Gray (grayscale), or Color. If you select Color, additional sliders will appear to let you control the gamma, brightness, and contrast of the scanned image, in that order. In addition, several other buttons will appear at the bottom of the program window, all of which you can leave at default settings. Remember that hovering the mouse cursor over each will explain what it does.

7. Next is the dots-per-inch (DPI) setting. Generally speaking, 300 DPI is acceptable for scanned photos, while 150 DPI will be acceptable for artwork such as diagrams.

8. To scan a preview, click the Acquire Preview button within the Preview window. The results should be something similar to what's shown in Figure 8-12.

Figure 8-12. *The XSane program works a little like TWAIN drivers under Windows and makes scanning easy.*

9. When the preview scan has finished, you can adjust the brightness/contrast settings using the sliders in the XSane program window (assuming you selected color scanning earlier). You should also click and drag to crop the image in the Preview window, if XSane doesn't do so automatically. When you're happy, click the Scan button in the main XSane program window. The image will then be scanned at your chosen resolution and saved to your /home directory, using the filename you specified earlier.

Installing 3D Graphics Card Drivers

Virtually all graphics cards are automatically supported and configured within Ubuntu, so you can stick with the default X.org drivers installed by Ubuntu. However, if you want to use their 3D functionality—usually to play 3D games, run 3D modeling software, or utilize Compiz/Beryl graphical desktops—then some extra steps may be necessary.

ATI and Nvidia 3D cards are well supported under Ubuntu, including the Radeon series and the GeForce series.

Adding 3D graphics support involves downloading and installing special driver software from the Ubuntu repositories via the Synaptic Package Manager. The drivers are provided by the manufacturer of the graphics card and are closed source (sometimes referred to as *binary only* or *proprietary*).

■**Note** If you experience seemingly random system-wide crashes or freezing after installing a 3D graphics driver, consider reverting to your old setup by using the Synaptic Package Manager to simply remove the new driver. If you find your system won't boot to the GUI after removing the drivers, type `sudo dpkg-reconfigure xserver-xorg` at the command prompt to reconfigure your graphics settings. See the guide in Chapter 6 for more information.

Installing an ATI Driver

To install support for ATI 3D cards, follow these steps:

1. Select System ➤ Administration ➤ Synaptic Package Manager.

2. Click the Search button, and enter `xorg-driver-fglrx` as a search term. Find your card among those listed in the Description box. Click the box next to the entry in the results list, and select Mark for Installation. Then click Apply. Ignore the `xorg-driver-fglrx-dev` entry.

3. When the Synaptic Package Manager has finished installing the driver, open a GNOME Terminal window (Applications ➤ Accessories ➤ Terminal), and type `sudo aticonfig --initial`. This will configure your X.org configuration file to work with the ATI drivers.

4. Once the configuration program has finished, reboot your system.

5. When the system is up and running, you will be able to further configure the card by opening a GNOME Terminal window and typing `fireflcontrolpanel`.

There are mixed reports about the effectiveness of the ATI drivers, and some people report they don't work very well. If you find that the new setup crashes X, or otherwise prevents you from running a GUI, try manually configuring the X server to use the new drivers by typing `sudo dpkg-reconfigure xserver-xorg`. When prompted to choose a driver for your graphics card, select `fglrx` from the list. Complete the X.org setup wizard, and then restart your computer.

If you find the drivers *still* don't work, then it's time to give up and restore the original settings. To do so, type the following at the command prompt:

```
sudo mv /etc/X11/xorg.conf.original-0 /etc/X11/xorg.conf
```

Installing an NVIDIA Driver

There are two NVIDIA drivers, which between them offer support for practically all NVIDIA 3D cards produced in recent times—everything from the latest GeForce cards to the oldest TNT cards from the mid-1990s. The `nvidia-glx` driver supports modern cards, while the `nvidia-glx-legacy` driver supports older GeForce 1 and 2 and TNT chipsets.

To install support for NVIDIA cards, follow these steps:

1. Open a terminal window (Applications ➤ Accessories ➤), and type the following in the terminal window; this will back up a vital configuration file:

   ```
   sudo cp /etc/X11/xorg.conf /etc/X11/xorg.conf.backup
   ```

2. Select System ➤ Administration ➤ Synaptic Package Manager.

3. Click the Search button, and enter `nvidia-glx` as a search term. In the list of results, click the check box next to `nvidia-glx` if you have a modern NVIDIA card or `nvidia-glx-legacy` if you have a GeForce 1 and 2 or TNT graphics card. Note that you can ignore the `nvidia-glx-dev` package. Then click Apply.

4. After the installation has completed, open a GNOME Terminal window (Applications ➤ Accessories ➤ Terminal), and type `sudo nvidia-glx-config enable`.

5. Reboot your system.

To further configure the NVIDIA card once your PC is back up and running, open a GNOME Terminal window, and type `nvidia-settings`.

If you find that the NVIDIA graphics driver doesn't work, for whatever reason, you can revert to the backed-up configuration file by typing the following at the command prompt:

```
sudo mv /etc/X11/xorg.conf.backup /etc/X11/xorg.conf
```

Testing 3D Capabilities

To test the 3D function of the graphics card, try running a 3D graphical screensaver. If the graphics drivers are correctly installed, the animations should run smoothly and with a high frame rate.

To select the screensaver, click System ➤ Preferences, and click the Screensaver icon. Select an option from the list that is preceded by GL, although you might also try some of the Ant screensavers, such as AntSpotlight.

Click the Preview button to see the screensaver in action. Note that these screensavers are visually very impressive. This is a good chance to show off your new Ubuntu setup to friends and colleagues! To stop the screensaver, click the Leave Fullscreen button at the top right.

Configuring Bluetooth

Bluetooth is the short-range networking facility that allows various items of hardware, usually those designed for mobile devices, to work with each other wirelessly. You can use Bluetooth for everything from file transfers between a mobile phone and computer to employing a wireless keyboard with your desktop computer.

For Bluetooth to work, both devices need to have Bluetooth support. Many mobile phones come with Bluetooth nowadays, and an increasing number of notebook computers do too. It's also possible to buy very inexpensive Bluetooth USB adapters.

Your PC's Bluetooth hardware is automatically recognized under Ubuntu, and the low-level driver software is installed by default. Therefore, all you normally need to do is install the software that provides the Bluetooth functionality you require.

Pairing Bluetooth Devices

When two pieces of Bluetooth-compatible hardware need to communicate on a regular basis, they can *pair* together. This means that they trust each other, so you don't need to authorize every attempt at communication between the devices. Indeed, some devices won't communicate unless they're paired in this way.

Pairing is very simple in practice and works on the principle of a shared personal ID number (PIN). The first Bluetooth device generates the PIN, and then asks the second Bluetooth device to confirm it. Once the user has typed in the PIN, the devices are paired.

Pairing is easily accomplished under Ubuntu and doesn't require any additional software. However, you will need to edit a configuration file. This only needs to be done once.

Start by opening the central Bluetooth configuration file, hcid.conf, in Gedit, using superuser powers:

```
gksu gedit /etc/bluetooth/hcid.conf
```

Look for the line that reads security user, and change it so that it reads security auto.

The default PIN needed to pair with Ubuntu is 1234. For security reasons, it's wise to change this, and the setting is contained further down in the hcid.conf file. Look for the line that reads passkey "1234"; and replace 1234 with the number you desire. For example, if I wanted a PIN of 9435, the line would read passkey "9435";.

When you've finished, save the file, and close Gedit. It's then necessary to restart the background Bluetooth service. To do this, at the command prompt, type the following

```
sudo /etc/init.d/bluetooth restart
```

Following this, I paired my Ubuntu test PC to a Nokia 6680 mobile phone. It's easiest to initiate pairing on the phone, which should then autosense the PC's Bluetooth connection. On the Nokia 6680, I opened the menu, and selected Connections ➤ Bluetooth. Then I pressed the right arrow key to select Paired Devices and selected Options ➤ New Paired Device ➤ More Devices. This made the phone autosense my Ubuntu PC, which was identified by its hostname, followed by -0. In my case, the Ubuntu PC was identified as keir-desktop-0, and I was then prompted to enter the PIN I set earlier. Following this, the two devices were paired.

Transferring Files Between Bluetooth Devices

If you own a Bluetooth-equipped camera phone, you might be used to transferring pictures to your computer using Bluetooth. It's by far the easiest way of getting pictures off the phone and avoids the need for USB cables or card readers.

To transfer files via Bluetooth, you'll need to install some additional software from the Ubuntu Universe repository, and change another configuration file. If you haven't yet configured the Synaptic Package Manager for additional repositories, see the "Setting Up Online Software Repositories" section earlier in this chapter. Then open Synaptic Package Manager (from the System ➤ Administration menu). Search for and install gnome-bluetooth.

Next, open a terminal window, and type the following, which will open the rc.local configuration file in Gedit:

```
gksu gedit /etc/rc.local
```

Scroll down to the blank line above exit 0, and type the following:

```
hciconfig hci0 inqmode 0
```

Note that the characters in the line after hci and inqmode are zeros and not the letter "O". Save the file, close Gedit, and then restart your computer.

Once logged in again, you should now find a new entry on the Applications ➤ Accessories menu: Bluetooth File Sharing. The following instructions detail how to transfer any kind of file to and from your PC using Bluetooth. Once again, I use a Nokia 6680 in the examples, but the instructions should work with any phone, or even any Bluetooth device capable of sending and receiving files.

■Note Some phones refuse to transfer files unless the phone and computer are paired, so follow the instructions in the previous section first. Phones like the Nokia 6680 don't need pairing for file transfer, although each transfer will need to be confirmed manually.

Sending Files to a Ubuntu PC

Follow these steps to send files from a Bluetooth device to your PC:

1. Select Applications ➤ Accessories ➤ Bluetooth File Sharing. Nothing will appear to have happened, but in fact, a new icon will have been added to the notification area. This does nothing apart from indicate your computer is ready for incoming Bluetooth connections.

2. On the Bluetooth device from which you wish to send the file, start the file transfer. On the Nokia 6680, I selected the file and clicked Send ➤ Via Bluetooth.

3. When the file transfer is initiated, a dialog box will appear on your computer asking if you wish to accept the file, as shown in Figure 8-13. Click OK. (If the two devices are paired, the file transfer may happen instantly without the confirmation dialog box.) The file will be saved to your /home directory.

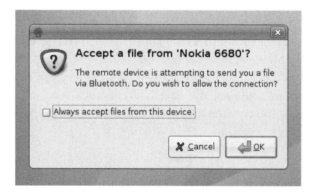

Figure 8-13. *If you send files from a Bluetooth device to your PC, you may be asked to authorize receipt.*

Sending Files from an Ubuntu PC to Another Device

The easiest way to send files from your PC to a Bluetooth device is to create a desktop shortcut onto which you can drag and drop files. Follow these steps to create the shortcut:

1. Right-click the desktop, and click Create Launcher.

2. In the Name field, type something like **Send file via Bluetooth**.

3. In the Command field, type gnome-obex-send.

4. You can also choose to give the new shortcut an appropriate icon. Click the No Icon button, and then type the following into the Path field:

   /usr/share/icons/gnome/48x48/stock/io/stock_bluetooth.png

5. Click OK.

After you've created the icon, you can send files as follows:

1. Drag and drop a file onto the launcher (icon) you just created.

2. The Choose Bluetooth Device dialog box appears. Click Refresh to make the computer detect any nearby Bluetooth devices. This may take a minute or two. Remember that your device will need to be set to be "visible," so that other Bluetooth devices can automatically detect it.

3. Select the device to which you want to transfer the file, and then click OK.

4. Check the device to see if the file transfer needs to be authorized. If the devices are paired, the transfer might take place automatically.

Using a Bluetooth Keyboard or Mouse

Your Bluetooth-equipped keyboard or mouse may work automatically under Ubuntu. However, if not, you may find the following instructions useful:

1. Open a GNOME Terminal window (Applications ➤ Accessories ➤ Terminal), and type hcitool scan.

2. Your Bluetooth keyboard or mouse should be identified in the results (ignore any other devices that might appear in the list). If not, make sure it isn't in sleep mode. You might also have to press a button on the device for it to be made visible to other Bluetooth devices.

3. Alongside the entry for the keyboard or mouse will be a MAC address—a series of numbers like 00:12:62:A5:60:F7.

4. In the GNOME Terminal window, type the following:

```
sudo hidd --connect xx:xx:xx:xx:xx:xx
```

Replace *xx:xx:xx:xx:xx:xx* with the series of numbers you discovered in the previous step.

5. You should find that your keyboard or mouse works under Ubuntu. You now need to make sure your mouse or keyboard works every time you boot your computer, so you'll need to edit the Ubuntu Bluetooth configuration file. Type the following in the GNOME Terminal window to open the configuration file in Gedit:

```
gksu gedit /etc/default/bluetooth
```

6. Search for the line that reads HIDD_ENABLED=0 (on its own, with no other text on the line), and change it to HIDD_ENABLED=1.

7. Beneath this will be a line that begins HIDD_OPTIONS=. Change this so it reads as follows, again replacing *xx:xx:xx:xx:xx:xx* with the MAC address you discovered earlier:

```
HIDD_OPTIONS="-i xx:xx:xx:xx:xx:xx --server"
```

8. Save the file and reboot.

■**Tip** If you want to quickly connect a Bluetooth keyboard or mouse to your computer, but don't need to make it permanent, just open a GNOME Terminal window (Applications ➤ Accessories ➤ Terminal), and type `sudo hidd --search`.

Configuring Sound Cards

Generally speaking, your sound card shouldn't require any additional configuration and should work immediately after you install Ubuntu. The icon for the volume control applet is located at the top right of the Ubuntu desktop, and it offers a quick way to control the master volume.

However, if your sound card offers more than stereo output, such as multiple-speaker surround sound, then it might be necessary to take some simple steps to allow full control of the hardware:

1. Right-click the volume control icon (the one that looks like a speaker), and select Open Volume Control.

2. In the dialog box that appears, click Edit, and then click Preferences.

3. The Volume Control Preferences dialog box appears, as shown in Figure 8-14. Select the sliders that you wish to be visible. For example, on my desktop computer that has 5.1 surround sound, I was able to add a slider for the center and back speakers. On my notebook that has a sound card featuring pseudosurround sound, I was able to add a control to alter the intensity of the effect.

4. When you've finished, click the Close button. The new controls should then be visible on the front panel of the Volume Control window.

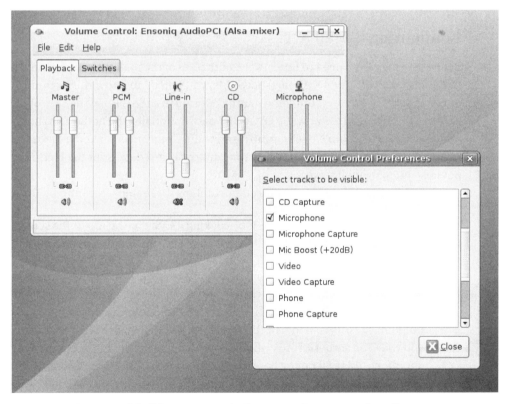

Figure 8-14. *You can add sliders to control all aspects of your sound card's output.*

Configuring E-Mail and Instant Messaging

Being online is all about staying in touch, and Ubuntu is no slouch in this regard. Ubuntu offers a full-featured e-mail program, called Evolution, as well as an instant messaging client called Gaim.

Unlike similar instant messaging clients, Gaim supports a wide variety of Internet chat protocols, such as AIM/ICQ, MSN, Yahoo, Jabber, and IRC. This means you can chat with friends and colleagues on different networks using this one program.

Evolution is able to work with both IMAP and the popular POP3 mail servers offered by ISPs and used within corporate environments. Additionally, it can work with the Microsoft Exchange protocol used by offices running the Outlook mail program and also Novell GroupWise. We'll look at the specifics of using Evolution in Chapter 27. Here, you'll learn how to configure the e-mail client to receive and send mail.

Configuring E-Mail Access

Before starting, you'll need to find out the addresses of the mail servers you intend to use. In the case of POP3 and IMAP mail accounts, you'll need to know the incoming and outgoing server addresses (outgoing may be referred to as SMTP). In the case of Microsoft Exchange, you'll need to know the OWA URL and, optionally, the Active Directory/Global Address List server. With Novell GroupWare, you'll simply need to know the server name.

You'll also need to know your username and password details for the incoming and possibly outgoing mail servers.

After gathering the necessary information, follow these steps to configure Evolution:

1. Start the Evolution e-mail client by clicking its icon at the top of the screen, to the right of the menus. Alternatively, you can select Applications ➤ Office ➤ Evolution.

2. When Evolution starts for the first time, you'll be invited to enter your configuration details via a wizard. After you click Forward, the first screen will ask for your name and the e-mail address you wish to use within Evolution. These are what will appear in outgoing messages. Beneath this is a check box that you should leave checked if you want the account you're about to create to be the default account. In nearly all situations, this will be the correct choice. You can also fill in the Reply-To and Organization information if you wish, but these fields can be left blank. They're not normally displayed by most e-mail clients. Click the Forward button to continue.

3. The next screen asks for details of the receiving (incoming) mail server that you want to use, as shown in Figure 8-15. First, select the server type from the drop-down list. If you don't know which option to go with, select POP. This is by far the most common type of incoming mail server currently in use.

4. Additional configuration fields will appear when you make the selection of server type. Enter the server address and username in the relevant fields. Click Check for Supported Types to find out what kind of authentication security, if any, your mail server uses. Following this, you should find the details are filled in automatically. Click Forward to continue.

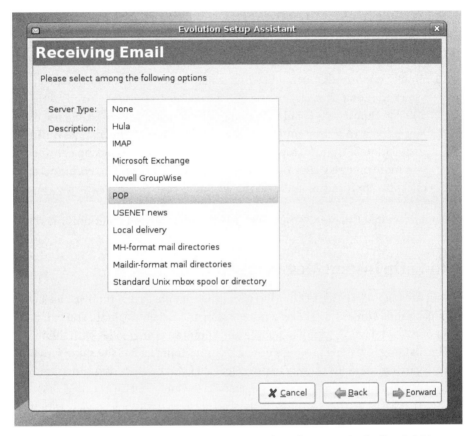

Figure 8-15. *Evolution can work with a variety of mail servers, including POP3, Microsoft Exchange, and IMAP.*

5. You might need to enter your mail password, depending on which server type you chose. In some cases, you'll need to type this later when you download your mail for the first time. Click Forward to continue.

6. You're given the chance to choose between various additional options, such as how often you want Evolution to check for new mail or if you want to delete mail from the server after it has been downloaded. Unless you have been told otherwise or have special requirements, it should be okay to leave the default settings as they are. If you use a Microsoft Exchange server, you may need to enter the Active Directory/Global Address List server details here. Click Forward to continue.

7. Depending on the server type you chose, you might now need to fill in the outgoing (SMTP) server address. Type this into the Server field. If your SMTP server requires authentication, put a check in the relevant box, and then enter your username. Once again, you can click the Check for Supported Types button to automatically fill in the authentication details. Once finished, click Forward to continue.

8. You're invited to enter a name for the account. This is the account name you will see when you use Evolution. The default is your e-mail address, but you can type something more memorable if you wish. Click Forward to continue.

9. Finally, choose your location, which will have the effect of automatically defining your time zone. This will ensure that e-mail messages are correctly time-stamped. You can choose your location from the Selection drop-down list (choose the nearest large city in your time zone), or click your location on the map. As during initial installation of Ubuntu, the map will zoom in when you click on continents, to let you more precisely click the place you live. Click Forward to continue, and then click the Apply button to finish the wizard.

Remember that Chapter 27 includes a full run-through of Evolution's main functions.

Setting Up Instant Messaging

Instant messaging is a way of chatting with other people in real time. It's as if you were having a phone conversation, but you're typing instead of speaking. You can talk to one other person or a whole group of people and sometimes share files with them.

The instant messaging program under Ubuntu, Gaim, offers the same functions and works in an almost identical way to programs that you might have used under Windows. It supports virtually all the popular chat standards, such as ICQ/AOL and MSN (Hotmail/ Passport). It assumes that you already have an account with each service, which will likely be the case if you've used instant messaging programs under Windows. You can have as many accounts as you wish and can select the one you want to use when you log in.

To transfer your instant messaging account over to Gaim, you just need your screen name and password. As with other instant messaging clients, you'll be able to choose an on-screen alias.

Follow these steps to set up Gaim:

1. Start Gaim by clicking Applications ➤ Internet ➤ Gaim Internet Messenger. When the program starts for the first time, it will automatically open the Accounts dialog box, although it might be behind the main login window. If so, click to bring it to the front of the desktop.

2. In the Accounts dialog box, click the Add button and, in the window that appears, select the account type you want to set up from the Protocol drop-down list.

3. Enter your screen name, password, and alias details, as required.

4. If you don't want to type your password each time you run Gaim, check Remember Password. However, be aware that someone else using the computer could abuse your account.

5. You can put a check in the New Mail Notifications box if you want to be notified of any mail sent to you via the address registered with your instant messaging service.

6. If you want to use a buddy icon (the icon that others will see when they connect to you), click the Open button and browse to a picture.

7. If you wish to connect to a specific instant messaging server or if your network uses a proxy, click the Advanced tab, and enter the details accordingly. In most cases, you won't need to do this.

8. When you've finished, click the Save button. Then, in the main Gaim login window, click Sign On.

After this, you should find the program works just like any other instant messaging program. You can double-click each contact in your list to start a conversation. To sign off, right-click the icon in the notification area, Change Status, and then select the option from the menu, as shown in Figure 8-16. To add another account, click Accounts ➤ Add/Edit, click the Add button in the Accounts window, and then follow the preceding step-by-step instructions.

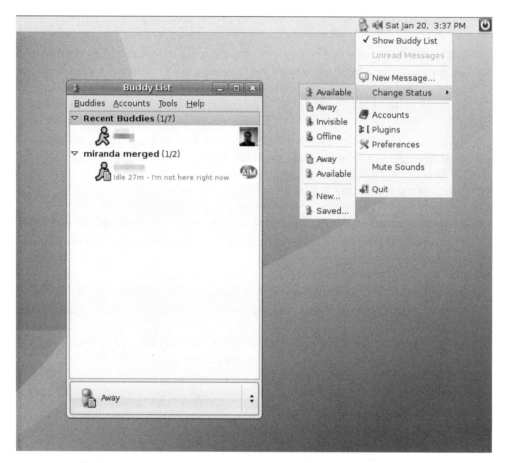

Figure 8-16. *You can control Gaim by right-clicking its notification area icon.*

Summary

In this chapter, you learned how to set up just about every piece of hardware you might have attached to your computer. Additionally, we looked at configuring various software components within your Ubuntu setup that are vital for its correct functioning.

We stepped through getting online with Ubuntu (including joining a wireless network), configuring e-mail, adding a printer, setting up online software repositories, setting up a digital camera, configuring a 3D graphics card, and much more.

In Chapter 9, we move on to look at how you can ensure that your system is secure and protected.

CHAPTER 9

■■■

How to Secure Your Computer

Linux is widely considered one of the most secure operating systems around. On a basic level, Linux is built from the ground up to be fundamentally sound, and it forces users to work with security in mind. For instance, it enforces the system of ordinary users who are limited in what they can do, thus making it harder for security breaches like virus infections to occur.

In addition, Linux contains a firewall that is hardwired into the kernel. It's called iptables (www.netfilter.org) and is considered among the best solutions by practically all computer security experts. Not only that, but it can protect your home PC just as well as it can protect the most powerful supercomputer.

But, as with many Linux kernel components, iptables is difficult to use. It requires in-depth knowledge of how networks operate and an ability to hack configuration files, both of which are beyond the skills of many ordinary computer users. Fortunately, several programs act as interfaces to iptables and make it simple to operate (or at least as simple as any equivalent Windows-based software firewall, such as Zone Labs's ZoneAlarm).

Perhaps surprisingly, Ubuntu doesn't install any firewall configuration program by default. This is because the developers consider Ubuntu to have no need for such a thing, and on a technical level they're correct—unlike with Windows, Ubuntu has no Internet-facing *services* (programs that wait for connections from the Internet or local area network). It was just such a service on Windows XP that allowed the Blaster worm to bring the Internet to its knees in 2003 (see http://en.wikipedia.org/wiki/Blaster_worm). Expressed meta-phorically, the theory is that without any windows or doors, Ubuntu will be difficult, if not impossible, for hackers to break into (or for viruses or worms to infect).

However, configuring the firewall with a program like Firestarter, which we examine later in this chapter, can be done so quickly and with such little effort that, in my opinion, there's no reason *not* to make use of the Linux firewall.

In addition, as with most versions of Linux, Ubuntu doesn't come with antivirus protection out of the box. This is because there are practically no viruses affecting Linux, and it is reasoned that there simply isn't a need for virus protection. However, as with a firewall configuration program, installing an antivirus program is easily done, and I explain how later in this chapter.

But first, you'll spend some time examining more basic security concepts. Following that, we'll look at some elementary steps that you can take to protect your system.

Windows Security vs. Linux Security

If you've switched to Ubuntu from Windows, there's a very good chance that the security failings of Windows featured in your decision. Windows Vista contains many improvements, but Microsoft's record on security over the past few years has been appalling. New and serious security warnings appeared on an ongoing basis, and even now new and devastating viruses make news headlines with worrying frequency (usually described as "a PC virus" rather than what it actually is—a Windows virus).

One argument is that Windows is the target of so many viruses merely because it's so popular. Although it's true that some of those who write viruses do so because they dislike Microsoft, there's also little doubt that Windows has more than its fair share of security issues.

Many people are still critical of Microsoft's approach to security. For example, Microsoft's latest operating system, Vista, features User Account Control (UAC) dialog boxes that appear whenever a system-affecting action is required. However, they are so common that many people stop reading what they warn about, and simply click OK by reflex. Compare this to Ubuntu. Similar dialog boxes appear whenever system-affecting action is required, but here the user's password must be entered. This forces the user to stop and think, rather than simply clicking a mouse button. However, perhaps more importantly, the password dialog boxes appear far less frequently than UAC dialog boxes.

While Vista offers reasonable security, Microsoft's previous operating system, Windows XP, is considered an easy target for hackers and virus writers. Upon installation, the default user is given root powers. True, a handful of tasks can be performed only by the genuine administrator, but the default user can configure hardware, remove system software, and even wipe every file from the hard disk. While you would never intentionally damage your own system, computer attackers use various techniques to get you to run malicious software (by pretending it's a different file, for example) or simply infect your computer across the Internet without your knowledge, which is how most worms work.

Viruses and worms also usually take advantage of security holes within Windows software. As just one example, a famous security hole within Outlook Express some years ago allowed a program attached to an e-mail message to run when the user simply clicked a particular message to view it. In other words, infecting a Windows machine was as easy as sending someone an e-mail message!

It's a different story with Linux. Viruses and worms are far rarer than they are on Windows. In fact, the total number of viruses and worms that have been found in the wild infecting Linux systems number far less than 100 (one report published in 2003 put the number at 40, and the number is unlikely to have grown much since then). Compare that to Windows, where according to the Sophos antivirus labs (www.sophos.com), approximately 1,000 new viruses are discovered *every month*! The Sophos antivirus product now guards against just under 120,000 viruses.

Note The high number of Windows viruses may be because of the quantity of Windows PCs out there. After all, for a virus to spread, it needs computers to infect, and it won't have trouble finding other Windows computers.

But while I would love to say that security holes are not found on Linux, the sad truth is that they're a fact of life for users of every operating system. Many so-called rootkits are available, which are specialized software toolkits that aim to exploit holes within the Linux operating system and its software.

The bottom line is that while writing a virus or worm for Linux is much harder than doing the same thing on Windows, all Linux users should spend time securing their system and *never* assume that they're safe.

Root and Ordinary Users

As I've mentioned in earlier chapters, Linux makes use of something called the *root* user account. This is sometimes referred to as the *superuser* account, and that gives you an idea of its purpose in life: the root user has unrestricted access to all aspects of the system. The root user can delete, modify, or view any file, as well as alter hardware settings.

Linux systems also have ordinary user accounts, which are limited in what they can do. Such users are limited to saving files in their own directory within the /home directory (although the system is usually configured so that an ordinary user can read files outside the /home directory, too). But an ordinary Ubuntu user cannot delete or modify files other than those that he created or for which he has explicitly been given permission to modify by someone else.

The user account you created during the installation of Ubuntu is a limited account, but on some Linux systems, it's possible to type `root` at the login prompt and, after providing the correct password, actually log in as root and perform system maintenance tasks. Ubuntu is slightly different in that the root account is disabled by default, and users are instead able to *borrow* superuser powers whenever they're required. For this to happen, they simply need to provide their own login password. With desktop programs, a password prompt dialog box will appear automatically, but at the command prompt, users need to preface commands with `sudo`.

Although the root account is disabled, most key operating system files "belong" to the root user, which is to say that only someone with superuser powers can alter them. Ordinary users are simply unable to modify or delete these system files, as shown in Figure 9-1. This is a powerful method of protecting the operating system configuration from accidental or even deliberate damage.

Note Along with the root and ordinary user accounts, there is a third type of Linux account, which is similar to a limited user account, except that it's used by the system for various tasks. These user accounts are usually invisible to ordinary users and work in the background. For example, the audio subsystem has its own user account that Ubuntu uses to access the audio hardware. The concepts of users and files are discussed in more depth in Chapter 14.

ARE YOU A CRACKER OR A HACKER?

Linux users are often described as *hackers*. This doesn't mean they maliciously break into computers or write viruses. It's simply using the word "hacker" in its original sense from the 1970s, when it described a computer enthusiast who was interested in exploring the capabilities of computers. Many of the people behind multinational computing corporations started out as hackers. Examples are Steve Wozniak, a cofounder of Apple Computer, and Bill Joy, cofounder of Sun Microsystems.

The word "hacker" is believed to derive from model train enthusiasts who "hacked" train tracks together as part of their hobby. When computing became popular in the early 1970s, several of these enthusiasts also became interested in computing, and the term was carried across with them.

However, in recent years, the media has subverted the term "hacker" to apply to an individual who breaks into computer systems. This was based on ignorance, and many true hackers find the comparison extremely offensive. Because of this, the term "cracker" was invented to clearly define an individual who maliciously attacks computers.

So, don't worry if an acquaintance describes herself as a Linux hacker, or tells you that she has spent the night hacking. Many Linux types use the term as a badge of honor.

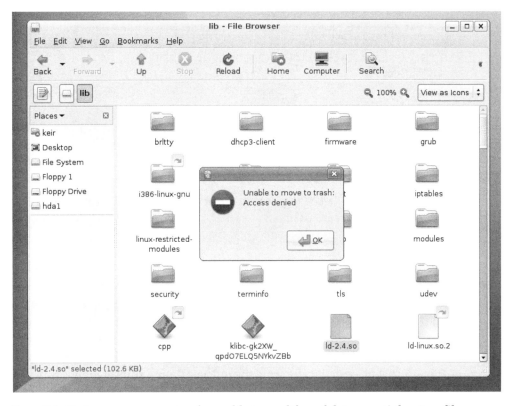

Figure 9-1. *Ordinary users are simply unable to modify or delete essential system files under Linux.*

Common-Sense Security

As you start to understand how Ubuntu works, you'll become more and more aware of common-sense methods that will protect your system. However, I'll outline a few of these now to get you started:

> **Entering your password:** Be very wary if you're asked to enter your password (outside of initial login, of course). You'll be asked to provide your password when following many of the configuration steps within this book, for example, and this is acceptable and safe. But if you're asked to do so out of the blue, then you should be suspicious. If the root password prompt dialog box (shown in Figure 9-2) appears when you run a file that shouldn't really need root permissions, such as an MP3 or OpenOffice.org file, you should treat the situation with caution.

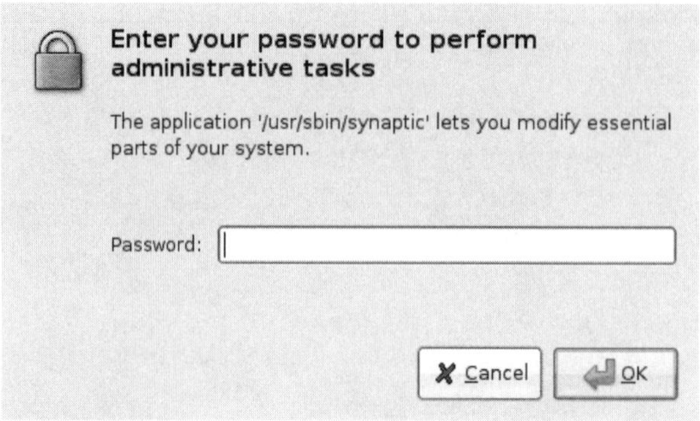

Figure 9-2. *Beware if you're asked to type your password out of the blue and for no apparent reason.*

Installing new software: Be careful in choosing programs to download and install. Because Linux works on the basis of open-source code, anyone can theoretically tamper with a program and then offer it for download by the unwary. This very rarely happens in real life. Even so, it's wise to avoid downloading programs from unofficial sources, such as web sites you find online via a search engine and whose authenticity you cannot totally trust. Instead, get software from the web site of the people who made it in the first place or, ideally, from the official Ubuntu software repositories (discussed in Chapter 8).

Updating your system: Always ensure your system software is completely up-to-date. As with Windows, many Ubuntu programs have bugs that lead to security holes. Crackers target such vulnerabilities. Downloading the latest versions of Ubuntu software ensures that you not only get the latest features, but also that any critical security holes are patched. As with most versions of Linux, updating Ubuntu is easy and, of course, it's also free of charge. You'll learn how to get online updates in the next section.

Locking up your PC: Limit who has physical access to your computer. Any Ubuntu system can be compromised by a simple floppy boot disk, or even by just selecting the Rescue Mode entry on the boot menu, which will provide the user with root access to the computer. This is for obvious reasons; the idea of a boot disk or the Rescue Mode is to let you fix your PC should something go wrong, and you cannot do this if you're blocked from accessing certain files. When Linux is used on servers that hold confidential data, it's not uncommon for the floppy and CD-ROM drives to be removed, thus avoiding booting via a boot disk. Such computers are also usually locked away in a room or even in a cupboard, denying physical access to the machine.

Online Updates

The Ubuntu notification area (the equivalent of the Windows system tray) at the top right of the screen contains a program that automatically monitors the package repositories and tells you when updates are available. This is an extension of the Synaptic Package Manager program called Software Updates. If you've already configured the Synaptic Package Manager, as described in Chapter 8, and haven't yet updated your system, this icon will have probably turned into an orange box with a white star in it. This is informing you that updates are available. In addition, each time you boot, you will see a speech bubble telling you that updates are available. When your system is completely up-to-date, the icon will not be visible.

Clicking the Update Manager icon opens the Software Updates window, as shown in Figure 9-3. To go online and grab the updated files, simply click the Install Updates button at the bottom-right side of the window. You will probably be asked to enter your root password, because system files will need to be altered.

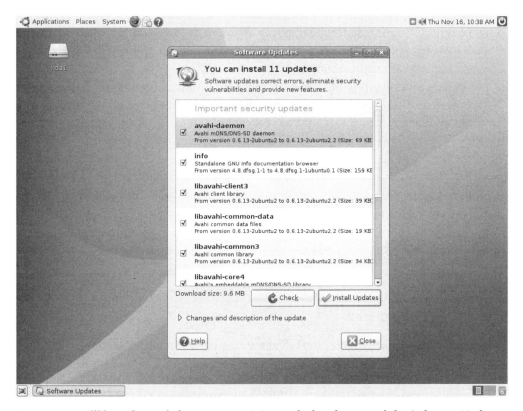

Figure 9-3. *You'll be informed if your system is in need of updates, and the Software Updates program can take care of everything for you.*

Be aware that some updates can be large and might take some time to download, particularly if you're doing it for the first time after installing Ubuntu.

Once the downloads have finished, you probably won't need to reboot unless the kernel file has been updated. If you do need to reboot, or the if the update requires you to take any other action (such as logging out and then back in again), the Software Update icon in the notication area will turn into an information icon, or into two encircled arrows. You should then click the icon to see what action you're advised to take.

Configuring the Ubuntu Firewall

A *firewall* is a set of programs that protects your PC when it's online. It does this by watching what data attempts to enter your PC from the Internet and allowing in only what it is sure is secure (which usually is what you've asked for). It also attempts to close off various aspects of your Internet connection, so that crackers don't have a way in should they target your system.

Although Ubuntu includes a powerful firewall in the form of iptables, you'll also need a program that can manage it. Here, I'll show you how to use Firestarter, available from the Ubuntu software repository, for this purpose. Together with the built-in firewall, this really does provide very strong protection.

The benefit of configuring the firewall is that even if your system has security vulnerabilities because of buggy software, crackers will find it a lot harder to exploit them across the Internet. When someone attempts to probe your system, it will appear to be virtually invisible.

■Caution Although software firewalls such as the one built into Linux offer a high level of protection, it's best to use them in concert with a hardware firewall, such as that provided by most DSL/cable broadband routers (curiously, some of these routers actually use Linux's iptables software as well). Many security experts agree that relying solely on a software firewall to protect a PC affords less than the optimal level of protection.

Installing Firestarter

Let's get started by downloading and installing Firestarter. Follow these steps:

1. Select System ➤ Administration ➤ Synaptic Package Manager. You'll need to enter your password when prompted. Click the Search button, and enter **firestarter** as a search term. In the list of results, locate the program, and click the check box. Then choose to install the package, and click Apply on the Synaptic toolbar.

■**Caution** Firestarter is contained in the Ubuntu "universe" repository, which isn't activated by default. If you haven't already, follow the instructions in Chapter 8, in the "Setting Up Online Software Repositories" section.

2. After installing Firestarter, log out and then back in again. This will update the menus to show Firestarter.

3. Once the desktop is back up and running, select System ➤ Administration ➤ Firestarter. When you run Firestarter for the first time, it will walk you through a wizard.

4. Click the Forward button to continue the wizard beyond the introductory page.

5. The first step asks which network interface Firestarter should configure, as shown in Figure 9-4. If you use an Ethernet card, have a wireless card, or attach a broadband modem directly to your computer, the answer will probably be eth0 or wlan0. However, if you use a modem, the answer is ppp0. Once you've made your choice, click Forward.

Figure 9-4. *Firestarter includes a wizard to walk you through the basics of firewall configuration.*

6. Put a check in the IP address is assigned via DHCP box, unless you're using a dial-up modem. If you are using a dial-up modem, select Start the Firewall on Dial-Out. However, don't activate this option otherwise. After making your choices, click the Forward button.

7. You're asked if you want to enable Internet connection sharing. This allows you to turn your computer into an Internet router and can be very useful in certain circumstances. You can activate this later on by running the wizard again (to rerun the wizard, simply click Firewall on Firestarter's main window, and then click Run Wizard). Click Forward to continue.

8. The wizard will finish, and you should click the Save button to save your settings to disk. In addition, ensure the Start Firewall Now box is checked. After this, the Firestarter main window opens.

Configuring Firestarter

Firestarter works by controlling the data that goes into and out of your computer via your Internet or network connection. By default, it blocks every type of uninvited inbound connection but allows every type of outbound connection.

Whenever you click a link on a web page, your computer sends a request for data to the web server hosting the web page. Within a few milliseconds, that data will be sent to your computer. This is an *inbound* data connection. The Linux firewall is clever enough to realize that the data was requested by you, so it is allowed through. However, any uninvited connections are turned away. If, out of the blue, someone attempts to connect to your computer via the popular Secure Shell (SSH) tool, as just one example, he won't be allowed to make that connection. This is a good thing, because it makes your computer secure. Crackers are turned away whenever they try to connect, no matter *how* they try to connect.

But in some circumstances, allowing uninvited connections is useful. For example, if you create a shared folder for other computers in your office to connect to, they will frequently make uninvited inbound connections to your computer whenever they want to grab a file. And if you want to make use of SSH to connect to your computer remotely, you will need to allow such incoming connections. Therefore, Firestarter lets you allow through certain types of inbound connections.

In the terminology of Firestarter (and many firewall programs), *outbound traffic* is any kind of data originating on your computer that is sent out on the network and/or Internet. By default, Firestarter allows out all data, no matter what it is. This is described as a *permissive* policy. But Firestarter can be configured to block all outgoing connections *apart from those you configure Firestarter to allow through*. This is described as a *restrictive* policy and can be useful in blocking certain types of programs that "phone home" with personal data about you, such as spyware.

■**Note** Unlike with Windows, I've never heard of a Linux program that contains spyware that "phones home" in this way. Nevertheless, a cautious attitude often pays dividends.

A restrictive policy can also prevent certain types of viruses and worms from spreading. The downside of a restrictive policy is that you must configure Firestarter to take into account every type of outgoing data connection that you *do* want to allow through, such as those for web browsers, instant messaging programs, and so on.

You can configure Firestarter by clicking the Policy tab in the main program window. Click the Editing drop-down list, and choose to configure either the inbound traffic policy or the outbound traffic policy.

■**Note** Firestarter is used only to configure the built-in firewall and doesn't need to be running for the firewall to work. Once you've finished configuration, you can quit the program. You'll need to use it again only if you wish to reconfigure the firewall.

Setting Inbound Rules

For most users, Firestarter's default inbound traffic policy will be perfectly acceptable. It configures the firewall to disallow all uninvited incoming data connection, apart from certain diagnostic tools, such as ping, traceroute, and so on. You can choose to disallow those as well, as described shortly in the "Turning Off Diagnostic Services" section.

You might wish to allow an incoming connection if you intend to connect to your computer via SSH from a remote location or if you have a shared folder created for other computers in your office. It's a must if you're running the BitTorrent file sharing application. Additionally, if you run a web, e-mail, or other type of server on your computer, you will need to allow the correct type of incoming connection here.

Here's how to set inbound connection rules:

1. In the Firestarter main window, click the Policy tab. Select Inbound Traffic Policy in the Editing drop-down list.

2. Right-click in the second box on the Policy tab (with the headings Allow Service/ Port/For), and then select Add Rule.

3. The Add New Inbound Rule dialog box appears. In the Name drop-down list, select the type of outgoing connection you want to allow, as shown in Figure 9-5. To allow others to access shared folders on your computer, select Samba (SMB). To allow SSH or BitTorrent connections to your computer, select the relevant entry from the list. Selecting the service will automatically fill in the Port box, which you shouldn't alter unless you know exactly what you're doing.

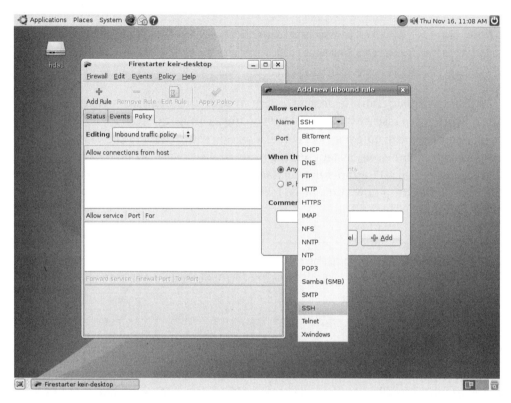

Figure 9-5. *Creating an inbound rule enables computers to connect to your PC uninvited.*

4. If you know the IP address of the computer that's going to make the incoming connection, you can click the IP, Host or Network radio button, and then type in that address. However, the default of Anyone will allow anyone using any IP address to connect to your computer.

5. Click Add. Back in the main Firestarter window, click the Apply Policy button on the toolbar.

Note You'll need to return to Firestarter whenever you activate new services on your computer. For example, in Chapter 12, we will look at accessing Windows shares across a network, and you'll need to enable SMB incoming and outgoing access for this to work. In Chapter 34, we will look at using the SSH service, which will have to be allowed through the firewall. In other words, securing your computer isn't something you can do once and then forget about. It's a continual process.

Setting Outbound Rules

By default, Firestarter allows all types of outgoing connections and, as with its incoming connections policy, this is by no means a bad choice for the average user. It's certainly the option that involves the least fuss. However, by opting to go with a restrictive traffic policy, you can completely control what kind of data leaves your computer. Any type of data connection that isn't authorized will be refused; as far as the program sending the data is concerned, it will be as if your computer did not have a network or Internet connection.

Here's how to set outbound connection rules:

1. In the Firestarter main window, click the Policy tab. Select Outbound Traffic Policy in the Editing drop-down list.

2. Click the Restrictive by Default, Whitelist Traffic radio button.

3. In the second empty box at the bottom of the Policy tab (which has the Allow Service/Port/For headings), right-click and select Add Rule.

4. The Add New Outbound Rule dialog box appears. In the Name drop-down list, select the type of data connection you wish to allow. At the very least, you should select HTTP. This will allow your web browser to operate correctly (it's also needed to allow the Synaptic Package Manager and Update Manager programs to work). HTTPS should also be allowed—this is the secure version of HTTP used to access the likes of online banking sites, and some online e-mail services. You should also add a rule for POP3 and another for SMTP, without which your e-mail program won't work. Selecting the type of service will fill in the Port box automatically. You shouldn't alter this unless you know what you're doing.

■**Note** You can only add one rule at a time. You'll have to repeat steps 3 and 4 several times to add rules for each service you want to allow.

---

5. Click the Add button to add the rule. Back in the Firestarter main window, click Apply Policy.

6. Test your settings with a program that uses the services you've just authorized.

■**Caution** If you created an inbound rule, you'll need to create a matching outbound rule. If you created an incoming rule for BitTorrent, for example, you'll need to create an outgoing rule for BitTorrent, too.

You can delete both incoming and outgoing rules by right-clicking their entries in the list.

Turning Off Diagnostic Services

Certain network tools can be misused by crackers to break into a computer or just cause it problems. In the past, the traceroute and ping tools, among others, have been used to launch denial-of-service (DoS) attacks against computers.

Ubuntu is set to allow these tools to operate by default. If you want to adopt a belts-and-suspenders approach to your computer's security, you can opt to disable them. If you don't know what ping and traceroute are, you're clearly not going to miss them, so there will be no harm in disallowing them. Here's how:

1. In the Firestarter main window, click Edit ➤ Preferences.

2. On the left side of the Preferences window, click ICMP Filtering. Then click the Enable ICMP Filtering check box, as shown in Figure 9-6. *Don't* put a check in any of the boxes underneath, unless you specifically want to permit one of the services.

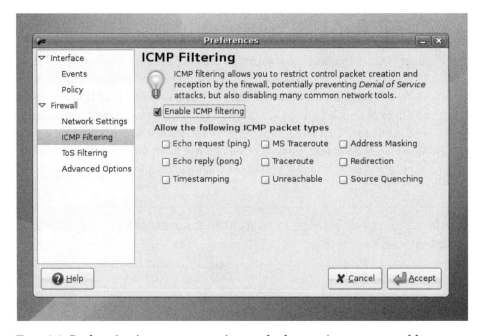

Figure 9-6. *By deactivating traceroute, ping, and other services, you can add extra protection to your PC.*

3. Click the Accept button to finish.

PARANOIA AND SECURITY

There's a fine line between security and paranoia. Using Firestarter gives you the opportunity to ensure your system is secure, without needing to constantly reassess your system for threats and live in fear.

When considering your system security, remember that most burglars don't enter a house through the front door. Most take advantage of an open window or poor security elsewhere in the house. In other words, when configuring your system's security, you should always select every option and extra layer of security, even if it might not appear to be useful. You should lock every door and close every window, even if you don't think an attacker would ever use them.

Provided a security setting doesn't impact your ordinary use of the computer, you should select it. For example, deactivating the ping response of your computer might sound like a paranoid action, but it's useful on several levels. First, it means your computer is less easy to detect when it's online. Second, and equally important, it means that if there's ever a security flaw in the ping tool (or any software connected with it), you'll be automatically protected.

This illustrates how you must think when configuring your system's security. Try to imagine every situation that might arise. Remember that you can never take too many precautions!

Adding Virus Scanning to Ubuntu

As mentioned in the chapter introduction, Linux (and therefore Ubuntu) are not currently affected by viruses. Nobody knows the true number of viruses affecting Linux, but the number is almost certainly less than 50, and that's the total number since Linux was created back in the early 1990s! At the time of this writing, there are no Linux viruses in the wild, which is to say, actually infecting computers.

However, there can be no room for complacency. It's very likely virus writers will turn their attention to Linux in the coming years as it becomes a popular desktop solution.

The following instructions describe how to install ClamTk, which is a graphical front-end for the Clam AntiVirus (ClamAV) antivirus program (www.clamav.net). Clam AntiVirus is an open source, industrial-strength antivirus scanner designed to work on all kinds of computers and operating systems. It detects Windows and even Macintosh viruses, as well as the minority Linux and Unix viruses. This has obvious benefits if you share files with Windows users—you can inform your friends and colleagues if any files they give you are infected (and bask in the warm feeling that arises when you realize the viruses can't affect your system!).

Clam AntiVirus's only drawback is that it is limited just to virus scanning. It isn't able to disinfect files, like the more-sophisticated virus scanners available for Windows. However, it should be noted that disinfection rarely works very well, as discussed in the Clam AntiVirus FAQ (`www.clamav.net/faq.html#pagestart`).

I discuss the options for dealing with infected files later, but first I discuss installing ClamTk and performing virus scans.

Installing ClamTk

You must install Clam AntiVirus first, and then install the ClamTk graphical front-end separately. This is because, at the time of this writing, there is a bug in the Clam AntiVirus software package that means a minor extra step is necessary to install it.

▓**Note** These bugs may have been fixed by the time you read this. However, the following instructions will still work fine.

Start by opening a terminal window (Applications ➤ Accessories ➤ Terminal). At the command prompt in the window that appears, type the following:

```
sudo apt-get install clamav
```

This will download and install not only Clam AntiVirus but also some of its dependencies. Once the download and installation have completed, look at the last lines of the command output. If they read similar to the following lines, then enter `sudo apt-get install clamav` once again to complete the installation successfully:

```
Errors were encountered while processing:
ClamAV-base
ClamAV-freshclam
ClamAV
E: Sub-process /usr/bin/dpkg returned an error code (1)
```

If you don't see the error message, then there's no need to repeat the command. Following this, install ClamTk using the following command:

```
sudo apt-get install clamtk
```

This will also install a number of additional dependency packages.

■**Caution** `clamav` and `clamtk` are contained in the Ubuntu "universe" repository, which isn't activated by default. If you haven't already, follow the instructions in Chapter 8, under the "Setting Up Online Software Repositories" heading.

Updating the Clam AntiVirus Database

Before you scan for viruses, you should update the virus database. This should be done every time you scan and can be done using the ClamTk program.

■**Note** When you installed Clam AntiVirus, it added a background service called `freshclam` that periodically downloads updates for Clam AntiVirus's database. However, manually updating before scanning is also a good idea, to ensure you're always using the very latest version of the database at the time of scanning.

However, in order to update the database, ClamTk needs to access system files, so it needs to be run with root powers. To do this, open a Terminal window by clicking Accessories ➤ Terminal. Then type `gksu clamtk`, and press Enter. Enter your password when prompted.

■**Note** `gksu` is like `sudo`, in that it gives the program you specify administrator powers, except that it's used for GUI applications.

Click Help ➤ Update Signatures. Updating can take a few moments, and you'll see a progress report in the ClamTk window beneath the toolbar.

■**Note** When Clam AntiVirus is first installed, it automatically grabs the latest database file, so ClamTk will probably report it's already up to date the first time an update is run.

It's also possible to update Clam AntiVirus without using ClamTk—just type `sudo` `freshclam` in a terminal window.

> **Note** When updating using the `freshclam` command, you might see a warning that your version of Clam AntiVirus is out of date. This is because the Ubuntu packages are sometimes a version or two behind the main release. However, this isn't a significant issue, and Clam AntiVirus will still be able to scan for viruses, and virus definitions will stay up to date.

Scanning for Viruses

With Windows virus scanners, you might be used to performing whole system scans. This isn't advisable with Clam AntiVirus, because it simply isn't designed for that task. Instead, Clam AntiVirus is designed to scan user files, such as documents.

> **Note** In actual fact, Clam AntiVirus is primarily designed to be used in concert with a mail server and to scan incoming or outgoing mail attachments. See the "about" page at the Clam AntiVirus web site: `www.clamav.net/abstract.html#pagestart`.

You can try performing a full system scan, but in my tests, several *false positives* were identified, meaning that Clam AntiVirus identified innocent files as containing viruses. For more details about this, see the "Dealing with Infections" section later in this chapter.

Because of this, it's best to use Clam AntiVirus simply to scan your personal files for viruses, which is to say, those within your `/home` directory. Bear in mind that this is where all files you import to your computer will likely to be installed, so this is where an infection is most likely to be found.

To scan your personal files, follow these instructions:

1. Start ClamTk by clicking Applications ➤ Accessories ➤ Virus Scanner.

2. Before starting the scan, it's useful to ensure hidden files are scanned. After all, a virus is likely to try to hide, rather than make its presence obvious! This can be done by clicking Options ➤ Scan Hidden Files (.*).

> **Note** Resist the temptation at this stage to select Delete Infected Files on the Options menu. This is because ClamTk might return a false positive—a file that it thinks contains a virus but that is actually perfectly safe. It's better to deal with viruses after they've been found on a one-by-one basis, rather than automatically.

3. Although there's a button on the toolbar that lets you scan your /home directory with a single click, it won't scan recursively, which is to say, it won't scan any folders (or folders of folders) within your /home directory. This isn't much use, so to perform a recursive scan of your /home directory, click File ➤ Recursive Scan. Then click the OK button on the Select a Directory (Recursive Scan) file open dialog box. This will select your /home directory. Of course, you can also select any other folder to scan at this stage.

4. The scan will start. Depending on the quantity of files in your /home directory and their sizes, it may take some time. You'll see a live status report beneath the toolbar, showing what file is currently being scanned. When the status line reads Scanning Complete, the scan has finished. Running along the bottom of the window will be a complete status report, showing the number of files scanned and the number of viruses found, if any. See Figure 9-7 for an example. If any viruses are found, move on to the "Dealing with Infections" section.

Figure 9-7. *You'll see a live status report of which files are being scanned below the toolbar in the ClamTk program window.*

Dealing with Infections

If any viruses are found they will be listed in the ClamTk program window. The type of virus that's allegedly infecting the file will be listed under the Status column. See Figure 9-8 for an example.

Be aware that ClamTk sometimes reports a virus when it simply can't access a particular file, perhaps because of file permission problems. If this is the case, you'll see Access Denied or Can't Open Directory in the Status column. You can ignore these files.

Tip If you really want to scan such files, run ScanTk with superuser powers: open a terminal window (Applications ➤ Accessories ➤ Terminal), and type `gksu scantk`.

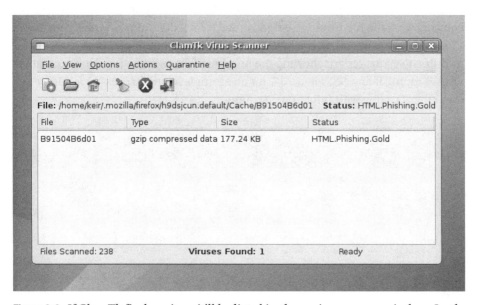

Figure 9-8. *If ClamTk finds a virus, it'll be listed in the main program window. Look under the Status column for the name of the virus.*

Entries in the list can be right-clicked and quarantined or deleted. *Quarantining* is where the file is moved to a special directory for inspection or deletion later on, and you can manage quarantined files using the Quarantine ➤ Maintenance menu.

While the impulse might be to simply delete the file, you should be cautious. Be aware that ClamTk might be reporting a *false positive*—a file that it thinks is infected with a virus, but which isn't. This is rare but can happen. If you do find a file you know is a false positive, right-click it and select Quarantine. Then click Quarantine ➤ Maintenance, and in the list, select the file, and click False Positive. This will ensure it's ignored next time you scan.

So what should you do if you find a file is infected? First, don't panic! Remember that practically all viruses that Clam AntiVirus is likely to find are targeted at Windows systems and don't affect Linux.

> **Note** If we assume there are 120,000 viruses for Windows and 50 for Linux, then in theory, there's 99.999% chance that any virus Clam AntiVirus finds will be a Windows virus!

Next, look at the name of the virus under the Status heading, and look it up online to learn more about it. This is the point at which you'll learn if it's a Linux virus and, if so, its potential impact on your system.

In the example in Figure 9-8, the virus ClamTk found is called HTML.Phishing.Gold, so I searched for this using Google. It transpires that this isn't a threat to Linux.

> **Note** In addition to searching for HTML.Phishing.Gold, I also added "ClamAV" to the search string to see if there was any specific information. This is where I might have learned if the report was a false positive.

If the file is located in your Firefox cache, as in my example (see Figure 9-8), then there's nothing to worry about, and the file can be deleted with impunity—just right-click and select Delete from the menu. In fact, this is where you're most likely to find virus infections, because this is where all the files are temporarily downloaded when you're browsing the web (including HTML files, images, and so on). But, once again, you should remember that most nefarious web sites that attempt to spread virus infections are targeted at Windows users, usually via security holes within Internet Explorer. As a Linux user using the Firefox web browser, you have far less to worry about.

Summary

In this chapter, we've looked at what threats your system faces and how security holes can be exploited by malicious interests. You learned about measures you can take to protect your system, such as updating it online, configuring the system's firewall, and installing an antivirus program. We also discussed some common-sense rules you can follow to keep your system safe.

In the next chapter, we move on to looking at how your Ubuntu system can be personalized and how to set up everything to suit your own preferences.

■ ■ ■

## CHAPTER 10

Personalizing Ubuntu: Getting Everything Just Right

If you've read this book from Chapter 1, by this stage you no doubt have become comfortable with Ubuntu. You've started to realize its advantages and are on the way to making it your operating system of choice.

But things might still not be quite right. For instance, you might find the color scheme is not to your tastes. Or perhaps the mouse cursor moves a little too fast (or too slowly). Maybe you simply want to stamp your individuality on your system to make it your very own.

That's what this chapter is all about. We look at personalizing Ubuntu, so that you're completely happy with your user experience. To do this, we will thoroughly examine the GNOME desktop and explore its potential.

Changing the Look and Feel

Ubuntu is similar to Windows in many ways, but the developers behind it introduced improvements and tweaks that many claim make the software easier to use. For example, Ubuntu offers multiple virtual desktops—long considered a very useful user-interface feature that seems to have passed Microsoft by. It also moves the programs menu to the top of the screen, leaving the whole width of the screen at the bottom to display taskbar buttons. This is very sensible, because the buttons don't look cramped when more than a handful of applications are open. However, if you're not satisfied with Ubuntu's out-of-the-box look and feel, you can change it.

You might be used to changing the desktop colors or wallpaper under Windows, but Ubuntu goes to extremes and lets you alter the look and feel of the entire desktop. Everything from the styling of the program windows to the desktop icons can be altered quickly and easily.

Altering the Theme

Ubuntu refers to the look of the desktop as a *theme*. Because it's built on the GNOME desktop, Ubuntu allows you to radically personalize your desktop theme. Several different themes come with the distribution, and you can download many more. Each lets you change the way the windows look, including the buttons and the icon set (although some themes come without additional icons).

However, unlike Windows themes, most GNOME themes don't change the fonts used on the desktop, and the wallpaper and color scheme will probably remain broadly the same. You can change these manually, as described in the "Setting Font Preferences" and "Changing the Wallpaper" sections a bit later in this chapter.

To alter the theme, select System ➤ Preferences ➤ Theme. Then it's simply a matter of choosing a theme from the list in the Theme Preferences dialog box, as shown in Figure 10-1. A useful hint is to open a Nautilus file browser window in the background (Places ➤ Home), so you can see how the changes will affect a typical window.

■**Note** The default Ubuntu theme is called Human and is designed to represent the skin tones of the world's population. This is intended to reflect Ubuntu's mission of being accessible to everyone, no matter where or who they are.

My favorite themes are Clearlooks and Mist, largely because they're simple and uncomplicated. Remember that you'll be working with the theme on a daily basis, so it should be practical and not too distracting. Those miniature close, minimize, and maximize buttons might look stylish, but they're useless if they're so small that you can't reliably click them with your mouse.

As well as changing the overall theme, you can also modify individual theme components and even download more theme components.

Figure 10-1. *Ubuntu comes with several theme choices.*

Changing Individual Theme Components

You can alter the three aspects that constitute a GNOME theme: the *controls* (sometimes known as *widgets*), the *window borders*, and the *icons*. Controls are simply the elements you click within dialog boxes and windows: buttons, scroll bars, and so on. Additionally, controls usually come with their own color schemes, which affect all components of the program windows.

The window borders are, as seems obvious, the borders of program windows and dialog boxes, with particular attention paid to the top of the window, where the program name appears along with the minimize, maximize, and close buttons.

Icons are, as is again obvious, all the icons on the desktop, within program windows (such as file browsing windows), and so on.

Note To make matters a little confusing, most window borders have their own selection of close, minimize, and maximize controls.

To make changes to a theme, click the Theme Details button in the Theme Preferences dialog box (see Figure 10-1), and then click each tab to see your choices, as shown in Figure 10-2. Unfortunately, there are no thumbnail previews of each style, but as soon as you click each option, it will be automatically applied to the currently open windows. To preview the effects fully, the best policy is to keep a Nautilus window open (Places ➤ Home).

Figure 10-2. *You can create a theme by choosing your own controls, window borders, and icons.*

When you've made your choices, you can save the theme for further use. Simply click the Save Theme button in the main Theme Preferences dialog box. You'll need to give the theme a name and, if you wish, a short description for future reference. By putting a check in the Save Background Image box, the theme will also remember the wallpaper that's in use. When you select the theme in the future, the wallpaper will be suggested at the bottom of the Theme Preferences window; to select it, just click Apply Background.

If you don't save the theme, as soon as you select another one, the changes you made will be lost.

Installing Additional Components

If you get tired of the built-in possibilities, you can download additional theme components, such as window borders and controls, to enhance your desktop experience. You have two ways of getting new themes:

- Download themes from the official Ubuntu repositories.

- Visit the GNOME Art or GNOME-Look web sites (http://art.gnome.org and http://gnome-look.org), and download items from there. Be warned that there is sometimes artistic nudity on some of the wallpapers available from GNOME-Look.

Downloading from Ubuntu Repositories

To get theme components from the Ubuntu software repositories, you use the Synaptic Package Manager. Setting up Synaptic Package Manager to use the online repositories is described in Chapter 8.

Select System ➤ Administration ➤ Synaptic Package Manager, click the Search button, and enter gtk2-engines as a search term (gtk2-engines is how Ubuntu refers to theme components). In the list of results will be those gtk2-engines already installed, indicated by a dark green check box, and several that are available for download.

Note In my tests I found a handful of dummy gtk2-engines packages (according to the description when you select them in Synaptic Package Manager). These are there for those upgrading from an older version of Ubuntu, and you can ignore them.

Icons rarely come in gtk2-engines packages, and instead are contained in their own packages. To find icons, use the Synaptic Package Manager to search for gnome icon theme (without any dashes).

Although each theme component comes with a description, you won't really know what it looks like until you see it. The best policy is to download all of them and audition them one by one. However, be aware that themes can be large, so they may take some time to download on a slower connection.

Don't forget that you're downloading theme components, rather than entire themes. To use your new theme components, select System ➤ Preferences ➤ Theme, click the Theme Details button, and choose from the various lists.

Downloading from the GNOME Art Web Site

Visiting the GNOME Art site (http://art.gnome.org), shown in Figure 10-3, gives you access to just about every theme ever created for GNOME. In fact, the site also contains wallpaper selections, icons, and much more besides. All of the offerings are free to use, and most of the packages are created by enthusiasts.

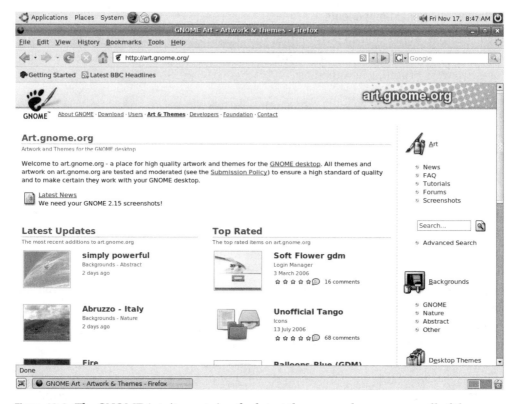

Figure 10-3. *The GNOME Art site contains the latest themes, and you can use all of them with Ubuntu.*

Installing new theme components is easy, and the instructions here work just as well for the GNOME-Look site too (`http://gnome-look.org`).

If you wish to install a new window border, for example, click the link to browse the examples, and when you find one you like, click to download it. It will be contained in a `.tar.gz` archive, but you don't need to unpack it. Simply select System ➤ Preferences ➤ Theme, and click the Install Theme button in the Theme Preferences dialog box. Then browse to the downloaded theme, and click Open. You'll be asked if you want to use the new theme component immediately, although it will also be available by clicking the Theme Details button.

You can delete the downloaded file when you're finished.

■Note The same principle of sharing that underlines the GPL software license is also usually applied to themes. This means that one person can take a theme created by someone else, tweak it, and then release it as a new theme. This ensures constant innovation and improvement.

Changing the Wallpaper

The default Ubuntu wallpaper is a love-it-or-hate-it affair. Some find its swirling skin-tone colors beautiful and appreciate its humanist metaphor. Others just don't like it. If you're one of those who prefer something different, it's easy to switch. Right-click the desktop, and click Change Desktop Background. You can then select from a short list of different wallpapers, including Dawn of Ubuntu, which shows the Ubuntu logo raining down on an African landscape.

If you want to use a picture of your own as wallpaper, click the Add Wallpaper button, and then browse to its location.

In the Style drop-down list, you can select from the following choices:

Centered: This option places the wallpaper in the center of the screen. If the wallpaper is not big enough to fill the screen, a border appears around the edge. If it's bigger than the screen, the edges of the wallpaper are cropped off.

Fill Screen: This option forces the picture to fit the screen, including squashing or expanding it if necessary (known as *altering its aspect ratio*). If the wallpaper isn't in the same ratio as the screen, it will look distorted. Most digital camera shots should be okay, because they use the same 4:3 ratio as most monitors (although if you have a wide-screen monitor, a digital camera picture will be stretched horizontally).

Scaled: Like the Fill Screen option, this option enlarges the image if it's too small or shrinks it if it's too big, but it maintains the aspect ratio, thus avoiding distortion. However, if the picture is in a different aspect ratio than the monitor, it may have borders at the edges.

Zoom: Like Fill Screen, this option forces the picture to fit the screen, without any borders at the top and bottom. However, it avoids altering the aspect ratio. If the wallpaper isn't the correct aspect ratio then parts of the top/bottom or left/right of the image may be cropped off.

Tiled: If the picture is smaller than the desktop resolution, this option simply repeats the picture (starting from the top left) until the screen is filled. This option is primarily designed for patterned graphics.

Don't forget that the GNOME Art web site (`http://art.gnome.org`) offers many wallpaper packages for download.

■Tip The default GNOME backgrounds include several wonderful nature pictures and some cool patterns. However, they aren't included out of the box with Ubuntu. To install them, search for `gnome-backgrounds` in Synaptic Package Manager. Note that the backgrounds are contained in the "universe" software repository, which should be enabled prior to installing the backgrounds; see the "Setting Up Online Software Repositories" section in Chapter 8.

Setting Font Preferences

Ubuntu lets you change the fonts that are used throughout Ubuntu (referred to as *system fonts*). You can also alter how they're displayed.

To change a system font, select System ➤ Preferences ➤ Font. In the Font Preferences dialog box, shown in Figure 10-4, click the button next to the system font you want to change, and then choose from the list. You can also set the font point size, so for example, you can make the labels beneath icons easier to read.

By clicking the entries under the Font Rendering heading in the Font Preferences dialog box, you can change how fonts look on your monitor. This will alter the *antialiasing* and *hinting* of the font. Antialiasing softens the edges of each letter to make them appear less jagged. Hinting affects the spacing and shaping of the letters. Used together, they can make the on-screen text look more pleasant. Try each Font Rendering setting in sequence to see which looks best to you (the text in the dialog box will update automatically to show the changes). Nearly everyone with a TFT-based screen, including notebook users, finds the Subpixel Smoothing option best.

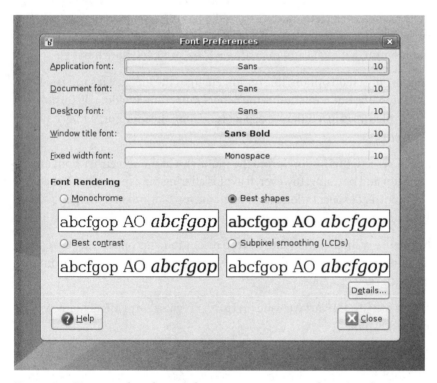

Figure 10-4. *You can alter the way fonts appear on screen by using the Fonts Preferences dialog box.*

BYTECODE HINTING

Two font hinting subsystems are available under Ubuntu: Autohinting and Bytecode Interpreting. There's a lengthy debate about which produces the best results. Personally, I prefer to use the Bytecode Interpreter, because I believe it leads to the cleaner fonts, but others say Autohinting is better in this regard.

It's easy to switch between Bytecode Interpreter and Autohinting. Follow these steps:

1. Open a GNOME Terminal window (Applications ➤ Accessories ➤ Terminal).

2. In the terminal window, type the following:

```
sudo dpkg-reconfigure fontconfig-config
```

3. On the first screen of the configuration program, select Native to activate the Bytecode Interpreter. Alternatively, you can choose Autohinting or even None, which will turn off the hinting system.

4. On the next screen, you can select whether subpixel rendering is activated. This is useful only for TFT screens (including notebooks), so ether select Automatic, or if you use a TFT monitor and want to ensure the option is activated, select Always.

5. The third screen offers the option of using bitmap fonts. These are fonts that, unlike the TrueType fonts used within the rest of Ubuntu, don't scale beyond their original sizes. There's no harm in enabling them, because they can sometimes be useful as system fonts.

6. After making this choice, the configuration program will quit. Then you must write the changes you've made using the following command:

```
sudo dpkg-reconfigure fontconfig
```

7. Once the program has finished configuring the software, restart your X server by logging out and then back in again.

Configuring Input Devices

Mouse and key repeat speeds are personal to each user, and you may find the default Ubuntu settings not to your taste, particularly if you have a high-resolution mouse such as a gaming model. Fortunately, changing each setting is easy. You'll find the relevant options under the System ➤ Preferences menu.

Configuring Mouse Options

Select System ➤ Preferences ➤ Mouse to open the Mouse Preferences dialog box, which has three tabs:

Buttons: This tab lets you set whether the mouse is to be used by a left-handed or right-handed person. Effectively, it swaps the functions of the right and left buttons. Beneath this is the double-click timeout setting. This is ideal for people who are less physically dexterous, because the double-click speed can be slowed down. On the other hand, if you find yourself accidentally double-clicking items, you can speed it up.

Pointers: On this tab, you can select from any mouse pointer themes that are installed. You can also activate the Locate Pointer option, which causes a box to appear around the mouse cursor when you press the Ctrl key. This can help you find the cursor on a busy desktop.

Motion: This tab, shown in Figure 10-5, lets you alter the speed of the mouse pointer, as well as the drag-and-drop threshold. Changes are made as each setting is adjusted, so to test the new settings, simply move your mouse. Here's what the settings do:

- The Acceleration setting controls how fast the mouse moves. Whenever you move the mouse, the pointer on screen moves a corresponding amount. However, the cursor actually increases in speed the more you move your hand (otherwise, you would need to drag your hand across the desk to get from one side of the screen to the other). This is referred to as acceleration. If you set the acceleration too high, the pointer will fly around the screen, seemingly unable to stop. If you set it too slow, you'll need to ramp the mouse several times to make it go anywhere.

- The Sensitivity setting controls how quickly the acceleration kicks in when you first move the mouse. Choosing a higher setting means that you can move the mouse relatively quickly before it starts to accelerate and cover more screen space. A low setting means that acceleration will begin almost as soon as you move the mouse. Higher sensitivity settings give you more control over the mouse, which can be useful if you use image-editing programs, for example.

- The Threshold setting determines the amount of mouse movement allowed in a click-and-drag maneuver before the item under the cursor is moved. This setting is designed for people who have limited dexterity and who might be unable to keep the mouse perfectly still when clicking or double-clicking an icon. In such cases, a large threshold value may be preferred.

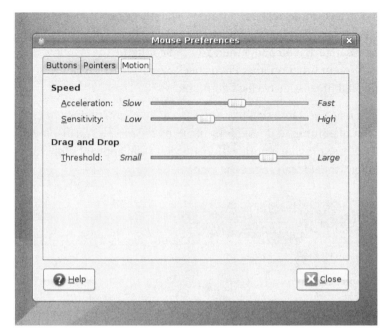

Figure 10-5. *The Mouse Preferences dialog box lets you tame that mouse.*

Changing Keyboard Settings

Select System ➤ Preferences ➤ Keyboard to open the Keyboard Preferences dialog box. This dialog box has four tabs:

Keyboard: Using the Keyboard tab, you can alter the rate of key repeat. This can be useful if you often find yourself holding down the Backspace key to delete a sentence; a shorter setting on the Delay slider and a faster setting on the Speed slider can help. However, if you get the settings wrong, you may find double characters creeping into your documents; typing an *f* may result in *ff*, for example. Beneath the Repeat Keys setting is the Cursor Blinking slider. Altering this may help if you sometimes lose the cursor in a document; a faster speed will mean that the cursor spends less time being invisible between flashes.

Layouts: On the Layouts tab, you can choose to add an alternative keyboard layout, as shown in Figure 10-6. For example, if you write in two different languages on your keyboard, it may be helpful to be able to switch between them. Click the Add button, and select the second language from the list.

Layout Options: This tab lets you select from a variety of handy tweaks that affect how the keyboard works. For example, you can configure the Caps Lock key to act like a simple Shift key, or you can turn it off altogether. You can configure the Windows key so that it performs a different function, too. Put a check alongside the option you want after reading through the extensive list of options.

Typing Break: This tab features a function that can force you to stop typing after a predetermined number of minutes. It does this by blanking the screen and displaying a "Take a break!" message. Note that a notification area icon will appear before the break time to give you advanced warning of the lockout.

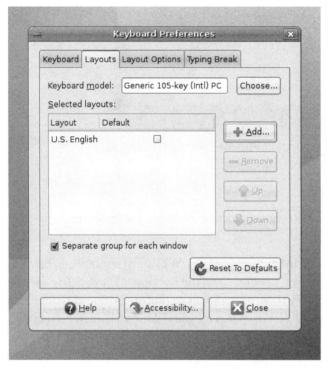

Figure 10-6. *You can have more than one language setting in place for a keyboard, which is handy if you need to type in a foreign language.*

Creating Keyboard Shortcuts

Ubuntu lets you define your own keyboard shortcuts for just about any action on the system. To create a shortcut, select System ➤ Preferences ➤ Keyboard Shortcuts. In the dialog box, search through the list for the action you want to create a shortcut for, click it, and then press the key (or key combination) you want to use. For example, you might locate the Volume Up and Volume Down entries in the list, click each, and press Ctrl+left arrow and Ctrl+right arrow. Then you will be able to turn the volume of your sound card up or down by holding down Ctrl and tapping the left or right arrow key, respectively.

■**Caution** Be careful not to assign a shortcut to a popular key. It might be nice to make Totem Media Player appear when you hit the spacebar, for example, but that will mean that it will start up several times whenever you type a sentence in a word processor! Also be aware that some key combinations are used by applications. Within OpenOffice.org's Writer, for example, the Ctrl+left/right arrow key combination moves you from word to word in a paragraph. If you define those combinations as shortcuts, you will no longer have this functionality.

I like to configure my /home folder to appear whenever I press the Home button on the keyboard. This can be done by locating the Home Folder option under the Desktop heading.

Personalizing Login Options

You can even personalize the login screen under Ubuntu. This is known technically as the GNOME Display Manager, or GDM. To access its configuration options, select System ➤ Administration ➤ Login Window. The dialog box that appears has five tabs:

> **Local**: The Login Windows Preferences dialog can configure settings for *remote* as well as *local* logins. Remote logins are those that take place over a network (or even the Internet), while local logins are the standard type that you use to access Ubuntu while sitting in front of it. In the Style drop-down list of the Local tab, you can choose the type of login screen people logging in locally will see: Themed, which is to say one that includes a pretty graphic such as the Ubuntu logo; Plain, which shows a simple plain color background with the GNOME logo; or Plain with Face Browser, which is like the Plain option but also shows user-selected photographs (see the next section). Assuming that you select Themed from the Style drop-down list, you can select the actual theme you want from the list. The default choice is Human, which features the Ubuntu logo and color scheme, but you can also select from a handful of other designs. By unchecking Show Actions Menu under the Menu Bar heading, you can deactivate the Actions menu on the login screen, which lets the user restart or shut down the computer. This can be useful for security purposes. By unchecking Include Hostname Chooser (XDMCP) Menu Item, you can remove the option from the Actions menu that allows users to log into a remote system. By selecting Custom under the Welcome Message heading, you can have the login screen display a custom sentence, but only if the Theme allows this—the default Human login screen doesn't. By clicking the Add button, you can install new login screen themes, which, as with other GNOME theme components, can be downloaded from http://art.gnome.org.

Remote: The Remote tab controls X Display Manager Control Protocol (XDMCP) logins. This is considered a very insecure method of remotely accessing Ubuntu and should be disabled. I discuss more secure options for remotely accessing Ubuntu in Chapter 34.

Accessibility: This tab lets you activate GNOME's Accessibility tools during login, which can aid those with physical disabilities. Additionally, you can alter the sound that is heard when the login prompt is ready to take input (by default, this is the sound of bongo drums). By putting a check alongside Login Successful and Login Failed, you can also choose sound effects to accompany both those two actions.

Security: This tab lets you alter login settings that might present a security risk to your system. The Enable Automatic Login check box lets you do away with the login screen completely when Ubuntu starts up and go straight to the desktop. Simply put a check in the box, and provide the login username. This presents obvious security issues, but if you're the only person using the computer and if it's located in a secure location, you might want to choose this option. The Enable Timed Login option lets you select a user who will be logged in by default after a given period. This is useful if you want to present the opportunity to log in as a different user but also want to have the fail-safe of logging in automatically, too. Under the Security header you can select Allow Local System Administrator Login, which controls if the root user is allowed to log in, something which is considered a security risk (this is only relevant if the root user account is enabled, which it isn't by default under Ubuntu). The Enable Debug Messages to System Log and Deny TCP Connections to X Server options relate to security, and it's unlikely you'll ever need to use them. The Login Retry Delay section controls how long Ubuntu will pause after an incorrect username or password has been entered on the login screen. Increasing this value can put an irritating block in the way of anybody who intends to try various random username or password combinations to break into your system, but it can also be annoying to you should you mistype and then have to wait! The Configure X Server button lets you configure the X server that starts by default. Changing these settings could stop your computer booting to a GUI, so you shouldn't alter the settings unless you know exactly what you're doing.

Users: Here, you can specify which users are offered as choices within GDM if the Face Browser option is activated in the Security tab. Bear in mind that Linux has many system user accounts that aren't designed to allow logins. By default, all users who have a password are displayed at login time, which is the best way of working (the system accounts don't have passwords, because they aren't login accounts).

ASSISTIVE TECHNOLOGY

You might know about the Accessibility tools under Windows, which help people with disabilities use the computer. It's possible to use an on-screen magnifier, so that users can better see what they're typing or reading, for example.

Under the GNOME desktop, the Accessibility tools are referred to as Assistive Technology. To use them, select System ➤ Administration ➤ Preferences ➤ Assistive Technology Preferences. Click the check box alongside Enable Assistive Technologies.

Here is what's offered:

- The Screenreader uses a speech synthesizer to announce whatever you click on, as well as whatever you type. To alter its settings, click the Settings button. Note that this also lets you configure any Braille output devices that might be connected to the computer, and it lets you configure the on-screen magnifier.

- The On-screen Keyboard can be used by a mouse, but is most useful when an alternative input device is used, such as a touch screen. As well as presenting a virtual keyboard, it shows the options on screen as a series of large and easy-to-activate buttons.

Changing Your Login Picture

If, when configuring the login options in the previous section, you selected the Happy GNOME with Browser theme, or activated the Plain with Face Browser option, the login screen will display a picture alongside your name, as shown in Figure 10-7. You can click this and type your password to log in. You might be familiar with a similar system under Windows XP or Mac OS X.

Users can choose their own login pictures by clicking System ➤ Preferences ➤ About Me. The About Me dialog is designed for users to enter their personal details, such as their addresses, but they can also simply use it to choose photographs of themselves. To do this, click the empty square alongside your name at the top of the dialog box. Ideally, the image you choose should be square and 96×96 pixels, although if the picture is too large, it will be automatically scaled down. Click OK when you've finished.

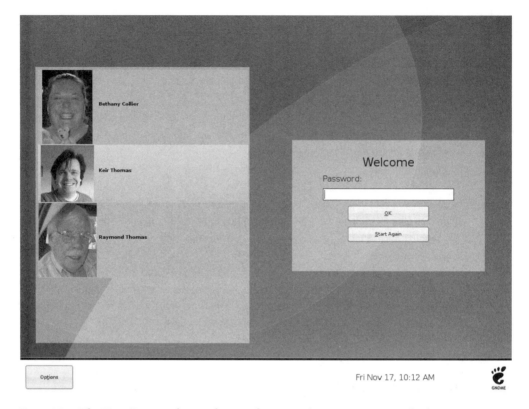

Figure 10-7. *The Face Browser lets each user choose an icon to appear on the login screen.*

Adding and Removing Desktop Items

Virtually the entire Ubuntu desktop can be redesigned and restructured. You can move the Applications menu from the top of the screen to the bottom to be more like Windows, for example, or you can add numerous desktop shortcuts to popular applications and/or files.

Adding a Shortcut

Ubuntu's nearest equivalent to a Windows-style desktop shortcut is a *launcher*, and you can create a launcher that points to a program or a file. If a launcher is created for a file, Ubuntu will automatically launch the correct program to display the file. If you create a launcher to a .jpg file, for example, Ubuntu will know to launch the Eye of GNOME image viewer when the launcher is double-clicked.

Creating a Launcher

You can create a launcher two ways. One way is to simply click and drag an icon from one of the main menus to the desktop. This effectively copies the menu's launcher to the desktop, rather than creating a new launcher, but the effect is the same. A little technique is required: when initially clicking the menu icon, click and hold for a second before dragging. This will let Ubuntu know that you intend to create a launcher, and that you haven't simply misclicked!

The other way to create a launcher is to right-click the desktop and select Create Launcher. In the dialog that appears, select whether you want to create a launcher to a file or application from the Type drop-down list (the third option, Application in Terminal, will open a terminal window and run the program within it; this is only for specialized use).

Then fill in the Name and Command fields. Alternatively, if you don't know the exact name and path of the file, clicking the Browse button will open a dialog box by which you can navigate to the file or program and click to select it.

■Tip If you want to create a launch to a program, bear in mind that most Linux programs you use from day to day are contained within /usr/bin.

The Comment field can be left blank. If it's filled in, it forms the tooltip text that will appear if you hover the mouse cursor over the launcher icon.

To choose an icon for your launcher, click the No Icon button. You can select from several predefined icons, as shown in Figure 10-8, or choose your own picture by clicking the Browse button. If you don't choose an icon, a stock GNOME icon is used.

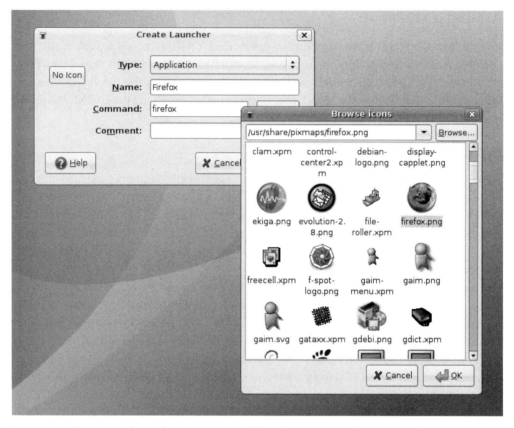

Figure 10-8. *Creating a launcher is easy. Just fill in the Name and Command fields, and choose an icon.*

Creating a Link

Launchers have one failing, and that is that they're only recognized by GNOME (and other desktop environments, such as KDE). You can't create a launcher to an application and use it from the command line, for example. In technical terms, a launcher isn't recognized by the underlying Linux file system.

The solution is to create a *link* to the file or program. This will actually create a *symbolic link* to the file. I explain more about file links in Chapter 14, but it's enough to know that this is very similar to a launcher, except it works on a file-system level.

Note Actually, Linux offers two types of link: a *symbolic link*, which is the most common type of link used under Linux, and a *hard link*, which is a cross between copying a file and creating a shortcut.

To create a link, locate the file you want to create the link to, right-click it, and select Make Link. The link will be created in the same directory as the original file, and you can then click and drag the new link to wherever you want it to appear, such as the desktop. You don't need to choose an icon, because the link inherits the icon of the original file. For example, if it's a picture link, it will inherit the thumbnail preview icon.

Note If you find the Make Link option grayed out, it's likely that you don't have sufficient permissions to write the link to the directory in question.

Personalizing the Panels

Panels are the long strips that appear at the top and bottom of the Ubuntu screen and play host to a choice of menus, applets, and icons. You can add a new panel by right-clicking a blank spot on an existing one and selecting New Panel, or you can remove a panel by right-clicking it and selecting Delete This Panel.

Caution If you delete a panel, the arrangement of items it contains will be lost. Of course, you can always re-create the collection on a different panel.

By right-clicking a panel and selecting Properties, you can change its size and dimensions. For example, by unchecking the Expand box, you can make the panel shrink to its smallest possible size. Then, when you add new components (or, in the case of a panel containing the Window List, a new program is run), the panel will expand as necessary. This can be a neat effect and also creates more desktop space.

Tip This effect is a little like the Mac OS X Dock and might help migrating OS X users feel at home!

Selecting the Autohide feature will make the panel slide off the screen when there isn't a mouse over it. Choosing Show Hide Buttons will make small arrows appear on either side of the panel so that you can click to slide it off the side of the screen when it's not in use. Both these two techniques create more desktop space.

Adding and Removing Menus

You can add either just the Applications menu or the entire set of menus (Applications, Places, and System) to the panel at the bottom of the screen. This can help those who long for the Windows Start button approach to access programs.

Adding All the Menus to a Panel

To add the Application, Places, and System menu to the Panel at the bottom of the Ubuntu desktop, follow these steps:

1. Right-click a blank spot on the bottom Panel, and select Add to Panel.

2. In the dialog box that appears, click the Menu Bar option to add all three menus. You'll find this under the Utilities heading in the list, and you'll have to scroll down to see it.

3. Click the Add button at the bottom of the dialog box.

4. Click the Close button.

Adding a Start-Like Button to a Panel

As an alternative to the Applications, Places, and System menu, you can add a Start-like button which offers submenus for all three menus. See Figure 8-9 for an example.

1. Right-click a blank spot on the bottom Panel, and select Add to Panel.

2. In the dialog box that appears, click the Main Menu option. You'll find this under the Utilities heading in the list, and you'll have to scroll down to see it.

3. Click the Add button at the bottom of the dialog box.

4. Click the Close button.

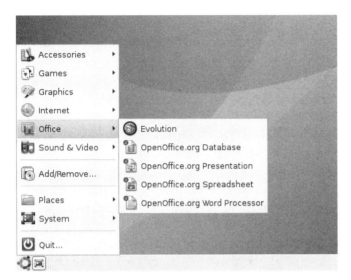

Figure 10-9. *If you just can't do without that Start button, you can re-create one on your Ubuntu desktop.*

Deleting a Menu

Creating new instances of the menus won't delete the old ones. If you create a new Applications menu at the bottom of the screen, for example, the old Applications menu will remain at the top of the screen. In fact, you can have as many instances of the menus on the desktop as you wish, although this won't be a good use of desktop space!

To delete any menu, simply right-click anywhere on that menu, and select Remove from Panel.

Moving Panel Items

To move a panel item, right-click it and select Move. Then drag the mouse to the new location, and click the mouse button once to set it in place. All panel items can be moved, including menus, and items can be moved between different panels. Any item that's in the way will be shifted to make space.

If an item refuses to move, right-click it and ensure that Lock to Panel doesn't have a check alongside it. This is especially relevant if you're trying to move an item into the space occupied by something else—if the other item is locked then it *won't* automatically shift out of the way!

GIVE ME MY TRASH CAN!

The developers who designed Ubuntu's desktop decided to keep the desktop largely clean of icons. This included relegating the Trash icon to its own applet at the bottom-right side of the screen. Many people find using the applet a little difficult and miss the desktop trash can icon, which has been present on Windows and Mac OS desktops for more than 20 years.

The good news is that it's easy to get the trash can back. Click Applications ➤ Accessories ➤ Terminal, and at the command prompt type `gconf-editor`. In the program window that appears, click the down arrows next to Apps, then Nautilus (you'll have to scroll down the list a little), and then click Desktop. On the right side of the program window, put a check in the `trash_icon_visible` entry. The Trash icon should then instantly appear on your desktop! To delete the old Trash icon at the bottom right, simply right-click it and select Remove from Panel.

You can also put a check in the `computer_icon_visible`, `home_icon_visible`, and `documents_icon_visible` entries if you wish to see Computer, Home, and Documents desktop icons. By putting a check alongside `network_icon_visible`, you can add a My Network Places–style icon to the desktop too.

Be careful when using the Configuration Editor program. It lets you configure just about every aspect of the GNOME desktop and doesn't warn you when you're about to do something devastating, so the potential for accidental damage is high!

Working with Applets

In actual fact, almost everything you see on the desktop is considered by the GNOME desktop to be an applet, with the exception of application/file icons and the panels. A menu is a form of applet, for example, as is the Workspace Switcher.

Ubuntu provides many more applets that you can choose to add to the desktop to provide a host of useful or entertaining functionality. To add an applet, right-click a blank spot on a Panel, and select Add to Panel. As shown in Figure 10-10, you have a wide choice of applets, divided into categories. Many require configuration when they've been created, so you may need to right-click them and select Properties. For example, you'll need to set your location in the Weather Report applet's properties, so it can provide accurate forecasting. For more details about each applet, and whether it needs additional configuration, see Table 10-1.

To remove an applet, simply right-click it and select Remove from Panel.

Figure 10-10. *A wide variety of applets are available. Some are informative; others are just fun.*

Table 10-1. *Ubuntu Desktop Applets*

Applet	Description	Configuration*
Address Book Search	Lets you quickly retrieve contact information from your Evolution address book.	None needed.
Battery Charge Monitor	Shows the battery level on notebooks and whether outlet power is in use.	None needed.
Character Palette	Displays a palette of accented or unusual characters; click a character to insert it into the text.	None needed.
Clock	Displays the time and date (active by default).	None needed.
Connect to Server	Lets you quickly connect to remote servers, such as FTP (equivalent of clicking Places ➤ Connect to Server).	None needed.

Table 10-1. *Ubuntu Desktop Applets (Continued)*

Applet	Description	Configuration*
CPU Frequency Scaling Monitor	Shows CPU frequency and, on compatible hardware and if correctly configured (see Chapter 8), lets you change CPU frequency.	Right-click to change frequency.
Deskbar	Adds a quick search text box by which Ubuntu software library or the Web can be searched.	None needed
Dictionary Lookup	Displays a text box that will look up words according to online dictionaries.	None needed.
Disk Mounter	Lets you quickly mount and unmount removable disks	None needed.
Drawer	Displays a drawer icon that, when clicked, "slides out" to reveal yet more applets.	Right-click the icon and click Add to Drawer to add applets.
Fish	Adds a couple of fish to the panel that, when clicked, will spout wisdom.	None needed.
Force Quit	Lets you quit a crashed program.	None needed.
Geyes	Displays two eyes whose pupils follow the mouse cursor.	None needed.
Invest	Adds a text-based scrolling stock ticker to the panel.	Right-click and select Preferences to add individual stock symbols to the list.
Keyboard Accessibility Status	Shows whether Sticky Keys or other accessibility functions are activated.	None needed.
Keyboard Indicator	Shows the current language settings of the keyboard.	None needed.
Lock Screen	Adds an icon that, when clicked, blanks the screen and displays password prompt.	None needed.
Main Menu	Lets you add a single icon Start-like system menu.	None needed.
Menu Bar	Adds a new Applications, Places, and Desktop menu bar to the panel.	None needed.
Modem Monitor	Displays virtual LEDs showing when modem data is sent/received and lets you quickly dial up with a single click.	None needed.
Network Monitor	Displays virtual LEDs showing data sent/received via networking devices.	None needed.
Notification Area	Adds a notification area to the panel (active by default).	None needed.

Table 10-1. *Ubuntu Desktop Applets (Continued)*

Applet	Description	Configuration*
Pilot Applet	Lets you quickly connect to Palm devices via gnome-pilot software.	If gnome-pilot hasn't already been set up, a configuration dialog box will appear.
Quit	Lets you log out or shut down.	None needed.
Run Application	Adds an icon that, when clicked, makes the Run Application dialog box appear.	None needed.
Search for Files	Provides one-click access to Nautilus's search mode.	None needed.
Separator	Simply inserts a graphical separator—useful for making several applets alongside each other look neater.	None needed.
Show Desktop	Minimizes all desktop windows (active by default).	None needed.
Sticky Notes	Lets you create virtual sticky notes.	None needed.
System Monitor	Adds a small graph that shows system resource usage.	Right-click and select Preferences to choose system areas to be monitored.
Terminal Server Client Applet	Provides one-click access to locations set up within the Terminal Server program (see Chapter 34).	None needed.
Tomboy Notes	Lets you add sticky notes to the desktop.	None needed.
Trash	Adds the Trash icon to the panel, where files can be dropped for removal to Trash.	None needed.
Volume Control	Adds volume controls (active by default).	None needed.
Weather Report	Adds an icon that shows current weather conditions.	Right-click, and select Preferences and then the Location tab to set your location.
Window List	Adds a list of windows, which you can use to switch between currently running programs (active by default).	None needed.
Window Selector	Adds an icon that, when clicked, switches between currently open windows (alternative to Window List).	None needed.
Workspace Switcher	Shows virtual desktop selector.	None needed.

* *Nearly all applets have configuration options that can be used to tweak them in various ways. This column only indicates if immediate configuration is needed.*

Summary

In this chapter, you've learned how to completely personalize Ubuntu to your own tastes. We've looked at changing the theme so that the desktop has a new appearance, and we've examined how to make the input devices behave exactly as you would like.

In addition, you've learned how to add and remove applets from the desktop in order to add functionality or simply make Ubuntu work the way you would like.

Finally, we looked at the power-saving functions under Ubuntu and how you can avoid your computer wasting energy.

In the next chapter, we will look at what programs are available under Ubuntu to replace those Windows favorites you might miss.

■■■

## CHAPTER 11

Ubuntu Replacements for Windows Programs

Ubuntu is a thoroughly modern operating system and, as such, includes a comprehensive selection of software for just about every day-to-day task. Regardless of whether you want to write letters, edit images, or listen to music, Ubuntu offers something for you.

This chapter introduces the software under Ubuntu that performs the tasks you might be used to under Windows. It's not a detailed guide to each piece of software. Instead, this chapter aims to get you up and running with the Ubuntu replacement as quickly as possible. The chapter will tell you the name of the software, where you can find it on Ubuntu's menus, and a few basic facts about how to use it. In many cases, these applications are covered in far more depth later in the book.

Available Software

Table 11-1 lists various popular Windows programs alongside their Ubuntu counterparts. You'll find most of the programs listed on the Applications menu. Table 11-1 also includes a number of other mainstream alternatives, most of which aren't installed by default under Ubuntu, but are available from the Ubuntu online software repositories. You might want to try these later on. As you might expect, they're all free of charge, so you have nothing to lose.

Note Table 11-1 lists only a fraction of the programs available under Linux. There are quite literally thousands of others. The programs listed here are those that work like their Windows equivalents and therefore provide an easy transition.

Table 11-1. *Ubuntu Alternatives to Windows Software*

Type of Program	Windows	Ubuntu	Alternative Choices
Word processor	Microsoft Word	OpenOffice.org Writer	AbiWord (www.abisource.com), KOffice KWord (www.koffice.org/kword)
Spreadsheet	Microsoft Excel	OpenOffice.org Calc	Gnumeric (www.gnome.org/projects/gnumeric/), KOffice KSpread (www.koffice.org/kspread)
Presentations	Microsoft PowerPoint	OpenOffice.org Impress	KOffice KPresenter (www.koffice.org/kpresenter)
Drawing (vector art)	Adobe Illustrator	OpenOffice.org Draw	Inkscape (www.inkscape.org), KOffice Karbon14 (www.koffice.org/ karbon)
Database	Microsoft Access	OpenOffice.org Base	Rekall (www.thekompany.com/products/rekall)
Web page creation	Microsoft FrontPage	OpenOffice.org Writer	Seamonkey (www.mozilla.org/projects/seamonkey/), Amaya (www.w3.org/Amaya)
E-mail	Microsoft Outlook	Evolution	Mozilla Thunderbird (www.mozilla.com), KMail (http://kmail.kde.org)
Contacts manager/ calendar	Microsoft Outlook	Evolution	Kontact (www.kontact.org)
Web browser	Microsoft Internet Explorer	Mozilla Firefox	Konqueror (www.konqueror.org), Opera (www.opera.com)[1]
CD/DVD burning	Nero	Nautilus[2]	K3B (www.k3b.org), X-CD-Roast (www.xcdroast.org)
MP3 player	Winamp	Rhythmbox	XMMS (www.xmms.org), Banshee (http://banshee-project.org)
CD player	Windows Media Player	Sound Juicer	XMMS (www.xmms.org)
Movie/DVD player	Windows Media Player	Totem Media Player	MPlayer (www.mplayerhq.hu/homepage)
Image editor	Adobe Photoshop	The GIMP	KOffice Krita (www.koffice.org/krita)
Zip files	WinZip	Archive Manager	TkZip (www.woodsway.com/TkZip)
MS-DOS prompt	cmd.exe/command.exe	GNOME Terminal	Xterm (www.x.org)[3]
Calculator	Calc	Calculator	Too many to mention!
Text editor/viewer	Notepad	Gedit	Kate (www.kate-editor.org)
Desktop games	Minesweeper/Solitaire	Mines/AisleRiot Solitaire	Too many to mention!

[1] *Opera is a proprietary project, rather than open source; however, it is free of charge.*

[2] *Nautilus is the file manager within Ubuntu; to activate its CD/DVD burning mode, click Go ➤ CD/DVD Creator.*

[3] *Xterm is part of the X.org package, so it is installed by default under Ubuntu. To use it, type* xterm *in a GNOME Terminal window. See Chapter 10 to learn how to create a permanent desktop launcher for Xterm.*

LINUX HAS IT ALL

The Ubuntu software archives contain thousands of programs to cover just about every task you might wish to do on your computer. Diversity is vitally important within the Linux world. For example, rather than offering just one e-mail program, you'll find many available. They compete with each other in a gentle way, and it's up to you which one you settle down with and use.

Part of the fun of using Linux is exploring what's available. Of course, the added bonus is that virtually all this software is free of charge, so you can simply download, install, and play around. If you don't like a program, just remove it from your system. However, don't forget to revisit the program's home page after a few months; chances are the program will have been expanded and improved in that short period, and it might be better at meeting your needs.

A Quick Start with Common Linux Programs

The remainder of this chapter outlines a handful of the programs listed in Table 11-1. My goal is to give you a head start in using each program, pointing out where most of the main functions can be found. You'll find more details about the The GIMP image editor, multimedia tools, and office applications in Parts 5 and 6 of this book.

Keep in mind that Linux doesn't aim to be an exact clone of other operating systems. Some of the programs will work in a similar way to what you're used to, but that's not true of all of them. Because of this, it's very easy to get frustrated early on when programs don't seem to work quite how you want or respond in strange ways. Some programs might hide functions in what seem like illogical places compared with their counterparts on other operating systems. Some patience is required, but it will eventually pay off as you get used to Linux.

Word Processing: OpenOffice.org Writer

OpenOffice.org is an entire office suite for Linux that was built from the ground up to compete with Microsoft Office. Because of this, you'll find much of the functionality of Microsoft Office is replicated in OpenOffice.org, and the look and feel are also similar. The major difference is that OpenOffice.org is open source and therefore free of charge.

OpenOffice.org Writer (Applications ➤ Office ➤ OpenOffice.org Word Processor), shown in Figure 11-1, is the word processor component. As with Microsoft Word, it's fully WYSIWYG (What You See Is What You Get), so you can quickly format text and paragraphs. This means the program can be used for elementary desktop publishing, and pictures can be easily inserted (using the Insert menu).

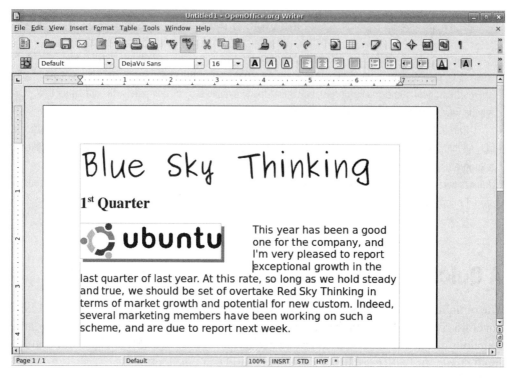

Figure 11-1. *OpenOffice.org Writer*

Writer's toolbars provide quick access to the formatting tools, as well as to other common functions. The vast majority of menu options match those found in Word. Right-clicking the text itself also offers quick access to text-formatting tools.

A number of higher-level functions are provided, such as mail merge and spell-checking, (found on the Tools menu). You can perform spell-checking on the fly, with incorrect words underlined in red as you type.

As with all OpenOffice.org packages, Writer is fully compatible with Microsoft Office files, so you can save and open .doc files. Just click File ➤ Save As, and click the arrow alongside File Type to choose a document format. The only exception is password-protected Word files, which cannot be opened. You can also export documents as PDF files (using File ➤ Export As PDF), so they can be read on any computer that has Adobe Acrobat Reader installed.

■**Note** Although compatible with Microsoft Office 2003 (and below) file formats, OpenOffice.org isn't compatible with Office 2007's new Open XML file format. However, this will almost certainly change in the future, which is why it's always a good idea to regularly update your Ubuntu system online.

OpenOffice.org Writer is covered in more detail in Chapter 23.

Spreadsheet: OpenOffice.org Calc

As with most of the packages that form the OpenOffice.org suite, Calc (Applications ➤ Office ➤ OpenOffice.org Spreadsheet) does a good impersonation of its Windows counterpart, Microsoft Excel, both in terms of powerful features and also the look and feel, as you can see in Figure 11-2. However, it doesn't run Excel Visual Basic for Applications (VBA) macros. Instead, Calc (and all OpenOffice.org programs) uses its own macro language called OpenOffice.org Basic (for more information, see `http://development. openoffice.org`).

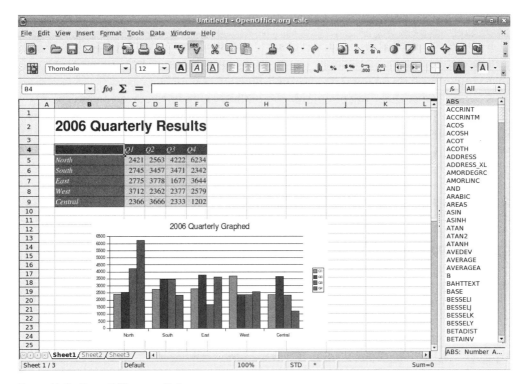

Figure 11-2. *OpenOffice.org Calc*

Calc has a vast number of mathematical functions. To see a list, choose Insert ➤ Function. The list on the left of the dialog box includes a brief explanation of each function to help you get started. Just as with Excel, you can access the functions via the toolbar (by clicking the Function Wizard button), or you can enter them directly into cells by typing an equal sign and then the formula code. Calc is intelligent enough to realize when formula cells have been moved and to recalculate accordingly. It will even attempt to calculate formulas automatically and can work out what you mean if you type something like sales + expenses as a formula.

As you would expect, Calc also provides automated charting and graphing tools (under Insert ➤ Chart). In Figure 11-2, you can see an example of a simple chart created automatically by the charting tool.

You can format cells using the main toolbar buttons, or automatically apply user-defined styles (choose Format ➤ Styles and Formatting).

Tip In all the OpenOffice.org applications, you can hover the mouse cursor over each button for one second to see a tooltip showing what it does.

If you're a business user, you'll be pleased to hear that you can import databases to perform serious number-crunching. Use Insert ➤ Link to External Data to get the data, and then employ the tools on the Data and Tools menu to manipulate it.

As with all OpenOffice.org programs, compatibility with its Microsoft counterpart— Excel files in this case—is guaranteed. You can also open other common data file formats, such as comma-separated values (CSV) and Lotus 1-2-3 files.

OpenOffice.org Calc is covered in more detail in Chapter 24.

Presentations: OpenOffice.org Impress

Anyone who has used PowerPoint will immediately feel at home with Impress, OpenOffice.org's presentation package (Applications ➤ Office ➤ OpenOffice.org Presentation), shown in Figure 11-3. Impress duplicates most of the common features found in PowerPoint, with a helping of OpenOffice.org-specific extras.

The program works via templates into which you enter your data. Starting the program causes the Presentation Wizard to appear. This wizard guides you through selecting a style of presentation fitting the job you have in mind. At this point, you can even select the type of transition effects you want between the various slides.

Once the wizard has finished, you can choose from the usual normal and outline view modes (look under the View menu). Outline mode lets you enter your thoughts quickly, while normal mode lets you type straight onto presentation slides.

You can format text by highlighting it and right-clicking it, by using the Text Formatting toolbar that appears whenever you click inside a text box, or by selecting an entry on the Format menu. Impress also features a healthy selection of drawing tools, so you can create even quite complex diagrams. These are available on the Drawing toolbar along the bottom of the screen. You can also easily insert pictures, other graphics, and sound effects.

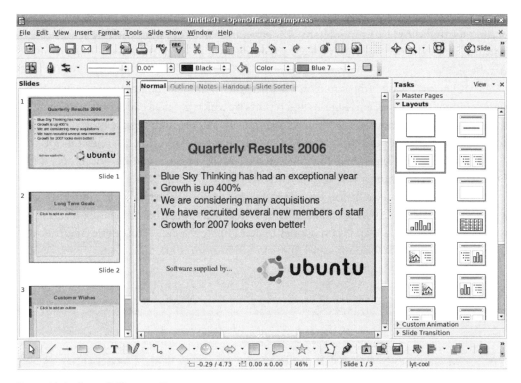

Figure 11-3. *OpenOffice.org Impress*

You can open and edit existing PowerPoint (PPT) files and, as with all OpenOffice.org packages, save your presentation as a PDF file. Unique to Impress is the ability to export your presentation as a Macromedia Flash file (SWF). This means that anyone with a browser and Macromedia's Flash plug-in can view the file, either after it's put online or via e-mail. Simply click File ➤ Export, and then choose Macromedia Flash from the File Format drop-down list.

Along with slide presentations, Impress also lets you produce handouts to support your work.

OpenOffice.org Impress is covered in more detail in Chapter 25.

Database: OpenOffice.org Base

Base, shown in Figure 11-4, is the newest component of OpenOffice.org, introduced with version 2. You can access it by clicking Applications ➤ Office ➤ OpenOffice Database. Base allows you to create relational databases using a built-in database engine, although it also can interface with external databases. It's very similar to Microsoft Access in look and feel, although it lacks some of Access's high-end functions. For most database uses, it should prove perfectly adequate.

If you know the fundamentals of database technology, you shouldn't have any trouble getting started with Base immediately. This is made even easier than you might expect because, when the program starts, a wizard guides you through the creation of a simple database.

As with Access, Base is designed on the principles of tables of data, forms by which the data is input or accessed, and queries and reports by which the data can be examined and outputted. Once again, wizards are available to walk you through the creation of each of these, or you can dive straight in and edit each by hand by selecting the relevant option.

Each field in the table can be of various types, including several different integer and text types, as well as binary and Boolean values.

Forms can contain a variety of controls, ranging from simple text boxes to radio buttons and scrolling lists, all of which can make data entry easier. Reports can feature a variety of text formatting and can also rely on queries to manipulate the data. The queries themselves can feature a variety of functions and filters in order to sort data down to the finest detail.

You'll learn more about Base in Chapter 26.

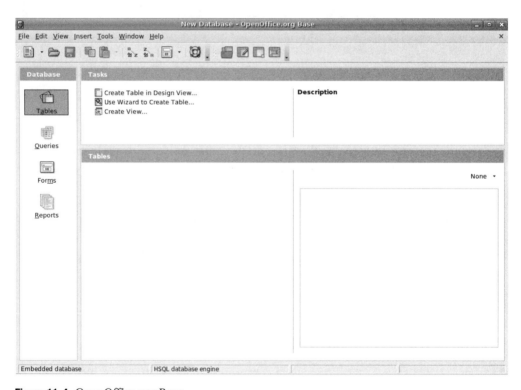

Figure 11-4. *OpenOffice.org Base*

E-Mail/Personal Information Manager: Evolution

Evolution is a little like Microsoft Outlook in that, in addition to being an e-mail client, it can also keep track of your appointments and contacts. You can Start Evolution by clicking Applications ➤ Office ➤ Evolution.

Before using the program, you'll need to set it up with your incoming and (if applicable) outgoing mail server settings, as detailed in Chapter 8. Evolution is compatible with POP/SMTP, IMAP, Novell GroupWise, Hula, Microsoft Exchange, and a handful of Unix-based mail formats rarely used nowadays.

Once the program is up and running, as shown in Figure 11-5, you can create a new message by clicking the New button on the toolbar. To reply to any e-mail, simply select it in the list, and then click the Reply or Reply To All button, depending on whether you want to reply to the sender or to all the recipients of the message.

To switch to Contacts view, click the relevant button on the bottom left. If you reply to anyone via e-mail, they're automatically added to this Contacts list. You can also add entries manually by either right-clicking someone's address in an open e-mail or right-clicking in a blank space in the Contacts view.

Clicking the Calendar view shows a day-and-month diary. To add an appointment, simply select the day, and then double-click the time you want the appointment to start. You can opt to set an alarm when creating the appointment, so that you're reminded of it when it it's scheduled.

Finally, by clicking the Tasks and Memos buttons, you can create a to-do list and jot down quick notes, respectively. To add a task, click the bar at the top of the list. Once an entry has been created, you can put a check in its box to mark it as completed. Completed tasks are marked with strike-through, so you can see at a glance what you still need to do. To add a memo, click the bar at the top of the memo list, and simply type what you want to remember.

In addition to the setup guide in Chapter 8, you'll find a full explanation of Evolution's features in Chapter 27.

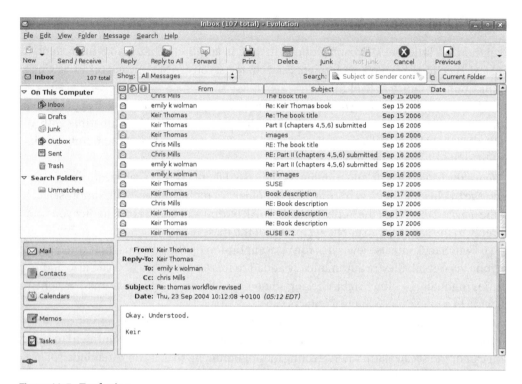

Figure 11-5. *Evolution*

Web Browser: Firefox

You might already know of Mozilla Firefox under Windows, where it's firmly established itself as the alternative browser of choice. The good news is that the Linux version of Firefox is nearly identical to its Windows counterpart. You'll find it on the Applications ➤ Internet ➤ Firefox Web Browser menu.

When the program starts, as shown in Figure 11-6, you can type an address into the URL bar to visit a web site. If you wish to add a site to your bookmarks list, click Bookmarks ➤ Bookmark This Page. Alternatively, you can press Ctrl+D.

Searching is very easy within Firefox, using its search bar at the top right of the window. By default, Firefox uses Google for searches. To choose from other search engines, click the small down arrow on the left side of the search box. You can even enter your own choice of site if your favorite isn't already in the list—click Manage Search Engines and then click the Get More Search Engines link in the dialog that appears.

Firefox popularized the principle of tabbed browsing, which means you can have more than one site open at once. To open a new tab, type Ctrl+T. You can move between the tabs by clicking each.

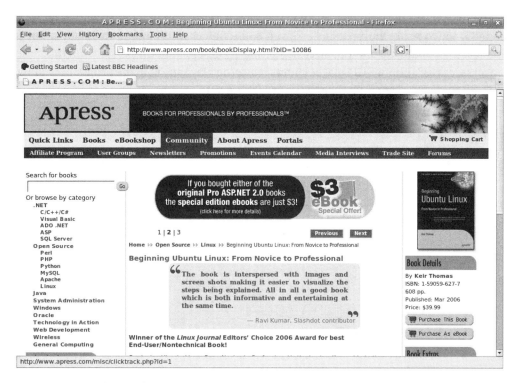

Figure 11-6. *Mozilla Firefox*

■**Tip** When Firefox starts, tabs aren't activated. If you would like to keep tabs in view all the time, click Edit ➤ Preferences, and then click the Tabs button. Then put a check alongside Always Show the Tab Bar.

Firefox is compatible with the same range of extensions you might have used under the Windows version of the browser. You can download new extensions from `https://addons.mozilla.org/extensions`. In addition, Firefox under Ubuntu can work with Flash animations, although you'll need to download the Flash Player software first. See the instructions in Chapter 19 to learn more.

Audio Playback: Rhythmbox and Sound Juicer

Ubuntu's multimedia software is basic but effective. It can play back the majority of audio files, as long as it's properly configured, which is to say after additional software has been installed. I'll describe how to set up this software in Chapter 18, and if you're thinking of playing audio files on your computer, you may want to read that chapter immediately.

Rhythmbox is the audio file player, which can be started by clicking Applications ➤ Sound & Video ➤ Rhythmbox Music Player. Sound Juicer will start automatically when you insert an audio CD into the drive. It's primarily designed to rip CD tracks to disk, but it also serves as Ubuntu's CD player (simply click the Play button in the program window to listen to tracks). Figure 11-7 shows both of these applications.

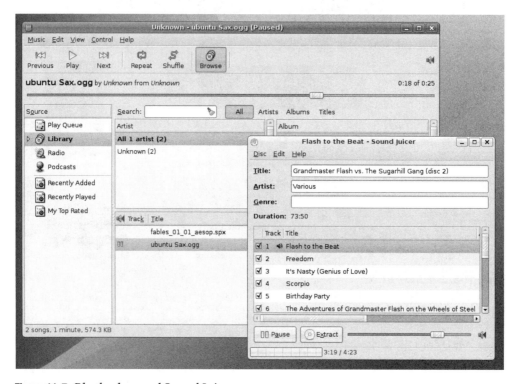

Figure 11-7. *Rhythmbox and Sound Juicer*

When Rhythmbox is run for the first time, it will attempt to find and then catalog your music collection. You might be used to this kind of functionality with Windows utilities like iTunes. After the initial file search has taken place, whenever Rhythmbox runs, you will find your tracks listed by artist or name, providing they have the relevant tag information embedded in them (such as ID3 tags in MP3 music).

■**Note** Unlike iTunes, Rhythmbox can't play Digital Rights Management (DRM)-protected files.

To start playing a music track, double-click it in the list. To make the player smaller so that it doesn't dominate the screen, click View ➤ Small Display.

Sound Juicer is very simple to operate. It will open automatically once a CD has been inserted, although to start playing you must select a track from the list and click the Play button (clicking Play without selecting a track will simply play the CD starting from track 1). While Sound Juicer is playing, you can switch to any other tracks by double-clicking them in the list. One nice feature of Sound Juicer is that it will automatically look up the artist and track information about most CDs online, and then save the information for future reference.

You can control the output volume within the applications themselves or use the volume control applet, which is located at the top-right side of the Ubuntu desktop, near the clock. Simply click and then drag the slider to alter the volume.

Movie Playback: Totem Movie Player

Totem Movie Player, which can be started by clicking Applications ➤ Sound & Video ➤ Movie Player, is able to handle the majority of video files you might own, as long as some additional software is installed. Totem can also play back DVD movies, which, again, requires the installation of software. I'll cover setting up this software in Chapters 18 and 19; if you intend to play back videos and DVDs, these chapters should be your first port of call.

As with Rhythmbox and CD Player, Totem is a simple and uncomplicated application, as shown in Figure 11-8. The video file will play in the top left of the window. A playlist detailing movies you have queued appears in the top-right area of the program window. You can remove this, to give the video window more room, by clicking the Sidebar button.

You can control video playback using the tape-recorder–like controls at the bottom left. In addition, provided a compatible video format is being played, you can use the Time bar to move backward and forward within the video file. You can switch to full-screen playback by clicking View ➤ Fullscreen. To switch back, simply press the Escape key (labeled Esc on some keyboards). If you're watching a program that has been ripped from TV, you might want to use the Deinterlace feature on the View menu to remove any interference patterns.

Provided the software described in Chapter 19 is installed, DVD playback will start automatically as soon as a disc is inserted, and you should be able to use the mouse with any on-screen menus. In addition, you can skip between chapters on the disc using the Go menu, and also return to the DVD's main or submenu systems. To switch between the various languages on a DVD (if applicable), click Sound ➤ Languages and choose from the list.

Figure 11-8. *Totem Movie Player*

CD/DVD Burning: Nautilus and Serpentine

As soon as you insert a blank writable disc, whether it's a CD or DVD, Ubuntu will detect it and offer you a range of choices. You can then create a data, music, or photo disc. If you choose to create a music CD, the Serpentine Audio CD Creator application will open. If you choose to create a data or photo CD/DVD, a Nautilus file browser window will open in CD/DVD Creator mode.

To use Serpentine to create an audio CD, simply drag-and-drop your music files onto the program window, and then click the Write to Disc button. Keep an eye on the disc graphic at the bottom left. This is like a pie chart; when the white portion is full, the disc is full. Note that you won't be able to write certain audio files, like MP3s, to CDs unless you have the relevant codecs installed. See Chapter 18 to learn more.

Using the Nautilus CD/DVD Creator, shown in Figure 11-9, is similar to using Serpentine. Just drag-and-drop files onto the window to create shortcuts to the files. When it comes time to burn, Nautilus will take the files from their original locations. When you've finished choosing files, click the Write to Disc button. Unfortunately, you won't see a warning if the disc's file size has been exceeded until you try to write to the disc. However, by right-clicking an empty space in the Nautilus window and selecting Properties, you can discover the total size of the files. Remember that most CDs hold 700MB, and most DVD+/-R discs hold around 4.7GB (some dual-layer discs hold twice this amount; see the DVD disc packaging for details).

▓**Tip** Most modern CD/DVD recorders utilize burn-proof technology, which helps ensure error-free disc creation. To activate this, open a terminal window (Applications ➤ Accessories ➤ Terminal), and type gconf-editor. When the program starts, Click Edit ➤ Find, and type burnproof. Make sure there's a check in Search Also in Key Names. In the search results at the bottom of the window, click the first result (/apps/nautilus-cd-burner/burnproof) and make sure there's a check in burnproof at the top right of the window. Then close the Configuration Editor.

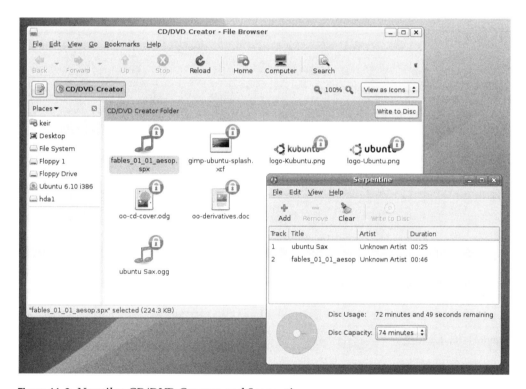

Figure 11-9. *Nautilus CD/DVD Creator and Serpentine*

Photo Editing: The GIMP

While many of the other programs introduced so far mirror the Windows look and feel in some way, The GIMP (Applications ➤ Graphics ➤ GIMP Image Editor) walks a different path. It has its own unique way of working, which takes a little getting used to. But it's very much worth the effort, because The GIMP offers photo-editing tools on par with professional products like Adobe Photoshop. It's certainly more than powerful enough for tweaking digital camera snapshots.

Once the program is running, you'll notice that it's actually little more than a large toolbar on the left side of the screen, as shown in Figure 11-10. Everything else that runs within The GIMP—whether it's a window containing the image you're editing or an additional configuration dialog box—uses its own program window. This also means that each program item that you activate gets its own button on the Panel at the bottom of the screen.

Figure 11-10. *The GIMP*

To open a picture, select File ➤ Open and select your image from the hard disk. Once an image file is opened, you can manipulate it using the tools on the toolbar (which are similar to those found in other image editors). On the bottom half of the main program window, you'll find the settings for each tool, which can be altered, usually via click-and-drag sliders.

To apply filters or other corrective changes, right-click anywhere on the image to bring up a context menu with a variety of options. Simple tools to improve brightness and contrast can be found on the Layer ➤ Colors submenu.

For an in-depth look at The GIMP package, see Chapter 20.

Other Handy Applications

Many additional applications might prove useful on a day-to-day basis. Here, I'll review some of the more common ones.

Calculator

The GNOME Calculator (also known as GCalctool) can be found on the Applications ➤ Accessories menu. In its default mode, shown in Figure 11-11, it shouldn't present any challenges to anyone who has ever used a real-life calculator, although the Bksp key might be new. This simply deletes the last number you typed (handy if you miskey during a calculation).

Figure 11-11. *GNOME Calculator*

Calculator also has three other modes that you can switch into using the View menu: Advanced, Financial, and Scientific. All offer calculator functions relevant to their settings. The Advanced mode is simply a more complicated version of the basic Calculator. It can store numbers in several memory locations, for example, and carry out less common calculations such as square roots and reciprocals.

Archive Manager

Archive Manager (also known as File Roller), shown in Figure 11-12, is Ubuntu's archive tool. It's the default program that opens whenever you double-click .zip files (or .tar, .gz, or .bzip2 files, which are the native archive file formats under Linux). If you want to start the program manually, click Applications ➤ Accessories ➤ Archive Manager.

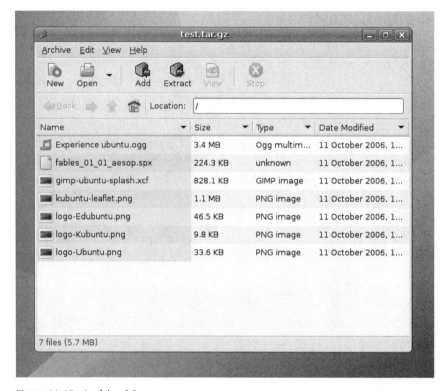

Figure 11-12. *Archive Manager*

To extract files from an archive, select them (hold down the Ctrl key to select more than one file), and then click the Extract button on the toolbar.

To create an archive, start Archive Manager and click the New button. Give the archive a name, and then drag-and-drop files onto the Archive Manager window. When you've finished, simply close the Archive Manager window.

Dictionary

You can use the Dictionary tool to look up the definition of words using the Collaborative International Dictionary of English. This is based on a 1913 edition of Webster's Revised Unabridged Dictionary, but with some additional modern definitions. The dictionary is useful for quick lookups, although if you want a precise and modern definition of a word, you might consider using a more contemporary source.

You'll find the Dictionary program, shown in Figure 11-13, on the Applications ➤ Accessories menu. As soon as you start typing, the program will begin to look up the word in the dictionary, and this can cause a momentary delay before the letters appear on your screen.

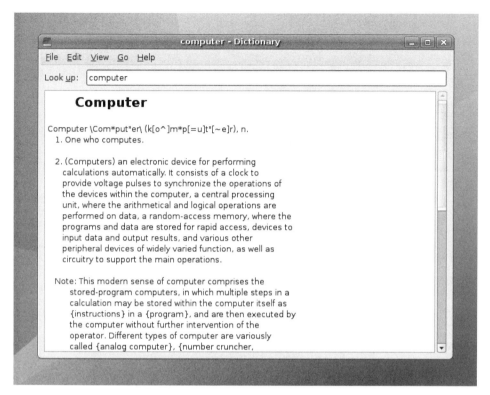

Figure 11-13. *Dictionary*

Gaim Internet Messenger

Gaim is the instant messaging software provided with Ubuntu. Unlike most other messaging programs, Gaim isn't exclusive to one chat protocol. In other words, you can use it to connect to MSN, AOL/ICQ, Yahoo!, and many other services. The program can be found on the Applications ➤ Internet menu.

Details for setting up Gaim are in Chapter 8. Once the program is up and running, you can chat with any of your buddies by double-clicking their icon, as shown in Figure 11-14. To set your status, click the Away icon at the bottom left and select an appropriate message.

The rest of the program can be administered by right-clicking the notification area icon that appears when the program starts. For example, you can initiate file transfers or sign off from there.

■**Note** If you're interested in learning more about how Gaim is built, check out *Open Source Messaging Application Development: Building and Extending Gaim*, authored by Gaim project leader Sean Egan (1-59059-467-3; Apress, 2005).

Figure 11-14. *Gaim Internet Messenger*

Mines

Mines is the Ubuntu equivalent of Minesweeper and, in fact, is almost exactly the same as the Windows program, as you can see in Figure 11-15. The rules are identical, too: on each grid are several hidden mines, and it's your job to locate them. After you've clicked one square at random, you'll see a series of empty squares and several with numbers in them. Those with numbers indicate that a bomb is near. Your job is to use logic to work out where the bombs are, and then mark them by right-clicking them. Oh, and you have to do this as quickly as possible because you're being timed.

To change the grid size, click Settings ➤ Preferences. Your choices are Small, Medium, Large, and Custom.

Figure 11-15. *Mines*

Ekiga

Ekiga provides Internet telephony (known as Voice over IP, or VoIP), via the SIP and H.323 protocols. It also provides video conferencing and is compatible with all major features specified within SIP and H.323, such as holding, forwarding, and transferring calls. Ekiga can be found on the Applications ➤ Internet menu.

To activate the video camera mode, in order to video conference, click the webcam icon on the left of the window. To text chat, click the first icon on the left side of the program window.

When the program starts, it will walk you through setup via a wizard. Simply answer the questions with the details of your setup. Once the program is up and running, as shown in Figure 11-16, type the URL of the person you would like to call into the address bar and click Call ➤ Call.

Note that Ekiga is not compatible with proprietary VoIP software, such as Skype. To learn how to install Skype under Ubuntu, see Chapter 18.

Figure 11-16. *Ekiga*

Summary

In this chapter, we've taken a look at some Ubuntu programs that provide vital functions that you might have used daily under Windows. The aim was to get you started with this software as quickly as possible by pointing out key features. You've seen how some programs mirror the look and feel of their Windows counterparts almost to the letter, while others resolutely strike out on their own path. It takes just a little time to become familiar with Ubuntu software, and then using these programs will become second nature.

In the next chapter, we'll move on to more fundamental Ubuntu tasks: manipulating files. However, once again, this is not too dissimilar from the Windows experience, which makes getting used to the system very easy.

CHAPTER 12

■■■

Managing Your Files

Files are what make the world of Linux go round. They're the currency of any kind of operating system, because every time you use your computer, you generate new files, even if they're only temporary.

How Linux views files, as well as the disks and partitions that contain them, varies somewhat from how Windows handles files. In many ways, the Linux system of file management is far simpler than that in Windows (which, ironically, was created as an attempt to make everything easy!). The Linux system is also much more established.

In this chapter, I will explain how you can manage your files under Ubuntu. This isn't a definitive guide; you'll need to wait until Chapter 14 to learn the technical ins and outs of the file system and the all-important system of user accounts that goes hand-in-hand with files. However, this chapter provides enough information for you to understand how the system works and where and how you should store your data.

Understanding File System Concepts

Just like Windows, Ubuntu has a file system that is shared among software components and your own personal data, which you generate within various applications, or perhaps download from the Internet. However, Ubuntu differs from Windows in a couple of important ways.

Drive References

Perhaps the most important differences between Linux and Windows are the following:

- The Linux file system doesn't use drive letters; and

- The Linux file system uses a forward slash (/) instead of a backslash (\) in filename paths.

In other words, something like /home/john/myfile is typical under Ubuntu, as opposed to C:\Documents and Settings\John\myfile under Windows. The root of the hard disk partition is usually referred to as C:\ under Windows. In Ubuntu, it's referred to simply with a forward slash (/).

If you have more than one drive, the drives are usually combined into the one file system under Linux. This is done by *mounting*, so that the any additional drives appear as virtual folders under the file system. In other words, you browse the other hard disks by switching to various directories within the main file system. I'll explain mounting in Chapter 14.

■**Note** If you're used to Mac OS X, then the Ubuntu file system shouldn't come as much of a surprise, because both OS X and Ubuntu are based on Unix and utilize similar concepts.

File Names

Another important difference between Ubuntu and Windows is that filenames in Ubuntu are case-sensitive. This means that MyFile is distinctly different from myfile. Uppercase letters are vitally important. In Windows, filenames might appear to have uppercase letters in them but, actually, these are ignored when you rename or otherwise manipulate files.

Because of this case-sensitivity, you could have two separate files existing in the same place, one called MyFile and another called myfile. In fact, you could also have myFile, Myfile, MYFILE, and so on, as shown in Figure 12-1.

However, as with Windows, filenames can have spaces within them. This means it's possible to have file or folder names like Pictures from Disneyland or party at bob's house.jpg.

■**Note** You might notice that some Linux old-hands avoid using spaces in filenames and use an underscore character (_) instead. There are two main reasons for this. The first is that it's tricky to manipulate filenames with spaces in them at the command prompt (discussed in Part 4 of this book). To manipulate a file with spaces in it at the command prompt, you have to put quotes around the whole thing or precede each space with a backslash (\). Secondly, the Internet is incompatible with files with spaces in them, which means that you would have to rename files to send them anywhere (unless you put them in an archive).

Unlike with Windows, filenames can include virtually any symbol, including an asterisk (*), backslash (\), question mark (?), lesser than/greater than signs (<>), and so on. The only symbol that's prohibited is the forward slash (/), and that's because it has a special use in file paths, described earlier. Be aware, however, that if you wish to share files with colleagues running Windows, you should stick to Windows conventions to avoid incompatibilities and avoid using the following symbols: \/:*?"<>|.

Figure 12-1. *Ubuntu filenames are case-sensitive, so many similar filenames can exist, differing only in which letters are capitalized.*

Note If you try to copy a file with illegal symbols to a Windows machine across a network, Ubuntu simply won't let you and will report an Invalid Parameters error.

File Access and Storage

Although Windows Vista tightens up security and stops users from writing files outside of the Users directory unless they have permission, under Windows XP you have access to the entire hard disk. You can write, read, or delete files anywhere (unless the system has specifically been configured otherwise). You can save your personal files in C:\Windows, for example.

Under Ubuntu, ordinary users can browse most of the hard disk, but they aren't able to write files to the majority of folders (in some cases, they won't even be able to access files).

Although we'll cover the file system in much more depth in Chapter 14, for the moment, it's enough to know that you've been given your own part of the hard disk in which to store your stuff. This is a directory located within the /home directory, and its name is taken from your username. If your login name is louisesmith, your place for storing files will be /home/louisesmith. Figure 12-2 shows an example of a user's home directory.

■**Note**   Linux generally uses the terms *directory* and *subdirectory* for the places you put files, whereas Windows refers to them as folders. It's merely a matter of semantics. However, within the Nautilus file browser, directories are pictured as folders and are referred to as such, thus furthering the confusion!

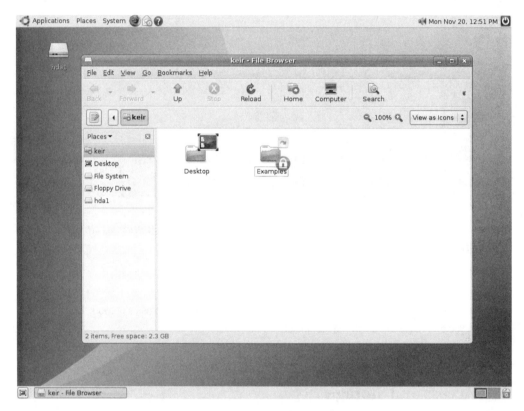

Figure 12-2. *Your personal area on the hard disk is in the /home directory and is named after your username.*

Some programs might create subdirectories in your home directory in order to store and organize their output. For example, a digital camera program might create a Pictures directory within your /home directory. It's up to you whether you use these. The standard practice within the Linux community is to simply save everything into your /home subdirectory (for example, /home/keir) and sort it out later!

Files within Ubuntu remember who owns them. If user johnsmith creates a file, he can make it so that only he can read or write the file (the default setting is that other users will be able to read the file but not write any new data to it). Directories, too, are owned by people, and the owner can set access permissions. By default, all users on a system can access each other's /home directories and read files, but they won't be able to change the files or write new files to any directory within /home that isn't theirs.

■**Note** Any user with superuser powers has access to all of the system and can create, edit, and delete files in all directories. This is so that user can perform essential system maintenance.

Using Nautilus

Nautilus is the name of the default file browser in Ubuntu. It's not dissimilar to My Computer/ Windows Explorer under Windows in that it presents a list of files on the right side of the window and a series of shortcuts to popular locations within the file system on the left side.

Starting Nautilus is simply a matter of clicking the Places menu and choosing a location, as shown in Figure 12-3.

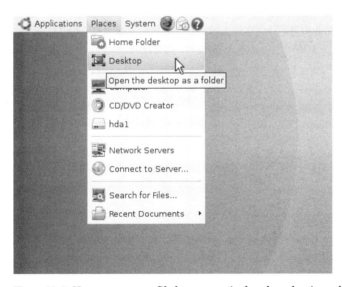

Figure 12-3. *You can open a file browser window by selecting a location under the Places menu.*

The Nautilus window (see Figures 12-1, 12-2, and 12-4) consists of several elements:

Menu bar: The menus offer options for controlling the way files are displayed in the Nautilus window, as well as the look and feel of Nautilus itself—look under the View menu in both instances. The Edit menu lets you manually cut, copy, and paste files, among other things. The Go menu lets you quickly jump to other locations in the file system, while the Bookmarks menu lets you create web-browser–like shortcuts to certain locations in your file system, so you can access them instantly.

Toolbar: As in a web browser, the toolbar allows you to quickly move backward and forward from place to place in your browsing history. In addition, you can reload the file listing, in order to reflect any changes that might have taken place since the Nautilus window opened, and quickly navigate to popular file system locations, such as your /home folder.

Location bar: This feature, located beneath the toolbar, is unique to Nautilus and works in two modes. The first mode, which we'll call button mode, is activated by default. This shows individual directories as buttons on the Location Bar and lets you see where you are in your file system at a glance, as well as quickly and easily move through your file-browsing history. For example, if you start in /home/keir and then browse to /home/keir/pictures/holiday/disneyworld, clicking the Pictures button will return you to /home/keir/pictures. The other folders listed on the location bar (holiday and disneyworld in this example) won't disappear and will still have buttons, so you can return to those as well. It's best demonstrated by example, so give it a try! The second mode, activated by clicking the icon to the left of the Location Bar buttons, switches the Location Bar into a more traditional, text-based bar, where you can type paths and filenames manually. To switch back to button mode, click the icon again.

Zoom controls: To the right of the location bar are the zoom controls. These make the icons representing the files bigger or smaller. When you're browsing a lot of files at once, shrinking them will fit more in the window. On the other hand, when you're viewing photo thumbnails, it can be handy to increase the zoom setting, so you can see more detail in the pictures.

View As Icons/List: To the right of the zoom controls is a drop-down list that switches between icon and list view. List view shows details about the files, such as file size, the type of file, its permissions, and so on. Icon view presents the files as a series of large icons. In many cases, the icons will give a clue as to the nature of the file; for example, audio files appear with musical note graphics. If the folder you're browsing contains image files (or certain document files, such as PDFs), these will be automatically thumbnailed—the icon will be a small version of the contents of the file, as shown in Figure 12-4. This is very handy when browsing pictures for printing or editing.

Places pane: The Places pane on the left lists the most popular locations within the file system, as well as any locations that you've bookmarked, which can be done by dragging a folder to the white space under the current bookmarked folders. Double-clicking each icon takes you to that location instantly. Clicking the File System entry takes you to the root of the file system (/).

Figure 12-4. *Whenever you view a folder full of pictures in icon view, they will be automatically thumbnailed.*

As under Windows, you can right-click each file in the file browser window to see a context menu with options to rename the file, delete it, open it with particular applications, and so on. The Properties option on the context menu lets you view information about the file and alter certain aspects of it, such as its access permissions (discussed in Chapter 14). You can even add some text notes about the file if you wish!

■**Caution** You should never delete your /home folder. Doing so will most likely destroy your personal Ubuntu configuration and prevent you from logging in, since all many personal system and program settings are also stored in your /home folder.

Searching for Files

Nautilus includes a powerful but easy-to-use search tool, and it can be accessed by clicking the Search button on the toolbar. This will present a text box below the toolbar into which you can type any part of the filename you're searching for. For example, typing beer will return any filenames with the word beer in them.

However, by clicking the plus sign icon next to the Reload button after a search has taken place, you specify an exact file type. To do this, click the Location drop-down list, and select File Type. Then click the Any drop-down list, and select only to search for the particular file type you're interested in.

Here's an example of where this might be useful: Suppose you're searching for a picture taken at a beer festival, and you know the filename contains the word beer. But you don't want to have returned in the search results the various documentation you created while booking your place at the festival, whose filenames also contain the word beer. In such a case, simply selecting Picture from the drop-down list, as shown in Figure 12-5, will ensure only images are returned in the search.

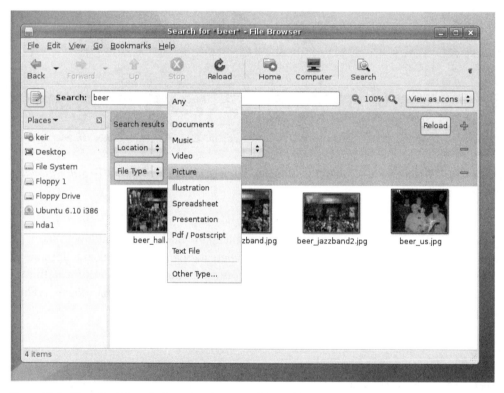

Figure 12-5. *Nautilus' Search function is powerful and lets you filter by file type.*

File and Folder Icons

Files and folders can have *emblems* applied to them. These are smaller icons that are "tagged on" to the larger icons in both list view and icon view. Emblems are designed to give you quick clues about the nature of the file. To apply an emblem, right-click the file or folder, select Properties, and then click the Emblems tab. As shown in Figure 12-6, a range of icons is available; in fact, any file or folder can have several emblems applied at once. Simply put a check in the box beside the icons you wish to apply.

The text alongside some emblems in the Properties window might not appear to be useful (a "cvs-conflict" will only be of interest to programmers, for example), but there's no reason why you can't still use them, provided you know what they mean for you!

Nautilus makes use of a handful of emblem icons for its own needs, too. For example, a file with a lock emblem attached to it indicates that you don't have the necessary file permissions to edit or delete that file. An X emblem means you don't have permissions to access that file or folder at all, not even to view it. In most cases, the file system emblems are self-explanatory.

▉**Tip** Want to have some fun with desktop icons? Right-click them, and select Stretch Icon. Then click and drag the handles at one of the corners. To restore an icon to its original size, right-click it, and select Restore Icon's Original Size.

Figure 12-6. *A variety of miniature emblems can be applied to an icon to aid recognition of the file.*

Special Nautilus Windows

As well as letting you view your files, Nautilus has a number of *object modes*. This is a complicated way of saying that Nautilus lets you view things other than files.

The most obvious example of this is the Computer view of your file system, which presents an eagle's eye view of your storage devices. To access this view, click Places ➤ Computer. If you have a card reader attached, it will appear here, as will any Windows partitions that may be on your hard disk. Double-clicking each item opens a standard Nautilus file browser window (for this to work with Windows partitions, they must be set up correctly, as described in the "Accessing Windows Files" section later in this chapter).

Another Nautilus object mode is the Fonts view, which lets you see at a glance any fonts installed on your computer. To access Fonts view, click Go ➤ Location in any open Nautilus window, and then type `fonts://`.

Object mode comes into its own when viewing network locations. Clicking Places ➤ Network Servers brings up the browsing network object view, for example, which is a little like Network Neighborhood/My Network Places under Windows. You can also browse to FTP sites by clicking Go ➤ Location in a file browser window and entering an FTP address (prefacing it with `ftp://`).

■**Note** You might be used to dragging and dropping files onto program windows or taskbar buttons within Windows in order to open the file. This works with only some programs within Ubuntu. Generally, the best policy is to try it and see what happens. If the program starts but your file isn't opened, it obviously didn't work.

HIDDEN FILES AND DIRECTORIES

When you view your /home directory via Nautilus, you're not seeing every file that's there. Several hidden files and directories relating to your system configuration also exist. You can take a look at them by clicking View ➤ Show Hidden Files in the Nautilus menu. Clicking this option again will hide the files and directories.

You might notice something curious about the hidden items: they all have a period before their file-names. In fact, this is all that's needed to hide any file or directory: simply place a period at the front of the filename. There's no magic involved above and beyond this.

For example, to hide the file `partypicture.jpg`, you could simply right-click it and rename it `.partypicture.jpg`. You'll need to click the Reload button on the toolbar for the file view to be updated and for the file to disappear. As you might expect, removing the period will unhide the file.

Files are usually hidden for a reason, and it's no coincidence that most of the hidden files are system files. In addition, every program that you install, or is installed by default, will usually create its own hidden folder for its system configuration data. Deleting such files by accident can be catastrophic.

Launching Files and Running Programs

As with Windows or Mac OS X, most of the programs on your Ubuntu system automatically associate themselves with various file types that they understand. For example, double-clicking a picture will automatically open the Eye of GNOME viewer application, and double-clicking a `.doc` file will start OpenOffice.org Writer.

Ubuntu is automatically set up to view common file types. However, you might find Table 12-1 useful. It shows which programs are required for viewing certain types of documents.

Note Whenever you install new software from the installation CD or the official software repositories, it should add an entry to the Applications menu. If for some reason this doesn't happen, you can create a shortcut using the techniques explained in Chapter 10.

Table 12-1. *Common File Types*

File Type	File Extension	Viewer	Location on Applications Menu
Word processor document	`.doc`, `.rtf`	OpenOffice.org Writer	Office ➤ OpenOffice.org Word Processor
Spreadsheet	`.xls`	OpenOffice.org Calc	Office ➤ OpenOffice.org Spreadsheet
Presentation	`.ppt`	OpenOffice.org Impress	Office ➤ OpenOffice.org Presentation
PDF file	`.pdf`	Evince	Not on Applications menu[1]
Compressed file	`.zip`, `.tar`, `.gz`, `.bz2`, and others	File Roller	Accessories ➤ Archive Manager
Image file	`.jpg`, `.gif`, `.bmp`, and others	Eye of GNOME	Not on Applications menu[2]
HTML file	`.htm`, `.html`	Firefox	Internet ➤ Firefox Web Browser
Text file	`.txt`, `.log`	Gedit	Accessories ➤ Text Editor
Audio file	`.wav`, `.mp3`, `.ogg`[3]	Rhythmbox	Sound & Video ➤ Rhythmbox Music Player
Video file	`.mpg`, `.mpeg`, `.avi`	Totem	Sound & Video ➤ Movie Player

---

[1] *For some reason, Evince is not present on the Applications menu, although it is installed by default and associated with PDF files. If you wish, you can add your own shortcut following the instructions in Chapter 10.*

[2] *Eye of GNOME is not present on the Applications menu; you can add your own shortcut following the instructions in Chapter 10. The program's filename is* eog.

[3] *Playback of many media files is only possible after extra software is installed; see Chapter 18 and 19.*

If you want to temporarily open a file type with a different program, right-click the file, select Open with Other Application, and choose the other program. From that point on, every time you right-click, you'll be offered the choice of the program to open the file.

To make GNOME automatically and permanently use the application to open the file type, right-click and select Properties, and then click the Open With tab. Click the Add button to locate the application you wish to use if it's not in the list. Finally, ensure the radio button alongside the program you wish to use is highlighted (you may need to click twice for this to happen), as shown in Figure 12-7, and then click the Close button.

■**Note** Under Windows, you can use Windows Explorer to launch program executables by just browsing to their locations within Program Files and double-clicking their .exe files. It's technically possible to run programs by browsing to their locations using Nautilus, but this is discouraged. One reason is that Ubuntu doesn't store all of its programs in one central folder, as does Windows. However, most programs that are used on a daily basis can be found in /usr/bin. If the program itself isn't stored in /usr/bin, it will contain a *symbolic link* (effectively, a shortcut) to the program's genuine location on the hard disk.

Figure 12-7. *You can change which program opens a file by right-clicking, selecting Properties, and clicking the Open With tab.*

Accessing Windows Files

Running Ubuntu on your PC makes you a relative stranger in a world of Windows users. It's likely that you'll need to access Windows files on a regular basis. If you've chosen to dual-boot with Windows, you might want to grab files from the Windows partition on your own hard disk. If your PC is part of a network, you might want to access files on a Windows-based server or workstation on which a shared folder has been created.

Working with Files in Windows Partitions

If you've chosen to dual-boot Ubuntu with Windows on the same hard disk, Ubuntu will probably make your Windows partitions available automatically, although I found during my tests across several different computers that it sometimes failed to do this.

■Note It's possible for an installation of Windows 2000 or XP to use FAT32 instead of NTFS, but this requires the user to make a deliberate choice during setup. Unless you know your Windows 2000 or XP system has been formatted with FAT32, it's very likely that it is NTFS.

If the drive has automatically been made available, an icon for it should appear on the desktop. Double-clicking this should show your Windows partition contents. On my system, the icon was identified by its partition designation, which is hda1.

If you find that your Windows partition isn't visible, you can follow these instructions to make it visible. This involves *mounting* the Windows partition under your Ubuntu file system. Mounting is explained in more detail in Chapter 14.

1. These instructions need to be carried out at the command prompt, so start by opening a GNOME Terminal Window—click Applications ➤ Accessories ➤ Terminal.

2. We need to identify the Unique Udev ID (UUID) number of your Windows partition. This is simply the hexadecimal number that Ubuntu uses to identify the drive internally. To find out the number, type the following at the command prompt:

   ```
   sudo vol_id -u /dev/hda1
   ```

   You'll be prompted to enter your password; do so. The preceding line assumes that your PC contains an IDE hard disk, which will probably be the case if your computer is over a year old. If you're using a SATA hard disk on a modern computer, then you will need to type the following:

   ```
   sudo vol_id -u /dev/sda1
   ```

These instructions also assume that the Windows partition is the first on the hard disk, which will almost certainly be the case for most users. If you know the Windows partition to be the second partition, replace /dev/hda1 and /dev/sda1 with /dev/hda2 and /dev/sda2.

3. You'll need to make a note of the output of the command. On my test PC, the line read FE3C2F103C2EC38D, but yours will almost certainly be different.

4. Next, you'll need to create a mount point. This is a dummy folder that's used to make the contents of the Windows partition magically available. The convention within Ubuntu is to create a directory within the /media directory, so type the following:

```
sudo mkdir /media/Windows
```

5. Following that, you need to edit the /etc/fstab file. This is the configuration file that tells Ubuntu where to find all of the file systems it uses. This includes the root file system, without which Ubuntu can't operate, so you should take extra care when editing this file. To load the file into the Gedit text editor, type the following:

```
gksu gedit /etc/fstab
```

6. The file looks complicated, but don't worry. Simply scroll to the bottom and create a new line. Then type the following:

```
UUID=<UUID>  /media/Windows  ntfs  defaults,nls=utf8,umask=007,gid=46  0  0
```

You should replace <UUID> with the hexadecimal number you noted earlier. For example, on my test PC, the line within fstab read as follows (see also Figure 12-8):

```
UUID=FE3C2F103C2EC38D  /media/Windows  ntfs  defaults,nls=utf8, ➡
umask=007,gid=46  0  0
```

7. Once you're finished, click File ➤ Save within Gedit.

8. From now on, the Windows file system will be automatically made available whenever you boot, and it should appear as an icon both on the desktop and within the Computer view of Nautilus (click Places ➤ Computer to see it). However, you can mount it immediately by typing the following command at the prompt:

```
sudo mount /media/Windows
```

■**Note** You cannot write to or edit files in an NTFS partition. Although it is *technically* possible, it's not advisable because of various technical limitations. Therefore, the NTFS partition is made read-only.

Figure 12-8. *By editing the* /etc/fstab *file, you can make your Windows partition available under Ubuntu.*

Accessing Networked Files

The easiest way to access servers or shared folders on Windows workstations or servers over a network is to click Places ➤ Network Servers. This will start Nautilus and attempt to search for Windows machines on your local network, just like Network Neighborhood and My Network Places on the various versions of Windows.

■Tip When using this method, if the icon for a computer or workgroup is a blank sheet of paper, click the Refresh button on the toolbar. The icon should then change to a computer. In my tests, I found that I couldn't access the network resource if the icon wasn't correctly set.

If you've ever used the network browsing services under Windows, you might already know how unreliable they can be—some computers simply don't appear in the list, others appear eventually after a wait, and others appear but then prove to be mysteriously inaccessible.

■Note Accessing shared printers attached to Windows computers is explained in Chapter 8 under the "Configuring a Windows/SMB Shared Printer" heading.

A far quicker and more reliable method of accessing a Windows shared folder is to manually specify its network name or IP address. The network name is simply the name of the computer that's used during networking. The IP address is the computer's identifying number and usually takes the form of four digits separated by periods, like this: 192.168.1.4.

You should try using the network name first when connecting to a computer. If that proves unreliable, try using the IP address instead.

Discovering the Network Name of a Windows Computer

This can be discovered within Windows Vista by clicking Start and right-clicking Network on the menu. Click Properties on the menu, and in the window that appears, look at the name of This Computer on the diagram beneath the Network and Sharing Center heading. The name of my test PC was keir-pc.

To discover the network name within Windows XP, right-click My Computer, select Properties, and then click the Computer Name tab in the window that appears. Look under the Full Computer Name heading.

Discovering the IP Address of a Windows Computer

Open an MS-DOS command prompt. To do this under Windows XP, click Start ➤ Run, and type cmd. Under Windows Vista, click the Start button, and type cmd into the Start Search text box.

Under both XP and Vista, type ipconfig at the prompt. Then, under XP, look for the line that reads "IP Address" and make note of the details. Under Windows Vista, look for the line that reads "IPv4 Address", and note the number (on my test computer, I had to scroll up the window to see the line).

Accessing the Shared Folder

Open a Nautilus file browser window (Places ➤ Home), and then click Go ➤ Location. In the box, type the following:

`smb://computer name/`

Alternatively, if you wish to use the IP address, type the following:

`smb://IP address/`

Obviously, in both cases, you should replace `computer name` and `IP address` with the details you noted down earlier.

You may also be prompted to enter a username and/or password to access the shared folder, as shown in Figure 12-9. To allow for password-free access in future, check the Remember Password for this Session box and the Save Password in Keyring box.

■**Note** If you're accessing a Windows 95, 98, or Me shared folder, only password protection will have been set (these versions of Windows are unable to specify a username). However, when prompted by Nautilus, you still need to type *something* into the Username box to gain access—anything will do, as long as the password is correct. You cannot leave the Username box blank.

To create a permanent desktop shortcut to the Windows folder, right-click a blank spot on the desktop and create a launcher. In the Command text box, enter `nautilus`, followed by the full network path to the share. You can discover this by browsing to the shared directory using Nautilus, as described previously, and then clicking the icon next to the Location Bar to switch to the text-mode view of the path. Then cut and paste the text into the Command box.

For example, on my Ubuntu setup, I created a shortcut to the `pictures` directory on the computer `keir-office-pc` by typing the following into the Command box:

`nautilus smb://keir-office-pc/pictures`

For more info about creating desktop launchers, see Chapter 10.

When using the launcher after rebooting your Ubuntu system, you might notice the folder takes a few seconds to appear. This is normal and merely the result of the time Ubuntu takes to log on to the computer sharing the files.

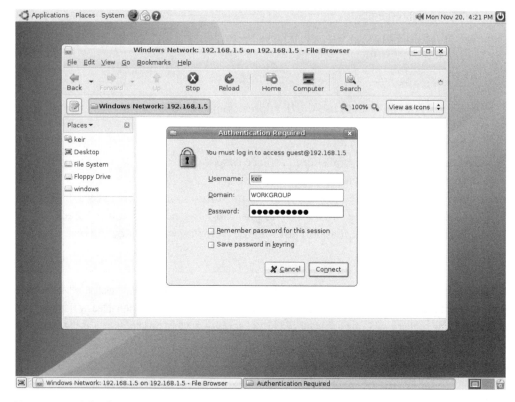

Figure 12-9. *If the share requires a username and/or password, you'll be invited to enter these.*

Sharing a Folder from Within Ubuntu

As well as accessing the shared files of other Windows users, you can also set up your own shared folder under Ubuntu for Windows users to access (or, indeed, other Ubuntu computers). To do this, follow these instructions:

1. Right-click the folder you wish to share, and select Share Folder from the menu.

2. If this is the first time you're sharing a folder, you'll be informed that you need to install either Unix Networks Support (NFS) or Windows Networks Support (SMB). Remove the check from the NFS box, and then click Install Services.

■**Note** NFS is an older form of file sharing used primarily on Unix computers. In most cases, even when sharing exclusively among Ubuntu computers, the SMB option is best, because it offers better security.

Synaptic Package Manager will automatically start in the background and will install the software. You'll be prompted for your password.

3. When Synaptic has finished, the Share Folder dialog will appear. In the Share Through drop-down list, select Windows Network.

4. You can leave the Name box with its default contents, but you might want to put a check in the Read Only box if you wish to stop users writing new files to the shared folder or from deleting existing files. Once finished, click the OK button.

5. If this is the first time you're creating a shared folder, you must manually set up a password, so that others can access the shared folders on the computer. This only needs to be done once for each user account that's sharing the folder. If you share any more folders in the future, there's no need to repeat this step. Click Applications ➤ Accessories ➤ Terminal, and at the command prompt, type the following:

```
sudo smbpasswd -a <username>
```

You should replace *<username>* with your username. First, you'll be invited to enter your password, because this operation requires a superuser; do so. Then, you'll be invited to enter *the SMB share password*. This can be anything you wish and doesn't have to match your login password. However, you'll need to enter it twice for confirmation purposes, as prompted.

6. Following this, Windows users can access the shared folder using My Network Places/Network Neighborhood, where it should be "detected" alongside other Windows computers (under Vista, click Start ➤ Network). Users should log in using your username but using the SMB password you specified in the previous step.

Note To access the shared folder from another Ubuntu computer, you'll need to specify its IP address. When I attempted to connect via Places ➤ Network Servers or by using the network name, I received an error message. To find out the IP address, open a GNOME Terminal window (Applications ➤ Accessories ➤ Terminal) and type `ifconfig`. Then look for the numbers alongside the `inet addr` entry.

Accessing Removable Storage Devices

Ubuntu automatically makes available any CDs or DVDs you insert into your computer, and they'll appear instantly as icons on the desktop. The same is true of any card readers or USB memory devices that you use.

Alternatively, you can access the storage devices by clicking Places ➤ Computer. Here, you'll find icons for all of the storage devices attached to your computer, including the floppy disk drive, as shown in Figure 12-10. However, because of the way floppy disk drives work, Ubuntu isn't able to automatically detect if a floppy has been inserted. Instead, you'll need to double-click the icon, as with Windows.

■Note In days of old, special tools were used to access MS-DOS floppies under Linux, and you might hear some Linux old-hands talking about them. Nowadays, you can simply use Nautilus without needing to take any special steps.

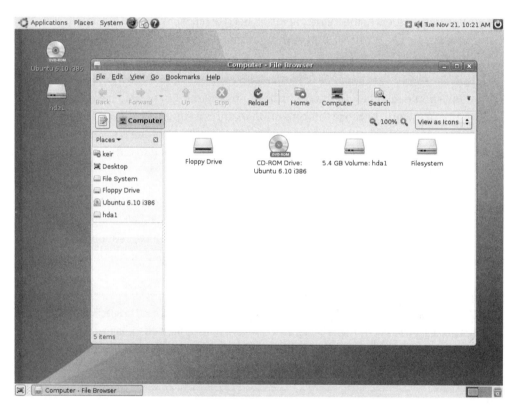

Figure 12-10. *Select Places ➤ Computer to access your removable storage drives.*

Whenever you double-click any entry in the Computer window, it will open a Nautilus file browser window. You can copy files by clicking and dragging, and right-clicking files offers virtually all the options you could need.

Tip You don't need to use Places ➤ Computer each time to access your floppy, CD, or DVD drive. These drives are mounted in the `/media` folder on your hard disk. Just browse to `/media/floppy`, and `/media/cdrom`.

Ejecting Media

Ubuntu isn't quite like Windows when it comes to ejecting or unplugging removable storage devices. In some cases, devices must be *unmounted*, which is to say that you need to tell Ubuntu that you're finished with the device in question and that you're about to unplug it.

In the case of CD or DVD discs, you can simply press the Eject button on the drive itself. Ubuntu is clever enough to realize that the disc is being ejected, so it will automatically unmount the drive. If the disc ever refuses to eject, right-click its icon on the desktop or within Computer and select Eject.

In the case of floppy disks, memory cards, and other USB storage devices, you should *always* right-click the icon and select Eject. Then you can then unplug and/or remove the device. This also applies when you're removing a memory card from a card reader—before pulling out the card from the reader, it needs to be ejected.

Note It's necessary to close any files that were open on the device before unmounting and even close any file browser windows that were accessing the device.

If you fail to unmount the device, Ubuntu will still believe the device is attached. This shouldn't cause too many problems, but it could crash any programs that were accessing the device. It might also mean the card isn't recognized properly when you reinsert it. In rare instances, data loss can occur.

Formatting Floppies

Formatting a floppy can be done by right-clicking the Floppy Drive icon in My Computer and selecting Format. You'll see the program window shown in Figure 12-11.

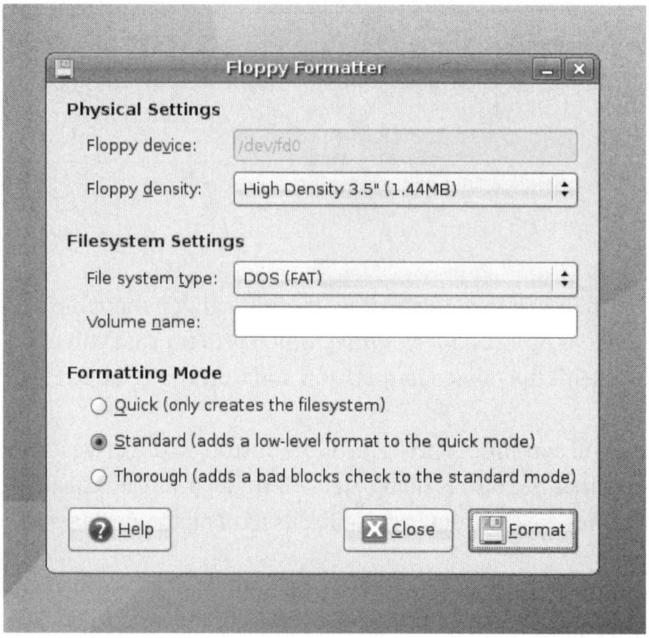

Figure 12-11. *Formatting floppy disks is done using the Floppy Formatter tool.*

Floppy Formatter is similar to the disk-formatting tool in Windows, and most of the options are self-explanatory. If you intend to share the disk with Windows users, make sure DOS (FAT) is selected in the File System Type box (it's possible to format a floppy using Ubuntu's own ext2 file system format, but there's little to be gained by doing so).

Summary

This chapter has led you on your first steps in exploring the Linux file system. The file system is vitally important to how Linux works, and we'll go into it in much depth in upcoming chapters.

Here, you were introduced to elementary concepts, such as where personal files are stored and the basic rules that govern what you can and cannot do with files. We also looked at the principal method of accessing files via the GUI: the Nautilus file manager. Additionally, you learned how to run programs manually, as well as how to access any Windows partition or files that may exist on your hard disk or across a network.

In Part 4 of this book, starting in the next chapter, we will look at some of the underlying technology that makes Ubuntu work and how you can gain more control over your computer. Chapter 13 introduces the BASH shell—perhaps the most powerful piece of software offered by Ubuntu to control your system.

The Shell and Beyond

CHAPTER 13

■■■

Introducing the BASH Shell

As you learned in Chapter 1, strictly speaking, the word *Linux* refers to just the kernel, which is the fundamental, invisible program that runs your PC and lets everything happen. However, on its own, the kernel is completely useless. It needs programs to let users interact with the PC and do cool stuff, and it needs a lot of system files (also referred to as *libraries*) to provide vital functions.

The GNU Project provides many of these low-level pieces of code and programs. This is why many people refer to the Linux operating system as GNU/Linux, giving credit to the fact that, without the GNU components, Linux wouldn't have gotten off the starting blocks.

The GNU Project provides various shell programs, too. A *shell* is what the user interacts with on a day-to-day basis, whether by mouse or keyboard. The word originates from the fact that the shell is the outer layer of the operating system, which encompasses the kernel (and in some instances protects it by filtering out bad user commands!). Some shells offer graphical functionality but, in general, the word *shell* is understood to mean text-only interfaces. These text shell programs are also known as *terminal programs*, and they're often colloquially referred to as *command-line prompts*, in reference to the most important component they provide. This kind of shell lets you take control of your system in a quick and efficient way.

By learning how to use the shell, you'll become the true master of your own system. In this part of the book, you'll learn all you need to know about using the shell. This chapter introduces the BASH shell, which is the default one in Ubuntu.

What Is the BASH Shell?

The best way of explaining the BASH shell to a Windows user is to compare it to the DOS command prompt. It lets you issue commands directly to the operating system via the keyboard without needing to mess around with the mouse and windows (although it is sometimes possible to use the mouse within a BASH shell to copy and paste text, and sometimes to control simple text-based menus). The big difference is that the BASH shell has commands for just about everything you might do on your system, whereas the DOS command prompt is restricted to tools capable of manipulating and viewing files and directories, and on Windows 2000/XP/Vista machines, configuring certain system settings.

In the old days, the DOS command prompt was also the visible layer of an entire operating system in which DOS programs were designed to be run. However, the shell is merely one of the many ways of accessing the Linux kernel and subsystems. It's true that many programs are designed to run via the BASH shell, but technically speaking, most actually run on the Linux operating system, and simply take input and show their output via the BASH shell.

■**Note** Linux purists will point out another reason why the shell isn't exactly the same as a DOS command prompt within Windows: it doesn't run in virtual machine mode, a CPU trick by which part of the memory is subdivided to let programs run as if they had the PC all to themselves.

Linux finds itself with the BASH shell largely because Linux is a clone of Unix. In the early days of Unix, the text-based shell was all that was offered as a way of letting users control the computer. Typing in commands directly is one of the most fundamental ways of controlling any type of computer and, in the evolutionary scale, comes straight after needing to set switches and watch blinking lights in order to run programs.

That the BASH shell can trace its history back to the early days of Unix might sound like a tacit indication that the BASH is somehow primitive—far from it. It's one of the most efficient and immediate ways of working with your computer. Many people consider the command-line shell to be a way of using a computer that has yet to be superseded by a better method.

■**Note** When you run a shell on a Linux system, the system refers to it as a `tty` device. This stands for teletypewriter, a direct reference to the old system of inputting data on what were effectively electronic typewriters connected to mainframe computers. These, in turn, took their names from the devices used to automate the sending and receiving of telegrams in the early part of the twentieth century.

Most Linux distributions come with a choice of different kinds of shell programs. However, the default shell is BASH, as is the case in Ubuntu. BASH stands for Bourne Again SHell. This is based on the Bourne shell, a tried-and-tested program that originated in the early days of Unix.

The other shells available include PDKSH (Public Domain Korn SHell, based on Korn Shell, another early Unix shell), and ZSH (Z SHell), a more recent addition. These are usually used by people who want to program Linux in various ways, or by those who simply aren't happy with BASH.

The BASH shell is considered by many to be the best of all worlds in that it's easy enough for beginners to learn, yet is able to grow with them and offer additional capabilities as necessary. BASH is capable of scripting, for example, which means you can even create your own simple programs.

Why Bother with the Shell?

You might have followed the instructions in Part 2 of this book and consider yourself an expert in Linux. But the real measure of a Linux user comes from your abilities at the shell.

In our modern age, the GUI is mistakenly considered "progress." For instance, users of the Microsoft and Apple-based operating systems are quite accustomed to using a mouse to navigate and perform various tasks. While it's handy in certain situations—it would be difficult to imagine image editing without a mouse, for example—in many other situations, such as when manipulating files, directly typing commands is far more efficient.

Most modern Linux distributions prefer you to use the GUI to do nearly everything. This is because they acknowledge the dominance of Windows and realize they need to cater to mouse users who might not even know the shell exists (and, of course, programs like web browsers would be unusable without a GUI!). To this end, they provide GUI tools for just about every task you might wish to undertake. Ubuntu is strong in this regard, and you can configure a lot of things from the desktop.

However, it's well worth developing at least some command-line shell skills, for a number of reasons:

> **It's simple and fast.** The shell is the simplest and fastest way of working with Ubuntu. As just one example, consider the task of changing the IP address of your network card. You could click the Systems menu, then the Administration option, then the Networking option, and then double-click the entry in this list relating to your network card. That will take at least a minute or two if you know what you're doing, and perhaps longer if it's new to you. Alternatively, you could simply open a shell and type this:

```
ifconfig eth0 192.168.0.15 up
```

> **It's versatile.** Everything can be done via the shell—from deleting files, to configuring hardware, to creating MP3s. A lot of GUI programs actually make use of programs you can access via the shell.

> **It's consistent among distributions.** All Linux systems have shells and understand the same commands (broadly speaking). However, not all Linux systems will have Ubuntu's graphical configuration programs. SUSE Linux uses its own GUI configuration tool, as does Mandriva Linux. Therefore, if you ever need to use another system, or decide to switch distributions, a reliance on GUI tools will mean learning everything from scratch. Knowing a few shell commands will help you get started instantly.

It's crucial for troubleshooting. The shell offers a vital way of fixing your system should it go wrong. Your Linux installation might be damaged to the extent that it cannot boot to the GUI, but you'll almost certainly be able to boot into a shell. A shell doesn't require much of the system other than the ability to display characters on the screen and take input from the keyboard, which most PCs can do, even when they're in a sorry state. This is why most rescue floppies offer shells to let you fix your system.

It's useful for remote access. One handy thing about the shell is that you don't need to be in front of your PC to use it. Programs like ssh let you log in to your PC across the Internet and use the shell to control your PC (as described in Chapter 34). For example, you can access data on a remote machine, or even fix it when you're unable to attend the machine's location. This is why Linux is preferred on many server systems when the system administrator isn't always present on the site.

It's respected in the community. Using a shell earns you enormous brownie points when speaking to other Linux users. It separates the wheat from the chaff and the men from the boys (or women from the girls). If you intend to use Linux professionally, you will most certainly need to be a master at the shell.

Seen in this light, learning at least a handful of shell commands is vital to truly mastering your PC.

The drawback when using a command-line shell is that it's not entirely intuitive. Take for instance the command to change the network card's IP address:

```
ifconfig eth0 192.168.0.15 up
```

If you've never used the shell before, it might as well be Sanskrit. What on earth does ifconfig mean? And why is there the word up at the end?

■**Note** If you're curious, the command tells the network card, referred to by Linux as eth0, to adopt the specified IP address. The word up at the end merely tells it to activate—to start working now. If the word down were there instead, it would deactivate! Don't worry about understanding all this right now; later in this chapter, I'll explain how you can learn about every Linux command.

Learning to use the shell involves learning terms like these. Hundreds of commands are available, but you really need to learn only around 10 or 20 for everyday use. The comparison with a new language is apt because, although you might think it daunting to learn new terminology, with a bit of practice, it will all become second nature. Once you've used a command a few times, you'll know how to use it in the future.

The main thing to realize is that the shell is your friend. It's there to help you get stuff done as quickly as possible. When you become familiar with it, you'll see that it is a beautiful concept. The shell is simple, elegant, and powerful.

When Should You Use the Shell?

The amount of use the Linux shell sees is highly dependent on the user. Some Linux buffs couldn't manage without it. They use it to read and compose e-mail, and even to browse the Web (usually using the Mutt and Lynx programs, respectively).

However, most people simply use it to manage files, view text files (like program documentation), and run programs. All kinds of programs—including GUI and command-line—can be started from the shell. As you'll learn in Chapter 29, unlike with Windows, installing a program on Ubuntu doesn't necessarily mean the program will automatically appear on the Applications menu. In fact, unless the installation routine is specifically made for the version of Linux you're running, this is unlikely. Therefore, using the shell is a necessity for most people.

■**Note** Unlike with DOS programs, Ubuntu programs that describe themselves as "command-line" are rarely designed to run solely via the command-line shell. All programs are like machines that take input at one end and output objects at the other. Where the input comes from and where the output goes to is by no means limited to the command line. Usually, with a command-line program, the input and output are provided via the shell, and the programmer makes special dispensation for this, but this way of working is why GUI programs often make use of what might be considered shell programs. You'll often find that a GUI program designed to, for example, burn CDs, will also require the installation of a command-line program that will actually do the hard work for it.

There's another reason why the shell is used to run programs: you can specify how a particular program runs before starting it. For example, to launch the Totem Movie Player in full-screen mode playing the `myvideofile.mpg` file, you could type this:

```
totem --fullscreen myvideofile.mpg
```

This saves the bother of starting the program, loading a clip, and then selecting the full-screen option. After you've typed the command once or twice, you'll be able to remember it for the next time. No matter how much you love the mouse, you'll have to admit that this method of running programs is more efficient.

When you get used to using the shell, it's likely you'll have it open most of the time behind your other program windows.

Getting Started with the Shell

You can start the shell in a number of ways. The most common is to use a terminal emulator program. As its name suggests, this runs a shell inside a program window on your desktop.

You can start GNOME Terminal, the built-in GNOME shell emulator, by clicking Applications ➤ Accessories ➤ Terminal, as shown in Figure 13-1.

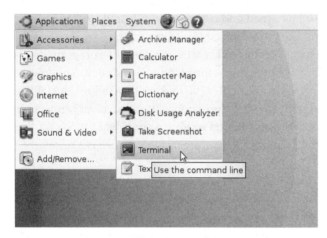

Figure 13-1. *Start the The GNOME Terminal program from the Accessories submenu.*

You'll see the terminal window—a blank, white window that's similar to a simple text editor window. When you run the terminal for the first time, at the top of the window will be a handful of lines telling you about the sudo command. I explain the importance of this in Chapter 14, but right now there's no need to worry about it.

Below this will be the most important component of the terminal window—the *command prompt*: a few words followed by the dollar symbol: $. On my test system, this is what I see:

```
keir@keir-desktop:~$
```

The first part is my username—the user account I created during installation and use to log in to the PC. After the @ sign is the hostname of the PC, which I also chose when installing Ubuntu. The hostname of the PC isn't important on most desktop PCs; it's a legacy from the days of Unix.

■**Note** What's with the @ sign? Again, it's a legacy from the days of Unix when the hostname referred to the site the computer was located at (such as the university or military facility). Reading the command prompt in this context, the line reads that the user keir is logged into the computer located at the location specified in the hostname! Like I said, this is a legacy of Unix's origins and doesn't mean much nowadays.

After the colon is the current directory you're browsing. In this example, the ~ symbol appears instead of an actual path or directory name. This is merely Linux shorthand for the user's home directory. In other words, wherever I see a ~ on my test PC, I read it as

/home/keir/. After this is the dollar symbol ($), which indicates that I'm currently logged in as an ordinary user, as opposed to the root user. However, unlike most other Linux distributions, Ubuntu doesn't use the root account during day-to-day operations, so this is a moot point. Finally, there is a cursor, and this is where you can start typing commands!

■**Note** If you were to log in as root, a hash (#) would appear instead of the dollar symbol prompt. This is important to remember, because often in magazines and some computer manuals, the use of the hash symbol before a command indicates that it should be run as root. In addition, if you use the rescue function of the install CD, you'll be running as root, and a hash will appear at the prompt. See Chapter 14 for more information about the root user.

Running Programs

When we refer to *commands* at the shell, we're actually talking about small programs. When you type a command to list a directory, for example, you're actually starting a small program that will do that job. Seen in this light, the shell's main function is to simply let you run programs—either those that are built into the shell, such as ones that let you manipulate files, or other, more complicated programs that you've installed yourself.

The shell is clever enough to know where your programs are likely to be stored. This information was given to it when you first installed Ubuntu and is stored in a system variable.

■**Note** A *variable* is the method Linux uses to remember things like names, directory paths, or other data. There are many system variables that are vital for the running of Ubuntu. These variables can be seen by typing set at the command prompt.

The information about where your programs are stored, and therefore where Ubuntu should look for commands you type in, as well as any programs you might want to run, is stored in the PATH variable. You can take a look at what's currently stored there by typing the following:

```
echo $PATH
```

Don't forget that the difference between uppercase and lowercase letters matters to Ubuntu, unlike with Windows and DOS.

The echo command merely tells the shell to print something on screen. In this case, you're telling it to "echo" the PATH variable onto your screen. On my test PC, this returned the following information:

```
/usr/local/sbin:/usr/local/bin:/usr/sbin:/usr/bin:/sbin:/bin:/usr/bin/X11: ➡
/usr/games
```

Several directories are in this list, each separated by a colon.

Don't worry too much about the details right now. The important thing to know is that whenever you type a program name, the shell looks in each of the listed directories in sequence. In other words, when you type ls, the shell will look in each of the directories stored in the PATH variable, starting with the first in the list, to see if the ls program can be found. The first instance it finds is the one it will run. (The ls command gives you a directory listing, as described in the "Listing Files" section later in this chapter.)

But what if you want to run a program that is not contained in a directory listed in your PATH? In this case, you must tell the shell exactly where the program is. Here's an example:

```
/home/keir/myprogram
```

This will run a program called myprogram in the /home/keir directory. It will do this regardless of the directory you're currently browsing, and regardless of whether there is anything else on your system called myprogram.

If you're already in the directory where the program in question is located, you can type the following:

```
./myprogram
```

So, just enter a dot and a forward slash, followed by the program name. The dot tells BASH that what you're referring to is "right here." Like the tilde symbol (~) mentioned earlier, this dot is BASH shorthand.

Getting Help

Each command usually has help built in, which you can query (a little like typing /? after a command when using DOS). This will explain what the command does and how it should be used. In most cases, you'll see an example of the command in use, along with the range of command options that can be used with it. For example, you can get some instant help on the ifconfig command by typing this:

```
ifconfig --help
```

You'll see the help screen shown in Figure 13-2.

The --help option is fairly universal, and most programs will respond to it, although sometimes you might need to use a single dash. Just type the command along with --help to see what happens. You'll be told if you're doing anything wrong.

In addition, most commands have manuals that you can read to gain a fairly complete understanding of how they work. Virtually every Ubuntu setup has a set of these man pages, which can be accessed by typing this:

```
man <command>
```

However, man pages are often technical and designed for experienced Ubuntu users who understand the terminology.

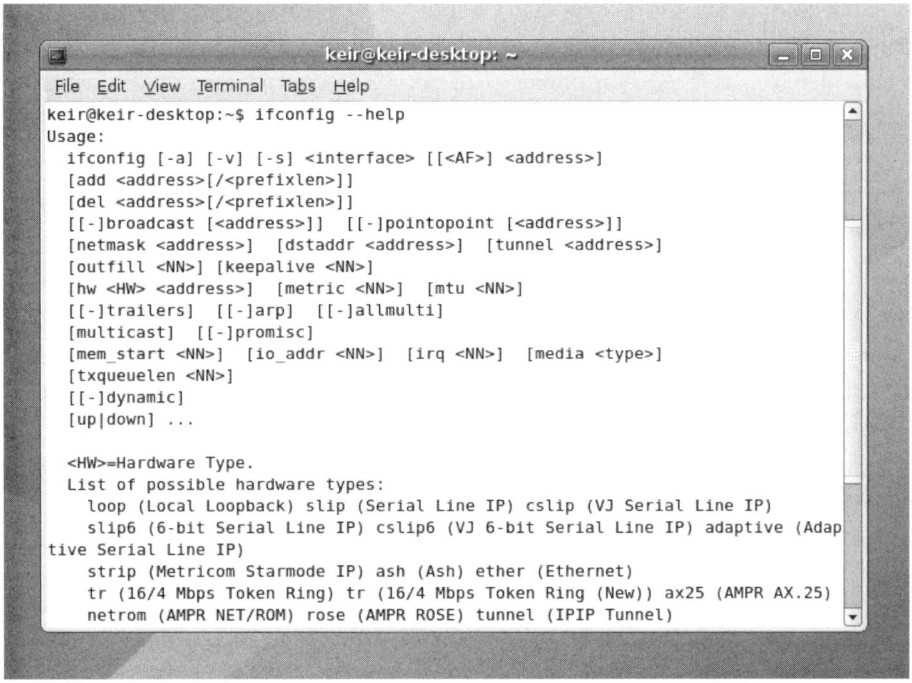

```
keir@keir-desktop: ~                                    _ □ x
File  Edit  View  Terminal  Tabs  Help
keir@keir-desktop:~$ ifconfig --help
Usage:
  ifconfig [-a] [-v] [-s] <interface> [[<AF>] <address>]
  [add <address>[/<prefixlen>]]
  [del <address>[/<prefixlen>]]
  [[-]broadcast [<address>]]  [[-]pointopoint [<address>]]
  [netmask <address>]  [dstaddr <address>]  [tunnel <address>]
  [outfill <NN>] [keepalive <NN>]
  [hw <HW> <address>]  [metric <NN>]  [mtu <NN>]
  [[-]trailers]  [[-]arp]  [[-]allmulti]
  [multicast]  [[-]promisc]
  [mem_start <NN>]  [io_addr <NN>]  [irq <NN>]  [media <type>]
  [txqueuelen <NN>]
  [[-]dynamic]
  [up|down] ...

  <HW>=Hardware Type.
  List of possible hardware types:
    loop (Local Loopback) slip (Serial Line IP) cslip (VJ Serial Line IP)
    slip6 (6-bit Serial Line IP) cslip6 (VJ 6-bit Serial Line IP) adaptive (Adap
tive Serial Line IP)
    strip (Metricom Starmode IP) ash (Ash) ether (Ethernet)
    tr (16/4 Mbps Token Ring) tr (16/4 Mbps Token Ring (New)) ax25 (AMPR AX.25)
    netrom (AMPR NET/ROM) rose (AMPR ROSE) tunnel (IPIP Tunnel)
```

Figure 13-2. *Most commands contain built-in help to give you a clue as to how they're used.*

Some commands also have info pages, which offer slightly more down-to-earth guides. You can read these by typing this:

`info <command>`

If a command isn't covered by the info system, you'll be shown the default screen explaining basic facts about how the info command works.

Note that both man and info have their own man and info pages, explaining how they work. Just type man man or info info. I explain how to read man and info pages in Appendix C.

Running the Shell via a Virtual Console

As noted earlier, you can start the shell in a number of ways. The most common way among Linux diehards is via a virtual console. To access a virtual console, press Ctrl+Alt, and then press one of the function keys from F1 through F6 (the keys at the top of your keyboard).

Using a virtual console is a little like switching desks to a completely different PC. Pressing Ctrl+Alt+F1 will cause your GUI to disappear, and the screen to be taken over by a command-line prompt (don't worry; your GUI is still there and running in the background). You'll be asked to enter your username and your password.

Any programs you run in a virtual console won't affect the rest of the system, unless they're system commands. (As discussed in Chapter 16, one way to rescue a crashed GUI program is to switch to a virtual console and attempt to terminate the program from there.)

You can switch back to the GUI by pressing Ctrl+Alt+F7. Don't forget to quit your virtual console when you're finished with it, by typing exit.

BOOTING INTO THE SHELL

If you're really in love with the shell, you can choose to boot into it, avoiding the GUI completely (although you can later start the GUI by typing startx at the command line).

Booting into the shell is done by defining a custom run level. A *run level* is how the operating mode that Ubuntu is currently running in is described. For example, one particular run level might start a GUI, while another might start only a command prompt.

There are usually seven run levels under Linux, numbered from 0 to 6. Not all of them do something interesting. On Ubuntu, run levels 2 through 5 are all the same. Each runs the GUI. Run level 1 runs a command prompt, so it might seem ideal for booting into the shell, but it also shuts down a few essential services. This means it isn't suitable for day-to-day use.

The trick is to take one of the existing run levels and alter it slightly so that it doesn't run a GUI by default. On many distributions, run level 3 is reserved for this purpose, so it makes sense to alter it under Ubuntu. (For what it's worth, the default Ubuntu run level is 2.)

Stopping Ubuntu from running a GUI upon booting is simply a matter of stopping the program that appears when Ubuntu boots—GDM. This provides the login window that appears and starts the whole graphical subsystem. Type the following command at the shell to remove the shortcut to GDM within the run level 3 configuration:

```
sudo rm /etc/rc3.d/S13GDM
```

After this, you'll need to tell Ubuntu to boot straight to run level 3, rather than the default of 2. You do this by creating the /etc/inittab file, which then becomes one of the first configuration files Ubuntu reads when booting. Issue the following command at the shell to create and then open the file in the Gedit text editor:

```
gksu gedit /etc/inittab
```

Then add the following line at the top of the file:

```
id:3:initdefault:
```

Then save the file. From now on, you'll always boot straight to a BASH prompt. To restore things to the way they were, simply delete the /etc/inittab file by typing the following at the prompt:

```
sudo rm /etc/inittab
```

Working with Files

So let's start actually using the shell. If you've ever used DOS, then you have a head start over most shell beginners, although you'll still need to learn some new commands. Table 13-1 shows various DOS commands alongside their Ubuntu equivalents. This table also serves as a handy guide to some BASH commands, even if you've never used DOS. In Appendix B, you'll find a comprehensive list of useful shell commands, together with explanations of what they do and examples of typical usage.

Table 13-1. *DOS Commands and Their Shell Equivalents*

Command	DOS Command	Linux Shell Command	Usage
Copy files	COPY	cp	cp ⟨*filename*⟩ ⟨*new location*⟩
Move files	MOVE	mv	mv ⟨*filename*⟩ ⟨*new location*⟩
Rename files	RENAME	mv	mv ⟨*old filename*⟩ ⟨*new filename*⟩[1]
Delete files	DEL	rm	rm ⟨*filename*⟩[2]
Create directories	MKDIR	mkdir	mkdir ⟨*directory name*⟩
Delete directories	DELTREE/RMDIR	rm	rm -rf ⟨*directory name*⟩
Change directory	CD	cd	cd ⟨*directory name*⟩
Edit text files	EDIT	vi	vi ⟨*filename*⟩
View text files	TYPE	less	less ⟨*filename*⟩[3]
Print text files	PRINT	lpr	lpr ⟨*filename*⟩
Compare files	FC	diff	diff ⟨*file1*⟩ ⟨*file2*⟩
Find files	FIND	find	find -name ⟨*filename*⟩
Check disk integrity	SCANDISK	fsck	fsck[4]
View network settings	IPCONFIG	ifconfig	ifconfig
Check a network connection	PING	ping	ping ⟨*address*⟩
View a network route	TRACERT	tracepath	tracepath ⟨*address*⟩
Clear screen	CLS	clear	clear
Get help	HELP	man	man ⟨*command*⟩[5]
Quit	EXIT	exit	exit

[1] The BASH shell offers a `rename` command, but this is chiefly used to rename many files at once.

[2] To avoid being asked to confirm each file deletion, you can add the -f option. Be aware that the `rm` command deletes data instantly, without the safety net of the Recycle Bin, as with the GNOME desktop.

[3] Use the cursor keys to move up and down in the document. Type Q to quit.

4 This is a system command and can be run only on a disk that isn't currently in use. To scan the main partition, you'll need to boot from the installation CD and select the rescue option. Then issue the `fsck` command.

[5] The `info` command can also be used.

CREATING ALIASES

If you've ever used DOS, you might find yourself inadvertently typing DOS commands at the shell prompt. Some of these will actually work, because most distribution companies create command aliases to ease the transition of newcomers to Linux.

Aliases mean that whenever you type certain words, they will be interpreted as meaning something else. However, an alias won't work with any of the command-line switches used in DOS. In the long run, you should try to learn the BASH equivalents.

You can create your own command aliases quickly and simply. Just start a BASH shell and type the following:

```
alias <DOS command>='<Linux shell command>'
```

For example, to create an alias that lets you type del instead of rm, type this:

```
alias del='rm'
```

Note that the Ubuntu command must appear in single quotation marks.

To make aliases permanent, you need to add them to your .bashrc file.

Open the file in the Gedit text editor by typing the following:

```
gedit .bashrc
```

At the bottom of the file, add new lines for all the aliases you want to make permanent. Simply type the command shown previously. Save the file when you've finished.

Note that the aliases won't go into effect until you open a new terminal window or reboot the computer.

Listing Files

Possibly the most fundamentally useful BASH command is ls. This will list the files in the current directory, as shown in Figure 13-3. If you have a lot of files, they might scroll off the screen. If you're running GNOME Terminal, you can use the scroll bar on the right side of the window to view the list.

Having the files scroll off the screen can be annoying, so you can cram as many as possible onto each line by typing the following:

```
ls -m
```

The dash after the command indicates that you're using a command option. These are also referred to as command-line *flags* or *switches*. Nearly all shell commands have options like this. In fact, some commands won't do anything unless you specify various options. In the case of the ls command, only one dash is necessary, but some commands need two dashes to indicate an option.

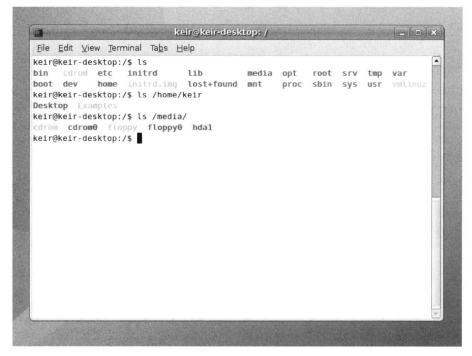

Figure 13-3. *The* ls *command lists the files in the current directory.*

You can see a list of all the command options for ls by typing the following (ironically, itself a command option):

```
ls --help
```

Once again, the output will scroll off the screen, and you can use the window's scroll bars to examine it. (In Chapter 17, you'll learn a trick you can use to be able to read this output without needing to fiddle around with the scroll bars, even if there's screen after screen of it.)

With most commands, you can use many command options at once, as long as they don't contradict each other. For example, you could type the following:

```
ls -lh
```

This tells the ls command to produce "long" output and also to produce "human-readable" output. The long option (-l) lists file sizes and ownership permissions, among other details (permissions are covered in the next chapter). The human-readable option (-h) means that rather than listing files in terms of bytes (such as 1029725 bytes), it will list them in kilobytes and megabytes. Notice that you can simply list the options after the dash; you don't need to give each option its own dash.

■**Caution** Don't forget that case-sensitivity is vitally important in Ubuntu! Typing ls −L is not the same as typing ls −l. It will produce different results.

Copying Files and Directories

Another useful command for dealing with files is cp, which copies files. You can use the cp command in the following way:

```
cp myfile /home/keir/
```

This will copy the file to the location specified.

One important command-line option for cp is −r. This stands for recursive and tells BASH that you want to copy a directory and its contents (as well as any directories within this directory). Most commands that deal with files have a recursive option.

■**Note** Only a handful of BASH commands default to recursive copying. Even though it's extremely common to copy folders, you still need to specify the −r command option most of the time.

One curious trick is that you can copy a file from one place to another but, by specifying a filename in the destination part of the command, change its name. Here's an example:

```
cp myfile /home/keir/myfile2
```

This will copy myfile to /home/keir, but rename it as myfile2. Be careful not to add a final slash to the command when you do this. In the example here, doing so would cause BASH to think that myfile2 is a directory.

This way of copying files is a handy way of duplicating files. By not specifying a new location in the destination part of the command, but still specifying a different filename, you effectively duplicate the file within the same directory:

```
cp myfile myfile2
```

This will result in two identical files: one called myfile and one called myfile2.

Moving Files and Directories

The mv command is similar to cp, except that rather than copying the file, the old one is removed. You can move files from one directory to another, for example, like this:

```
mv myfile /home/keir/
```

You can also use the `mv` command to quickly rename files:

```
mv myfile myfile2
```

Figure 13-4 shows the results of using `mv` to rename a file. The `mv` command can be used to move a directory in the same way as with files. However, there's no need to use a command option to specify recursivity, as with other commands.

For instance, to move the directory `daffodil` into the directory `flowers`, you could type the following (assuming both directories are in the one you're currently browsing):

```
mv daffodil/ flowers/
```

Note the use of the slash after each directory.

To rename directories, simply leave off the slashes. To rename the directory `daffodil` to `hyacinth`, for example, you could type the following:

```
mv daffodil hyacinth
```

■**Note** Getting technical for a moment, moving a file in Linux isn't the same as in Windows, where a file is copied and then the original deleted. Under Ubuntu, the file's absolute path is rewritten, causing it to simply appear in a different place in the file structure. However, the end result is the same.

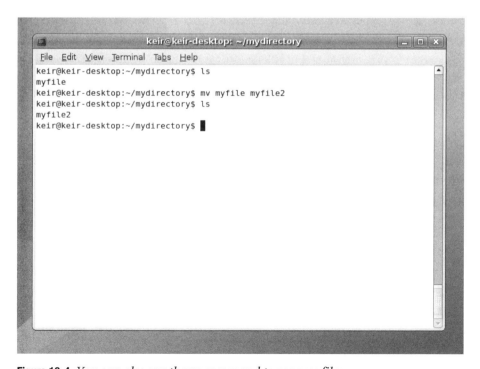

Figure 13-4. *You can also use the* mv *command to rename files.*

Deleting Files and Directories

But how do you get rid of files? Again, this is relatively easy, but first a word of caution: the shell doesn't operate any kind of Recycle Bin. Once a file is deleted, it's gone forever. (There are utilities you can use to recover files, but these are specialized tools and aren't to be relied on for day-to-day use.)

Removing a file is achieved by typing something like this:

```
rm myfile
```

It's as simple as that.

In some instances, you'll be asked to confirm the deletion after you issue the command. If you want to delete a file without being asked to confirm it, type the following:

```
rm -f myfile
```

The f stands for force (that is, force the deletion).

If you try to use the rm command to remove a directory, you'll see an error message. This is because the command needs an additional option:

```
rm -rf mydirectory
```

As noted earlier, the r stands for recursive and indicates that any folder specified afterward should be deleted, in addition to any files it contains.

■**Tip** You might have used wildcards within Windows and DOS. They can be used within Ubuntu, too. For example, the asterisk (*) can be used to mean any file. So, you can type rm -f * to delete all files within a directory, or type rm -f myfile* to delete all files that start with the word myfile. But remember to be careful with the rm command. Keep in mind that you cannot salvage files easily if you accidentally delete them!

WORKING WITH FILES WITH SPACES IN THEM

If, at the command prompt, you try to copy, move or otherwise manipulate files that have spaces in their names, you'll run into problems. For example, suppose you want to move the file picture from germany.jpg to the directory mydirectory. In theory the following command should do the trick:

```
mv picture from germany.jpg mydirectory/
```

But when I tried it on my test Ubuntu setup, I got the following errors:

```
mv: cannot stat 'picture': No such file or directory
mv: cannot stat 'from': No such file or directory
mv: cannot stat 'germany.jpg': No such file or directory
```

In other words, BASH had interpreted each word as a separate file and tried to move each of them! The error messages tell us that BASH cannot find the file `picture`, `from`, or `germany.jpg`.

There are two solutions. The easiest is to enclose the filename in quotation marks ("), so the previous command would read as follows:

```
mv "picture from germany.jpg" mydirectory/
```

The other solution is to precede each space with a backslash. This tells BASH you're including a *literal character* in the filename. In other words, you're telling BASH not to interpret the space in the way it normally does, which is as a separator between filenames or commands. Here's how the command looks if you use backslashes:

```
mv picture\ from\ germany.jpg mydirectory/
```

The backslash can also be used to stop BASH from interpreting other symbols in the way it normally does. For example, the less than and greater than symbols (`<>`) have a specific meaning in BASH, which I discuss in Chapter 17, but they're allowed in filenames. So to copy the file `<bach>.mp3` to the directory `mydirectory`, you could type:

```
cp \<bach\>.mp3 mydirectory/
```

Generally speaking, however, simply enclosing filenames in quotation marks is the easiest approach.

Changing and Creating Directories

Another handy command is `cd`, for change directory. This lets you move around the file system, from directory to directory. Say you're in a directory that has another directory in it, named `mydirectory2`. Switching to it is easy:

```
cd mydirectory2
```

But how do you get out of this directory once you're in it? Try the following command:

```
cd ..
```

The `..` refers to the "parent" directory, which is the one containing the directory you're currently browsing. Using two dots to indicate this may seem odd, but it's just the way that Ubuntu (and Unix before it) does things. It's one of the many conventions that Unix relies on and that you'll pick up as you go along.

You can create directories with the `mkdir` command:

```
mkdir mydirectory
```

What if you want to create a new directory and, at the same time, create a new directory to contain it? Simply use the -p command option. The following command will create a new folder called flowers and, at the same time, create a directory within flowers called daffodil:

```
mkdir -p flowers/daffodil
```

Summary

This chapter introduced the command-line shell, considered by many to be the heart of Linux. We've discussed its similarities to MS-DOS, and shown that these are only cursory; knowledge of DOS doesn't equate to skill within BASH. In the long run, you should work to polish your BASH skills.

This chapter also introduced some elementary commands used within BASH, such as those used to provide directory listings and to copy files. We looked at how you can use command-line options to control BASH tools. In many cases, these are mandatory, so you learned how the BASH shell itself can be used to investigate a command and find out vital information about how it works.

At this point, your newfound knowledge will have no doubt caused you to venture into the Ubuntu file system itself, which can be a confusing, if not terrifying, place for the inexperienced. But don't worry. The next chapter explains everything you need to know about the file system and what you'll find in it.

■ ■ ■

## CHAPTER 14

Understanding Linux Files and Users

Most of us are used to dealing with files—the things that live on our hard disks, floppies, and DVD-ROMs, and contain data and program code. It should come as no surprise that Linux has its own file structure, which is different from Windows, in terms of where data is stored and also the underlying technology.

Taking a page from Unix, Ubuntu takes the concept of the file system to an extreme. To Ubuntu, almost everything is treated as a file: your PC's hardware, network computers connected to your PC, information about the current state of your computer—almost everything finds a home within the Linux file system.

Linux places an equal emphasis on the users of the system. They own the various files and can decide who can and cannot access various files that they create or that are transferred to their ownership.

In this chapter, we'll delve into users, files, and permissions. You'll be introduced to how Ubuntu handles files and how files are tied into the system of user accounts.

Real Files and Virtual Files

Linux sees virtually everything as a series of files. This might sound absurd and certainly requires further explanation.

Let's start with the example of plugging in a piece of hardware. Whenever you attach something to a USB socket, the Linux kernel finds it, sees if it can make the hardware work, and if everything checks out okay, it will usually make the hardware available as a file under the /dev directory on your hard disk (dev is short for devices). Figure 14-1 shows an example of a /dev directory.

The file created in the /dev directory is not a real file, of course. It's a file system shortcut plumbed through to the input and output components of the hardware you've just attached.

■**Note** As a user, you're not expected to delve into the /dev directory and deal with this hardware directly. Most of the time, you'll use various software packages that will access the hardware for you or use special BASH commands or GUI programs to make the hardware available in a more accessible way for day-to-day use.

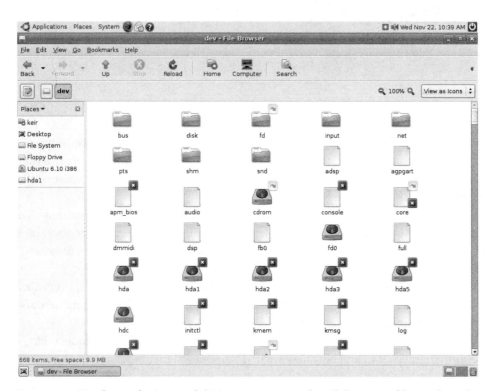

Figure 14-1. *Hardware devices under Linux are accessed as if they were files and can be found in the /dev folder.*

Here's another example. Say you're working in an office, and you want to connect to a central file server. To do this under Linux, you must *mount* the files that the server offers, making it a part of the Ubuntu file system. Doing this involves creating an empty directory (or using one that already exists) and using the mount command at the BASH shell to make the server's contents magically appear whenever that directory is accessed. We'll discuss how this is done later in this chapter, in the "Mounting" section.

■**Note** Bear in mind that, in most cases, Ubuntu takes care of mounting automatically, as discussed in Chapter 12. For example, when you try to connect to a shared folder by clicking Places ➤ Network Servers, Ubuntu will automatically handle the mounting of the shared folder.

Once the network server is mounted, it is treated exactly like a directory on your hard disk. You can copy files to and from it, just as you would normally, using the same tools as you use for dealing with any other files. In fact, less knowledgeable users won't even be aware that they're accessing something that isn't located on their PC's hard disk (or, technically speaking, within their Ubuntu partition and file system).

By treating everything as a file, Linux makes system administration easier. To probe and test your hardware, for example, you can use the same tools you use to manipulate files.

So how do you know which files are real and which are virtual? One method is to use the following command, which was introduced in the previous chapter:

```
ls -l
```

The -l option tells the ls command to list nearly all the details about the files. If you do this in GNOME Terminal, you'll see that the listing is color-coded. There are many different combinations of colors, but Table 14-1 shows some typical examples that you're likely to come across.

The ls -l command returns a lot of additional information, including who owns which file and what you and others can do with it. This requires an understanding of users and file permissions, which we'll discuss next.

■**Tip** The command ls -la will give you even more information—perhaps too much for general use. In most instances, ls -l should show enough information.

Table 14-1. *Color-Coding Within GNOME Terminal*

Color	Type of File
Black text	Standard file
Light-blue text	Directory
Black outline with yellow text	Virtual device[1]
Green text	Program or script[2]
Cyan text	Symbolic link to another file[3]
Pink text	Image file
Red text	Archive[4]

[1] *This is found only in the /dev directory.*
[2] *Technically speaking, green text indicates a program or script that has merely been marked as being executable.*
[3] *This is similar to a Windows desktop shortcut.*
[4] *Installation files are also marked red, because they're usually contained in archives.*

Users and File Permissions

The concept of users and permissions is as important to Ubuntu as the idea of a central and all-encompassing file system. In fact, the two are implicitly linked.

When initially installing Linux, you should have created at least one user account. By now, this will have formed the day-to-day login that you use to access Linux and run programs.

Although you might not realize it, as a user, you also belong to a group. In fact, every user on the system belongs to a group. Under Ubuntu, ordinary users belong to a group based on their usernames (under other versions of Linux, you might find that you belong to a group called users).

■**Note** Groups are yet another reminder of Ubuntu's Unix origins. Unix is often used on huge computer systems with hundreds or thousands of users. Putting each user into a group makes the system administrator's job a lot easier. When controlling system resources, the administrator can control groups of users rather than hundreds of individual users. On most home user PCs, the concept of groups is a little redundant, because there's normally a single user, or at most, two or three. However, the concept of groups is central to the way that Linux handles files.

A standard user account under Ubuntu is normally limited in what it can do. As a standard user, you can save files to your own private area of the disk, located in the /home directory, but usually nowhere else. You can move around the file system, but some directories are strictly out of bounds. In a similar way, some files can be opened as read-only, so you cannot save changes to them. All of this is enforced using file permissions.

Every file and directory is owned by a user. In addition, files and directories have three separate settings that indicate who within the Linux system can read them, who can write to them, and, if the file in question is "runnable" (usually a program or a script), who can run it (execute it). In the case of directories, it's also possible to set who can browse them, as well as who can write files to them. If you try to access a file or directory for which you don't have permission, you'll be turned away with an "access denied" error message.

ROOT VS. SUDO

Most versions of Linux have two types of user accounts: standard and root. Standard users are those who can run programs on the system but are limited in what they can do. Root users have complete run of the system, and as such, are often referred to as "superusers." They can access and/or delete whatever files they want. They can configure hardware, change settings, and so on.

Most versions of Linux create a user account called root and let users log in as root to perform system maintenance. However, for practical as well as security reasons, most of the time the user is logged in as a standard user.

Ubuntu is different in that it does away with the root account. Instead, it allows certain users, including the one created during installation, to temporarily adopt root-like powers. You will already have encountered this when configuring hardware. As you've seen, all you need to do is type your password when prompted in order to administer the system.

This way of working is referred to as *sudo*, which is short for "superuser do." In fact, the command sudo will let you adopt root powers at the shell prompt—simply preface any command with sudo in order to run it with root privileges. (A different command is normally used if you want to run graphical applications from the shell prompt—gksu. However, the effect is the same.) Ubuntu remembers when you last used sudo too, so that it won't annoy you by asking you again for your password wtihin 15 minutes of its first use. You can avoid this grace period by typing sudo -k.

In some ways, the sudo system is slightly less secure than using a standard root account. But it's also a lot simpler. It reduces the chance of serious errors, too. Any command or tweak that can cause damage will invariably require administrative powers, and therefore require you to type your password or preface the command with sudo. This serves as a warning and prevents mistakes.

If you're an experienced Linux user and want to invoke the root account, simply type the following at the command prompt:

```
sudo passwd root
```

Then, type a password. If you subsequently want to deactivate the root account, type this:

```
sudo passwd -l root
```

If you ever want to slip into the root account for a short period, even if you haven't followed the previous instructions to activate the root account login, you can do so by typing the following:

```
sudo su
```

You'll be prompted to type your password; do so. When you've finished, type exit to return to your standard user account.

Viewing Permissions

When you issue the ls -l command, each file is listed on an individual line. Here's an example of one line of a file listing from my test PC:

```
-rw-r--r--   2 keir keir 673985982 2006-11-31 17:19 myfile
```

The r, w, and – symbols on the very left of the listing indicate the file permissions. The permission list usually consists of the characters r (for read), w (for write), x (for execute), or - (meaning none are applicable).

They're followed by a number indicating the link count, which indicates how many hard/soft links have been made to the file, but you can ignore this for the moment (for more information about file links, see the "Creating File Links" sidebar).

After this is listed the owner of the file (keir in the example) and then the group that also has permission to access the file (in this case, the group is also called keir). This is followed by the file size (in bytes), the date and time the file was last accessed, and finally, the filename itself appears.

The file permissions part of the listing might look confusing, but it's actually quite simple. To understand what's going on, you need to split it into groups of four, as illustrated in Figure 14-2.

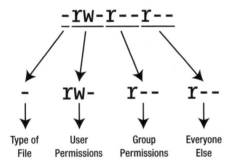

Figure 14-2. *The file permissions part of a file listing can be broken down into four separate parts.*

The four groups are as follows:

Type of file: This character represents the file type. A standard data file is indicated with a dash (-). Most files on your system fall into this category. A d shows that the entry is not a file but a directory. Table 14-2 lists the file type codes.

User permissions: Next come the permissions of the person who owns the file. The three characters indicate what the person who owns the file can do with it. The owner of a file is usually the user who created it, although it's also possible to change the owner later on. In this example, you see rw-. This means that the owner of the file can read (r) and write (w) the file. In other words, he can look at it and also save changes to it. However, there's a dash afterward, and this indicates that the user cannot execute the file. If this were possible, there would be an x in this spot instead.

Group permissions: After the owner's permissions are the permissions given to the specified group. This is indicated by another three characters in the same style as those for user permissions. In the example, the group's permission is r--, which means that the members of the specified group can read the file but don't have permission to write to it, since there's a dash where the w would normally appear. In other words, as far as they're concerned, the file is read-only.

Everyone else's permissions: The last set of permissions indicates the permissions of everyone else on the system (other users in other groups). In the example, they can only read the file (r); the two dashes afterward indicate that they cannot write to the file nor execute it.

Table 14-2. *File Type Codes*

Code	File Type
-	Standard file
d	Standard directory
l	Symbolic link (a shortcut to another file)
p	Named pipe (a file that acts as a conduit for data between two programs)
s	Socket (a file designed to send and receive data over a network)
c	Character device (a hardware device driver, usually found in /dev)
b	Block device (a hardware device driver, usually found in /dev)

As you might remember from Windows, programs are stored as files on your hard disk, just like standard data files. On Linux, program files need to be explicitly marked as being executable. This is indicated in the permission listing by an x. Therefore, if there's no x in a file's permissions, it's a good bet that the file in question isn't a program or script (although this isn't always true for various technical reasons).

To make matters a little more confusing, if the entry in the list of files is a directory (indicated by a d), then the rules are different. In this case, an x indicates that the user can access that directory. If there's no x, then the user's attempts to browse to that directory will be met with an "access denied" message.

File permissions can be difficult to understand, so let's look at a few real-world examples. These examples assume that you're logged in to Linux as the user keir.

> ### LESS COMMON FILE PERMISSIONS
>
> Instead of the x or dash in the list of permissions for a directory, you might sometimes see a t. This is referred to as the "sticky bit" and means that the only people who can delete or alter a file in that directory are the users who created the file in the first place. This is a useful option to have in some circumstances. It's used with the /tmp (temporary) folder, for example, to ensure that one user can't delete another user's temporary files but is able to delete his own temporary files. To set the sticky bit for a directory, type chmod +t *directoryname*.
>
> You might sometimes see a set of permissions like rws. The s stands for "set user id" and is often referred to as the "suid bit". Like x, it indicates that the file is executable, except in this case, it means that the file will be run with the permissions of the person who owns it, rather than the user who is executing it. In other words, if user frank tries to run a program owned by keir that has the execute permission set as s, that program will be run as if keir were running it. This is very useful, because it can make programs that require root powers usable by ordinary users, although this brings with it obvious security risks.
>
> To set the suid bit, type chmod +s *filename*. However, it's very unlikely you'll ever need to use this command.

Typical Data File Permissions

Here's the first example:

```
-rw-rw----  2 keir keir 1450 2006-07-07 09:19 myfile2
```

You see immediately that this file is owned by user keir, because that username appears directly after the permissions. You also see that the group keir has access to the file, although precisely how much depends on the permissions.

Reading the file permissions from left to right, you see that the initial character is a dash. That indicates that this is an ordinary file and has no special characteristics. It's also not a directory.

After that is the first part of the permissions, rw-. These are the permissions for the owner of the file, keir. You're logged in as that user, so this file belongs to you, and these permissions apply to you. You can read and write the file but not execute it. Because you cannot execute the file, you can infer that this is a data file rather than a program (there are certain exceptions to this rule, but we'll ignore them for the sake of simplicity).

Following this is the next part of the file permissions, rw-. This tells you what members of the group called keir can do with the file. It's fairly useless information if you're the only user of your PC, but for the record, you're told that anyone else belonging to the group called keir can also read and write the file but not execute it. If you're not the only user of a computer, group permissions can be important. The "Altering Permissions" section, coming up shortly, describes how to change file permissions to control who can access files.

Finally, the last three characters tell you the permissions of everyone else on the system. The three dashes (---) mean that they have no permissions at all regarding the file. There's a dash where the r normally appears, so they cannot even read it. The dashes afterward tell you they cannot write to the file or execute it. If they try to do anything with the file, they'll get a "permission denied" error.

Permissions on a User's Directory

Here's example number two:

```
drwxr-xr-x   7  keir  keir  824  2006-07-07  10:01  mydirectory
```

The list of permissions starts with d, which tells you that this isn't a file but a directory. After this is the list of permissions for the owner of the directory (keir), who can read files in the directory and also create new ones there. The x indicates that you can access this directory, as opposed to being turned away with an "access denied" message. You might think being able to access the directory is taken for granted if the user can read and write to it, but that's not the case.

Next are the permissions for the group members. They can read files in the directory but not write any new ones there (although they can modify files already in there, provided the permissions of the individual files allow this). Once again, there's an x at the end of their particular permission listing, which indicates that the group members can access the directory.

Following the group's permissions are those of everyone else. They can read the directory and browse it, but not write new files to it, as with the group users' permissions.

Permissions on a Directory Owned by Root

Here's the last example:

```
drwx------   25  root  root  1000  2004-08-06  15:44  root
```

You can see that the file is owned by root. Remember that in this example, you're logged in as keir and your group is keir.

The list of permissions starts with a d, so you can tell that this is actually a directory. After this, you see that the owner of the directory, root, has permission to read, write, and access the directory.

Next are the permissions for the group: three dashes. In other words, members of the group called root have no permission to access this directory in any way. They cannot browse it, create new files in it, or even access it.

Following this are the permissions for the rest of the users. This includes you, because you're not the user root and don't belong to its group. The three dashes means you don't have permission to read, write, or access this directory. In other words, it's out of bounds to you, probably because it contains files that only the root user should access!

SWITCHING USERS

If you have more than one user set up on your system, it's possible to switch users on the fly while you're working at the shell. On my test PC, I have an additional user account called frank. While logged in as any user, I can temporarily switch to this user by typing the following command, which stands for substitute user:

```
su frank
```

I'll then be asked for user frank's password. Once this is typed, I will effectively have logged in as user frank. Any files I create will be saved with frank's ownership.

If you created a root account (by using the command sudo passwd root), you can temporarily switch into it by typing just su, without any username afterward.

To return to your own account from any other account, type exit.

Altering Permissions

You can easily change permissions of files and directories by using the chmod command. For example, if you want to change a file so that everyone on the system can read and write to it, type the following:

```
chmod a+rw myfile
```

In other words, you're adding read and write (rw) permissions for all users (a), including the owner, the group, and everybody else. Here's another example:

```
chmod a-w myfile
```

This tells Linux that you want to take away (-) the ability of all users (a) to write (w) to the file. However, you want to leave the other permissions as they are.

■Tip If you leave out the a, chmod assumes you mean "all". In other words, commands like chmod a+r myfile and chmod +r myfile do the same thing.

If you specify u, you can change permissions just for the owner (u is for "user", which is the same as "owner"):

```
chmod u+rw
```

This will add (+) read/write (rw) permissions for the owner.

As you might already have guessed, you can substitute a g to change group permissions:

```
chmod g-rw
```

This will configure the file so that members of the group that owns the file can't read or write to it. Using an o, which is for "others", will configure the file permissions for those who aren't the owner of the file or who are not in the group that owns the file—the last three digits of the permission list.

A typical day-to-day use of chmod is in making a program file that you've downloaded executable. Because of the way the Internet works, if you download a program to install on your computer, it can lose its executable status while in transit. In this case, issue the following command:

```
chmod u+x myprogram
```

This will configure the file so that the owner (u) can execute (x) it.

Changing the Ownership of a File

To change the owner of a file, use the chown command. For security reasons, this must be prefaced with the sudo command, which is to say that chown and chgrp (to change the group ownership) require superuser powers.

For example, to set the owner of myfile as frank, type this command:

```
sudo chown frank myfile
```

You can also change the owner *and* the group of a file using chown. Simply type each separated by a period:

```
sudo chown frank.mygroup myfile
```

This will change myfile so that its owner is frank and its group is mygroup.

To change just the group of a file, you can use the chgrp command in exactly the same way as chown:

```
sudo chgrp mygroup myfile
```

CREATING FILE SHORTCUTS

I touched upon the idea of file system shortcuts in Chapter 12, when I discussed creating launchers on the GNOME desktop. The problem with launchers is that they are only recognized within GNOME. In other words, they mean nothing when you're using the command prompt (or virtually every other program that loads/saves files, with the exception of some programs created specially for the GNOME desktop environment).

The Ubuntu file system offers two types of genuine shortcuts, which it refers to as *file links*. They are *symbolic links* and *hard links*. Both are created using the `ln` command.

Symbolic links are the most commonly used. A symbolic link is the most similar to a Windows shortcut in that a small file is created that "points toward" another file. Unlike a Windows shortcut, the symbolic link file exists at the file system level, so it can't be viewed in a text editor, for example.

You can spot a symbolic link in a file listing, because it will be followed by an arrow and then the name and path (if necessary) of the file it links to. For example, in your `/home` directory, the directory `Examples` is symbolically linked to `/usr/share/example-content`. When you type `ls -l`, it appears as follows:

```
Examples -> /usr/share/example-content
```

A hard link is more complex and needs some understanding of how files work. In simple terms, all files consist of a pointer and actual data. As you might expect, the pointer tells the file system where on the disk to find the data. Creating a hard link effectively creates an additional pointer to the data that has exactly the same attributes as the original pointer, except with a different name. Performing any operation on the linked file will perform that operation on the original file. Additionally, there will be no obvious sign the hard link isn't actually a genuine file, apart from the fact that the *link count*—the number after the file permissions—will be more than 1. This indicates that more than one file *links* to the data. Maybe now you can see why people prefer to use the more obviously detectable symbolic links!

To create a symbolic link, the `-s` command option is used with the `ln` command. First, specify the original file and then the new link's name. Here's an example, followed immediately by the output of the `ls -l` command, which shows the results:

```
ln -s original_file link
ls -l
lrwxrwxrwx 1 keir keir 13 2006-11-22 12:05 link -> original_file
-rw-r--r-- 1 keir keir  0 2006-11-21 15:30 original_file
```

The new link has odd file permissions. It claims to have read/write/execute permissions for everybody (`rwxrwxrwx`) but actually, because it's a link, it mirrors the permissions of the file it links to. So if you attempt to access a shortcut that links to a file you don't have permission to access, you'll see the appropriate error message.

To create a hard link, simply use `ln` on its own:

```
ln original_file link
```

As mentioned, apart from the link count, there will be no obvious sign the new link is, in fact, a link:

```
-rw-r--r--   2 keir keir  0 2006-11-21 15:30 original_file
-rw-r--r--   2 keir keir  0 2006-11-21 15:30 link
```

The hard link adopts all the properties of the file, including its permissions and date/time of creation. It even has the same link count!

The File System Explained

Now that you understand the principles of files and users, we can take a bird's-eye view of the Linux file system and start to make sense of it.

You might already have ventured beyond the /home directory and wandered through the file system. You no doubt found it thoroughly confusing, largely because it's not like anything you're used to. The good news is that it's not actually very hard to understand. If nothing else, you should be aware that nearly everything can be ignored during everyday use.

■**Note** The Ubuntu file system is referred to as a *hierarchical* file system. This means that it consists of a lot of directories that contain files. Windows also uses a hierarchical file system. Ubuntu refers to the very bottom level of the file system as the root. This has no connection with the root user.

You can switch to the root of the file system by typing the following shell command:

```
cd /
```

When used on its own, the forward slash is interpreted as a shortcut for root.

If I do this on my PC and then ask for a long file listing (ls -l), I see the following:

```
total 108
drwxr-xr-x   2 root root  4096 2006-11-14 04:29 bin
drwxr-xr-x   3 root root  4096 2006-11-14 04:27 boot
lrwxrwxrwx   1 root root    11 2006-11-14 04:20 cdrom -> media/cdrom
drwxr-xr-x  12 root root 13500 2006-11-22 05:44 dev
drwxr-xr-x 102 root root  4096 2006-11-22 11:35 etc
drwxr-xr-x   3 root root  4096 2006-11-14 04:26 home
drwxr-xr-x   2 root root  4096 2006-10-25 09:26 initrd
lrwxrwxrwx   1 root root    33 2006-11-14 04:27 initrd.img -> boot/ ➡
```

```
initrd.img-2.6.17-10-generic
drwxr-xr-x  17 root root  4096 2006-11-14 04:29 lib
drwxr-xr-x   2 root root 49152 2006-11-14 04:20 lost+found
drwxr-xr-x   5 root root  4096 2006-10-25 09:26 media
drwxr-xr-x   2 root root  4096 2006-10-19 18:49 mnt
drwxr-xr-x   2 root root  4096 2006-10-25 09:26 opt
dr-xr-xr-x  94 root root     0 2006-11-22 00:43 proc
drwxr-xr-x   7 root root  4096 2006-11-22 11:14 root
drwxr-xr-x   2 root root  4096 2006-11-14 04:28 sbin
drwxr-xr-x   2 root root  4096 2006-10-25 09:26 srv
drwxr-xr-x  11 root root     0 2006-11-22 00:43 sys
drwxrwxrwt  12 root root  4096 2006-11-22 11:00 tmp
drwxr-xr-x  11 root root  4096 2006-10-25 09:26 usr
drwxr-xr-x  15 root root  4096 2006-10-25 09:39 var
lrwxrwxrwx   1 root root    30 2006-11-14 04:27 vmlinuz -> boot/ ➡
vmlinuz-2.6.17-10-generic
```

The first thing you'll notice from this is that the root of the file system contains largely directories and that all files and directories are owned by root.

Only users with administrative powers can write files to the root of the file system. That means if you wanted to write to the root of the file system or otherwise access those files, you would need to use the sudo command. This is to prevent damage, since most of the directories in the root of the file system are vital to the correct running of Linux and contain essential programs or data.

■**Caution** It's incredibly easy to slip up when using the command-line shell and thereby cause a lot of damage. For example, simply mistyping a forward slash in a command can mean the difference between deleting the files in a directory and deleting the directory itself. This is just another reason why you should always be careful when working at the command line, especially if you use the sudo command.

As you can see from the file permissions of each directory in the root of the file system, most directories allow all users to browse them and access the files within (the last three characters of the permissions read r-x). You just won't be able to write new files there or delete the directories themselves. You might be able to modify or execute programs contained within the directory, but this will depend on the permissions of each individual file.

Table 14-3 provides a brief description of what each directory and file in the Ubuntu root file system contains. This is for reference only; there's no need for you to learn this information. The Ubuntu file system broadly follows the principles in the Filesystem Hierarchy Standard, as do most versions of Linux, but it does have its own subtleties.

Table 14-3. *Directories and Files in the Ubuntu Root File System*

Directory	Contents
bin	Vital tools necessary to get the system running or for use when repairing the system and diagnosing problems
boot	Boot loader programs and configuration files (the boot loader is the menu that appears when you first boot Linux)
cdrom -> media/cdrom	Symbolic link (shortcut) to the entry for the CD- or DVD-ROM drive in the /dev folder (accessing this file will let you access the CD- or DVD-ROM drive)
dev	Virtual files representing hardware installed on your system
etc	Central repository of configuration files for your system
home	Where each user's personal directory is stored
initrd	Used during booting to mount the initial ramdisk
initrd.img -> boot/ initrd.img-2.6.17-10-generic	Symbolic link to the initial ramdisk, which is used to boot Linux
lib	Shared system files used by Linux as well as the software that runs on it
lost+found	Folder where salvaged scraps of files are saved in the event of a problematic shutdown and subsequent file system check
media	Where the directories representing various mounted storage systems are made available (including Windows partitions on the disk)
mnt	Directory in which external file systems can be temporarily mounted
opt	Software that is theoretically optional and not vital to the running of the system (many software packages you use daily can be found here)
proc	Virtual directory containing data about your system and its current status
root	The root user's personal directory
sbin	Programs essential to administration of the system
srv	Configuration files for any network servers you might have running on your system
sys	Mount point of the sysfs file system, which is used by the kernel to administer your system's hardware
tmp	Temporary files stored by the system

Table 14-3. *Directories and Files in the Ubuntu Root File System (Continued)*

Directory	Contents
usr	Programs and data that might be shared with other systems (such as in a large networking setup with many users)[1]
var	Used by the system to store data that is constantly updated, such as printer spooling output
vmlinuz -> boot/ vmlinuz-2.6.17-10-generic	Symbolic link to the kernel file used during bootup

[1] *The usr directory contains its own set of directories that are full of programs and data. Many system programs, such as the X11 GUI software, are located within the /usr directory. Note that the /usr directory is used even if your system will never act as a server to other systems.*

TYPES OF FILE SYSTEMS

Linux is all about choice, and this extends to the technology that makes the file system work. Unlike with Windows, where the only choice is NTFS, Linux offers many different types of file system technology. Each is designed for varying tasks. Most are scalable, however, which means that they will work just as happily on a desktop PC as on a massive cluster of computers.

Ubuntu uses the ext3 file system. This is a popular choice among distros, and nearly all home- or office-oriented distros use it. That said, people are constantly arguing about which file system is best. The principal measuring stick is performance. Your computer spends a lot of time writing and reading files, so the faster a file system is, the faster your PC will be overall (although, in reality, the hardware is of equal importance).

Note that what we're talking about here is the underlying and invisible technology of the file system. In day-to-day use, the end user won't be aware of any difference between ext3, reiserfs, or another file system technology (although when things go wrong, different tools are used to attempt repairs; their selection is automated within Ubuntu).

Here are the various types along with notes about what they offer:

- **ext2:** Fast, stable, and well established, ext2 was once the most popular type of file system technology used on Linux. It has now been eclipsed by ext3.

- **ext3:** An extension of ext2, ext3 allows journaling, a way of recording what has been written to disk so that a recovery can be attempted when things go wrong.

- **reiserfs:** This is another journaling file system, which claims to be faster than others and also offers better security features.

- **jfs:** This is a journaling file system created by IBM. It's used on industrial implementations of Unix.

- **xfs:** This is a 64-bit journaling file system created by Silicon Graphics, Inc. (SGI) and used on its own version of Unix, as well as Linux.

Mounting

Described in technical terms, mounting is the practice of making a file system available under Linux. Whereas Windows uses drive letters to make other file systems available within Windows Explorer, Linux integrates the new file system within the root file system, usually by making the contents appear whenever a particular directory is accessed. The mounted file system can be a partition on your hard disk, a CD-ROM, a network server, or many other things.

Mounting drives might seem a strange concept, but it actually makes everything much simpler than it might be otherwise. For example, once a drive is mounted, you don't need to use any special commands or software to access its contents. You can use the same programs and tools that you use to access all of your other files. Mounting creates a level playing field on which everything is equal and can therefore be accessed quickly and efficiently.

Using the mount Command

At the command line, mounting is done via the mount command. Under Ubuntu, you must have administrator powers to use the mount command, which means prefacing it with sudo and providing your password when prompted.

With most modern versions of Linux, mount can be used in two ways: by specifying all the settings immediately after the command or by making reference to an entry within the fstab file. fstab stands for File System Table, and that gives an indication of what it's used for—it's a look-up file stored in the /etc directory that contains details of all file systems on the PC that are regularly mounted. Figure 14-3 shows an example of a typical fstab file.

■**Note** The root file system is itself mounted automatically during bootup, shortly after the kernel has started and has all your hardware up and running. If you look within /etc/fstab, you'll see that it too has its own entry, as does the swap partition. Every file system that Linux uses must be mounted at some point.

Let's say that you insert a CD or DVD into your computer's DVD-ROM drive. To mount the CD or DVD and make it available to Linux (something that is actually done automatically as soon as you put a disk in the drive, so this example is for demonstration purposes only), you would type the following:

```
sudo mount /media/cdrom
```

The mount command first looks in your fstab file to find what you're referring to. It then matches up the directory you've specified as the mount point against the hardware details, in the form of a UUID number, which is then translated by Ubuntu into a file within the /dev directory. The two are then magically connected together.

Note that the contents of the mounted file system are made available in a virtual way. The files are not literally copied into the directory. The directory is merely a conduit that allows you to read the CD's contents.

There aren't any special commands used to work with drives that have been mounted. The shell commands discussed in Chapter 13 should do everything you need, and Nautilus will have no trouble browsing its contents.

The mount command doesn't see widespread usage by most users nowadays, because most removable storage devices like CDs, and even memory card readers, are mounted automatically under Ubuntu, and an icon for them appears on the desktop. However, there may be occasions when you need to mount a drive manually.

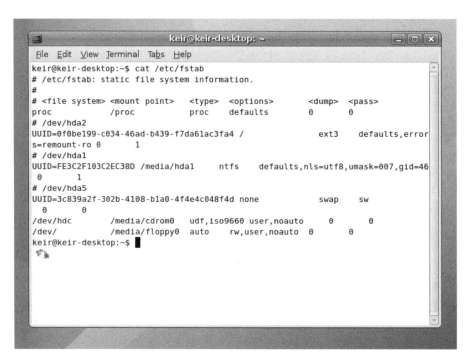

Figure 14-3. *Details of all frequently mounted file systems are held in the* /etc/fstab *file.*

Mounting a Drive Manually

Let's look at an example of when you might need to mount a drive manually. Suppose that you've just added a second hard disk to your PC that has previously been used on a Windows system, and you want to salvage some data before formatting the disk. Let's also assume the new disk has been added as the slave on the primary IDE channel, which is the usual method of adding a second disk to an IDE-based computer.

■Tip To learn more about installing hard disks, see `www.computerhope.com/issues/ch000413.htm`.

Here are the steps you would typically follow:

1. The first thing to do is create a *mount point*, which is a directory that will act as a location where you can tell `mount` to make the disk accessible.

■Note The mount point doesn't necessarily have to be empty or new! You can use any directory as a mount point, and as long as the file system is mounted, the original contents of the directory will be invisible. However, to avoid confusion, it's best to create a new independent mount point.

You can create the new directory anywhere, but under Ubuntu, the convention is to create it in the `/media` directory. Therefore, the following command should do the trick (note that you need to use the `sudo` command, because writing to any directory other than your `/home` directory requires administrator privileges):

```
sudo mkdir /media/newdisk
```

2. You now need to know what kind of partition type is used on the disk, because you need to specify this when mounting. To find this out, use the `fdisk` command. Type the following exactly as it appears:

```
sudo fdisk -l /dev/hdb
```

3. This will list the partitions on the second disk drive (assuming an average PC system). With most hard disks used under Windows, you should find a single partition that will be either NTFS or FAT32. The examples here assume that this is `hdb1`.

■Caution Be aware that `fdisk` is a dangerous system command that can damage your system. The program is designed to partition disks and can wipe out your data if you're not careful!

---

4. With this information in hand, you're now ready to mount the disk. For a FAT32 disk, type the following:

```
sudo mount -t vfat –o umask=000 /dev/hdb1 /media/newdisk
```

For an NTFS disk, type the following:

```
sudo mount -t ntfs -o umask=0222 /dev/hdb1 /media/newdisk
```

The -t command option is used to specify the file system type. The -o flag indicates that you're going to specify some more command options, and you do so in the form of umask, which tells mount to ensure that the directory is readable (and writable in the case of the FAT32 drive). After this, you specify the relevant file in the /dev directory (this file is only virtual, of course, and merely represents the hardware), and then specify the directory that is acting as your mount point.

▪Note Although the fstab file refers to UUID numbers, for a temporary mount, it's fine to refer specifically to the hardware within the /dev directory.

Now when you browse to the /mnt/newdisk directory by typing cd /mnt/newdisk, you should find the contents of the hard disk accessible. You should also have found that a new icon appeared on the desktop for the file system which you can double-click to access the new disk via Nautilus.

For more information about the mount command, read its man page (type man mount).

Removing a Mounted System

To unmount a system, you use the special command umount (notice there's no n after the first u). Here's an example of using the command to unmount the hard disk we mounted previously:

```
sudo umount /media/newdisk
```

All you need to do is tell the umount command the mount point. Alternatively, you can specify the file in the /dev directory that refers to mounted resource, but this is a little complicated, so in most cases, it's better to simply specify the file system location of the mount.

If you're currently browsing the mounted directory, you'll need to leave it before you can unmount it. The same is true of all kinds of access to the mounted directory. If you're browsing the mounted drive with Nautilus or if a piece of software is accessing it, you won't be able to unmount it until you've quit the program and closed the Nautilus window (or browsed to a different part of the file system).

USEFUL BASIC SHELL COMMANDS

Here are some additional shell commands that you might find useful on a day-to-day basis. Don't forget you can view the man pages of these commands to learn more. Note that commands for manipulating text files are dealt with in the next chapter.

- `clear`: Clear the terminal window, and put the cursor at the top of the window.

- `date`: Display current date and time.

- `dmesg`: Show the output of the kernel, including error messages (useful for problem solving).

- `eject`: Eject a CD/DVD.

- `exit`: Log out of current user account being accessed at the command line (if issued in a terminal window, the window will close).

- `file`: Display useful information about the specified file; the filename should be stated immediately afterward (that is, `file myfile.txt`).

- `free`: Display information about memory usage; add `-m` command option to see output in megabytes.

- `halt`: Shut down the computer (needs to be run as root, so prefeace with `sudo`).

- `help`: Show a list of commonly used BASH commands.

- `last`: Show recent system logins.

- `pwd`: Print Working Directory; this will simply tell you the full path of where you're currently browsing.

- `reboot`: Reboot the computer (needs to be run as root, so preface with `sudo`).

- `shred`: Destroy the specified file beyond recovery by overwriting with junk data; the filename should be specified immediately afterward.

- `touch`: Give the specified file's current date and time; if the specified file doesn't exist, then create an empty file. The filename should be specified immediately afterward.

- `uptime`: Display how long the computer has been booted, plus various CPU usage statistics.

- `whatis`: Display a one-line summary of the specified command; the command name should follow immediately afterward.

File Searches

Files frequently get lost. Well, technically speaking, they don't actually get lost. We just forget where we've put them. But because of this, the shell includes some handy commands to search for files.

Using the find Command

The find command manually searches through all the files on the hard disk. It's not a particularly fast way of finding a file, but it is reliable.

Here's an example:

```
find /home/keir -name "myfile"
```

This will search for myfile using /home/keir as a starting point (which is to say that it will search all directories within /home/keir, any directories within those directories, and so on, because it's recursive). To search the entire file system, type / as the path. Remember that / is interpreted by BASH as the root of the file sytem.

If the file is found, you'll see it appear in the output of the command. The full path will be shown next to the filename.

If you give find a try, you'll see that it's not a particularly good way of searching. Apart from being slow, it will also return a lot of error messages about directories it cannot search. This is because, when you run the find command, it takes on your user permissions. Whenever find comes across a directory it cannot access, it will report it to you, as shown in the example in Figure 14-4. There are frequently so many of these warnings that the output can hide the instances where find actually locates the file in question!

You can avoid these error messages in various ways, but perhaps the quickest solution is to preface the find command with sudo to invoke superuser powers. In this way, you'll have access to every file on the hard disk, so the find command will be unrestricted in where it can search and won't run into any directories it doesn't have permission to enter.

■**Caution** Using the sudo command with find may represent an invasion of privacy if you have more than one user on your system. The find command will search other users' /home directories and report any instances of files found there, too.

However, an even better solution for finding files is to use the locate command.

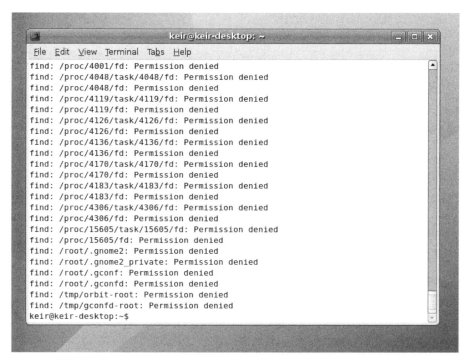

```
find: /proc/4001/fd: Permission denied
find: /proc/4048/task/4048/fd: Permission denied
find: /proc/4048/fd: Permission denied
find: /proc/4119/task/4119/fd: Permission denied
find: /proc/4119/fd: Permission denied
find: /proc/4126/task/4126/fd: Permission denied
find: /proc/4126/fd: Permission denied
find: /proc/4136/task/4136/fd: Permission denied
find: /proc/4136/fd: Permission denied
find: /proc/4170/task/4170/fd: Permission denied
find: /proc/4170/fd: Permission denied
find: /proc/4183/task/4183/fd: Permission denied
find: /proc/4183/fd: Permission denied
find: /proc/4306/task/4306/fd: Permission denied
find: /proc/4306/fd: Permission denied
find: /proc/15605/task/15605/fd: Permission denied
find: /proc/15605/fd: Permission denied
find: /root/.gnome2: Permission denied
find: /root/.gnome2_private: Permission denied
find: /root/.gconf: Permission denied
find: /root/.gconfd: Permission denied
find: /tmp/orbit-root: Permission denied
find: /tmp/gconfd-root: Permission denied
keir@keir-desktop:~$
```

Figure 14-4. *The* find *command is useful for finding files but isn't problem-free.*

Using the locate Command

The alternative to using find is to use the locate command. This is far quicker than find, because it relies on a central database of files, which is periodically updated. In other words, it doesn't literally search the file system each time.

The problem is that if you've saved a file recently and are hoping to find it, there's a chance that it won't yet appear in locate's database, so it won't turn up in the list of results.

Using locate is easy. You can use the following command to search for a file (you don't need to precede the command with sudo):

```
locate myfile
```

It's possible to update the locate database manually, although this might take a few minutes to work through. Simply issue the command:

```
sudo updatedb
```

After this, all files in the system should be indexed, making your search results more accurate.

Using the whereis Command

One other command worth mentioning in the context of searching is whereis. This locates where programs are stored and is an excellent way of exploring your system. Using it is simply a matter of typing something like this:

```
whereis cp
```

This will tell you where the cp program is located on your hard disk. It will also tell you were its source code and man page are located (if applicable). However, the first path returned by the search will be the location of the program itself.

File Size and Free Space

Often, it's necessary to know how large files are and to know how much space they're taking up on the hard disk. In addition, it's often handy to know how much free space is left on a disk.

Viewing File Sizes

Using the ls -l command option will tell you how large each file is in terms of bytes. Adding the -h option converts these file sizes to kilobytes, megabytes, and even gigabytes, depending on how large they are.

In order to get an idea of which are the largest files and which are the smallest, you can add the -S command option. This will order the files in the list in terms of the largest and smallest files.

The following will return a list of all the files in the current directory, in order of size (largest first), detailing the sizes in kilobytes, megabytes, or gigabytes:

```
ls -Slh
```

There's another, more powerful way of presenting this information: using the du command, which stands for "disk usage." When used on its own without command switches, du simply presents the size of directories alongside their names (starting in the current directory). It will show any hidden directories (directories whose names start with a period) and will also present a total at the end of the list. This will probably be quite a long list. Once again, you can add the -h command option to force the du command to produce human-readable measurements of kilobytes and megabytes.

If you specify a file or directory when using the du command, along with the -s command option, you can find out its total file size:

```
du -sh mydirectory
```

This will show the size taken up on the disk by mydirectory, adding to the total any files and/or subdirectories it contains.

However, du is limited by the same file permission problems as the find tool, as shown in Figure 14-5. If you run du as an ordinary user, it won't be able to calculate the total for any directories you don't have permission to access. Therefore, you might consider prefacing the command with sudo.

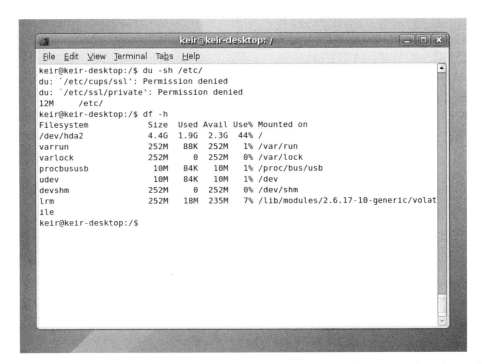

Figure 14-5. *The* du *command shows the size of a file, and the* df *command can be used to gauge the amount of free space on the disk.*

Finding Out the Amount of Free Space

What if you want to find out how much free space is left on the disk? In this case, you can use the df command. This command is also demonstrated in Figure 14-5.

The df command reports the free space in *all* mounted file systems, as well as just the root file system. This can lead to confusing results, because you'll also see results for the /var directory, for example, or /dev. You'll see results for your Windows file system too!

To make sense of it all, look under the Mounted On heading for /, which always indicates the root file system. If you have a memory card inserted and want to find out its free space, look under this list for its mount point (which will probably be in /media).

Once again, you can add the -h option to the df command to have the file sizes returned in megabytes and gigabytes (and even terabytes if your hard disk is big enough!).

Note There is as much space free in any directory as there is space on the disk, which is why df displays data about the entire partition. If you're using a system managed by a system administrator within a business environment, you might find that quotas have been used to limit how much disk space you can take up. However, if you're using a desktop PC and are the only user, this won't be activated.

Summary

In this chapter, we examined how the Ubuntu file system lies at the heart of an understanding of how the operating system works. We also discussed how the file system and user accounts go hand-in-hand and are inextricably linked. This involved discussing the concept of file ownership and usage permissions, plus how these can be manipulated using command-line shell tools.

We also discussed the overall structure of the Ubuntu file system and how external file systems can be mounted and made available within Ubuntu. Finally, we looked at how to find files and how to gauge how much free space there is within the file system.

In the next chapter, we'll look at how the BASH shell can be used to view and otherwise manipulate text files, which are also important to the way Ubuntu works.

■ ■ ■

## CHAPTER 15

Working with Text Files

Windows views text files as just another file type, but to Ubuntu, they can be essential components that make the system work. Configuration files are stored as plain text, and program documentation is also stored as text. This is clearly different from Windows, where it's very likely any information you're supposed to read will be contained in a Windows Help file, a rich text format (RTF) file, or even a Microsoft Word document.

Because of the reliance on text files, the shell includes several commands that let you display, edit, and otherwise manipulate text files in various ways. Learning to use the shell, and therefore learning how to administer your Ubuntu system, involves having a good understanding of these text tools. You'll use text tools for editing configuration files and viewing log files, as just two examples.

Viewing Text Files

You can easily view files using command-line tools, including cat, less, head, and tail. The simplest command for dealing with text files is cat.

Using the cat Command

When followed with a filename, the cat command will display the text file on screen:

```
cat mytextfile
```

cat is short for concatenate, and it isn't designed just to display text files. That it can do so is simply a side effect of its real purpose in life, which is to join two or more files together. However, when used with a single file, it simply displays its contents on screen.

If you try to use cat, you'll realize that it's good for only short text files; large files scroll off the screen.

Using the less Command

Because cat works well only with short files, and to give you more control when viewing text files, the less and more commands were created. The more command came first but was considered too primitive, so someone came up with less, which is preferred by many Linux users. However, both are usually available on the average Linux installation.

■**Note** The less and more commands are sometimes known as *pagers* because of their ability to let you scroll through pages of text. You might still hear them referred to as such in the wider Linux community, although the term has fallen out of use.

Let's look at using less to read the Eye of Gnome README file, which contains information about the current release of the default Ubuntu image viewer. The file is located at /usr/share/doc/eog/README, so to use less to read it, type the following:

```
less /usr/share/doc/eog/README
```

You can scroll up and down within the less display by using the cursor keys. If you want to scroll by bigger amounts of text, you can use the Page Up and Page Down keys. Alternatively, you can use the spacebar and B key, both of which are commonly used by old-hand Linux users for the same function. In addition, the Home and End keys will take you to the start and end of the document, respectively.

A useful command option to use with less is -M, which adds a short status bar to the bottom left. Alongside the filename, you'll see how many lines the document has and which line you're currently up to. In addition, you'll see, as a percentage, the amount of document you've already read through, so you'll know how much is left.

less lets you search forward through the file by typing a slash (/) and then entering your search term. Any words that are matched will be highlighted on screen. To repeat the search, type n. To search backward in a file from your current point, type a question mark (?). To quit less, simply type q.

Although it's supposedly a simple program, less is packed with features. You can see what options are available by reading its man page or by typing less --help.

Using the head and tail Commands

A couple of other handy commands that you can use to view text files are head and tail. As their names suggest, these let you quickly view the beginning (head) of a file or the end (tail) of it.

Using the commands is simple:

```
tail mytextfile
```

or

```
head mytextfile
```

By default, both commands will display ten lines of the file. You can override this by using the -n command option followed by the number of lines you want to see. For example, the following will show the last five lines of mytextfile:

```
tail -n5 mytextfile
```

These two commands are very useful when viewing log files that might contain hundreds of lines of text. The most recent information is always at the end, so tail can be used to see what's happened last on your system, as shown in the example in Figure 15-1.

Although they're powerful, all of these shell commands don't let you do much more than view text files. If you want to edit files, you'll need to use a text editor such as vim.

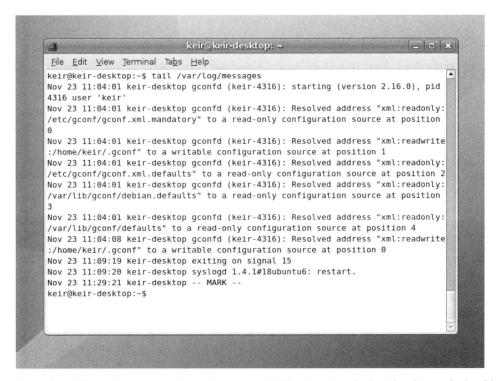

Figure 15-1. *The tail command can be very useful for viewing the last few lines of a log file.*

STANDARD INPUT AND OUTPUT

If you've read any of the Ubuntu man pages, you might have seen references to *standard input* and *standard output*. Like many things in Linux, this sounds complicated but is merely a long-winded way of referring to something that is relatively simple.

Standard input is simply the device that programs running under Ubuntu normally take input from. In other words, on the majority of desktop PCs when you're using the command-line shell, standard input refers to the keyboard. However, it's important to note that it could also feasibly refer to the mouse or any other device on your system capable of providing input; even some software can take the role of providing standard input.

Standard output is similar. It refers to the device to which output from a command is usually sent from software. In the majority of cases at the command line, this refers to the monitor screen, although it could feasibly be any kind of output device, such as your PC's sound card and speakers.

The man page for the `cat` command says that it will "concatenate files and print on the standard output." In other words, for the majority of desktop Ubuntu installations, it will combine (concatenate) any number of files together and print the results on screen. If you specify just one file, it will display that single file on your screen.

In addition to hardware devices, input can also come from a file containing commands, and output can also be sent to a file instead of the screen, or even sent directly to another command. This is just one reason why the command-line shell is so flexible and powerful.

Using a Command-Line Text Editor

A variety of text editors can be used within the shell, but three stand out as being ubiquitous: ed, vim, and Emacs. The first in that list, ed, is by far the simplest. That doesn't necessarily mean that it's simple to use or lacks powerful features, but it just doesn't match the astonishing power of both vim and Emacs. To call vim and Emacs simple text editors is to do them a disservice, because both are extremely powerful interactive environments. In particular, Emacs is considered practically an operating system in itself, and some users of Linux treat it as their shell, executing commands and performing everyday tasks, such as reading and sending e-mail from within it. There are entire books written solely about Emacs and vim.

Tip A fourth shell-based text editor found on many Linux systems is nano. This offers many word processor–like features that can be helpful if you've come to Linux from a Windows background.

The downside of all the power within Emacs and `vim` is that both packages can be difficult to learn to use. They're considered idiosyncratic by even their most ardent fans. Both involve the user learning certain unfamiliar concepts, as well as keyboard shortcuts and commands.

Although there are debates about which text editor is better and which is best, it's generally agreed that `vim` offers substantial text-editing power but isn't too all-encompassing. It's also installed by default on Ubuntu. On Ubuntu, Emacs must be installed as an optional extra. Both text editors are normally available on virtually every installation of Linux or Unix. We'll concentrate on using `vim` here.

It's important to understand that `vim` is an update of a classic piece of software called `vi`. In fact, there are many versions and updates of `vi`. The original program, once supplied with Unix, is rarely used nowadays. `vim` is the most commonly used clone; `vim` stands for vi improved. Other versions include `elvis` (`http://elvis.the-little-red-haired-girl.org/`). However, most people still refer to `vim` and `elvis` as `vi`, despite the fact they are entirely new pieces of software.

■**Note** There's always been a constant flame war between advocates of `vi` and Emacs, as to which is better. This could be quite a vicious and desperate debate, and the text editor you used was often taken as a measure of your character! Nowadays, the battle between the two camps has softened, and the Emacs versus `vi` debate is considered an entertaining cliché of Linux and Unix use. Declaring online which text editor a user prefers is often followed by a smiley symbol to acknowledge the once-fevered emotions.

Understanding vim Modes

The key to understanding how `vim` works is to learn the difference between the various modes. Three modes are important: Command mode, Insert mode, and Command-Line mode.

Command Mode

Command mode is `vim`'s central mode. When the editor starts up, it's in Command mode, as shown in Figure 15-2. This lets you move around the text and delete words or lines of text. `vim` returns to Command mode after most operations. In this mode, the status bar at the bottom of the screen shows information such as the percentage progress through the document. Although you cannot insert text in this mode, you can delete and otherwise manipulate words and lines within the file. You can also move through the text using the cursor keys and the Page Up and Page Down keys.

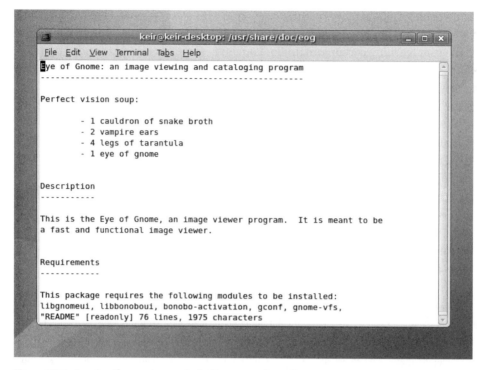

Figure 15-2. *In* vim, *the main mode is Command mode.*

Table 15-1 shows a list of the commands you can use in Command mode (consider photocopying it and sticking it to the side of your monitor as a handy reference).

Table 15-1. vim *Command Mode Commands*

Command	Description
Delete Text	
dd	Delete current line
ndd	Delete n number of lines (for example, 5dd will delete five lines)[1]
dw	Delete the current word under the cursor [2]
db	Delete the word before the cursor[2]
D	Delete everything from the cursor to the end of the line[1]
Search	
/	Search forward (type the search text directly after the slash)
?	Search backward
n	Repeat search in a forward direction
N	Repeat search in a backward direction

Table 15-1. *vim Command Mode Commands*

Command	Description
Cut and Paste	
yy	Copy the current line[3]
*n*yy	Copy *n* number of lines into the buffer from the cursor downwards (for example, 5yy copies five lines of text)
p	Paste the contents of the clipboard[3]
Insert Text	
i	Switch to Insert mode at the cursor
o	Switch to Insert mode, placing the cursor below current line
O	Switch to Insert mode, placing the cursor above current line
A	Append text to end of line
Navigation[4]	
$	Move the cursor to the end of the current line
w	Move the cursor to the next word
b	Move the cursor to beginning of the current or previous word
Miscellaneous	
.	Repeat the last command
u	Undo the last command

[1] *A line ends where a line-break control character occurs in the file. Because of this, a line of text may actually take up several lines of the on-screen display.*

[2] *This will delete the remainder of current word before/after the cursor if the cursor is in the middle of a word.*

[3] *The standard documentation refers to copying as "yanking" and the clipboard as the "buffer."*

[4] *You can also use the cursor keys to move around the file and the Page Up and Page Down keys to move up and down a page at a time. Additionally, press 0 (zero) on the main keyboard, not the numeric keypad, to move the cursor to the start of the current line, or Shift+0 to move forward one sentence (until the next full stop).*

Insert Mode

To type your own text or edit text, you need to switch to Insert mode. This is normally done by typing i, but you can also type O or o to change to Insert mode, which is indicated by the word *INSERT* appearing at the bottom of the screen, as shown in Figure 15-3. The difference between the commands required to switch into Insert mode is that some let you insert before or after the cursor. Generally, i is most useful, because what you type will appear before the character under the cursor, as with most word processors. The commands that activate Insert Mode are listed in Table 15-1, under "Insert Text."

■Tip By typing A (Shift+A), you can add text to the end of the line on which the cursor currently resides.

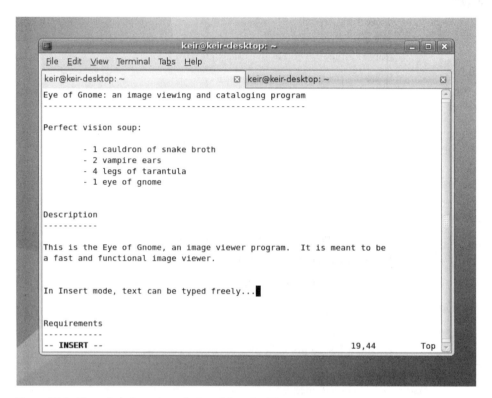

Figure 15-3. *Use* vim's *Insert mode to add and edit text.*

In Insert mode, you can still move around the text using the cursor keys. Anything you type will appear the point of the cursor. To quit this mode, press the Esc key. This will return you to Command mode.

Command-Line Mode

The third mode you should be aware of is Command-Line mode (note that, irritatingly, this is not the same as the Command mode). As its name suggests, this is the mode in which you can enter commands to save and load files, as well as perform other fundamental tasks to control vim or to quit the program. You can enter Command-Line mode by typing a colon (:), although if you're in Insert mode, you'll first need to leave it by pressing the Esc key. You can identify when vim is in this mode, because the cursor will be at the bottom of the screen next to a colon symbol, as shown in Figure 15-4. To quit Command-Line mode, press the Esc key. You'll be returned to Command mode. Note that you'll automatically leave Command-Line mode after each command you issue has completed.

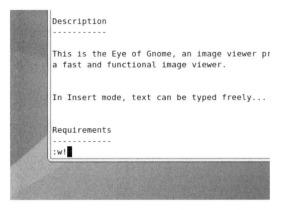

Figure 15-4. *Use* vim's *Command-Line mode to issue commands.*

For a list of basic Command-Line mode commands, see Table 15-2.

Table 15-2. *Some* vim *Command-Line Mode Commands*

Command	Description
:w	Save the file
:w!	Save the file and ignore errors such as an existing file with the same filename
:q	Quit vim
:q!	Quit vim and ignore errors such as an unsaved file
:s/word/replacement/	Search from the cursor downwards and replace any instances of the word with the replacement [1]
:help	View help documentation

[1] *The search tool is very powerful and uses a number of command options for additional flexibility. Read the vim help file to learn more.*

Using vim to Edit a File

As an example, let's use vim to edit the Nautilus README file. You don't want to actually alter this file, so start by making a copy of it in your /home directory:

```
cp /usr/share/doc/nautilus/README ~
```

This will copy the file README to your /home directory, which you indicate using the ~ symbol.

Then fire up vim with the file, like this:

```
vim README
```

■**Note** Windows makes a lot of use of file extensions in order to recognize files and therefore know what program to use to run them. By default, a file with a .doc extension tells Windows that it should use Microsoft Word to open the file, for example. Linux uses a different system based on the first few bytes of each file. Because of this, file extensions are used within Linux simply to let the users know what type of file they're dealing with. Often, they're not used at all. If a file is called README, you can be fairly certain that it's a text file, for example.

Once the file is opened, you'll find yourself automatically in Command mode and will be able to move around the file using the cursor keys. Altering the text is achieved using various commands (see Table 15-1). For example, typing dd will delete the line of text that the cursor is currently within. Typing x will delete the letter under the cursor. Typing dw will delete the current word under the cursor. Try some of these to see how they work.

To actually edit a file and type text, you'll need to switch to Insert mode. Type i to do this. Insert mode is fairly easy to understand. You can move around the text using the cursor keys, and then simply start typing wherever you want. The Backspace key will delete text behind the cursor, and the Delete key will delete text in front of the cursor.

When you're finished, press the Esc key to return to Command mode. Once back in Command mode, you can page through the text. The Page Up and Page Down keys will move a screenful of text at a time. Pressing the up and down cursor keys will cause the screen to scroll when the cursor reaches the top or bottom.

After you're finished editing, you'll need to save the file. This is done in Command-Line mode. You can enter this mode by typing a colon (:). You'll see a colon appear at the bottom of the screen, and this is where you type the commands. Note that after you type a command, you'll immediately exit Command-Line mode, so if you want to issue another command, you'll need to type a colon again.

To save a file, in Command-Line mode, type :w (which stands for "write"). If you want to save the current file with a different name, you'll need to enter a filename after the w command, like this:

```
:w mytextfile
```

To quit vim, type :q. However, if you've edited a file, you won't be able to quit until the file has been saved. If you want to save the file and then quit, you can type :wq. If you don't want to save the file, type :q!. The exclamation point tells vim to override any objections it might have. You can also use it with the save command—:w!—to force the overwriting of a file that already exists.

Note If you don't have the correct permissions to write a file, `vim` might tell you that you can use `:w!` to override. In this case, it's wrong. The only way to write to a file for which you don't have permissions is to change its permissions.

Creating a New Text File Using vim

Creating and editing a new file with `vim` is easy. From any command-line shell, simply type this:

`vim myfile`

This will start `vim` and give your new file a name. However, the file won't be saved until you manually issue the save command (`:w`) in `vim`. This means that if your computer crashes before you save, the file will be lost!

Note `vim` includes some elementary file-save protection. If, for any reason, `vim` is not shut down properly, there's a chance you'll be able to recover a version of file the next time `vim` starts. However, as with all such protection in any kind of program, you shouldn't rely on this. You should use the `:w` command to save your file periodically.

As always with `vim`, you start out in the default Command mode. To start typing immediately, enter Insert mode by typing `i`. You'll notice when typing that although the text is wrapped on each line, words are not carried over, and they often break across lines in an ugly way. This is because `vim` is primarily a text editor, not a word processor. For people who create text files, like programmers, having line breaks shown in this way can be useful.

When you're finished typing a sentence or paragraph, you can press the Enter key as usual to start a new line. You should then be able to move between lines using the up and down cursor keys. You'll notice an odd thing when you try to do this, however: unlike with a word processor, moving up a line of text that spreads across more than one line on screen will take the cursor to the start of the line, rather than into the middle of it. This again relates to `vim`'s text editor focus, where such a feature is useful when editing documents such as program configuration files.

When you're finished, press the Esc key to switch to Command mode. Then type a colon to enter Command-Line mode. Type `:w` to save the file using the filename you gave it earlier. If you started `vim` without specifying a filename, you'll need to specify a filename with the save command, such as `:w myfile`.

USING GEDIT TO EDIT TEXT FILES

If all this talk of vim sounds like too much hard work, don't forget that the GNOME desktop includes an excellent text editor in the form of Gedit. In fact, to describe Gedit as merely a text editor is to do it something of a disservice, because it includes many handy word processor–like features.

You can call Gedit and open a file in it from the command-line prompt as follows:

gedit <*filename*>

If you need to adopt superuser powers to edit the likes of configuration files, simply preface it with gksu:

gksu gedit <*filename*>

You'll find Gedit fairly straightforward to use.

Searching Through Files

You can search for particular words or phrases in text files by loading the file into less or vim (see Table 15-1). The maneuverability offered by both programs lets you leap from point to point in the text, and their use is generally user-friendly.

However, using vim or less can take precious seconds. There's a quicker command-line option that will search through a file in double-quick speed: grep.

Using grep to Find Text

grep stands for Global Regular Expression Print. grep is an extremely powerful tool that can use pattern-based searching techniques to find text in files. Pattern-based searching means that grep offers various options to loosen the search so that more results are returned.

The simplest way of using grep is to specify some brief text, followed by the name of the file you want to search. Here's an example:

```
grep 'hello world' myfile
```

This will search for the phrase hello world within myfile. If it's found, the entire line that hello world is on will be displayed on screen.

If you specify the * wildcard instead of a filename, grep will search every file in the directory for the text. Adding the -r command option will cause grep to search all the files, and also search through any directories that are present:

```
grep -r 'hello world' *
```

Another handy command option is -i, which tells grep to ignore uppercase and lower-case letters when it's searching. Figure 15-5 shows an example of using grep.

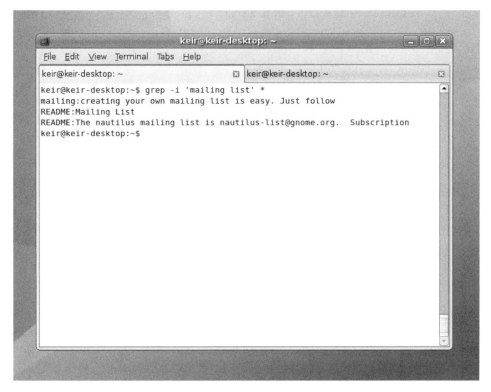

Figure 15-5. *grep is a powerful tool that can search for text within files.*

■**Tip** You might never choose to use grep for searching for text within files, but it can prove very handy when used to search through the output of other commands. This is done by "piping" the output from one command to another, as explained in Chapter 17.

Using Regular Expressions

The true power of grep is achieved by the use of search patterns known as *regular expressions*, or *regexes* for short. Put simply, regexes allow you to be vague rather than specific when searching, meaning that grep (and many similar tools that use the system of regexes, such as the find command discussed in Chapter 14) will return more results.

For example, you can specify a selection or series of characters (called a *string* in regex terminology) that might appear in a word or phrase you're searching for. This can be

useful if you're looking for a word that might be spelled differently from how you anticipate, for example.

The most basic form of regex is the bracket expansion. This is where additional search
terms are enclosed in square brackets within a search string. For example, suppose you
want to find a file that refers to several drafts of a document you've been working on. The
files are called myfile_1draft.doc, myfile_2draft.doc, and so on. To find any document
that mentions these files, you could type this:

```
grep 'myfile_[1-9]draft\.doc' *
```

The use of square brackets tells grep to fill in details within the search string based on
what's inside the square brackets. In this case, 1-9 means that all the numbers from one
to nine should be applied to the search string. It's as if you've told grep to search for
myfile_1draft.doc, and then told it to search for myfile_2draft.doc, and so on. Notice
that the example has a backslash before the period separating the file extension from the
filename. This indicates to grep that it should interpret the period as an element of the
string to be searched for, rather than as a wildcard character, which is how grep usually
interprets periods.

You don't need to specify a range of characters in this way. You can simply enter whatever selection of characters you want to substitute into the search string. Here's an example:

```
grep 'myfile[12345]\.doc' *
```

This will attempt to find any mention of myfile1.doc, myfile2.doc, myfile3.doc, and so
on, in any file within the directory.

Here's another example:

```
grep '[GgNn]ome' *
```

This will let you search for the word Gnome within files but takes into account any possible
misspelling of the word by people who forget to use the silent G, and any use of uppercase
or lowercase.

This is only scratching the surface of what regexes can do. For example, many regexes
can be combined together into one long search string, which can provide astonishing
accuracy when searching. Table 15-3 contains some simple examples that should give you
an idea of the power and flexibility of regexes.

Table 15-3. *Some Examples of Regular Expressions*

Search String	Description
'document[a-z]'	Returns any lines containing the string "document" followed by any single letter from the range *a* through *z*.
'document[A-Za-z]'	Returns any lines containing the string "document" followed by the letters *A* through *Z* or *a* through *z*. Note that no comma or other character is needed to separate possibilities within square brackets.

Table 15-3. *Some Examples of Regular Expressions*

Search String	Description
`'document.'`	Returns any lines containing the string "document" followed by any other character. The period is used as a wildcard signifying any single character.
`'document[[:digit:]]'`	Returns any lines containing the string "document" followed by any number.
`'document[[:alpha:]]'`	Returns any lines containing the string "document" followed by any character.
`'^document'`	Returns any lines that have the string "document" at the beginning. The caret symbol (^) tells grep to look only at the beginning of each line.
`'document$'`	Returns any line that has the string "document" at the end of the line. The dollar sign symbol ($) tells grep to look for the string only at the end of lines.
`'document[^1-6]'`	Returns lines that have the string "document" in them but not if it's followed by the numbers 1 through 6. When used in square brackets, the caret character (^) produces a nonmatching list—a list of results that don't contain the string.

grep is very powerful. It can be complicated to master, but it offers a lot of scope for performing extremely precise searches that ensure you find only what you're seeking. It's well worth reading through its man pages. You can also refer to books on the subject, of which there are many. A good example is *Regular Expression Recipes: A Problem-Solution Approach*, by Nathan A. Good (1-59059-441-X; Apress, 2004).

Comparing Text Files

If you want to compare the differences between two text files, one way to do this is to use the diff command. This is designed primarily to uncover small changes in otherwise identical documents, such as revisions made by another person. Of course, it can also be used to prove that two files are identical. If you run the files through diff, and it shows no output, it has been unable to spot any differences.

diff is ordinarily used like this:

```
diff mytextfile1 mytextfile2
```

If diff spots any differences between the files, the results are a little more complicated than you might be used to. Any lines that are different within the files will appear on screen. Those lines that are identical won't be displayed. Lines preceded with a left angle bracket (<) are from the first file, while those with a right angle bracket (>) are from the second file.

For a different display, you could type something like this:

```
diff -y mytextfile1 mytextfile2
```

This places the two lists side-by-side and highlights lines that are different with a pipe symbol (|). However, it requires a lot more screen space than using `diff` without the `-y` option.

■**Note** When you use the `-y` command option with `diff`, it will struggle to fit the output in a standard GNOME Terminal window. If it is maximized on a 1024×768 resolution screen, it should be just large enough to fit the information in, depending on the complexity of the files being compared.

By specifying the `-a` command option, you can make `diff` process binary files, too. This is a handy way of comparing virtually any kind of files, including program files, to see if they're identical. If there's no output from `diff`, then the two files are identical. If your screen fills with gibberish, then the files are clearly different.

Incidentally, if you want to compare three documents, you can use a very similar command: `diff3`. Check the command's man page to learn more about how it works.

More Text Tools

BASH is an incredibly capable tool when it comes to text manipulation, and some of its toolset offers modest word-processing–like functionality. It's no wonder that some people live their lives working at the BASH prompt and have no need of sophisticated GUI tools!

Table 15-4 lists some more text-processing tools that you can use on the command line. Along with the commands are listed any command options needed to make them work in a useful way. Some commands rely on redirection and piping, which are explained in depth in Chapter 17.

■**Note** Most text-processing tools under BASH were created for programmers, so some options might seem a little odd when you read the man pages. However, all the tools all extremely flexible and offer functions for every kind of user.

Table 15-4. *Useful Text-Processing Commands*

Function	Command	Notes
Spell-check	aspell -c *filename*	Any questionable words within *filename* are highlighted, and a choice of replacements is offered, rather like a standard word processor's spell check. Press X if you wish to exit after spell-checking starts.
Single word spell-check	look *word*	Looks up *word* in the dictionary; if the word is displayed in output, the word has been found. If not, then the word hasn't been found. Note that this command returns loose matches—searching for test, for example, will return every word beginning with test (testing, testimony, testosterone, and so forth).
Word count	wc -w *filename*	Outputs the number of words in *filename*. Used without the -w command switch, wc outputs the number of lines, followed by the word count, followed by the number of bytes in the file.
Remove line breaks	fmt *filename* > *newfile*	Creates *newfile*, removing breaks at the end of lines in *filename*. Double-line breaks between paragraphs aren't affected. Adding the -u command switch removes instances of double spaces too.
Remove duplicate lines	uniq *filename* > *newfile*	Creates *newfile* from *filename* but removes duplicate lines.
Join two files	paste *file1* *file2* > *file3*	Creates *file3* by joining *file1* and *file2* side-by-side (effectively creating two columns of text). Each line is separated by a tab.
Word wrap	fold -sw20 *filename* > *newfile*	Creates *newfile* from *filename*, wrapping lines at the specified 20 characters (increase/decrease this value for shorter/longer lines). Note that the -s switch ensures lines don't break across words, even if this means exceeding the specified character count.
Add line numbers	nl *filename* > *newfile*	Creates *newfile* from *filename*, adding line numbers to the beginning of each line.
Sort list	sort file1 > file2	Creates file2 from file1, sorting its contents alphanumerically (technically, it sorts according to ASCII, so some symbols appear above numbers). For obvious reasons, this command works best on lists.

Summary

In this chapter, we examined how text files can be manipulated. In many ways, the BASH shell is built around manipulating text, and we explored various tools created with this goal in mind. We started with the commands that can display text files (or part of them).

We then looked at how the vim text editor can be used to both edit and create documents. Next, we explored how regexes can be used with the grep command to create sophisticated search strings, which can uncover any text within documents. Finally, you saw how to compare text files.

In the next chapter, we'll look at how you can use various command-line tools to take control of your system.

CHAPTER 16

■■■

Taking Control of the System

By now, you should be starting to realize that the shell offers an enormous amount of power when it comes to administering your PC. The BASH shell commands give you quick and efficient control over most aspects of your Linux setup. However, the shell truly excels in one area: controlling the processes on your system.

Controlling processes is essential for administration of your system. You can tidy up crashed programs, for example, or even alter the priority of a program so that it runs with a little more consideration for other programs. Unlike with Windows, this degree of control is not considered out of bounds. This is just one more example of how Linux provides complete access to its inner workings and puts you in control.

Without further ado, let's take a look at what can be done.

Viewing Processes

A process is something that exists entirely behind the scenes. When the user runs a program, one or many processes might be started, but they're usually invisible unless the user specifically chooses to manipulate them. You might say that programs exist in the world of the user, but processes belong in the world of the system.

Processes can be started not only by the user, but also by the system itself to undertake tasks such as system maintenance, or even to provide basic functionality, such as the GUI system. Many processes are started when the computer boots up, and then they sit in the background, waiting until they're needed (such as programs that send mail). Other processes are designed to work periodically to accomplish certain tasks, such as ensuring system files are up-to-date.

You can see what processes are currently running on your computer by running the top program. Running top is simply a matter of typing the command at the shell prompt.

As you can see in Figure 16-1, top provides very comprehensive information and can be a bit overwhelming at first sight. However, the main area of interest is the list of processes (which top refers to as *tasks*).

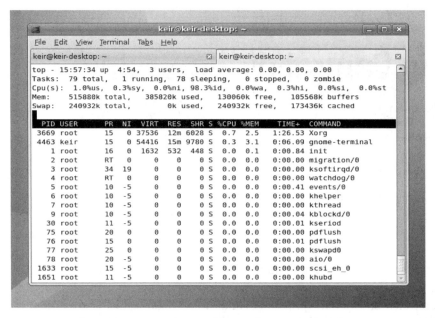

Figure 16-1. *The top program gives you an eagle-eye view of the processes running on your system.*

Here's an example of a line taken from top on my test PC, shown with the column headings from the process list:

PID	USER	PR	NI	VIRT	RES	SHR	S	%CPU	%MEM	TIME+	COMMAND
5499	root	15	0	78052	25m	60m	S	2.3	5.0	6:11.72	Xorg

A lot of information is presented here, as described in Table 16-1.

Table 16-1. *The top Program Process Information*

Column	Description
PID	The first number is the process ID (PID). This is the unique number that the system uses to track the process. The PID comes in handy if you want to kill (terminate) the process (as explained in the next section of this chapter).
USER	This column lists the owner of the particular process. As with files, all processes must have an owner. A lot of processes will appear to be owned by the root user. Some of them are system processes that need to access the system hardware, which is something only the root user is allowed to do. Other processes are owned by root for protection; root ownership means that ordinary users cannot tamper with these processes.

Table 16-1. *The top Program Process Information*

Column	Description
PR	This column shows the priority of the process. This is a dynamic number, showing where the particular process is in the CPU queue at the present time.
NI	This column shows the "nice" value of the process. This refers to how charitable a process is in its desire for CPU time. A high figure here (up to 19) indicates that the process is willing to be interrupted for the sake of other processes. A negative value means the opposite: the process is more aggressive than others in its desire for CPU time. Some programs need to operate in this way, and this is not necessarily a bad thing.
VIRT	This column shows the amount of virtual memory used by the process.[1]
RES	This column shows the total amount of physical memory used.[1]
SHR	This column shows the amount of shared memory used. This refers to memory that contains code that is relied on by other processes and programs.
S	This column shows the current status of the task. Generally, the status will either be sleeping, in which case an S will appear, or running, in which case an R will appear. Most processes will be sleeping, even ones that appear to be active. Don't worry about this; it just reflects the way the Linux kernel works. A Z in this column indicates a zombie process (a child of a process that has been terminated).
%CPU	This column shows the CPU use, expressed as a percentage.[2]
%MEM	This column shows the memory use, again expressed as a percentage.[2]
TIME+	This column shows a measure of how long the process has been up and running.
COMMAND	This shows the actual name of the process itself.

[1] *Both VIRT and RES are measured in kilobytes unless an m appears alongside the number; in which case, you should read the figure as megabytes.*

[2] *The %CPU and %MEM entries tell you in easy-to-understand terms how much of the system resources a process is taking up.*

This list will probably be longer than the screen has space to display, so top orders the list of processes by the amount of CPU time the processes are using. Every few seconds, it updates the list. You can test this quite easily. Let your PC rest for a few seconds, without touching the mouse or typing. Then move the mouse around for a few seconds. You'll see that the process called Xorg leaps to the top of the list (or appears very near the top). Xorg is the program that provides the graphical subsystem for Linux, and making the mouse cursor appear to move around the screen requires CPU time. When nothing else is going on, moving the mouse causes Xorg to appear as the number one user of CPU time on your system.

■**Tip** Typing d while top is running lets you alter the update interval, which is the time between screen updates. The default is three seconds, but you can reduce that to one second or even less if you wish. However, a constantly updating top program starts to consume system resources and can therefore skew the diagnostic results you're investigating. Because of this, a longer, rather than shorter, interval is preferable.

It's possible to alter the ordering of the process list according to other criteria. For example, you can list the processes by the quantity of memory they're using, by typing M while top is up and running. You can switch back to CPU ordering by typing P.

RENICING A PROCESS

You can set how much CPU time a process receives while it's actually running. This is done by *renicing* the process. This isn't something you should do on a regular basis, but it can prove very handy if you start a program that then uses a lot of system resources and makes the system unbearably slow.

The first thing to do is to use top to spot the process that needs to be restrained and find out its PID number. This will be listed on the left of the program's entry on the list. Once you know this, type r, and then type in the PID number. You'll then be asked to specify a renice value. The scale goes from –20, which is considered the highest priority, to 19, which is considered the lowest. Therefore, you should type 19. After this, you should find some responsiveness has returned to the system, although how much (if any) depends on the nature of the programs you're running.

You might be tempted to bump up the priority of a process to make it run faster, but this may not work because of complexities in the Linux kernel. In fact, it might cause serious problems. Therefore, you should renice with care and only when you must.

Renicing can also be carried out via the renice command at the prompt, avoiding the need to use top. Also useful is the nice command, which can be used to set the initial priority of a process before it starts to run. To learn more, see the man pages for renice and nice.

Controlling Processes

Despite the fact that processes running on your computer are usually hidden away, Linux offers complete, unrestricted, and unapologetic control over them. You can terminate processes, change their properties, and learn every item of information there is to know about them.

This provides ample scope for damaging the currently running system but, in spite of this, even standard users have complete control over processes that they personally started (one exception is zombie processes, described a bit later in this section). As you might expect, the root user (or any user who adopts superuser powers) has control over all processes that were created by ordinary users, as well as those processes started by the system itself.

The user is given this degree of control over processes in order to enact repairs when something goes wrong, such as when a program crashes and won't terminate cleanly. It's impossible for standard users to damage the currently running system by undertaking such work, although they can cause themselves a number of problems.

■Note This control over processes is what makes Linux so reliable. Because any user can delve into the workings of the kernel and terminate individual processes, crashed programs can be cleaned up with negligible impact on the rest of the system.

Killing Processes

Whenever you quit a program or, in some cases, when it completes the task you've asked of it, it will terminate itself. This means ending its own process and also that of any other processes it created in order to run. The main process is called the *parent*, and the ones it creates are referred to as *child* processes.

■Tip You can see a nice graphical display of which parent owns which child process by typing pstree at the command-line shell. It's worth piping this into the less command so you can scroll through it: type pstree | less. I explain what piping is in the next chapter.

While this should mean your system runs smoothly, badly behaved programs sometimes don't go away. They stick around in the process list. Alternatively, you might find that a program crashes and so isn't able to terminate itself. In very rare cases, some programs that appear otherwise healthy might get carried away and start consuming a lot of system resources. You can tell when this happens because your system will start slowing down for no reason, as less and less memory and/or CPU time is available to run actual programs.

In all of these cases, the user usually must kill the process in order to terminate it manually. This is easily done using top.

The first task is to track down the crashed or otherwise problematic process. In top, look for a process that matches the name of the program, as shown in Figure 16-2. For example, the Firefox web browser generally runs as a process called firefox-bin.

```
EM     TIME+   COMMAND
3.0  14:09.19  Xorg
).7   0:01.16  firefox-bin
!.9   0:00.73  metacity
3.8   0:00.54  wnck-applet
5.0   0:07.73  gnome-terminal
3.5   0:00.70  gnome-settings-
).0   0:01.22  kblockd/0
).0   0:00.12  kswapd0
3.7   0:00.71  gnome-panel
5.0   0:00.96  nautilus
3.7   0:00.33  update-notifier
```

Figure 16-2. *You can normally identify a program by its name in the process list.*

■**Caution** You should be absolutely sure that you know the correct process before killing it. If you get it wrong, you could cause other programs to stop running.

Because top doesn't show every single process on its screen, tracking down the trouble-causing process can be difficult. A handy tip is to make top show only the processes created by the user you're logged in under. This will remove the background processes started by root. You can do this within top by typing u and then entering your username.

Once you've spotted the crashed process, make a note of its PID number, which will be at the very left of its entry in the list. Then type k. You'll be asked to enter the PID number. Enter that number, and then press Enter once again (this will accept the default signal value of 15, which will tell the program to terminate).

With any luck, the process (and the program in question) will disappear. If it doesn't, the process you've killed might be the child of another process that also must be killed. To track down the parent process, you need to configure top to add the PPID field, for the parent process ID, to its display. To add this field, type f, and then b. Press Enter to return to the process list. The PPID column will appear next to the process name on the right of the window. It simply shows the PID of the parent process. You can use this information to look for the parent process within the main list of processes.

The trick here is to make sure that the parent process isn't something that's vital to the running of the system. If it isn't, you can safely kill it. This should have the result of killing the child process you uncovered prior to this.

■**Caution** In both the PPID and PID fields, you should always watch out for low numbers, particularly one-, two- or three-digit numbers. These are usually processes that started early on when Linux booted and that are essential to the system.

Controlling Zombie Processes

Zombie processes are those that are children of processes that have terminated. However, for some reason, they failed to take their child processes with them. Zombie processes are rare on most Linux systems.

Despite their name, zombie processes are harmless. They're not actually running and don't take up system resources. However, if you want your system to be spick-and-span, you can attempt to kill them.

In the top-right area of top, you can see a display that shows how many zombie processes are running on your system, as shown in Figure 16-3. Zombie processes are easily identified because they have a Z in the status (S) column within top's process list. To kill a zombie process, type k, and then type its PID. Then type 9, rather than accept the default signal of 15.

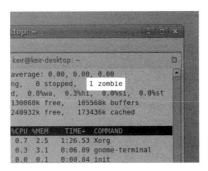

Figure 16-3. *You can see at a glance how many zombie processes are on your system by looking at the top right of top's display.*

■**Note** No magic is involved in killing processes. All that happens is that top sends them a "terminate" signal. In other words, it contacts them and asks them to terminate. By default, all processes are designed to listen for commands such as this; it's part and parcel of how programs work under Linux. When a program is described as *crashed*, it means that the user is unable to use the program itself to issue the terminate command (such as Quit). A crashed program might not be taking input, but its *processes* will probably still be running.

In many cases, zombie processes simply won't go away. When this happens, you have two options. The first is to restart the program that is likely to be the zombie's owner, in the hope that it will reattach with the zombie, and then quit the program. With any luck, it will take the zombie child with it this time. Alternatively, you can simply reboot your PC. But it's important to note that zombie processes are harmless and can be left in peace on your system!

Using Other Commands to Control Processes

You don't always need to use top to control processes. A range of quick and cheerful shell commands can diagnose and treat process problems.

The first of these is the ps command. This stands for Process Status and will report a list of currently running processes on your system. This command is normally used with the -aux options:

```
ps -aux
```

This will return a list something like what you see when you run top.

If you can spot the problematic process, look for its PID and issue the following command:

```
kill <PID number>
```

For example, to kill a process with a PID of 5122, you would type this:

```
kill 5122
```

If, after this, you find the process isn't killed, then you should use the top program, as described in the previous sections, because it allows for a more in-depth investigation.

Another handy process-killing command lets you use the actual process name. The killall command is handy if you already know from past experience what a program's process is called. For example, to kill the process called firefox-bin, which is the chief process of the Firefox web browser, you would use the following command:

```
killall firefox-bin
```

■**Caution** Make sure you're as specific as possible when using the killall command. Issuing a command like killall bin will kill all processes that might have the word bin in them!

CLEARING UP CRASHES

Sometimes, a crashed process can cause all kinds of problems. The shell you're working at may stop working, or the GUI itself might stop working properly.

In cases like this, it's important to remember that you can have more than one instance of the command-line shell up and running at any one time. For example, if a process crashes and locks up GNOME Terminal, simply start a new instance of GNOME Terminal (Applications ➤ Accessories ➤ Terminal). Then use top within the new window to kill the process that is causing trouble for the other terminal window.

If the crashed program affects the entire GUI, you can switch to a virtual console by pressing Ctrl+Alt+F1. Although the GUI disappears, you will not have killed it, and no programs will stop running. Instead, you've simply moved the GUI to the background while a shell console takes over the screen. Then you can use the virtual console to run top and attempt to kill the process that is causing all the problems. When you're ready, you can switch back to the GUI by pressing Ctrl+Alt+F7.

If you know the name of the program that's crashed, a quick way of getting rid of it is to use the pgrep command. This searches the list of processes for the program name you specify and then outputs the PID number. So if, say, Nautilus had frozen, you could type pgrep nautilus. Then you would use the kill command with the PID number that's returned.

Controlling Jobs

Whenever you start a program at the shell, it's assigned a job number. *Jobs* are quite separate from processes and are designed primarily for users to understand what programs are running on the system.

You can see which jobs are running at any one time by typing the following at the shell prompt:

```
jobs
```

When you run a program, it usually takes over the shell in some way and stops you from doing anything until it's finished what it's doing. However, it doesn't have to be this way. Adding an ampersand symbol (&) after the command will cause it to run in the background. This is not much use for commands that require user input, such as vim or top, but it can be very handy for commands that churn away until they're completed.

For example, suppose that you want to decompress a large zip file. For this, you can use the unzip command. As with Windows, decompressing large zip files can take a lot of time, during which time the shell would effectively be unusable. However, you can type the following to retain use of the shell:

```
unzip myfile.zip &
```

When you do this, you'll see something similar to the following, although the four-digit number will be different:

```
[1] 7483
```

This tells you that unzip is running in the background and has been given job number 1. It also has been given process number 7483 (although bear in mind that when some programs start, they instantly kick off other processes and terminate the one they're currently running, so this won't necessarily be accurate).

■**Tip** If you've ever tried to run a GUI program from the shell, you might have realized that the shell is inaccessible while it's running. Once you quit the GUI program, the control of the shell will be returned to you. By specifying that the program should run in the background with the & (ampersand symbol), you can run the GUI program and still be able to type away and run other commands.

You can send several jobs to the background, and each one will be given a different job number. In this case, when you wish to switch to a running job, you can type its number. For example, the following command will switch you to the background job assigned the number 3:

`%3`

You can exit a job that is currently running by pressing Ctrl+Z. It will still be there in the background, but it won't be running (officially, it's said to be *sleeping*). To restart it, you can switch back to it, as just described. Alternatively, you can restart it but still keep it in the background. For example, to restart job 2 in the background, leaving the shell prompt free for you to enter other commands, type the following:

`%2 &`

You can bring the command in the background into the foreground by typing the following:

`fg`

When a background job has finished, something like the following will appear at the shell:

```
[1]+  Done                    unzip myfile.zip
```

Using jobs within the shell can be a good way of managing your workload. For example, you can move programs into the background temporarily while you get on with something else. If you're editing a file in vim, you can press Ctrl+Z to stop the program. It will remain in the background, and you'll be returned to the shell, where you can type other commands. You can then resume vim later on by typing fg or typing % followed by its job number.

■**Tip** Also useful is Ctrl+C, which will kill a job that's currently running. For example, if you previously started the unzip command in the foreground, hitting Ctrl+C will immediately terminate it. Ctrl+C is useful if you accidentally start commands that take an unexpectedly long time to complete.

NOHUP

What if you want to start a command running in a terminal window, but then want to close that terminal window? As soon as you close the window, any processes started within it are also closed. Try this now—type gcalctool at the prompt to start the Calculator application and then quit the terminal window.

To get around this, you can use the nohup command. This stands for "no hangup," and in simple terms, it tells the command you specify to stick around, even after the process that started it has ended (technically, the command is told to ignore the SIGHUP signal). However, commands run via nohup can still be killed.

To use nohup, simply add it before the command, for example:

```
nohup unzip myfile.zip
```

If the command requires sudo or gksu powers, add either of these after the nohup command.

Any command output (including error messages) is sent to the file nohup.out, which you can then view in a text editor. Note that if you run a command via nohup using sudo or gksu, the nohup.out file will have root privileges. If that's the case, you will also have to delete the nohup.out file via sudo before you can use nohup again as an ordinary user, because otherwise, nohup will be unable to over-write the root-owned nohup.out.

Summary

This chapter has covered taking complete control of your system. We've looked at what processes are, how they're separate from programs, and how they can be controlled or viewed using programs such as top and ps. In addition, we explored job management under BASH. You saw that you can stop, start, and pause programs at your convenience.

In the next chapter, we'll take a look at several tricks and techniques that you can use with the BASH shell to finely hone your command-line skills.

CHAPTER 17

■■■

Cool Shell Tricks

The BASH shell is the product of many years of development work by a lot of people. It comes from the old days of Unix and was an important step in computer software evolution. It's a program that retains complete simplicity, yet packs in more features than most users could ever hope to use.

One of the best things about the shell is its sheer power. If you ever wonder if you can do a task differently (and more efficiently), you'll probably find that one of the many BASH developers has implemented a method to do so. Once you learn these techniques, you'll find you can whiz around the shell at blinding speed. It's just a matter of exploring the far reaches of the shell, and that's what you'll do in this chapter. Hold onto your hats, because it's an exciting ride!

Using Autocompletion

The Tab key is your best friend when using the shell, because it will cause BASH to automatically complete whatever you type. For example, if you want to run Ubuntu's web browser, you can enter firefox at the command line. However, to save yourself some time, you can type fir, and then press Tab. You'll then find that BASH fills in the rest for you. It does this by caching the names of the programs you might run according to the directories listed in your $PATH variable (see Chapter 13).

Of course, autocompletion has some limitations. On my Ubuntu test system, typing loc didn't autocomplete locate. Instead, it caused BASH to beep. This is because on a default Ubuntu installation, there is more than one possible match. Pressing Tab again shows those matches. Depending on how much you type (how much of an initial clue you give BASH), you might find there are many possible matches.

In this case, the experienced BASH user simply types another letter, which will be enough to distinguish the almost-typed word from the rest, and presses Tab again. With any luck, this should be enough for BASH to fill in the rest.

Autocompletion with Files and Paths

Tab autocompletion also works with files and paths. If you type the first few letters of a folder name, BASH will try to fill in the rest. This also obviously has limitations. There's no point in typing cd myfol and pressing Tab if there's nothing in the current directory that starts with the letters myfol. This particular autocomplete function works by looking at your current directory and seeing what's available.

Alternatively, you can specify an initial path for BASH to use in order to autocomplete. Typing cd /ho and pressing Tab will cause BASH to autocomplete the path by looking in the root directory (/). In other words, it will autocomplete the command with the directory home. In a similar way, typing cd myfolder/myfo will cause BASH to attempt to autocomplete by looking for a match in myfolder.

If you want to run a program that resides in the current directory, such as one you've just downloaded for example, typing ./, followed by the first part of the program name, and then pressing Tab should be enough to have BASH autocomplete the rest. In this case, the dot and slash tell BASH to look in the current directory for any executable programs or scripts (programs with X as part of their permissions) and use them as possible autocomplete options.

BASH is clever enough to spot whether the command you're using is likely to require a file, directory, or executable, and it will autocomplete with only relevant file or directory names.

Viewing Available Options

The autocomplete function has a neat side effect. As I mentioned earlier, if BASH cannot find a match, pressing Tab again causes BASH to show all the available options. For example, typing ba at the shell, and then pressing Tab twice will cause BASH to show all the possible commands starting with the letters *ba*. On my test PC, this produces the following list of commands:

```
badblocks   banner   baobab   basename   bash   bashbug   batch
```

This can be a nice way of exploring what commands are available on your system. You can then use each command with the --help command option to find out what it does, or browse the command's man page.

When you apply this trick to directory and filename autocompletion, it's even more useful. For example, typing cd in a directory, and then pressing the Tab key twice will cause BASH to show the available directories, providing a handy way of retrieving a brief directory listing. Alternatively, if you've forgotten how a directory name is spelled, you can use this technique to find out prior to switching into it.

Figure 17-1 shows a few examples of using this technique with BASH.

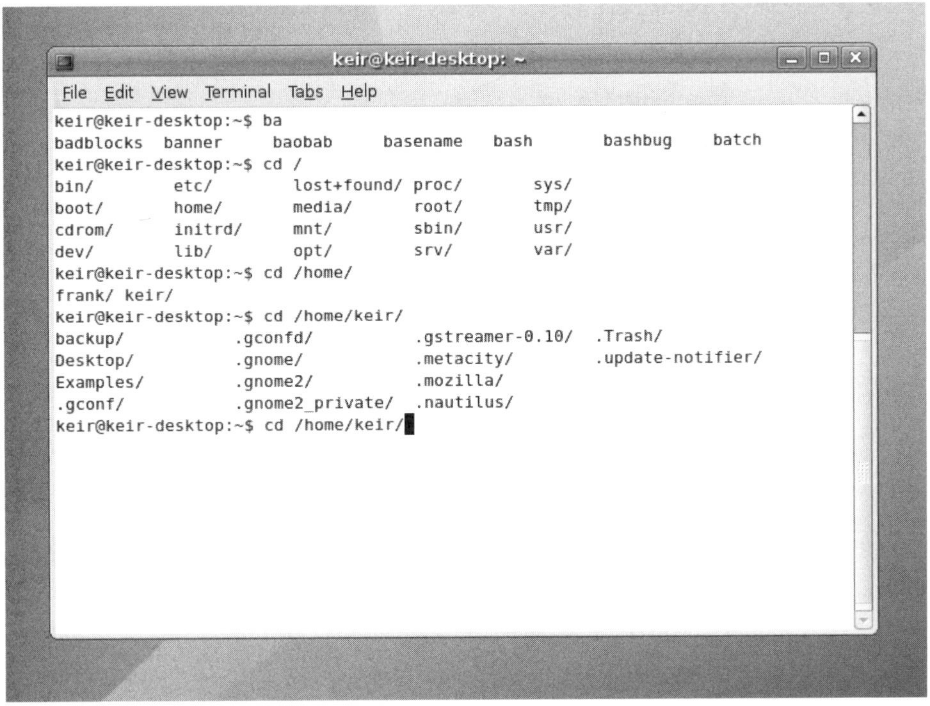

Figure 17-1. *Autocompletion makes using BASH much easier.*

Using Keyboard Shortcuts

Your other good friends when using BASH are the Ctrl and Alt keys. These keys provide shortcuts to vital command-line shell functions. They also let you work more efficiently when typing by providing what most programs call keyboard shortcuts.

Shortcuts for Working in BASH

Table 17-1 lists the most common keyboard shortcuts in BASH (there are many more; see BASH's man page for details). If you've explored the Emacs text editor, you might find these shortcuts familiar. Such keyboard shortcuts are largely the same across many of the software packages that originate from the GNU Project. Often, you'll find an option within many Ubuntu software packages that lets you use Emacs-style navigation, in which case, these keyboard shortcuts will most likely work equally well.

Table 17-1. *Keyboard Shortcuts in BASH*

Shortcut	Description
Navigation	
Left/right cursor key	Move left/right in text
Ctrl+A	Move to beginning of line
Ctrl+E	Move to end of line
Ctrl+right arrow	Move forward one word
Ctrl+left arrow	Move left one word
Editing	
Ctrl+U	Delete everything behind cursor to start of line
Ctrl+K	Delete from cursor to end of line
Ctrl+W	Delete from cursor to beginning of word
Alt+D	Delete from cursor to end of word
Ctrl+T	Transpose characters on left and right of cursor
Alt+T	Transpose words on left and right of cursor
Miscellaneous	
Ctrl+L	Clear screen (everything above current line)
Ctrl+U	Undo everything since last command[1]
Alt+R	Undo changes made to the line[2]
Ctrl+Y	Undo deletion of word or line caused by using Ctrl+K, Ctrl+W, and so on[3]
Alt+L	Lowercase current word (from the cursor to end of word)

[1] *In most cases, this has the effect of clearing the line.*

[2] *This is different from Ctrl+U, because it will leave intact any command already on the line, such as one pulled from your command history.*

[3] *This allows primitive cutting and pasting. Delete the text and then immediately undo, after which the text will remain in the buffer and can be pasted with Ctrl+Y.*

Shortcuts for System Control

In terms of the control over your system offered by keyboard commands, as mentioned in Chapter 16, pressing Ctrl+Z has the effect of stopping the current program. It suspends the program until you switch back into it or tell it to resume in another way, or manually kill it.

In the same style, pressing Ctrl+C while a program is running will quit it. This sends the program's process a termination signal, a little like killing it using the top program. Ctrl+C can prove handy if you start a program running by accident and quickly want to end it, or if a command takes longer than you expected to work and you cannot wait for it to complete.

It's also a handy way of attempting to end crashed programs. Some complicated programs don't take too kindly to being quit in this way, particularly those that need to save data before they terminate. However, most should be okay.

Ctrl+D is another handy keyboard shortcut. This sends the program an end-of-file (EOF) message. In effect, this tells the program that you've finished your input. This can have a variety of effects, depending on the program you're running. For example, pressing Ctrl+D on its own at the shell prompt when no program is running will cause you to log out (if you're using a GUI terminal emulator like GNOME Terminal, the program will quit). This happens because pressing Ctrl+D informs the BASH shell program that you've finished your input. BASH then interprets this as the cue that it should log you out. After all, what else can it do if told there will be no more input?

While it might not seem very useful for day-to-day work, Ctrl+D is vital for programs that expect you to enter data at the command line. You might run into these as you explore BASH. If ever you read in a man page that a program requires an EOF message during input, you'll know what to press.

Using the Command History

The original hackers who invented the tools used under Unix hated waiting around for things to happen. After all, being a hacker is all about finding the most efficient way of doing any particular task.

Because of this, the BASH shell includes many features designed to optimize the user experience. The most important of these is the *command history*. BASH remembers every command you enter (even the ones that don't work!) and stores them as a list on your hard disk.

During any BASH session, you can cycle through this history using the up and down arrow keys. Pressing the up arrow key takes you back into the command history, and pressing the down arrow key takes you forward.

The potential of the command history is enormous. For example, rather than retype that long command that runs a program with command options, you can simply use the cursor keys to locate it in the history and press Enter.

■**Tip** Typing !-3 will cause BASH to move three paces back in the history file and run that command. In other words, it will run what you entered three commands ago.

On my Ubuntu test system, BASH remembers 1000 commands. You can view all of the remembered commands by typing history at the command prompt. The history list will scroll off the screen because it's so large, but you can use the scroll bars of the GNOME Terminal window to read it.

Each command in the history list is assigned a number. You can run any of the history commands by preceding their number with an exclamation mark (!), referred to as a *bang*, or sometimes a *shriek*. For example, you might type !923. On my test system, command number 923 in the BASH history is cd .., so this has the effect of switching me into the parent directory.

Command numbering remains in place until you log out (close the GNOME Terminal window or end a virtual console session). After this, the numbering is reordered. There will still be 1000 commands, but the last command you entered before logging out will be at the end of the list, and the numbering will work back 1000 places until the first command in the history list.

■Tip One neat trick is to type two bangs: !!. This tells BASH to repeat the last command you entered.

Rather than specifying a command number, you can type something like !cd. This will cause BASH to look in the history file, find the last instance of a command line that started with cd, and then run it.

Pressing Ctrl+R lets you search the command history from the command prompt. This particular tool can be tricky to get used to, however. As soon as you start typing, BASH will autocomplete the command based on matches found in the history file, starting with the last command in the history. What you type appears before the colon, while the auto-completion appears afterwards.

Because BASH autocompletes as you type, things can get a little confusing when you're working with the command history, particularly if it initially gets the match wrong. For example, typing cd will show the last instance of the use of cd, as in the example in Figure 17-2. This might not be what you're looking for, so you must keep typing the command you do want until it autocompletes correctly.

Figure 17-2. *BASH history completion is very useful but can also be confusing.*

Piping and Directing Output

It's not uncommon for a directory listing or output from another command to scroll off the screen. When using a GUI program like GNOME Terminal, you can use the scroll bars to view the output, but what if you are working at the bare command-line prompt?

By pressing Shift+Page Up and Shift+Page Down, you can "scroll" the window up to take a look at some of the old output, but very little is cached in this way, and you won't see more than a few screens. A far better solution is to pipe the output of the directory listing into a text viewer. Another useful technique is to redirect output to a file.

Piping the Output of Commands

Piping was one of the original innovations provided by Unix. It simply means that you can pass the output of one command to another, which is to say the output of one command can be used as input for another.

This is possible because shell commands work like machines. They usually take input from the keyboard (referred to technically as *standard input*) and, when they've done their job, usually show their output on the screen (known as *standard output*).

The commands don't need to take input from the keyboard, and they don't need to output to the screen. Piping is the process of diverting the output before it reaches the screen and passing it to another command for further processing.

Let's assume that you have a directory that is packed full of files. You want to do a long directory listing (`ls -l`) to see what permissions various files have. But doing this produces reams of output that fly off the screen. Typing something like the following provides a solution:

```
ls -l | less
```

The | symbol between the two commands is the pipe. It can be found on most US keyboards next to the square bracket keys (near the Enter key; you'll need to hold down the Shift key to get it).

What happens in the example is that `ls -l` is run by the shell, but rather than sending the output to the screen, the pipe symbol (|) tells BASH to send it to the command that follows—to `less`. In other words, the listing is displayed within `less`, where you can read it at your leisure. You can use Page Up and Page Down or the arrow keys to scroll through it. Once you quit `less`, the listing evaporates into thin air; the piped output is never actually stored as a file.

In the previous section, you saw how you can use the `history` command to view the command history. At around 1000 entries, its output scrolls off the screen in seconds. However, you can pipe it to `less`, like so:

```
history | less
```

Figure 17-3 shows the result on my test PC.

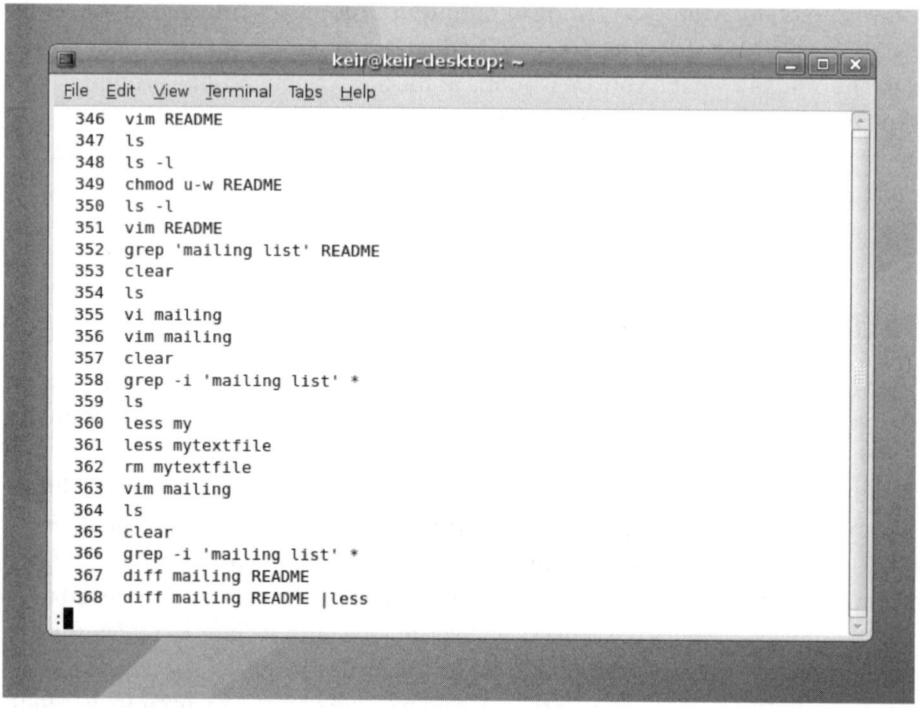

```
          keir@keir-desktop: ~                        _ □ x
File  Edit  View  Terminal  Tabs  Help
   346  vim README
   347  ls
   348  ls -l
   349  chmod u-w README
   350  ls -l
   351  vim README
   352  grep 'mailing list' README
   353  clear
   354  ls
   355  vi mailing
   356  vim mailing
   357  clear
   358  grep -i 'mailing list' *
   359  ls
   360  less my
   361  less mytextfile
   362  rm mytextfile
   363  vim mailing
   364  ls
   365  clear
   366  grep -i 'mailing list' *
   367  diff mailing README
   368  diff mailing README |less
:
```

Figure 17-3. *Piping the output of the history command into the less command lets you read the output fully.*

You can pipe the output of any command. One of the most common uses is when searching for a particular string in the output of a command. For example, let's say you know that, within a crowded directory, there's a file with a picture of some flowers. You know that the word *flower* is in the filename, but can't recall any other details. One solution is to perform a directory listing, and then pipe the results to grep, which is able to search through text for a user-defined string (see Chapter 15):

```
ls -l | grep -i 'flower'
```

In this example, the shell runs the ls -l command, and then passes the output to grep. The grep command then searches the output for the word *flower* (the -i option tells it to ignore uppercase and lowercase). If grep finds any results, it will show them on your screen.

The key point to remember is that grep is used here as it normally is at the command prompt. The only difference is that it's being passed input from a previous command, rather than being used on its own.

You can pipe more than once on a command line. Suppose you know that the filename of the picture you want involves the words *flower* and *daffodil*, yet you're unsure of where they might fall in the filename. In this case, you could type the following:

```
ls -l | grep -i flower | grep -i daffodil
```

This will pass the result of the directory listing to the first grep, which will search the output for the word *flower*. The second pipe causes the output from grep to be passed to the second grep command, where it's then searched for the word *daffodil*. Any results are then displayed on your screen.

Redirecting Output

Redirecting is like piping, except that the output is passed to a file rather than to another command. Redirecting can also work the other way: the contents of a file can be passed to a command.

If you wanted to create a file that contained a directory listing, you could type this:

```
ls -l > directorylisting.txt
```

The angle bracket (>) between the commands tells BASH to direct the output of the ls -l command into a file called directorylisting.txt. If a file with this name exists, it's overwritten with new data. If it doesn't exist, it's created from scratch.

You can add data to an already existing file using two angle brackets:

```
ls -l >> directorylisting.txt
```

This will append the result of the directory listing to the end of the file called directorylisting.txt, although, once again, if the file doesn't exist, it will be created from scratch.

Redirecting output can get very sophisticated and useful. Take a look at the following:

```
cat myfile1.txt myfile2.txt > myfile3.txt
```

As you learned in Chapter 15, the cat command joins two or more files together. If the command were used on its own without the redirection, it would cause BASH to print myfile1.txt on the screen, immediately followed by myfile2.txt. As far as BASH is concerned, it has joined myfile1.txt to myfile2.txt, and then sent them to standard output (the screen). By specifying a redirection, you have BASH send the output to a third file. Using cat with redirection is a handy way of combining two files.

It's also possible to direct the contents of a file back into a command. Take a look at the following:

```
sort < textfile.txt > sortedtext.txt
```

The sort command simply sorts words into alphanumeric order (it actually sorts them according to the ASCII table of characters, which places symbols and numbers before alphabetic characters). Directly after the sort command is a left angle bracket, which directs the contents of the file specified immediately after the bracket into the sort command. This is followed by a right angle bracket, which directs the output of the command into another file.

Tip To see a table of the ASCII characters, type man ascii at the command-line prompt.

There aren't many instances in day-to-day usage where you'll want to use the left angle bracket. It's mostly used with the text-based mail program (which lets you send e-mail from the shell), and in shell scripting, in which a lot of commands are combined together to form a simple program.

REDIRECTING STANDARD ERROR OUTPUT

Standard input and standard output are what BASH calls your keyboard and screen. These are the default input and output methods that programs use unless you specify something else, such as redirecting or piping output and input.

When a program goes wrong, its error message doesn't usually form part of standard output. Instead, it is output via *standard error*. Like standard output, this usually appears on the screen.

Sometimes, it's very beneficial to capture an error message in a text file. This can be done by redirecting the standard error output. The technique is very similar to redirecting standard output:

```
cdrecord --scanbus 2> errormessage.txt
```

The cdrecord command is used to burn CDs, and with the --scanbus command option, you tell it to search for CD-R/RW drives on the system, something which frequently results in an error message if your system is not properly configured.

After the initial command, you see the redirection. To redirect standard error, all you need to do is type 2>, rather than simply >. This effectively tells BASH to use the second type of output: standard error.

You can direct both standard output and standard error to the same file. This is done in the following way:

```
cdrecord --scanbus > error.txt 2>&1
```

This is a little more complicated. The standard output from cdrecord --scanbus is sent to the file error.txt. The second redirect tells BASH to include standard error in the standard output. In other words, it's not a case of standard output being written to a file, and then standard error being added to it. Instead, the standard error is added to standard output by BASH, and then this is written to a file.

Summary

In this chapter, we've looked at some tricks and tips to help you use the BASH shell more effectively. You've seen how BASH can help by autocompleting commands, filenames, and directories. You also learned about keyboard shortcuts that can be used to speed up operations within the shell.

This chapter also covered the command history function and how it can be used to reuse old commands, saving valuable typing time. Finally, we looked at two key functions provided by BASH: redirection and piping. This involved the explanation of standard input, output, and error.

In Part 5 of the book, starting with the next chapter, we move on to discuss the multimedia functionality within Ubuntu.

Multimedia

## CHAPTER 18

Digital Audio

Today's PC is a multimedia powerhouse, and it's hard to come across a home computer that doesn't have at least a set of speakers attached. Some people take this to extremes and have surround-sound speakers on their computers, as well as large monitors for crystal-clear video playback.

The people behind Ubuntu aren't blind to this and include not only an audio player but also a video player with the distribution. In this chapter, you'll learn how to listen to MP3s, CDs, and Internet radio on your Ubuntu system. You'll also learn how to configure Skype, the most popular Internet telephony application. In the next chapter, you'll learn how to manage video playback.

Issues Surrounding Multimedia Playback

As you might have read in the press, multimedia playback on computer devices, and Linux in particular, is hindered by a number of issues, including the following:

Software patents: Audio and video playback technologies such as MP3 and MPEG are patented in countries that allow software to be patented, such as the United States. A *patent* protects the implementation of an idea, as opposed to *copyright*, which protects the actual software. Patents are designed to restrict distribution of the technology utilizing a particular idea, unless permission is granted, usually via a payment to the license holder. Because Linux is based on the sharing of computing technology and knowledge, organizations like Ubuntu are fundamentally and philosophically opposed to any kind of software patenting. As such, they try to avoid distributing such software, which is why MP3 playback is not supported natively within Ubuntu, for example. This doesn't make playback of popular music and video files impossible, but it means that extra software must be downloaded and installed. Additionally, the use of patented software raises ethical issues, such as the fact that using patented software runs counter to the aims of Linux and the open source movement.

▥**Note** It isn't the job of this book to dictate a position for you on the ethics of using software that has been patented. That's something you must do on your own. It's a very complicated issue, but Wikipedia has a good summary of the arguments: `http://en.wikipedia.org/wiki/Software_patent`.

Digital Rights Management (DRM): Much more devastating than patenting is DRM, a technology tied into audio or video playback software. It's designed to control how, where, when, and on what device you can play certain media. For example, Apple's iTunes DRM scheme means you can play back MP3s bought from iTunes only on their iPod range of devices (including the Apple TV and iPhone range of devices) phone) or using the iTunes software. DVD movie players include a form of DRM called Content Scrambling System (CSS), which prevents users from playing DVDs on computers unless special software is purchased. Perhaps it goes without saying that the Linux community, including the Ubuntu project, is also fundamentally opposed to DRM. Because of this, practically no DRM software has been officially ported to Linux, so you can't, for example, play music purchased via the iTunes or Napster online stores.

Linux and other open source programmers are very resourceful and are often able to reverse-engineer technology formats in order to get around DRM or patent issues. But the laws in many countries—with the United States as a particularly strident example—prohibit reverse engineering in this way. In addition, the laws in some countries seek to prohibit use of software resulting from this process.

▥**Note** You may be wondering why music and movie corporations are so intent on enforcing DRM and patenting if these schemes give their customers such a hard time. To learn more, and to find out what you can do to help halt the progress of such technology, visit the Electronic Frontier Foundation's web site: `www.eff.org`.

Programmers have also come up with Free Software alternatives to proprietary formats. Examples include the Ogg media format, which is every bit as good as MP3 but is unencumbered by patent issues. We'll look at using Ogg later in this chapter, in the "Choosing a Format" section; it's an excellent way of avoiding issues surrounding patenting. However, at the moment, there's no ideal open source video format, or at least not one that's in widespread use.

As an end-user migrating from Windows or Mac OS X, it's likely you'll want to add support for MP3 and popular video file playback formats, at least until you can switch yourself over to open source file formats. Throughout this and the next chapter, we'll examine installing media playback software and using it in concert with Ubuntu's built-in playback software, even though some of that software may have issues surrounding patenting. In one case, the software is designed to bypass the DRM scheme that protects DVD movie discs.

■**Note** The United States and Japan both have laws allowing software to be patented. Most other countries, including those within the European Union, do not currently allow software patents.

AUTOMATING MULTIMEDIA SETUP

Despite the fact that it comes with limited multimedia support out of the box, Ubuntu is capable of comprehensive audio and video playback so long as the right software packages are installed. Additionally, in many cases, some additional configuration stages are necessary.

I cover this in this chapter and the next, but if all that hard work fills you with dread, you might want to download either Automatix (`www.getautomatix.com`) or EasyUbuntu (`http://easyubuntu.freecontrib.org`). These are two programs that automate the installation of third-party software, such as audio codecs, as well as other useful software such as Adobe Acrobat and several items of open source software not installed under Ubuntu by default. Also worth investigating is Bumps, which installs just the multimedia codec software. For more information, see `http://ubuntuforums.org/showthread.php?t=181248`.

Personally, I avoid using programs like these, because they automate things too much. Although Bumps is a little more transparent in its operation, both Automatix and EasyUbuntu download and install packages with a single click, and it's not entirely clear where these packages come from or what additional configuration changes are being made to my system. Although these are very well established and trusted by thousands of users, I consider it a risk to hand over complete control of my system to third-party software packages, none of which are official or affiliated in any way with the main Ubuntu project.

Playing Audio Files: Overview

Audio playback under Ubuntu is normally handled by the Rhythmbox player. This is a simple but feature-packed piece of software that can play back audio files, podcasts, Internet radio, and even CDs. However, Totem, the Ubuntu movie player, can also play back digital audio files. Additionally, Sound Juicer is the default application for playback of audio CDs.

Like many modern music players, Rhythmbox can also manage your music collection, arranging it into a library so you can locate songs easily. This makes it a better choice for playback if you have many digital audio files, although Totem is good for quick playback of individual files, such as auditioning those you've just downloaded.

Out of the box, Ubuntu supports playback of Ogg Vorbis and FLAC across all its audio playback applications. These are two open source audio file formats, and I explain more about these in the "Choosing a Format" section later in this chapter.

To use Rhythmbox or Totem to play back the most ubiquitous audio file format—MP3— you need to download and install additional software, which is explained in the next section.

Installing Codecs

Software that handles the decoding (and also encoding) of digital music files is called a *codec*. The word is a shortened version of *coder-decoder*. For any digital multimedia file type you want to play on your computer, you'll need an appropriate codec. This includes both audio and video files. In addition, if you wish to create your own multimedia files, you might need to download an additional codec that allows the *encoding* of files, such as if you create MP3s from CD audio tracks.

The necessary audio codec software for MP3 playback and encoding can be found in Ubuntu's online software repositories, although you'll need to ensure that the Universe and Multiverse repositories are added—see Chapter 8 for details.

■Note The software required for video playback *can't* be found in the Ubuntu repositories, and you must add additional repositories. This is covered in the next chapter.

There are two possible paths to follow when installing audio codecs. As mentioned previously, the issue of patenting has had a large impact on the distribution of codecs. What's more, the issue has not been resolved with 100% clarity, leaving many end uers in a legal gray area.

Several audio codecs available for Linux, contained primarily in the `gstreamer-plugins-ugly` software packages, are not licensed with the patent holders. This is of little issue to you, as an end user. It's a practical concern only for the distributors of the codecs, because the laws of some countries state that it's their duty to pay patent licensing fees. But it's something you should be aware of.

If you wish to avoid using such software, you'll be pleased to hear that one audio codec available for Ubuntu *is* licensed with the MP3 patent holder: the Fluendo MP3 codec. In an act of generosity, the Fluendo company paid the MP3 technology license and made their own decoder freely available for all Linux users. For more info, see `www.fluendo.com/resources/fluendo_mp3.php`.

The Fluendo codec doesn't avoid the ethical considerations surrounding using patented technology, as discussed early in this chapter, but it does leave you in the best possible position. However, the Fluendo codec can only be used to *decode* MP3 audio. It can't be used to *encode* MP3s, so if you wish to rip tracks to MP3 from audio CDs, you will have to use the less legally precise `gstreamer-plugins-ugly` packages (or, better still, use the open source Ogg Vorbis format, which avoids patenting issues).

I would advise you to install the Fluendo codec if you simply want to listen to your existing MP3 tracks and would like to embrace open source audio file formats from this point onward. If you are not yet ready to abandon MP3 technology, which might be the case if you have a portable MP3 player, for example, then you should follow the instructions explaining how to install the `gstreamer-plugins-ugly` software packages.

Installing the Fluendo MP3 Codec

Before installing the Fluendo codec, ensure that the Universe software repository is activated. You can read how to do this in Chapter 8 in the "Setting Up Online Software Repositories" section.

Open Synaptic Package Manager, and click the Search button. Then search for `gstreamer0.10-fluendo-mp3`. In the results, click the check box alongside the entry, and click Mark for Installation. Then click the Apply button on the toolbar.

Once the software is installed, MP3 files should play in both Totem and Rhythmbox.

Installing the gstreamer-plugin-ugly Packages

The `gstreamer-plugin-ugly`, `gstreamer-plugin-ugly-multiverse`, and `liblame` software packages install a variety of codecs that allow the playback of the majority of audio file types under Ubuntu. Chief among the codecs are the MAD decoder and the LAME encoder. MAD allows MP3 playback, while LAME allows MP3 encoding, which you'll need later on in the "Ripping Music from CDs" section (if you wish to encode tracks as MP3 files; it's not necessary if you wish to encode in Vorbis or FLAC formats).

Perhaps it goes without saying that, because of the patent issues, the software packages are in the Universe and Multiverse repositories. Ensure these package repositories are enabled if they aren't already—see the "Setting Up Online Software Repositories" section in Chapter 8.

To install the packages, open the Synaptic Package Manager (Settings ➤ Administration), click Search, and type the following in the Search box:

```
gstreamer0.10-plugins-ugly
```

In the list of results, click the check box alongside `gstreamer0.10-plugins-ugly` and `gstreamer0.10-plugins-ugly-multiverse`. Mark both for installation, and click the Apply button on the toolbar.

You'll be informed that several dependencies will be included, including `liblame`. See Figure 18-1 for an example. Once the packages are installed, MP3 playback will be possible under Totem and Rhythmbox.

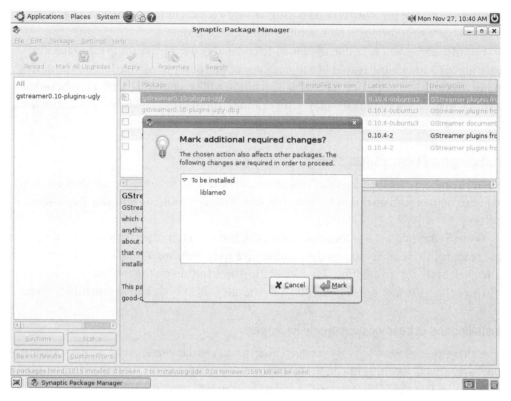

Figure 18-1. *Installing the* liblame *package will allow you to encode MP3s.*

Playing Audio Files

Both Rhythmbox and Totem can be used for audio file playback under Ubuntu. Rhythmbox is best if you have a lot of MP3 tunes, because it is able to catalog and manage your collection. You'll find it on the Applications ➤ Sound & Video menu.

The first time you start the program, it runs through a wizard that will ask you where your music files are stored. Simply click the Browse button, and then double-click the folder that holds those files. Click OK, and then click Apply to finish the wizard.

Unlike iTunes, or some other comparable programs, Rhythmbox doesn't copy your music to its own library folders when cataloging it. Instead, it merely creates an index of the files you already have. Therefore, if you move or delete any files, Rhythmbox might get confused. This can be alleviated by clicking Music ➤ Import Folder and reimporting the files (for single files, click Music ➤ Import File).

The program starts in the Browse mode, which means that your music files are listed at the bottom of the program window, and in roughly the middle-left of the program window, you'll find a listing of the artists behind the MP3s in your collection. On the right, you'll see the album that the music track is taken from (provided that information is included in the music file itself, such as the MP3 ID3 tags). Figure 18-2 shows an example of a Rhythmbox window.

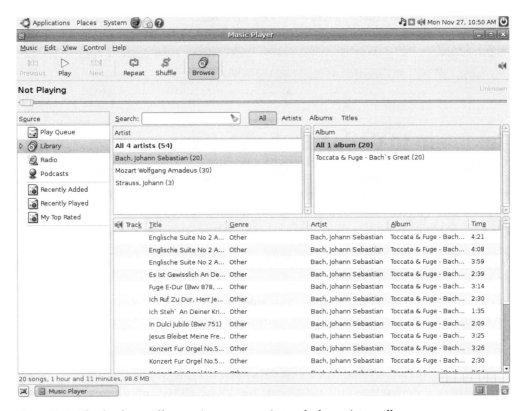

Figure 18-2. *Rhythmbox will organize your music tracks by artist or album.*

Clicking the Browse button on the toolbar will turn off the Browse view and simply present a list the tracks in your collection, which can be ordered by clicking the headings in the list. The default sort order is by artist.

Playing a track is simply a matter of double-clicking it in the list at the bottom. Once the track is finished, Rhythmbox will play the next track in the MP3 file list. At the top of the Rhythmbox window are transport controls that let you pause or play the track, skip tracks, repeat tracks, or switch to shuffle play (that is, random track selection). Beneath this is a slider that shows the progress through the current song and lets you cue forward and backward by clicking and dragging.

To create a new playlist, right-click under the Source heading in the pane on the far left side of the program window, and select New Playlist. Then type its name. To add tracks to the playlist, click Library in the Source pane, and then drag-and-drop files onto your new playlist entry. To start playing the tracks in the playlist, select it and double-click the first track in the list.

■Note I noticed that whenever I double-clicked an an audio file in a Nautilus window, Ubuntu would try to start the Totem Movie Player rather than Rhythmbox. This is good if you want to preview tracks, but to have them imported into Rhythmbox when you double-click them, you'll need to change the Open With preferences. This is easily done. Right-click any MP3 file, select Properties, and click the Open With tab. Ensure that the radio button alongside its entry in the list is selected, and then click the Close button. Curiously, however, the track will only be imported if Rhythmbox is already up and running!

Tuning In to Online Radio Stations

By clicking the Radio heading in the Source pane of the Rhythmbox, you can listen to a number of predefined Internet radio stations or add your own. Provided the MP3 codec software is installed, as discussed previously, Rhythmbox is compatible with streaming MP3-based playlists, such as those listed at `http://shoutcast.com` or `http://live365.com`.

To listen to a radio station within Rhythmbox, simply double-click its entry in the list. To stop playback, deselect the Play button on the toolbar by clicking it.

To add a new station, right-click in some blank space below the list of existing stations, and click New Internet Radio Station. Then enter its URL.

A much easier way of adding a station is to open its playlist (`.pls`) within Rhythmbox by downloading it directly from a web site. For example, browsing to the Shoutcast web site and clicking the Tune In button alongside a station listed there will open a dialog box whereby you can download and open the `.pls` file within Rhythmbox. Similarly, clicking the Play button alongside a site listed on the Live365 web site will offer a `.pls` file that you can then choose to open within Rhythmbox (although the site will first open a pop-up window). Note that Rhythmbox has to be already running in the background for the station to be successfully imported into its list.

Once the station has been imported into the list of stations, you'll then need to double-click its entry to tune in.

■Note Some online radio station playback utilizes RealPlayer or Windows Media Player format. These usually stream directly from a station's web site. You'll be able to tune in to these too by following the instructions in the next chapter, which discusses installing video playback codecs and software.

Some people prefer to use the Streamtuner program to find online radio stations to listen to. This acts as a station cataloging program, and it can be downloaded using Synaptic Package Manager. You should also search for and download xmms, which is a media player that's needed by Streamtuner for the actual playback. See Figure 12-3 to see Streamtuner in action.

■**Note** XMMS utilizes mpg123 for its MP3 playback. Like LAME and MAD, this is an unlicensed implementation of MP3 technology.

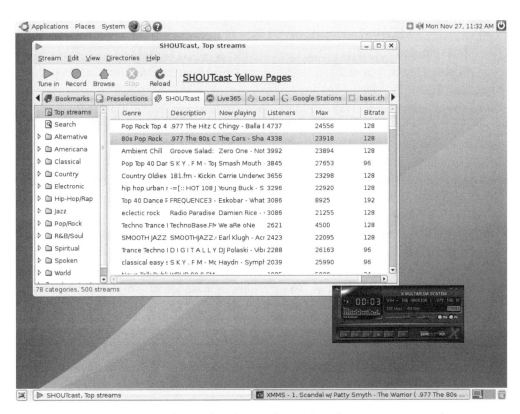

Figure 18-3. *Rhythmbox can play back online radio stations, but some users prefer to use Streamtuner and XMMS.*

Listening to Podcasts

Podcasts are audio files that are distributed by RSS (Real Simple Syndication). This sounds complicated, but it's actually quite simple. It means that, once you're subscribed to a particular podcast, the audio files are always downloaded automatically in the background, so that the latest episodes will always be available. This makes keeping up with the latest episodes effortless. Most podcasts take the form of MP3 files, but any audio file format can be used.

In terms of content, podcasts range from simple spoken blog entries, usually created by individuals, to podcasts that are more akin to radio shows and involve interviews. Some professional radio stations even release entire shows as podcasts, with the British Broadcasting Corporation (BBC) leading the charge (`www.bbc.co.uk/radio/downloadtrial`).

Rhythmbox is able to handle podcast subscriptions under Ubuntu, and you can add a new subscription by clicking the Podcast heading under the Sources pane of Rhythmbox, right-clicking a blank spot in the track listing area, and selecting New Podcast Feed. Then enter the URL.

However, a much easier way of adding a podcast is to use Firefox. Ensure Rhythmbox is open in the background, and using Firefox, browse to the page where the podcast is made available. Then click the Subscribe link. This will open the `.xml` or `.rss` file within Firefox, and at the top of the window will be a drop-down list from which you can select the program you wish to use to subscribe. Click Choose Application in the drop-down list, and navigate to `/usr/bin/rhythmbox`, as shown in Figure 18-4. Click OK in the file dialog, and then click Subscribe Now in the Firefox window.

Switch back to Rhythmbox, and click the Podcasts heading on the left of the window, and you should see the latest episode of the podcast being downloading automatically, with a progress meter alongside the entry in the list (remember that some podcasts can be long, which makes for large file sizes). To start listening to a podcast, simply double-click it.

If you want to download a particular episode, right-click it, and select Download Episode.

■**Tip** You can start listening to a podcast before it's completely downloaded.

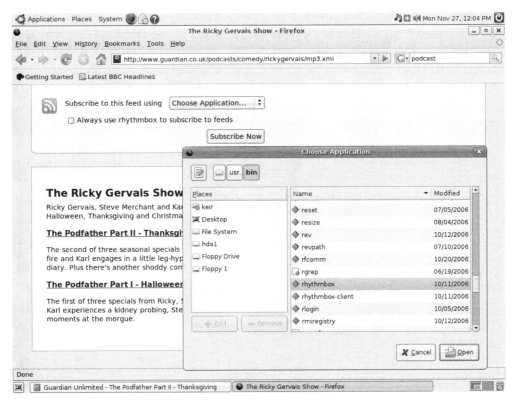

Figure 18-4. *The best way of subscribing to a podcast is to select it within Firefox and then choose to subscribe using Rhythmbox.*

Listening to Audio CDs

Playing back audio CDs is simple. Just insert the CD, and you should find that Sound Juicer starts automatically. Alternatively, click Applications ➤ Sound & Video ➤ Sound Juicer CD Extractor.

However, you can also listen to audio CDs using Rhythmbox. Simply close Sound Juicer, and then start Rhythmbox. Click the name of the CD in the Sources list on the left of the window, and click the Play button on the toolbar.

Figure 18-5 shows Sound Juicer alongside Rhythmbox in audio-CD mode.

In both Sound Juicer and Rhythmbox, provided you're online, the track and artist information will be looked up online, so you should find a complete listing. To start playing the CD in
either application, simply click the Play button. This is located at the bottom of the window in
Sound Juicer or the top of the window within Rhythmbox. Both applications also offer a slider
by which you can cue backward and forward in the track by clicking and dragging.

To eject the disk, press the button on the front of the drive. If this doesn't work, right-
click the Audio CD desktop icon, and select Eject.

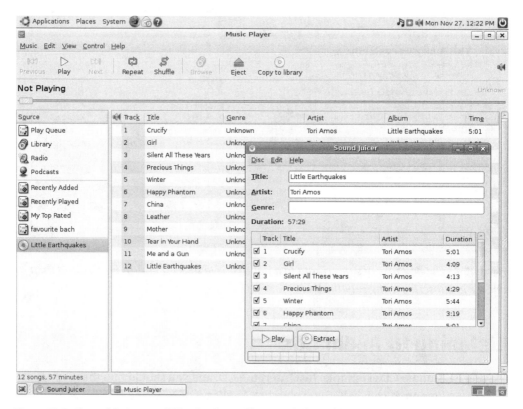

Figure 18-5. *Sound Juicer and Rhythmbox offer simple but effective CD playback, and both
look up artist and track information online.*

■**Tip** As with all GNOME applications, hover the mouse cursor over each button to display a tooltip that
describes what it does.

If you find the track listing information is incorrect, as can sometimes happen with online lookups, you can correct it within Sound Juicer by slowly double-clicking the track name— click once and then, half a second later, click again (a little like renaming files within Windows/Mac). Then type the new name. To rename a track in Rhythmbox, right-click the track, and select Properties.

Under Sound Juicer, you can then submit the revised track names to the online database by clicking Disc ➤ Submit Track Names.

Ripping Music from CDs

Converting audio tracks on a CD into digital music files you can store on your hard disk for personal use is informally known as *ripping*. It's handled under Ubuntu using the Sound Juicer application, which can be found on the Applications ➤ Sound & Video menu.

■**Note** Because of the way audio CDs work, you can't simply insert the disc and then drag-and-drop the tracks onto your hard disk. They must be converted first.

Before you start to rip CDs, however, you'll need to decide the format in which you wish to store the audio files.

Choosing a Format

You have three basic choices for audio file formats: *Ogg Vorbis*, *FLAC*, and *MP3*. Let's look at what each has to offer.

> **Ogg Vorbis:** This is the Free Software alternative to MP3. Unless you have a trained ear, you won't be able to tell the difference between a Vorbis and MP3 file (if you *do* have a trained ear, then you may find Vorbis better!). The two technologies generate files of around the same size, an average of 4MB to 5MB per song. The advantage of Vorbis is that it's completely open source technology, so you there isn't the ethical burden of using patented MP3 software and, therefore, working against the interests of the open source software movement. The downside of Vorbis is that not many portable audio players support it (although this situation is slowly changing), and other operating systems like Windows won't be able to play back Vorbis files unless some additional software is installed (see `www.vorbis.com/setup`). Therefore, Vorbis is perhaps best if you're ripping files solely for use on your computer.

FLAC: This stands for Free Lossless Audio Codec, and it's the choice of the audiophile. Vorbis and MP3 are lossy formats, which means that some of the audio data is lost in order to significantly shrink the file. FLAC doesn't lose any audio data but still manages to compress files to a certain degree (although they're still much larger than an equivalent MP3 or Ogg file). FLAC scores points, because it's open source, like Vorbis, but you'll face the same lack of support in portable audio players and other operating systems (unless additional software is installed; see `http://flac.sourceforge.net/download.html`).

MP3: This is by far the most ubiquitous music file format, and practically everyone who owns a computer has at least a handful of MP3 tracks. This means software support for MP3 playback is strong, and of course, portable audio players are built around the MP3 standard. The only problem for you, as a Linux user, is the issue of surrounding patents, as explained at the beginning of this chapter. Using the MP3 format goes against a lot of what the Linux and open source movement stands for. But in the end, the choice is up to you.

Adding MP3-Ripping Support to Sound Juicer

Not only does Sound Juicer play back audio CDs, but it's also used to rip the tracks to disk. Support for Ogg and FLAC is built into Sound Juicer, but if you wish to encode CD tracks as MP3s, you'll need to enter some configuration details into Sound Juicer. Remember that this will only work if you installed the `gstreamer-plugins-ugly` packages earlier. If you installed the Fluendo codec, you won't be able to rip tracks to MP3 files.

Follow these steps to configure MP3 support:

1. Select Applications ➤ Sound & Video ➤ Sound Juicer to start the program.

2. Click Edit ➤ Preferences. In the dialog box that appears, click the Edit Profiles button.

3. Click New, and then type MP3 in the Profile Name box. Then click Create.

4. Select the new MP3 entry in the list, and click Edit.

5. In the Profile Description box, type MP3.

6. In the GStreamer Pipeline box, type the following:

    ```
    audio/x-raw-int,rate=44100,channels=2 ! lame name=enc bitrate=160 ! id3v2mux
    ```

■**Tip** If you're an experienced MP3 ripper, you might notice that `rate=44100` and `bitrate=160` refer to the sampling frequency and bit rate, respectively. You can vary these as you see fit for higher quality audio—you might want to increase the `bitrate` number of `192`, for example, or the `rate` to `48000`. However, this will result in larger file sizes.

7. In the File Extension box, type `mp3`.

8. Put a check in the Active? box.

9. Click OK, and Close in the Edit GNOME Audio Properties window.

10. Restart Sound Juicer.

11. Click Edit ➤ Preferences again, and select your new MP3 entry from the Output Format drop-down list. Then click Close.

Ripping Tracks

When you're ready to rip some music, insert the audio CD, and then start Sound Juicer. If the CD isn't read immediately, click Disc ➤ Re-read Disc.

Click Edit ➤ Preferences. In the Output Format part of the dialog box, choose the type of audio files you want to create—Ogg Vorbis, FLAC, or, if configured, MP3. In addition, you can select where you would like the files to be saved to by clicking the drop-down list under the Music Folder heading. Once finished, click the Close button.

■**Note** Audio tracks will be saved in a directory named after the artist and in a subdirectory named after the album title.

Back in the main Sound Juicer window, any track in the listing with a check in its box will be ripped. When you insert a CD, Sound Juicer assumes that all the tracks are to be ripped. If this isn't the case, remove the checks from the tracks you don't want to rip, as shown in Figure 18-5. By selecting a track and clicking the Play button, you'll be able to audition it. This can be helpful if you're deciding on exactly which tracks to rip. Finally, check that the Title and Artist information is correct.

Figure 18-6. *Audio tracks can be ripped from CDs using the Sound Juicer program.*

To begin the process, click the Extract button. It can take up to a minute or so to rip each track, so ripping an entire CD may take some time. However, it's safe to leave Sound Juicer working in the background.

■**Tip** You can also use Rhythmbox to rip tracks. This has the advantage that the tracks are automatically imported into your music library. Simply select the CD from under the Source heading, and click Copy to Library on the toolbar. To change the file format (that is, Vorbis, MP3, etc.), click Edit ➤ Preferences, and then click the Library tab on the dialog that appears. Select from the Preferred Format drop-down list. The files will be saved into your /home directory.

MAKING MUSIC AND RECORDING AUDIO

Most PCs come with sound cards that are capable of making music. You can use many open source programs, designed for both amateurs and professionals alike, to create music or record and edit audio.

In terms of musical sequencers, Muse (www.muse-sequencer.org), Rosegarden (www.rosegardenmusic.com), and Jazz++ (www.jazzware.com/zope) are well worth investigating. Like all modern MIDI sequencers, all three programs let you record audio tracks, effectively turning your PC into a recording studio.

It's also possible to run virtual synthesizers on your PC, which effectively turn even the most basic sound card into a powerful musical instrument. Examples include Bristol (`www.slabexchange.org`) and FluidSynth (`www.fluidsynth.org`).

If you're interested in only audio recording and processing, Sweep (`www.metadecks.org/software/sweep/`) and Audacity (`http://audacity.sourceforge.net`) are worth a look. In addition to audio recording and playback, both feature graphical waveform editing and powerful filters.

Most of the packages mentioned here are available from the Ubuntu software repositories, and you can download them with the Synaptic Package Manager.

Creating Your Own CDs

You can create audio CDs by using the Serpentine Audio-CD Creator program, found on the Applications ➤ Sound & Video menu.

Start by inserting a blank CD. Almost immediately, Ubuntu will ask what you want to do with the disc via a dialog box. If you choose Make Audio CD, Serpentine will open automatically.

The program is very simple to use. Click the Add button on the toolbar, and then browse to your store of files (these can be Ogg, FLAC, or MP3, if you installed the MP3 playback sofware earlier; both the Fluendo and `gstreamer-plugins-ugly` packages will work fine).

Then select the tracks you wish to go onto the CD. As with Windows, Shift-click to select many tracks at once, or hold down Ctrl and click multiple individual tracks.

After clicking Open to add the tracks, you'll see the track listing build up in the Serpentine program window. In addition, a small graphic of a CD will also fill up, like a pie chart, showing how much space is left on the CD. You can rearrange the track listing by clicking and dragging the tracks to new locations.

When you're happy with the track listing, click the Write to Disc button to start the write procedure. First, the tracks are converted to pure audio files, and then they're actually burned to disc, as shown in Figure 18-7. This can take some time. When Serpentine finishes with the burning, the CD will be ejected.

■**Tip** Depending on the quality of the blank CD, you might not be able to write audio CDs at full speed. If this is the case, Serpentine will stop during the writing process with an error message. Click Edit ➤ Preferences on the menu, and click the radio button next to Choose Writing Speed. Then enter a more conservative speed.

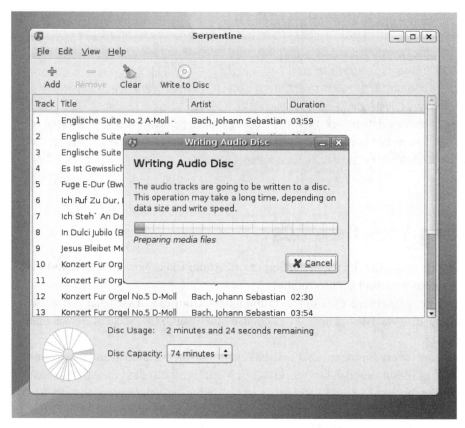

Figure 18-7. *Serpentine Audio-CD Creator makes it easy to create CDs from digital audio files.*

Installing Skype

Skype is used by millions of people around the world to make Internet telephone calls via Voice over IP (VoIP). This is a complicated way of saying that voice calls are transmitted across the Internet. Using Skype, it's possible to call other Skype users for free, or to call various phone numbers around the world, usually for a small charge.

Installing Skype is easy, and the developers at Skype have even created a software repository from which it can be installed. This means that you'll be informed via Software Update whenever a new version of Skype becomes available.

To add the Skype repository, click System ➤ Administration ➤ Software Sources. Click the Third Party tab in the window that appears, and then click the Add button. In the APT Line text box, type the following:

```
deb http://download.skype.com/linux/repos/debian/ stable non-free
```

Note the spaces between debian/ and stable and between stable and non-free.

Then click the Add Source button. Click Close, and click the Reload button on the dialog box that appears.

To install Skype, open Synaptic Package Manager (System ➤ Administration), click Search, and type skype into the search box. Then click Search. In the list of results, put a check alongside the entry, and click Mark for Installation. You'll see an error message about Skype not being authenticated and that an additional package needs to be installed, but this is acceptable, so click the Mark button on the dialog box. Then click Apply on the toolbar to install the software.

Once the software has installed, click Applications ➤ Internet ➤ Skype to start it. Using Skype under Linux is almost exactly the same as using the same program under Windows or Macintosh, as shown in Figure 18-7. You'll find excellent documentation at www.skype.com.

Tip To configure your audio input devices, such as the microphone, right-click the Speaker icon at the top-right of the desktop, and select Open Volume Control. Then click and drag the slider on the Microphone entry as necessary. You may have to unmute the input by removing the red check next to the speaker icon below the microphone sliders.

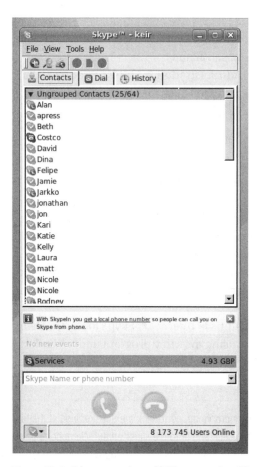

Figure 18-8. *It's easy to install Skype under Ubuntu and it works in almost exactly the same way as it does under Windows or Macintosh.*

Summary

This chapter has covered the audio functions built into Ubuntu and how, by downloading a few extra system files, you can play back the majority of audio files in existence. We started by discussing the moral and legal dilemmas associated with multimedia play-back on a computer. Then we moved on to look at how to install the necessary codec files on your computer, before discussing how you can listen to music files, CDs, and online radio stations.

We examined how you can convert CDs into music files, and then the inverse of this: how you can create CDs using audio files. Finally, we examined how you can install Skype on your computer.

In Chapter 19, we'll look at how you can play back movies and online animations using Ubuntu.

CHAPTER 19

■ ■ ■

Movies and Multimedia

Movie playback is becoming increasingly popular on computers. Modern PCs come equipped with DVD-ROM drives and, coupled to the right software, these can play DVD movie discs. In addition, many web sites feature streaming movie clips or offer them for download.

Ubuntu provides support for movie playback but, as with audio support, you'll need to install additional codecs in order to enjoy the broadest range of playback options. This chapter explains how to set up Ubuntu for watching videos, DVDs, and TV on your computer, as well as playing web site Flash animations and videos.

Installing Playback Software

You use the Totem Movie Player application to play back video under Ubuntu, as shown in Figure 19-1. Like the other multimedia software provided with Ubuntu, it's basic but effective and does the job well. However, because of licensing and patenting issues, Totem doesn't support all video formats out of the box. In fact, it supports very few of those you might be used to using under Windows or Macintosh.

If you wish to play back the most common video files, such as those listed in Table 19-1, you must install additional software. First, you must download the w32codecs software package. This contains codecs that allow you to play Windows Media Player, RealPlayer, QuickTime, and DivX movie files under Ubuntu, as well as a handful of other file formats.

In addition, you'll need to download the totem-xine package. This will switch the Totem Movie Player package to use the Xine multimedia framework, rather than Gstreamer. See the "Multimedia Frameworks" sidebar for an explanation of this.

You'll also need to download the libxine-extracodecs package, which will provide a handful of vital extra codecs that allow the w32codecs package to work correctly with Totem.

The files within the w32codecs package are quite literally lifted straight from a Windows installation. In fact, they're simply the .dll system files that constitute the codecs under Windows.

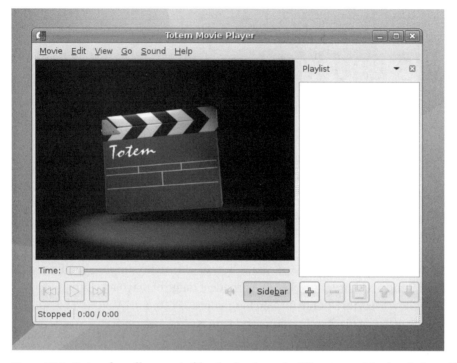

Figure 19-1. *Totem handles movie file playback under Ubuntu and is simple but effective.*

As you might expect, this makes for another legally gray situation. It's unlikely that the companies who created the codecs sanction their distribution in this way. In fact, distributing them in this way is certainly breaching their copyright. But, on the other hand, none of the companies behind the codecs have made any attempt to stop distribution of the package, despite the fact that it's been openly and freely available for many years.

There's an untested theory that using the w32codecs package is legally OK if you fulfil the following three requirements: you own a license for Windows; you have installed the relevant media player applications under Windows (if you dual-boot); and you agreed to their license agreements. After all, you're simply using the system files in a different way and on a different operating system. But this is far from a cast-iron defense in legal terms.

There's even a cynical theory that the reason the companies whose software is in the w32codecs package haven't attempted to stop distribution is because they *want* Linux users to use their playback software! Competition within the world of multimedia codecs is fierce and Windows Media Player, QuickTime, and RealPlayer are all fighting to become the *de facto* multimedia format. By turning a blind eye to the distribution of the w32codecs package, the companies behind the codecs can add the millions of Linux users to their user bases with zero effort!

However, while the fact remains that nobody has even got in trouble for distributing or installing the w32codecs package, there's no guarantee that this situation won't change in the future.

■**Note** Video and audio playback within Firefox are handled via the Totem browser plug-in, in exactly the same way as the Windows Media Player and QuickTime browser plug-ins work under Windows. This is set up automatically and is also compatible with the `w32codecs` package once it's installed. However, many web sites offering streaming content attempt to probe your setup to ensure you have the required media player software and balk when unable to find Windows Media Player or QuickTime. This makes playback difficult, although more and more sites are switching to video playback via Flash Player. Installing this is covered later in the chapter.

Table 19-1. *Popular Movie File Formats*

Format	Typical File Extensions	Web Site	Notes
Windows Media Player 9	`.wmv, .wma, .asx, .asf`	`www.microsoft.com/ windows/windowsmedia`	Default format for Windows Media Player and, therefore, for most Windows users. Although it's possible to play Windows Media Player files under Ubuntu, you won't be able to play DRM-restricted files (those that rely on the download and installation of a certificate).
Real Video	`.rm, .ram`	`www.real.com`	By downloading the `w32codecs` package, you can play back Real Video files in Totem. However, you can also download a Linux version of RealPlayer. Both approaches are described in this chapter.
QuickTime	`.mov, .qt`	`www.quicktime.com`	QuickTime is Apple's default media format and has gained ground on both Windows and Macintosh computers. As with Windows Media Player, you won't be able to play DRM-restricted files.
DivX	`.avi, .divx`	`www.divx.com`	The DivX format is one of the most popular formats for those in the Internet community who like to encode their own movies. It's renowned for its ability to shrink movies to very small sizes.

MULTIMEDIA FRAMEWORKS

In simple terms, there are three software components needed for multimedia playback under Ubuntu: a player application, the multimedia framework, and codecs.

- **Player application:** This is the software that's actually used to listen to music or display videos. It's the part of the multimedia system that you interact with. Under Ubuntu, Totem Movie Player is used to play back video, and Rhythmbox is used to handle audio. However, if you install the KDE desktop, Kaffeine will be used to play back movies, and armaroK will be used to handle audio playback.

- **Multimedia framework:** This is like the behind-the-scenes middleman who puts the player application in touch with the codecs, which are explained next. The multimedia framework preferred by Ubuntu is called Gstreamer, while the multimedia framework preferred by KDE is called Xine. The multimedia framework is a background component of your system, and you won't come into direct contact with it apart from when you're initially configuring your system for media playback. However, it's important to note that more than one multimedia framework can be installed, as is described in this chapter, because this is sometimes necessary to utilize certain codecs.

- **Codecs:** Short for coder-decoder, codecs are the small pieces of software that handle multimedia file decoding. Codecs do all the hard work. Most multimedia file formats are compressed, to make for smaller file sizes, and the codec's job is to expand the files again, so that they can be played back on your computer (some codecs also work the other way around by shrinking files).

Under Ubuntu, the Gstreamer multimedia framework is installed by default, along with a handful of codecs. However, to play back common video formats used in the world at large—such Windows Media and QuickTime—the installation of additional codecs and the Xine framework is necessary. The installation of the `totem-xine` package configures the Totem movie player to use Xine instead of Gstreamer.

Installing Codecs

To install the `w32codecs` package, you'll need to subscribe to a new software repository that is provided by Debian Multimedia (`www.debian-multimedia.org`). This is a simple third-party project created to package multimedia software in Debian installation file formats (Ubuntu is based on Debian). It primarily consists of the aforementioned software repository.

Note Subscribing to the repository, rather than manually downloading the files, has the advantage that you'll be informed via Software Update if the package is updated in the future.

You'll also need to install the `totem-xine` and `libxine-extracodecs` packages, which are contained in Ubuntu's Universe and Multiverse software repositories. If you haven't already, you should follow the instructions in Chapter 8, describing how to add these to Synaptic Package Manager. Look under the heading "Setting Up Online Software Repositories."

Here are the steps to install all the necessary software packages. After following the instructions in this section, you will be able to play video files on your hard disk and stream video from web sites within Firefox:

1. Click System ➤ Administration ➤ Software Sources. Then click the Third Party tab in the window that appears.

2. Click the Add button, and in the Apt Line text box, type the following:

   ```
   deb http://www.debian-multimedia.org etch main
   ```

▓Note Etch is the version of Debian that the version of Ubuntu supplied with this book, Edgy (6.10), is based on. In theory, most software designed for Etch should also work with Edgy, as is the case with the Debian Multimedia software.

---

3. Click the Add button and then the Close button in the Software Sources window. You'll be informed that the information about the available software is out of date, so click the Reload button. At the end of the procedure, you'll see an error message along the lines of "W: GPG error: http//www.debian-multimedia.org . . ." This can be ignored. It means that the security key of the new repository hasn't been imported into Ubuntu and that the veracity of the packages can't be confirmed. However, there's no need to worry about this when installing just a handful of packages, as here.

4. Open Synaptic Package Manager (it's on the System ➤ Administration menu). Click the Search button, and in the Find dialog box, type `w32codecs`. Click the Search button.

5. In the results, put a check in the box next to the package, and click Mark for Installation. You'll see a warning about the package not being authenticated, but this is fine. Click the Mark button to close the dialog box.

6. Click the Search button again, and in the Search text box, type `totem-xine`. Click the check box alongside its entry in the results list, and click Mark for Installation. You'll be told that several additional packages need to be installed, and that `totem-gstreamer` needs to be removed. This is fine, so click the Mark button in the dialog box.

7. Click Search again, and this time, enter `libxine-extracodecs`. Mark it for installation as before. Once again, you'll be told an extra package needs to be installed, and this is fine.

8. To install all the software packages, click the Apply button on the toolbar. In the Summary dialog box, you'll be informed that you're about to install Not Authenticated packages, and that some other packages are to be removed. This is all fine. Click the Apply button in the dialog.

9. Once the software has downloaded and installed, log out and then back into Ubuntu. Following this, file playback should work fine within Totem, and streaming video/audio should work fine within Firefox.

Installing RealPlayer

If you wish to install RealPlayer, follow steps 1-3 under the "Installing Codecs" heading to subscribe to the Debian Multimedia repository, if you haven't already. Next, open Synaptic Package Manager, and search for `realplayer`. Put a check in the box alongside the package in the list of results, and click Mark for Installation. You'll be warned that the package isn't authenticated, but this is fine, so click the Mark button. Then click Apply to start the installation. You'll be warned again that the package isn't authenticated, but click the Apply button in the dialog box.

Once installation within Synaptic has finished, start RealPlayer by clicking Applications ➤ Sound & Video ➤ RealPlayer. This will run the first-time setup wizard that will install the browser plug-ins, so that you can watch streaming RealPlayer video (or listen to RealPlayer audio) within Firefox. Simply click the Forward button. See Figure 19-2 for an example.

One final step is necessary after this, but only if you've installed the `w32codecs` package. Open a terminal window (Applications ➤ Accessories ➤ Terminal), and type the following:

```
sudo rm -rf /usr/lib/firefox/plugins/libtotem-complex-plugin.*
```

This will delete the `w32codecs` version of the RealPlayer plug-in, allowing the native Linux RealPlayer to handle Real video and audio streams. Bear in mind that RealPlayer audio and video streams won't work until you close down and restart Firefox (ensure that all instances of Firefox are closed, including the Download window).

■**Tip** To see what plug-ins are installed under Firefox, type `about:plugins` in the address bar.

Figure 19-2. *After RealPlayer has been installed via Synaptic, you must run through its setup program to install the browser plug-in.*

Installing Adobe Flash Player

Flash Player is a standard fixture on most modern browsers. It allows access to not only animation but also to interactive web sites and games. Increasingly Flash Player is used for online video, such as that provided at YouTube (www.youtube.com), as shown in Figure 19-3.

Adobe makes a player especially for Linux, and you can download it from the Ubuntu software repositories.

To install Flash Player, open Synaptic Package Manager (System ➤ Administration), and search for flashplugin-nonfree.

■**Note** Flash Player is contained in the Multiverse repository—see the "Setting Up Online Software Repositories" heading in Chapter 8.

Mark it for installation, and click Apply. This will download a handful of packages and start the Flash Player installation routine. You'll be asked if you agree to the software license and want to complete downloading the plug-in. The license isn't displayed but can be viewed at www.adobe.com/products/eulas/players. Assuming you agree, put a check in the box, and click the Forward button. Following this, the software will be set up, and the actual plug-in software downloaded and automatically configured.

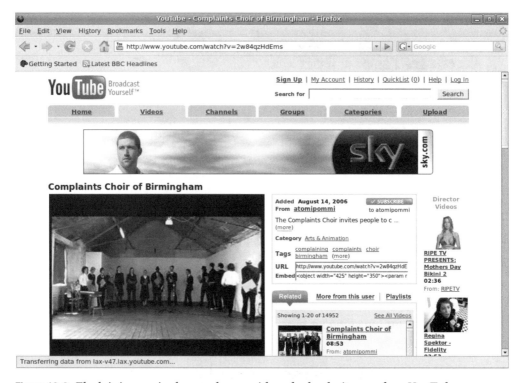

Figure 19-3. *Flash is increasingly popular on video playback sites, such as YouTube.*

Once installation has finished, log out of Ubuntu and then back in again. Configuration is automatic, and you should now be able to visit any Flash site with Firefox.

Sadly, there isn't a Linux version of the Shockwave Director browser plug-in. If you really need to have access to Shockwave sites under Linux, consider using CrossOver Office (`www.codeweavers.com`) to install the Windows version. But be aware that CrossOver Office is commercial product, and you'll need to pay for it.

Installing the Java Runtime Engine

Some sites use Java to present interaction, animation, and even movies. You can install the Sun Java Runtime program by searching for `sun-java5-plugin` within Synaptic Package Manager. In the list of results, check the check box, and select Mark for Installation. Several additional packages will have to be installed too, and this is fine. When the packages have finished downloading via Synaptic, you'll see the Java setup screen, where you'll be able to agree to the license. Put a check in the Do You Agree box, and click the Forward button. This will complete installation.

When everything is installed, log out and then back in again.

■**Note** At the time of this writing, the Java Runtime sofware is contained in the Multiverse repository—see the "Setting Up Online Software Repositories" heading in Chapter 8 if you don't already have this set up.

Watching Movies

To play a movie file on your hard disk, simply double-click its icon. This will automatically start Totem, as shown in Figure 19-4.

■**Note** By default, all video files will play in Totem, including RealMedia. To change this so that RealPlayer handles its own file types, right-click any RealPlayer movie file, select Open With, and click Add. Locate Real-Player in the list, click the Add button, and then make sure the radio button alongside RealPlayer is selected.

Figure 19-4. *Properly configured, Totem can play just about every kind of movie file, such as QuickTime, Windows Media Player, or DivX, as here.*

Using Totem is easy, and the interface only has a handful of options. At the bottom-left of the screen are the transport controls that allow you to pause, play, or move forward and backward in the video file. Alternatively, you can right-click the video window and select the controls from there.

Above the controls is the Time bar. With certain types of video, you can drag the slider to move through the video, but not all files support this function.

At the right of the program window is a playlist. You can queue several video files to be played in sequence by simply dragging and dropping movies from a Nautilus file browser window. You can hide the playlist by clicking the Sidebar button. This gives nearly all of Totem's program window to the playback window.To play the video full screen, thereby hiding the desktop and Totem controls, press the F key. To return to the program window, press Escape. In full-screen mode, you can start and stop the video by pressing the space bar.

To adjust the image quality, click Edit ➤ Preferences, and click the Display tab in the Preferences dialog box. Click and drag the Brightness, Contrast, Saturation, and Hue sliders as you see fit. If a video is playing in the background, the changes will be shown as you make them.

■**Tip** If you find you have problems with video playback, such as Totem showing an error message about another application using the video output, try the following: click System ➤ Preferences ➤ Terminal, and at the prompt, type `gstreamer-properties`. Click the Video tab, and in the Output drop-down list, select Xwindows (No XV).

OPEN-SOURCE MOVIE FILE FORMATS

A number of promising open-source movie file formats are in development. Some are more mature than others, but few see widespread use at the moment. All promise much for the future. Many consider the following three formats the chief contenders:

- XviD (www.xvid.org) is a reworking of the popular DivX MPEG-4-based file format. As such, it is able to encode movies to relatively small files sizes (a 90-minute movie can fit on a CD). Despite small file sizes, it can maintain good image and sound quality. In theory, it should also be possible to play XviD movies using any MPEG-4 codec, such as DivX or QuickTime. Unfortunately, XviD uses technology covered by patents in some parts of the world, so the project exists in a legally gray area. Additionally, it's only possible to download a Windows version of the codec, although if you follow the instructions at the beginning of this chapter, you will be able to download the ported Windows version of the codec so you can play XviD files under Ubuntu.

- Ogg Theora (`www.theora.org`) is being developed by the Xiph.org Foundation, the people behind the Ogg Vorbis audio codec project that's a favorite among Linux users. As such, it promises to be a completely open-source project. Although the technology is covered by patents, Xiph.org has promised never to enforce them, meaning that anyone in the world can use Theora without charge. At the time of this writing, Theora is still in the alpha development phase, but it will almost certainly become the open-source video codec of choice in the future.

- The British Broadcasting Corporation (`www.bbc.co.uk`), the UK's largest public service broadcaster, is sponsoring development of the Dirac codec (see `http://dirac.sourceforge.net`). Dirac is less developed than both Theora and XviD at present, and it is aimed more at the broadcast/enthusiast market. For example, it is designed to support high-definition TV. However, it's certainly one to watch.

Watching DVDs

DVD movie discs are protected by a form of Digital Rights Management (DRM) called Content Scrambling System (CSS). This forces anyone who would like to create DVD playback software or hardware to pay a fee to the DVD Copy Control Association, an industry organization set up to protect DVD movie technology.

Nearly all Linux advocates are scornful of any kind of DRM system. It isn't possible to buy standalone licensed DVD playback software for Linux, but even if it were, few would be willing to support what they see as prohibitive software technology.

Some open-source advocates reverse-engineered DVD protection and came up with the *DeCSS* software. This bypasses the CSS system and allows the playback of DVD movies under practically any operating system. Sadly, DeCSS is caught in a legal quagmire. The Motion Picture Association of America (MPAA) has attempted to stop its distribution within the United States but has failed. Some experts suggest that distributing DeCSS breaks copyright laws, but there has yet to be a case anywhere in the world that proves this. Nor has there been a case proving or even suggesting that using DeCSS is in any way illegal.

Ubuntu doesn't come with DeCSS installed by default, but you can download and install the software by issuing a simple command, following the installation of a software package. Here is the procedure:

1. If you haven't already, follow the instructions under the previous "Installing Codecs" heading to install the `w32codecs` package as well as `totem-xine` and `libxine-extracodecs`.

2. Select System ➤ Administration ➤ Synaptic Package Manager.

3. Click Search, and search for libdvdread3. This might already be installed if you followed the instructions to install the gstreamer-plugins-ugly packages in the previous chapter. If the package isn't already installed, click its check box, and mark it for installation. Then click Apply. Once the package has installed, close Synaptic Package Manager.

4. Ensure Synaptic Package Manager and Software Update are closed, and then open a GNOME Terminal window (Applications ➤ Accessories ➤ Terminal). Type the following in the terminal window to download and install the DeCSS component:

```
sudo /usr/share/doc/libdvdread3/install-css.sh
```

Once the command has completed, you can close the terminal window.

After you've installed DeCSS, just insert a DVD, and Totem will automatically start playing it. Alternatively, if Totem is already open, you can play the DVD by clicking its entry on the File menu.

Playing a DVD is not dissimilar to watching movie files on your hard disk. The main difference is that you can now navigate from chapter to chapter on the DVD by clicking the relevant entry under the Go menu, as shown in Figure 19-5. You can also return to the DVD's menu this way. You can use your mouse to click entries in DVD menus.

MOVIE EDITING

The field of Linux movie-editing software is still young, and only a handful of programs are available for the nonprofessional user. One of the best is Kino (www.kinodv.org), which is available in the Ubuntu software archives. Although far from being a professional-level program, Kino allows competent users to import and edit videos, apply effects, and then output in either MPEG-1 or MPEG-2 format.

If you're looking for something more powerful, but also more complicated, then Cinelerra is well worth a look (http://heroinewarrior.com/cinelerra.php3). To quote the web site, Cinelerra is "the same kind of compositing and editing suite that the big boys use," except it's made for Linux! Sadly, Cinelerra isn't in the Ubuntu repository, and at the time of this writing, there wasn't a Ubuntu-compatible package at the web site. However, a sister project that is based on Cinelerra—Cinelerra-CV—contains a Debian package that should work fine on Ubuntu. See http://cvs.cinelerra.org for details.

MainActor (www.mainconcept.com) is the Linux version of a commercial Windows project. Although it's not free, most people agree that it's one of the most comprehensive video editors available for Linux at the moment, and possibly the easiest to use, too.

Incidentally, professional moviemakers use Linux all the time, particularly when it comes to adding special effects to movies. Movies like *Shrek 2*, *Stuart Little*, and the *Harry Potter* series all benefited from the CinePaint software running under Linux! For more details, see www.cinepaint.org.

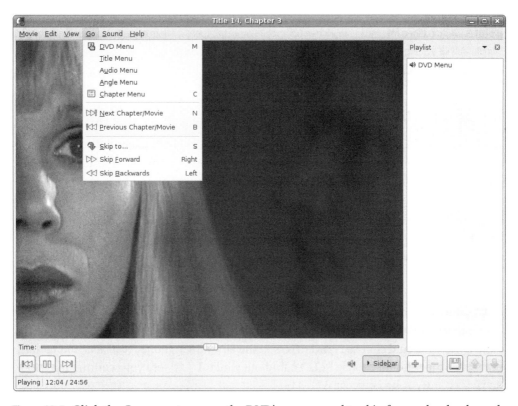

Figure 19-5. *Click the Go menu to access the DVD's menus and to skip forward or backward.*

Watching TV

If you have a TV card, you may be able to use it to watch TV under Ubuntu. Ubuntu doesn't come with a TV tuner application by default, but you can download the tvtime program from the software repositories using the Synaptic Package Manager.

Checking for Video Input

Ubuntu includes the Video for Linux project, an extension to the Linux kernel to allow many popular TV and video-capture cards to work. You can find out if yours is compatible by opening a comand prompt (Applications ➤ Accessories ➤ Terminal) and typing gstreamer-properties. Then, in the dialog box that appears, click the Video tab, and click the Test button in the Default Input Plugin part of the window. If you see a video window without an error message, then your TV card is compatible. If you receive an error message, then your card probably isn't compatible.

■Note Getting Video for Linux to work can be troublesome, but there are lots of resources out there to help. I would advise visiting the following site first: www.exploits.org/v4l/.

Installing tvtime

To download and install tvtime, open Synaptic Package Manager (System ➤ Administration), click the Search button, and enter tvtime as a search term. In the list of results, click the entry for tvtime, and mark it for installation. Then click Apply.

■Note tvtime is in the Universe repository. If you haven't already added this to your system, see the "Setting Up Online Repositories" heading in Chapter 8.

When the download has completed, you'll be asked a number of questions during the configuration process. First, you need to choose your TV picture format. Users in the United States should choose NTSC. Users in the United Kingdom, Australia, and certain parts of Europe should choose PAL. To find out which TV system your country uses, look up your country at www.videouniversity.com/standard.htm. You also need to choose your geographical area from the list so that tvtime can set the correct radio frequency range for your TV card.

Once the program is installed, you'll find it on the Applications ➤ Sound & Video menu. Using the program is straightforward, but if you need guidance, visit the program's web site at http://tvtime.sourceforge.net.

Summary

In this chapter, we looked how you can watch movies on your PC. You've seen how you can update Ubuntu to work with the most popular digital video technologies, such as Windows Media Player and QuickTime.

In addition, we looked at how you can view online multimedia such as Flash animations on your computer, and discussed how you can watch TV on your PC.

In the next chapter, we take a look at image editing under Ubuntu. You'll learn about one of the crown jewels of the Linux software scene: The GIMP.

CHAPTER 20

■ ■ ■

Digital Photos

The PC has become an increasingly useful tool in the field of photography. In fact, these days it's hard to find a professional photographer who doesn't use a computer in some way, either to download digital camera images or to scan in images taken using traditional film-based cameras.

Ubuntu includes several photo manipulation and cataloging tools. Chief among these is a professional-level image-editing program called The GIMP. The title stands for GNU Image Manipulation Program. This chapter introduces this jewel in the crown of Linux software, but first discusses how to use the gThumb and F-Spot Photo Manager software to import and manage your image collection.

Downloading and Cataloging Images

Before you can undertake any image editing, you need to transfer the images to your PC. Depending on the source of the pictures, there are a variety of methods of doing this, but in nearly every case, the work of importing your photos is handled by gThumb Image Viewer (Applications ➤ Graphics ➤ gThumb Image Viewer). After using gThumb, you can use the F-Spot Photo Manager program (Applications ➤ Graphics ➤ F-Spot Photo Manager) to organize the collection.

But first, let's briefly recap the various methods of transferring images to your PC, some of which were outlined in Chapter 8.

Connecting Your Camera

Most modern cameras use memory cards to store the pictures. If you have such a model, when you plug the camera into your PC's USB port, you should find that Ubuntu instantly recognizes it. An icon should appear on the desktop, and double-clicking it should display the memory card's contents in a Nautilus window. You will also see a dialog box explaining that a photo card has been detected and offering to import the photos. Clicking this button will start gThumb, with which you can copy the images to your hard disk. See the "Importing Photos Using gThumb" section to learn more about this procedure. Of course, you can click Cancel on the Import dialog box, and simply copy the pictures to your hard disk manually using Nautilus.

■**Note** You don't *have* to use gThumb if importing pictures, unless your camera is one that isn't recognized automatically by Ubuntu (such as older cameras that connect via the serial port). In fact, in my opinion, copying pictures from the card to your hard disk via Nautilus is quicker and easier than using gThumb.

If your camera doesn't appear to be recognized by Ubuntu, you should consider buying a USB card reader. These devices are typically inexpensive and usually can read a wide variety of card types, making them a useful investment for the future. Some new PCs even come with card readers built in. Most generic card readers should work fine under Linux, as will most new digital cameras. Attaching them to your computer will be the same as previously— a desktop icon and import dialog box will appear whenever a card is inserted.

■**Caution** Before detatching your camera or removing a photo card, you should right-click the desktop icon and select Eject. This tells Ubuntu that you've finished with the device. Failing to eject in this way could cause data errors.

If your camera isn't recognized, perhaps if it's a few years old and uses the serial port to connect to your PC, you can use gThumb's special import function.

Start gThumb by clicking Applications ➤ Graphics ➤ gThumb Image Viewer. Attach and activate your camera (ensure you select the data transfer mode on the camera, if applicable), and then click File ➤ Import Photos within gThumb. Your camera should be probed and detected automatically. If not, click the camera icon, and choose both its make and model from the list, as shown in Figure 20-1. The Port drop-down list refers to how the camera attaches to your PC and will normally be filled in automatically once you select the model. Note that `serial:/dev/ttyS0` refers to the first serial port. If your computer has two serial ports and if the camera refuses to work, you might need to return to this step and select `serial:/dev/ttys1`.

If you're working with print photos, negative film, or transparencies, you can use a scanner to scan them in using the XSane image scanning program, as explained in Chapter 8. XSane can be started by clicking Applications ➤ Graphics ➤ XSane Image Scanner. This works in a virtually identical way to the TWAIN modules supplied with Windows scanners, in that you need to set the dots per inch (DPI) figures, as well as the color depth. Generally speaking, 300 DPI and 24-bit color should lead to a true-to-life representation of most photos (although because of their smaller size, transparencies or negative film will require higher resolutions, on the order of 1,200 or 2,400 DPI).

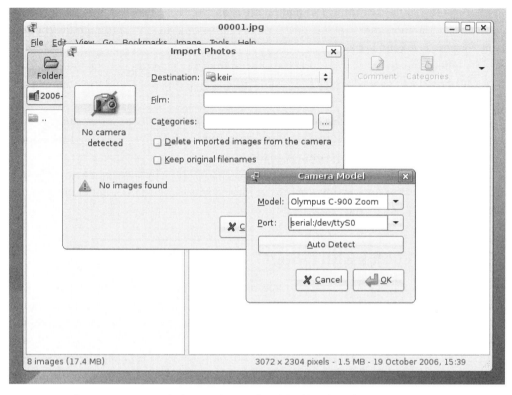

Figure 20-1. *If your camera isn't detected, you should tell gThumb its make and model, as well as how it attaches to your computer.*

Importing Photos Using gThumb

Once your camera is set up within gThumb, or after you click the Import Photos button that appears when you insert a memory card or attach your digital camera, the main gPhoto import window will appear.

This window has two panes. On the left is the directory structure contained on the camera or memory card. On the right is an area where thumbnail previews of the images appear. Normally gThumb will automatically find and open the directory on the camera/card containing your photographs, but you may have to navigate to it manually. This is done as with any file manager—double-click directories to open them.

Once the folder is open, the images it contains will be thumbnailed. Depending on the size of the images, this might take some time.

To save the images to your hard disk, click File ➤ Import Photos. Following this, if you wish to import all the photographs, simply click the Import button at the bottom of the dialog box. If you wish to selectively import a handful of photographs, hold down Ctrl, click those you are interested in, and click the Import button.

By default, gThumb will import your photos to a directory it creates in your /home directory, which will be named after the date and time of import (*not* the date and time the photos were originally taken!).

If you plan to use F-Spot to catalog the photos, this folder should be seen as temporary storage; later on, F-Spot will copy the photos into its own directory, and the original can then be deleted.

If you don't intend to use F-Spot, I strongly suggest that you create a directory called Pictures and save all your images into it within gThumb. Creating a special directory in this way will avoid clogging up your /home directory.

You can select this directory within gThumb when importing by clicking the drop-down list alongside Destination, within the Import Photos window. Click the Other entry in the list, and manually locate the Pictures directory.

Cataloging Photos with F-Spot

F-Spot Photo Manager is styled after image cataloging programs you might have used under Windows or Macintosh, such as iPhoto or Picasa. It allows you to tag photographs, aiding searching later on, and lets you view the images using a time line of when they were taken.

You'll find the program on the Applications ➤ Graphics menu. When the program is run for the first time, the Import dialog box will open automatically. (In the future, whenever you have any new photos you want F-Spot to know about, you should click File ➤ Import.)

In the Import dialog box, click the Import Source drop-down list, and then click Select Folder. Next, highlight the directory containing your images, and click OK. It's vital to note that you shouldn't double-click the directory, because this will cause F-Spot to open the directory in the file browser.

After you've selected the folder, F-Spot will present thumbnail previews of the images, and this might take some time. Keep your eye on the orange status bar. Once this reads Done Loading, you can click the Import button to import all the images, or Ctrl+click to selectively select photos in the left-hand side of the window and then click the Import button.

■**Tip** The Import window can be resized by clicking and dragging its edges. This can be very useful when importing many photographs at one time.

By default, F-Spot copies the images into a directory it creates within your /home directory, called Photos. Therefore, once you've imported the photos, you can delete the originals.

The F-Spot Program Window

Once the photos have been imported, the main F-Spot window will appear. On the left are the default tags, which I'll explain in a moment. On the right is the picture preview window, which can be set to either Browse or Edit Photo mode. You can switch between these two modes using the buttons on the toolbar, where you can also view an image full screen or start a slide show that will cycle through the images in sequence.

Above the picture window is the time line. By clicking and dragging the slider, you can move backward and forward in the photograph collection, depending on when the pictures were taken. Each notch on the time line represents a month within the year marked beneath the time line. The graphs on the time line give an imprecise idea of how many photographs were taken during that particular month (or, indeed, if *any* were taken during a particular month).

Tweaking Photos

By either double-clicking an image or selecting an image and clicking Edit Photo on the toolbar, you can trivially adjust images by cropping them, adjusting brightness contrast, or adjusting the color saturation/balance. In addition, you can convert images to black and white or sepia tone, and you can remove red-eye caused by an indoor flash. All of this can be achieved by clicking the buttons under the image. All changes to the image are made live, as shown in Figure 20-2, so it's a good idea to drag the dialog box out of the way to allow full viewing of the image underneath.

Tip Remember that hovering the mouse cursor over an icon will cause a tooltip to appear, explaining what the button does.

You can also add a comment in the text field below the image. This will then be attached to the image for future reference and can act as a useful memory aid.

A note of caution is required when tweaking images. Once changes have been made, there doesn't appear to be any way of undoing them. The Edit menu lacks an Undo option, and pressing Ctrl+Z doesn't do anything. However, F-Spot keeps a copy of the original image alongside the modified one. To access the original unedited image, click File ➤ Version ➤ Original.

■**Tip** By clicking File ➤ Create New Version, the currently selected image will be copied and made available on the File ➤ Version menu. You can do this as many times as you want, perhaps to record various image tweaks to choose the best later.

Figure 20-2. *Any edits to the image are made live, so it's a good idea to move the adjustment dialog box out of the way.*

Tagging Images

F-Spot's cataloging power comes from its ability to tag each image. However, tagging is one of those simple concepts that can be a little hard to grasp.

A tag is simply a word or short phrase that can be attached to any number of images, rather like a real-life tag that you might find attached to an item in a shop. Once images have been tagged, you can then filter the images using the tag word. For example, you could create a tag called German vacation, which you would attach to all images taken on a trip to Germany. Then, when you select the German vacation tag, only those images will be displayed. Alternatively, you could be more precise with tags—you could create the tags Dusseldorf and Cologne to subdivide pictures taken on the vacation.

If your collection involves lots of pictures taken of your children at various stages during their lives, you could create a tag for each of their names. By selecting to view only photos tagged with a particular child's name, you could then view only pictures of that child, regardless of when or where they were taken.

Images can have more than one tag. A family photo could be tagged with the words thanksgiving, grandma's house, family meal, and the names of the individuals pictured. Then, if you searched using any of the tags, the picture would appear in the list.

A handful of tags are provided by default, and they are Favorites, Hidden, People, Places, and Events. These are rather generic, so to create your own tags, right-click under the tag list on the left of the F-Spot program window and select Create New Tag. Tags can have "parents," which can help organize them, but I wouldn't recommend this unless you have a great many tags. Simply type in the name of the new tag in the dialog box and click OK.

Tags can also have icons attached to them. A tag will automatically assign an icon based on the first photo it's assigned to, but to manually assign a tag an icon, right-click it in the list and select Edit. Next, in the Edit Tag dialog box, click the icon button, and select from the list of icons under the Predefined heading.

▪Note On my test computer, the icons under the Predefined heading didn't show up, although when I clicked on where they *should* have been, a preview appeared at the top of the dialog box! Hopefully, this bug will have been fixed by the time you read this. Getting fixes for bugs like this is yet another good reason why you should regularly update online.

To attach a tag to a picture, simply right-click it (in either the Browse or Edit Photo mode), and click its entry on Attach Tag.

To filter by tag, put a check alongside its entry in the tag list, as shown in Figure 20-3. To remove the filtering, remove the check.

Figure 20-3. *To filter images by tag, put a check alongside the tag in the list on the left.*

Image Editing Using The GIMP

The GIMP is an extremely powerful image editor that offers the kind of functions usually associated with top-end software like Adobe Photoshop. Although it's not aimed at beginners, those new to image editing can get the most from of it, provided they put in a little work.

The program relies on a few unusual concepts within its interface, which can catch many people off guard. The first of these is that each of the windows within the program, such as floating dialog boxes or palettes, gets its own Panel entry. In other words, The GIMP's icon bar, image window, settings window, and so on have their own buttons on the Panel alongside your other programs, as if they were separate programs.

■**Note** The GIMP's way of working is referred to as a *Single Document Interface*, or SDI. It's favored by a handful of programs that run under Linux and seems to be especially popular among programs that let you create things.

Because of the way that The GIMP runs, before you start up the program, it's a wise idca to switch to a different virtual desktop (virtual desktops are discussed in Chapter 7), which you can then dedicate entirely to The GIMP.

Click Applications ➤ Graphics ➤ GIMP Image Editor to run The GIMP. You'll be greeted by what appears to be a complex assortment of program windows. Now you need to be aware of a second unusual aspect of the program: its reliance on right-clicking. Whereas right-clicking usually brings up a context menu offering a handful of options, within The GIMP, it's the principal way of accessing the program's functions. Right-clicking an image brings up a menu offering access to virtually everything you'll need while editing. Ubuntu includes the latest version of The GIMP, 2.2, and this features a menu bar in the main image-editing window. This is considered sacrilege by many traditional The GIMP users, although it's undoubtedly useful for beginners. However, the right-click menu remains the most efficient way of accessing The GIMP's tools.

The main toolbar window, shown in Figure 20-4, is on the left. This can be considered the heart of The GIMP, because when you close it, all the other program windows are closed, too. The menu bar on the toolbar window offers most of the options you're likely to use to start out with The GIMP. For example, File ➤ Open will open a browser dialog box in which you can select files to open in The GIMP. It's even possible to create new artwork from scratch by choosing File ➤ New, although you should be aware that The GIMP is primarily a photo editor.

■**Tip** To create original artwork, a better choice is a program like Inkscape (www.inkscape.org), which can be downloaded via Synaptic Package Manager (to learn about software installation, see Chapter 28).

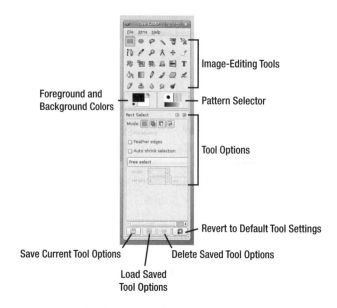

Figure 20-4. *The GIMP's main toolbar window*

Beneath the menu bar in the main toolbar window are the tools for working with images. Their functions are described in Table 20-1, which lists the tools in order from left to right, starting at the top left.

Table 20-1. *The GIMP Image-Editing Tools*

Tool	Description of Use
Rectangular selection tool	Click and drag to select a rectangular area within the image. This selected area can then be copied and pasted into a different part of the image or turned into a new layer.
Elliptical selection tool	Create an oval or circular selection area within the image, which you can then copy and paste.
Hand-drawn selection tool	Click and draw with the mouse to create a hand-drawn selection area. Your selection should end where it started. If not, The GIMP will draw a straight line between the start and end of the selection.
Contiguous regions selection tool	Known as the "magic wand" in other image editors, this tool creates a selection area based on the color of the pixels where you click. For example, clicking on a red car hood will select most, if not all of the hood, because it is mostly red.
Color region selection tool	This tool works like the contiguous region selection tool, but will create a selection across the entire image based on the color you select. In other words, selecting a black T-shirt will also select a black signpost elsewhere in the picture if the shades are similar.

Table 20-1. *The GIMP Image-Editing Tools (Continued)*

Tool	Description of Use
Shape selection tool	Another "magical" tool, the shape selector lets you create a selection by clicking on various points within an image, with the program joining the points together based on the color differences between the two points. This means that you can select the outline of a car by clicking a few points around the edge of the car and, provided the color of the car is different from the background, The GIMP will work out the color differences and select the car's shape automatically.
Path creation tool	This tool draws Bezier curves in order to create paths. Paths are akin to selections and can be saved for use later on in the image-editing process. Creating a Bezier curve is not too hard to do: just click and drag to draw a curve. Each extra click you make will define a new curve, which will be joined to the last one. To turn the path into a selection, click the button at the bottom of the toolbar.
Color picker	This lets you see the RGB, HSV, or CMYK values of any color within the image. Simply click the mouse within the image.
Zoom tool	Click to zoom into the image, right-click to see various zoom options, and hold down the Alt key while clicking to zoom out.
Measurer	This tool measures distances between two points (in pixels) and also angles. Just click and drag to use it. The measurements will appear at the bottom of the image window.
Move tool	Click and drag to move any selection areas within the image, as well as rearrange the positioning of various layers.
Crop tool	Click and drag to define an area of the image to be cropped. Anything outside the selection area you create will be discarded.
Rotate tool	This tool rotates any selections you make and can also rotate entire layers. It opens a dialog box in which you can set the rotation manually. Alternatively, you can simply click and drag the handles behind the dialog box to rotate by hand.
Scale tool	Known in some other image editors as "transform," this tool lets you resize the selection area or layer. It presents a dialog box where you can enter numeric values, or you can click and drag the handles to resize by hand.
Shear tool	This tool lets you transform the image by shearing it. Slant a selection by clicking and dragging the corners of the selection area (if the selection area isn't square, a rectangular grid will be applied to it for the purposes of transformation).
Perspective tool	This tool lets you transform a selection by clicking and dragging its four corners and independently moving them without affecting the other corners. In this way, a sense of perspective can be emulated.
Flip tool	This tool flips a selection or image so that it is reversed on itself, either horizontally (click) or vertically (hold down Ctrl and click).
Text tool	Click on the image to add text.
Fill tool	Fill a particular area with solid color, according to the color selected in the color box below.
Gradient fill	This tool will create a gradient fill based on the foreground and background colors by clicking and dragging.

Table 20-1. *The GIMP Image-Editing Tools (Continued)*

Tool	Description of Use
Pencil tool	This tool lets you draw individual pixels when zoomed in, or hard-edge lines when zoomed out. Simply click and drag to draw freehand, and hold down Shift to draw lines between two points.
Brush tool	This tool lets you draw on the picture in a variety of brush styles to create artistic effects. A brush can also be created from an image, allowing for greater versatility.
Erase tool	Rather like the Brush tool in reverse, this tool deletes whatever is underneath the cursor. If layers are being used, the contents of the layer beneath will become visible.
Airbrush tool	This tool is also rather like the Brush tool, in that it draws on the picture in a variety of styles. However, the density of the color depends on the length of time you press the mouse button. Tap the mouse button, and only a light color will appear. Press and hold the mouse button, and the color will become more saturated.
Ink tool	This tool is like the Brush tool except that, rather like an ink pen, the faster you draw, the thinner the brush stroke is.
Pattern stamp	Commonly known as the clone tool, this is a popular image-editing tool. It is able to copy one part of an image to another via drawing with a brush-like tool. The origin point is defined by holding down Ctrl and clicking.
Blur/sharpen tool	Clicking and drawing on the image will spot blur or sharpen the image, depending on the settings in the tool options area in the lower half of the toolbar.
Smudge tool	As its name suggests, clicking and drawing with this tool will smudge the image, rather like rubbing a still-wet painting with your finger (except slightly more precise).
Burn and dodge tool	This tool lets you spot lighten and darken an image by clicking and drawing on the image. The results depend on the settings in the tool options part of the window.

Directly beneath the image-editing tool icons, on the left, is an icon that shows the foreground and background colors that will be used when drawing with tools such as the Brush. To define a new color, double-click either the foreground (top) or background (bottom) color box. To the right is the brush selector, which lets you choose the thickness of the brush strokes and patterns that are used with tools such as the Brush. Simply click each to change them.

Beneath these icons, you'll see the various options for the selected tool. By using the buttons at the bottom of the window, you can save the current tool options, load tool options, and delete a previously saved set of tool options. Clicking the button on the bottom right lets you revert to the default settings for the tool currently being used (useful if you tweak too many settings!).

Next to the toolbar window is the Layers dialog box. This can be closed for the moment, although you can make it visible again later, if you wish.

The Basics of The GIMP

After you've started The GIMP (and assigned it a virtual desktop), you can load an image by selecting File ➤ Open. The browser dialog box offers a preview facility on the right of the window.

You will probably need to resize the image window so that it fits within the remainder of the screen. You can then use the Zoom tool (see Table 20-1) to ensure that the image fills the editing window, which will make working with it much easier. Alternatively, you can click the zoom drop-down list in the lower left-half of the image window.

You can save any changes you make to an image by right-clicking it and selecting File ➤ Save As. You can also print the image from the same menu.

Before you begin editing with The GIMP, you need to be aware of some essential concepts that are vital to understand in order to get the most from the program:

Copy, cut, and paste buffers: Unlike Windows programs, The GIMP lets you cut or copy many selections from the image and store them for use later. It refers to these saved selections as *buffers*, and each must be given a name for future reference. A new buffer is created by selecting an area using any of the selection tools, then right-clicking within the selection area and selecting Edit ➤ Buffer ➤ Copy Named (or Cut Named). Pasting a buffer back is a matter of right-clicking the image and selecting Edit ➤ Buffer ➤ Paste Named.

Paths: The GIMP paths are not necessarily the same as selection areas, although it's nearly always possible to convert a selection into a path and vice versa (right-click within the selection or path, and look for the relevant option on the Select menu—Select ➤ To Path for a selection or Select ➤ From Path for a path). In general, the tools used to create a path allow the creation of complex shapes rather than simple geometric shapes, as with the selection tools. You can also be more intricate in your selections, as shown in the example in Figure 20-5. You can save paths for later use. To view the Paths dialog box, right-click the image and select Dialogs ➤ Paths.

▓**Tip** Getting rid of a selection or path you've drawn is easy. In the case of a path, simply click any other tool. This will cause the path to disappear. To get rid of a selection, select any selection tool, and quickly click once on the image, being careful not to drag the mouse while doing so.

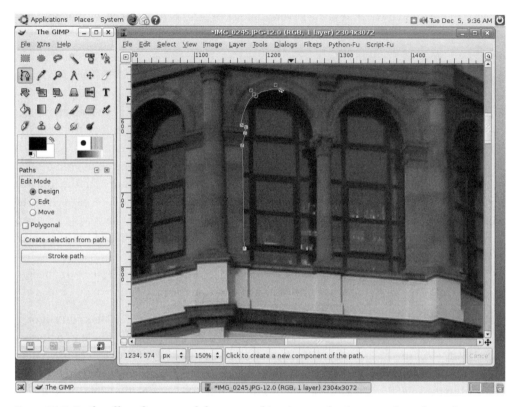

Figure 20-5. *Paths allow for more elaborate and intricate selections, such as those that involve curves.*

Layers: In The GIMP (along with most other image-editing programs), layers are like transparent sheets of plastic that are placed on top of the image. Anything can be drawn on each individual transparent sheet, and many layers can be overlaid in order to create a complicated image. Layers also let you cut and paste parts of the image between them. It's also possible to apply effects and transformations to a single layer, rather than to the entire image. The Layers dialog box, shown in Figure 20-6, appears by default, but if you closed it earlier, you can open it again by right-clicking the image and selecting Dialogs ➤ Layers. The layers can be reordered by clicking and dragging them in the dialog box. In addition, the blending mode of each layer can be altered. This refers to how it interacts with the layer below it. For example, its opacity can be changed so that it appears semitransparent, thereby showing the contents of the layer beneath.

Figure 20-6. *Set the opacity of various layers by clicking and dragging the relevant slider in the Layers dialog box.*

Making Color Corrections

The first step when editing most images is to correct the brightness, contrast, and color saturation. This helps overcome some of the deficiencies that are inherent in digital photographs or scanned-in images. To do this, right-click the image and select Layers ➤ Colors. You'll find a variety of options to let you tweak the image, allowing you a lot of control over the process.

For trivial brightness and contrast changes, selecting the Brightness-Contrast menu option will open a dialog box where clicking and dragging the sliders will alter the image. The changes you make will be previewed on the image itself, so you should be able to get things just right.

Similarly, the Hue-Saturation option will let you alter the color balance and the strength of the colors (the saturation) by clicking and dragging sliders. By selecting the color bar options at the top of the window, you can choose individual colors to boost. Clicking the Master button will let you once again alter all colors at the same time.

The trouble with clicking and dragging sliders is that it relies on human intuition. This can easily be clouded by a badly calibrated monitor, which might be set too dark or too light. Because of this, The GIMP offers another handy option: Levels.

To access the Levels feature, right-click the image and select Layer ➤ Colors ➤ Levels. This presents a chart of the brightness levels in the photo and lets you set the dark, shadows, and highlight points, as shown in Figure 20-7. Three sliders beneath the chart represent, from left to right, the darkest point, the midtones (shadows), and the highlights within the picture. The first step is to set the dark and light sliders at the left and right of the edges of the chart. This will make sure that the range of brightness from the lightest point to the darkest point is set correctly. The next step is to adjust the middle slider so that it's roughly in the middle of the highest peak within the chart. This will accurately set the midtone point, ensuring an even spread of brightness across the image.

Figure 20-7. *The Levels function can be used to accurately set the brightness levels across an image.*

A little artistic license is usually allowed at this stage, and depending on the effect on the photo, moving the midtone slider a little to the left and/or right of the highest peak might produce more acceptable results. However, be aware that the monitor might be showing incorrect brightness/color values.

Cropping and Cloning

After you've adjusted the colors, you might want to use the Crop tool (see Table 20-1) to remove any extraneous details outside the focus of the image. For example, in a portrait of someone taken from a distance away, you might choose to crop the photo to show only the person's head and shoulders, or you might separate a group of people from their surroundings, as shown in Figure 20-8.

Figure 20-8. *You can use the Crop tool to remove any irrelevant details surrounding the subject of your photo.*

You might also want to use the Clone tool to remove facial blemishes. Start by using the Zoom tool to close in on the area. If the blemish is small, you might need to zoom in quite substantially. Then try to find an area of skin that is clear and from which you can copy. Hold down Ctrl and click in that area. Then click and draw over the blemish. The crosshair indicates the area from which you're copying.

Sharpening

One final handy trick employed by professional image editors to give their photos a shot in the arm is to use the Sharpen filter. This has the effect of adding definition to the image and negating any slight blur caused by things such as camera shake or poor focusing. To apply the Sharpen filter, right-click the image and select Filters ➤ Enhance ➤ Sharpen.

As shown in Figure 20-9, a small preview window will show the effect of the sharpening on the image (you might need to use the scroll bars to move to an appropriate part of the image). Clicking and dragging the slider at the bottom of the dialog box will alter the severity of the sharpening effect. Too much sharpening can ruin a picture, so be careful. Try to use the effect subtly.

Figure 20-9. *Sharpening an image can give it a professional finish by adding definition.*

The Sharpen filter is just one of many filters you can apply in The GIMP, as explained in the next section.

Applying Filters

Like other image-editing programs, The GIMP includes many filters to add dramatic effects to your images with little, if any, user input. Filters are applied either to the currently selected layer or to a selection within the layer. To apply a filter, right-click the image and choose the relevant menu option. If you don't like an effect you've applied, you can reverse it by selecting Edit ➤ Undo, or by pressing Ctrl+Z.

The submenus offer filters grouped by categories, as follows:

Blur: These filters add various kinds of blur to the image or selection. For example, Motion Blur can imitate the effect of photographing an object moving at speed with a slow shutter. Perhaps the most popular blur option is Gaussian Blur, which has the effect of applying a soft and subtle blur.

Color: This option includes many technical filters, mostly of interest to image technicians or those who want to uncover and otherwise manipulate the color breakdown within an image. However, Filter Pack might appeal to the general user. This filter can quickly adjust the hue, saturation, and other values within the image, and relevant dialog boxes will appear when you put a check alongside the headings beneath the Windows heading. Also of interest is Colorify, which can tint the image to any user-defined color. Figure 20-10 shows an example of using the Colorify filter.

Noise: This collection of filters is designed to add speckles or other types of usually unwanted artifacts to an image. These filters are offered within The GIMP for their potential artistic effects, but they can also be used to create a grainy film effect—simply click Scatter RGB.

Edge-Detect: This set of filters can be used to automatically detect and delineate the edges of objects within an image. Although this type of filter can result in some interesting results that might fall into the category of special effects, it's primarily used in conjunction with other tools and effects.

Enhance: The Enhance effects are designed to remove various artifacts from an image or otherwise improve it. For example, the Despeckle effect will attempt to remove unwanted noise within an image (such as flecks of dust in a scanned image). The Sharpen filter discussed in the previous section is located here, as is the Unsharp Mask, which offers a high degree of control over the image-sharpening process.

Figure 20-10. *The Colorify filter can be used to add a sepia-like effect to a picture.*

Generic: In this category, you can find a handful of filters that don't seem to fall into any other category. Of particular interest is the Convolution Matrix option, which lets you create your own filters by inputting numeric values. According to The GIMP's programmers, this is designed primarily for mathematicians, but it can also be used by others to create random special effects. Simply input values and then preview the effect.

Glass Effects: As the name suggests, these filters can apply effects to the image to imitate the effects that come about when glass is used to produce an image. For example, the Apply Lens filter will apply the same kind of distortion caused by various wide-angle lenses used on cameras, as shown in Figure 20-11.

Light Effects: Here, you will find filters that imitate the effects that light can have on a picture, such as adding sparkle effects to highlights or imitating lens flare caused by a camera's lens.

Figure 20-11. *The Glass Effects ➤ Apply Lens filter can be used to imitate a fish-eye lens.*

Distorts: As the name of this category of filters suggests, the effects here distort the image in various ways. For example, Whirl and Pinch allow you to tug and push the image to distort it (to understand what is meant here, imagine printing the image on rubber and then pinching or pushing the surface). This category also contains other special effects, such as Pagecurl, which imitates the curl of a page at the bottom of the picture.

Artistic: These filters allow you to add painterly effects to the image, such as making it appear as if the photo has been painted in impressionistic brushstrokes or as if it were painted on canvas by overlaying the texture of canvas onto the picture. Figure 20-12 shows an example of applying the "Oilify" filter for an oil painting effect.

Map: These filters aim to manipulate the image by treating it like a piece of paper that can be folded in various ways and also stuck onto 3D shapes (a process referred to as *mapping*). Because the image is treated as if it were a piece of paper, it can also be copied, and the copies placed on top of each other to create various effects.

Figure 20-12. *The Artistic effects can be used to give images an oil painting effect.*

Render: Here, you'll find filters designed to create new images from scratch, such as clouds or flame effects. They obliterate anything that was previously underneath on that particular layer or within that selection, and the original image has no bearing on what is generated by the filter.

Web: Here, you can create an image map for use in a web page. An *image map* is a single image broken up into separate hyperlinked areas, typically used on a web page as a sophisticated menu. For example, an image map is frequently used for a geographical map on which you can click to get more information about different regions.

Animation: These filters aim to manipulate and optimize GIF images, which are commonly used to create simple animated images for use on web sites.

Combine: Here, you'll find filters that combine two or more images into one.

Toys: These are so-called "Easter Eggs"; they aren't designed to manipulate the image but are present in the program as harmless animations for the user to enjoy. They're created by the programmers of The GIMP as a way of thanking you for using their program.

■**Tip** If you like The GIMP, you might be interested in another book published by Apress: *Beginning GIMP: From Novice to Professional* by Akkana Peck (1-59059-587-4; 2006). This offers a comprehensive, contemporary and highly readable guide to The GIMP, and goes into far more detail than I'm able to here.

GIMPSHOP

The GIMP is one of the most powerful items of software available for Linux, but not everybody is enamored of its user interface. A special bone of contention for many is that The GIMP uses almost completely different terminology compared to Adobe Photoshop, considered by most the king of image editors.

One developer became so annoyed by this that he created a new version of The GIMP called GIMPShop (`www.gimpshop.net`). This is ostensibly exactly the same as The GIMP, but the names of the tools have been changed to match those of Photoshop (or its home-user brother, Photoshop Elements). In a similar way, many of the right-click menu entries have also been changed so that they're identical.

Of course, the freedom to adapt software in this way is one of the benefits of open source software. There's nothing wrong in doing so, and the ability to take program code and create your own version is the foundation of Linux.

GIMPShop isn't available via Synaptic Package Manager, and the Linux version offered for download at the GIMPShop web site is an RPM file, designed for other versions of Linux. However, searching Google for an Ubuntu package should pay dividends. Once you've downloaded the package, see Chapter 29 to learn how software installation works under Ubuntu.

Summary

In this chapter, we took a look at image cataloging and editing under Ubuntu. This has involved an examination of one of the best programs available for the task under any operating system, The GIMP, but first we started by looking at the gThumb and F-Spot importing and cataloging tools.

Then, you learned how to start The GIMP and about some of the basic principles behind it. Next, we discussed some of the functions contained within The GIMP, including the image filters provided with the program.

In the next part of the book, we move on from multimedia to look at another core component of Ubuntu: the OpenOffice.org suite, which provides word processing, spreadsheet, presentation, and other functions.

PART 6

∎∎∎

Office Tasks

■ ■ ■

## CHAPTER 21

Making the Move to OpenOffice.org

Y ou might be willing to believe that you can get a complete operating system for no cost. You might even be able to accept that this offers everything Windows does and much more. But one stumbling block many people have is in believing a Microsoft Office–compatible office suite comes as part of the zero-cost bundle. It's a step too far. Office costs hundreds of dollars—are they expecting us to believe that there's a rival product that is free?

Well, there is, and it's called OpenOffice.org. It comes preinstalled with Ubuntu, as well as most other Linux distributions, making it the Linux office suite of choice. It's compatible with most Microsoft Office files, too, and even looks similar and works in a comparable way, making it easy to learn. What more could you want?

Office Similarities

OpenOffice.org started life as a proprietary product called Star Office. Sun Microsystems bought the company behind the product and released its source code in order to encourage community development. This led to the creation of the OpenOffice.org project, a collaboration between open-source developers and Sun. This project has released several new versions of OpenOffice.org, and at the time of this writing, the current version is 2.0. This is the version supplied with Ubuntu.

Note For what it's worth, Sun still sells Star Office. This is based on the OpenOffice.org code, so it's effectively the same program. However, in addition to the office suite itself, Sun includes several useful extras such as fonts, templates, and the all-important technical support, which you can contact if you get stuck trying to undertake a particular task.

OpenOffice.org features a word processor, spreadsheet program, presentation package, drawing tool (vector graphics), web site creation tool, database program, and several extras. As such, it matches Microsoft Office almost blow-for-blow in terms of core functionality. See Table 21-1 for a comparison of core packages.

Table 21-1. *How the Office and OpenOffice.org Suites Compare*

Microsoft Office	OpenOffice.org	Function
Word	Writer	Word processor
Excel	Calc	Spreadsheet
PowerPoint	Impress	Presentations
Visio	Draw[1]	Technical drawing/charting
FrontPage	Writer[2]	Web site creation
Access	Base[3]	Database

[1] *Draw is a vector graphics creation tool akin to Adobe Illustrator. Creating flow charts or organizational diagrams is one of many things it can do. For some reason, it is not on the Ubuntu Applications menu; to start Draw, open any OpenOffice.org application, and click File ➤ New ➤ Drawing.*

[2] *Writer is used for word processing and HTML creation; when switched to Web mode, its functionality is altered appropriately.*

[3] *Writer and Calc can be coupled to a third-party database application such as MySQL or Firebird; however, Office.org also comes with the Base relational database.*

You should find the functionality within the packages is duplicated, too, although some of the very specific features of Microsoft Office are not in OpenOffice.org. But OpenOffice.org also has its own range of such tools not yet found in Microsoft Office!

OpenOffice.org does have a couple of notable omissions. Perhaps the main one is that it doesn't offer a directly comparable Outlook replacement. However, as I will discuss in Chapter 27, the Evolution application offers a highly capable reproduction of Outlook, with e-mail, contacts management, and calendar functions all in one location. In Ubuntu, you'll find Evolution on the Applications ➤ Internet menu. Evolution isn't directly linked to OpenOffice.org, but it retains the overall Ubuntu look, feel, and way of operating.

OpenOffice.Org Key Features

Key features of OpenOffice.org include the ability to export documents in Portable Document Format (PDF) format across the entire suite of programs. PDF files can then be read on any computer equipped with PDF display software, such as Adobe Acrobat Reader.

In addition, OpenOffice.org features powerful accessibility features that can, for example, help those with vision disabilities use the programs more effectively. For those who are technically minded, OpenOffice.org can be extended very easily with a variety of plug-ins, which allow the easy creation of add-ons using many different programming languages.

Although OpenOffice.org largely mirrors the look and feel of Microsoft Office, it adds its own flourishes here and there. This can mean that some functions are located on different menus, for example. However, none of this poses a challenge for most users, and OpenOffice.org is generally regarded as very easy to learn.

File Compatibility

As well as core feature compatibility, OpenOffice.org is also able to read files from Microsoft Office versions up to and including Office 2003, the latest version of Office at the time of this writing. Currently OpenOffice.org doesn't support Office 2007 files, although several projects are working on adding support, and it's likely it will be added soon. This is just one more reason why you should regularly update Ubuntu online in order to make sure you're running the very latest versions of each program.

■**Note** It's fair to say that many people still use the older Office file formats, even if they're using the latest version of Office. This is done to retain compatibility with other users who may not yet have upgraded.

Although file compatibility problems are rare, two issues occasionally crop up when opening Microsoft Office files in OpenOffice.org:

VBA compatibility: OpenOffice.org isn't currently compatible with Microsoft Office Visual Basic for Applications (VBA), although work is being undertaken to allow this functionality. OpenOffice.org uses a similar but incompatible internal programming language. This means that Microsoft macros within a document probably won't work when the file is imported to OpenOffice.org. Such macros are typically used in Excel spreadsheets designed to calculate time sheets, for example. In general, however, only high-end users use VBA.

Document protection: OpenOffice.org is unable to open any Office files that have a password, either to protect the document from changes or to protect it from being viewed. Theoretically, it would be easy for OpenOffice.org's programmers to include such functionality, but the laws of many countries make creating such a program feature illegal (it would be seen as a device to overcome copy protection). The easiest solution is to ask whoever sent you the file to remove the password protection. For what it's worth, OpenOffice.org's has its own form of password protection.

If you find that OpenOffice.org isn't able to open an Office file saved by your colleagues, you can always suggest that they, too, make the switch to OpenOffice.org. They don't need to be running Ubuntu to do so. Versions are available to run on all Windows platforms, as well as on the Apple Macintosh.

■**Note** Two versions of OpenOffice.org are available for Mac OS X: the standard release, which runs in an X window and is available from the main OpenOffice.org web site, and NeoOffice, which has been adapted to run natively within OS X. For more details, see www.neooffice.org.

As with the Ubuntu version, versions of OpenOffice.org available for other operating systems are entirely free of charge. Indeed, for many people who are running versions of Office they've installed from "borrowed" CDs, OpenOffice.org offers a way to come clean and avoid pirating software. For more details and to download OpenOffice.org, visit www.openoffice.org.

Once your colleagues have made the switch, you can exchange files using OpenOffice. org's native format, or opt to save files in the Microsoft Office file formats (.doc, .xls, .ppt, and so on). Figure 21-1 shows the file type options available in OpenOffice.org's word processor component's Save As dialog box.

■**Note** OpenOffice.org also supports Rich Text Format (RTF) text documents and comma-separated value (CSV) data files, which are supported by practically every office suite program ever made.

When it comes to sharing files, there's another option: save your files in a non-Office format such as PDF or HTML. OpenOffice.org is able to export documents in both formats, and most modern PCs equipped with Adobe Acrobat or a simple web browser will be able to read them. However, while OpenOffice.org can open and edit HTML files, it can export documents only as PDF files, so this format is best reserved for files not intended for further editing.

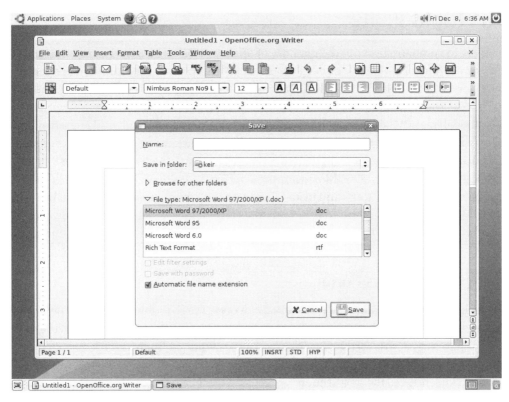

Figure 21-1. *All the OpenOffice.org components are fully compatible with Microsoft Office file formats.*

OPEN DOCUMENT FORMAT

One of the principles behind all open-source software is the idea of open file formats. This means that if someone creates a new open-source word processor, she also makes sure that the technology behind the file format is explained, so that other people can adapt their programs to read and/or save in that file format.

To meet the goals of open-source software, the OASIS OpenDocument Format (ODF) was created, and this is utilized in OpenOffice.org 2.0. This is a completely open and free to use office document file format that all software suites can adopt. The idea is that ODF will make swapping files between all office suites easy.

Sadly, Microsoft has decided not to support ODF and is sticking with its own proprietary file formats, although it has recently opened up the file formats and made a promise not to sue anybody who implements them in non-Microsoft software.

However, several local governments in countries all around the world have adopted ODF, and there's little doubt that ODF will become one of the main ways of disseminating and sharing documents online.

The Right Fonts

One key to compatibility with the majority of Microsoft Office files is ensuring you have the correct fonts. This is an issue even when using Windows. It's very common to open an Office document to find the formatting incorrect, because you don't have the fonts used in the construction of the document.

Although most Windows systems have many fonts, most people tend to rely on a handful of core fonts, which are default on most Windows installations: Arial, Tahoma, Verdana, Trebuchet MS, and Times New Roman (MS Comic Sans might also be included in that list, although it isn't often used within business documents).

You can obtain these fonts and install them on your Ubuntu system in several ways. Here, we'll cover two methods: copying your fonts from Windows, and installing Microsoft's TrueType Core Fonts. The latter method is by far the easier way of undertaking this task.

Copying Windows Fonts

If you dual-boot Ubuntu with Windows, you can delve into your Windows partition's font folder and copy across every font you have available under Windows. This method is useful if you wish to copy across *all* the fonts you use under Windows, such as those installed by third-party applications. If you wish to get just Arial and Times New Roman, you might want to skip ahead to the next section.

■**Caution** Installing Windows fonts under Ubuntu is a legally gray area. Technically speaking, there's no reason why you shouldn't be able to use the fonts under Ubuntu. Purchasing Windows as well as any software running on it should also have meant you purchased a license to use the fonts. But the situation is far from clear. You'd be well-advised to read the Windows End-User License Agreement (EULA) for more guidance. This can be found in the packaging for your computer.

---

1. Click Applications ➤ Accessories ➤ Terminal. In the window that appears, type the following:

   ```
   nautilus /media/hda1/;nautilus fonts://
   ```

   This will cause two Nautilus file browsing windows to appear: one displaying the directories in your Windows partition and the other displaying Ubuntu's collection of fonts. If your computer uses SATA discs, you should replace /media/hda1 with /media/sda1. Also note that these instructions assume that the Windows partition is the first on the disk, as that is the most likely setup. If you know the partition to be second on the disk, replace hda1 (or sda1) with hda2 (or sda2).

2. In the Nautilus window displaying the Windows directories, navigate to your Windows fonts folder. The location of this varies depending on which version of Windows you're using. On my Windows Vista test computer, it was located in the `Windows/Fonts` directory, but on my Windows XP Home test machine, it was located in the `WINDOWS/Fonts` directory. Remember that case sensitivity is important under Ubuntu!

3. Still in the window displaying your Windows font directory, click View ➤ View As List and then click the Type column header in the window, so that the list is sorted according to file extensions. Scroll down to the list of TrueType fonts, and select them all. This can be done by clicking the first, holding down Shift, and then clicking the last.

4. Click and drag all the TrueType fonts to the Nautilus window displaying your Ubuntu font collection. The fonts will be copied across and installed automatically. In some of my tests, this happened instantly, and there was no indication copying had happened (such as a dialog box).

5. Close all the windows, log out of Ubuntu (System ➤ Quit), and log back in again. You should find your Windows fonts are now available.

Installing TrueType Core Fonts

If you don't want to undertake the font-copying maneuver, you can download and install Microsoft's TrueType Core Fonts. This package contains common Windows fonts, including Arial and Times New Roman.

Note The fonts were made legally available by Microsoft in 1996 for use under any operating system—for more details, see `http://en.wikipedia.org/wiki/Core_fonts_for_the_Web`.

To install the fonts, you'll need to enable the Multiverse software repository, as described under the "Setting Up Online Software Repositories" heading in Chapter 8.

1. Click System ➤ Administration ➤ Synaptic Package Manager. Enter your password to continue.

2. Click the Search icon, type `msttcorefonts`, and click the Search button. Click the check box alongside the entry in the results list, and select Mark for Installation. You'll be warned an additional program needs to be installed; this is fine. Then click Apply on the main toolbar to install the fonts.

3. Close all program windows, click System ➤ Quit, and opt to log out of the system. Then log back in again. You should now find the Windows fonts are available in all applications, including OpenOffice.org, as shown in Figure 21-2.

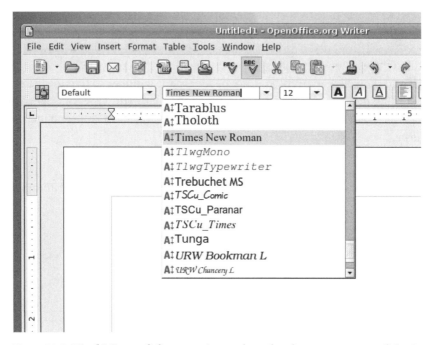

Figure 21-2. *Vital Microsoft fonts are just a download away courtesy of the Synaptic Package Manager.*

OTHER LINUX OFFICE SUITES

OpenOffice.org is widely regarded as one of the best Linux office suites, but it's not the only one. Its main competitor is KOffice. KOffice tightly integrates into the KDE desktop and mirrors much of its look and feel. It includes a word processor, spreadsheet, presentation package, flow-charting tool, database-access tool, and much more. As with OpenOffice.org, in most cases, you can load and save Microsoft Office files. For more details, see its home page at www.koffice.org. It's available with Ubuntu, too. Just use the Synaptic Package Manager to search for and install it.

In addition, there are several open-source office applications that aren't complete office suites. For example, AbiWord is considered an excellent word processor, which packs in a lot of features but keeps the user interface very simple. It's partnered by Gnumeric, a spreadsheet application that is developed separately (although both aim to be integrated into the GNOME desktop environment). For more details, see www.abisource.com and www.gnome.org/projects/gnumeric/, respectively. You can also find both of these programs in the Ubuntu software repositories (use the Synaptic Package Manager to search for them).

Summary

This chapter was a general introduction to OpenOffice.org, providing an overview of what you can expect from the programs within the suite. In particular, we focused on the extent of the suite's similarities with Microsoft Office and discussed issues surrounding file compatibility with Microsoft Office. We also looked at how Windows fonts can be brought into Ubuntu, which aids in successfully importing and creating compatible documents.

In the next chapter, you'll learn about the configuration options globally applicable to the suite, as well as common functions provided across all the programs.

■ ■ ■

## CHAPTER 22

OpenOffice.org Overview

All the programs in the OpenOffice.org suite rely on a common interface, and therefore look and operate in a similar way. They are also configured in an identical way, and all rely on central concepts such as wizards, which guide you through the creation of particular types of documents. In addition, many components within the suite are shared across the various programs. For example, the automatic chart creation tool within Calc can also be used within Writer.

In this chapter, we'll look at the OpenOffice.org suite as a whole, and explain how it's used and configured. In the following chapters, we'll examine some specific programs in the suite.

Introducing the Interface

If you've ever used an office suite, such as Microsoft Office, you shouldn't find it too hard to get around in OpenOffice.org. As with Microsoft Office, OpenOffice.org relies primarily on toolbars, a main menu, and separate context-sensitive menus that appear when you right-click. In addition, OpenOffice.org provides floating palettes that offer quick access to useful functions, such as paragraph styles within Writer.

Figure 22-1 provides a quick guide to the OpenOffice.org interface, showing the following components:

- **Menu bar:** The menus provide access to most of the OpenOffice.org functions.

- **Standard toolbar:** This toolbar provides quick access to global operations, such as saving, opening, and printing files, as well as key functions within the program being used. The Standard toolbar appears in all OpenOffice.org programs and also provides a way to activate the various floating palettes, such as the Navigator, which lets you easily move around various elements within the document.

- **Formatting toolbar:** As its name suggests, this toolbar offers quick access to text-formatting functions, similar to the type of toolbar used in Microsoft Office applications. Clicking the B icon will boldface any selected text, for example. This toolbar appears in Calc, Writer, and Impress.

- **Ruler:** The ruler lets you set tabs and alter margins and indents (within programs that use rulers).

- **Status bar:** The status bar shows various aspects of the configuration, such as whether Insert or Overtype mode is in use.

- **Document area:** This is the main editing area.

Most of the programs rely on the Standard and Formatting toolbars to provide access to their functions, and some programs have additional toolbars. For example, applications such as Impress (a presentation program) and Draw (for drawing vector graphics) have the Drawing toolbar, which provides quick access to tools for drawing shapes, adding lines, and creating fills (the blocks of color within shapes).

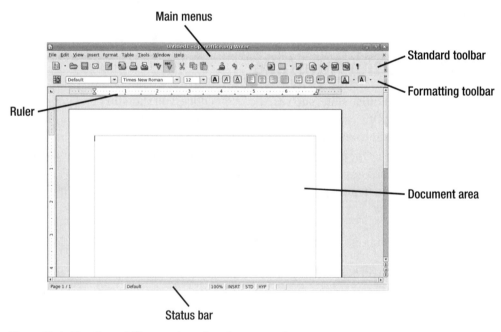

Figure 22-1. *The OpenOffice.org interface has several components.*

Customizing the Interface

You can select which toolbars are visible on your screen, as well as customize those that are already there. You can also add new toolbars and customize the OpenOffice.org menus.

Adding Functions to Toolbars

The quickest way to add icons and functions to any toolbar is to click the two small arrows at the right of a toolbar and select the Visible Buttons entry on the menu that appears. This will present a list of currently visible icons and functions, along with those that might prove useful on that toolbar but are currently hidden. Any option already visible will have a check next to it.

Additionally, you can add practically any function to a toolbar, including the options from the main menus and many more than those that are ordinarily visible. Here are the steps:

1. Click the two small arrows to the right of a toolbar, and select the Customize Toolbar option.

2. In the Customize dialog box, click the Add button in the Toolbar Content section to open the Add Commands dialog box, as shown in Figure 22-2.

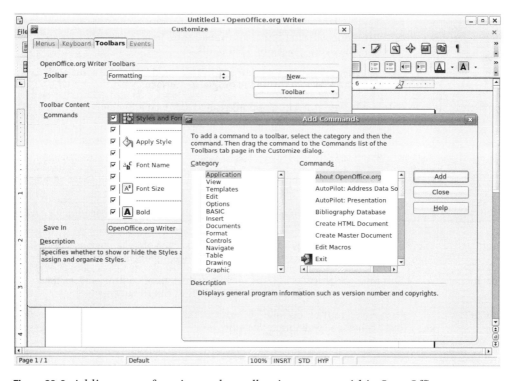

Figure 22-2. *Adding a new function to the toolbar is very easy within OpenOffice.org.*

3. Choose a category from the list on the left to see the available commands in the list on the right. The categories of functions are extremely comprehensive. For example, under the Format category, you'll find entries related to specific functions, such as increasing font sizes or setting a shadow effect behind text. Table 22-1 provides brief descriptions of each of the categories listed in the Add Commands dialog box.

4. Select the function you want to add on the right side of the Add Commands dialog box, and then click the Add button.

5. Click the Close button. You'll then see your new function in the list of icons in the Customize dialog box, under the Toolbar Content heading. The new icon will be automatically selected.

6. Click and drag to move the new function left or right on the toolbar itself (you'll see the toolbar itself update when you release the mouse button). Alternatively, you can highlight the icon and click the up and down arrows next to the list. To temporarily hide the new icon, or any other icon, remove the check from alongside it.

Table 22-1. *OpenOffice.org Toolbar Customization Categories*

Category	Description
Application	These options relate to the specific OpenOffice.org application you're using. For example, if you select to customize a toolbar within Writer, the Application category menu will offer functions to start AutoPilots (effectively wizards) that will build word processor documents.
View	This category offers options related to the look and feel of the suite, such as which items are visible within the program interface.
Templates	In this category, you'll find options related to the creation and use of document templates.
Edit	This category contains options related to cutting, pasting, and copying items within the document, as well as updating elements within it.
Options	These are various options that relate to configuration choices in OpenOffice.org, allowing you to control how it works.
BASIC	Options under this category relate to the creation and playback of OpenOffice.org macros.
Insert	This category includes options related to inserting objects, such as sound, graphics, and elements from other OpenOffice.org documents.
Documents	This category provides options specific to document control, such as those related to exporting documents as PDF files or simply saving files.
Format	Here, you'll find a range of options related largely to text formatting, but also some concerned with formatting other elements, such as drawings and images.

Table 22-1. *OpenOffice.org Toolbar Customization Categories (Continued)*

Category	Description
Controls	Under this heading, you'll find widgets that can be used in conjunction with formulas or macros, such as check boxes, buttons, text box creation tools, and so on.
Navigate	This category offers tools that let you move around a document quickly, such as the ability to quickly edit headers and footers, or move from the top of the page to the end very quickly.
Table	Here, you'll find options related to the creation of tables.
Drawing	Here, you'll find tools related to drawing objects, such as shapes and lines, and also tools for creating floating text boxes.
Graphic	This category presents a handful of options related to manipulating bitmap graphics that are inserted into the document.
Data	Here, you'll find a couple of options related to working with information sources, such as databases.
Frame	These options relate to any frames inserted into the document, such as how elements within the frame are aligned and how text is wrapped around the frame.
Numbering	These are various options related to creating automatic numbered or bulleted lists.
Modify	These options relate to the drawing components within OpenOffice.org and let you manipulate images or drawings in various ways by applying filters.
OpenOffice.org BASIC Macros	Here, you can select from various ready-made macros, which provide some of OpenOffice.org's functions.

Many functions that can be added are automatically given a relevant toolbar icon, but you can choose another icon for a function by selecting the icon in the list in the Customize dialog box, clicking Modify, and then selecting Change Icon. You can also use this method to change an icon that already appears on a toolbar.

■**Note** To delete an icon from a toolbar, click the two small arrows to the right of a toolbar, and select the Customize Toolbar option. Select the icon you want to remove, click the Modify button, and choose to delete it.

Adding a New Toolbar

If you want to add your own new toolbar to offer particular functions, you'll find it easy to do. Here are the steps:

1. Click the two small arrows to the right of any toolbar and select Customize Toolbar from the list of options. Don't worry—you're not actually going to customize that particular toolbar!

2. In the Customize dialog box, click the New button at the top right.

3. Give the toolbar a name. The default entry for the Save In field is correct, so you don't need to alter it.

4. Populate the new toolbar, following the instructions in the previous section.

5. Once you've finished, click the OK button.

You should see your new toolbar beneath the main toolbars. To hide it in the future, click View ➤ Toolbars, and then remove the check alongside the name of your toolbar.

Customizing Menus

You can also customize the OpenOffice.org menus. Here are the steps:

1. Select Tools ➤ Customize from the menu bar.

2. In the Customize dialog box, select the Menus tab at the top left.

3. Choose which menu you wish to customize from the Menu drop-down list.

4. Select the position where you wish the new function to appear on the menu, by selecting an entry on the menu function list, and then click the Add button.

5. Add commands to the menu, as described earlier in the "Adding Functions to Toolbars" section.

The up and down arrows in the Customize dialog box allow you to alter the position of entries on the menu. You could move those items you use frequently to the top of the menu, for example.

You can remove an existing menu item by highlighting it in the Customize dialog box, clicking the Modify button, and then clicking Delete.

If you make a mistake, simply click the Reset button at the bottom right of the Customize dialog box to return the menus to their default state.

Configuring OpenOffice.org Options

In addition to the wealth of customization options, OpenOffice.org offers a range of configuration options that allow you to make it work exactly how you wish. Within an OpenOffice.org program select Tools ➤ Options from the menu to open the Options dialog box, as shown in Figure 22-3.

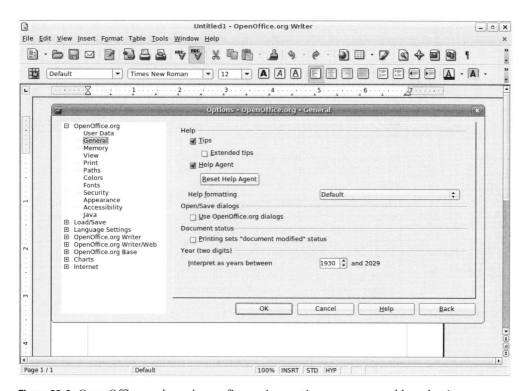

Figure 22-3. *OpenOffice.org's main configuration options are accessed by selecting Tools ➤ Options.*

Most of the configuration options offered within each program apply across the suite, but those under the heading of the program's name apply only to the program in use. In other words, to set the options specific to Calc, you need to use the Calc Options dialog box. But to set global options for the entire suite, you can use any program's Options dialog box.

A variety of options are offered, allowing you to tweak everything from the default file format to the colors used by default within the software. Table 22-2 briefly describes each of the OpenOffice.org configuration options.

Table 22-2. *OpenOffice.org Configuration Options*

Option	Description
OpenOffice.org	
User Data	This is the personal data that will be added to the documents you create. You can leave this area blank if you wish.
General	This offers a handful of miscellaneous options, such as how to handle two-digit dates, when the help system should step in to offer tips, how the help system should be formatted (such as in high resolution for people with vision problems), and whether printing a document is interpreted by OpenOffice.org as modifying it.
Memory	This entry relates to how much system memory OpenOffice.org can use. You can limit the number of undo steps, for example, and alter the cache memory used for holding graphical objects.
View	Here, you can alter the look, feel, and operation of OpenOffice.org. You can define whether the middle mouse button performs a paste operation (which is consistent with how Ubuntu works), or whether it should perform a scrolling function, as with Windows. You can also alter elements such as whether icons appear in menus and if fonts are previewed in the toolbar menu.
Print	This option lets you adjust how printing is handled within OpenOffice.org. The functions relate to those that can stop documents from printing incorrectly, such as reducing any transparency effects within the documents so on-page elements don't appear faint or completely disappear in the final output. (Note that specific print functions are handled within the Print dialog box when you actually print a document.)
Paths	This is where the file paths for user-configured and vital system tools are handled. Generally, there's little reason to edit this list, although you might choose to alter the default location where your documents are saved (simply double-click the My Documents entry to do this).
Colors	Here, you can define the default color palette that appears in the various programs in the suite.
Fonts	By creating entries here, you can automatically substitute fonts within documents you open for others on your system. If you don't have the Microsoft core fonts installed, this might prove useful. For example, you might choose to substitute Arial, commonly used in Microsoft Office documents, for Luxi Sans, one of the sans serif fonts used under Ubuntu.
Security	This option controls which types of functions can be run within OpenOffice.org. For example, you can choose whether macros created by third parties should be run when you open a new document.
Appearance	Here, you can alter the color scheme used within OpenOffice.org, in a similar way to how you can alter the default Ubuntu desktop color scheme. Individual elements within documents and pages can be modified, too.

Table 22-2. *OpenOffice.org Configuration Options (Continued)*

Option	Description
Accessibility	This option relates to features that might help people with vision disabilities to use OpenOffice.org. For example, you can define whether animated graphics are shown on the screen.
Java	This option lets you control whether you use the Java Runtime Environment, which may be necessary to use some of OpenOffice.org's features.
Load/Save	
General	Options here relate to how files are saved. You can select whether the default is to save in OpenOffice.org or Microsoft Office format. Choosing the latter is useful if you share a lot of documents with colleagues who are not running OpenOffice.org.
VBA Properties	This option relates to how Visual Basic for Applications (VBA) code is handled when Microsoft Office documents are opened. Specifically, it ensures that the code isn't lost when the file is saved again.
Microsoft Office	This option provides functions specifically needed to convert or open Microsoft Office files within OpenOffice.org.
HTML Compatibility	Here, you can set options that affect the compatibility of HTML files saved within OpenOffice.org.
Language Settings	
Languages	Here, you can set your local language so that documents are spell-checked correctly. In addition, Asian language support can be activated, which allows for more complex document layout options.
Writing Aids	Under this option, you can activate or deactivate various plug-ins designed to help format documents, such as the hyphenator or the spell-checking component. In addition, you can alter how the spell-checker works, such as whether it ignores capitalized words.
OpenOffice.org Writer	
General	Here, you can alter various options related to the editing of word processor documents, such as which measurements are used on the ruler (centimeter, inches, picas, and so on).
View	Under this option, you can configure the look and feel of the Writer program, such as which scroll bars are visible by default. You can also turn off the display of various page elements, such as tables and graphics.
Formatting Aids	This option lets you choose which symbols appear for "invisible" elements (such as the carriage return symbol or a dot symbol to indicate where spaces have been inserted) in Writer.
Grid	This controls whether page elements will snap to an invisible grid. You can also define the dimensions and spacing of the grid cells here.
Basic Fonts (Western)	This controls which fonts are used by default in the various text styles, such as for the default text and within lists.
Print	This option offers control over printing options specific to Writer, such as which page elements are printed (you might choose to turn off the printing of graphics, for example).

Table 22-2. *OpenOffice.org Configuration Options (Continued)*

Option	Description
Tables	Here, you can control how tables are created and how you interact with them within Writer. For example, you can control what happens when a table is resized, such as whether the entire table responds to the changes or merely the cell you're resizing.
Changes	This option lets you define how changes are displayed when the track changes function is activated.
Compatibility	Here, you can set specifics of how Writer handles the import and export of Microsoft Word documents.
AutoCaption	This offers settings for the AutoCaption feature within Writer.
Mail Merge E-Mail	This option lets you control the sending of e-mail mail merge messages.

OpenOffice.org Writer/Web

Option	Description
View	Here, you can control the HTML editor component of OpenOffice.org (effectively an extension of Writer). You can control the look and feel of the HTML editor, including which elements are displayed on the screen.
Formatting Aids	As with the similar entry for Writer under Text Document, this option lets you view symbols in place of usually hidden text elements.
Grid	This lets you define a grid that on-screen elements are able to "snap to" in order to aid accurate positioning.
Print	Here, you can define how HTML documents created within OpenOffice.org are printed.
Table	Similar to the Tables entry under Text Document, this controls how tables are created and handled within HTML documents.
Background	This lets you set the default background color for HTML documents.

OpenOffice.org Calc

Option	Description
General	Here, you can modify miscellaneous options related to Calc, such as which measurement units are used within the program and how the formatting of cells is changed when new data is input.
View	This option relates to the look and feel of Calc, such as the color of the grid lines between cells and which elements are displayed on the screen. For example, you can configure whether zero values are displayed, and whether overflow text within cells is shown or simply truncated at the cell boundary.
Calculate	This option relates to how numbers are handled during certain types of formula calculations, such as those involving dates.
Sort Lists	This option lets you create lists that are applied to relevant cells when the user chooses to sort them. Several lists are predefined to correctly sort days of the week or months of the year.
Changes	This option relates to the on-screen formatting for changes when the track changes function is activated.
Grid	This option lets you configure an invisible grid that stretches across the sheet and which page objects can be set to snap to the grid for correct alignment.

Table 22-2. *OpenOffice.org Configuration Options (Continued)*

Option	Description
Print	This option relates to printing specifically from Calc, such as whether Calc should avoid printing empty pages that might occur within documents.

OpenOffice.org Impress

Option	Description
General	This option refers to miscellaneous settings within the Impress program, such as whether the program should always start with a wizard and which units of measurement should be used.
View	This option relates to the look and feel of Impress, and, in particular, whether certain on-screen elements are displayed.
Grid	This controls whether an invisible grid is applied to the page and whether objects should snap to it.
Print	This option controls how printing is handled within Impress and, in particular, how items in the document will appear on the printed page.

OpenOffice.org Draw

Option	Description
General	This option relates to miscellaneous settings within Draw (the vector graphics component of OpenOffice.org).
View	Here, you can set specific preferences with regard to which objects are visible on the screen while you're editing with Draw.
Grid	This option relates to the invisible grid that can be applied to the page.
Print	This option lets you define which on-screen elements are printed and which are not printed.

OpenOffice.org Base

Option	Description
Connections	This option lets you control how any data sources you attach to are handled.
Databases	Here, you can configure which databases are registered for use within Base.

Chart

Option	Description
Default Colors	Here, you can set the default color palette that should be used when creating charts, usually within the Calc program.

Internet

Option	Description
Proxy	Here, you can configure network proxy settings specifically for OpenOffice.org, if necessary.
Search	Certain functions within various OpenOffice.org programs let you search the Internet. Here, you can configure how these search functions work.
E-mail	This option lets you specify which program you wish OpenOffice.org to use for e-mail.
Mozilla Plug-in	This function allows integration of OpenOffice.org into the Mozilla and/or Netscape browsers, to allow the viewing of OpenOffice.org documents within the browser window.

Using OpenOffice.org Core Functions

Although the various programs within OpenOffice.org are designed for very specific tasks, they all share several core functions that work in broadly similar ways. In addition, each program is able to borrow components from other programs in the suite.

Using Wizards

One of the core functions you'll find most useful when you're creating new documents is the wizard system, which you can access from the File menu. A wizard guides you through creating a new document by answering questions and following a wizard-based interface. This replaces the template-based approach within Microsoft Office, although it's worth noting that OpenOffice.org is still able to use templates.

A wizard will usually offer a variety of document styles. Some wizards will even prompt you to fill in salient details, which they will then insert into your document in the relevant areas.

Getting Help

OpenOffice.org employs a comprehensive help system, complete with automatic context-sensitive help, called the Help Agent, which will appear if the program detects you're performing a particular task. Usually, the Help Agent takes the form of a light bulb graphic, which will appear at the bottom-right corner of the screen. If you ignore the Help Agent, it will disappear within a few seconds. Clicking it causes a help window to open. Alternatively, you can access the main searchable help file by clicking the relevant menu entry.

Inserting Objects with Object Linking and Embedding

All the OpenOffice.org programs are able to make use of Object Linking and Embedding (OLE). This effectively means that one OpenOffice.org document can be inserted into another. For example, you might choose to insert a Calc spreadsheet into a Writer document.

The main benefit of using OLE over simply copying and pasting the data is that the OLE item (referred to as an *object*) will be updated whenever the original document is revised. In this way, you can prepare a report featuring a spreadsheet full of figures, for example, and not need to worry about updating the report when the figures change. Figure 22-4 shows an example of a spreadsheet from Calc inserted into a Writer document.

Whenever you click inside the OLE object, the user interface will change so that you can access functions specific to that object. For example, if you had inserted an Impress object into a Calc document, clicking within the object would cause the Calc interface to temporarily turn into that of Impress. Clicking outside the OLE object would restore the interface back to Calc.

You can explore OLE objects by selecting Insert ➤ Object ➤ OLE Object. This option lets you create and insert a new OLE object, as well as add one based on an existing file. To ensure the inserted OLE object is updated when the file is, check the Link To File box in the Insert OLE Object dialog box.

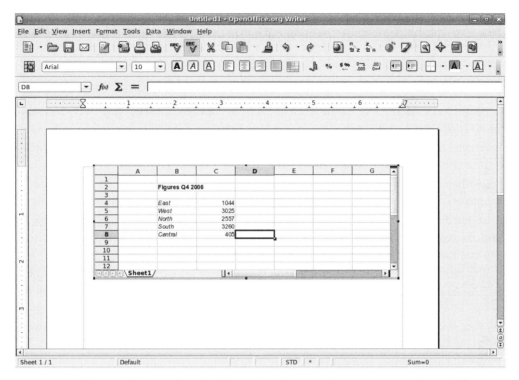

Figure 22-4. *Object Linking and Embedding (OLE) lets you incorporate one OpenOffice.org document into another.*

Creating Macros

OpenOffice.org employs a powerful BASIC-like programming language, which you can use to create your own functions. Although this language is called BASIC, it is several generations beyond the BASIC you might have used in the past. OpenOffice.org's BASIC is a high-level, object-oriented environment designed to appeal to programmers who wish to quickly add their own functions to the suite.

However, it's possible for any user to record a series of actions as a macro, which is then automatically turned into a simple BASIC program. This can be very useful if you wish to automate a simple, repetitive task, such as the insertion of a paragraph of text, or even something more complicated, such as searching and replacing text within a document.

To record a macro, select Tools ➤ Macros ➤ Record Macro. After you've selected this option, any subsequent actions will be recorded. All keyboard strokes and clicks of the mouse will be captured and turned automatically into BASIC commands. To stop the recording, simply click the button on the floating toolbar. After this, you'll be invited to give the macro a name (look to the top left of the dialog box). Once you've done so, a dialog box will appear, into which you can type a name for the macro (in the Macro Name text box). Then, click Save. You can then run your macro in the future by choosing Tools ➤ Macros ➤ Run Macro. Simply expand the My Macros and Standard entries at the top left of the dialog box, click Module1, select your macro in the list on the right, and click Run.

Saving Files

As mentioned in Chapter 21, OpenOffice.org uses the OpenDocument range of file formats. The files end with an .ods, .odt, .odp, or .odb file extension, depending on whether they've been saved by Calc, Writer, Impress, or Base, respectively. The OpenDocument format is the best choice when you're saving documents that you are likely to further edit within OpenOffice.org. However, if you wish to share files with colleagues who aren't running Ubuntu or OpenOffice.org, the solution is to save the files as Microsoft Office files. To save in this format, just choose it from the Save As drop-down list in the Save As dialog box. If your colleague is running an older version of OpenOffice.org or StarOffice, you can also save in those file formats.

Alternatively, you might wish to save the file in one of the other file formats offered in the Save As drop-down list. However, saving files in an alternative format might result in the loss of some document components or formatting. For example, saving a Writer document as a simple text file (.txt) will lead to the loss of all of the formatting, as well as any of the original file's embedded objects, such as pictures.

To avoid losing document components or formatting, you might choose to output your OpenOffice.org files as Portable Document Format (PDF) files, which can be read by the Adobe Acrobat viewer. The benefit of this approach is that a complete facsimile of your document will be made available, with all the necessary fonts and on-screen elements included within the PDF file. The drawback is that PDF files cannot be loaded into OpenOffice.org for further editing, so you should always save an additional copy of the file in the native OpenOffice.org format. To save any file as a PDF throughout the suite, select File ➤ Export As PDF. Then choose PDF in the File Type drop-down box, as shown in Figure 22-5.

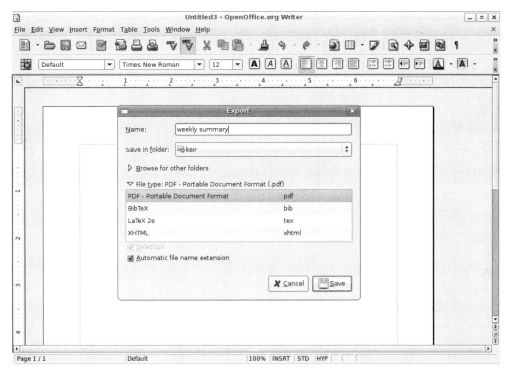

Figure 22-5. *All the programs in the suite can export files in Adobe PDF format.*

Summary

In this chapter, we looked at the configuration options provided with OpenOffice.org. You were introduced to the user interface, which is shared across all the programs within the suite, and learned how it can be customized. We also examined some common tools provided across the suite of programs, such as macro generation.

Over the following chapters, we will look at each major component of the suite, starting with Writer.

■ ■ ■

## CHAPTER 23

In Depth: Writer

The word processor is arguably the most popular element within any office suite. That said, you'll be happy to know that OpenOffice.org's Writer component doesn't skimp on features. It offers full text-editing and formatting functionality, along with powerful higher-level features such as mail merge.

In this chapter, we'll take a look at some of Writer's most useful features. As with all of the components in the OpenOffice.org suite, describing the features within Writer could easily fill an entire book. You should do some exploring on your own by clicking around to discover new features, as well as make judicious use of the help system. To start Writer, click Applications ➤ Office ➤ OpenOffice.org Word Processor.

Formatting Text

You can format text within Writer using several methods. Here, we'll look at using the Formatting toolbar, the context menu, and the Style and Formatting palette.

The Formatting Toolbar

Formatting text is easy to do via the Formatting toolbar, which is just above the ruler and main document area. Using the toolbar buttons, you can select the type of font you wish to use, its point size, and its style (normal, bold, italics, and so on). The range of fonts is previewed in the Font drop-down list, making it easy to select the right typeface.

In addition, the Formatting toolbar lets you justify text so that it's aligned to the left or right margin, centered, or fully justified. You can also indent text using the relevant icons. As with elsewhere in Ubuntu, a tooltip will appear over each icon when you hover the mouse cursor over it, as shown in Figure 23-1. To the right of the indentation buttons are tools to change the text background and foreground colors, and also a tool to create highlighter pen-style effects.

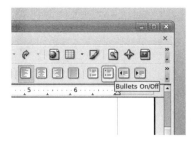

Figure 23-1. *When you hover your mouse over an icon, a tooltip appears to explain what it does.*

Context Menu

Rather than use the Formatting toolbar, you can format text using the context menu. Right-click the text you want to format, and a context menu will present options for the font, size, style, alignment, and line spacing. The context menu also allows you to change the case of the highlighted characters—from uppercase to lowercase, and vice versa.

By selecting the Character option from the context menu, you get ultimate control over the font formatting. This will present a dialog box that includes every possible option, such as rotating the text and altering the individual character spacing (look under the Position tab for these options).

■**Tip** The Character dialog box lets you create interesting typographical effects. The Paragraph dialog box has many options for formatting paragraphs. These tools open up the possibility of using Writer for simple desktop publishing work.

Selecting Paragraph from the context menu displays the Paragraph dialog box, as shown in Figure 23-2. This gives you control over paragraph elements, such as line spacing, indentation, and automatic numbering. Here, you will also find an option to automatically create drop caps, so you can start a piece of writing in style!

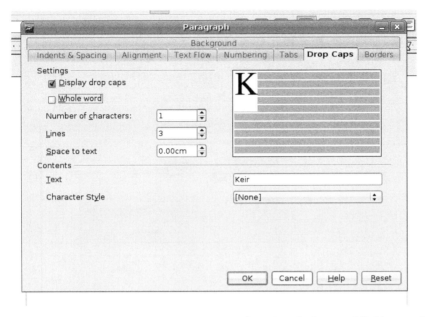

Figure 23-2. *Writer includes many elements found in desktop publishing packages, such as the ability to create drop caps.*

The Style and Formatting Palette

The Style and Formatting palette offers a variety of predefined formatting styles that you can apply to selected text or enable before you begin adding text. To make it appear, click Formatting ➤ Styles and Formatting, or press F11. You can simply click the palette's close button to get rid of it.

You can easily add your own text styles to the Style and Formatting palette. Simply select some text that has the formatting applied, click the top-right button (denoted by a paragraph symbol next to a block of text), and then select New Style from Selection in the list. You'll be invited to give the style a name, and when you click OK, it will appear in the list.

Spell-Checking

Writer is able to automatically spell-check as you type. Any words it considers misspelled will be underlined in red. You can choose from a list of possible corrections by right-clicking the word and selecting from the context menu. If you're sure the word is spelled correctly but it doesn't appear to be in the dictionary, you can select Add ➤ Standard.dic from the context menu, as shown in Figure 23-3. This will add the word to your own personal dictionary extension (other users won't have access to your dictionary and will need to create their own list of approved words).

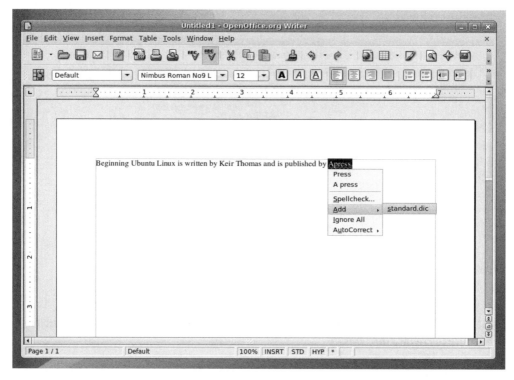

Figure 23-3. *Any words you're going to use frequently, but which Writer doesn't recognize, can be added to your personal dictionary.*

■**Tip** You might find that the spell-checker is set for US English. If you live outside the United States, or need to create documents for readers in other countries, you can choose a dictionary tailored to your locality or needs. To change the language, select Tools ➤ Options. In the list on the left, select Language Settings, and then Languages. In the Default Languages for Documents list, select your local variation. This will then become the default for all new documents.

If you find live spell-checking invasive or distracting, you can deactivate it by selecting Tools ➤ Spellcheck, clicking the Options button, and removing the check next to Check Spelling As You Type.

You can manually spell-check the document at any time by clicking Tools ➤ Spellcheck. This will scan through the document and prompt you for corrections for words the program considers misspelled.

Inserting Pictures

Writer includes quite substantial desktop publishing–like functions, such as the ability to insert pictures into text documents and to have text flow around pictures.

Inserting any kind of graphic—a graph, digital camera photo, drawing, or any other type of image—is easy. Simply choose Insert ➤ Picture ➤ From File.

Tip If you have a scanner, you can also scan pictures directly into Writer documents. Simply click Insert ➤ Picture ➤ Scan ➤ Select Source.

After you've inserted a picture, you can place it anywhere on the page. When you select the picture, a new toolbar appears. This toolbar contains various simple image-tweaking tools, such as those for altering the brightness, contrast, and color balance of the image. Additionally, by clicking and dragging the blue handles surrounding the image, you can resize it.

Graphics that are imported into Writer must be anchored in some way. In other words, they must be linked to a page element so that they don't move unexpectedly. By default, they're anchored to the nearest paragraph, which means that if that paragraph moves, the graphic will move, too. Alternatively, by right-clicking the graphic, you can choose to anchor it to the page, paragraph, or character it is on or next to, as shown in Figure 23-4. Selecting to anchor it to the page will fix it firmly in place, regardless of what happens to the contents of the surrounding text. The As Character option is slightly different from the To Character option. When you choose As Character, the image will be anchored to the character it is next to, and it is actually inserted in the same line as that character, as if it were a character itself. If the image is bigger than the line it is anchored in, the line height will automatically change to accommodate it.

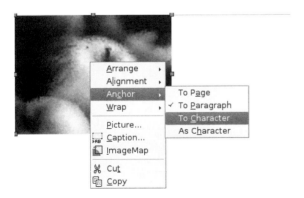

Figure 23-4. *A picture can be "anchored" to the page, paragraph, or a character. This affects how it responds to the paragraphs surrounding it.*

As you can see in Figure 23-4, the context menu also includes a Wrap option, which lets you set the type of text wrap you want to use. By default, Optimal Page Wrap is selected. This causes the text to wrap down just one side of the picture—the side on which the picture is farthest from the edge of the page. Alternatives include No Wrap, which will mean that the graphic will occupy the entire space on the page; no text is allowed on either side of it. However, Page Wrap is the best option if you're looking for a desktop publishing–style effect, because the text will wrap around both sides of the picture. Alternatively, if you wish the image to appear in the background of the page with text flowing across it, you can select the relevant option from the context menu.

As always within OpenOffice.org, ultimate control is achieved by opening the relevant dialog box. You can set up how graphics are treated on the page by right-clicking the image and selecting Picture. In the dialog box that appears, you can select the wrap effect, specify the invisible border around the wrap (which governs how close the text is to the image), and give the image a border frame.

Working with Tables

Often, it's useful to present columns of numbers or text within a word processor document. To make it easy to align the columns, OpenOffice.org offers the Table tool. This lets you quickly and easily create a grid in which to enter numbers or other information. You can even turn tables into simple spreadsheets, and tally rows or columns via simple formulas.

To insert a table, click and hold the Table icon on the Standard toolbar (which runs across the top of the screen beneath the menu). Then simply drag the mouse in the table diagram that appears until you have the desired number of rows and columns, and release the mouse button to create the table, as shown in Figure 23-5.

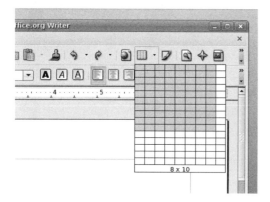

Figure 23-5. *Just select the Table icon on the Main toolbar and drag the mouse to define the size of the table. Release the mouse button when you're finished.*

Whenever your cursor is inside the table, a new toolbar will appear, offering handy options. Once again, simply hover your mouse over each button to find out what it does via a tooltip.

As with spreadsheets, tables consist of cells arranged into rows (running horizontally) and columns (running vertically). Altering the size of a column is easy. Just hover the mouse over the edge of a cell until it changes to a resizing cursor, and then click and drag. You can do the same on a horizontal bar to alter a cell's height, but a far better method is to right-click within the cell, select Row ➤ Height, and enter a value. This will ensure that subsequent cells are shifted down to make space for the newly enlarged cell, which doesn't happen when you click and drag the cell's border.

░**Tip** An alternative way of resizing cells is to click in a cell and press the Enter key, which inserts a carriage return. Cells expand in size to fit their contents.

Once the cursor is within a table, you can move from cell to cell using the Tab key. Alternatively, you can move backward through the cells by pressing Shift+Tab.

To add more rows or columns, click the relevant icon on the Table toolbar (the fourth and fifth buttons on the bottom row). To split an existing cell, ensure your cursor is inside it, right-click, select Cell from the menu, and then click Split.

If you want to total figures within a table, click in an empty cell, and then click the Sum icon on the Table toolbar (the Greek sigma symbol on the right side of the bottom row). This is similar to inserting a function in a spreadsheet. The cell holds the formula for the sum and clicking additional cells, or a range of cells, adds them to the sum.

░**Note** Only correctly formatted cells can be summed using the Sum icon on the Table toolbar. Cells with spaces or text within them cannot be added to the formula.

You can alter the styling of any cell using various icons on the Table toolbar, as well as the standard text formatting tools on the Formatting toolbar. The Table toolbar allows you to add borders to the cells and change the background colors. Alternatively, you can choose to remove all borders from the cells by clicking the Borders icon and then the No Borders option (note that gray borders will remain in place, but these are only for your convenience and won't appear in printouts).

Mail Merging

Mail merging refers to automatically applying a database of details, such as names and addresses, to a document, so that many personalized copies are produced. It's ordinarily used to create form letters for mailings.

OpenOffice.org makes the procedure very easy, but it requires source data that will be merged into the document. As with Microsoft Word, you can either enter this data within Writer itself or choose to import data from a separate document. Unless you have enough knowledge of databases to connect one to OpenOffice.org (the program works with dBase and MySQL files, among others), you may want to input existing data in the form of a comma-separated value (CSV) text file. This is the simplest form of data file that is understood by the majority of office programs and databases.

Here, we're going to look at entering the data within Writer, which is the best policy for smaller mail merge operations. You can then output the data as a CSV file, so you can use it again later. Here are the steps for using mail merge (click the Next button after each step):

1. Select Tools ➤ Mail Merge Wizard to start the wizard, as shown in Figure 23-6.

2. Specify your starting document, which is the document in which the merged data will appear. You can opt to use the current document, create a new document, open a document from file, or use a template as the basis for your file.

3. Choose the mail merge type. You can choose to create a merged e-mail (for sending to multiple recipients) or a merged letter.

4. You're asked to tell Writer about your data. Writer needs to know where to find the addresses that will be merged into the document. Click the Select Address List button.

5. In the window that appears, you have a number of options. You can raid your Evolution e-mail address book for the data, click Add to select an already existing data source (such as a database or CSV file), or create a data source from scratch. Click the Create button to create a data source to enter the data in Writer.

■**Note** The fourth option for choosing a mail merge data source, Filter, allows you to filter the database source you select after clicking Add, so that you can import only specific data. To learn more about this technique, browse the OpenOffice.org Help file (click Help ➤ OpenOffice.org Help) and search for Filtering ➤ Data in Databases.

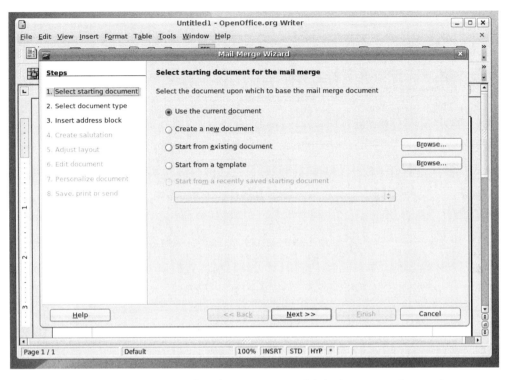

Figure 23-6. *The Mail Merge Wizard makes creating multiple documents from a data source incredibly easy.*

6. You're presented with a form for entering the data for each individual you want to receive the mail-merged letter, as shown in Figure 23-7. You don't need to fill in each field; you'll be able to choose which data fields to use in the document later on. If you wish to enter your own specific data types in addition to address details, you can click the Customize button to add your own field to the list. Using the up and down arrows in the window that appears, position the highlight where you would like the data to appear. Then click the Add button (alternatively, if there's a data field you're not using, you can highlight it and select Rename to reuse it). Obviously, you should add any new data fields you want *before* you begin to enter data!

7. Type in the data and press Enter at the end of each line. When you get to the last field, click the New button at the top right. When you've finished entering all the data, click OK. Then accept Writer's offer to save the data as a CSV file.

8. You're returned to the data-selection screen, and your just-saved file will be in the list. Click OK.

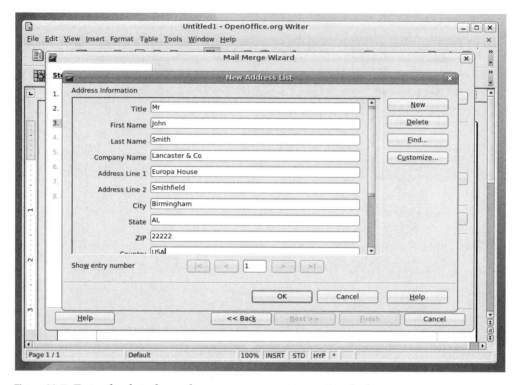

Figure 23-7. *Enter the data for each person you want to receive the letter.*

9. You're returned to the main Mail Merge Wizard window, where you can select whether or not to include an address block. All this means is that Writer will automatically add the merge fields to your document in what it considers the correct format (for example, title, followed by first and last name, with each line of the address underneath, and so on). You can insert the merge fields manually later on if you wish; in that case, remove the check from the "This document shall contain an address block" check box. Click Next.

10. You're invited to create the salutation that will head the letter. This will contain the merge data as well, so that you can personalize the letter. Again, you can accept the default, tweak it slightly, or choose not to have an automated salutation (so that you can create your own later).

11. Depending on your previous choices, and whether you accepted the automatic address block and salutation, you are now given the choice to adjust the layout of the document in a rough way or to actually edit it (note that even if you accepted the address block and/or salutation, you'll get a chance to edit the document in the next step anyway).

12. If you opt to edit the document, you can insert your choice of merge fields by clicking Insert ➤ Fields ➤ Other. Select the Database tab in the window that appears, and then select Mail Merge Fields on the left side of the window. Click the small plus symbol next to the data file you created earlier, which should be listed on the right, and you can then select and insert the merge fields. Once you've finished, click the Return to Mail Merge Wizard button.

13. Click Next to perform the merge. You're then given a chance to edit the actual mail-merged documents (which, depending on the quantity of data entries you created earlier, could number in the tens, hundreds or even thousands!).

14. You can save or print the *merged* document containing the data. To save the document creating the merge fields, click Save Starting Document.

Adding Headers and Footers

You may want to add headers and footers to long documents to aid navigation. They appear at the top and bottom of each page, respectively, and can include the document title, page number, and other information. Headers and footers are created and edited independently of the main document.

As you might expect, inserting both headers and footers takes just a couple of clicks. Select Insert ➤ Header ➤ Default or Insert ➤ Footer ➤ Default, depending on which you wish to insert (documents can have both, of course). Writer will then display an editing area where you can type text to appear in the header or footer. For more options, right-click in the area, select Page, and then click the Header or Footer tab. Here, you can control the formatting and nature of the header or footer. Clicking the More button will let you apply borders or background colors.

You might wish to insert page numbers that will be updated automatically as the document progresses. OpenOffice.org refers to data that automatically updates as a *field*. You can insert a wide variety of fields by selecting Insert ➤ Fields, as shown in Figure 23-8. For example, along with the page number, you can insert the document title and author name (which is read from the details entered into the Options configuration dialog box, accessed from the Tools menu). In addition, you can enter mail merge fields by clicking Other (see the previous section for a description of how to associate mail merge data with a document).

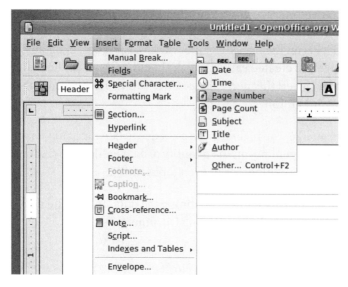

Figure 23-8. *Automatically updating data, such as page numbers, can be inserted into headers and footers.*

Summary

In this chapter, we've examined Writer, one of the core components of OpenOffice.org. We've looked at the some of the key tools, which enable quick and easy document creation. In particular, you've learned how to format text, use the spell-checking component, insert pictures, create and edit tables, mail merge, and add headers and footers.

In the next chapter, we move on to another vital part of OpenOffice.org: Calc, the spreadsheet component.

■■■

## CHAPTER 24

In Depth: Calc

Calc is the spreadsheet component of OpenOffice.org. Like most modern spreadsheet programs, it contains hundreds of features, many of which few average users will ever use. However, it doesn't abandon its user-friendliness in the process and remains very simple for those who want to work on modest calculations, such as home finances or mortgage interest payments. In many regards, Calc is practically a clone of Excel, and anyone who has used Microsoft's spreadsheet program will be able to get started with it immediately.

In this chapter, you'll learn about some of the best features of Calc, as well as the basics of spreadsheet creation. To start Calc, click Applications ➤ Office ➤ OpenOffice.org Spreadsheet.

Entering and Formatting Data

As with all spreadsheets, entering data into a Calc document is simply a matter of selecting a cell and starting to type. You can enter practically anything into a cell, but a handful of symbols are not allowed. For example, you cannot enter an equals sign (=) in a cell, because Calc will assume that this is part of a formula.

■**Tip** To enter any character into a cell, including an equals sign followed by a digit, precede it with an apostrophe ('). The apostrophe itself won't be visible within the spreadsheet, and whatever you type won't be interpreted in any special way; it will be seen as plain text.

Entering a sequence of data across a range of cells can be automated. Start typing the sequence of numbers (or words), highlight them, and then click and drag the small handle to the bottom right of the last cell. This will continue the sequence. You'll see a tooltip window, indicating what the content of each cell will be. Figure 24-1 illustrates this process.

Cells can be formatted in a variety of ways. For trivial formatting changes, such as selecting a different font or changing the number format, you can use the Formatting toolbar. For example, to turn the cell into one that displays currency, click the Number Format: Currency icon (remember that hovering the mouse cursor over each icon will reveal a tooltip). You can also increase or decrease the number of visible decimal places by clicking the relevant Formatting toolbar icon.

For more formatting options, right-click the individual cell, and select Format Cells from the menu. This displays the Format Cell dialog box, where you can change the style of the typeface, rotate text, place text at various angles, and so on. The Border tab of the Format Cell dialog box includes options for cell gridlines of varying thicknesses, which will appear when the document is eventually printed out.

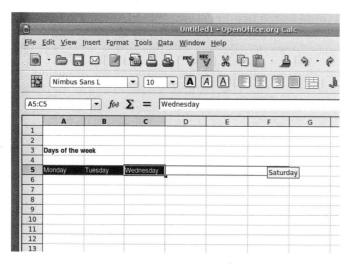

Figure 24-1. *You can automate the entering of data sequences by clicking and dragging.*

Deleting and Inserting Data and Cells

Deleting data is also easy. Just highlight the cell or cells with the data you want to delete, and then press the Delete key. If you want to totally eradicate the cell along with its contents, right-click it and select Delete Cells. This will cause the data to the sides of the cell to move in. You'll be given a choice on where you want the cells to shift from to fill the space: left, right, above, or below.

To insert a new cell, right-click where you would like to it to appear and select Insert Cells. Again, you'll be prompted about where you want to shift the surrounding cells in order to make space for the new cell.

Working with Formulas

Calc includes a large number of formulas. In addition to simple and complex math functions, Calc offers a range of logical functions, as well as statistical and database tools. Certain formulas can also be used to manipulate text strings, such as dates.

You can get an idea of the available functions by clicking the Function Wizard button on the Formula bar (which is just below the Formatting toolbar). This will bring up a categorized list of formulas, along with brief outlines of what function the formula performs. If you would like more details, use the help system, which contains comprehensive descriptions of most of the formulas, complete with examples of the correct syntax.

■**Note** The Function Wizard is actually a continuation of the wizard system you've seen in other OpenOffice.org programs, and some of the functions are also available elsewhere in the suite.

You can reuse formulas simply by cutting and pasting them. Calc is intelligent enough to work out which cells the transplanted formula should refer to, but it's always a good idea to check to make sure the correct cells are referenced.

Using the Function Wizard

To use the Function Wizard to add a function, click the relevant button on the Formula bar, select the desired type of formula from the Category drop-down list, and then double-click an entry in the Function list to select it. Following this, you'll be prompted to input the relevant figures or define the appropriate data sources. Next to each text-entry box is a "shrink" button, which temporarily hides the wizard window, so you can select cells to be used within the formula.

Let's look at a quick example of using the wizard to work out an average value of a number of cells.

1. Select the cell in which you want the result of the formula to appear.

2. Start the Function Wizard by clicking the button on the Formula bar. In the left-hand list of functions, double-click AVERAGE. The wizard will then present a list of fields on the right side of the dialog box, where you can enter the values to be averaged. You could type numeric values directly into these fields, but it's more likely that you'll want to reference individual cells from the spreadsheet.

3. Click and drag the top of the dialog box to move it so that the spreadsheet underneath is at least partially visible.

4. Click the cursor in the "number 1" field of the dialog box, and then click the first cell you want to include in the calculation. This will automatically enter that cell reference into the field. By clicking the button to the right of the field, you can roll up the dialog box to allow better access to the spreadsheet. This will then display only the dialog box field you're entering data into. To unroll the dialog box, click the button again.

5. Click the next field in the dialog box, and then click the next cell you wish to include.

6. Repeat step 5 until all the fields you wish to include have been added to the fields in the dialog box (up to 30 can be selected; use the scroll bar on the right side of the wizard dialog box to reveal more fields).

7. Once you've finished, click the OK button. Calc will insert the formula into the cell you selected at the start, showing the result of the formula.

After you've added a formula with the wizard, you can edit it manually by clicking it and overtyping its contents in the Formula bar editing area. Alternatively, you can use the Function Wizard once again, by clicking the button on the Formula bar.

Summing Figures

To add the values of a number of cells, you could use the Function Wizard and select the SUM function, as shown in Figure 24-2. The procedure for choosing the cells is the same as described in the previous section.

However, Calc provides a far easier method of creating the sum formula. After positioning the cursor in an empty cell, simply click the Sum icon (the Greek sigma character) on the Formula bar, and then select the cells you wish to include in the sum. Then press Enter to see the results. If you place the cursor in a cell directly beneath a column of numbers, Calc may be clever enough to guess what you want to add and automatically select them. If it's incorrect, simply highlight the correct range of cells.

■**Tip** You can select more than one cell by holding down the Ctrl key. You can select a range of cells in succession by clicking and dragging the mouse.

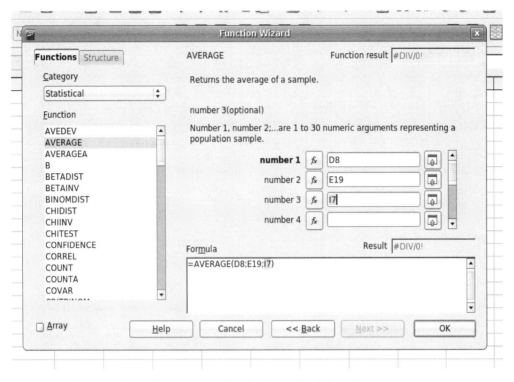

Figure 24-2. *Creating formulas is easy using the Function Wizard.*

Sorting Data

Within a spreadsheet, you may want to sort data according to any number of criteria. For example, you might want to show a list of numbers from highest to lowest, or rearrange a list of names so that they're in alphabetical order. This is easy to do within Calc.

Start by highlighting the range of data you wish to sort. Alternatively, you can simply select one cell within it, because Calc is usually able to figure out the range of cells you want to use. Then select Data ➤ Sort from the main menu. Calc will automatically select a sort key, which will appear in the Sort By drop-down list, as shown in Figure 24-3. However, you can also choose your own sort key from the drop-down menu if you wish, and you can choose to further refine your selection by choosing up to two more sort subkeys from the other drop-down menus.

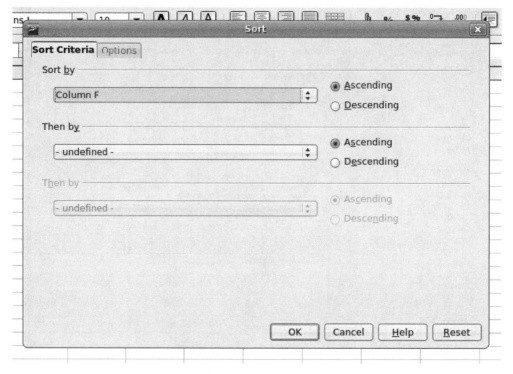

Figure 24-3. *Data can be sorted so that it's in alphabetical or numerical order.*

Creating Charts

Charts are useful, because they present a quick visual summary of data. Calc produces charts through a step-by-step wizard, so it becomes very easy indeed. Here are the steps:

1. Highlight the data you want to graph. Be careful to include only the data itself and not any surrounding cells, or even the cell that contains the title for the array of data.

2. Select the Insert ➤ Chart menu option, or click the Insert Chart button on the Standard toolbar.

3. The cursor turns into a target with a small graph next to it. Click and drag on the spreadsheet itself to define the area of the graph. This can be any size. Also, you can resize it later.

4. The wizard starts. The first step is to define the range of cells to be used for the chart. By highlighting the cells before you started, you've already done this, so you can click the Next button. However, first make sure that the First Row As Label option is selected.

5. Choose the type of chart you wish to use. For most simple data selections, a bar graph is usually best. However, you might also choose to select a horizontal bar graph. Then click Next.

6. The wizard presents a subselection of graph types. You can also select whether gridlines are used to separate the various areas of the graph. Make your selections and click Next.

7. The last step allows you to give the chart a title and also choose whether you want a legend (a key that explains what the axes refer to) to appear next to it.

8. Click Create, and the chart will be created. Figure 24-4 shows an example.

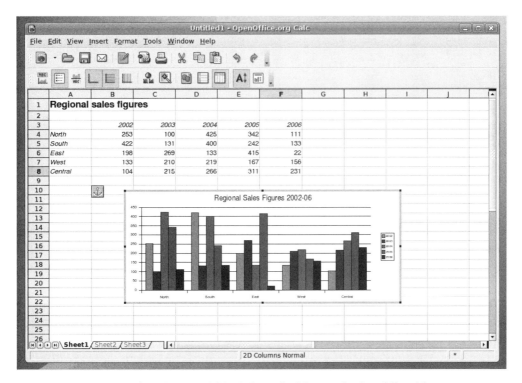

Figure 24-4. *Creating a chart is easy within Calc and adds a professional flourish to your spreadsheet.*

Once you've created a chart, you can alter its size by clicking and dragging the handles. You can also change various graphical aspects by double-clicking them. However, keep in mind that the graph is actually a picture, so the properties you edit are limited to changing the color and size of various elements.

The chart is linked to your data. Whenever your data changes, so will your chart. This is done automatically and doesn't require any user input.

Using Filters

The Filter function in Calc lets you selectively hide rows of data. The spreadsheet user then selects which of the rows of data to view from a drop-down list that appears in the cell at the top of the rows, as shown in the example in Figure 24-5.

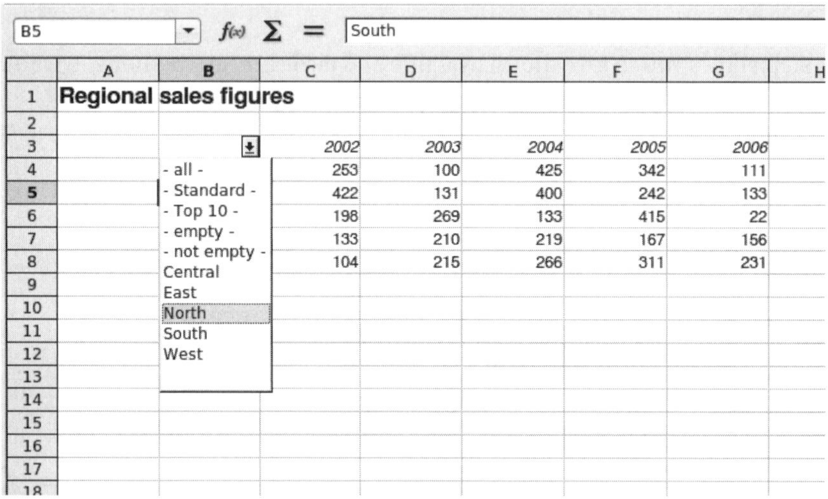

	A	B	C	D	E	F	G	H
1	**Regional sales figures**							
2								
3		⬇	2002	2003	2004	2005	2006	
4		- all -	253	100	425	342	111	
5		- Standard -	422	131	400	242	133	
6		- Top 10 -	198	269	133	415	22	
7		- empty -	133	210	219	167	156	
8		- not empty -	104	215	266	311	231	
9		Central						
10		East						
11		North						
12		South						
13		West						
14								
15								
16								
17								
18								

Figure 24-5. *Filters allow you to selectively hide or show rows of data in a spreadsheet.*

> ■**Note** A Calc filter is a little like an Excel pivot chart, especially when it's combined with an automatically generated chart.

Using filters in this way can be useful when you're dealing with a very large table of data. It helps isolate figures so you can compare them side by side in an easy-to-follow format. For example, you could filter a table of sales figures by year.

To use the Filter function, start by highlighting the data you wish to see in the drop-down list. Make sure the column header for the data is included, too. If you're using the Filter feature on a table of data, this selection can be any column within the table, although it obviously makes sense to use a column that is pertinent to the filtering that will take place. After you've selected the data to filter, select Data ➤ Filter ➤ Autofilter. You should find that, in place of the column header, a drop-down list appears. When a user selects a various entry in the list, Calc will display only the corresponding row of the spreadsheet beneath.

To remove a filter, select Data ➤ Filter ➤ Remove Filter.

Summary

In this chapter, we examined OpenOffice.org Calc. We looked at the basics of how data can be entered into a cell and how it can be formatted. Then you learned how to create formulas. This is easy to do with the Function Wizard function, which automates the task.

Next, you saw how to sort data in a spreadsheet. We also went through the steps for creating charts using a Calc wizard. Finally, we looked at creating data filters, which work rather like pivot charts in Microsoft Excel.

In the next chapter, we move on to Impress, the presentations component of OpenOffice.org.

## CHAPTER 25

In Depth: Impress

Impress is the presentation package within OpenOffice.org. At first glance, it appears to be the simplest of the key OpenOffice.org components, and also the one that borrows most the look and feel from Microsoft Office. However, delving into its feature set reveals more than a few surprises, including sophisticated animation effects and drawing tools. Impress can also export presentations as Adobe Flash–compatible files, which means that many Internet-enabled desktop computers around the world will be able to view the files, even if they don't have Impress or PowerPoint installed on their computers.

In this chapter, you'll learn about the main features of Impress, as well as the basics of working with presentations. You can start the program by clicking Applications ➤ Office ➤ OpenOffice.org Presentation.

Creating a Quick Presentation

As soon as Impress starts, it will offer to guide you through the creation of a presentation using a wizard. This makes designing your document a matter of following a few steps.

You'll initially be offered three choices: Empty Presentation, From Template, or Open Existing Presentation. When Impress refers to *templates*, it means presentations that are both predesigned and also contain sample content. Only two templates are supplied with Impress, so this option is somewhat redundant. However, you might choose to look at them later, if only to get an idea of what a presentation consists of and how it's made.

Tip When you become experienced in working with Impress, you can create your own templates or download some from the Internet. To create your own template, simply select to save your document as a template in the File Type drop-down list in the Save As dialog box. Make sure you place any templates you download or create in the `/usr/lib/openoffice/share/template/en-US/presnt/` directory (you will need to have superuser powers to do this and should make sure the file permissions are readable for all users).

The standard way of getting started is to create an empty presentation. This sounds more daunting than it actually is, because the Presentation Wizard will start, asking you to choose from a couple of ready-made basic designs, as shown in Figure 25-1. You'll also be given a chance to choose which format you want the presentation to take: whether it's designed primarily to be viewed on-screen or printed out.

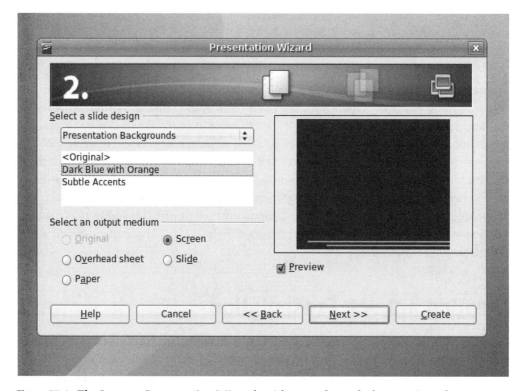

Figure 25-1. *The Impress Presentation Wizard guides you through the creation of a new presentation.*

After this, you'll be invited to choose the presentation effects, including the transition effect that will separate each slide when the presentation is viewed and the speed of the transition. If you wish, you can set the pause between slides, too, as well as the length of time each slide stays on the screen.

After clicking the Create button in the wizard, Impress will start, and you'll be invited to choose a layout for your initial slide. These are previewed on-screen on the right side of the program window. A variety of design templates are available, ranging from those that contain mostly text to those that feature pictures and/or graphs.

Depending on which template you choose, you should end up with a handful of text boxes on your screen. Editing the text in these is simply a matter of clicking within them. The formatting of the text will be set automatically.

Tip You can move and shrink each text box by clicking the handles surrounding the box. To draw a new text box, select the relevant tool on the Drawing toolbar, which runs along the bottom of the screen. Simply click and drag to draw a box of whatever size you want.

Working in Impress

When the Presentation Wizard has finished and Impress has started, you'll notice three main elements in the program window, from left to right, as shown in Figure 25-2. You work in these panes as follows:

Slides pane: This pane shows the slides in your presentation in order, one beneath the other. Simply click to select whichever slide you want to work on, or click and drag to reorder the slides. To create a new slide, right-click in a blank area on the Slides pane. Right-clicking any existing slide will present a range of options, including one to delete the slide.

Main work area: This is in the middle of the program window and lets you edit the various slides, as well as any other elements attached to the presentation, such as notes or handout documents. Simply click the relevant tab.

Tasks pane: Here, you can access the elements that will make up your presentation, such as slide templates, animations, and transition effects. Select the slide you wish to apply the elements to in the Slides pane, and then click the effect or template you wish to apply in the Tasks pane. In the case of animations or transitions, you can change various detailed settings relating to the selected element.

In addition, Impress has a Drawing toolbar, which appears at the bottom of the screen. This lets you draw various items on screen, such as lines, circles, and rectangles, and also contains a handful of special-effect tools, which I'll discuss later in this chapter, in the "Applying Fontwork" and "Using 3D Effects" sections.

You can hide each on-screen item by clicking the View menu and then removing the check next to it. Alternatively, by clicking the vertical borders between each pane, you can resize the pane and make it either more or less prominent on screen. This is handy if you wish to temporarily gain more work space but don't want to lose sight of the previews in the Slides pane, for example.

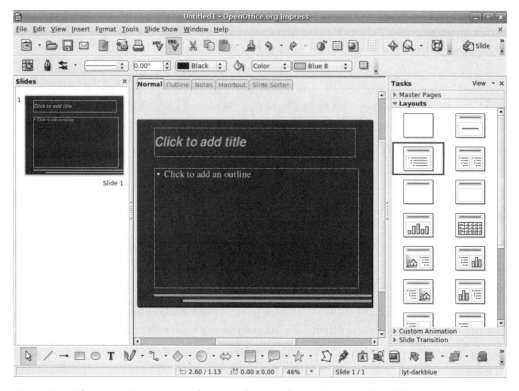

Figure 25-2. *The main Impress window is split into three elements: the Slides pane, main work area, and the Tasks pane.*

Animating Slides

All elements within Impress can be animated in a variety of ways. For example, you might choose to have the contents of a particular text box fly in from the edge of the screen during the presentation. This can help add variety to your presentation, and perhaps even wake up your audience!

Setting an animation effect is simply a matter of clicking the border of the object you wish to animate in the main editing area so that it is selected, selecting Custom Animation in the Tasks pane, and then clicking the Add button. In the dialog box that appears, select how you want the effect to work. As shown in Figure 25-3, you have four choices, each with its own tab within the dialog box:

> **Entrance:** This lets you animate an appearance effect for the selected object. For example, you can choose to have a text box dissolve into view or fly in from the side of the screen. When you select any effect, it will be previewed within the main editing area.

Emphasis: This gives you control over what, if anything, happens to the object while it's on screen. As the name suggests, you can use this animation to emphasize various elements while you're giving the presentation. Some emphasis effects are more dramatic than others, and this lets you control the impact. If you want to make an important point, you can use a dramatic effect, while more moderate information is presented with a more subdued effect.

Exit: As you might expect, this lets you add an exit animation to the object. You might choose to have it fly off the side of the screen or spin away off the top of the screen. The animation choices here are identical to the Entrance choices.

Motion path: This makes the selected element fly around on screen according to a particular path. For example, selecting Heart will cause the element to fly around describing the shape of a heart, eventually returning to its origin. A motion path is effectively another way of emphasizing a particular object.

■**Note** You can apply only one effect at a time to an object, although several separate effects can be applied to any object.

Figure 25-3. *A wide variety of animation effects is available for on-screen elements.*

With each animation, you can select the speed you wish it to play at, ranging from Very Slow to Fast. Simply make the selection at the bottom of the dialog box.

Once the animation has been defined and you've clicked OK, it will appear in a list at the bottom of the Custom Animation pane. You can choose to add more than one animation to an object by clicking the Add button again (ensuring the object is still selected in the main editing area). The animations will play in the order they're listed. You can click the Change Order up and down arrows to alter the order.

To fine-tune an effect you've already created, double-click it in the list to open its Effect Options dialog box (you can even add sound effects here). Under the Timing tab, you can control what cues the effect, such as a click of a mouse, or whether it will appear in sequence with other effects before or after in the list.

Applying Fontwork

The Fontwork tool lets you manipulate text in various playful ways, such as making it follow specific curved paths. You can find this tool on the Drawing toolbar, located at the bottom of the program window. It's the icon that's an A in a picture frame.

When you click the icon, the Fontwork Gallery dialog box appears, offering a choice of predefined font effects. Don't worry if they're not quite what you want, because after you make a choice, you'll be invited to fine-tune it.

Once you've made the selection, the dummy text "Fontwork" will appear on screen. Editing the text is simple: just double-click the "Fontwork" text and type your own words. When you've finished, click outside the Fontwork selection.

Whenever the new Fontwork item is selected, one or two floating toolbars will appear, as shown in Figure 25-4. You can use these toolbars to alter various options. For example, you can select a completely different Fontwork selection from the gallery or, by clicking the second icon on the left on the Fontwork toolbar, select your own path that you want the Fontwork item to follow. If the Fontwork type is three-dimensional, the 3D-Settings toolbar will let you alter the perspective, texture, and lighting. For more info on the options available, see the "Using 3D Effects" section.

You'll also see that the Formatting toolbar running along the top of the program window changes to allow you to alter the formatting of the Fontwork element. You can alter the thickness of the letter outlines, for example, or the color of the letters. Once again, the best way to learn how the tool works is to play around with the options and see what you can achieve.

To remove a Fontwork item, just select its border and press the Delete key on your keyboard.

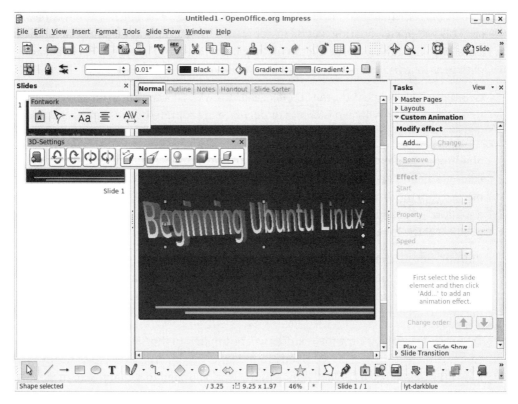

Figure 25-4. *The Fontwork tool can add some special effects to your presentations.*

Using 3D Effects

In addition to Fontwork effects, Impress includes a powerful 3D tool, which can give just about any on-screen element a 3D flourish (this tool is also available in some other OpenOffice.org applications). To use it, create a text box or shape using the Drawing toolbar at the bottom of the screen. Then right-click the text box or shape and select Convert ➤ 3D.

■**Note** The 3D option is designed simply to give your object depth. If you want to create a genuine 3D object that you can rotate in 3D space, select the 3D Rotation Object.

You can gain much more control over the 3D effect by right-clicking it and selecting 3D Effects. This will open a floating palette window with five configuration panels, as shown in Figure 25-5. Click the icons at the top of the palette to adjust the type of 3D effect and its lighting, as follows:

Geometry: This defines how the 3D effect will look when it's applied to on-screen selections. For example, you can increase or decrease the rounded-edges value, and this will make any sharp objects on the screen appear softer when the 3D effect is applied.

Shading: This affects not the actual texture of the 3D object, but instead alters its color gradient. This is best demonstrated in action, so select the various shading modes from the drop-down list to see the effect. In addition, you can choose whether a shadow is applied to the effect, as well as the position of the virtual camera (the position of the hypothetical viewer looking at the 3D object).

Illumination: This lets you set the lighting effect. All 3D graphics usually need a light source, because this helps illustrate the 3D effect; without a light source, the object will appear flat. Various predefined light sources are available. You can click and drag the light source in the preview window.

Textures: This affects how the textures will be applied to the 3D object. A texture is effectively a picture that is "wrapped around" the 3D object. Clever use of textures can add realism to a 3D object. A map of the world applied to a sphere can make it look like a globe, for example, or you could add wood or brickwork textures to make objects appear as tabletops or walls.

Material: This lets you apply various color overlays on the texture. This can radically alter the texture's look and feel, so it is quite a powerful option. To change the texture itself, right-click the object and select Area. This will present a list of predefined textures. Alternatively, you can select to use a color or pattern.

To apply any changes you make, click the check button at the top right of the palette. As with the other presentation effects, the best policy is simply to experiment until you're happy with the results.

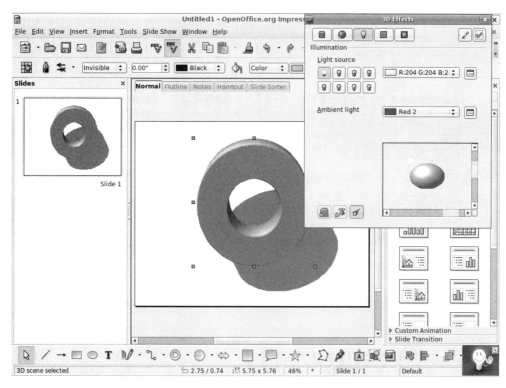

Figure 25-5. *You can fine-tune 3D objects to quite a high degree using the 3D Effects palette.*

Exporting a Presentation As a Flash File

If you plan to put your presentation online, or you want to send it to a colleague who doesn't have Impress or PowerPoint installed, outputting your presentation as a Flash animation could be a good idea. The process is simple. Just select File ➤ Export, and then select Macromedia Flash (SWF) in the File Format drop-down list (SWF is the Flash file type, which stands for Shockwave Flash). No further configuration is necessary.

In order to play the file, it needs to be opened within a web browser that has the Flash Player installed. This can be done by selecting File ➤ Open on most browsers, although you can also drag-and-drop the SWF file onto the browser window under Microsoft Windows. There shouldn't be much of a problem with compatibility, since the Flash Player is ubiquitous these days. If the web browser doesn't already have Flash installed, it's easy to download and install it (see www.adobe.com/shockwave/download/download.cgi? P1_Prod_Version=ShockwaveFlash).

When the Flash file is opened in a web browser, the presentation starts, as shown in Figure 25-6. You can progress through it by clicking anywhere on the screen.

Figure 25-6. *You can save any presentation as a Flash animation, which can be played back in a suitably equipped web browser.*

Summary

In this chapter, we examined Impress, which is the presentations component within OpenOffice.org. We started by looking at how you can use the Presentation Wizard function to automate production of a basic Impress document. Then you saw how various effects can be added to the presentation, including 3D effects. Finally, we looked at how the presentation can be exported as a Shockwave Flash file for playback on virtually any web browser.

In the next chapter, we will explore the database component within OpenOffice.org: Base.

## CHAPTER 26

In Depth: Base

OpenOffice.org includes a number of tools to both interface with database servers and perform tasks such as enter and edit data. However, for most day-to-day users who have humble needs, creating such a setup is rather complicated. It requires some knowledge of how databases work on a technical level. For this reason, a new component was added to OpenOffice.org 2.0: Base.

Base is a relational database along the lines of Microsoft Access and is perfect for database applications of all sizes, including more modest efforts. For example, you could use it to create an inventory database to produce a report showing all products added for a certain geographical region on a certain date, or you could use it to catalog items in your personal stamp collection.

Relational databases such as those created by Base are ideal for quickly creating catalogs of information, such as inventory lists. In addition to making database creation simple and quick, relational databases let you easily query data to produce reports tailored to individual needs.

Base works on a number of levels depending on the knowledge of the user, but in its most basic form, it offers a design-based approach to the creation of tables and forms. Anyone who has previously created a database under Access will feel right at home.

In this chapter, we'll work through an example of using Base to create a simple database cataloging a collection of music. You can use the same techniques to create any kind of relational database.

Getting Started with Base

You'll find Base under the Applications ➤ Office menu. When the program first starts, the Database Wizard guides you through either creating a new database or opening an existing one, as shown in Figure 26-1. Once you've made your choice, click Next to continue.

The first step in creating a new database is to register it within OpenOffice.org. This means that it will be made available in other OpenOffice.org programs, such as Calc or Writer. Although the knowledge needed to use a database in this way is quite advanced, there's no harm in agreeing to this option. It might prove useful in the future as you learn more about OpenOffice.org.

Following this, you can choose to open the database for editing and/or start the Table Wizard. Once you click the Finish button, you'll be invited to give the database a name and save it immediately.

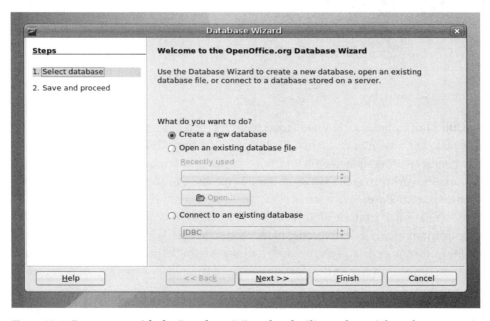

Figure 26-1. *Base starts with the Database Wizard to facilitate the quick and easy creation of new databases.*

▮Note Databases aren't like other office files in that they automatically save and update themselves. When using the finished database, you can simply enter data and then quit the program, without needing to deliberately opt to save the file.

Assuming that you did not opt to go directly to the Table Wizard, you'll now see the main Base program window. The right of the Base program window contains the Tasks and Data panes. The Tasks pane allows you to create new database elements, depending on what's selected in the Database pane. The Data pane shows any elements you've already created, and its content changes depending on whether you have the Tables, Queries, Forms, or Reports mode selected in the Database pane, on the left. The components of the Database pane relate to the four typical elements of a database, and they are as follows:

Tables: A table is what holds the actual data you'll eventually input. Therefore, a table is the first thing that needs to be created within a new database. Creating a table involves defining the types of data that you want to store and giving the individual data fields easy-to-understand names.

Forms: Although it's possible to enter data directly into a table, it isn't particularly intuitive or easy. Because of this, forms are used to make the data fields presentable. As the name suggests, in terms of layout these are not unlike the paper forms that you fill in to facilitate the collection of data by businesses. As with tables, forms must be created from scratch in a new database. Forms have *controls*, which are used to facilitate data entry, or to allow users to navigate the database or otherwise manipulate it. The most common type of control is a text-entry field, which is then tied to a data field within the table, but you can also have controls that perform certain functions, such as deleting a record in the database.

Queries: A query is a way of filtering the database so that you see only a subset of it. For example, in a database detailing sales figures from across the country, you might create a query to show only the data from a particular state.

Reports: A report is a way of presenting data for human consumption, usually in a printed format. For example, you could create a report that details sales figures in the form of a letter, or you might make a report to produce address labels using addresses stored in the database.

■**Note** The usefulness of both queries and reports are that they can be saved and used over and over again, so you could use the same query each month to examine just a small section of the data. Base offers wizards to automate the creation of both queries and reports.

Double-clicking an item in the Database pane displays or activates that item. Right-clicking a Database pane item displays a variety of options related to editing the file.

Now, let's work through an example of using Base. First, you'll create a table, and then you'll create a form.

Creating a Database

As an example of using Base, you'll build a database, ready for data entry. The first step in the creation of a database is to make a table. This will hold the data that you will eventually enter using a form.

Adding a Table

As with all components within Base, you can use a wizard to create the table. The Table Wizard offers a number of predefined data fields corresponding to typical databases. It is fine for general use, but if you have a specific and unusual database in mind, you will need to create the table manually.

Here, you'll create a database to catalog CDs. This is easily accomplished with the Table Wizard, as follows:

1. Click the Tables icon in the Database pane, and then click the Use Wizard to Create Table icon. The Table Wizard starts.

2. You're given a choice between creating a business or personal database. As you would expect, business databases are likely to contain fields relating to business matters, such as accounting, and the fields in the personal section relate more to domestic matters. Choose Personal for this example.

3. Choose an entry from the Sample Tables drop-down list. For this example, select CD Collection.

4. In the Available Fields box, you now see a number of data fields that would prove handy for a CD collection. You don't need to use all of these. Instead, select only those you want in your table, and then click the single right-facing arrow button to transfer them to the Selected Fields box. For this example, select AlbumTitle, Artist, ReleaseYear, and Review, as shown in Figure 26-2. Then click the Next button. (Don't worry if you find the fields lacking or if you want to add your own—you'll see how to do just that in step 6).

5. Check to make sure the fields you selected are of the correct type. Click each to see the information in the right area of the dialog box. Fields can take various forms depending on what kind of data they're supposed to hold. For example, one field might be designed to contain text, while another might need to contain numbers. Yet another might need to contain dates, and some can even contain pictures. As you might expect, the wizard has automatically selected the correct data types for the predefined fields.

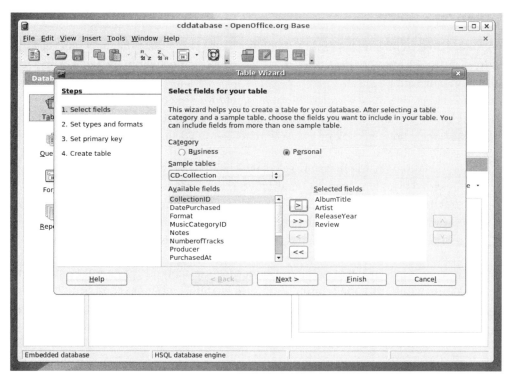

Figure 26-2. *The Table Wizard contains ready-made data fields for a wide variety of uses.*

6. For this example, you want to add a check box that shows whether the CD is scratched. If the CD in question is scratched, the user can click in a check box. If the CD isn't scratched, the box can be left blank. To create a check box, you need a special kind of data field called a Boolean. This means that the data field can be either true or false or, to put it a simpler way, it can hold either yes or no. To create a yes/no data field, click the plus button at the bottom of the Selected Fields box. This allows you to add another field. In the Field Name box, type **Scratched**. For the Field Type, click the drop-down list and locate the entry marked Yes/No [BOOLEAN]. The other options can remain as they are. Click Next to continue.

7. You're asked if you want to create a primary key. This is the unique numeric field that the database uses to keep track of each entry in the database. It's a must in a database like this one. The default choices are correct, so you can click Next again.

8. You've completed the Table Wizard. The next step is to create a form, so select Create a Form Based on This Table, and then click the Finish button.

Creating a Form

Forms are present in databases for the benefit of users to facilitate the quick-and-easy entry of data. They present data fields that you've just created within the table in an easy-to-understand form.

Base is able to walk you through the creation of forms via the Form Wizard. If you didn't select to run the Form Wizard previously, you can start it by clicking Forms in the Database pane, and then clicking Use Wizard to Create Form. Then follow these steps:

1. In the Form Wizard's first step, select which fields you want to appear on the form. As with the Table Wizard, this is simply a matter of selecting the fields and then clicking the right-arrow button so that they appear under the Fields on the Form heading. Alternatively, by clicking the double-arrow button, you can select all of them in one fell swoop, which is what you want for this example. Click Next.

2. You're asked if you want to create a subform. As its name suggests, this is effectively a form within your main form. A subform is useful with more complicated databases, where it might be necessary to view other data while filling in the form. For this simple example, leave the Add Subform box unchecked and click Next.

3. Choose a general layout for the data fields. The default is the table view, which many find ugly, so you might choose one of the first two options (in my database I chose the second option, as can be see in Figure 26-3). These arrange the data fields in a spacious manner and make the form much more usable. If you look behind the wizard dialog box, you'll see a preview of how the form will look. Once finished, click Next.

4. You're asked whether or not you want existing data to be displayed on the form. You can choose to treat the form as one created only for entering new data, so that you can't use it to navigate through the database and see existing data you've already entered. This might be useful in applications where you don't want users to see the other data in the database. However, for a database for your own personal use, being able to see the existing data is very handy, which is why The Form Is to Display All Data option is selected by default. For this example, simply click the Next button to accept the default.

5. Choose a look and feel for your form from the variety of color schemes available, as shown in Figure 26-3. Again, you can see them previewed behind the wizard dialog box. Feel free to experiment with the options under the Field Border heading. I prefer the 3D Look option, which gives the form elements a slight interior shadow, a common feature on most modern user interfaces. The Flat option simply adds a black border to the boxes, and the No Border option removes the border completely. Once you've made your choices, click Next.

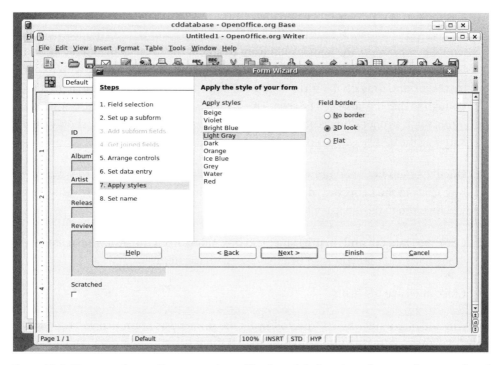

Figure 26-3. *You can choose from a variety of look and feel options for your form, and each will be previewed behind the wizard dialog box.*

6. You're invited to give the form a name. Enter a suitable name, such as **CD-Collection**. You are also given the option of entering data directly into the form or modifying it manually. Once you've made your choice, click the Finish button. The database is almost ready for use. You just need to take one more step to modify the table. However, first we'll take a brief look at adding custom controls to forms.

■**Note** There are no rules governing form names, and you can use virtually any symbols and also insert spaces into the name. However, it's a good idea to keep the form name simple and concise.

Adding Controls to the Form Manually

Although the form created by the wizard is good enough for our needs, there might be some instances where you want to edit the form manually to add your own controls. The following instructions describe how:

1. Double-click the form to edit it and then ensure the Form Controls toolbar is visible—click View ➤ Toolbars ➤ Form Controls. Then, on the Form Control toolbar, click the icon that represents the control you want to add to the form. Don't forget, you can hover your mouse over each icon to see a tooltip explaining what the icon is for. Next click and drag on the form to add the item. You need to make the item big enough so that the label can be seen. This is especially relevant in the case of smaller items, such as check boxes. If you release the mouse button too early, simply click and drag the handles at the edges to resize the control.

2. Once the item has been drawn, double-click it. This will open Properties dialog box. Click in the Label box, delete what's there already, and type the word(s) that will help the database users identify the item.

3. Click the Data tab and, in the Data Field box, select from the drop-down list the table data field that you wish to asssociate with the item.

4. Close and save the form.

You can add many custom controls following the same basic approach you used here. Simply draw them on to the form, and then match them up with an entry in the table using the Data tab.

Editing the Database Table

Before you can use the CD database we created earlier, you need to make a small change to the table you created. Although the Table Wizard created a primary key, it didn't make it into an automatically updating number. Without this option activated, the user will need to manually number each entry in the database as it's created.

Follow these steps to edit the table and activate automatic numbering for the ID field:

1. Click the Tables icon in the Database pane of the main program window, right-click the table you created earlier, and select Edit.

2. Look for the entry in the table list labeled ID. It should be first in the list. Make sure that the cursor is on the ID line, and click the Autovalue drop-down list at the bottom of the window. Make sure that it reads Yes, as shown in Figure 26-4.

3. Close the window and opt to save the table.

That's it! Your database is now ready to use.

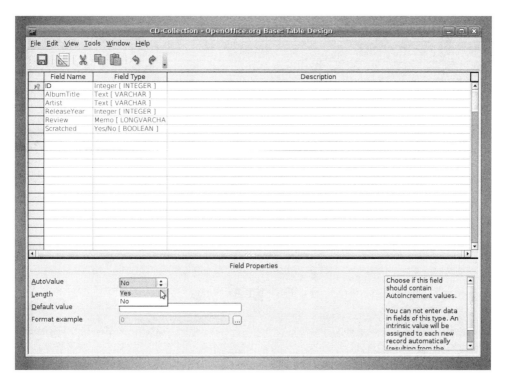

Figure 26-4. *Set the primary key to automatically update by editing its value in the table.*

Using the Database

Entering data into the finished database is easy. Click the Forms icon in the Database pane, and then double-click the form you created earlier.

The Form Control toolbar will still be visible. To hide it, click its close button at the top-right corner of the toolbar. After this, you can start to enter data into the form, as shown in the example in Figure 26-5. Note that you do not need to enter data in the ID field, because this will automatically be filled with the primary key number.

Once you've filled in the form, you can click the Next Record button in the Form Navigation toolbar running along the button of the window (don't forget that hovering the mouse cursor over each button reveals a tooltip explaining what the button does). This will move you on to the next blank form, where you can enter more data. Repeat this as many times as necessary.

The Form Navigation toolbar contains other handy tools. For example, the first button—a magnifying glass—lets you search the database for a particular entry. It's well worth investigating the functions.

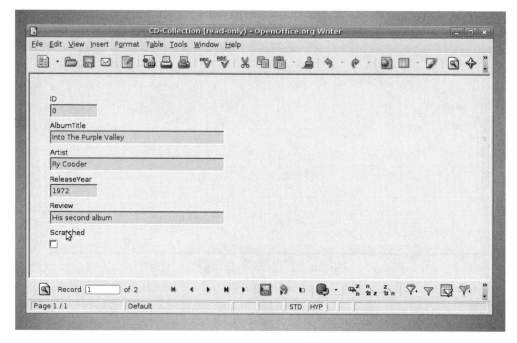

Figure 26-5. *The finished database form lets you enter data into the input fields and navigate using the toolbar at the bottom.*

Summary

In this chapter, we looked at the Base database component of OpenOffice.org and how to use it to easily create and edit simple databases. We stepped through an example of setting up a database table and creating a database form that users can employ to enter and edit data.

In the next chapter, we will look at Evolution, the powerful e-mail and personal information manager offered under Ubuntu.

■ ■ ■

## CHAPTER 27

In Depth: Evolution

Evolution isn't part of the OpenOffice.org suite. It was originally created by Ximian, an organization founded by the creators of the GNOME Desktop Project and acquired by Novell in August 2003. Even long after the acquisition, Evolution is still developed by many of the key GNOME desktop developers.

Although it's not explicitly described as such by its developers, Evolution is considered the "official" GNOME desktop e-mail program. Nearly every Linux distribution that uses the GNOME desktop system also uses Evolution. Evolution even retains the same look and feel as many elements of the Ubuntu desktop.

In terms of functionality, Evolution is similar to Microsoft Outlook, in that as well as being a powerful e-mail client, it incorporates contacts management, a calendar, and a to-do list. Evolution is even able to connect to Microsoft Exchange (2000 and above) groupware servers and synchronize with contact and calendar data, in addition to fetching e-mail. Of course, it can also connect to standard POP3/SMTP e-mail servers, as well as IMAP, Novell GroupMail, and a handful of other mail server technologies. This means it is compatible with practically every e-mail system in use today. For more details about how to set up Evolution, see Chapter 8.

Although Evolution offers many of the functions of Microsoft Outlook, it differs in some key ways. Therefore, this chapter describes how to perform basic tasks as well as more advanced everyday jobs.

Evolution Modes

Evolution consists of five components: Mail, Contacts, Calendars, Memos, and Tasks. These are interconnected but operate as separate modes within the program. Each mode can be selected using the switcher located at the bottom-left side of the program window. Simply click the button for the mode you wish to use. The program window, toolbar, and menu system will change to accommodate whichever mode is selected. Figure 27-1 shows the program in the default Mail mode.

■Tip   You can shrink the switcher component to small icons by clicking View ➤ Switcher Appearance ➤ Icons Only.

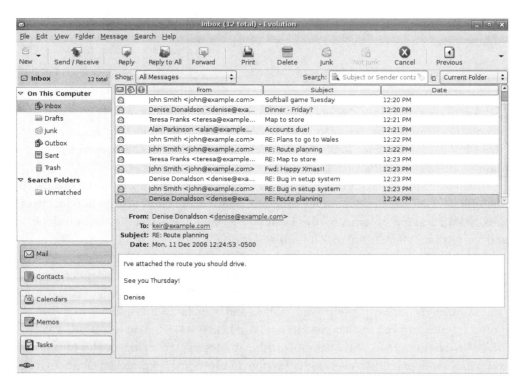

Figure 27-1. *You can switch between Evolution's modes by clicking the buttons at the bottom left of the program window.*

The five Evolution modes work as follows:

Mail: The e-mail component is at the heart of Evolution, and all the functions you might be used to are provided. Once the Mail mode is selected, at the top left of the program window, you'll find the mail folders. These include the Inbox and Sent folders, along with any other mail folders you create. On the right is the list of e-mail messages, and beneath this is the message preview pane, where the body of any message you select will be displayed. Above the message list is the search box, which works like most e-mail search routines: type the relevant word(s) and click Find Now. Notable icons running along the top of the window include the New button, which will let you compose an e-mail message, and the Send/Receive button, which will download new messages and also send any messages in the Outbox folder.

Contacts: Tied in with the mail function but acting as a separate and very powerful entity on its own, the contacts mode lets you store every pertinent detail about colleagues, friends, and others. Once the mode is selected, at the left side of the program window, you'll see the various contact folders. For most users, there will be just one, named Personal, but if you specified a groupware server during setup, you will also be able to connect to this by clicking its entry. At the top right is the list of contacts. Clicking any contact displays that individual's information at the bottom of the window, in the contact information area. The search bar at the top of the window beneath the toolbar lets you quickly search for contacts by name. The New button on the toolbar lets you create a new contact, where you can enter a wealth of data. To edit an existing entry, double-click its entry, and fill in the additional details.

Calendars: The Calendar mode is arguably Evolution's second most useful function. You can add events in a half-hourly increments, and view your schedule in day, week, and month views by clicking the relevant button on the toolbar. Once the mode is selected, at the top left of the program window you'll find the various calendars you can access. For most users, the Personal calendar will be the principal one, but you can also access shared calendars here. Assuming the default day view is in operation, beneath this you'll see the monthly calendar and, in the middle of the program window, the appointment list, with half-hour entries covering the working day. By default, the current day is shown. To select a different day, simply double-click the day in the month view. You can switch among day, week, and month appointment views by clicking the Day, Work Week, and Month buttons on the toolbar. On the right of the window, any tasks and memos that have been created are displayed, as described next.

Memos: The best way to think of Evolution's Memos mode is as a personal notepad. Once the Memos mode is selected, the list of memos will appear on the right side of the screen, and the contents of the memo at the bottom. Memos can consist of virtually any amount of text, along with attachments. They're ideal for jotting notes during phone calls, for example.

Tasks: Effectively, this is a simple To Do list. Once the mode is selected, your tasks will be listed on the right side of the program window. Beneath this will be details of any selected task.

Basic E-Mail Tasks

Evolution's e-mail functionality is arguably the heart of the program. Although it offers a lot of features, it is quite simple to use. If you've ever used any other mainstream e-mail client, such as Microsoft Outlook, you have a head start.

This section describes how to accomplish several everyday tasks within the e-mail component of Evolution. When you start Evolution, the e-mail mode is selected automatically. However, if it isn't, or if you've switched to a different mode within the program, simply click the Mail button at the bottom left of the program window.

Sending and Receiving E-Mail

Once Evolution has been set up correctly to work with your e-mail servers, as outlined in Chapter 8, you can simply click the Send/Receive button on the toolbar to connect to the server(s) and both send and receive e-mail.

You may need to enter your password if you didn't enter it during setup. You can check the Remember Password box to avoid having to type it again, but this will mean the password is then stored on your hard disk, possibly posing a security risk.

■Note Although e-mail is normally sent as soon as you click the Send button when composing it, if the sending has been delayed for any reason (such as because you were offline at the time), it will be sent as soon as you click the Send/Receive button. Until that point, it will be held in the Outbox folder on the left side of the program window.

Any outstanding mail is sent first, and then the receiving procedure is started. As shown in Figure 27-2, a status dialog box will tell you how many messages there are and the progress of the download. Clicking the Cancel button will stop the procedure (although some messages may already have been downloaded).

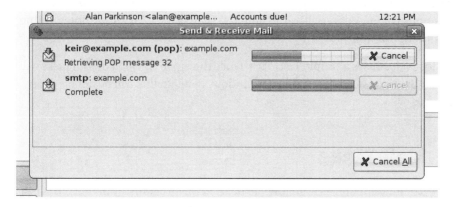

Figure 27-2. *You'll see a progress display whenever you click the Send/Receive button.*

Reading E-Mail

Simply click an e-mail message to view it in the preview pane at the bottom of the screen. Alternatively, you can double-click a message to open it in its own program window (selecting a message and pressing Enter will have the same effect).

As with most e-mail clients, any unread messages in the list appear in bold, and messages that have been read appear in ordinary type. By default, each message is marked as read after 1.5 seconds, but you can alter this value. To change it, click Edit ➤ Preferences, click the Mail Preferences icon in the Preferences dialog box, and then change the value under the Message Display heading. A value of 0 will cause the mail to switch to read status as soon as it's clicked, which can be useful if you want to quickly clear a lot of messages.

You can also mark many messages as read by highlighting them all, right-clicking an individual one, and selecting Mark As Read from the menu that appears. You can select multiple messages in the usual way: Shift-click to select a consecutive list or Ctrl-click for nonconsecutive selections.

Deleting Messages

You can delete messages by highlighting them and pressing the Delete key. Alternatively, right-click any message (or a selection of them) and select Delete. The message will then be moved to the Trash folder. To empty the Trash folder, simply right-click the folder, and select Empty Trash.

If you move any messages from folder to folder, as described later in the "Sorting and Filtering Messages" section, a copy of the mail will end up in the Trash folder. This is because Evolution doesn't literally move messages. Instead, it copies them from the old to the new location and deletes the original. This can be a little disconcerting at first, but there's nothing to worry about. The mail message will remain wherever you moved it, and it won't disappear when you expunge any folders.

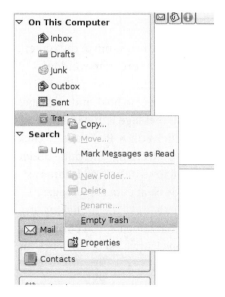

Figure 27-3. *To permanently delete messages, right-click the Trash folder, and select Empty Trash.*

Flagging Messages

You can flag messages in a variety of ways to help remind you of their status or purpose. The simplest form of flagging is to mark a message as important: right-click the message and select Mark As Important, or click in the space beneath the Important column (this is located to the left of the From column). This will add an exclamation mark symbol alongside the message.

Alternatively, you can add several different flags by right-clicking a message and selecting Mark for Follow Up. The choices, which can be selected from the Flag drop-down list in the dialog box that appears, range from Do Not Forward to No Response Necessary and Review. This heading will then appear in the message preview at the bottom of the window whenever the mail is selected.

If you prefer a simple color-coding scheme, you can mark up a message by right-clicking it and selecting Label. Then assign a color. As you'll see, each color relates to a key word or phrase. You can edit both the colors and the key phrases by clicking Edit ➤ Preferences, clicking Mail Preferences on the left of the dialog box, and clicking the Colors tab.

IMPORTING OUTLOOK E-MAIL VIA THUNDERBIRD

Back in Chapter 4, I discussed a method of exporting e-mail from various Microsoft e-mail programs, which use proprietary formats, so that it can be imported under Ubuntu. To recap, you can install the Mozilla Thunderbird e-mail client under Windows, import your e-mail into it from Outlook or Outlook Express, and then export Thunderbird's mailbox (`.mbox`) files for *importing* within Evolution.

If you followed these instructions and now have the `.mbox` files ready for use with Evolution, it's easy to import them. Click File ➤ Import. In the Import dialog box, click the Forward button, and select Import a Single File. Click Forward again, and click the Filename drop-down list. This will open a file browsing dialog box, in which you can locate the `.mbox` file, and click Open. If you have more than one `.mbox` file, you'll need to import each one manually.

Composing a Message

Creating a new e-mail is as simple as clicking the New button at the top left of Evolution's program window. Fill in the To and Subject details as usual, and then type in the main body of the message.

To add a CC or BCC, click the To button, and select addresses from your contacts list in the dialog box that appears (selecting the CC or BCC button as appropriate). Alternatively, if you would like to have the CC and BCC fields visible and available at all times, click their entries under the View menu of the Compose a Message window.

As with most Microsoft mail programs, new e-mail can be sent either as plain text or as HTML. Plain text mode is the default. To switch to HTML, click the entry on the Format menu. The advantage of HTML mail is that you can vary the style, size, and coloring of text, so you can emphasize various words or paragraphs, as illustrated in Figure 27-4. In addition, if you click Insert ➤ Image, you can insert pictures from the hard disk. Other options on the Insert menu let you insert tables, dividing lines (click the Rule menu entry), and hyperlinks.

The disadvantage of HTML e-mail is that the person receiving the message will need an HTML-compatible e-mail program to be able to read it.

Tip Many people in the Linux community frown on HTML-formatted e-mail and prefer plain text messages.

Words are automatically spell-checked in the new e-mail and are underlined in red if the spell checker thinks they are misspelled. To correct the word, right-click it, click Check Word Spelling, and then select the correctly spelled word from the list.

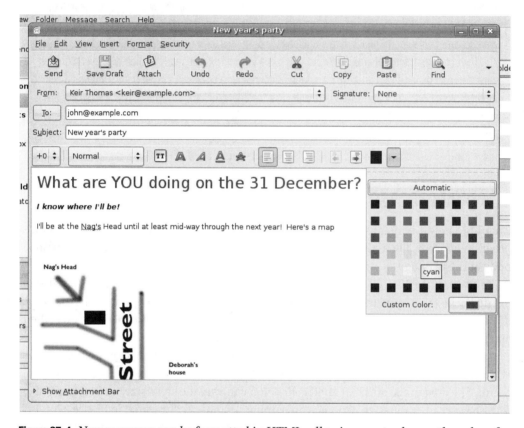

Figure 27-4. *New messages can be formatted in HTML, allowing you to change the color of text as well as its size.*

Creating an E-Mail Signature

E-mail signatures are the blocks of text that appear automatically at the end of new e-mail messages you compose. They save you the bother of typing your name and contact details each time. To create an e-mail signature, follow these steps:

1. Click Edit ➤ Preferences. Select Composer Preferences from the left-hand side of the window, and click the Signatures tab.

2. Click the Add button at the top right of the window.

3. In the Edit Signature dialog box, type what you wish to appear as your signature. The signature can either be in plain text or HTML (click Format ➤ HTML). Don't forget that in HTML mode you can insert lines (Insert ➤ Rule), which can act as a natural divider at the top of your signature to separate it from the body of the e-mail, as shown in the example in Figure 27-5.

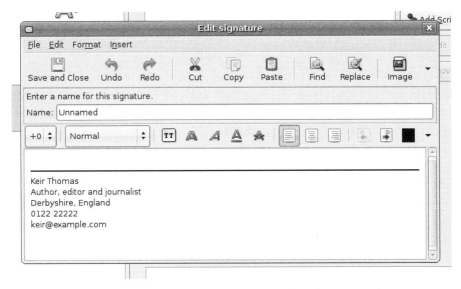

Figure 27-5. *Creating an e-mail signature saves you from having to type your contact details each time.*

4. Click the Save and Close icon at the top left.

5. Click Mail Accounts in the Preferences window, and double-click your mail account in the list on the right-hand side.

6. In the dialog that appears, click the Identity tab, and in the Signature drop-down list, click the signature you just created.

7. Click OK and then Close on the preferences dialog box. Your new signature will then automatically appear in new messages.

■**Tip** Enter a few carriage returns at the top of your signature so that, when you create a new e-mail, you have enough space to click and type without accidentally clicking within the signature.

Advanced E-Mail Tasks

Evolution offers several features that can help you to organize your e-mail. You can create new folders, as well as filter, sort, and search through your messages.

Creating New Folders

If you want to better organize your e-mail, you can create your own folders, which will then appear in the list on the left side of the program window.

To create a new top-level folder, which will appear in the list alongside the standard folders (Inbox, Junk, Outbox, and so on), right-click On This Computer, and select New Folder. Then make sure that On This Computer is selected in the folder view of the dialog box that appears. Type a name and click Create.

You can also create second-level folders, which will effectively be "inside" other folders and will appear indented below their parent folder within the list. For example, you might want to create a series of folders within the main Inbox folder to sort your mail from various individuals or organizations. To do this, right-click Inbox, select New Folder, and give the folder a name in the dialog box that appears, as shown in Figure 27-6. Once the new folder has been created, you'll have to click the arrow next to Inbox to "unfold" the display, so the new entry is visible.

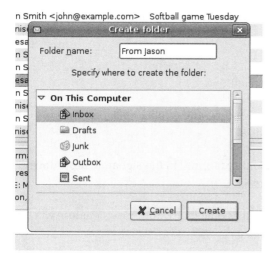

Figure 27-6. *You can create your own folders to better organize your mail.*

You can then drag-and-drop messages into the new folders, or simply right-click them, select Move to Folder, and select the folder from the dialog box that appears. This can be useful if you wish to select a handful of messages by holding down the Ctrl key. All you need to do then is right-click one of them and select Move to Folder.

You can also copy messages from one location to another, thus producing two copies of the same message. Simply right-click the message, and select Copy to Folder. Then select the folder from the list. Alternatively, you can hold down the Ctrl key while you drag the message to the new location.

Dealing with Junk E-Mail

Evolution includes intelligent junk mail filtering. Any mail that Evolution thinks is spam or junk mail will end up in the Junk folder. When you first start using Evolution, you should check the folder regularly, because there's a chance Evolution might have made a mistake. However, this is a good thing, because by right-clicking the message and selecting Mark As Not Junk, the Evolution junk mail filter will be able to better understand what to consider as junk in your particular Inbox.

In a similar way, if you find that Evolution misses a junk e-mail, and it ends up in your Inbox, you can right-click it and select Mark As Junk. Alternatively, select it and click the Junk icon on the main toolbar.

To empty the Junk folder, select all the messages (Ctrl+A), right-click, and select Delete. Bear in mind that, as with any folder, once the messages are deleted, they will appear in the Trash view where, if necessary, they can be restored.

Sorting and Filtering Messages

You can filter incoming messages according to practically any criteria, including who sent the message, its subject line, words within the body of the mail, its size, or even if it has attachments. Coupled with the ability to create folders, this allows you to automatically sort messages as soon as they're received.

To set up filters, click Edit ➤ Message Filters. Click the Add button and, in the Rule Name box, start by giving the new rule a descriptive name by which you'll be able to recognize it in the future. You might think this isn't important, but you may create tens, if not hundreds of filters, so being able to identify filters will be very helpful.

As shown in Figure 27-7, the Add Rule dialog box is split into two halves: Find Items That Meet The Following Criteria and Then. This is rather like a sentence: If the selected conditions are met, *then* the selected actions will take place.

The Find Items part is used to identify the mail. You can select to filter based on almost any criteria, such as who appears in the Sender field of the message, words that appear in the Subject line, the date sent, and so on. Simply select what you require from the drop-down list directly beneath the Add button. In most cases, you'll then need to specify details for the filter. For example, if you select to filter by the address of the individual sending the e-mail, you'll need to provide that e-mail address.

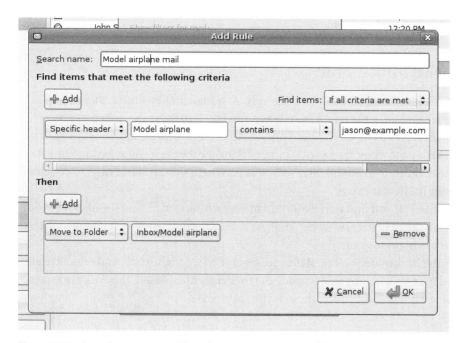

Figure 27-7. *Creating message filters lets you automatically organize your e-mail as soon as it's received.*

■**Tip** Several If rules can be created. For example, you could create a rule to filter by the address of the sender, and then click the Add button to create another rule to filter by text in the Subject line. By clicking If All Criteria Are Met in the Find Items drop-down list, the mail will be filtered only if both conditions are met. By selecting If Any Criteria Are Met from the drop-down list, the mail will be filtered if either condition is met.

Once you've set the Find Items conditions, you need to select from the Then section of the dialog box. This tells Evolution what to do with the filtered mail. The obvious course of action is to move the e-mail to a particular folder, which is the default choice, but you can also delete the e-mail, set a particular flag, beep, or even run a particular program! As with the Find Items rules, you can set more than one condition here, so you can have Evolution beep and then delete the message, for example.

TIPS FOR USING EVOLUTION E-MAIL

In many ways, Evolution is similar to e-mail programs you might have used in the past, but it also has a few of its own quirks and idiosyncratic ways of working. Here are a handful of preferences you might want to set to have Evolution behave in a more familiar way:

- **Forward e-mail inline:** If you attempt to forward a message, Evolution will attach it to a new message as a file. The person receiving the e-mail will then need to double-click the file to view the forwarded e-mail, which can be confusing. The solution is to make Evolution forward the message *inline*, which is to say that Evolution will quote it beneath the new mail message, like Microsoft e-mail programs. To do this, click Edit ➤ Preferences, click Composer Preferences on the left side of the dialog box, click the Forward Style drop-down list, and select Inline.

- **Change the plain text font:** Any messages sent to you in plain text format, rather than HTML, will appear in the message preview pane in a Courier-style font. To have messages display in a more attractive and readable typeface, click Edit ➤ Preferences, select Mail Preferences on the left side of the dialog box, and then remove the check from Use the Same Fonts As Other Applications. In the Fixed Width Font drop-down list, select an alternative font. The standard Ubuntu font is called Sans and is a good choice.

- **Always create HTML e-mail:** Evolution defaults to plain text e-mail for any new messages you create. If you want to always create HTML messages, click Edit ➤ Preferences, click Composer Preferences on the left side of the dialog box, and then put a check alongside Format Messages in HTML.

- **Empty Trash on exit:** To automatically get rid of deleted messages each time you quit Evolution, click Edit ➤ Preferences, click Mail Preferences on the left side of the program window, and put a check alongside Empty Trash Folders on Exit.

- **Vertical message window:** As an alternative to positioning the message preview window beneath your messages, Outlook lets you position the message at the right of the message list, thus forming three vertical columns (folders, messages, preview). To switch to this view under Evolution, click View ➤ Preview ➤ Vertical View.

Creating Search Folders

Evolution's search folder feature is a more powerful alternative to message filters. Using search folders, you can filter mail based on a similar set of criteria, but you can choose to include messages in the results that might be *associated* with the filtered messages. For example, if you choose to filter by a specific individual's e-mail address, you can select to have any replies you sent to that person included in the results, rather than simply messages received from her. In addition, you can apply search folders to specific e-mail folders on an ongoing basis, rather than all incoming e-mail.

It's important to note, however, that a Search Folder isn't a filter. The messages aren't moved into the new folders. They stay where they are in the Inbox, or any other folder they might be contained in. Despite the name, Search Folders are actually little more than saved searches. They just *act* like filters. In spite of this, Search Folders are dynamically updated—if a message is deleted from the Inbox, for example, it will also stop appearing in any relevant Search Folder.

You can create a new Search Folder by clicking Edit ➤ Search Folders and then clicking the Add button. As with creating message filters, clicking the drop-down box beneath the Add button will let you select a criteria by which you can filter. The choices are broadly similar to those for message filters, in that you can filter by e-mail address, size of e-mail, message body, and so on.

In the Include Threads drop-down box, you can select what kind of results you would like the search filter to return:

- None simply returns e-mail messages matching the criteria.

- All Related returns every single message that is associated with the criteria.

- Replies returns results that include replies to the messages returned via the filter.

- Replies and Parents returns results that include replies and also any initial message that you or others might have sent that inspired the message included in the filter results.

Search folder results are listed under the relevant heading on the left side of the Mail mode window. The Unmatched Search Folder, present by default, simply shows any messages that *aren't* included in any of the Search Folders.

The search folder feature is very powerful and worth spending some time investigating.

Contacts

Evolution includes a powerful contacts manager component that can catalog information about individuals. At its most basic, the contact manager stores e-mail addresses for use within the e-mail component of Evolution, but you can enter significant additional data about each individual, including addresses, phone numbers, fax numbers, and even a photograph for easy identification. This should allow Evolution to become your sole personal information manager.

To switch to the Contacts mode, click the button at the bottom-left side of the program window. Once in the Contacts mode, you can view information in several ways. Click View ➤ Current View to choose from the following views:

Address Cards: This is the default view and shows the contacts as virtual index cards arranged alongside each other at the top of the program window. Click the scroll bar beneath the cards to move through them.

Phone List: This shows the contact information as a simple list, arranged vertically, with various elements of the contact's personal information listed alongside, such as phone numbers and e-mail addresses.

By Company: This organizes the data in a similar way to Phone List view but sorted by the company the contacts work for (if such data has been entered into the contact entries).

Adding or Editing Contact Information

By far, the best way of initially building up your contacts list is to right-click e-mail addresses at the head of messages, in Mail mode, and select Add to Addressbook. This will add a simple contact record consisting of the individual's name and e-mail address.

When using Microsoft mail applications, simply replying to an e-mail from an individual is enough to add that contact to your address book. Evolution is capable of this behavior, too, but the feature isn't activated by default. To set this up, click Edit ➤ Preferences, click Mail Preferences on the left side of the dialog box, and click the Automatic Contacts tab. Next, put a check in the box marked Automatically Create Entries in the Addressbook When Responding to Mail.

You can then edit the contact details by double-clicking the entry in Contacts mode. This will let you enter a variety of information, as shown in Figure 27-8. To import a photo for this contact, click the top-left icon. You can use any picture here, and you don't need to worry about its size, because it will be resized automatically by Evolution (although its aspect ratio will be preserved). The imported photo will appear on the contact's virtual card.

Figure 27-8. *A lot of information can be entered for each contact and, by clicking the button at the top left, you can also add a photograph.*

Creating a Contact List

Contact lists are simply lists of e-mail addresses. Once a list is created, you can right-click its entry in the contacts list, and then choose to send a message to the list or forward it to someone else as a vCard. The obvious use of contact lists is for sending group e-mail messages.

■**Note** A vCard is a virtual business card. Effectively, it's a small file that contains personal information. As well as personal data, vCards can contain pictures and audio clips. They're understood by practically all business-level e-mail programs, including Microsoft Outlook and Apple Mail.

To create a contact list, click the small down arrow next to the New button in Contacts mode, and select the option from the list. Give the list a name in the relevant box, and simply click and drag contacts from the main program pane onto the bottom of the Contact List Editor pane. This will automatically add their names and e-mail addresses. Alternatively, you can type their e-mail addresses manually into the field under the Members heading, and then click the Add button, which can be useful if the individual isn't in your contact list.

By checking the Hide Addresses When Sending Mail to This List option, you can ensure that the e-mail addresses are added to the BCC field of a new message, so people on the list don't see the others on the list.

Calendars

The Calendars mode of Evolution allows you to keep an appointments diary. Entries can be added in half-hour increments to the working day, and you can easily add events to days that are weeks, months, or even years in advance. Viewing a day's appointments is as simple as clicking its entry in the monthly view at the top right of the program window.

Specifying Appointment Types

You can make the following three types of diary entries:

Appointments: These are events in your diary that apply to you only. You might have a meeting with a colleague, for example, or might simply want to add a note to your diary to remind you of a particular fact.

All Day Events: These are appointments that take the entire day. For example, a training day or a holiday could be entered as an all day event. However, all day events don't block your diary, and you can still add individual appointments (after all, just because your day is taken up with an event, it doesn't mean you won't need to make individual appointments during the event). All day events appear as a blue bar at the top of the day's entry in your diary.

Meetings: Meetings are like appointments, but you also have the option of inviting others to attend. The invitations are sent as iCal attachments to e-mail, so users of Microsoft Outlook should be able to reply to them (provided Outlook is properly configured; see the program's documentation for details, and note that iCal is sometimes referred to as RFC 2446/2447). Once an individual receives a meeting invitation, he can click to accept or decline. Once Evolution receives this response, the individual's acceptance or declination will be automatically added to the diary entry.

Adding or Editing a Diary Entry

These instructions assume the Calendar mode is set to Day view, which shows a full working day diary alongside a monthly calendar. To ensure Day view is selected, click the Day icon on the main toolbar running across the top of the screen. Day view is the default calendar view under Evolution, but if you switch to Week/Month view, Evolution will remember and always work in that view until you change back again.

To add a new diary entry, simply select the day in the monthly view on the left, and then select the time the appointment is to start in the day viewer. Then right-click and choose either an appointment, all day event, or meeting. To edit an already existing diary entry, double-click its entry in the list.

Note In the right-click menu, you'll also see an option to add a task. The Tasks functionality of Evolution is dealt with later in this chapter, but rather surprisingly, adding a task in calendar view doesn't automatically link it to the selected day or time. Therefore, there's not much to be gained creating tasks this way, and you might as well create them by switching to Tasks mode.

At its most basic, all an appointment needs in order to be entered into your diary is some text in the Summary field, as shown in Figure 27-9. By default, appointments and meetings are assumed to last for half an hour, but you can change this by clicking the down arrow in the Minutes or even Hours fields. For what it's worth, appointments can go on for days—just select a sufficient quantity of hours!

Note In fact, you're allowed practically an unlimited number of hours for the meeting. Put it this way—in my tests, when I got to 9999 hours, the counter roled over to 10,000 hours. At this point, I could no longer see the increments, because there wasn't space! Wouldn't that be the meeting from hell?!

By clicking the Recurrence button, you can set the appointment to be booked into your diary according to certain intervals. Start by putting a check in the This Appointment Recurs box, and then select a time interval. For example, selecting 1 week will mean that the appointment is booked into your diary automatically on a weekly basis. After this, select a day of the week for the recurring appointment. Following this, you must specify the number of recurrences. In the calendar view at the bottom of the dialog, you'll be able to see how this looks. Days in bold are those that have appointments.

It's also possible to set exceptions, as when the meeting might skip a week. This could be useful to work around holidays, for example. Simply click the Add button, and then type a date.

Once you're done, click the Close button to add the details of the recurring event to the appointment.

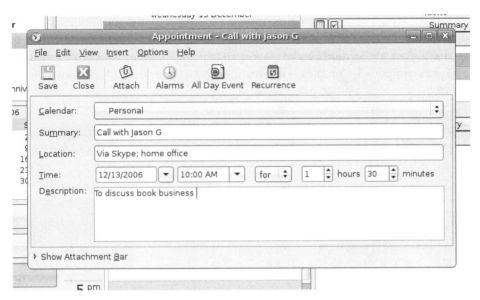

Figure 27-9. *When creating a new appointment, you can add all the details you need, but don't forget to set how long it lasts!*

In the case of meeting appointments, you can click the Add button to invite others to the meeting via iCal invitations, which will be sent out by e-mail as soon as you've finished creating the appointment. Simply click the Add button, and in the empty field that appears, start typing the contact name of the individual you want to invite. If the person is already in your contacts list, the name will be automatically completed, but you can also type individual e-mail addresses. By selecting the entry and clicking Edit, you can alter the Role of the individual. The choices are Chair, Required Participant, Optional Participant, Non-Participant (that is, somebody you want to inform about the meeting but who doesn't need to attend), and Unknown (for all other instances).

Clicking the Free/Busy button will open a new dialog box showing who can and can't attend, according to replies to the invitations sent out (obviously, this is a feature you'll be using after you initially created the appointment). On the left side of the dialog box, you will see the list of attendees and also their status: whether they've accepted, declined, or sent a busy/tentative reply (in which case, you might choose to reschedule the meeting).

Memos and Tasks

The Memos and Tasks modes are the simplest components within Evolution. Memos mode allows you to jot down simple notes, and Tasks mode allows you to create a to-do list.

In both modes, which can be selected by clicking their buttons at the bottom left of the screen, the program window consists simply of an area where you can click to add a new memo/task, a list area, and a preview area, which will show an details of the currently selected task.

In the case of Task mode, after you've made an entry, clicking the check box alongside it will mark it as completed. Completed items appear with strike-through, as shown in Figure 27-10.

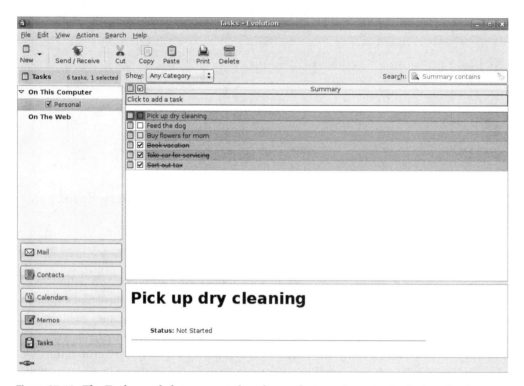

Figure 27-10. *The Tasks mode lets you catalog chores that you have to do during the day.*

To add a new memo or task, click the bar that reads Click to Add a New Memo (or Task). Type a description, and then press Enter. You will then be able to enter further tasks or memos in the same field.

Double-clicking a task or memo allows you to fine-tune its details. For example, you can add a due date for a task, so you'll know when the task must be completed. You can also add a description for future reference and attach any relevant files by clicking the relevant button on the toolbar.

By clicking the Status Details button in the Task Details dialog box, you can also set a percentage figure for completion of the task, as well as its priority, ranging from Low to High.

Summary

This chapter has been a whistle-stop tour of Evolution's main features. We've looked at e-mail creation and organization, contacts management, working with the appointments calendar, and editing the task list.

Evolution is a powerful program. Be sure to take a look at its help documentation (Help ➤ Contents) to learn more about it.

In the next part of the book, we look at keeping your system running. As a first step, the next chapter explains how to install, remove, and otherwise manage the software installed under Ubuntu.

PART 7

∎∎∎

Keeping Your System Running

■ ■ ■

## CHAPTER 28

Installing and Removing Software

One of the fun things about running any operating system is the ability to expand it—to add in new software over time to improve your workflow or just for entertainment value.

Linux is blessed in this regard, because there are tens of thousands of software titles available to meet just about every need. However, even if you've tracked down the ideal software title, there's just one barrier to overcome: actually installing it on your system.

Installing software under Ubuntu isn't the same as with Windows. Users are afforded a lot more power over what happens to their systems, but this comes at the expense of needing to take a little time to understand the terminology and techniques. That is what you'll learn in this chapter.

Software Installation Basics

Installing programs on Windows is relatively easy. If you wish to use the WinZip archive tool, for example, you can browse to the web site, download the installer .exe file, and install the software.

Although you might not realize it, a lot of work goes into making this seemingly simple task possible. Once the original software has been created by the programmers, it must be made into a form that you, the end user, can deal with.

The first thing to happen is that the software is *compiled*. This is the process of turning the source code created by programmers into an actual file (or set of files) that can be used on a daily basis. On most systems, compiling source code involves a lot of number crunching. This takes time—whole days, in some cases— and this is why it isn't normal practice to compile the source code every time you want to run the program.

Once the program files have been compiled, there needs to be a way they can be installed on various systems and easily transported across the Internet. This is where *packaging* comes into the equation. Programs usually consist of many files. To make each program file individually available would mean that some are sure to get lost or corrupted, and the program wouldn't work. Therefore, the files are usually combined into a single archive file. In addition, third-party system files are added to ensure compatibility on all computers and an extra program, called an installer, is added so that users can quickly get the files onto their systems.

All of this means that, to be able to install a program like WinZip on Windows, all you need to do is download the installer .exe file and run it once. No more work is necessary.

Linux is a little more involved, largely because it never assumes that the user wants her environment to be simplistic and with limited options. However, most Linux distributions still embrace the paradigm of packaging software into a single, easily-transported file. I explain how software packages under Ubuntu work in a moment, but first it's necessary to understand other typical software distribution file formats used in the world of Linux.

The Formats of Linux Installation Files

If you visit the web site of a particular Linux application, you may find that it's available to download in a number of different formats. The program will almost certainly be available as *source code*—the original listing that the developer created. But it might also be available as a binary or a package file.

■**Tip** Linux isn't the only operating system for which open-source programs are created and used. There are open-source projects for both Windows and Apple Macintosh, many of which are hosted at the http:// sourceforge.net web site. Many other, less widely used operating systems also rely on open-source software to a greater or lesser extent.

Here are the formats by which Linux software is normally distributed:

Source code: Programmers write their software in various programming languages, such as C and C++, and the code that results is known as *source code*. To make source code usable, it must be *compiled* into a *binary file*. Because the cornerstone of the Linux philosophy is the sharing of source code, you'll almost always find the source code of a program available at the developer's web site. You can then download and compile this on your own system (or, if you're so inclined, study the source code to further your understanding). Although compiling source code isn't very hard to do, it's more convenient to download either a binary version of the program or a package.

Binary files: You might find ready-made binary files are available at the developer's web site. In other words, the programmer has taken his or her own source code and, as a service to users of the program, compiled it so that it's ready for use as soon as it's downloaded. For example, this is how Linux versions of the Mozilla Foundation software, like Thunderbird and Firefox, are currently distributed should you download them directly from www.mozilla.com. Sometimes binary files come with scripts to help you install them. However, in most cases, you simply place the files in a convenient location on your hard disk, and then run them from there.

■**Note** In the cases of both source code and binary files, the files usually come in a *tarball*, which is a single archive file containing other files. A tarball isn't, by definition, compressed, but usually either the `bzip2` or `gzip` tools are used to shrink the file to ease transportation across the Internet.

Self-installing binaries: Some larger programs are made available as self-installing binary files. This comes very close to the way Windows works, because when the file is executed, a GUI-based installation wizard takes you through installation. If you download OpenOffice.org from the official web site (`www.openoffice.org`), for example, you'll end up with a single 80MB+ file, which you then simply execute from the command line.

Package files: In many cases, you'll find that a package file of the program is available. In this case, somebody has compiled the software files and put them all together in a single, easily transportable file. Ubuntu package files end with `.deb` file extensions, but other Linux distributions use other package formats, such as `.rpm` (Fedora/Red Hat, SUSE Linux, and Mandriva, among others).

■**Note** As a blanket rule, an installation package created for one distribution won't be compatible with another. It's possible to use a program called `alien` under Ubuntu, which aims to convert packages between distributions and different package formats, but this should be seen as a last resort. You'll be better off simply obtaining a package specifically designed for your Linux distribution.

Package Management

Of all the preceding formats, packages are by far the most common and popular in the world of Linux. Ubuntu utilizes packages, as do nearly all other distributions. In fact, the Ubuntu DVD-ROM contains hundreds of packages.

A well-implemented package management system is able to install programs, upgrade them, and uninstall them, all with just a few keystrokes or clicks of the mouse. It vastly reduces the amount of work required to get new software onto your system and makes maintenance tasks such as upgrading software easy too.

It's important to understand what an Ubuntu package file actually is and what it contains. With Windows, an installation `.exe` file is effectively a piece of software combined with an archive of files. When you run the executable, it triggers a small program contained within it that then unpacks the contents of the file and installs them to the hard disk.

In contrast, packages files used by Ubuntu merely contain the program files along with a handful of configuration files to ensure the software is set up correctly. Package files are useless without the various pieces of software already installed on the system that are used to manipulate them and that do the hard work of installing, removing, and querying them. This software is known as the *package management system*. In the case of Ubuntu, the package management system has two components: dpkg and *APT*.

The use of a package management system has a number of benefits. The package management system builds its own database, so it knows exactly what programs are installed at any one time. Therefore, you can simply query the database rather than search the applications menu or hard disk. The package system also keeps track of version numbers. This gives the user much more control over the software on the system, and it makes updating easy.

The use of a package management system also means that if a program starts to act strangely its configuration files can simply be refreshed using the package manager. There's no need to uninstall and reinstall the software as is so often the case with Windows programs.

Dependency Management

One of the key features offered by any package management system is *dependency management*. Put simply, the package manager has to ensure that if you install a piece of software, any additional software it relies on to work properly is already present on the system. It the software isn't present, the package manager must either resolve the situation automatically or ask you what to do.

Sometimes, the software you want to install might depend on other programs on your system, but more often, the dependencies take the form of system libraries. It helps if you realize that not all packages contain software that you, as a user, will make direct use of. Some packages contain nothing but library files—shared pieces of code that are equivalent to .dll files under Windows. The key library on an Ubuntu system is the GNU C Library, without which the Linux kernel couldn't function and which is provided by the libc6 package. But practically every program has its own needs when it comes to library files, and these requirements must be handled by the package manager software.

■**Note** This is one reason why Windows installation files are often so large—they typically come with all the system files they need, in case they're not already present on the system. In other words, dependency isn't an issue under Windows, because everything comes supplied. Windows isn't alone in this regard: installation files for the Apple Mac are similar.

Dependency management doesn't just mean adding in packages that a piece of software needs. It might also mean *removing* packages already present on your system. This might need to happen if they're incompatible with new software you want to install, something that's referred to as *package conflict*. In addition, sometimes you might want to remove a package that other packages rely upon, a situation known as *reverse dependency*. In such a case, the package manager has to either stop you from removing that software, to avoid breaking the software that depends on it, or remove the reverse-dependency packages too. In most cases, it will ask you what you wish to do.

DEPENDENCY HELL

If you try to install certain software packages, you will very likely find that they depend on other packages, such as software libraries. These must be either already present on the system or installed at the same time for the software to work correctly. Ubuntu will attempt to take care of the latter automatically.

In a similar way, removing software also means that other packages that rely upon that particular software must also be removed, a situation known as *reverse dependency*.

Dependency hell comes about when chains of dependencies arise, which is to say, when a program you install or remove involves the installation or removal of several other, apparently unrelated pieces of software. For example, let's say you decide to manually install a program called Oscar. You download it, and type the command to install it, but you are then told that this depends on another program called BigBird, which isn't installed. Fine, you think, I'll just download and add BigBird to the same installation command. But it then transpires that BigBird has its own dependency of Snuffleupagus. You download and add that too. Alas! Snuffleupagus has its own dependency of MrHooper.

This can carry on for some time, and this is why it's not advised to manually install or remove software without using something like Synaptic Package Manager. In the preceding example, Synaptic would add in all the dependencies automatically and download and install them at the same time.

However, even with Synaptic Package Manager, dependency hell can still arise when you try to *uninstall* software. Here's a real-life example. Try to remove Firefox, and you'll find out that, along with several other packages, the Ekiga Internet phone software must also be removed. Why? What component of a web browser could a telephony application possibly need? The answer is that it doesn't directly need any Firefox component. Instead, it relies on a program called Yelp, a help system, and *this* is what relies on Firefox, which it uses to display text and graphics.

Dependency chains like this are a by-product of any package management system. The solution is often simple—just don't remove the software package. After all, hard disks are extremely large nowadays, and space is rarely an issue, so there's little reason to not have software packages you no longer need hanging around.

Package Management System Components

As mentioned previously, dpkg and APT take care of package management within Ubuntu. These tools are taken from Debian, which Ubuntu is based on.

Debian Package, or dpkg, is the most basic part of the system. It's used to install and uninstall software, and it can also be used to query any individual software packages. It's like the manager in a warehouse who is tasked with knowing exactly what boxes have been stored where. The manager doesn't know where the boxes come from, and he doesn't know anything about packages outside of his warehouse. He just manages the boxes that are delivered to him and that are stored in his warehouse.

dpkg is aware of dependency issues and will refuse to fully install a package if the others it needs aren't already installed, or supplied at the same time. But it hasn't got the means to fix the situation automatically. This is akin to the warehouse manager's inability to order more boxes if he needs them. That's not his job. He'll just tell you if boxes delivered to him are missing some of their components.

Because of this, there's an additional layer of software that sits on top of dpkg called the Advanced Package Tool, or APT. APT is very sophisticated. Its job is to handle dependency management. Try to install some software using APT, and any dependency issues will be worked out for you.

APT can do this because it's designed to work with software repositories. These are collections of software that the user can search and install packages from. More often than not, these software repositories are online, but that's not always the case. The DVD supplied with this book contains the base installation software repository, for example.

▪Note As you might already have guessed, the Synaptic Package Manager is simply a GUI front-end for the APT system. You can see this clearly when you're installing or removing a package. In the Apply Changes dialog box that appears after software has downloaded, click Terminal, and you'll see the output of various APT commands.

It's important to note that APT relies on the dpkg system to take care of the actual installation. Effectively, dpkg and APT are two sides of the same coin.

As you might have realized, the package management system means that software installation/removal is a fundamentally different proposition compared to Windows or Mac OS. If you want to install new software, the first place to look is the Ubuntu software repositories. The online repositories contain most of the popular software available for Linux right now, all packaged for installation under Ubuntu.

It's comparatively rare for an Ubuntu user to visit a web site and download a package file for installation, as is often the case for Windows users, and the only time this normally happens is if you can't find what you're looking for in the official repositories.

■Tip Software repositories don't have to be "official," or sanctioned by Ubuntu, to be used under Ubuntu. Sometimes, you might opt to add additional repositories that contain particular software. For example, you might recall that in Chapters 18 and 19 I described how to add the Debian Multimedia repositories, so you could access multimedia playback software. This was necessary, because the playback software is licensed under terms that Ubuntu doesn't agree with, and Ubuntu, therefore, declines to offer this software from its official repositories.

SOFTWARE VERSIONS

Because most Linux software is open source, a curious thing happens when it comes to software versions. Rather than there being just one "official" version of a program, such as with most Windows software (where you must download the official version of the file), many individuals and organizations take the source code, compile it, and make their own package files available for others to use.

For example, virtually all the software installed with Ubuntu has been compiled by Ubuntu developers. This means it can be quite different from what's "officially" available at the programmer's web site. In some cases, the source code is tweaked, to fix notorious bugs or apply a different look and feel to the software, so it integrates with the distribution. Often, the configuration files are changed so that the software works properly under Ubuntu, such as integrating with other software packages.

The programmer behind the software doesn't mind when such things happen, because this way of working is part and parcel of open-source software. In fact, the programmer is likely to encourage such tweaking.

Because of this, the first place to look if you want any additional software is not the developer's web site but the Ubuntu software repositories. This way, you'll get an officially sanctioned Ubuntu release that will fit in with the rest of your system and won't require much, if any, additional work to get it up and running.

Package Repositories

Out of the box, Ubuntu comes with a couple of software repositories already configured. These allow the user to download new software and also update the system online. Moreover, back in Chapter 8, you might recall that we used the Software Sources tool to set up additional online software repositories. This enabled you to install useful extra software packages not contained in the main repository.

Ubuntu software repositories are subdivided into various categories and components, as follows.

Categories of Repositories

Regardless of whether they're online or on a CD/DVD, Ubuntu repositories are strictly categorized according to the type of software they contain:

Main Distribution: This repository contains the packages that are required to install Ubuntu. This repository usually takes its name from the code name for the release. For Ubuntu 6.10, the main distribution repository is called edgy, after the code name for the 6.10 release (Edgy Eft). In the previous release, the main distribution repository was called dapper (for more details on Ubuntu code names, see https://wiki. ubuntu.com/DevelopmentCodeNames).

Security Updates: Sometimes security flaws need to be fixed almost immediately, within as little as 24 hours of being discovered. If so, the packages concerned will be placed on this server. The Security Updates server isn't about new versions or functionality. It's about fixing security holes rapidly.

Recommended Updates: This repository contains newer versions of the packages in the Main Distribution repository. Like Security Updates, this category also offers bug fixes, but these fixes aren't urgent and are often more substantial than quick patches to fix a critical bug.

Proposed Updates: This is a special category by which testing releases of updates are made available. There's no reason to use this category unless you want to test packages and help fix bugs (for more information, see https://wiki.ubuntu.com/ HelpingWithBugs).

Backported Updates: The Backports server allows access to software that's intended to go into the next version of Ubuntu but has been packaged for the current version. This software might not have been tested thoroughly and so is only suitable for neophiliacs or those who absolutely need the latest version (perhaps because of a vital new feature it offers).

Repository Components

In addition to the categories listed in the previous section, the Ubuntu repositories are further split into *components* (effectively subsections) according to how essential the software is to a basic Ubuntu installation or the license that the software uses.

Here are the components under which software is filed within a repository:

Main: This section contains nearly all the software that's featured in a basic Ubuntu installation. As such, it's all Free Software, and every package is supported by Canonical, the company that oversees the Ubuntu project. That means that updates are frequently provided to fix security holes or simply to keep up with latest releases.

■**Note** *Free Software* refers to software that's licensed under the GNU Public License (GPL). It doesn't mean that the software is free of charge, although that's nearly always the case.

Restricted: Although Ubuntu is mostly Free Software, it must include some drivers released only in binary form (that is, closed source) and that, therefore, have license agreements that are not compatible with the goals of Free Software. That's what you'll find in this section. Some Ubuntu installations simply won't work fully without software from the Restricted section.

Universe: This section might be referred to as "the rest," because it contains the majority of Free Software available at the present time. Much of it is raided from the massive Debian software library, although the packages are sometimes tweaked to work correctly under Ubuntu before being made available (many of the people who create Debian packages also create the Ubuntu equivalents). Unlike Main and Restricted, the Universe section is not officially supported by the Ubuntu project, which means there's no guarantee that security flaws will be fixed. Nor is there any guarantee of updates, although its usually the case that most packages are updated regularly.

Multiverse: As with the Restricted section, here you'll find software that's released under a software license incompatible with either the word or spirit of Free Software. However, unlike the software in the Restricted section, none of the software in Multiverse is considered essential to a default Ubuntu installation.

Source Code: This section contains source code packages. Unless you're a software developer, or are thinking of becoming one, this section won't be of much interest.

Now that the theory is done with, it's time to talk about the tools used to manage software. First we'll look at graphical software that can be used to manage software, and then we'll look at the command-line tools you can use.

The Synaptic Package Manager in Depth

The Synaptic Package Manager is effectively a graphical front end for the APT system. Later on in this chapter, we'll look at the command-line APT tools. Here, we'll take a closer look at using the Synaptic Package Manager. This can be started by clicking System ➤ Administration ➤ Synaptic Package Manager.

Searching for Software

Before searching for software, it's nearly always a good idea to refresh the package databases. These are the lists of software contained in the repositories, and they are held on your hard disk. Just click the Reload button on the Synaptic Package Manager toolbar to grab the latest package lists from the various repositories you're subscribed to (that are in your `sources.list` file). Reloading can take a few minutes on a slow connection, but it ensures that you have access to the latest software within the repositories.

There are two ways to search for software: quick and in-depth. For a quick search, click any entry in the list of packages and then simply start typing. This will match what you type against the package names and sort the list dynamically, as you type. For an in-depth search, click the Search button the toolbar. By default, this searches through both package names and the descriptions, for a higher chance of a match. You can type either the specific program name or a keyword that may be within the description. For example, if you were looking for graphics drivers for your ATI Radeon card, but you didn't know the name of the package that contains them, you could type radeon.

■Tip You don't need to type whole words in the search field. You can type part of a word or, more commonly, the word in a shortened or alternate form. For example, if you're looking for an e-mail client, it might be more fruitful to simply type "mail client," or even just "mail." This will then return results containing e-*mail*, *mail*, *mailing*, and so on.

By clicking the Settings ➤ Filters button, you can enhance your search results by filtering out any packages that don't meet your requirements. You can filter by criteria such as whether the software is already installed, whether it's new in the repository, and much more. It's advisable to click the New button to create your own filter before starting, as shown in Figure 28-1, rather than editing one that's already there. Once a filter has been created, you can apply a filter to search results by clicking the Custom Filters button at the bottom left of the main program window and then clicking the name of your filter in the list.

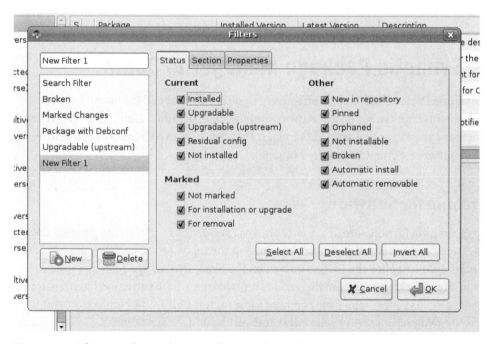

Figure 28-1. *Filters can be used to trim the list of search results according to certain criteria.*

One use of filtering is to remove the check alongside Installed so that you can remove from the search list any packages that might be already on your system.

Note Filtering can help reduce the number of search results if you use a generic search term, but don't forget to deactivate it when you've finished. To do so, click All at the top of the filters list.

In the search results, any packages with an Ubuntu symbol next to them are supported packages, which is to say, they're from the Main or Restricted software repositories, as opposed to a third-party repository or Universe/Multiverse. Therefore, future updates are likely to be offered.

If the check box is green, that means the package is already installed. A star next to the check box means the package is new.

You can view the complete range of Synaptic icons by clicking Help ➤ Icon Legend.

Installing Software

When you click the check box next to a piece of software in the search results and select Mark for Installation, the program will be queued for installation, which will take place as soon as you click the Apply button on the toolbar. In addition, when you click Mark for Installation, a dialog box will appear informing you of any uninstalled dependencies that the program needs. If you agree, these will be automatically added to the list of packages to be installed. Everything a package needs might already be installed, of course, in which case you won't see this dialog box.

Additionally, if you right-click the file and select Mark Suggested for Installation or Mark Recommended for Installation, you'll see a list of programs that, although not essential to the running of the program in question, will enhance its features to some degree.

For example, if you choose to install the `mutt` e-mail program, it's also recommended that you install `locales` and `mime-support`, so Mutt will have multiple language support and will be able to better handle file attachments. You don't have to install these recommended programs; the software will run fine without them. But it can often be rewarding if you do so.

Note If the software in the recommended and suggested lists is grayed out, that means it's already installed, or that the package doesn't have any recommended/suggested packages.

Once you click the Apply button on the toolbar (bear in mind that you can install more than one piece of software at once), you'll see the Summary dialog box, as shown in Figure 28-2.

Here, you're once again asked to confirm what needs to be installed. If any software needs to be removed in order to meet dependency issues, you'll be told about this, too. Additionally, you'll be shown the total size of the files that will be downloaded, as well as the anticipated impact on your hard disk in terms of size after the programs are installed. At the very bottom of the Summary dialog box, you'll see a check box marked Download Package Files Only. As it suggests, this will download but not install the packages. If you then select the package for installation again in the future, you won't need to download it, and installation will be instantaneous (unless a newer version of the package has been released; in which case, the newer version will be downloaded and installed).

If you see an Unchanged heading in the dialog box, this means that there are several system updates available that you haven't selected for installation. To install the system updates, click Cancel and then click Edit ➤ Mark All Upgrades. Then click Apply again. You will then see two separate headings—one listing the upgrades, and one listing the new packages you've selected to install.

■**Note** Of course, you can opt to ignore the fact that updates are available and simply go ahead with installation. Installing updates as soon as possible is advised but not enforced.

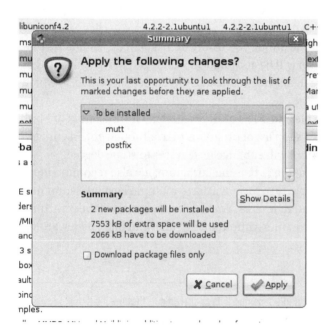

Figure 28-2. *Before any software is installed by the Synaptic Package Manager, you'll be told what it is and asked to confirm the choice.*

METAPACKAGES

Software such as the GNOME desktop actually consists of a number of programs and system libraries, rather than one single piece of software. Therefore, you might be wondering how, as just one example, you might install the KDE desktop under Ubuntu 6.10. Is it necessary to install each component's package manually?

In theory, dependency management should be able to help, and you should be able to select one key part of the KDE desktop system, such as the Konqueror file browser, and have the Synaptic Package Manager take care of the rest. After all, Konqueror will be dependent on other KDE packages.

Alas, this rarely works in reality. Installing Konqueror in this way will indeed install much of the KDE desktop suite, but not everything. Konqueror isn't reliant on Kate, for example, which is the default text editor under KDE. Perhaps more important, although the packages will be installed, there's no guarantee that they'll be configured to work correctly as a desktop environment.

Metapackages provide the solution. These are packages that contain configuration files to ensure the full range of software is installed and configured correctly, and they also have extensive lists of dependencies that include the complete set of packages for the software in question. (For what it's worth, the metapackage for KDE is kdebase.)

Alongside desktop suites, other examples of Ubuntu metapackages include the OpenOffice.org office suite, where the metapackage ensures all the components of the suite can be easily installed, and the X.org graphical subsystem. To see what metapackages are available, simply search for metapackage using the Synaptic Package Manager.

Removing Software

To remove a piece of software, search for it by name, click the check box alongside it, and then select Mark for Removal. This will remove the software but leave behind any configuration files it created. This means you can install it again in the future, and it will function as it did before removal. However, you can also select Mark for Complete Removal, which will remove the configuration files.

As with installing software, the Synaptic Package Manager will attempt to manage dependencies when you remove software, but in this case, it will enforce the removal of any software that explicitly relies on that software.

This isn't an issue most of the time, but unfortunately, some packages have major reverse dependencies. For example, if you decide that you've had enough of the Base database program and want to remove it, you'll find that you'll also need to remove the entire OpenOffice.org suite, as well as the ubuntu-desktop metapackage.

Often the solution is simply not to remove the software package. After all, modern hard disks have huge capacities, and it's unlikely the package will take up too much room.

Package Management from the Command Prompt

Synaptic is one of the best examples of package-management programs around, and there's little reason to shun it and choose to install packages from the command line. However, you may find occasions to use dpkg or the APT tools. For example, if you're already working at the command line, then this method is quicker than starting up the Synaptic Package Manager.

Using dpkg

The most basic package-manipulation command is dpkg. dpkg allows you to perform a lot of package-related tasks, such as building packages from scratch. Here, we'll look at just simple package installation, removal, and query functions.

Note dpkg requires superuser powers to install or remove software, so must be preceded with sudo. But it can be run without superuser powers if you simply wish to query the package database. The same is true of the APT tools discussed later.

Installing Packages

dpkg is useful when you've already downloaded a specific .deb package and would like to install it. Here is the command:

```
sudo dpkg -i packagename.i386.deb
```

You must specify the entire filename, rather than just the name of the program.

Note Be careful when downloading .deb package files. Not all of them are guaranteed to be 100% compatible with Ubuntu, because the .deb package format is used within a variety of distros, such as Debian and Xandros. In the first instance, you should download packages that are specifically created for Ubuntu. These will probably have the word ubuntu in their file names. In the second instance, you should try downloading those created for Debian. Those created for other distros might work, but should only be tried as a last resort.

---

dpkg is quick and dirty, and although it will warn you about any dependency issues, it will still go ahead and install the package. After installation, it will run the package's configuration scripts. But if there are missing dependencies, it won't be able to configure the program to work on your system, because it probably won't be in a usable state, as shown in the example in Figure 28-3.

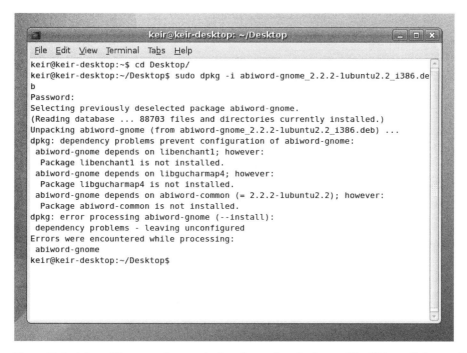

Figure 28-3. *dpkg will warn about missing dependencies but will still install the package.*

If this situation arises, it's up to you to install the dependencies that dpkg lists (several packages can be specified with the dpkg command, in any order; dpkg will sort them out itself).

Of course, some of these will have their own dependencies, which will also need to be installed. This cascade situation is informally known as *dependency hell* and is the main reason why the APT system was invented. As you'll see in the next section, APT effortlessly handles dependency issues like this.

If the dependencies aren't met after a dpkg installation, whenever you run the Synaptic Package Manager or attempt to use the APT tools, you'll be told of "broken" packages or unmet dependencies. APT will refuse to install any other software until the problem is fixed, while Synaptic Package Manager will attempt to fix the problem automatically—the missing packages will be selected for installation and will be installed alongside any software you choose. At the console, you can type sudo apt-get -f install. This will install all of the missing dependencies on the system.

■Tip Within the Synaptic Package Manager, you can click the Custom Filters button at the bottom left and then click the Broken entry in the filter list in order to see any packages that have unmet dependencies.

Uninstalling Packages

To remove a package, type the following:

```
sudo dpkg -r packagename
```

Note that you simply need to type the name of the program, without its version number or the `.i386.deb` file extensions.

In this case, `dpkg` is slightly better behaved than when installing software. If there are any reverse dependencies (other packages that depend on the one you're trying to remove), you'll be stopped in your tracks with a couple of error messages. You'll need to resolve the reverse dependencies first but, of course, they might also have their own reverse dependencies. Welcome back to dependency hell!

Note The `dpkg -r` command will remove the package but leave behind its configuration files. This is handy if you install the software again in the future. In order to remove the configuration files in addition to the software, type `sudo dpkg -P packagename`.

Querying Packages

`dpkg` includes a couple of query facilities that display details about packages. You can find out if a package is installed by typing this:

```
dpkg -l packagename
```

If you want to find out every bit of information about an installed package, including what dependencies it has, use the following command:

```
dpkg -s packagename |less
```

This example pipes the output of `dpkg` into `less` so you can read it more easily, because it's likely to fill several terminal window screens.

You can also use `dpkg` to query an installation file you've just downloaded:

```
dpkg -I packagename.i386.deb |less
```

All said, `dpkg` is an often undervalued tool that's capable of some handy low-level package-management tasks. Take a look at its man page to learn more.

Using the APT Tools

`dpkg` is the only option if you want to install a package file you've just downloaded. However, if you wish to utilize software repositories at the command line, you'll need to use the APT tools—namely `apt-get` and `apt-cache`. These still use `dpkg` in the background to install and remove packages, but they also feature intelligence to handle dependency management.

▪**Note** If, while using dpkg or APT, you get an error message along the lines of, "Can't get a lock," make sure that the Synaptic Package Manager or Software Updates programs aren't open. Only one piece of software can access the package database at any one time.

Installing and Removing Packages

The most basic APT command is apt-get. You can use this command to install or remove packages contained within the repositories as follows:

```
sudo apt-get install packagename
sudo apt-get remove packagename
```

You should specify the program name without the version number. To install the links web browser, for example, you just need to type the following command:

```
sudo apt-get install links
```

Figure 28-4 shows the results. There's no need to specify a full file name or even a version number.

▪**Note** On very rare occasions, there are several different versions of the same software in the repository; in such cases, version numbers sometimes *are* used. But this isn't something you should worry about.

As you can see in Figure 28-4, apt-get will check dependencies, download the software, and then install it. It's a much better way of working compared with dpkg.

▪**Note** You can specify two or more programs to be installed and/or removed at the same time. Just separate the package names with a space: apt-get install *package1 package2 package3*, and so on.

It's a similar situation when it comes to uninstalling software. For example, suppose you tried to remove the Firefox web browser, like so:

```
sudo apt-get remove firefox
```

apt-get would also mark for removal gnome-app-install and yelp, two packages that depend on the browser. But before doing anything, it will tell you what it is about to do and ask you to confirm it.

Similarly, if you tried to install the AbiWord word processor, like so:

```
sudo apt-get install abiword-gnome
```

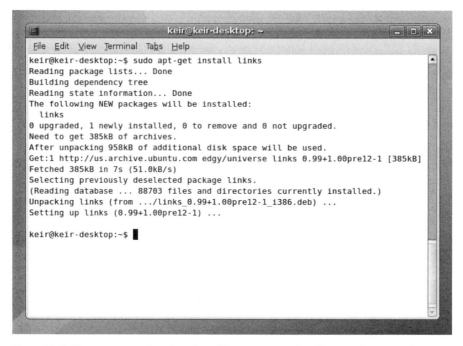

Figure 28-4. *You can use* apt-get *to install, remove, and update packages at the command line.*

You would be informed that an additional package need to be installed: abiword-common. It will be automatically added to the list of packages that are to be installed.

As with the Synaptic Package Manager, apt-get will also list suggested and recommended packages that will complement the software you wish to install but aren't vital. However, if you wish to install those packages, you'll need to do that later in a separate apt-get command.

■**Tip** An alternative to the command-line APT tools is aptitude. This can be used like APT tools such as apt-get, but can also take into account suggested and recommended packages. For more information, see its man page.

Querying Packages and Repositories

To search the repository databases for particular software packages, use the apt-cache command:

apt-cache search *packagename*

Both descriptions and package names are searched. The list of results will show the package name on the left and a description on the right. Sometimes, the results can scroll off the screen, so it's useful to pipe the output into less (that is, apt-cache search *packagename* |less).

You can also find out about dependencies and suggested packages using apt-cache:

```
apt-cache depends packagename |less
```

Once again, it's a good idea to pipe the output into less, because the dependency list may run off the screen.

You can read the program description for a package file by typing the following (see Figure 28-5 for an example):

```
apt-cache show packagename |less
```

None of these commands makes a distinction between packages that are installed or otherwise—you're accessing the details held in the repository databases.

Before searching for packages, it's a good idea to make sure you have the latest package lists from the databases (the equivalent of clicking the Reload button in the Synaptic Package Manager). To refresh the lists, use this command:

```
sudo apt-get update
```

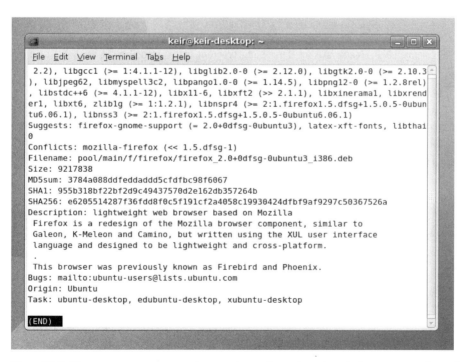

Figure 28-5. *You can query any package using* apt-cache *show to learn more about it.*

Updating the System

apt-get can also perform various types of system updates. To update all the packages on your system to the latest versions contained within the repositories, type the following:

```
sudo apt-get upgrade
```

This is the command-line equivalent of using the Software Updates function of the Ubuntu desktop.

To upgrade the system to the latest version of Ubuntu, if there is one, type this:

```
sudo apt-get dist-upgrade
```

Perhaps it goes without saying that updating your system can take a long time, depending on the number and size of files to be downloaded. In addition, each package will need to configure itself during installation, and this can also take a long time.

DECODING PACKAGE FILENAMES

Although the filenames of packages might seem like cryptic mumbo-jumbo, they actually tell you a great deal about the file. Let's take a look at the package file of the Eye of GNOME image viewer to explain this:

```
eog_2.17.2-0ubuntu2_i386.deb
```

The first element of the filename is the name of the program. In this case, Eye of GNOME has been abbreviated to eog. Abbreviations like this are quite common, because they decrease the length of the filename. But it's important to note that they will be consistent. For as long as Eye of GNOME is supported as a package under Ubuntu, its package filename will always begin with eog.

Following the name of the package is the version number of the program in question: 2.17.2-0. This is the version number that will appear if you click Help ➤ About when the program is running and is the version number decided on by the developer who created the software.

After the version number is the word ubuntu, which indicates that this is a package that's been created specifically for the Ubuntu distribution of Linux. Then you see the build version number of the package: 2. This is Ubuntu's own version number, indicating how many times the package has been built (created) by the Ubuntu team. Sometimes, it's necessary to release an updated build of the same version of a program in order to correct an error that was accidentally introduced in the last build version. Sometimes, the program is patched by the Ubuntu team to support a new function.

After the version numbers is the platform on which the package will run. In this case, i386 indicates that the package will run on all x86-based processors from the 80386 upwards (the 486, Pentium, Pentium II, AMD processors, and so on). Sometimes, you might see i686, which means that the package has been optimized for Pentium Pro chips and above (Pentium II, III, IV, and AMD's Athlon range of chips). If the package is created for 64-bit desktop processors, then amd64 will appear there.

Optimized versions of packages for particular processors are used only when they might bring a performance boost. For example, there are i686 versions of the Linux kernel and the libc6 library. But it's rare for ordinary programs, like OpenOffice.org, to be optimized. This means the majority of packages that are used under Ubuntu have the i386 designation.

Managing Software Repositories

It's unlikely that, in general use, you'll need to add, remove, or otherwise manipulate the list of software repositories, above and beyond what's described in Chapter 8, when you enabled the Universe and Multiverse repositories.

The list of repositories is held within the /etc/apt/sources.list file. You can administer this either by using the Software Sources program or by directly editing it. Although it's not a complicated file to understand, I don't advise making manual edits—in most cases, the Software Sources program will do all you need. However, I explain both approaches in the following sections.

Using Software Sources

The Software Sources program can be found on the System ➤ Administration menu. Although it can be used to add and remove third-party repositories, it's designed to let you tweak settings relating to the official repositories, which are set up by default.

The program contains five tabs, which offer the following functionality:

Ubuntu 6.10: This tab lets you choose the repository *components* (see the "Package Repositories" heading for a definition). You can choose to activate Universe, Main, Multiverse, Restricted, and Source Code. Additionally, under this tab, you can choose whether Ubuntu connects to a regional repository server (that is, one in or near your country) or the main Ubuntu server. Simply select the one you want from the Download From drop-down list. Connecting to a regional server is likely to result in faster service.

Internet Updates: This tab lets you select the types of updates you'd like to download. Effectively, it lets you choose which *category* of repository you want to connect to, as explained previously, although it's not possible to add/remove the main category, because it's always assumed that you'll want to be connected to that in order to download new software. But here, you can choose to connect to Proposed Updates and Backported Updates, in addition to Security Updates and Recommended Updates, as shown in Figure 28-6. This tab also lets you set how often the Software Updates program automatically checks for updates. Additionally, you can select to automatically install security updates without prompting you. This is not a bad idea considering many are considered vital for the safety of your system.

Third Party: This tab lets you add your own list of repositories. These can be either those that are online or those that are on a CD/DVD-ROM. When you click Add, you'll be asked to supply the APT Line, and this should be the line as it would appear in the sources.list file, which I discuss later. However, once a line has been added, you can double-click it in the list to see a more user-friendly dialog box that splits out the category and component fields into separate text boxes.

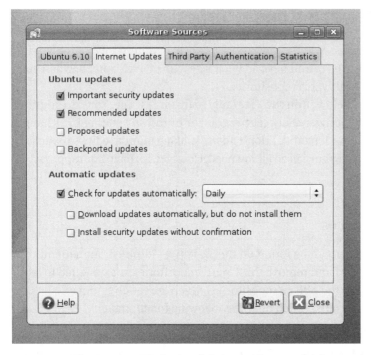

Figure 28-6. *The Internet Updates tab lets you choose which repository categories you wish to use.*

Authentication: Package files within repositories are usually digitally signed by their creators. This is a way of proving that they haven't been tampered with. Your computer can check the digital signature, but it needs a copy of the Signing Key for the relevant repository. If the key is missing, you'll be warned within Synaptic Package Manager that the package can't be authenticated when you try to install it (although it's still possible to install the package after this). Two Signing Keys are added to Ubuntu by default—one for the installation DVD-ROM and one for the online archive—but you can add more, such as those for third-party repositories that you've added manually. The Authentication tab lets you do this. Using a web browser, download the key file from the server (right-click the file and select Save As), and then click the Import Key File button. With the Open dialog box, select the file and click OK. The key will then be instantly imported.

Statistics: Here you can opt into an attempt by the Ubuntu developers to monitor which packages are most popular. This can help with future releases of Ubuntu. Simply put a check in the Submit Statistical Information box.

Adding/Removing a Repository at the Command Line

The `/etc/apt/sources.list` file is at the heart of the APT system and contains details of all the package repositories you're subscribed to, as well as the individual categories within each repository.

You can edit the file within `vim` by opening a terminal window (Applications ➤ Accessories ➤ Terminal) and typing the following:

```
sudo vim /etc/apt/sources.list
```

The `sources.list` file usually contains two types of entry: those beginning with `deb`, which indicate a standard repository containing binary files, and `deb-src`, which indicates a source file repository. `deb-src` entries are largely for developers and can be ignored.

Here's an example line from `sources.list` on my test system:

```
deb http://us.archive.ubuntu.com/ubuntu/ edgy main restricted universe multiverse
```

As you can see, the first component of the line is the address of the server. Then the repository category is listed—edgy. If the server offered updates, this might read `edgy-security` or `edgy-updates`. Following this, the repository components are listed—`main`, `restricted`, `universe`, and `multiverse`.

A hash at the beginning of a line in `sources.list` means that it's ignored. This can be useful for disabling a repository in a situation where you don't necessarily want to remove it from the file. In addition, as you can see within the file, some explanatory comments from Ubuntu developers are inserted into the file and are preceded by a hash, so that APT doesn't attempt to interpret them.

Adding a new repository is easy. For example, to add the Skype repository, in order to download the Skype VoIP software, you would find a new line, switch to insert mode within `vim` (that is, type i), and then type the following:

```
# added by Keir, 20 Feb 07
deb http://download.skype.com/linux/repos/debian/ stable non-free
```

As you can see, I've added a comment, so that I'll know later on who added the line and when.

You'll notice something interesting about the actual `deb` line. The Skype server's repository category and components aren't like the others in the `sources.list` file. The category is `stable`, and the component is `non-free`. In this case, the Skype server uses the Debian method of naming repository categories and components, which is different from Ubuntu's way. This is quite common.

Once you've added a new repository, don't forget to refresh your local list of packages. If you don't do this, APT won't be aware of the software contained on the new repository. Refreshing can be done by typing the following at the command prompt:

```
sudo apt-get update
```

This should also be done should you remove or disable a repository within `sources.list`.

Installing from Source

Back in the old days of Unix, the only way to install software was from source code, a process known as *compiling*. This was because most people edited the source code themselves, or at least liked to have the option of doing so. Nowadays, innovations such as the Debian package-management system make compiling all but redundant for the average user. But knowing how to compile a program from source is still a good Linux skill to have. In some cases, it's your only option for installing certain programs, because you may not be able to find a packaged binary.

It goes without saying that program compilation is usually handled at the command prompt. It's not the kind of thing you would do via a GUI program.

Installing the Compiler Tools

Before you can compile from source, you need to install several items of software: the `make` program, which oversees the process of creating a new program, and the GNU Compiler Collection (GCC), which does the hard work of turning the source code into a binary. In addition, if the software relies on certain library files, you'll need to install development (dev) versions of them, as well as the libraries themselves if they're not already installed. For example, if you're compiling a program to run under the GNOME desktop, you'll need development versions of the GTK2+ libraries.

Under Ubuntu, it's possible to install all the program-compilation tools you need by installing the `build-essential` metapackage. You can use the Synaptic Package Manager or the following `apt-get` command at the command prompt:

```
sudo apt-get build-essential
```

Unpacking the Source Tarball and Solving Dependencies

Let's take a look at installing a program from source. Dillo is a stripped-down web browser that's designed for speed and small file size. It's a fun little program that's good to have around in the event of your main browser developing a glitch that you can't fix. The Dillo home page is `www.dillo.org`, so head over there, and choose to download the latest version of the source code.

■Note Okay, you got me. If you use `apt-cache` or the Synaptic Package Manager to look through the repositories, you'll see that Dillo is available as a ready-to-install package. But Ubuntu's package repositories are so comprehensive that, frankly, I couldn't find anything to demonstrate program compilation that wasn't already in there!

The first thing to do is to unpack and uncompress the tarball (if you wish to learn more about the `tar` command, see Chapter 31):

```
tar jxf dillo-0.8.6.tar.bz2
```

Of course, you should replace the filename with that of the version you downloaded.

Next, you'll need to switch into the source code directory and take a look at the README file. This will tell you what dependencies Dillo has and also any caveats you may need to take into account in order to compile Dillo on a Linux system:

```
cd dillo-0.8.5
less README
```

■Note Unlike binary files, source code is rarely designed with one specific computer platform in mind. For example, Dillo is able to compile on all types of Unix, including Linux, Solaris, BSD, and others. With a little work, it might even be possible to compile it under Windows!

First, you see that Dillo needs the `glib` libraries. This is a given on nearly all Linux systems, but in order to compile, Dillo will need the `dev` version of `glib`, which isn't part of the default Ubuntu installation.

Next, you read that it also needs the GTK+ 1.2 libraries. These are present on the majority of GNOME-based Linux desktop systems, but once again, the `dev` versions will need to be installed.

Beneath that in Dillo's list of requirements is support for JPEG and PNG image formats, which are definitely installed on the average Linux system, and the WGET download tool, which is also included with most versions of Linux (although it's a good idea to use the Synaptic Package Manager or `apt-cache search` to check that it's installed).

After finding out about dependencies, you should scroll down the README to look for any notes about compiling under Linux. It turns out there might be some issues with older 2.4 versions of the Linux kernel, but Ubuntu uses 2.6, so this isn't an issue.

So, in short, before you can compile Dillo, you need to install dev versions of the `glib` and GTK+ 1.2 libraries. You can install these via the Synaptic Package Manager or `apt-get`. It will help cut down the search results if you realize that system library packages under Ubuntu are usually prefaced with `lib`. So, search for the dev versions of `libgtk` and `libglib`. Doing so on my test system returned three likely packages: `libglib1.2-dev`, `libglib2.0-dev`, and `libgtk1.2-dev`. There are two `libglib` entries, because my system has both `glib2` and the older `glib1.2`. To ensure compatibility, I decided to install dev versions of both. Since you're working at the command prompt, install the packages via `apt-get`:

```
sudo apt-get install libglib1.2-dev libglib2.0-dev libgtk1.2-dev
```

As soon as I typed this, it turned out that `libgtk1.2-dev` came with a host of dependencies in the form of X server dev libraries. The reasoning is that if the GTK+ dev library files are needed, these other libraries are often needed, too. Whatever the case, there's no harm in installing them.

Compiling

Now comes the exciting process of compiling the program! This is done via three commands, issued in sequence:

```
./configure
make
sudo make install
```

The first command starts the `configure` script, created by the Dillo programmer, which checks your system to ensure that it meets Dillo's requirements. In other words, it checks to make sure the `glib` and GTK+ libraries are present. It also checks to make sure you have the correct software that's required to actually compile a program, such as GCC and `make`.

It's when the `configure` script is running that something is most likely to go wrong. In that case, more often than not, the error message will tell you that you're missing a dependency, which you must then resolve.

■**Note** Some `configure` scripts are very thorough and check for components that the program you're trying to install might not even need. Because of this, you shouldn't worry if, as the text scrolls past, you see that various components are missing. Unless `configure` complains about it, it's not a problem.

The next command, `make`, takes care of the actual program compilation. When it's run, the screen will fill with what might look like gibberish, but this is merely the output of the GNU compiler. It provides a lot of valuable information to those who know about such things, but you can largely ignore it. However, you should keep your eyes peeled for any error messages. It's possible that the `configure` script might not have checked your system thoroughly enough, and you might be missing an important system component; in which case, `make` will halt.

Note I saw an error message at the end of the `make` session when compiling Dillo. I was able to follow up with the `sudo make install` command, which also reported error messages. However, I found that Dillo worked fine! The moral of the story is that software compilation is something of a black art, with error messages designed for programmers, and not all error messages are fatal.

Alternatively, the program simply might not be able to compile on your system without some tweaking to the `makefile` (the file that `make` uses). If such a situation arises, the best plan is to visit the web site of the developer of the software and see if there's a forum you can post to. Alternatively, check if the developer has an e-mail address you can contact to ask for help.

Eventually, the compilation will stop with a number of exit messages. Then the final command must be run: `make install`. This needs to be run with superuser powers, because its job is to copy the binary files you've just created to the relevant system directories. In addition, any documentation that comes with the program is also copied to the relevant location on your system.

Once the three commands have completed, you should be able to run the program by typing its name at the command prompt. If you've been playing along at home and have compiled Dillo, you can run it by typing `dillo`, as you can see in Figure 28-7.

Note Perhaps it goes without saying that you'll have to add your own icon to the desktop or Applications menu. Source packages are usually designed to be installed on any version of Unix running a variety of desktop managers. It is impossible, therefore, for the developer to know where to create desktop shortcuts.

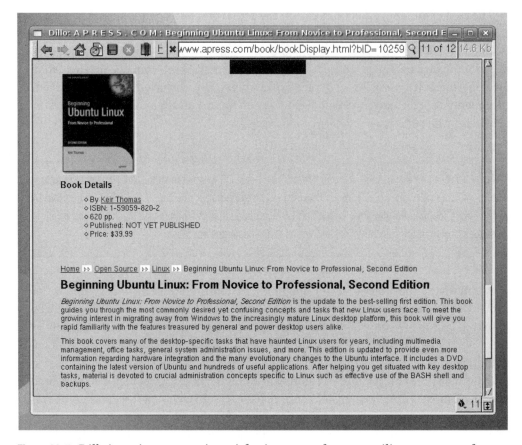

Figure 28-7. *Dillo in action—a certain satisfaction comes from compiling a program from source code.*

Summary

This chapter described how to install software under Ubuntu. We've looked at how this differs from Windows software installation, and how the Debian package-management system is designed to make life easier.

You learned how to use the Synaptic Package Manager to install software under the GUI, and how to use the dpkg and APT tools to install software at the command-line prompt. Finally, we looked at how programs can be compiled from their source code, which is a fundamental process of all versions of Linux.

In the next chapter, we'll look at how to administer the system of users under Ubuntu.

CHAPTER 29

■ ■ ■

Managing Users

Linux was designed from the ground up to be a multiuser system. When it is deployed on huge mainframe computers, it's capable of serving hundreds, if not thousands, of users at the same time, provided there are enough terminal computers for them to log in. In a more domestic setting, such as when Ubuntu is installed on a desktop PC, it usually means that more than one family member can have their very own account on the PC. They'll get their own desktop environment that is separate from that of the other users, and their own file storage area.

And even if you're the only person using your PC, you can still take advantage of Ubuntu's multiuser capabilities. Consider creating user accounts for various aspects of your life—perhaps one for work and one for time spent browsing the Web. Each user account can be tailored to a specific need.

In this chapter, you'll learn how to administer multiple user accounts.

Understanding User and Group Accounts

The concept of users and file ownership was explained in Chapter 14, but let's take a moment to recap and elaborate on some important points.

Users and Groups

Each person who wishes to use Ubuntu must have a user account. This will define what that user can and cannot do on the system, with specific reference to files and folders. Because Ubuntu is effectively one large file system, with even hardware devices seen as individual files (see Chapter 14), this means that user permissions lie at the heart of controlling the entire system. They can limit which user has access to which hardware and software, and therefore control access to various PC functions.

Each user also belongs to a group. Groups have the same style of permissions as individual users. File or folder access can be denied or granted to a user, depending on that person's group membership.

■**Note** As in real life, a group can have many members and can be based around various interests. In a business environment, this might mean that a group is created for members of the accounting department, for example, or for the human resources department. By changing the permissions on files created by the group members, each group can have files that only the group members can access (although, as always, anyone with superuser powers can access all files).

On a default Ubuntu system with just a handful of users, the group concept might seem somewhat redundant. However, the concept of groups is fundamental to the way Ubuntu works and cannot be avoided. Even if you don't make use of groups, Ubuntu still requires your user account to be part of one.

In addition to actual human users, the Ubuntu system has its own set of user and group accounts. Various programs that access hardware resources or particular sets of files normally use these. Setting up system users and groups in this way makes the system more secure and easier to administer.

Root User

On most Linux systems, the root user has power over the entire system. Root can examine any file and configure any piece of hardware. Root typically belongs to its own unique group, also called root.

Ubuntu is different in that the root account isn't utilized by default. Instead, certain users, including the one set up during installation, can "borrow" root-like powers by simply typing their login password. This is done by preceding commands with sudo/gksu at the command-line prompt or as needed when using GUI programs that affect system settings.

If you wish, you can activate the root user account on your system and then log in to it when necessary. To activate the root account, use the following command:

```
sudo passwd root
```

After typing your own login password, you'll be invited to define a password for the root user.

Because of its power, the root user can cause a lot of accidental damage, so it's rare for anyone to log in as root on bootup. Instead, you can switch to root user temporarily from an ordinary user account by typing the following:

```
su
```

This will prompt you for the root password and then log you in as root for as long as you need. When you've finished, type `exit`, and you'll be returned to your ordinary user account.

Tip You can tell when you're logged in as root user because the command prompt will end with a hash (#). When logged in as an ordinary user, it ends with a dollar sign ($). The hash symbol should be seen as a warning that you now have unrestricted control over the system, so be careful what you type and double-check everything before hitting Enter!

As an alternative to setting the root password, you can simply type the following whenever you want to switch to the root user account:

```
sudo su
```

You'll be prompted for your login password, in exactly the same way as if you had just preceded a command with `sudo`. After this, you'll be logged in as the root user. To quit the root user account, type `exit`.

UIDs and GIDs

Although we talk of user and group names, these are only used for the end user's benefit. Ubuntu uses a numerical system to identify users and groups. These are referred to as user IDs (UIDs) and group IDs (GIDs), respectively.

For various reasons, under Ubuntu, all the GID and UID numbers under 1000 are reserved for the system to use. This means that the first non-root user created on a system during installation will probably be given a UID of 1000. In addition, any new groups created after installation are numbered from 1000. On my system, the default user of `keir` had a UID of 1000 and a GID of 1000. The second user I added was given a UID of 1001.

Note UID and GID information isn't important during everyday use, and most commands used to administer users and file permissions understand the human-readable usernames. However, knowing UIDs and GUIDs can prove useful when you're undertaking more complicated system administration.

Adding and Deleting Users and Groups

The easiest and quickest way to add a new user or group is to use the Users and Groups tool under the System ➤ Administration menu. Of course, you can also perform these tasks through the command line.

Adding and Deleting Users via the GUI

To add a new user, select System ➤ Administration ➤ Users and Groups and click Add User. You'll see the User Account Editor dialog box, as shown in Figure 29-1.

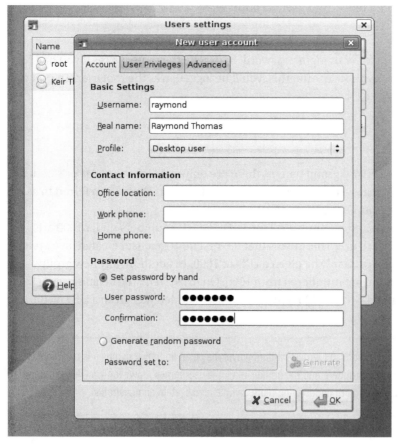

Figure 29-1. *Adding new users and groups is easy courtesy of the Users and Groups program.*

Fill out the fields on the Account tab, and optionally the Advanced and User Privileges tabs, as follows:

Account: As during initial installation (see Chapter 5), you're invited to enter a username for the user as well as the real name. The username is how the user is identified to the system, while the real name is how the user will be identified to other users. Beneath this, you can select the profile you want the user to have—Administrator, Desktop User, or Unprivileged. This relates to the user privileges the user has (although these can also be set manually using the User Privileges tab). Users with the Administrator profile can use sudo/gksu to administer the system. While Desktop Users can't, they do have access to most other system resources. The Unprivileged profile removes access to virtually all resources, including sound and external storage devices. Effectively, this is a lockdown account, although such users are still allowed to go online. For most users, the Desktop User profile is a good choice. Following this, you can enter contact information under the relevant heading if you wish, but this isn't strictly necessary. However, you do need to set an initial password for the user. To ensure accuracy, enter it twice. Alternatively, the system can generate a random password from letters and numbers, but this may be harder for the user to remember.

User Privileges: The settings on this tab offer much more control over what a user can and cannot do on the system. Here, you can prevent users from using certain hardware, such as scanners or modems. You can also control whether the user is able to administer the system. Simply put a check alongside any relevant boxes.

Advanced: Here, you can alter additional settings for the user. These are various technical settings that can remain unchanged. However, you might like to change the main group for the user. By default, he will belong to the group of the *first* user on the system. For example, when I added the user john, he was added to the group keir. This group was created during installation when the first user was added. To enforce a more stringent privacy policy regarding personal file access, you could create a separate group for each user (or perhaps a single group for all other users who aren't you), and assign the user to that group here. I discuss adding/removing groups in a moment.

■**Caution** Many groups are listed in the Main Group drop-down list. Nearly all of these relate to the way the Linux operating system operates and can be ignored. You should never, ever delete any of these, or add a user to them!

Deleting a user is simply a matter of highlighting the username in the list and clicking the Delete button. Note that the user's /home directory won't be deleted. You must do this manually with superuser powers, and it's best accomplished from the command-line prompt (see Chapter 13 for an introduction to basic file-manipulation shell commands).

Creating and Deleting Groups via the GUI

Adding a group is simply a matter of clicking the Manage Groups button in the Users and Groups program window (System ➤ Administration ➤ Users and Groups). After clicking the Add Group button, you'll be prompted to give the group a name. The group ID (GID) will be automatically filled in for you, but you could choose a different number if you have good reason to do so (remember to keep it above 1000 to keep in line with the way Ubuntu operates).

It isn't essential that you add users to the group there and then, but a list of users is provided at the bottom of the dialog box. Put a check alongside any to grant them access to your group.

■**Note** Bear in mind that users can be members of more than one group, although all users have a main group that they belong to, which is the group assigned to files they create.

As with user accounts, deleting a group is simply a matter of highlighting it in the list and clicking the Delete button. You should ensure that the group no longer has any members before doing this because, perhaps surprisingly, Ubuntu won't prevent you from doing so (although it will warn you that this is a bad thing to do).

■**Note** Ubuntu appears to offer protection against the havoc caused by deleting a group that is the main group of users on your system. When I deleted an entry that was the main group of a different user, and then logged in as that user, the group was automatically recreated! You shouldn't rely on this kind of protection, however, and should always check before deleting a group.

Adding and Deleting Users and Groups at the Command Line

You can create new users at the command-line shell by using the useradd command. This command must be run with superuser powers, which is to say that it must be prefaced with the sudo command.

The command to add a user is normally used in the following way:

```
sudo useradd -m <username>
```

The -m command option tells the command to create a home directory for the user. Used on its own, useradd merely updates system files with the new user's details and nothing else. There are several other useful command options, which can be discovered by a quick browse of the command's man page.

Creating a new user this way will automatically create a new group, which will have a title that's exactly the same as his username, and add him to it.

Adding a new group is just as easy as adding a new user:

```
sudo groupadd <groupname>
```

To specify a different main group when creating a new user, use the -g switch:

```
sudo useradd -m -g <username> <groupname>
```

For example, the following command creates a user called raymond and adds him to the main group users:

```
sudo useradd -m -g raymond users
```

It has to be said that creating users and groups at the command line is not advised, because there are a handful of annoying issues. Firstly, the new user is assigned the sh shell environment, rather than BASH, as is the default under Ubuntu. This can be overcome by the user simply typing bash at the command line after he has logged in.

▓**Note** For a permanent change, edit the /etc/passwd file. You'll need administrator powers to do this. Look for the line that begins with the name of the new user, and change the end of the line to read /bin/ bash, rather than /bin/sh. Be *extremely careful* editing this file! It's a central file without which your system could not operate. Ensure you only make the edit described here.

But there's another, more annoying issue relating to groups when you're creating a user account at the command line. Most users are members not only of their own group, but also of several system groups. These groups relate to various hardware and software functions. For example, membership of the audio group is required if the user wants to be able to use the sound card and hear audio. This is necessary because of the way Linux works. Therefore, you need to add new users to these groups if they're to make full use of the system. These groups are described as *supplementary groups*, as opposed to the main group that is assigned to files the user creates.

Use the id command to display user and group information. On my test system, typing the following:

```
id keir
```

revealed the following groups:

```
uid=1000(keir) gid=1000(keir)
groups=1000(kcir),4(adm),20(dialout),24(cdrom),25(floppy),29(audio),30(dip),44
(video),46(plugdev),109(lpadmin),111(scanner),114(admin)
```

All those after my main group, 1000(keir), are supplementary groups. For a list of what they do, see Table 29-1.

Table 29-1. *System Groups Within Ubuntu*

Group	Definition
adm	Used for system logging
dialout	Required for use of serial port devices, such as older modems
cdrom	Allows user to access CD/DVD-ROM
floppy	Allows user to access floppy disk drive
audio	Enables sound output for user
dip	Required for use of dial-up modems
video	Activates video acceleration for the user
plugdev	Allows user access to removable storage, such as card readers, digital cameras, and so on
lpadmin	Allows user to access the printer
scanner	Allows user to access the scanner
tape	Allows user to access tape storage devices (used for backup purposes)
fax	Allows user to access the fax facility
admin	Gives user system administration abilities (superuser powers)

As you might have guessed, to manually add a user under Ubuntu, you must not only create a group and then add the user to it, but you must also add that user to the required selection of supplementary groups. Some are mandatory for effective use of the computer, such as audio, while others are optional, depending on how much freedom you want to afford the new user.

You can add a user to supplementary groups by using the -G switch with adduser. Here's how to add a new user called raymond to the system so that he is able to make full use of the system (having first created a group called raymond):

```
sudo useradd -m -g raymond -G adm,dialout,cdrom,floppy,audio,dip,video,plugdev,
lpadmin,scanner,tape,fax,admin raymond
```

Additionally, creating a new user using `useradd` won't automatically apply a password to the account. Ubuntu can't work with passwordless accounts, so until one is applied, the new account will be locked. A user with administrative powers can assign a password using the `passwd` command, as discussed in the next section.

Deleting a user is mercifully simple compared to this! Use the `userdel` command, as follows:

```
sudo userdel <username>
```

This won't remove the user's `/home` directory, however. That must be done manually. Similarly, to delete a group, use the `groupdel` command:

```
sudo groupdel <groupname>
```

Note that you won't be able to remove a group if it's a user's main group.

Adding and Changing Passwords

On a default Ubuntu installation, ordinary users are able to change their passwords at the shell. The command for any user to change his password is simple:

```
passwd
```

The user will be asked to confirm his current password, and then to enter the new password twice, to confirm that it has been typed correctly.

Alternatively, by adopting superuser powers, a user can change the password of another account:

```
sudo passwd <username>
```

This is necessary just after you create a new user account because it isn't given a password automatically. For obvious security reasons Ubuntu won't allow blank passwords.

You can enter just about anything as a password, but you should bear in mind some common-sense rules. Ideally, passwords should be at least eight characters long and contain letters, numbers, and even punctuation symbols. You might also want to include both uppercase and lowercase letters.

A number of command options can be specified along with the `passwd` command when it used with superuser powers. For example, the `-l` option will lock the specified account so that it can't be accessed (the `-u` option will unlock it).

■**Tip** You can temporarily switch into any user account by typing `su <username>`. When you've finished, simply type `exit` to return to your own account.

Summary

In this chapter, we looked at the principles behind user and group accounts under Ubuntu. We've examined how user and group accounts can be created, edited, and deleted using the GUI, as well as the command-line prompt. We also looked at how passwords can be manipulated by the individual users themselves and by a user with superuser powers.

In the next chapter, we'll look at how the system can be optimized. You'll also learn about several interesting and important system tools.

CHAPTER 30

■ ■ ■

Optimizing Your System

Ubuntu should prove to be as responsive in day-to-operation as Windows, if not more so. But if you run into any performance issues, or if you simply want to get the most out of your system, then this chapter is for you. The chapter doesn't cover essential knowledge and can be skipped if need be. More often than not it discusses hacks—clever methods of making things work in a nonstandard fashion. But as your experience of Ubuntu might have already taught you, such hacks are the lifeblood of Linux. One of the strengths of Linux is the ability to delve under the hood and change absolutely any aspect of the way it works.

Speeding Up Booting

The previous edition of this book included a lengthy examination of how the Ubuntu boot process can be streamlined. However, Ubuntu 6.10 (Edgy Eft) introduced a new boot routine called Upstart that, effectively, optimizes itself. You can learn more about Upstart at `http://upstart.ubuntu.com`.

Therefore, to salvage further optimizations from the boot process, we need to look elsewhere.

Note In actual fact, in Ubutnu Edgy, Upstart emulates the older SysVinit boot routine. However, all versions after Edgy will include Upstart optimizations, making manually editing the boot procedure for performance redundant.

Reducing the Boot Menu Delay

Getting rid of the GRUB boot menu delay can save some waiting around in the early stages of the boot process. The delay can be reduced to a second or even eradicated completely. Of course, in such a case, you won't be able to choose which operating system you want to load if you're dual-booting with Windows. Even if Ubuntu is the only operating system on your computer, without the boot delay, you won't have the chance to boot into recovery mode, as offered on the GRUB menu. So you need to consider whether this is a worthwhile time-saving measure.

The boot menu delay is stated in the /boot/grub/menu.lst file. You can load this into the Gedit text editor by typing the following:

```
gksu gedit /boot/grub/menu.lst
```

Look for the line that begins with timeout, shown in Figure 30-1, and change the value to whatever you wish. The units are counted in seconds, so a value of 3 equates to three seconds. A value of 0 (zero) will mean the boot menu won't appear at all. Generally speaking, a delay of one second (1) gives you just enough time to press a key at the appropriate time, and this will cancel the countdown, meaning the boot menu will stay on your screen until you select an option.

When you've finished, save the file, and quit Gedit.

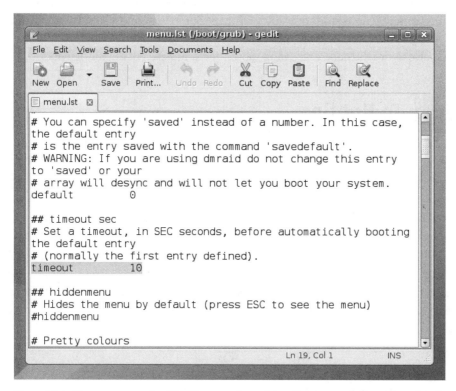

Figure 30-1. *You can stop the GRUB menu from hanging around for so long by changing the timeout value in its configuration file.*

Automatic Login

The first component of user interaction Ubuntu requires is the input of a username and password. In fact, Ubuntu will pause at the login screen indefinitely until the details are entered. Following this, the GNOME desktop will load, which can take another minute or two.

It's possible to make Ubuntu log in to any particular account automatically, which will save time during boot (and also allow you to activate your computer, leave the room, and come back to a computer ready for instant use).

However, you should only do this if you're confident your computer is in a secure location. After all, enabling automatic login will mean that anybody who has physical access to your computer will be logged in automatically and will have access to your data.

Note Once automatic login is enabled, you will still be able to log out by clicking System ➤ Quit, and clicking the Log Out button. This will then show the login screen, which you can use to switch to other user accounts and so on.

To enable automatic login, click System ➤ Administration ➤ Login Window. In the Login Window Preferences window that appears, click the Security tab, and put a check alongside Enable Automatic Login. Then choose the account that you'd like to log in automatically from the User drop-down list, shown in Figure 30-2 (if there's only one user on your system, there will only be one entry in this list). Once finished, click the Close button at the bottom right of the Login Window Preferences window.

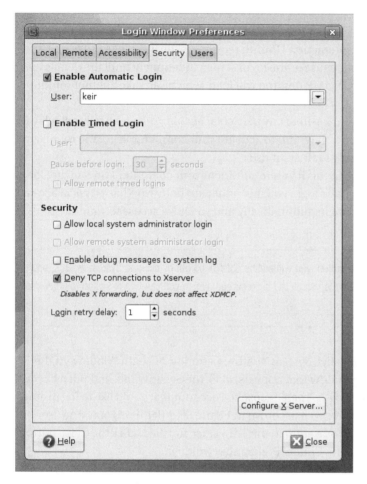

Figure 30-2. *Automatic login can save precious seconds when booting but represents a security risk to your data.*

Managing GNOME Sessions

Under Windows you might be used to controlling what programs start up with the desktop. This can be done by deleting entries from the Start menu's Startup program group.

To control what programs start up with the GNOME desktop, you'll need to use the Sessions program. To start this, open a terminal window (Applications ➤ Accessories ➤ Terminal), and type gnome-session-manager.

The Session Options tab lets you stop the splash screen from appearing on bootup, which some people say speeds up boot times a little (although I suspect it merely makes boot times *seem* quicker!). Clicking the Startup Programs tab shows what programs start when GNOME does, as shown in Figure 30-3. On my system, four entries were in the list: update-notifier, evolution-alarm-notify, gnome-power-manager, and gnome-volume-manager --sm-disable. Your computer might have more entries in the list.

Figure 30-3. *gnome-session-manager lets you control what programs start when GNOME does.*

update-notifier is the Software Updates tool. I don't advise that you disable this, because it performs the essential task of checking, each time you boot, if any system updates are available. It runs in the background once started and hardly impacts startup time at all. However, if you absolutely must prune valuable milliseconds from startup, you can select it and click the Disable button. You can then check for updates manually, whenever you desire, by clicking System ➤ Administration ➤ Update Manager.

evolution-alarm-notify is, as its name suggests, a background process that ties into Evolution's calendar function in order to notify you of events. If you don't use Evolution, or don't use its calendar function, then this can be disabled. Simply select its entry in the list and click Disable.

gnome-power-manager is another background service, except this time it controls all aspects of GNOME's power management, including the useful hibernate feature that can save the contents of the system's RAM to disk and then shut down the computer, to make for quicker subsequent startup. If yours is a notebook computer, then gnome-power-manager should be considered essential. If yours is a desktop PC and you never use hibernate, suspend, or screen blanking after a period of inactivity, then you might consider deactivating gnome-power-manager. To do so, select it in the list, and click Disable. However, I would advise against this.

▓Note Disabling gnome-power-manager will remove the Suspend and Hibernate functions from the System ➤ Quit dialog box.

---

gnome-volume-manager isn't, as you might think, related to the sound system. Instead it allows the automounting of removable storage (known in Linux lingo as *volumes*), such as digital cameras and CD/DVD-ROM discs. This is a critical function of Ubuntu and, without it running, you face the uphill struggle of manually mounting removable storage devices at the command prompt. You can disable it if you want, but I definitely wouldn't advise such a move.

■**Tip** As you might see, the Startup Programs tab also features an Add button. By clicking this, you can add any program you like to the GNOME startup. You could add Evolution, for example, so that it starts automatically whenever your computer boots.

STOP WAITING FOR AN ADDRESS

If you use an ethernet or Wi-Fi connection to access your network, you might find that Ubuntu spends a few seconds each boot acquiring an Internet address. This will be characterized by a long pause while nothing seems to be happening. Therefore, one way to provide an instant speed boost is to give your computer a static IP address. I explained in Chapter 8 how to configure your network interface.

However, to assign a static address, you'll have to find out what IP address range your router (or other DHCP server) uses. This can be discovered by looking at the router's configuration software. Sometimes, this is accessed via a web browser. Look for the configuration section headed DHCP Configuration or similar.

Normally, the addresses are in the 192.168.*x.x* range, where *x.x* can be any series of numbers from 1.1 to 255.255. For instance, the router within my test setup uses the 192.168.1.2-255 range.

In my case, choosing a static IP address that will work with the router is, therefore, simply a matter of choosing an IP address in this range. However, I know that the router hands out addresses sequentially from 2 upward, so it's best if I choose an address it's unlikely to reach, even if I happen to have many computers connected to the network. Starting at 50 is a good idea, so on my test PC I can assign the address 192.168.1.50.

Don't forget that, when defining static IP addresses, you'll need to manually supply the gateway, subnet, and DNS addresses. In most cases, the subnet address will be 255.255.255.0. The DNS addresses will be the same as the gateway address.

Optimizing Hard Disk Settings

The hard disk is one of the key elements in the modern PC. Because most of your PC's data must travel to and from it, speeding up your hard disk means that your entire PC will be faster.

Ubuntu provides a powerful command-line tool that you can use to control every aspect of your hard disk: hdparm. This is a power user's tool. Not only must it be run with superuser powers (preceded by sudo at the command line), but you also must be careful not to mistype the commands. All changes are made instantly, so if you make a mistake, your system may crash or at least suffer from serious problems. There's even the risk of data loss, although this is minimized by making sure that you have no other programs running at the same time you run hdparm.

The good news is that changes made via hdparm will last for only the current session, so there's no risk of permanent damage. Any changes that are beneficial can be made permanent later.

In the context of optimization, hdparm lets you both benchmark the disk and change various technical settings, such as the sector multcount value. These adjustments can bring speed boosts.

Note that most of hdparm's optimization commands only work on older EIDE hard disks, and not newer SATA hard disks. Because of the way SATA works, it is in less need of this kind of optimization.

■**Note** EIDE hard disks were used in practically all desktop computers up until a year or so ago. SATA is a replacement technology that's slowly pushing aside EIDE, but it's still the case that many new computers come with EIDE hard disks, particularly at the budget end of a manufacturer's range. For an explanation of SATA, see http://en.wikipedia.org/wiki/SATA.

Benchmarking Your Hard Disk

Because experimenting with hdparm can cause crashes, and because its benchmarking feature needs almost exclusive access to the hard disk, hdparm is best run with as few as possible additional programs up and running. Therefore, killing the GUI is a good idea. To stop the GUI, open a GNOME Terminal window (Applications ➤ Accessories ➤ Terminal), and type the following:

```
sudo /etc/init.d/gdm stop
```

You'll then need to log in again; do so.

■**Note** Technically speaking, switching to run level 1 is an even better idea, because this will deactivate all unnecessary services. Run level 1 is akin to the Windows Safe Mode, except without the GUI. However, you want realistic benchmark results to test the changes you make via hdparm, and it's debatable whether the confines of run level 1 will provide such results.

Let's start by benchmarking your hard disk to see its performance based on the current settings. Type the following (assuming Ubuntu is installed on the first hard disk in your system; if it's on the second hard disk, change /dev/hda to /dev/hdb):

```
sudo hdparm -tT /dev/hda
```

This will benchmark your disk in two ways. The first tests the PC's memory throughput, measuring the data rate of the memory, CPU, and cache. The second actually tests the disk's data rate. The second test affects the outcome of the first, which is why the two are used together. Between them, these two methods of benchmarking present the standard way your disk is used on a day-to-day basis. Figure 30-4 shows the results on my system.

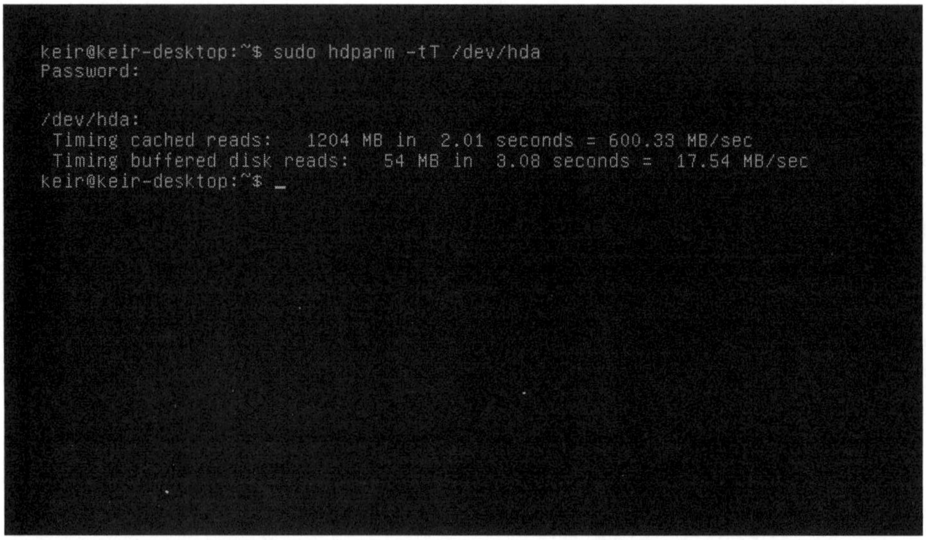

Figure 30-4. *The hdparm program can be used to both benchmark and optimize your hard disk.*

Make a note of the figures, so that you can compare them to the results of these tests after you change hard disk settings.

Changing Hard Disk Settings

You can use hdparm to view your current hard disk settings by entering the following at the command prompt:

```
sudo hdparm /dev/hda
```

On my test PC, these are the results I got:

```
/dev/hda:
 multcount     = 0 (off)
 IO_support    = 0 (default 16-bit)
 unmaskirq     = 0 (on)
 using_dma     = 1 (on)
 keepsettings  = 0 (off)
 readonly      = 0 (off)
 readahead     = 256 (on)
 geometry      = 65535/16/63, sectors = 160086528, start = 0
```

Let's take a look at what these settings mean.

The multcount Setting

The first, multcount, refers to how many sectors can be read from the hard disk at any one time. The theory is that the highest possible value here is best. Most modern hard drives support a value of up to 64. You can find out by issuing the following command:

```
sudo hdparm -i /dev/hda
```

Look for MaxMultSect in the results. On my test PC, this read MaxMultSect=64.

Ironically, although higher values are thought best, sometimes a lower value can speed up hard disk access. You can experiment with the multcount setting on your hard disk by using the -m hdparm command option:

```
sudo hdparm -m16 /dev/hda
```

You can then follow this by another benchmark to see if there is an improvement:

```
sudo hdparm -tT /dev/hda
```

If there isn't any improvement, you could try a lower value by simply swapping the -m16 for -m8.

The IO_Support Setting

The IO_support line refers to the input/output (I/O) mode used by the hard disk controller. There are three possible settings: 0 to disable 32-bit support, 1 to enable 32-bit support, and 3 to enable 32-bit support with a special sync signal.

You can change the IO_support setting with the -c hdparm command option, and the 32-bit support with sync option (3) is generally considered the best choice:

```
sudo hdparm -c3 /dev/hda
```

The unmaskirq Setting

The third setting, umaskirq, allows Ubuntu to attend to other tasks while waiting for your hard disk to return data. This won't affect hard disk performance very much, and generally it's a good idea for the health of your system to activate it if isn't already switched on. This command activates umaskirq:

```
sudo hdparm -u1 /dev/hda
```

The Using_Dma Setting

The fourth setting refers to whether Direct Memory Access (DMA) is in use. Hard disks are sold on the basis of their DMA modes, such as UltraDMA Burst 2 and the like. DMA is considered an indicator as to the speed of a hard disk, but the truth is that, like any specification, it is only a guide.

DMA is activated by default under Ubuntu, but you can alter the DMA mode using the -X command option. However, on most modern PCs, this isn't necessary, because the computer's BIOS defaults to the fastest DMA mode.

Other Settings

The last three settings, which are above the summary of the geometry and sector information of the disk, are those you shouldn't change. The readahead setting controls how many hard disk blocks are loaded in advance. It doesn't affect the performance of modern IDE-based hard disks, because the drive electronics contain buffers that perform this task themselves.

The keepsettings setting refers to the ability of the drive to remember hdparm settings over a reboot, which isn't necessary, because you intend to use the hdparm.conf file to change the disk settings at each boot. The readonly setting sets whether or not the hard disk is read-only (so that no data can be written to it). Changing this setting is not advisable!

Making Disk Optimizations Permanent

The /etc/hdparm.conf file is read at each bootup, and any settings it contains are applied to the hard disk. You can edit this file in the Gedit text editor by typing the following:

```
gksu gedit /etc/hdparm.conf
```

The simplest way of using this file is to edit the hdparm command string at the end of the file. To do so, start by finding the line that reads as follows:

```
#command_line {
```

Delete the hash mark from the beginning of the line. Then delete the next line (the one that starts with a hash mark, followed by hdparm -q -m16 . . .), and type your own version of the hdparm command, complete with the command options you discovered previously. For example, if your benchmarking has shown that the multcount and IO_support command options bring dividends, you might type something like the following:

```
hdparm -m16 -c3 /dev/hda
```

There's no need to type a hash mark at the beginning, as with the line you deleted. Then delete the hash mark from in front of the line beneath this, so that it's simply a bracket (}) on its own, as shown in Figure 30-5.

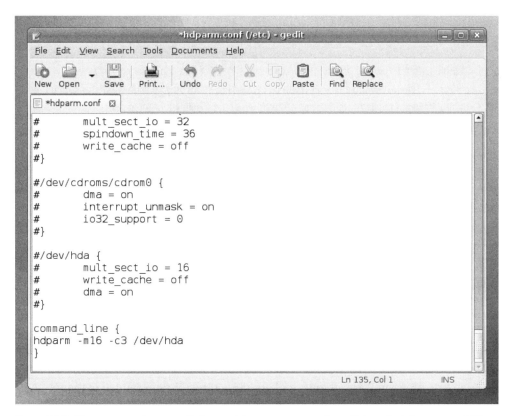

Figure 30-5. *You can make your disk tweaking permanent by editing the* hdparm.conf *file.*

When you've finished, save the file, and reboot to test your settings.

BUILD YOUR OWN READAHEAD PROFILE

Ubuntu includes a feature called readahead, which is able to order the list of files to be loaded during bootup by their locations on the hard disk. A default readahead list is installed on a standard Ubuntu installation. This is created on a generic PC, but you can build your own version of the list, customized for your own computer.

Here are the steps needed to create your own readahead list:

1. Reboot Ubuntu, and at the boot menu, highlight the Ubuntu entry and press E. If Ubuntu is the only operating system on your computer (that is, your computer doesn't dual-boot with Windows), you might need to press Esc to see the boot menu when prompted.

2. Highlight the second line, beginning with the word `kernel`, and press E again.

3. Using the right arrow key, move the cursor to the end of the line. Insert a space and then type `profile`. This is how the entire line read on my test PC; yours may be slightly different (note that the beginning of the line was cropped off because of the resolution of the screen):

```
< quiet splash profile
```

4. Press B to boot the computer. This boot will take longer than usual, because the boot profile is being rebuilt. When the computer has booted up, and all disk activity has stopped (which might take a minute or two after the desktop has appeared), reboot your computer. You should find that bootup is faster.

Prelinking

A lot of Ubuntu software relies on other pieces of code to work. These are sometimes referred to as *libraries*, which is a good indicator of their purpose: to provide functions that programs can check in and out whenever they need them, as if they were borrowing books from a library.

Whenever a program starts, it must look for these other libraries and load them into memory, so they're ready for use. This can take some time, particularly on larger and more complicated programs. Because of this, the concept of *prelinking* was invented. By a series of complicated tricks, the `prelink` program makes each bit of software you might run aware of the libraries it needs, so that memory can be better allocated.

Prelinking claims to boost program startup times by up to 50% or more, but the problem is that it's a *hack*—a programming trick designed to make your system work in a nonstandard way. Because of this, some programs are incompatible with prelinking. In fact, some might simply refuse to work unless prelinking is deactivated. At the time of this writing, such programs are in the minority. However, keep in mind that prelinking can be easily reversed if necessary. Alternatively, you might want to weigh whether it's actually worth setting up prelinking in the first place.

■**Note** Many of the GNOME programs under Ubuntu aren't compiled in a way that's compatible with prelinking. Therefore, you might not see much of a speed boost using the GNOME desktop.

Configuring Prelinking

If you decide to go ahead with prelinking, you'll need to download the relevant software from the Ubuntu software repositories. (If you haven't already set up the Synaptic Package Manager to use the additional online repositories, see Chapter 8). Open Synaptic Package Manager (System ➤ Administration), click the Search button, and type prelink into the search box. Mark prelink for installation, and then click Apply.

Before you can run a prelinking sweep of your system, you need to enable it in one of its configuration files. To do this, type the following in a GNOME Terminal window:

```
gksu gedit /etc/default/prelink
```

Change the line that reads PRELINKING=unknown to PRELINKING=yes. Then save the file and quit Gedit.

To run a prelinking scan of your system, simply issue this command:

```
sudo prelink -a
```

This will prelink practically all the binary files on your system and may take some time to complete. You may also see some error output, but you don't need to pay attention to it.

Prelinking was automatically added as a daily cron job when you installed it (see Chapter 32 for a description of cron), so any new programs you add will be automatically prelinked.

Deactivating Prelinking

Should you find prelinking makes a particular application malfunction or simply stop working, you can try undoing prelinking. To do this, find out where the main binary for the program resides, and issue the prelink command with the --undo command option. For example, to remove prelinking from the Gedit text editor program, you could type the following:

```
whereis gedit
sudo prelink --undo /usr/bin/gedit
```

However, this may not work, because some programs might rely on additional binaries on the system. Therefore, the solution might be to undo prelinking for the entire system, which you can do by typing the following:

```
sudo prelink -ua
```

After this, you should remove the `prelink` package, via Synaptic, to stop it from running again in the future (or manually remove its `cron` entry, as explained in Chapter 32).

OPTIMIZING THE KERNEL

You can download the Linux kernel source code and compile your own version of it. This gives you total control over the kernel configuration, so you can leave out parts you don't want in order to free memory. You can also set certain optimization settings, such as creating a version of the kernel specifically built for your model of CPU.

Although compiling a kernel is a simple procedure, there are many complex questions that you'll need to answer, and an in-depth knowledge of the way Linux works is necessary.

In addition, compiling your own kernel brings with it several issues. The first is that it may not work with any binary modules that you have installed, such as graphics cards or wireless drivers. You can opt to install these yourself from scratch, but this adds to the complexity.

The second problem is that Ubuntu is built around precompiled kernels. Several software packages expect to work with the precompiled kernel, and in addition, Ubuntu may occasionally download an updated prepackaged kernel automatically as part of the system update feature and override the one you've created.

If there are any security problems with the kernel version you compiled, you'll need to recompile a new kernel from scratch (or patch the one you have). This means you'll have to keep an eye on the security news sites and take action when necessary.

That said, compiling a kernel is an excellent way of learning how Linux works, and if it all goes well, the sense of achievement is enormous.

Some people choose to download the kernel source code from the official Linux kernel site, `www.kernel.org`. However, it makes more sense to download the official Ubuntu release, because this will be tailored for the way your system works. Using the Synaptic Package Manager, simply search for `linux-source`.

You can find several guides to compiling your own kernel online, but I recommend the following posting on the Ubuntu forums web site, which looks at compiling a kernel under Ubuntu: `http://doc.gwos.org/index.php/Kernel_Compilation_Dapper`.

Freeing Up Disk Space

After using Ubuntu for some time, you might find that the disk begins to get full. You can keep an eye on disk usage by using the following command in a GNOME Terminal window:

```
df -h
```

This will show the free space in terms of megabytes or gigabytes, and also expressed as a percentage figure.

If the disk does start to get full, you can take steps to make more space available.

Emptying the /tmp Folder

An easy way to regain disk space is to empty the /tmp folder. As with the Windows operating system, this is the folder in which temporary data is stored. Some applications clean up after themselves, but others don't, leaving behind many megabytes of detritus.

Because the /tmp folder is accessed practically every second the system is up and running, to empty it safely, it's necessary to switch to run level 1. This ensures few other programs are running and avoids the risk of deleting data that is in use. The following series of commands will switch to run level 1, empty the /tmp folder, and then reboot afterwards:

```
sudo killall gdm
[log in with your username and password]
sudo init 1
rm -rf /tmp/*
rm -rf /tmp/.*
reboot
```

▨**Tip** On a similar theme, don't forget to empty the desktop Trash. This can hold many megabytes of old data. If you see an error message about permissions when emptying the Trash, you can do so manually from a terminal window. Simply type `sudo rm -rf ~/.Trash/*`.

Emptying the Cache of Package Files

You might also choose to clear out the Advanced Packaging Tool (APT) cache of old `.deb` package files. On a system that has been very frequently updated, this can free many megabytes (possibly gigabytes) of space.

You can empty the cache by typing the following command in a GNOME Terminal window:

```
sudo rm -f /var/cache/apt/archives/*.deb
```

▓**Caution** Be careful to type the command to empty the APT cache exactly as it's written. Even inserting an additional space can lead to very bad consequences!

If you want to restore any packages later on, simply locate them in the Synaptic Package Manager list, click the check box, and click Mark for Reinstallation. This will cause the package to be downloaded, installed, and configured.

Removing Unused Software

If you still need disk space, consider uninstalling unused programs. As you've learned, you manage software through the Synaptic Package Manager (System ➤ Administration).

To remove a package, click its check box, and select Mark for Removal. However, it's not a good idea to simply scroll down the list and remove anything that seems dispensable. Because of the way Linux works, many seemingly insignificant packages are actually vital to the running of the system. Instead, it's a better idea to look for programs on the Applications menu, and then return to the Synaptic Package Manager to remove them by searching for their names.

As always, removing software can create dependency problems, so you might find yourself limited in what software you can actually remove.

▓**Tip** If you want to remove all the desktop games, simply search for gnome-games and gnome-games-data in the Synaptic Package Manager, and mark them for removal.

Summary

In this chapter, we looked at streamlining your installation of Ubuntu. This involved speeding up the boot procedure by decreasing the boot menu delay, along with a handful of other tricks. We also looked at optimizing your hard disk settings to allow for greater efficiency in loading and saving files.

Additionally, we investigated prelinking programs so that they load faster, recompiling the kernel so that it's optimized for your system, and freeing disk space by various means.

In the next chapter, you'll learn how to perform backups to safeguard your data.

CHAPTER 31

■■■

Backing Up Data

Every computer user knows that backing up data is vital. This is usually because every computer user has lost data at some point, perhaps because of a corrupted file or accidental deletion.

Some of the people behind Unix were highly aware of such occurrences and built in several advanced and useful backup tools. These have been mirrored within Linux, with the result that creating and maintaining backups is easy.

In this chapter, we'll first look at what data should be backed up, and then explore two ways to make backups: using the Simple Backup utility and from the command line.

What Data Should You Back Up?

Data on your system can be classified into three broad types: program data, configuration data, and personal data. It's traditionally reasoned that backing up all types of data is inefficient and difficult, largely because it would mean backing up practically the entire hard disk. Because of this, you usually want to back up the latter two types of data: configuration and personal. The theory is that if your PC is hit by a hard-disk-wrecking disaster, you can easily reinstall the operating system from the CD/DVD. Restoring your system from backup is then simply a matter of ensuring the configuration files are back in place, so your applications work as you would like them to, and making sure that your personal data is once again made accessible.

Practically all the personal configuration data for programs you use every day, as well as your personal data, is stored in your /home folder (although the configuration files for software used system-wide are stored in the /etc folder). If you take a look in your /home directory, you might think that previous sentence is incorrect. On a freshly installed system, the directory appears largely empty. However, most, if not all, of the configuration files are hidden; their directory and filenames are preceded with a period (.), which means that Linux doesn't display them during a standard directory listing.

To view hidden files and folders in the Nautilus file manager, select View ➤ Show Hidden Files. This can be quite an eye-opener when you see the masses of data you didn't even realize were there, as shown in the example in Figure 31-1. To view hidden files at the shell prompt, simply use the -a command option with the ls command:

```
ls -a
```

Figure 31-1. *Most of the configuration files for programs are hidden—literally—in your /home folder.*

The configuration files held in your /home folder relate solely to your user account. Any other users will have their own configuration files, entirely independent of yours. In this way, all users can have their own configuration settings for various applications, which can be backed up independently.

Under Ubuntu, you can back up both configuration data and personal files using Simple Backup, which can be downloaded from the Ubuntu software repositories.

Keep in mind that there's little point in making backups if you leave the resultant archive files on your hard disk. For full backup protection, the archives should be stored elsewhere, such as on an external hard disk, network mount or CD/DVD-ROM. Consider using GNOME CD/DVD Creator (click Go ➤ CD/DVD Creator on the menu of any open Nautilus window).

Using Simple Backup

Simple Backup is a series of programs that enables the quick and easy backup and also restoration of files. Simple Backup can back up personal data as well as system configuration files. Its output, which takes the form of backup directories containing an archive of the files, plus configuration data, can be written to your hard disk (or a network mount attached to it), or in a remote Internet location, such as an FTP server.

Simple Backup was created courtesy of the Google Summer of Code sponsorship scheme and was designed with the help of Ubuntu developers. It's a new member of the Ubuntu software family, and it's likely that new features will be added all the time, so be sure to regularly update your system (see Chapter 9).

To install Simple Backup, open Synaptic Package Manager (System ➤ Administration), and then search for sbackup. Click its entry in the list of results, mark it for installation, and click Apply. Log out and back in again in order to update the system menus. You'll then find entries for the backup and restoration components of Simple Backup on the System ➤ Administration menu.

▪Note Simple Backup is in the "universe" software repository. If you haven't already, follow the instructions under the "Setting Up Online Software Repositories" heading in Chapter 8.

Backing Up Data via Simple Backup

To configure a backup, select System ➤ Administration ➤ Simple Backup Config. You'll see the Backup Properties dialog box, as shown in Figure 31-2. Using this dialog box, you can choose the files that Simple Backup backs up, as well as when it does so. Once you've made your changes, click the Save button to write the configuration changes to disc. This should be done before making a backup. If scheduled backups are set, it's sufficient to save the changes and quit the program. The backup jobs will take place automatically, in the background, at the set times.

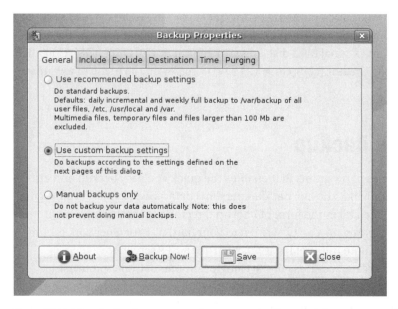

Figure 31-2. *Simple Backup can work automatically or with custom settings you specify.*

As listed on the General tab of the Backup Properties dialog box, Simple Backup can operate in three different modes:

Use Recommended Backup Settings: This is by far the best choice for fuss-free operation. Simple Backup will perform a daily backup of your /home folder, as well as the vital system data held in /etc, /usr/local, and /var. However, it will deliberately exclude any multimedia files (because of their large size), along with any temporary files and files of any type that exceed 100MB (again for size reasons). By default, the backup directory created is placed in /var/backup.

Use Custom Backup Settings: This is effectively the same as the recommended backup, and includes the same list of file inclusions and exceptions, but you are able to edit the settings manually. For example, you might choose to include MP3 files, rather than excluding them, as with the recommended backup. The custom backup option lets you alter where the eventual backup directory is saved and also lets you alter the time when the backup is made.

Manual Backups Only: This effectively deactivates Simple Backup, so that it no longer periodically backs up files. However, you can still click the Backup Now! button to manually perform a backup according to the settings on the other Backup Properties dialog box tabs.

■Note Simple Backup doesn't create a new backup each time it runs, because that would take too long. The first time it runs, a full backup is taken, but those created afterwards are *incremental backups*, and only files that are new or that have changed are backed up. The backup directory created during the first run is given the file extension `.ful`, while the backup directories created after this have the extension `.inc`. As you might expect, if the original `.ful` backup directory can't be found, a new full backup will be created.

Including Files and Folders in the Backup Job

Assuming that you've chosen a custom backup, and so are able to alter the backup settings, clicking the Include tab allows you to specifically define directories and files that you wish to include in the backup. Simply click the Add File or Add Directory button, and then browse to the relevant location (to add a directory, you'll need to click to open it before clicking the Open button).

Bear in mind that adding a directory does so recursively, which means that any directories contained within that directory are also backed up. For this reason, you don't need to specifically add your /home/<*username*> folder, because the entire /home folder is included in the backup by default. This means the backup will also include all other users' directories within /home, too.

Excluding Files and Folders from the Backup Job

You have a wide range of choices when it comes to excluding files and folders from the list. While directories can be excluded based on location, files can be excluded based on location, type of file, or size.

Clicking the Exclude tab reveals a set of side tabs on the left side of the program window, which allow you to exclude items from the backup as follows:

Paths: To exclude a specific file or folder, click this side tab. As with including files, click the Add File or Add Directory button, and then browse to the relevant location.

File Types: To exclude certain types of files, click this side tab, as shown in Figure 31-3. After clicking the Add button, you'll see that you can choose from a brief list of standard file types or filter by file extension (such as mp3 for MP3 files or zip for compressed Zip files).

Regex: If you're competent at using regular expressions, as outlined in Chapter 15, you can use them to specify extremely precise rules by clicking this side tab.

Max Size: Any files larger than the stated size on this tab aren't backed up. By removing the check next to the Do Not Backup line, you can deactivate this feature (although that could lead to massive backup files).

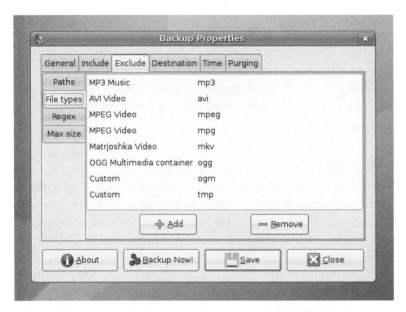

Figure 31-3. *Excluding certain types of large files will lead to far smaller backup files.*

Changing the Backup Directory Destination

By default, the backup directory created by Simple Backup is stored in the /var/backup directory. By clicking the Destination tab, you can choose to save it in a different location on your hard disk. Of course, if you have a network mount, you can also opt to save it there. In most cases, I would advise that you use /var/backup to store the newly created backup files, however, and copy the files to their permanent store destinations later. You might even choose to do this periodically and automatically—by following the instructions in Chapter 32, which explain how to schedule tasks, you could setup a cron job to automatically copy the files to a network mount or removable storage device.

■**Note** Remember that Simple Backup creates incremental backups, so you should copy *all* the backup directories and files within /var/backup to the external storage device, rather than just the latest one.

You can even transfer the backup directory across the Internet via SSH file transfer or the older FTP standard. To do so, simply enter the protocol, username, password, and URL in the following format:

```
ftp://username:password@myftpsite.com/remotedirectory
```

It's important to precede the address with the protocol you intend to use, whether it's SSH or FTP.

Changing the Time Period Between Backups

Clicking the Time tab lets you set the frequency of the backup. You can opt to back up hourly, daily, weekly, or monthly, You can also set the exact time of the backup if necessary. For example, you could set a backup to take place every week on a Tuesday at 12.30 p.m. Simply select the interval period from the Do Backups drop-down list, and then select from the Day of Month, Day of Week, Hour, and Minute lists, as necessary. Simple Backup uses the system scheduler, `cron`. I discuss `cron` in more detail in Chapter 32. The use of `cron` means that Simple Backup doesn't need to be running for the backup to take place— Simple Backup is started and stopped automatically in the background when needed.

You can also elect to perform a full backup after a certain number of days have passed (up to 1,000). A full backup means that Simple Backup creates a new complete backup, rather than incremental ones.

Purging Old Backup Files

By clicking the Purging tab, you can opt to automatically delete old backup directories. This can save on storage space. Purging can be done either by specifying a cutoff date, so that any backup archive older than the specified number of days is deleted, or it can be done logarithmically. This means that the program keeps just one backup out of the many that might be created in a week, month, and so on. All others are deleted. For obvious reasons, you should use the purging option with care!

Restoring Data via Simple Backup

If the worst happens and you need to restore any number of files from the backup, you can click System ➤ Administration ➤ Simple Backup Restore.

The first step is to select the location of the backup directories. If the backups aren't contained in /var/backup, then click Use Custom, and either type the path into the field or click the file browse button and locate the backup directories. Then click the Available Backups drop-down list to choose a backup directory from which to restore. The directory names contain the dates and times the backups were made, and it makes sense to choose the latest (unless you want to revert to an older version).

Once the backup has been selected, the files the actual backup archive contains will be displayed beneath. Each directory will have a small triangle to its left, which you can click to expand the directory to show its contents.

After you've found the file(s) or directories you want to restore, highlight them and then click the Restore button. But beware, because this will rewrite the files and directories to their original locations—files or directories already there with matching filenames will be overwritten!

If you want to restore the files to a different location, click the Restore As button, and then choose a folder.

■**Caution** Restored files and directories are owned by root. This is because Simple Backup runs with superuser powers. Therefore, one of the first things you'll have to do is use the chown command, preceded by sudo, to change the ownership and group of the file to what they were originally. See Chapter 14 for more details about file ownership and how the chown command works.

Making Backups from the Command Line

Although Simple Backup allows the uninitiated to make quick backups, the tar program is preferred by Linux old-timers. This creates .tar files and is one of the original carry-overs from Unix. tar stands for Tape ARchive and refers to backing up data to a magnetic tape backup device. Although tar files are designed for backup, they've also become a standard method of transferring files across the Internet, particularly with regard to source files or other installation programs.

A tar file is simply a collection of files bundled into one. By default, the tar file isn't compressed, although additional software can be used to compress it. tar files aren't very sophisticated compared to modern archive file formats. They're not encrypted, for example, but this can also be one of their advantages.

■**Note** Linux comes with a couple more backup commands, which you might choose to use. They are cpio and pax. Both aim to improve on tar in various ways, but neither is broadly supported at the moment. cpio is installed by default under Ubuntu, and pax can be found via the Synaptic Package Manager. Examine their man pages for more details.

Creating tar Files

Perhaps unsurprisingly, tar files are created at the console using the tar command. Usually, all that's needed is to specify a source directory and a filename, which can be done like so:

```
tar -cf mybackup.tar /home/keir/
```

This will create a backup called mybackup.tar based on the contents of /home/keir/. tar is automatically recursive so, in this example, it will delve into all subdirectories beneath /home/ keir. The -c command option tells tar you're going to create an archive, and the -f option indicates that the filename for the archive will immediately follow. If you don't use the -f option, tar will send its output to standard output, which means that it will display the contents of the archive on the screen.

If you typed in a command like the preceding example, you would see this message:

```
Removing leading '/' from member names.
```

This means that the folders and files added to the archive will all have the initial forward slash removed from their paths. So, rather than store a file in the archive as this:

```
/home/keir/Mail/file1
```

The file will be stored as follows:

```
home/keir/Mail/file1
```

The difference between the two forms concerns when the files are later extracted from the archive. If the files have the initial slash, tar will write the file to /home/keir/Mail/file1. If there's already a file of that name in that location, it will be overwritten. On the other hand, with the leading slash removed, tar will create a new directory wherever you choose to restore the archive. In this example, it will create a new directory called home, and then a directory called keir within that, and so on.

Because of the potential of accidentally overwriting data by specifying absolute paths in this way, a better way of backing up a directory is simply to change into its parent and specify it without a full path:

```
cd /home/
tar -cf mybackup.tar keir
```

When this particular archive is restored, it will simply create a new folder called keir wherever it's restored.

Compressing tar Archives

You can also compress the archive from within tar, although it actually calls in outside help from either bzip2 or gzip, depending on which you specify.

To create a tar archive compressed using bzip2, the following should do the trick:

```
tar -cjf mybackup.tar.bz2 keir
```

This will create a compressed backup from the directory keir. The -j command option passes the output from tar to the bzip2 program, although this is done in the background. Notice the change in the backup filename extension to indicate that this is a bzip2 compressed archive.

The following command will create an archive compressed with the older `gzip` compression:

```
tar -czf mybackup.tar.gz keir
```

This uses the `-z` command option to pass the output to `gzip`. This time, the filename shows it's a `gzip` compressed archive, so you can correctly identify it in the future.

Extracting Files from a tar Archive

Extracting files using `tar` is as easy as creating them:

```
tar -xf mybackup.tar
```

The `-x` option tells `tar` to extract the files from the `maybackup.tar` archive.

Extracting compressed archives is simply a matter of adding the `-j` or `-z` option to the `-x` option:

```
tar -xjf mybackup.tar.bz2
```

■**Note** Technically speaking, `tar` doesn't require the preceding hyphen before its command options. However, it's a good idea to use it anyway, so you won't forget to use it with other commands in the future.

Viewing tar Archive Information

To view the contents of a `tar` archive without actually restoring the files, use the `-t` option:

```
tar -tf mybackup.tar |less
```

This example adds a pipe into `less` at the end, because the listing of files probably will be large and scroll off the screen. Just add the `-j` or `-z` option if the `tar` archive is also compressed.

In addition, you can add the `-v` option to all stages of making, extracting, and viewing an archive to see more information (chiefly the files that are being archived or extracted).

Typing `-vv` provides even more information:

```
tar -cvvf mybackup.tar keir
```

This will create an archive and also show a complete directory listing as the files and folders are added, including permissions.

Saving the File to a CD-R/RW

Once the `tar` file has been created, the problem of where to store it arises. As I mentioned earlier, storing backup data on the same hard disk as the data it was created to back up is foolish, since any problem that might affect the hard disk might also affect the archive. You could end up losing both sets of data!

If the archive is less than 700MB, it might be possible to store it on a CD-R or CD-RW. To do this from the command line, first the file must be turned into an ISO image, and then it must be burned.

■**Note** Remember that the Ubuntu desktop has a very capable CD/DVD burning tool that can save the hassle of working at the command-line prompt. To access it, click Places ➤ CD/DVD Creator. Simply drag the backup file(s) onto the Nautilus window, and then click the Write To Disc button.

To turn it into an ISO image, use the `mkisofs` command:

```
mkisofs -o backup.iso mybackup.tar.bz2
```

You can then burn the ISO image to a CD by using the `cdrecord` command. Before using this, you must determine what device name your CD writer uses. In an average system, the CD-R/RW drive is attached to the master connection on the secondary IDE channel, and in that case, the device name is `/dev/hdc`. You must specify this using the `dev=` command option with `cdrecord`, and you must also specify the speed at which you wish the burn to take place using the `speed=` command option. This is the writing spin-speed of the drive, which is usually mentioned in the drive's documentation.

Put together, to burn the backup image, all you need to do is enter a command in this format:

```
cdrecord dev=<device name> speed=<speed of your drive> mybackup.iso
```

On my test system, this took the following form:

```
cdrecord dev=/dev/hdc speed=24 mybackup.iso
```

You'll need to eject and then reinsert the newly burned disc before you can examine its contents.

Saving the File to a DVD Disc

If the backup file is larger than a CD-R/RW disc, you might want to burn the backup file to DVD, using a DVD+-R/RW drive. You can use the `growisofs` command for this. You don't need to create an ISO file for this command, because one is created automatically in the background. Instead, you simply specify the file(s) you want to back up.

Apart from this difference, `growisofs` works along the same lines as `cdrecord`, and the following command should do the trick (again assuming the DVD writer is connected to the master connection of the secondary IDE channel: `/dev/hdc`):

```
growisofs -Z /dev/hdc -R -J mybackup.tar.bz2
```

If the DVD disc has any space left, then you can simply add your next backup to the disc, alongside the older file. To do this, use the -M command option, instead of -Z:

```
growisofs -M /dev/hdc -R -J mybackup2.tar.bz2
```

In both cases, you'll have to eject the DVD-ROM and then reinsert it in order to read its contents.

■**Note** Remember that you can use the man command to learn about any commands, including those detailed here. In the case of cdrecord and growisofs in particular, this is worthwhile, because they are very powerful pieces of software.

Summary

In this chapter, we looked at making backups. First, you saw how to verify where your personal and other vital data is stored. Then we looked at how the Simple Backup tool can be used to back up system configuration and personal data. Finally, you learned how to use tar at the command line to back up any kind of data.

In the next chapter, we'll look at how tasks can be scheduled to occur at various times under Ubuntu.

CHAPTER 32

███

Scheduling Tasks

In this book, you've learned about various tasks you can perform to keep Ubuntu running smoothly. You may decide that you want some of these tasks to occur on a regular basis. For example, perhaps you want your /home folder to be backed up every day, or perhaps you want to clean the /tmp folder to ensure that you always have enough free disk space. You could carry out each task individually, but human nature would no doubt step in, and you would forget, or you might perform the action twice, because you've forgotten that you've already done it.

As you might expect, Linux is able to automate the running of particular tasks. They can be run either periodically at scheduled times or as one-time tasks. Using Linux's scheduling features is explained in this chapter.

Scheduling with crontab

Under Ubuntu, the main way of scheduling tasks is via the cron daemon. This works on behalf of the user in order to schedule individual tasks, and it is also used by the system to run vital system tasks, although a different way of working is used in each case.

For cron to run user-scheduled tasks, it reads a file called crontab. Each user has her own version of this file, which is stored in the /var/spool/cron/crontabs directory. This file can be edited in a text editor, but a special command should be used to do so.

Note System-wide tasks are handled by the /etc/crontab/ file. This runs scripts contained in /etc/cron.hourly, /etc/cron.daily, and so on, depending on when the tasks are meant to be run (every hour, day, week, or month). The average user never needs to bother with system-wide cron jobs. These are handled by the internal system, and programs create their own entries as and when necessary.

The cron daemon starts at bootup and simply sits in the background while you work, checking every minute to see if a task is due. As soon as one comes up, it commences the task, and then returns to a waiting status.

Creating a Scheduled Task

Adding a scheduled task is relatively easy and is done via the shell. Entering the following command will cause your personal crontab file to be loaded into the GNU nano text editor, ready for editing:

```
crontab -e
```

If this is the first time you've edited your crontab file, you'll see a comment line at the top. Comments in configuration files are nearly always preceded by hash symbols, as here. The hash tells Ubuntu not to try and interpret that line and to ignore it. This particular comment line outlines the protocol for adding an entry to the file, which I also explain later. You can delete the comment line if you want. Adding a new entry is relatively easy and normally takes the form of something like this:

```
01 12 15 * * tar -cjf /home/keir/mybackup.tar.bz2 /home/keir
```

Let's examine the line piece by piece. The first part—the numbers and asterisks—refers to when the task should be run. From left to right, the fields refer to the following:

- Minutes, from 0 to 59

- Hours, in 24-hour time, so from 0 to 23

- Day dates, for the day of the month, from 1 to 31 (assuming the month has that many days)

- Months, from 1 to 12

- Day, for a particular day, either from 0 to 6 (0 is Sunday), or specified as a three-letter abbreviation (mon, tue, wed, and so on)

In the example, the task is set to run at the first minute at the twelfth hour (midday) on the fifteenth day of the month. But what do the asterisks stand for? They're effectively wildcards and tell cron that every possible value applies. Because an asterisk appears in the month field, this task will be run every month. Because an asterisk appears in the day field, the task will be run every day.

You might have noticed a logical contradiction here. How can you specify a day if you also specify a date in the month? Wouldn't this seriously limit the chances of the task ever running? Yes, it would. If you were to specify sat, for example, and put 15 in the date field, the task would run on only the fifteenth of the month if that happened to be a Saturday. This is why the two fields are rarely used in the same crontab entry, and an asterisk appears in one if the other is being used.

After the time and date fields comes the command itself: `tar`. As you learned in the previous chapter, `tar` is designed to back up your personal data.

Only standard BASH shell commands can be used in the command section. `cron` isn't clever enough to interpret symbols such as the tilde (~) as a way of referring to your `home` directory. For this reason, it's best to be very thorough when defining a `cron` job and always use absolute paths.

Let's take a look at another example (shown in Figure 32-1):

```
59 23 * * 0-3 tar -cjf /home/keir/mybackup.tar.bz2 /home/keir
```

Figure 32-1. *Editing* `crontab` *lets you schedule tasks using the nano text editor.*

The first field says that this task will run at the fifty-ninth minute of the twenty-third hour (that is, one minute before midnight). The date and month fields have asterisks, so this implies that the task should run every day and every month. However, the day field contains `0-3`. This says that the task should run on only days 0 through to 3, or Sunday through Wednesday.

You can have as many `cron` entries as you like; simply give each a separate line. You don't need to put them in date or time order. You can just add them as and when you see fit.

When you're finished, save the file and quit GNU nano in the usual way (by pressing Ctrl+X). You'll be prompted to save the file to the `/tmp` directory, but this is fine. Just hit Enter. The `cron` file will be copied into the correct location as soon as nano quits.

Scheduling with anacron

If cron has an Achilles' heel, it is that it expects your computer to be up and running all the time. If you schedule a task for around midnight, as in one of the previous examples, and your computer isn't switched on at that time, the task simply won't run.

anacron was created to fix this problem (see Figure 32-2). It also can run scheduled tasks, but unlike cron, it doesn't rely on exact times or dates. Instead, it works on the principle of time periods. For example, tasks can be set to run every day. In fact, tasks can be set to run every *x* number of days, regardless of whether that's every two days or every hundred thousand. It also doesn't matter if the computer is shut down and rebooted during that time; the task will be run only once in the specified time period. In addition, tasks can be specifically set to run at the beginning of each month, regardless of the length in days of each month.

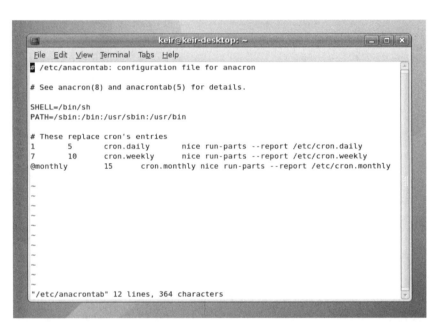

Figure 32-2. *anacron is used to run tasks periodically, such as every couple of days.*

anacron is primarily designed to be used for system maintenance, and the /etc/anacrontab file holds the details of the tasks. Unlike as with crontab, each user doesn't have his own anacrontab file. However, there's no reason why you can't add your own commands to the main anacrontab file. This file can be edited in any text editor, and you don't need to use a special command to edit it (as with crontab), although you'll need to adopt superuser powers to do so.

Each line in `anacrontab` takes the following form:

days   *delay*   `name of task`   *command*

The days field holds the number of days in between the running of the task. To set the task to run every day, you would enter 1. To make the task run every nine days, you would add 9. To set it to run monthly, you should type `@monthly`.

The delay field tells `anacron` how long to wait after it's run before running the task, specified in minutes. It is necessary because `anacron` is usually run at bootup, and if it were to run the scheduled tasks instantly, the machine would grind to a halt because it is already busy. A delay of five minutes is usually adequate, although if some tasks are already scheduled to run on the same day before that task, you should allow enough time for them to finish.

The name of task field is for your personal reference and shouldn't contain either slashes or spaces (hint: separate words using underscores or periods).

The command field is, as with `crontab`, the shell command that should be run.

■**Note** `anacron` is run as the root user, so if you do add your own entry to `anacrontab`, any files it creates will be owned by root, too. If you use `anacron` to create a backup of your /home directory, for example, the resultant backup file will be owned by root, and you'll need to use the `chown` command to change its owner-ship so you can access it. See Chapter 14 for more information about the `chown` command.

Let's look at an example of an `anacrontab` entry:

```
1    15    backup_job    tar -cjf /home/keir/mybackup.tar.bz2 /home/keir
```

This will run the specified `tar` command every day (because 1 is in the days field), and with a delay of 15 minutes after `anacron` is first run.

`anacron` is run automatically every time you boot, but you can also run it manually by simply typing it at the command prompt (with superuser powers):

```
sudo anacron
```

Using at to Schedule One-Off Tasks

What if you quickly want to schedule a one-time-only task? For this, you can use the `at` command.

Adding a job with `at` is very easy, largely because the `at` command accepts a wide variety of time formats. For example, typing the following at the command prompt will run a job at lunchtime tomorrow:

```
at noon tomorrow
```

It really is as simple as that!

Alternatively, you can specify a time, date, and even a year:

```
at 13:00 jun 25 2008
```

This will run the job at 1 p.m. on June 25, 2008. The various time and date formats are explained in the at command's man page.

Once the at command containing the date has been entered, you'll be presented with a mock shell prompt. Here, you can type the commands you want to run. Many shell commands can be entered, one after the other; just press Enter between them. Then press Ctrl+D to signal that you're finished editing. At this point, at will confirm the time and write the task into its list.

You can view the list at any time by typing atq. This will show a list of numbered jobs. You can remove any job by typing atrm, followed by its atq job number. For example, the following will remove the job numbered 9 in the atq list:

```
atrm 9
```

Summary

In this brief chapter, we looked at how you can schedule tasks under Ubuntu, which is essentially making programs run at certain times. We examined the crontab and anacron facilities, which can schedule tasks to run periodically, and we also examined the at service, which can schedule one-off tasks to run at certain times.

In the final chapter of this book, we will look at how you can access your Ubuntu computer remotely—theoretically, from any Internet-equipped location in the world.

■■■

## CHAPTER 33

Accessing Computers Remotely

One area where Linux particularly excels is in its support for networking, including the Internet. If you wish to learn about how networks operate on a fundamental level, then Linux is an ideal choice, because it puts you in virtually direct contact with the technology.

The widespread integration and support for networking extends to several useful system tools, which let you access Linux across any kind of network, including the Internet. In fact, it's even possible to access a Linux machine running on a different continent, just as if you were sitting in front of it!

This chapter looks at the many ways you can access your Ubuntu computer remotely. In addition, we look at the ways that you can use Ubuntu to access almost any other computer, including Windows PCs.

Using Secure Shell

The history of Unix has always featured computers connecting to other computers in some fashion, whether they were dumb terminals connecting to a mainframe computer or Unix machines acting as nodes on the fledgling Internet. Because of this, a wide variety of techniques and protocols were invented to allow computers to communicate and log in to each other across networks. However, while these still work fine over the modern Internet, we're now faced with new threats to the privacy of data. In theory, any data transmitted across the Internet can be picked up by individuals at certain key stages along the route. If the data isn't protected in any way, it can be easily intercepted and read.

To counter such an occurrence, the ssh suite of programs was created. Although these programs started as open source, they gradually became proprietary. Therefore, several newer open-source versions were created, including the one used on the majority of Linux distributions (including Ubuntu): OpenSSH.

The goal of ssh is to create a secure connection between two computers. You can then do just about any task, including initiating a shell session so you can use the remote computer as if you were sitting in front of it, or copying files to and from. ssh uses various techniques at both ends of the connection to encrypt not only the data passing between the two machines, but also the username and password.

■**Note** This chapter refers to *remote* and *local* machines. The *remote* machine is the computer you're connecting to across the network or Internet. The *local* machine is the one you're actually sitting in front of. These two terms are widely used within documentation describing networking.

Logging In to a Remote Computer

The most basic type of ssh connection is a remote login. This will give you a command prompt on the remote computer, as if you had just sat down in front of it and opened GNOME Terminal.

But before you can log in to any machine via ssh, you'll need to be sure the remote computer is able to accept ssh connections. This means that it needs to be running the ssh server program (referred to as a *service*), and also that its firewall has an open port for incoming connections.

The two major components of OpenSSH are the client and server. Most distributions install both items and run the server component all the time. However, only the client component of SSH is installed under Ubuntu. To install the server component, and therefore access your Ubuntu system remotely, you'll need to open Synaptic Package Manager (System ➤ Administration) and search for openssh-server. Click to install it. Configuration will be automatic, although if you're using the Ubuntu firewall (see Chapter 9), you will need to configure an incoming rule to open port 22.

■**Tip** If you use Firestarter, as described in Chapter 9, you can simply select the default incoming SSH rule. There's no need to manually specify a port number.

Initiating an ssh remote shell session with a remote machine is usually achieved by typing something similar to the following at a command prompt on the local machine:

```
ssh <username>@<IP address>
```

In other words, you specify the username you want to log in as, as well as the IP address of the machine. If there's a fully qualified domain name (FQDN) for the system you want to access, you could specify that instead of the IP address.

■**Note** An FQDN is the hostname of a system plus its Internet address, such as `mycomputer.example.com`. Unless you have had this function specifically set up for you by a system administrator, you'll probably have to connect via IP addresses. However, if you rent a web server, you might be able to `ssh` into it using the domain name of the server.

You'll be prompted for your password which, obviously, is the password for the account you're trying to log in to on the *remote* computer.

When you log in for the first time, you'll see the following message:

```
The authenticity of the host <host IP address> can't be established
```

Figure 33-1 shows an example. This means that the remote computer's encryption key hasn't yet been added to your PC's store file. However, once you agree to the initial login, the encryption key will be added, and it will be used in the future to confirm that the remote computer you're connecting to is authentic.

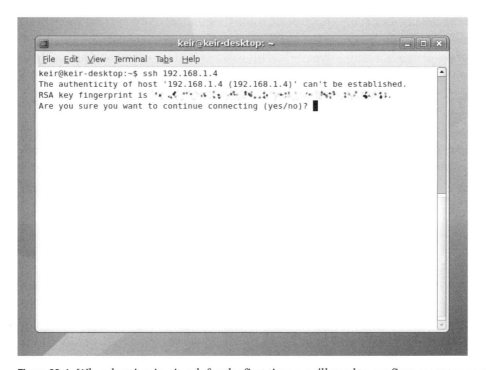

Figure 33-1. *When logging in via ssh for the first time, you'll need to confirm acceptance of the encryption key.*

■**Note** There's a fine line between security concern and paranoia. Connecting to a remote machine for the first time and accepting its ssh key is considered insecure by some people, because you cannot be 100% sure that the remote machine is the one you want to connect to. It might have been swapped for a different machine by hackers (or some such theory). In addition, the key might be intercepted on its journey to you. Because of this, those who are highly security conscious can use the ssh-keygen program to create a key on the remote machine first, and then import it to the local machine via floppy disk before logging in. See the ssh-keygen man page for more details.

After confirming that you want to make the connection, you'll be invited to enter the password for the user account under which you initiated the ssh connection. Once this is done, you should find yourself with a shell login on the remote computer. You can run the same commands as usual and perform identical tasks.

The machine you're logged in to will show no symptoms of being used remotely. This isn't like the movies, where what you type on your local machine is somehow mirrored on the remote machine for all to see. However, obviously, if a user of the remote machine were to view her network connections using something similar to the netstat command, then she would see another computer attached via ssh.

To end an ssh session, simply type exit. This will then return you to the command prompt on your own machine.

■**Tip** There's a version of the ssh client that runs on a variety of non-Linux operating systems, making it possible to log in to your Ubuntu machine from a Windows computer. The program is called PuTTY and can be downloaded from www.chiark.greenend.org.uk/~sgtatham/putty/.

MANAGING REMOTE SESSIONS

Whenever you open any kind of shell to enter commands and run programs, you might have noticed that any commands you start running last only as long as the shell window is open. When the shell window is closed, any task running within it ends, too. This is because the shell is seen as the "owner" of the process, and when the owner dies, any processes it started also die.

When using ssh to start a remote shell session, this also applies. Whenever you log out, any tasks you were running are ended. This can be annoying if, for example, you've started a lengthy download on the remote machine. Effectively, you must remain logged in via ssh until the download has finished.

To get around this, you can use the handy screen program. This isn't specifically designed to be an aid to remote logins, but there's no reason why it cannot be used in such a situation.

The `screen` program effectively starts shell sessions that stick around, even if the shell window is closed or the `ssh` connection is ended or lost. After logging in to the remote computer via `ssh`, you can start a `screen` session by simply typing the program name at the prompt:

```
screen
```

After pressing the spacebar as prompted to start the program, there won't be any indication that you're running a `screen` session. There's no taskbar at the bottom of the terminal window, for example. `screen` works completely in the background.

Let's consider what happens when you detach and then reattach to a `screen` session. To detach from the `screen` session, press Ctrl+A and then Ctrl+D. You'll then be returned to the standard shell and, in fact, you could now disconnect from your `ssh` session as usual. However, the `screen` session will still be running in the background on the remote computer. To prove this, you could log back in, and then type this:

```
screen -r
```

This will resume your `screen` session, and you should be able to pick up quite literally where you left off; any output from previous commands will be displayed.

To quit a screen session, you can either type `exit` from within it or press Ctrl+A, and then Ctrl+\ (backslash).

The `screen` program is very powerful. To learn more about it, read its man page. To see a list of its keyboard commands, press Ctrl+A, and then type a question mark (?) while `screen` is running.

Transferring Files Between Remote Computers

The `ssh` utility brings with it two basic ways of transferring files between machines: `scp` and `sftp`. `scp` is fine for smaller file transfers, but if you want to copy a lot of files, `sftp` is probably a better choice.

Using scp

Strictly speaking, `scp` is merely a program that copies files from one computer to another in a secure fashion using the underlying `ssh` protocol. You don't have to be logged in to another computer via `ssh` to use it. For example, if I were merely browsing my own computer and wanted to transfer a file to a remote computer, I could type:

```
scp myfile keir@<IP address>:/home/keir/
```

I would replace `<IP address>` with the IP address of the computer to which I wanted to send the file. In other words, you must first specify the local file you want to copy across, and then provide the login details for the remote computer in the same format as with an `ssh` login. Then, after a colon, you specify the path on the *remote* computer where you would like the file to be copied.

Note If it helps, consider the latter part of the scp command after the filename as one large address: first you provide your username, then the computer address, and then the path.

Using the command when you *are* logged in to another computer via ssh works in exactly the same way. Let's consider an example.

Assume there are two computers: A and B. I have a user account on each one. So sitting at the keyboard of A, I establish an ssh connection with B by typing the following:

```
ssh keir@computer_B
```

This lets me log in to B as if I were sitting in front of it. I spot a file called spreadsheet.xls that I want to copy to my local machine (A). I therefore issue the following command:

```
scp spreadsheet.xls keir@computer_A:/home/keir/
```

This will copy the file from computer B to computer A and place it in the /home/keir/ directory.

Tip With scp, you can copy entire directories, too. Simply add the -r command option, like so: scp -r *mydirectory <username>@<IP address>:/path/*.

Using sftp

To copy a lot of files to or from a remote computer, the sftp program is the best solution. If you've ever used a shell-based ftp program, you'll feel right at home, because sftp isn't very different.

You can initiate a sftp session by using this command format:

```
sftp <username>@<IP address>
```

The same rules as when you're logging in with ssh apply, both in terms of formatting the login command and also confirming the encryption key if this is the first time you've logged in.

The sftp commands are fairly basic. For example, to copy a file from the remote machine, simply type this:

```
get <filename>
```

This will copy the file into the directory you were in on the local machine before you started the sftp session.

By specifying a path after the filename, the file will be copied to the specified local directory:

```
get spreadsheet.xls /home/keir/downloaded_files/
```

Sending files from the local machine to the remote machine is just as easy:

```
put <filename>
```

By specifying a path after the filename, you can ensure the file is saved to a particular remote path.

One useful thing to remember is that any command preceded by an exclamation mark (!, called a bang in Linux-speak) is executed on the local machine as a shell command. So, if you wanted to remove a file on the local machine, you could type this:

```
!rm -rf <filename>
```

Simply typing a bang symbol on its own starts a shell session on the local machine, so you can perform even more tasks. When you're finished, type exit to return to the sftp program.

For a list of popular sftp commands, see Table 33-1.

Table 33-1. *sftp Commands*

Command	Function
cd	Change the remote directory
lcd	Change the local directory
get	Download the specified file
ls	List the remote directory
lls	List the local directory
mkdir	Create a directory on the remote machine
lmkdir	Create a directory on the local machine
put	Upload the specified file to the remote machine
pwd	Print the current remote directory
rmdir	Delete the remote directory
rm	Delete the remote file
exit	Quit sftp
!command	Execute the specified command on the local machine
!	Start a temporary local shell session (type exit to return to sftp)
help	Show a list of commands

Accessing GUI Applications Remotely

So far, we've looked at connecting to a remote machine using command-line tools. But Ubuntu is based around the graphical desktop, so is there any way of running, say, a Nautilus file browser window so you can manipulate files on the remote machine? Yes!

The graphical subsystem of Linux, X, is designed to work across a network. In fact, if you run Linux on your desktop PC, X *still* works via a loopback network within your machine (meaning that network commands are sent out but addressed to the very same machine on which they originated). Because of this, it's possible to make programs on a remote machine run on a local machine's X server. The actual work of running the application is handled by the *remote* machine, but the work of displaying the graphics is handled by the *local* machine.

■**Caution** X connections across a network can be a little slow and certainly not as snappy as running the same application on the local machine. This lag can become irritating after a while.

Running X Applications on a Remote Computer

Unfortunately, X server communications aren't normally encrypted, so if one machine were to simply connect to an X server over a network (or even the Internet), the data transfer would be unencrypted and open to eavesdroppers.

But ssh once again comes to the rescue. You can configure ssh so that X applications on the remote computer can be run on the local machine, with the data sent through the ssh connection. Log in to the remote machine using ssh, but also specify the -X flag:

```
ssh -X <username>@<IP address>
```

When you're logged in, you can simply start any application by typing its name as usual. The only difference is that the program will appear on the screen of the local machine, rather than on the remote machine, as shown in Figure 33-2.

Using X across the Internet or even a local network isn't very fast, and you can expect delays when you open menus or if the screen must frequently redraw. However, it can prove very useful.

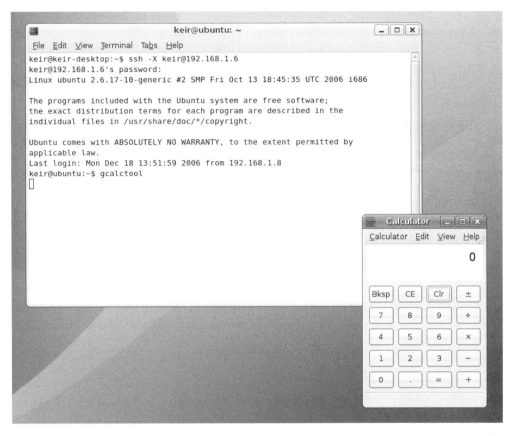

Figure 33-2. *Although the calculator application appears on the local computer's display, it's actually running on the remote machine.*

Accessing Ubuntu via Remote Desktop

A less secure but more convenient way to access your Ubuntu PC's desktop applications across a network is to use Ubuntu's Remote Desktop feature. The advantage of this method is that the entire desktop of the remote computer appears in a window on the local computer's desktop.

Remote Desktop uses the Virtual Network Computing (VNC) software to share the desktop. *Sharing* is the key word because, effectively, anyone who connects will take control of the main desktop. They will control the mouse and keyboard input.

However, there are a couple of important differences compared to accessing X across an ssh connection:

- Although the password is sent encrypted, the rest of the VNC data transfers aren't. Complete encryption is possible using special versions of VNC, or via an OpenSSH tunnel, but this can be difficult to set up on the Windows end of the connection.

- The remote desktop isn't blanked, so anyone standing in front of the computer will be able to see what you're doing. This could present a security/privacy risk.

If you're prepared to put up with these caveats, then allowing remote desktop access on a computer is easy. Here's the procedure:

1. Click System ➤ Preferences and then click Remote Desktop. Put a check alongside Allow Other Users to View Your Desktop and ensure there's a check in the box alongside Allow Other Users to Control Your Desktop, as shown in Figure 33-3. Beneath this option, you can choose whether the user can confirm each connection and whether you want to set a password. Both options add to the security of your system, although the confirmation option will mean that someone will have to be at the computer to authorize an incoming connection.

Figure 33-3. *Ubuntu's Remote Desktop feature lets you share your desktop but isn't as secure as making an X server connection across SSH.*

Note Ignore the information in the dialog box about how users can view your desktop. Instead, you should find out your computer's IP address and use that.

---

2. On the computer from which you want to connect to the remote desktop, click Applications ➤ Internet ➤ Terminal Server Client. In the Computer field, enter the IP address of the computer you wish to connect to. In the Protocol drop-down list, select VNC. Then click Connect.

3. You'll be prompted to enter the password, if one is applicable, and you should then see the remote computer's desktop in a window. Once you've finished, simply close the window to terminate the connection.

Connecting to Remote Windows Computers

The Terminal Server Client program allows you to connect to a variety of remote desktop server programs and, in particular, Windows Vista, XP, or 2000 computers via the Remote Desktop Protocol (RDP). Unfortunately, Windows XP Home, Me, 98, and 95 don't support RDP connections, which means that they aren't able to run an RDP server and allow other computers to access their desktops. However, there is a way to access the desktop of these computers remotely using some add-in software.

Connecting to Windows Vista

The Terminal Server Client program is actually the graphical front-end for a handful of command-line programs, including rdesktop, which is used to connect to Windows Vista, XP, and 2000 computers. Unfortunately, the version of rdesktop supplied with Ubuntu needs to be updated in order to connect to Windows Vista. This involves downloading a third-party package created by an Ubuntu community member. Visit www.getdeb.net/ search.php?release=Edgy&keywords=rdesktop, and click to download the package to the desktop. Open a terminal window (Applications ➤ Accessories ➤ Terminal), and type the following to install the package:

```
sudo dpkg -i rdesktop_1.5.0-1getdeb1_i386.deb
```

Obviously, you should substitute the filename for the one you downloaded.

Before initiating the connection, you should ensure the Windows Vista computer is set for incoming remote connections, if you haven't already. Start by ensuring that your Vista account has a password—Terminal Server Client won't be able to connect otherwise. Next, ensure that Vista's remote desktop feature is activated. Click the Start button, and then right-click Computer. Click Properties, and in the window that appears, click the Remote Settings link on the left-hand side. In the dialog that appears, click Allow Connections from Computers Running Any Version of Remote Desktop (Less Secure), and click Apply.

■**Note** These instructions assume that you intend to connect using a Vista administrator username and password. If not, you'll need to click the Select Users button and add the user accounts you wish to use.

Back on the Ubuntu computer, click Applications ➤ Internet ➤ Terminal Server Client. Once the program is running, in the Computer field, type either the IP address of the machine or its FQDN (if applicable). You don't need to type the username, password, or any other details. Click Connect, and a new window should appear, in which you should see a login prompt. You should then log in to Windows using your username and password.

Connecting to Windows XP Professional, 2000, and NT

Here, I use an XP Professional machine as an example, but the instructions are valid for 2000 and NT, too.

You'll find the Terminal Server Client program on the Applications ➤ Internet menu. Once it's running, in the Computer field, type either the IP address of the machine or its FQDN (if applicable). You don't need to type the username, password, or any other details. Click Connect, and a new window should appear in which you should see an XP login prompt. You should then log in to Windows using your username and password.

■**Caution** If you haven't set a password for your user account on the Windows machine, you won't be able to log in. This is a quirk of the Windows XP RDP system. The solution is simple: use the User Accounts applet within the Windows Control Panel to assign yourself a password.

Of course, the XP computer will need be configured to allow incoming RDP connections. To configure it, right-click My Computer, selecting Properties, click the Remote tab, and make sure Allow Users to Connect Remotely to This Computer is checked, as shown in Figure 33-4. The Windows computer to which you want to connect may also need to be updated with the latest service packs, particularly in the case of a Windows 2000 computer.

Figure 33-4. *You can access remote Windows XP Professional machines using RDP and the Terminal Server Client program.*

If this is the first time you've accessed the Windows computer over an RDP connection, you might be wondering why the graphics look so bad. This is because they're heavily compressed in order to transmit efficiently across networks.

Connecting to Other Windows Computers

You can download a VNC server for just about any operating system. Windows and Linux are supported, as is Macintosh OS X. In fact, a VNC server will run on any Windows computer, from 95 upwards. Once it's installed, you can then use the Terminal Server Client program within Ubuntu to connect to that computer's remote desktop.

Note In fact, any computer that's running the VNC Viewer program can access a computer running a VNC server (including the one set up by Ubuntu's Remote Desktop feature). Various VNC Viewer programs are available for Linux, Windows, Macintosh OS X, and other operating systems, including the likes of PocketPC. Just search the Web using "VNC Viewer" as a search string to find viewer programs.

Of course, you'll have the same insecurities and lack of desktop blanking that plague VNC connections to a Ubuntu desktop, as described previously. But if you're prepared to accept this, you'll be pleased to hear that setting up the VNC server on the Windows machine is easy. TightVNC, available from `www.tightvnc.com`, is one of the best variations of VNC around. You should download the Self-Installing Package for Windows. During installation, you'll be asked if you want to register TightVNC as a system service. Click the check box alongside this option. This will activate the VNC server every time the computer starts.

Once the program has installed, the server configuration program will appear. You should change the password by overtyping the default in the Password field.

Connecting to the remote Windows machine is also a piece of cake. On the Ubuntu system, open Terminal Server Client (Applications ➤ Internet) and type the remote computer's IP address into the Computer field. In the Protocol drop-down list, select VNC. Then click Connect. There's no need to fill in any of the other details. You'll be prompted for the remote computer's VNC server password and, once you enter this, the remote desktop will appear in a window. Figure 33-5 shows an example of connecting to a Windows 98 computer.

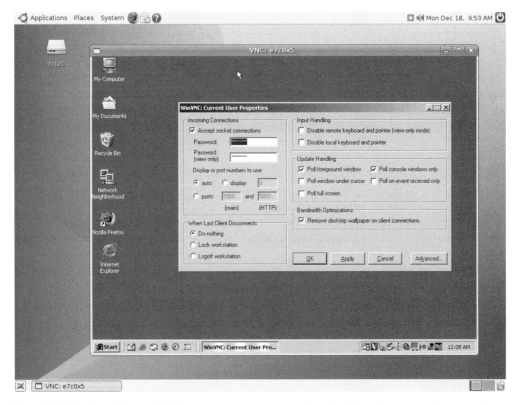

Figure 33-5. *By installing a VNC server, you can connect to just about any remote operating system, including Windows 98 (as here).*

Summary

In this chapter, we looked at how you can access your Ubuntu computer remotely across the Internet. We examined how you can access the computer as if you were sitting in front of it, using the ssh program. This allows you to start a command-line prompt and even run GUI programs on the remote computer.

In addition, we discussed how the screen program can be used to keep sessions alive across various logins, and how you can transfer files using the sftp and scp programs. Then we looked at how to use the Terminal Server Client tool to access the desktop of remote Windows computers.

PART 8

■■■

Appendixes

■ ■ ■

Glossary of Linux Terms

This appendix provides brief explanations of common terms used in the Linux and Unix environments. These include technical terms, as well as conventions used within the Linux community. Because of space limitations, this glossary is somewhat selective, but still should prove a lasting reference as well as a helpful guide for those new to Linux.

Cross-referenced terms are highlighted in italics.

Symbols

.

Symbol that, in the context of file management, refers to the current directory.

..

Symbol that, in the context of file management, refers to the parent directory of that currently being browsed.

/

Symbol that, in the context of file management, refers to the *root* of the file system; also separates directories in a path listing.

~

Symbol that, in the context of file management, refers to a user's home directory.

|

Pipe symbol; used at the *command prompt* to *pipe* output from one *command* to another.

>

Symbol that, when used at the *command prompt*, indicates output should *redirect* into a file.

<

Symbol that, when used at the *command prompt*, indicates a *command* should accept input from a file (see *redirect*).

#

Symbol that, when it appears on the *command prompt*, usually indicates the user is currently logged in as *root*.

$

Symbol that, when it appears on the command prompt, usually indicates the user is currently logged in as an ordinary user. (Note that some versions of *Linux/ Unix* use % or > instead of $.)

?

Wildcard character indicating that any character can be substituted in its place.

*

Wildcard character indicating that zero or more characters can appear in its place.

*nix

Popular but unofficial way of describing the family tree that comprises *Unix* and its various clones, such as *Linux* and *Minix*.

A

administrator

Another word for either the *root* user or one who has adopted that user's powers temporarily.

AIX

IBM's *proprietary* form of *Unix* that runs on the company's proprietary hardware, as well as *commodity* hardware based around AMD and Intel processors. Nowadays, IBM is slowly deprecating AIX in favor of *Linux*.

alias

Method of creating a user-defined *command* that, when typed, causes another command to be run or a *string* to be expanded.

Apache

Popular *Open Source* web server software that runs on *Unix*, *Linux*, and other operating system platforms. Considered responsible in part for the rise in popularity of Linux in the late 1990s.

applet

Small program that, in the context of the *Ubuntu* desktop, runs as part of a larger program and offers functions that complement the main program. The *GNOME* desktop incorporates several applets in its notification area.

APT

Advanced Packaging Tool; the underlying system by which software is managed and installed on *Ubuntu* and *Debian Linux* systems. *Shell* commands beginning with apt, such as apt-get, are used to install new software from various repositories. Under Ubuntu, the Synaptic Package Manager program provides a *GUI* method of using APT.

archive

Any file containing a collection of smaller files, compressed or otherwise (see also *tar*).

B

BASH

Bourne Again SHell. The most common *shell* interpreter used under *Linux* and offered as default on many Linux systems.

binary executable

Another way of referring to a program that has been compiled so that it can be used day-to-day. See also *compile*.

block device

How the *Linux kernel* communicates with a *device* that sends and receives blocks of data; usually a hard disk or removable storage device. See also *character device*.

BSD Unix

Berkeley Software Distribution Unix; form of *Unix* partially based on the original Unix *source code* but also incorporating recent developments. BSD is *open source* and free for all to use and share with practically no restrictions. There are various forms of BSD Unix, such as FreeBSD, NetBSD, and OpenBSD. BSD doesn't use the *Linux kernel*, but it runs many of the same programs. Some of the programs offered within the Linux operating system come from BSD.

bzip2

Form of file compression. Together with the older and less efficient *gzip*, it is a popular form of file compression under *Linux* and the equivalent to Zip compression under Windows. Files employing bzip compression are usually given a .bz2 file extension. See also *tar*.

C

C

Programming language in which much of the *Linux kernel* is written, as were later versions of *Unix* before it. C was created by some of the same people who created Unix, and its development mirrors that of Unix.

C++

Object-oriented programming language; originally designed to be an enhancement to *C*, but now seen as a popular alternative.

C#

Modern programming language, which uses similar syntax to *C*, created by Microsoft and re-created on *Linux* via the Mono project.

character device

How Linux refers to a *device* that sends/receives data asynchronously. For various technical reasons, this typically refers to the *terminal* display. See also *block device*.

checksum

Mathematical process that can be applied to a file or other data to create a unique number relative to the contents of that file. If the file is modified, the checksum will change, usually indicating that the file in question has failed to download correctly or has been modified in some way. The most common type of checksum program used under *Linux* is md5sum.

client

Shorthand referring to a computer that connects to a *server*.

closed source

The reverse of *Open Source* in which the *source code* is not available for others to see, share, or modify. See also *proprietary*.

code

See *source code*.

command

Input typed at the *shell* that performs a specific task, usually related to administration of the system and/or the manipulation of files.

command-line prompt

See *shell*.

commodity

In the context of hardware, describes PC hardware usually based around Intel or AMD processors that can be bought off the shelf and used to create sophisticated computer systems (as opposed to buying specially designed hardware). One reason for *Linux*'s success is its ability to use commodity hardware.

community

The general term for the millions of *Linux* users worldwide, regardless of what they use Linux for or their individual backgrounds. By using Linux, you automatically become part of the community.

compile

The practice of creating a binary file from *source code*, usually achieved using the `./configure`, `make`, `make install` series of commands and scripts.

config file

Configuration file; any file that contains the list of settings for a program. Sometimes it's necessary to edit config files by hand using programs like *vi* or *Emacs*, but often the program itself will write its config file according to the settings you choose.

copyleft

The legal principle of protecting the right to share a creative work, such as a computer program, using a legally binding license. Copyleft also ensures future iterations of the work are covered in the same way.

cracker

Someone who breaks into computer systems to steal data or cause damage. The term is not necessarily linked to *Linux* or *Unix* but was created by the *community* to combat the widespread use of hacker in this sense. The word *hacker* has traditionally defined someone who merely administers, programs, and generally enjoys computers.

cron

Background *service* that schedules tasks to occur at certain times. It relies on the crontab file.

CUPS

Common Unix Printing System; set of programs that work in the background to handle printing under *Unix* and *Linux*.

curses

Library that lets software present a semigraphical interface at the *shell*, complete with menu systems and simple mouse control (if configured). The version of curses used under *Linux* and *Unix* is called ncurses.

CVS

Concurrent Versioning System; application that allows the latest version of software packages to be distributed over the Internet to developers and other interested parties.

D

daemon

See *service*.

Debian

Voluntary organization that produces *distributions* of *Free Software* operating systems, including *Linux*. Because it is a nonprofit organization run by passionate Free Software advocates, it is considered the most ethically sound of all Linux outfits. Many *distributions*, including *Ubuntu*, use Debian as the basis for their software because of its claimed reliability and relative simplicity.

dependency

A way of referring to system files that a program requires in order to run. If the dependencies are not present during program installation, a program might refuse to install.

device

Linux shorthand describing something on your system that provides a function for the user or that the system requires in order to run. This usually refers to hardware, but it can also describe a virtual device that is created to provide access to a particular Linux function.

directory

What Windows refers to as a folder; areas on a hard disk in which files can be stored and organized.

distribution

A collection of software making up the *Linux* operating system; also known as a *distro*. The software is usually compiled by either a company or organization. A distribution is designed to be easy to install, administer, and use by virtue of it being an integrated whole. Examples include *Ubuntu*, *SUSE Linux*, *Red Hat*, and *Debian*.

distro

Shorthand for *distribution*.

documentation

Another way of describing written guides or instructions; can refer to online sources of help as well as actual printed documentation.

dpkg

Shell command that can be used to administer software under *Ubuntu* and *Debian*. However, the *APT* system, which uses dpkg, is the preferred method of installing software.

E

Emacs

Seminal text editor and pseudo-*shell* beloved by *Unix* aficionados; can be used for programming tasks, simple word processing, and much more. This editor has cultural significance as one of the core pieces of software offered by *GNU Project, The*. Emacs was originally developed principally by *Stallman, Richard*. See also *vi*.

environment

Shorthand referring to a user's unique *Linux* configuration, such as variables that tell the *shell* where programs are located.

F

FAT32

File Allocation Table 32-bits; file system offered by Windows 98, Me, 2000, and XP. *Linux* can both read and write to FAT32 file systems. See also *NTFS* and *VFAT*.

Firefox

Web browser program used under *Ubuntu* and produced by the *Mozilla Foundation*.

FLOSS

Free, Libre, or Open Source Software; used within the *community* to describe all software or technology that, broadly speaking, adheres to the ethical approach of *Open Source* software and/or *Free Software*, as well as its legal guidelines.

FOSS

Free or Open Source Software; alternative term for *FLOSS*.

free

When used to describe software or associated areas of technology, "free" indicates that the project abides by the ethical (if not legal) guidelines laid down by *GNU Project, The.* It doesn't indicate that the software is free in a monetary sense; its meaning is quite different from "freeware."

Free Software

Software in which the *source code*—the original listing created by the programmer—is available for all to see, share, study, and adapt to their own needs. This differs from the concept of *open source,* because the right of others to further modify the code is guaranteed via the *GNU Public License* (GPL) software license (or a compatible license). For various reasons, Free Software sometimes does not include the source code (although the software can still be legally decompiled), but this is rare.

G

gcc

GNU Compiler Collection; programs used when creating *binary executable* files from *source code.*

GID

Group ID; numbering system used by the operating system to refer to a *group.*

GIMP

GNU Image Manipulation Program; high-powered image-editing program that runs under *Linux, Unix,* Windows, and other operating systems. Often preceded by the definite article: "The GIMP."

GNOME

GNU Network Object Model Environment; a *GUI*-based desktop environment used by *Ubuntu,* as well as several other *distributions.* It uses the GTK+ *libraries.* See also *KDE.*

GNU

GNU's Not Unix; see *GNU Project, The.*

GNU/Linux

Another name for the operating system referred to as *Linux.* The name GNU/Linux gives credit to the vast quantity of *GNU Project, The* software that is added to the *Linux kernel* within a *distro* to make a complete operating system. As such, GNU/Linux is the preferred term of many *Free Software* advocates.

GNU Project, The

Organization created by *Stallman, Richard* in order to further the aims of *Free Software* and create the body of software that makes up the *GNU* operating system.

GNU Public License

Software license principally created by *Stallman, Richard* in order to protect software *source code* against *proprietary* interests and ensure that it will always be shared. It does this by insisting that any source code covered by the GNU Public License (GPL) must remain licensed under the GPL, even after it has been modified or added to by others. The *Linux kernel*, as well as much of the software that runs on it, uses the GPL.

GPL

See *GNU Public License.*

grep

Global Regular Expression Print; powerful *shell command* that lets you search a file or other form of input using *regular expressions.* Because of the ubiquity of the grep program, many *Linux* and *Unix* users refer to searching as "grepping." To "grep a file" is to search through it for a *string.*

group

Collection of users under one heading (group name) to facilitate system administration.

GRUB

GRand Unified Bootloader; boot manager program that offers a menu from which you can choose which operating system you wish to boot. It's needed to load the *kernel* program and thereby initiate the *Linux* boot procedure.

GUI

Graphical user interface; describes the software that provides a graphical system to display data and let you control your PC (usually via a mouse).

guru

One who is experienced and knowledgeable about *Linux/ Unix* and is willing to share his or her knowledge with others. In a perfect world, every *newbie* would have his or her own guru.

gzip

One of the two preferred forms of file compression used under *Linux.* Files employing gzip compression usually have a `.gz` file extension. See also *bzip2.*

H

hack

Ingenious and/or extremely efficient solution to a problem, particularly within the programming world.

hacker

Term used within the *community* to describe anyone who enjoys computers and possesses some skill therein, either in a professional capacity or as a hobby. This term is distinct from connotations of maliciously breaking into computers propagated by the media. See also *cracker*.

host

Shorthand referring to any computer that acts as a *server* to another computer. See also *client*.

HP-UX

Hewlett-Packard's *proprietary* form of *Unix* designed to work on its own hardware platform.

Hurd

Kernel being developed by *GNU Project, The*. It's not associated with the *Linux* kernel in any way.

I

info

Source of *documentation* accessible from the *shell*; an alternative to the more established *man page* system. Also known as Texinfo.

init

The program that is automatically run after the *kernel* has finished loading, and therefore early in the boot procedure. It's responsible for effectively starting the operating system.

init.d

Collection of startup *scripts* that make up the components of a *run level*. Under *Ubuntu*, these are found at /etc/init.d. *Symbolic links* to selected init.d scripts are contained in folders within /etc/init.d that are named after *run level* numbers, such as rc0.d, rc1.d, rc2.d, and so on.

initrd

Initial RAM disk; system used by the *Linux kernel* to load *modules* that are essential for the kernel to be able to boot, such as disk controllers.

inode

Part of the usually invisible file system structure that describes a file, such as its ownership permissions or file size.

ipchains

Now deprecated component of version 2.2 of the *Linux kernel* that allows the creation of network security setups, such as firewalls or port-forwarding arrangements. Note that some *distros* still prefer to use ipchains. See also *iptables*.

iptables

Component of versions 2.4 and 2.6 of the *Linux* kernel that allows powerful network security setups. Chiefly used in the creation of firewalls, but can be used for more elementary arrangements such as network address translation (NAT) routers.

J

job

How the *BASH shell* refers to a running program in order to facilitate administration by the user.

journaling

File system technology in which integrity is maintained via the logging of disk writes.

K

KDE

K desktop environment; *GUI* and set of additional programs used on various distros, such as *Mandriva* and a variation of *Ubuntu* called *Kubuntu*.

kernel

Essential but ordinarily invisible set of programs that run the computer's hardware and provide a platform on which to run software. In the *Linux* operating system, the kernel is also called Linux, after its creator, *Torvalds, Linus*.

kernel panic

Error message that appears when the *kernel* program in *Linux* cannot continue to work. In other words, a polite way of indicating a crash or, more often, a problem arising from user misconfiguration. This is most often seen when booting up after making incorrect changes to the system.

kludge

Community slang describing an inelegant way of making something work, usually not in a way that is generally accepted as being correct. Pronounced "kloodge."

Kubuntu

Version of *Ubuntu* that substitutes the *GNOME* desktop environment for *KDE*.

L

LAMP

Acronym describing a series of programs that work together to provide a complete *Linux*-based web-hosting environment. Stands for *Linux, Apache, MySQL,* and Perl, PHP, or Python (the last three in the list are scripting languages; see *script*).

LGPL

Lesser GPL; version of the *GNU Public License* (GPL) in which some use restrictions are slackened at the expense of various freedoms laid down by the main GPL. The LGPL is mostly used for *library* files.

library

General term referring to code that programs need to run and that, once in memory, is frequently accessed by many programs (leading to the phrase "shared library"). The most common and vital library is glibc (GNU C Library), created by *GNU Project, The* and the fundamental building block without which *Linux* could not operate. *GNOME* relies on the GTK+ libraries, among others.

link

File system method of assigning additional filenames to a file; also known as a "hard link." See also *symbolic link*.

Linux

You mean you don't know by now? Linux is what this book is all about. It is a *kernel* program created by *Torvalds, Linus* in 1991 to provide an inexpensive operating system for his computer, along with other components. These days, Linux is used to describe the entire operating system discussed in this book, although many argue (perhaps quite rightly) that this is inaccurate, and use the term *GNU/Linux* instead.

local

Shorthand referring to the user's PC or a device directly attached to it (as opposed to *remote*).

localhost

(1) Network name used internally by *Linux* and software to refer to the *local* computer, distinct from the network.

(2) Default name given to a Linux-based PC when no other name is defined during installation. However, under Ubuntu, the name ubuntu is assigned if no name is defined by the user.

M

man page

Documentation accessible from the *shell* that describes a *command* and how it should be used.

Minix

Operating system that is a rough clone of *Unix*, created by Professor Andrew Tanenbaum. It was the inspiration for *Linux*.

module

Program code that can be inserted or removed from the *kernel* in order to support particular pieces of hardware or provide certain kernel functions. Drivers under Windows perform the same function.

mount

To add a file system so that it is integrated (and therefore accessible) within the main file system; applies to external file systems, such as those available across networks, as well as those on the *local* PC, such as the hard disk or CD/DVD-ROMs.

Mozilla Foundation

Organization founded by Netscape to create *open source* Internet software, such as web browsers and e-mail clients; originally based on the Netscape *source code*. At the time of this writing, it produces the *Firefox* and Camino web browsers, the Thunderbird e-mail and Usenet client, the Bugzilla bug-tracking software, as well as other programs.

MySQL

Popular and powerful *open source* database application. See also *LAMP*.

N

newbie

Term used to describe anyone who is new to *Linux* and therefore still learning the basics. It's not a derogatory term! See also *guru*.

NFS

Network File System; reliable and established method of sharing files, printers, and other resources across a network of *Unix*-based operating systems. See also *Samba*.

NTFS

NT File System; file system offered by Windows NT, 2000, and XP. It can be read by *Linux*, but usually writing is prohibited because it is considered unsafe. See also *FAT32*.

O

OpenOffice.org

Open Source office suite project created with the continuing input of Sun Microsystems and based on code Sun contributed to the Open Source *community*. Its commercial release is in the form of Star Office (although Star Office has several *proprietary* components added).

open source

(1) Method and philosophy of developing software whereby the *source code*—the original listing created by the programmer—is available for all to see. Note that open source is not the same as *Free Software*, describing software as open source doesn't imply that the code can be shared or used by others (although this is often the case).

(2) A community of users or any project that adheres to open-source values and/or practices.

P

partition

Subdivision of a hard disk into which a file system can be installed.

PID

Process ID; the numbering system used to refer to a *process*.

pipe

Method of passing the output from one *command* to another for further processing. Piping is achieved within the *shell* by typing the | symbol.

POSIX

Portable Operating System Interface; various technical standards that define how *Unix*-like operating systems should operate and to which the *Linux* operating system attempts to adhere.

PPP

Point-to-Point Protocol; networking technology that allows data transfer across serial connections like telephone lines. In other words, it's the technology that lets you connect to your Internet service provider using a modem.

process

The way the system refers to the individual programs (or components of programs) running in memory.

proprietary

Effectively, software for which a software license must be acquired, usually for a fee. This usually means the *source code* is kept secret, but it can also indicate that the source code is available to view but not to incorporate into your own projects or share with others.

R

Red Hat

Well-known company that produces distributions of *Linux*.

redirect

To send the output of a *command* into a particular file. This also works the other way around: the contents of a particular file can be directed into a command. Redirection is achieved within the *shell* using the left and right angle brackets (< and >), respectively.

regex

See *regular expression*.

regular expression

Powerful and complex method of describing a search *string*, usually when searching with tools such as *grep* (although regular expressions are also used when programming). Regular expressions use various symbols as substitutes for characters or to indicate patterns.

remote

Indicates a computer or *service* that is available across a network, including but not limited to computers on the Internet (as opposed to *local*).

root

(1) The bottom of the *Linux* file system directory structure, usually indicated by a forward slash (/).

(2) The user on some versions of *Unix* or *Linux* who has control over all aspects of hardware, software, and the file system.

(3) Used to describe a user who temporarily takes on the powers of the root user (via the sudo command, for example).

RPM

Red Hat Package Manager; system used to install and administer programs under *Red Hat*, *SUSE Linux*, and some other *distributions*. See also *APT*.

RTFM

Read the freaking manual/ *man page*; exclamation frequently used online when a *newbie* asks for help without having undertaken basic research.

run level

Describes the current operational mode of *Linux* (typically, the *services* that are running). Run level 1 is single-user mode (a stripped-down system with minimal running services); run levels 2 through 5 provide a *GUI*; run level 6 is reboot mode (switching to it will cause the computer to terminate its processes and then reboot); run level 0 is shutdown (switching to it will cause the PC to shut down.

S

Samba

Program that re-creates under *Unix* or *Linux* the Microsoft *SMB*-based system of sharing files, printers, and other computer resources across a network. It allows Linux to become a file or printer server for Linux and Windows computers, and also allows a Linux client to access a Windows-based server.

scalable

Term describing the ability of a single computer program to meet diverse needs, regardless of the scale of the potential uses. The *Linux kernel* is described as being scalable, because it can run supercomputers, as well as handheld computers and home entertainment devices.

script

Form of computer program consisting of a series of *commands* in a text file. Most *shells* allow some form of scripting, and entire programming languages such as Perl are based around scripts. In the context of the Linux operating system, shell scripts are usually created to perform trivial tasks or ones that frequently interact with the user. Shell scripts have the advantage that they can be frequently and easily modified. The *Linux* boot process relies on several complex scripts to configure essential system functions such as networking and the *GUI*. See also *init*.

server

(1) Type of computer designed to share data with other computers over a network.

(2) Software that runs on a computer and is designed to share data with other programs on the same PC or with other PCs across a network.

service

Background program that provides vital functions for the day-to-day running of *Linux*; also known as a *daemon*. Services are usually started when the computer boots up and as such are constituent parts of a *run level*.

shell

Broadly speaking, any program that creates an operating environment in which you can control your computer. The *GNOME* desktop can be seen as a shell, for example. However, it's more commonly understood within *Unix* and *Linux* circles as a program that lets you control the system using *command*s entered at the keyboard. In this context, the most common type of shell in use on Linux is *BASH*.

Shuttleworth, Mark

Entrepreneurial South African businessman who, as a long-term *Debian hacker*, devised and financially supports *Ubuntu* via his company, Canonical Ltd.

SMB

Server Message Block; network technology for sharing files, printers, and other resources. See also *Samba*.

Solaris

Form of *Unix* sold by Sun Microsystems; runs on *proprietary* hardware systems as well as on *commodity* systems based on Intel and AMD processors.

source code

The original program listing created by a programmer. Most programs that you download are precompiled—already turned into *binary executables* ready for general use—unless you specifically choose to download and *compile* the source code of a program yourself.

SSH

Secure SHell; program that lets you access a *Linux/ Unix* computer across the Internet. SSH encrypts data sent and received across the *link*.

SSL

Secure Sockets Layer; form of network data transfer designed to encrypt information for security purposes. It's used online for certain web sites and also within *Linux* for certain types of secure data exchange.

Stallman, Richard M.

Legendary *hacker* who founded *GNU Project, The* and created the concept of *copyleft*, as well as the software license that incorporates it: the *GNU Public License* (GPL). See also *Torvalds, Linus*.

standard error

Linux and *Unix* shorthand for the error output provided by a *command*.

standard input

Linux and *Unix* shorthand for the *device* usually used to provide input to the *shell*. For the majority of desktop PC users, this refers to the keyboard.

standard output

Linux and *Unix* shorthand for the *device* usually used to display output from a *command*. For the majority of desktop PC users, this refers to the screen.

string

A word, phrase, or sentence consisting of letters, numbers, or other characters that is used within a program and is often supplied by the user.

sudo

Program that runs under *Unix* and *Linux* by which ordinary users are temporarily afforded *administrator* rights. Ubuntu relies on sudo as the exclusive way for users to administer the system.

SVG

Scalable Vector Graphics; vector graphics technology. SVG is actually an XML markup language designed to create 2D graphics, increasingly used for *Linux* desktop icons and web graphics.

swap

Area of the hard disk that the *Linux kernel* uses as a temporary memory storage area. Desktop or *server* Linux differs from Windows in that it usually requires a separate hard disk *partition* in which to store the swap file.

symbolic link

Type of file akin to a Windows shortcut. Accessing a symbolic link file routes the user to an actual file. See also *link*.

sysadmin

Systems administrator; a way of describing the person employed within a company to oversee the computer systems. In such an environment, the sysadmin usually is the *root* user of the various computers.

System V

Variant of *Unix* used as a foundation for modern forms of *proprietary* Unix.

T

tainted

Describes a *kernel* that is using *proprietary modules* in addition to *Open Source* modules. Can also refer to insecure software.

tar

Tape ARchive; software able to combine several files into one larger file in order to back them up to a tape drive or simply transfer them across the Internet. Such files are usually indicated by a `.tar` file extension. Note that a tar file isn't necessarily compressed; the *bzip2* and *gzip* utilities must be used if this is desired.

TCP/IP

Transmission Control Protocol/Internet Protocol; standard protocol stack used by most modern operating systems to control and communicate across networks and also across the Internet (as opposed to NetBEUI, commonly available on older versions of Windows, and IPX/SPX, used on Novell's NetWare operating system).

terminal

Another word for *shell*.

TeX

Method and set of programs for typesetting complex documents. Invented prior to word processors and desktop publishing software, and now considered a specialized tool for laying out scientific texts. An updated version of the program called LaTeX is also available.

Torvalds, Linus

Finnish programmer who, in 1991, created the initial versions of the *Linux kernel*. Since then, he has taken advantage of an international network of volunteers and staff employed by various companies who help produce the kernel. Torvalds himself contributes to and oversees the efforts.

tty

TeleTYpewriter; shorthand referring to underlying *Linux* virtual *devices* that allow programs and users to access the *kernel* and thereby run programs.

Tux

The name of the penguin character that is the *Linux* mascot. The original Tux graphic was drawn by Larry Ewing.

U

Ubuntu

Linux distribution with several unique characteristics. Ubuntu is designed primarily for desktop use, although several server versions are available. It is intended for use by individuals in any location in the world, so it has strong multiple language support. It's run by the *Ubuntu Foundation*, which is financially backed by *Shuttleworth, Mark*. Each release is guaranteed to be supported for 18 months (5 years in the case of server releases).

Ubuntu Foundation

Organization set up by *Shuttleworth, Mark* and his company, Canonical, Ltd., to administer and provide support for the *Ubuntu* distribution of *Linux*.

UID

User ID; numbering system used by the operating system to refer to a *user*.

Unix

Seminal operating system created as a research project in 1969 by Kenneth Thompson and Dennis Ritchie at Bell Labs (later AT&T). Because it was initially possible to purchase the *source code* for a fee, subsequent revisions were enhanced by a variety of organizations and went on to run many mainframe and minicomputer systems throughout the 1980s, 1990s, and up to the present. Nowadays, Unix is fragmented and exists in a variety of different versions. Perhaps most popular is its *Open Source* rendition, *BSD Unix*, which has seen many developments since the source code was first released. This means that BSD Unix no longer exists but has instead diversified into a number of separate projects. *Proprietary* versions are also available, including *Solaris, HP-UX*, and *AIX*.

user

The way the operating system refers to anyone who accesses its resources. A user must first have a user account set up, effectively giving that user his or her own private space on the system. In addition to actual human users, an average *Linux* system has many other user accounts created to let programs and *services* go about their business. These are usually not seen by human users.

V

variable

A changeable value that stores a certain data type (such as a number, date, or *string*), remembering it for future reference by the system or *script* it is defined by. Variables defined by and for the *Linux kernel* are vital to it.

verbose

Command option that will cause it to return more detailed output (or, in some cases, to return actual output if the command is otherwise "quiet"); usually specified by adding the -v command option.

VFAT

Virtual File Allocation Table; technical name of Microsoft's FAT file system offered under Windows and also on removable storage devices such as flash memory cards.

vi

Arcane text editor and pseudo-*shell* beloved by *Unix* aficionados that can be used for creation of text files or for creating programs. Traditionally, Unix users either love or hate vi; some prefer *Emacs*. Nowadays new and improved versions of vi are available, such as vim, used under Ubuntu.

W

Wine

Short for Wine Is Not an Emulator; software that re-creates the Windows Application Programming Interface (API) layer within *Linux* and lets users run Windows programs.

workspace

X terminology referring to a *GUI* desktop.

X

X

Short for X Window; software that controls the display and input devices, thereby providing a software foundation on top of which desktop managers like *GNOME* are able to run.

X11

Version 11 of the *X* software, currently in use on most desktop *Linux* systems.

XFree86 Project

Organization that creates *X* software. At one time, every *distribution* of *Linux* used XFree86 software, but most now use similar software from the *X.org* organization.

xinetd

The *service* responsible for starting various network servers on the computer.

XMMS

Audio player program.

X.org

Organization that produces the X Window software and, in particular, a set of programs called X11. X11 is used on most modern distributions of *Linux*. It is backed by a number of *Unix* and Linux industry leaders.

xterm

Simple program that allows you to run a shell under X. This program has the advantage of being available on most *Linux* systems that offer a *GUI*.

APPENDIX B

■■■

BASH Command Index

This appendix provides a whistle-stop tour of commands that can be used at the BASH shell. This is a highly selective listing, intended to provide a guide to commands that see day-to-day use on average desktop systems. In a similar fashion, although some command options are listed, they're strictly limited to those that receive regular deployment.

The descriptions of each command are deliberately simple. Note that the quantity of space a command is given is not an indication of its importance or usefulness. To this end, commands in the list with an asterisk after their name offer far more than hinted at by its brief description hints. In such cases, I strongly advise that you refer to the command's man page for more information.

Various conventions are used in the list:

- You should substitute your own details wherever italicized words appear.

- Commands that can and might be run by ordinary users are preceded with a dollar sign ($).

- Commands that require root privileges (the use of sudo) are preceded with a hash symbol (#).

Commands that present dangers to the system through misuse are clearly marked. Such commands should not be used without research into the command's usage and function.

Command	Description	Typical Command Options	Examples of Use
`$ alias`	Create or display command aliases		`alias list=ls`
`$ alsamixer`	Alter audio volume levels		`alsamixer`
`$ apropos`	Search man pages for specified words/phrases		`apropos "word or phrase"`
`$ apt-cache`	Search, query, and otherwise manipulate the APT database cache (see `apt-get`)	`search`: Search for specified package (regexes may be used; see Chapter 15)	`apt-cache search packagename`
		`showpkg`: Show information about specified package	
		`depends`: Show package dependencies of specified package, and show other packages that can meet that dependency	
`# apt-get`	Multifunction tool use to install, remove, and otherwise administer software packages, according to the APT database	`install`: search for and install specified package from repositories (as specified in `/etc/apt/sources.list`)	`apt-get install packagename`
		`update`: Update or build package database by contacting package repositories	
		`upgrade`: Attempt to upgrade all current installed packages with new versions	
		`dist-upgrade`: Attempt to upgrade all currently installed packages, automatically and aggressively resolving package conflicts; often used to upgrade entire distro to new version	
		`remove`: Opposite of `install`; removes packages	
		`clean`: Remove any old package installation files that are stored on hard disk	
		`-f`: Attempt to fix broken package dependencies (used with `install` or `remove`)	
		`--force-yes`: Override any errors and thereby bypass apt-get's protective measures. Dangerous option—use with care!	

Command	Description	Typical Command Options	Examples of Use
$ bzip2	Compress specified file (replaces original file with compressed file and gives it .bz2 file extension)	-d: Decompress specified file -k: Don't delete original file -t: Test; do a dry run without writing any data	bzip2 *myfile*
$ bzip2recover	Attempt recovery of specified damaged .bz2 file		bzip2recover *myfile.tar.bz2*
$ cal	Display calendar for current month (or specified month/year)		cal *4 2005*
$ cat	Display a file on screen or combine and display two files together		cat *myfile*
$ cd	Change to specified directory		cd */usr/bin*
$ cdparanoia *	Convert CD audio tracks to hard disk files	-B: Batch mode; convert all tracks to individual files -S: Set CD read speed (2, 4, 8, 12, and so on; values relate to CD-drive spin speed; used to avoid read errors)	cdparanoia -S 8 -B
# cdrecord *	Burn audio or CD-R/RW data discs (the latter usually based on an ISO image; see mkisofs)	-dev=: Specify the drive's device number (can be discovered by running cdrecord with the scanbus option) --scanbus: Scan to see which CD-R/RW drives are present and return device numbers -speed=: Specify the write speed (2, 4, 6, 8, and so on) -v: Verbose output; obligatory for feedback on cdrecord's progress	cdrecord *dev=0,0,0* *-speed=16 -v* *myfile.iso*
# cfdisk *	DANGEROUS! Menu-based disk-partitioning program		cfdisk */dev/hda*
# chgrp	Change group ownership of a file/directory	-R: Recursive; apply changes to subdirectories	chgroup *mygroup* *myfile*
$ chmod	Change permissions of a file/directory (where a=all, u=user, g=group; and r=read, w=write, x=executable)	-R: Recursive; apply to subdirectories --reference=: Copy permissions from specified file	chmod a+rw *myfile*
$ chown	Change file ownership to specified username	-R: Recursive; apply to subdirectories	chown *username* *myfile1*

Command	Description	Typical Command Options	Examples of Use
# chroot	Change the root of the file system to the specified path		chroot /home/mydirectory
# chvt	Switch to the specified virtual terminal (equivalent of holding down Ctrl+Alt and pressing F1–F6)		chvt 3
$ clear	Clears terminal screen and places cursor at top		clear
$ cp	Copy files	-r: Recursive; copy subdirectories and the files therein	cp myfile1 directory/
		-s: Create symbolic link instead of copying	
$ crontab	Edit or display the user's crontab file (scheduled tasks)	-e: Edit the crontab file (create/amend)	crontab -e
		-l: List crontab entries	
		-r: Delete the crontab file	
		-u: Specify a user and edit their crontab file	
$ date	Display the date and time		date
$ df	Display free disk space within file system	-h: Human readable; display sizes in KB, MB, GB, and TB, as appropriate	df -h
		-l: Restrict to local file systems, as opposed to network mounts	
$ diff	Display differences between specified files	-a: Consider all files text files (don't halt when asked to compare binary files)	diff myfile1 myfile2
		-i: ignore lowercase and uppercase differences	
$ diff3	Display differences between three specified files		diff3 myfile1 myfile2 myfile3
$ dig	Look up IP address of specified domain		dig mysite.com
$ dmesg	Display kernel message log		dmesg
# dosfsck *	Check and repair MS-DOS–based file hard disk partition (see also fsck)	-a: Repair without asking user for confirmation	dosfsck -rv /dev/hda4
		-r: Repair file system asking user for confirmation when two or more repair methods are possible	
		-v: Verbose; display more information	

Command	Description	Typical Command Options	Examples of Use
# dpkg	Install, remove, and otherwise administer local installation packages (on your hard disk); see also apt-get	-i: Install specified package -r: Remove (uninstall) specified package -I: Show info about specified package --ignore-depends= *packagename.deb*: Don't halt on package dependency issues (dangerous!)	dpkg -i *packagename.deb*
# dpkg-reconfigure	Reconfigure an already installed package		dpkg-reconfigure *packagename*
$ du	Show sizes of files and folders in kilobytes	-h: Human readable; produce output in MB, GB, and TB -s: Summary; display totals only for directories rather than for individual files	du -h */home/myuser*
$ eject	Eject a removable storage disk	-t: Close an already open tray	eject */media/ dvd-rom*
$ ex *	Start a simple text-editor program used principally within shell scripts		ex *myfile.txt*
$ exit	Log out of shell (end session)		exit
$ fdformat	Low-level format a floppy disk (this won't create a file system; see also *mkfs*)		fdformat */dev/fd0*
# fdisk *	DANGEROUS! Hard-disk partitioning program	-l: List partition table	fdisk */dev/hda*
$ fg	Brings job running in background to foreground		fg *1*
$ file	Display information about specified file, such as its type		file *myfile*
$ find *	Find files by searching directories (starting in current directory)	-maxdepth: Specify the number of subdirectories levels to delve into, starting from 1 (current directory) -name: Specify name of file to search for -type: Specify file types to be returned; -type d returns directories and -type f returns only files	find -name "*myfile*"

Command	Description	Typical Command Options	Examples of Use
$ free	Display information about memory usage	-m: Show figures in MB -t: Total the columns at bottom of table	free -m
# fsck *	Check file system for errors (usually run from rescue disc)		fsck /dev/hda1
$ ftp *	FTP program for uploading/downloading to remote sites		ftp ftp.mysite.com
$ fuser	Show which processes are using a particular file or file system	-v: Verbose; detailed output	fuser -v myfile
$ grep *	Search specified file for specified text string (or word)	-i: Ignore uppercase and lowercase differences -r: Recursive; delve into subdirectories (if applicable) -s: Suppress error messages about inaccessible files and other problems	grep "phrase I want to find" myfile.txt
# groupadd	Create new group		groupadd mygroup
# groupdel	Delete specified group		groupdel mygroup
$ groups	Display groups the specified user belongs to		groups myuser
$ gzip	Compress files and replace original file with compressed version	-d: Decompress specified file -v: Verbose; display degree of compression	gzip myfile
# halt	Initiate shutdown procedure, ending all processes and unmounting all disks	-p: Power off system at end of shutdown procedure	halt -p
# hdparm *	DANGEROUS! Tweak or view hard disk settings		hdparm /dev/hda
$ head	Print topmost lines of text files (default is first 10 lines)	-n: Specify number of lines (such as -n 5)	head myfile.txt
$ help	Display list of common BASH commands		help
$ history	Display history file (a list of recently used commands)		history

Command	Description	Typical Command Options	Examples of Use
`$ host`	Query DNS server based on specified domain name or IP address	`-d`: Verbose; return more information `-r`: Force name server to return its cached information rather than query other authoritative servers	`host 82.211.81.166`
`$ hostname`	Display localhost-style name of computer		`hostname`
`$ id`	Display username and group info of specified user (or current user if none specified)		`id myuser`
`# ifconfig *`	Display or configure settings of a network interface (assign an IP address, subnet mask, and activate/deactivate it)	down: Disable interface (used at end of command chain) netmask: Specify a subnet mask up: Enable interface (used at end of command chain)	`ifconfig eth0 192.168.0.10 netmask 255.255.0.0 up`
`$ info *`	Display info page for specified command		`info command`
`# init`	Change current run level		`init 1`
`$ jobs`	Display list of jobs running in background		`jobs`
`$ kill`	Kill specified process		`kill 1433`
`$ killall`	Kill process(es) that have specified name(s)	`-i`: Confirm before killing process `-v`: Verbose; report if and when successful	`killall processnumber`
`$ last`	Display details of recent logins, reboots, and shutdowns		`last`
`$ ldd`	Display system files (libraries) required by specified program		`ldd /usr/bin/program`
`$ less`	Interactively scroll through a text file	`-q`: Quiet; disable beeps when end of file is reached or other error encountered `-i`: Ignore case; make all searches case-insensitive unless uppercase letters are used	`less myfile.txt`

Command	Description	Typical Command Options	Examples of Use
$ ln	Create links to specified files, such as symbolic links	-s: Create symbolic link (default is hard link)	ln -s *myfile1 myfile2*
$ lpr	Print file (send it to the printer spool/queue)	-V: Verbose; print information about progress of print job	lpr *myfile.txt*
$ lpstat	Display print queue		lpstat
$ ls	List directory	-a: List all files, including hidden files	ls -h *mydirectory*
		-d: List only directory names rather than their contents	
		-h: Human readable; print figures in KB, MB, GB, and TB	
		-l: Long list; include all details, such as file permissions	
		-m: Show as comma-separated list	
# lsmod	Display currently loaded kernel modules		lsmod
$ lsof	Display any files currently in use	-u: Limit results to files used by specified user	lsof -u *username*
$ man	Display specified command's manual		man *command*
$ md5sum	Display MD5 checksum (normally used to confirm a file's integrity after download)		md5sum *myfile*
# mkfs *	DANGEROUS! Create specified file system on specified device (such as a floppy disk)	-t: Specify type of file system	mkfs -t *vfat /dev/fd0*

Command	Description	Typical Command Options	Examples of Use
$ mkisofs *	Create ISO image file from specified directory (usually for burning to disc with cdrecord)	-o: Options; this must appear after command to indicate that command options follow	mkisofs -o isoimage.iso -R -J -v mydirectory
		-apple: Use Mac OS extensions to make disc readable on Apple computers	
		-f: Follow symbolic links and source actual files	
		-J: Use Joliet extensions (make ISO compatible with Windows)	
		-R: Use Rock Ridge extensions (preferred Linux CD-ROM file system)	
		-v: Verbose; display more information (-vv for even more info)	
# modinfo	Display information about kernel module		modinfo modulename
# modprobe	Insert specified module into the kernel, as well as any others it relies on	-k: Set module's autoclean flag so it will be removed from memory after inactivity	modprobe modulename
		-r: Remove specified module as well as any it relies on to operate	
$ more	Interactively scroll through text file (similar to less)		more myfile.txt
# mount *	Mount specified file system at specified location	-o: Specify command options, such as rw to allow read/write access; various types of file systems have unique commands	mount /dev/hda4 /mnt
$ mv	Move (or rename) specified files and/or directories	-b: Back up files before moving	mv myfile mydirectory/
		-v: Display details of actions carried out	
$ netstat *	Show current network connections		netstat -a
$ nice	Run specified command with specified priority	-n: Specify priority, ranging from the highest priority of –20, to 19, which is the lowest priority	nice -n 19
$ nohup	Run specified command and continue to run it, even if user logs out		nohup command

Command	Description	Typical Command Options	Examples of Use
$ passwd	Change user's password		passwd
$ ping	Check network connectivity between local machine and specified address	-w: Exit after specified number of seconds (such as -w 5)	ping *mydomain.com*
$ printenv	Display all environment variables for current user		printenv
$ ps *	Display currently running processes	a: List all processes (note that command options don't require preceding dash)	ps aux
		f: Display ownership of processes using tree-style graphics	
		u: Limit results to processes running for and started by current user	
		x: Include processes in results not started by user but running with the user ID	
$ pwd	Display current directory		pwd
# reboot	Reboot computer		reboot
$ renice	Change a process's priority while it's running (see nice)		renice *19 10704*
$ rm	Delete single or multiple files and/or directories	-r: Recursive; delete specified directories and any subdirectories	rm -rf *mydirectory*
		-f: Force; don't prompt for confirmation before deleting (use with care!)	
# rmmod	Delete module from kernel		rmmod *modulename*
# route *	Add and create (or view) entries in routing table (see ifconfig)		route add default gw *192.168.1.1*
$ runlevel	Display current run level		runlevel
$ screen *	Program that runs pseudo shell that is kept alive regardless of current user login	-ls: Display list of currently running screen sessions	screen
		-R: Reattach to already running screen session or start new one if none available	
$ sftp *	Secure Shell FTP; like FTP but running over an ssh connection (see ssh)		sftp *username @192.168.1.14*

Command	Description	Typical Command Options	Examples of Use
$ shred	Overwrite data in a file with gibberish, thereby making it irrecoverable	-u: Delete file in addition to overwriting -v: Verbose; show details of procedure -f: Force permissions to allow writing if necessary	shred -fv *myfile*
$ sleep	Pause input for the specified period of time (where s=seconds, m=minutes, h=hours, d=days)		sleep *10m*
$ smbclient *	FTP-style program with which you can log in to a SMB (Windows)-based file share		smbclient *//192.168.* *1.1/*
$ sort	Sort entries in the specified text file (default is ASCII sort)		sort *myfile.txt* -o *sorted.txt*
$ ssh *	Log in to remote computer using secure shell		ssh *username@* *192.168.1.15*
$ startx	Start GUI session (if GUI isn't already running)		startx
$ su	Temporarily log in as specified user; log in as root if no user specified (provided root account is activated)	-: Adopt user's environment variables, such as $PATH	su
$ sudo	Execute specified command with root privileges		sudo *command*
$ tac	Display specified text file but in reverse (from last to first line)		tac *myfile.txt*
$ tail	Display final lines of specified text file	-n: Specify number of lines to display (such as -n4)	tail *myfile.txt*
$ tar *	Combine specified files and/or directories into one larger file, or extract from such a file	-c: Create new archive -j: Use bzip2 in order to compress (or decompress) files -f: Specifies filename (must be last in chain of command options) -r: Add files to existing archive -x: Extract files from existing archive -z: Use gzip to compress (or decompress) files	tar -zcf *myfile.* *tar.gz mydirectory*

Command	Description	Typical Command Options	Examples of Use
$ tee	Display piped output and also save it to specified file		ls -lh| tee *listing.txt*
$ top *	Program that both displays and lets the user manipulate processes		top
$ touch	Give specified file current time and date stamp; if it doesn't exist, create a zero-byte file with that name		touch *myfile*
$ tracepath	Discover and display network path to another host		tracepath *192.168.1.20*
$ umask	Set default permissions assigned to newly created files		umask u=rwx,g=r,o=
# umount	Unmount a file system		umount */media/cdrom*
# useradd	Add new user	-m: Create home directory for user	useradd -m *username*
# userdel	Delete all mention of user in system configuration files (effectively deleting the user, although files owned by the user might remain)	-r: Remove user's home directory	userdel -r *username*
$ unalias	Remove specified alias	-a: Remove all aliases (use with care!)	unalias *command*
$ uname	Display technical information about current system	-a: Display all basic information	uname -a
$ unzip	Unzip a Windows-compatible Zip file	-l: Display archive content but don't actually unzip	unzip *myfile.zip*
$ uptime	Display uptime for system, as well as CPU load average and logged-in users		uptime
$ vim *	Text editor program		vim
$ wc	Count the number of words in a file		wc *myfile.txt*
$ whatis	Display one-line summary of specified command		whatis *command*
$ whereis	Display information on where a binary command is located, along with its source code and man page (if applicable)	-b: Return information only about binary programs	whereis -b *command*

Command	Description	Typical Command Options	Examples of Use
$ xhost	Configure which users/systems can run programs on the X server	+: When followed by a username and/or system name, gives the user/system permission to run programs on the X server; when used on its own, lets *any* user/system use the X server	xhost +
		-: Opposite of +	
$ xinit	Start elementary GUI session (when not already running a GUI)		xinit
$ zip	Create Windows-compatible compressed Zip files	-r: Recursive; includes all subdirectories and files therein	zip -r *myfile*.zip *mydirectory*
		-u: Updates Zip with specified file	
		-P: Encrypts Zip with specified password	
		-v: Verbose; display more information	
		-#: Set compression level (from 0, which is no compression, to 9, which is highest)	
$ zipgrep	Searches inside Zip files for specified text string		zipgrep *"search phrase"* *myfile*.zip

APPENDIX C

■■■

Getting Further Help

So you've read through this book and have a good working knowledge of Linux. Ubuntu is running exactly as you want it to, and things are going okay. But then you hit a brick wall. Perhaps you want to perform a task but simply don't know how. Or maybe you know roughly what you need to do but don't know the specifics. Although this book tries to be as comprehensive as possible, it can't cover every eventuality.

You need to find some help, but where do you turn? Fortunately, many sources of information are available to those who are willing to help themselves. Linux contains its own series of help files in the form of man and info pages, and these are good places to start. In addition, some programs come with their own documentation. If neither of these sources provides the help you need, you can head online and take advantage of the massive Linux community around the world.

Read the Manual!

Before asking for help online, it's important that you first attempt to solve your problems by using Linux's built-in documentation. If you go online and ask a question so simple that it can be answered with a little elementary research, you might find people reply with "RTFM." This stands for Read the Freaking Manual. In other words, do some basic research, and then come back if you're still stuck.

It's not that people online don't want to help. It's that they don't like people who are too lazy to help themselves and expect others to do the hard work for them. Although not all Linux people you encounter will take such a hard line, doing a little homework first can provide answers to a lot of questions, removing the need to ask others. This is particularly true when it comes to the fundamentals.

Documentation typically comes in three formats: man pages, info pages, and README files.

Man Pages

Man pages are the oldest form of Unix documentation. In the old days, once an individual had created a piece of software, he would write a brief but concise man page in order to give others a clue as to how to operate it. The programmer would come up with a few screens of documentation that could be called up from the command prompt. This documentation would outline what the software did and list all the ways in which it could be used.

Nowadays, depending on the software package, man pages are usually created by technical writers, but the concept of providing essential information still applies. Man pages under Linux provide all the information you need about how to use a particular command or piece of software.

Sounds great, doesn't it? Alas, there's a problem: man pages are written by software engineers *for* software engineers. They expect you to already understand the technology being discussed. This is illustrated very well by the man page for cdrecord, software that can be used to burn CD images to disc. You can view this man page by typing man cdrecord at the command prompt.

The first line of the man page states, "Cdrecord is used to record data or audio Compact Discs on an Orange Book CD-Recorder or to write DVD media on a DVD-Recorder."

Most of that is clear, but what do they mean by "Orange Book"? They don't explain. (If you're curious, head over to http://searchstorage.techtarget.com/sDefinition/ 0,,sid5_gci503648,00.html.)

Further down in the man page, you see, "Cdrecord is completely based on SCSI commands . . . Even ATAPI drives are just SCSI drives that inherently use the ATA packet interface as [a] SCSI command transport layer."

What's SCSI, or ATAPI for that matter? Again, the man page doesn't explain. (They're methods of interfacing with storage devices attached to your computer.)

But why should man pages explain as they go along? Their function is to describe how to use a piece of software, not to provide a beginner's introduction to technology. If they did that, a single man page could run to hundreds of pages.

In other words, man pages are not for complete beginners. This isn't always the case and, because Linux sees widespread usage nowadays, man pages are sometimes created with less knowledgeable users in mind. But even so, the format is inherently limited: man pages provide concise guides to using software. Luckily, there are some tips you can bear in mind to get the most from a man page. But before you can use those tips, you need to know how to read a man page.

How to Read a Man Page

To read a man page, you simply precede the command name with man. For example, to read the man page of cdrecord, a piece of software used to write ISO images to CD-R/RW discs, type the following command:

```
man cdrecord
```

This opens a simple text viewer with the man page displayed. You can move up and down line by line with the cursor keys, or move page by page using the Page Up and Page Down keys (these are sometimes labeled Pg Up and Pg Down). You can search by hitting the forward slash key (/). This will highlight all instances of the word you type. You can search for other examples of the word in the document by hitting the n key.

The average man page will include many headings, but the following are the most common:

Name: This is the name of the command. There will also be a one-sentence summary of the command.

Synopsis: This lists the command along with its various command options (sometimes known as *arguments* or *flags*). Effectively, it shows how the command can be used. It looks complicated, but the rules are simple. First is the command itself. This is in bold, which indicates it is mandatory. This rule applies to anything else in bold: it must be included when the command is used. Anything contained within square brackets ([ ]) is optional, and this is usually where you will find the command options listed. A pipe symbol (|) separates any command options that are exclusive, which means that only one of them can be used. For example, if you see [apple|orange|pear], only one of apple, orange, or pear can be specified. Usually at the end of the Synopsis listing will be the main argument, typically the file(s) that the command is to work on and/or generate.

Description: This is a concise overview of the command's purpose.

Options: This explains what the various command options do, as first listed in the Synopsis section. Bearing in mind that command options tell the software how to work, this is often the most useful part of the man page.

Files: This lists any additional files that the command might require or use, such as configuration files.

Notes: If this section is present (and often it isn't), it sometimes attempts to further illuminate aspects of the command or the technology the command is designed to control. Unfortunately, Notes sections can be just as arcane as the rest of the man page.

See Also: This refers to the man pages of other commands that are linked to the command in question. If a number appears in brackets, this means the reference is to a specific section within the man page. To access this section, type: man *<section no> command*.

Although there are guidelines for the headings that should appear in man pages, as well as their formatting, the fact is that you may encounter other headings, or you may find nearly all of them omitted. Some man pages are the result of hours if not days of effort; others are written in ten minutes. Their quality can vary tremendously.

Tips for Working with Man Pages

The trick to quickly understanding a man page is decoding the Synopsis section. If you find it helps, split the nonobligatory command options from the mandatory parts. For example, `cdrecord`'s man page says that you *must* specify the `dev=` option (it's in bold), so at the very least, the command is going to require this:

```
cdrecord dev=X filename
```

Then you should skip to the Options section and work out which options are relevant to your requirements. While you're there, you'll also need to figure out what the `dev=` command option requires.

Although the command options contained in square brackets in the Synopsis section are, in theory, nonobligatory, the command might not work satisfactorily without some of them. For example, with `cdrecord`, I use the `-speed` command option, which sets the burn speed, and also the `-v` option, which provides verbose output (otherwise, the command runs silently and won't display any information on screen, including error messages!).

Another handy tip in decoding man pages is understanding what standard input and standard output are. In very simple terms, standard input (stdin) is the method by which a command gets input—the keyboard on most Linux setups. Standard output (stdout) is where the output of a command is sent, which is the screen on most Linux setups. (See Chapter 15 for more details about standard input and standard output.)

Often, a man page will state that the output of a command will be sent to standard output. In other words, unless you specify otherwise, its output will appear on screen. Therefore, it's necessary to specify a file to which the data will be sent, either by redirecting the output (see Chapter 17), or by specifying a file using a command option. For example, the `mkisofs` command can be used to create ISO images from a collection of files for subsequent burning to CD. But unless the -o option is used to specify a filename, `mkisofs`'s output will simply be sent to standard output—it will appear on the screen.

Finally, here's the best tip of all for using man pages: don't forget that man has its own man page. Simply type `man man`.

Info Pages

Man pages date from the days of relatively primitive computers. Back then, most computers could only display page after page of text, and allow the user to scroll through it. In addition, memory and disk space were scarce, which is why some man pages are incredibly concise— fewer words take up less memory!

The *Texinfo* system is a valiant by the GNU Project attempt to overcome the shortfalls of man pages. Often, this is referred to as *info*, because that's the command used to summon Texinfo pages (normally, you type `info command`).

For starters, info pages are more verbose than the equivalent man pages, and that gives the author more space to explain the command or software. This doesn't necessarily mean that info pages are easier to understand, but there's a better chance of that being the case.

Secondly, info pages contain hyperlinks, just like web pages. If you move the cursor over a hyperlinked word, which is usually indicated by an asterisk (*), you can proceed to a related page. In a similar sense, pages are linked together so that you can move back and forth from topic to topic.

The bad news is that the man page system is far more popular and established than Texinfo. If a programmer creates a new application, for example, it's unlikely he'll bother with an info page, but he will almost certainly produce a man page.

In fact, in many cases, typing `info` *command* will simply bring up the man page, except in the software used to browse info pages.

However, nearly all the GNU tools are documented using info pages, either in their own pages or as part of the `coreutils` pages. For example, to read about the `cp` command and how to use it, you can type this:

```
info coreutils cp
```

To browse through all sections of the `coreutils` pages, type this:

```
info coreutils
```

Because man pages are so established, everyone expects to find one for every utility. So most utilities that have info pages will also have man pages. But in such a case, the man page will state near the end that the main documentation for the utility is contained in an info page, and you may find it more fruitful to use that instead.

Navigating through info pages is achieved via the keyboard and is something of an art. But, as you might expect, there's a user-friendly guide to using info: just type `info info`. Remember that words preceded with an asterisk are hyperlinks, and you can jump from link to link using the Tab key.

README Files and Other Documentation

Some programs come with their own documentation. This is designed to give users the information they need to get started with the program (as opposed to the man page, which is a concise and complete guide to the software). Alternatively, program documentation sometimes gives a brief outline of the program's features.

The files are usually simple text, so they can be read in any text editor or word processor, and are normally called README. Under Ubuntu, these documents are usually stored in a program-specific directory within /usr/share/doc (although a small minority of programs use /usr/doc).

Not all programs are friendly enough to provide such documentation, but even so, you'll still find a directory for the software in /usr/share/doc. This is because the software might also come with a getting started guide written by the Ubuntu package maintainer. Such guides detail specifics of using the software under Ubuntu, such as where configuration files are located or how the program interoperates with other software on the system. Sometimes, this documentation is written by a Debian package maintainer because nearly all Ubuntu software has its origins in the Debian project (www.debian.org).

In addition, the directory will probably contain copyright information, explaining the software license used by the software, as well as a CHANGELOG, which is a text file listing features that have been added to each release of the software. The directory might contain some other files, too, detailing where to send information about bugs, for example.

Viewing the README documentation is easy. For example, for the sudo command, you could type this:

```
cd /usr/share/doc/sudo
less README
```

Sometimes, the README documentation is in a compressed tarball, in which case it will have either a .tar.gz or a .tar.bz2 file extension. However, less is clever enough to realize this and extract the document for reading.

Getting Help Online

If you can't figure out the answer by referring to the documentation, then there's little choice other than to look online. Linux benefits from a massive community of users, all of whom are usually willing to help each other.

The best way of getting help is to visit a forum. Here, you can post messages for others to reply to. Alternatively, you might choose to sign up for a mailing list. This is a way of sending e-mail to several hundreds, if not thousands, of people at once. Any individual can then reply. Mailing lists often have the benefit of allowing personal attention and interaction, but this comes at the expense of each subscriber receiving a whole lot of mail.

Forums

The official Ubuntu project forums are located at www.ubuntuforums.org. You'll find forums for just about every need, from security to beginner's issues, but by far, the most popular is the one devoted to the current release of Ubuntu, which is under the heading Ubuntu Release Assistance. Look in the General Help forum if your question isn't specifically related to one of the other technology areas listed.

Before you can post, you need to register by providing an e-mail address. This is designed to keep down the quantity of unwanted junk postings to the forum.

You might think it fine to post a new question immediately after registering, but don't forget the simple rules mentioned at the beginning of this appendix: if you don't do elementary research first and try to solve your own problem, you may elicit a hostile response from the other posters, especially if your question is one that comes up time and time again and has been answered several times.

So, first make use of the comprehensive search facility provided with the forums. For example, if you're looking for advice on getting a Foomatic D1000 scanner working, use this as a search term and see what comes up. The chances are that you won't be the first person who has run into problems with that piece of hardware, and someone else may have already posted a solution.

Often, you'll need to read the full thread to find an answer. Someone may start by asking the same question as you but, with the help and guidance of the forum members, they might find a solution, which they then post several messages later.

In addition, some individuals write their own HOWTO guides when they figure out how to do something. These are normally contained in the Faqs, Howto, Tips & Tricks forum, under the Other Support Categories heading.

If you're unable to find a solution by searching, then consider posting your own question. Keep your question simple, clear, and concise, because no one likes reading through acres of text. If possible, provide as many details about your system as you can. You will almost certainly want to provide the version number of the Linux kernel you're using, for example. You can find this version number by typing the following in a GNOME Terminal window:

```
uname -sr
```

In addition, any other details you can provide may prove handy. You definitely should mention the version of Ubuntu you're using, which is Edgy Eft (often referred to simply as "Edgy"). If you're asking about hardware, give its entire model name and/or number. Don't just ask for help with a Foomatic scanner. Ask for help with a Foomatic D1000 scanner, model number ADK1033, Revision 2. If you're asking about a piece of software, provide its version number (click Help ➤ About).

Sometimes in their replies, other forum members may ask you to post further details or to provide log files. If you don't understand the question, simply ask the poster to give you more details and, if necessary, instructions on what to do. Just be polite. Explain that you're a newbie. If you think the question is extremely obvious, then say so—apologize for asking what may be a stupid question, but explain that you've tried hard to answer it yourself but have failed. Don't forget that the Ubuntu forums include the Absolute Beginner Talk forum, where fundamental questions are asked all the time.

Mailing Lists

Using the forum's search function also has the advantage of searching the archives of the mailing lists.

Mailing lists have a number of advantages and disadvantages. The advantages are that a mailing list provides an excellent way to learn about Ubuntu. All you have to do is read through the e-mail messages you receive in order to partake of a constant information drip-feed. In addition, some mailing lists are designed to make public announcements, so you'll find it easy to learn about the latest happenings in the Ubuntu community.

Mailing lists also have a terrific sense of community. They offer a neat way of getting to know other Ubuntu users and talking to them. E-mails often drift off topic into humor and general discussion.

The disadvantages of mailing lists are that you can easily receive in excess of 200 messages a day, depending on which mailing list you join. Even if you have a moderately fast Internet connection, that quantity of messages can take a long time to download. In addition, you'll need to sort out any personal or business e-mail from the enormous quantity of mailing list traffic (although the mailing list messages usually have the list title in square brackets in the subject field; you can therefore create a mail rule that sorts the mail according to this).

You can sign up to the Ubuntu mailing lists at `https://lists.ubuntu.com/mailman/listinfo/ubuntu-users`.

Other Official Sites

The Ubuntu Document Storage Facility (`http://doc.gwos.org/index.php/Main_Page`) is a guide put together by the individuals who maintain the Ubuntu forums. It contains a lot of information culled from the forums, not least of which is the Hardware Compatibility Guide. This lists hardware that is known to work with Ubuntu, or at least hardware that can be made to work with Ubuntu with a little effort, which often is also detailed.

The official Ubuntu web site contains a Documentation section that features FAQs and a glossary of terms. It's located at `www.ubuntu.com/support/documentation`.

In addition, you might want to take a look at the Ubuntu wiki: `https://wiki.ubuntu.com`. This contains a whole world of fascinating information about Ubuntu, but can be somewhat difficult to navigate and tends to aimed at higher-level Ubuntu users, such as developers.

Third-Party Sites

Of course, the Ubuntu project doesn't have a monopoly on sites that discuss Ubuntu. Several third-party web sites are worth at least an occasional visit, and other forum web sites are devoted to Linux.

One I visit on a regular basis is the Ubuntu blog: `http://ubuntu.wordpress.com`. This is written by a relative newcomer to Ubuntu who has chosen the Ubuntu distribution for his computer. It details discoveries that Carthik Sharma has made about Ubuntu, such as configuration options, online sources of software, how to overcome hardware issues, and so on.

In addition, I like to visit `http://linuxhelp.blogspot.com`, which is a similar blog written by a Linux user who uses Ubuntu and likes to share tips and techniques.

Perhaps the king of third-party Ubuntu sites is Ubuntu Guide: `http://ubuntuguide.org`. This contains brief instructions on how to do a variety of common tasks under Ubuntu, such as installing certain types of software or administering particular hardware. It covers a lot of the same ground as this book, but is still worth investigating if you wish to browse through some excellent tips and advice.

Finally, one of the best Linux forums and general advice sites can be found at `www.linuxquestions.org`. This has a forum dedicated specifically to Ubuntu, but also contains hundreds more devoted to just about every aspect of Linux, including forums for beginners.

APPENDIX D

■■■

Exploring the DVD-ROM: Other Versions of Ubuntu

The DVD-ROM supplied with this book is double-sided. Side A contains the current version of the main Ubuntu release, 6.10, plus ISO images of several Ubuntu derivations, including Kubuntu, Edubuntu, and Xubuntu. Side B contains the previous release, 6.06.1, along with the 6.06.1 releases of Kubuntu, Edubuntu, and Xubuntu. In addition, both sides of the disc contain the alternate install versions of Ubuntu, as well as the PowerPC releases.

Version 6.06.1 of Ubuntu is included because of the advantages it offers to corporate users, as is explained in the following section. This appendix also lists details about each of the Ubuntu derivations, along with instructions on how to utlize them.

Ubuntu 6.10 or 6.06 LTS?

Each version of Ubuntu has a version number and also a code name. The version number is simply the year of release, followed by the month. The release made in June of 2006 has the version number 6.06, for example. The code name is how Ubuntu is referred to informally, especially among community members, and is set by Mark Shuttleworth, the creator of Ubuntu. Code names tend to be based around animals and are usually humorous. The 6.06 version of Ubuntu is code-named Dapper Drake, for example.

This book was written using version 6.10 as a base. This was released in October 2006 and is code-named Edgy Eft. It was the most recent version at the time of this writing.

■**Note** As authoring of this book progressed, Shuttleworth announced plans for the 7.04 release, which is code-named Feisty Fawn.

Each successive version of Ubuntu brings improvements, such as newer versions of software packages. However, not all versions of Ubuntu are created equal when it comes to online updates. All versions of Ubuntu come with free software updates for a set period, usually 18 months, after which users are expected to upgrade (for free) to the most recent version at that time.

However, the 6.06 release, code-named Dapper Drake, also has the epithet LTS, which stands for Long Term Support. The freely available software updates for 6.06 will last until 2009, some *three years* after the initial release. In contrast, the 6.10 release will only receive software updates until February 2008.

■**Note** If you use the 6.06 release on a server system, support will last for five years, until 2011.

The intention behind the 6.06 release is that it should be used by those who want a proven and stable Linux operating system but who don't care about newer features provided by the latest releases of Ubuntu. If Ubuntu is used in a corporate environment, some of the new features provided in more recent versions of Ubuntu might require additional staff training, so it is clear why an unchanging 6.06 release proves appealing to some.

Booting your computer from Side B of the DVD will start Ubuntu 6.06 LTS in live distro mode; from there, you can install it by following the instructions in Chapter 5.

If using a consistent version of Ubuntu that will be supplied with bug-fix updates until 2009 is important to you, and *if you don't intend to upgrade to a more recent version of Ubuntu before that point*, then you should investigate using 6.06.

However, most users will want to use the newer release of Ubuntu on Side A of the DVD-ROM and update to the latest versions as and when they become available. How to do this is described in the "Updating to a Newer Version of Ubuntu" sidebar. Following this policy will ensure you always use the latest versions of the Ubuntu software packages and still have the benefit of the latest bug-fix updates for 18 months after the initial release.

■**Note** The release included with this book on Side B of the DVD-ROM is 6.06.1 LTS. The .1 simply means that the disc is an updated version of the original release, with some bug fixes included.

Other Versions of Ubuntu

In addition to the main Ubuntu releases, several Ubuntu derivations are available. You might refer to these as "spin-off projects." They are created by taking the main Ubuntu release as a base and then adding additional software, usually in the form of an alternative desktop environment.

I detail some of the most popular alternative versions of Ubuntu next. All of these are included on the DVD-ROM supplied with this book in the form of *ISO images*. These are single files that contain the entire contents of the bootable install CDs. They're designed to be burned to blank CD-R or CD-RW discs. To learn how to do this, see the "Creating Bootable CDs from ISO Images" heading later in the chapter.

Versions of the 6.10 and 6.06 releases are provided on Side A and B of the DVD respectively in the `ubuntu_alternatives` directories.

Kubuntu

The standard Ubuntu release, as supplied with this book, relies on the GNOME Desktop Project for its graphical interface (see `www.gnome.org`). Many other desktop projects exist in the wider Linux world, but perhaps the only one that ranks alongside GNOME in terms of popularity is the K Desktop Environment project (`www.kde.org`), usually referred to as KDE. Kubuntu is simply a version of Ubuntu that eschews GNOME in favor of KDE.

Kubuntu (`www.kubuntu.org`) retains the same philosophy as Ubuntu, in both its humanitarian aims of being available to all as well as its more pragmatic aspects, such as always including the latest versions of applications. It also shares many technical features, such as the use of `sudo` to invoke superuser powers.

■**Note** Rather than use `gksu` to invoke `sudo` powers for graphical applications, Kubuntu uses `kdesu`. It's used in the same way, however.

The main difference is the software bundled with this variant. When it comes to e-mail, KDE's KMail program is used instead of Evolution, for example, and Konqueror is used for browsing instead of Firefox (although, of course, Evolution and Firefox can easily be installed via the Synaptic Package Manager after Kubuntu has been installed). The system configuration software is radically different, too, with several KDE tools used instead of the GNOME software described in this book.

Kubuntu is supplied in the `ubuntu_alternatives` directory on the DVD-ROM provided with this book—version 6.10 is on Side A, and version 6.06 is on Side B. To learn how to create a bootable installation CD from either version, see the "Creating Bootable CDs from ISO Images" section.

From an already-installed Ubuntu system you can install Kubuntu by searching for and installing the `kubuntu-desktop` package using the Synaptic Package Manager. This is a metapackage that ensures all the Kubuntu components are installed alongside the current desktop environment. Once the Kubuntu components have been installed, you can opt to boot into Kubuntu by clicking the Options button on the login screen and clicking the Select Session entry. Then select the KDE entry from the list. To boot to the standard Ubuntu desktop after this, simply select GNOME from the list.

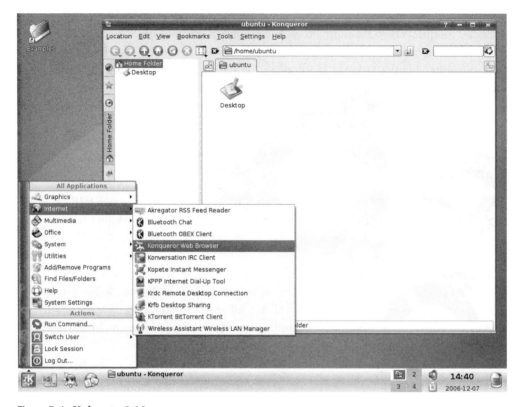

Figure D-1. *Kubuntu 6.10*

Edubuntu

The Ubuntu philosophy is to make an operating system accessible by everyone, no matter who they are or where they live in the world. Of course, young people are included in this vision, and Edubuntu (www.edubuntu.org) is a version of Ubuntu specifically geared toward their needs. It's a rendition of the standard Ubuntu release that's been bolstered by many educational software titles. In addition, it has a friendlier and simpler interface that's designed to appeal to youngsters.

The chief education titles are KDE Edutainment Suite, GCompris, and Tux4Kids. KDE Edutainment Suite (http://edu.kde.org) contains games involving mathematics, languages, science, and other miscellaneous topics. Teachers might also appreciate the inclusion of KEduca, a program designed to create form-based tests and exams.

GCompris (http://gcompris.net) is for children of kindergarten age and introduces them to computer use as well as elementary math and reading skills. Tux4Kids (www.tux4kids.com) includes a typing tutor, publishing program, and a handful of games geared toward math and literacy skills.

The main benefit of Edubuntu for educational establishments is that it's both free of charge and comes with the same kind of update support as Ubuntu. As with Ubuntu, although newer releases are available, it's possible to install the 6.06 release, meaning security updates will be available up until 2009. This provides a consistent experience for students and teachers alike.

Edubuntu is supplied in the `ubuntu_alternatives` directory on the DVD-ROM provided with this book—version 6.10 is on Side A, and version 6.06 is on Side B. To learn how to create a bootable installation CD from either version, see the "Creating Bootable CDs from ISO Images" section.

You can also update any Ubuntu system to Edubuntu by searching for and installing the `edubuntu-desktop` package within Synaptic Package Manager. Because Edubuntu is built on the Ubuntu base, there is no way to "switch between" Edubuntu and Ubuntu—effectively Edubuntu is a reconfiguration of Ubuntu with the addition of some education software and a more kid-friendly theme. To return to a standard Ubuntu setup and deactivate the Edubuntu theme, simply select the Human entry from the Theme chooser list. See Chapter 10 for more details on how to switch themes.

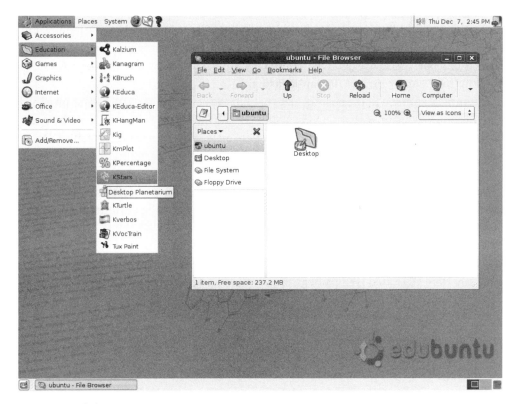

Figure D-2. *Edubuntu 6.10*

Xubuntu

While GNOME and KDE dominate the desktop interface landscape of Linux and are used in the main Ubuntu and Kubuntu releases, respectively, other projects take a different approach to the graphical desktop. XFCE Desktop Environment (www.xfce.org) is one of these. It's a streamlined desktop that retains the good looks of GNOME but is much smaller in terms of memory footprint. This means that a system running XFCE is faster than an equivalent GNOME system. It also means that XFCE can be used on many older computers that don't have the powerful hardware we take for granted nowadays and which would struggle with the latest GNOME and KDE releases of Ubuntu.

Because a key component of the Ubuntu Foundation's philosophy is to create an operating system that can be used by anyone, regardless of where they are in the world, a version of Ubuntu that can run on older hardware makes a lot of sense. It's unlikely that less developed countries will have access to the latest expensive computer hardware, for example.

Xubuntu (www.xubuntu.org) is simply a version of Ubuntu that replaces GNOME with XFCE. Despite XFCE's claim to be lightweight, it still offers a high degree of usability and shouldn't be seen as a second-best choice for stripped-down hardware. It's certainly worth trying out. It also uses many modern GUI aspects we take for granted, such as theming (see Chapter 10) and font antialiasing.

Xubuntu is supplied in the ubuntu_alternatives directory on the DVD-ROM provided with this book—version 6.10 is on Side A, and version 6.06 is on Side B. To learn how to create a bootable installation CD from either version, see the "Creating Bootable CDs from ISO Images" section.

Alternatively, you can install Xubuntu from any Ubuntu release by opening Synaptic Package Manager and searching for and installing xubuntu-desktop. This is a metapackage that ensures all the XFCE components are installed alongside the current desktop environment.

To use the XFCE desktop once it's installed, click the Options button on the login screen and then click the Select Session entry. Next, select XFCE from the list. To boot to the standard Ubuntu desktop after this, simply select GNOME from the list.

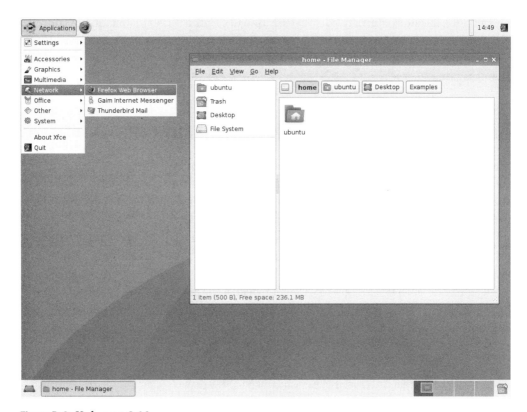

Figure D-3. *Xubuntu 6.10*

PowerPC and Alternate Install Ubuntu

Also within the `ubuntu_alternatives` directory on both sides of the disc are the PowerPC and Alternate Install/Server versions of Ubuntu.

The PowerPC version of Ubuntu is designed for Apple Macintosh computers that utilize the PowerPC processor. Using Ubuntu on older Macintosh computers that struggle to cope with OS X can give them a new lease on life, and many people have reported high satisfaction levels when installing Ubuntu on G3- and G4-powered notebooks and desktop computers.

The alternate install disc serves two main purposes. First, it's ideal if you find that the Ubuntu live distro mode and subsequent installation simply won't work on your computer. The alternate install disc employs a proven text-mode installation routine. Select Install in Text Mode when booting from the disc.

Secondly, the alternate install disc can be used to create a server installation of Ubuntu. Simply select Install a Command-Line System from the boot menu. To learn more about the Ubuntu Server project and the possible uses of Ubuntu in server environments, see www.ubuntu.com/server.

Creating Bootable CDs from ISO Images

The Ubuntu derivatives are supplied on the DVD-ROM disc as ISO images within the ubuntu_alternatives directories on Side A and Side B of the disc, depending on whether you want to utilize the 6.10 or 6.06 releases, respectively. It should be obvious from the individual filenames what each ISO file contains.

ISO images are designed to be burned to blank CD-R or CD-RW discs that you boot from in order to install the operating system. Alternatively, you can use them within virtual machines.

Of course, to burn ISO images to CD, you'll need a CD or DVD drive capable of burning discs. These have been available for many years and are standard features on nearly all desktop and notebook computers.

Note DVD burners are also capable of burning CD-R or CD-RW discs.

You'll also need a blank CD-R or CD-RW disc and perhaps one or two spares in case your first attempt doesn't work. If you opt to use CD-RW discs, these should be blanked prior to use. This can be done within most burning software packages.

A couple of rules should be followed whenever burning ISO images. First, copy the ISO image to your computer's hard disk. Don't try to burn an ISO image straight from a DVD/CD or a network share. The burning software requires quick access to the ISO file, and this isn't possible when it's not on your hard disk.

Second, always burn at the slowest speed possible, even if your CD/DVD burner is capable of much faster speeds. For some reason, ISO images burned quickly onto discs often fail to work. Even worse, sometimes the discs appear to work until it becomes apparent that one particular file is corrupted and the installation halts.

It's also not a good idea to use your computer for heavy tasks while burning ISO images. You should refrain from game playing or video editing, although light computer use should be fine (that is, word processing, web browsing, and so on).

The instructions in the following sections describe how to burn ISO images to CDs using Ubuntu, Windows, and Mac OS X.

DECODING ISO FILENAMES

ISO filenames for Linux distributions can be a little hard to understand, so here's a quick guide. Let's take the Xubuntu 6.10 ISO filename as a guide. Here it is:

```
xubuntu-6.10-desktop-i386.iso
```

The first part is the name of the distribution. In this case, it's `xubuntu`, but this could read `edubuntu` or maybe just `ubuntu`. The second part is the version number of the distribution—6.10. The third part is the platform the distro is designed for. In this case, this version of Xubuntu is designed for the desktop, but this could read `server` or `alternate`, to indicate an alternate install disc.

The final part, before the `.iso` file extension, is a description of the computer architecture the distro is made for. `i386` means the distro will run on all 32-bit PCs, but you might also see `amd64` here, which means the distro is designed to work on 64-bit processors, such as recent Intel Pentium 4 and AMD Athlon 64–based computers. If you see `PowerPC` here, it means the distro is designed to run on PowerPC-based computers, primarily older Apple Macintoshes.

Burning CDs Using Ubuntu

Copy the ISO image to the desktop, and then right-click it. Select Write to Disc from the menu that appears, and under the Write Speed drop-down list in the dialog box that appears, select the lowest value possible. If you have more than one CD/DVD writer drive installed on your computer, ensure the correct model is selected from the Write Disc To list too.

Insert a blank CD-R or CD-RW, and then click the Write button.

Burning CDs Using Windows Vista/XP

Unlike Ubuntu and Mac OS X, Windows Vista and XP don't contain any built-in ISO burning software. For the purpose of burning ISO images, I recommend you download and install the freeware ISO Recorder tool from `http://isorecorder.alexfeinman.com/isorecorder.htm`. Versions are available for both Windows XP and Vista.

Copy the ISO file to your desktop, and then insert a blank CD-R or CD-RW disc into your drive. Right-click the `.iso` file on the desktop, and select Open With ➤ ISO Recorder.

Click the Properties button on the ISO Recorder program window, and click and drag the recording speed slider so that the middle number under the slider is 1 (or to the lowest possible number if 1 isn't available). Click OK on the Properties dialog box, and then click the Next button on the main ISO Recorder program window. This will start the burning procedure, which might take some time, during which you should avoid using your PC.

Burning CDs Using Mac OS X

Copy the ISO file to the desktop, and then insert a blank CD-R or CD-RW disc. Next, using Finder, click Applications ➤ Utilities ➤ Disc Utility. When the program starts, click Images on the menu and then Burn. Navigate to the ISO file on the desktop, and then click the Burn button in the dialog box that appears.

UPDATING TO A NEWER VERSION OF UBUNTU

Ubuntu works to a six-month release cycle, and this means a new version of Ubuntu comes out every half year. The version of Ubuntu offered with this book is 6.10, code-named Edgy Eft. This was the latest release available as this book was written. By the time you read this, it's very likely there will be a new release of Ubuntu available.

You can update to the latest version of Ubuntu in two ways.

The first is to download the ISO image of the latest release from www.ubuntu.com/downloads and burn it to CD. If you then insert the CD when Ubuntu is up and running, you'll be asked if you want to upgrade to the latest version using Synaptic Package Manager. This process is automated. Of course, you can then use the same CD to install Ubuntu afresh on any other computer.

The other way of upgrading is to do so online. Open a GNOME Terminal window (Applications ➤ Accessories ➤ Terminal), and type the following two lines, after each other (pressing Enter after each):

```
sudo apt-get update
sudo apt-get dist-upgrade
```

This will download all the packages for the latest release of Ubuntu, if one is available, and attempt to update your system. Updating in this way involves less downloading, because your computer will only get the packages it needs, although it's still likely that several hundred megabytes will need to be downloaded.

Index

Find it faster at http://superindex.apress.com

Find it faster at http://superindex.apress.com

Find it faster at http://superindex.apress.com

You Need the Companion eBook

Your purchase of this book entitles you to buy the companion PDF-version eBook for only $10. Take the weightless companion with you anywhere.

We believe this Apress title will prove so indispensable that you'll want to carry it with you everywhere, which is why we are offering the companion eBook (in PDF format) for $10 to customers who purchase this book now. Convenient and fully searchable, the PDF version of any content-rich, page-heavy Apress book makes a valuable addition to your programming library. You can easily find and copy code—or perform examples by quickly toggling between instructions and the application. Even simultaneously tackling a donut, diet soda, and complex code becomes simplified with hands-free eBooks!

Once you purchase your book, getting the $10 companion eBook is simple:

❶ Visit **www.apress.com/promo/tendollars/**.

❷ Complete a basic registration form to receive a randomly generated question about this title.

❸ Answer the question correctly in 60 seconds, and you will receive a promotional code to redeem for the $10.00 eBook.

2560 Ninth Street • Suite 219 • Berkeley, CA 94710

eBookshop

THE EXPERT'S VOICE™

Offer valid through 9/07.